OBSERVER'S HANDBOOK 2018

USA EDITION

The Royal Astronomical Society of Canada is dedicated to the advancement of astronomy and its related sciences; this Handbook espouses the scientific method, and supports dissemination of information, discoveries, and theories based on that well-tested method.

EDITOR
JAMES S. EDGAR

ONE-HUNDRED-AND-TENTH YEAR OF PUBLICATION

© THE ROYAL ASTRONOMICAL SOCIETY OF CANADA
203–4920 DUNDAS STREET WEST, TORONTO ON M9A 1B7
2017

ISSN 0080-4193
ISBN 978-1-927879-12-2

MIX
Paper from
responsible sources
FSC® C004071

PRINTED IN CANADA
BY WEBCOM INC.

TABLE OF CONTENTS

Key to Marginal Chapter Symbols

Basic Data

Time

Optics and Observing

The Sky Month by Month

Eclipses

The Moon

The Sun

Planets and Satellites

Dwarf & Minor Planets

Meteors, Comets, and Dust

Stars

The Deep Sky

(N) New content   (R) Revised significantly

LIST OF CONTRIBUTORS

JAY ANDERSON, Prairie Storm Prediction Centre, Winnipeg, Manitoba......................................
(Frequency of Nighttime Cloud Cover)

J. RANDY ATTWOOD, Mississauga, Ontario...............................(Voyages in the Solar System)

CHRIS BECKETT, Regina, Saskatchewan ....(Feature Star Field, Wide-Field Wonders)

ROY BISHOP, Avonport, Nova Scotia..............................(Astronomical Precession, Binoculars,
Eclipse Patterns, Electromagnetic Spectrum, Expired Stars,
Filters, Interplanetary Dust, Mars oppositions diagram, Map of the Moon,
Maps of the Night Sky, Orbital Motion, Rainbows, Saturn Ring Diagram,
Sky Brightness at Midnight, Some Astronomical and Physical Data, Telescope Exit Pupils,
Telescope Parameters, Tides and the Earth–Moon System, Time and Time Scales)

LARRY D. BOGAN, Brooklyn Corner, Nova Scotia........... (Configurations of Jupiter's Galilean
Satellites, Configurations of Saturn's Brightest Satellites)

DEREK BREIT (IOTA*), Morgan Hill, California....................................(Planetary Occultations)

RANDALL BROOKS, Windsor, Nova Scotia ....(Astronomical Twilight and Sidereal Time)

PETER BROWN, Western University, London, Ontario ....(Meteors)

IAN CAMERON, University of Manitoba, Winnipeg, Manitoba ....(Finder Charts)

MARGARET CAMPBELL–BROWN, Western University, London, Ontario................(Meteors)

CHRIS CORBALLY, Vatican Observatory, Vatican City State.....................(The Brightest Stars;
Spectroscopy of Stars)

DAVID L. CRAWFORD, Tucson, Arizona ....(Light Pollution)

DAVID W. DUNHAM (IOTA*), Greenbelt, Maryland ....(Lunar Occultations, Planetary
Occultations)

MICHEL DUVAL, Montréal, Québec..(Coloured Double Stars)

ALAN DYER, Strathmore, Alberta ....(Deep-Sky Challenge Objects, Deep-Sky Observing Hints,
The Finest NGC Objects, The Messier Catalogue)

JAMES EDGAR, Melville, Saskatchewan..(Eclipse History)

LOUISE EDWARDS, California Polytechnic University, San Luis Obispo, California.......................
(The Deep Sky—From Near to Far)

FRED ESPENAK, Portal, Arizona...(Eclipses in 2018)

JOHN J. GOSS, Fincastle, Virginia ....(Guest Editorial)

PAUL GRAY, South Greenwood, Nova Scotia...(Dark Nebulae)

RICHARD GRAY, Appalachian State University, Boone, North Carolina...... (The Brightest Stars,
Spectroscopy of Stars)

DANIEL W.E. GREEN, Harvard University, Cambridge, Massachusetts ....
(Minor Planet Ephemerides, Comets in 2018)

KIM HAY, Yarker, Ontario ....(Solar Observing)

TODD J. HENRY, Georgia State University, Atlanta, Georgia ....(The Nearest Stars)

DAVID HERALD (IOTA*), Murrumbateman, Australia ....(Lunar Occultations, Planetary
Occultations)

CHRISTOPHER D.K. HERD, Univ. of Alberta, Edmonton, Alberta............(Meteorite Identification)

RICHARD K. HERD, Geological Survey of Canada, Ottawa, Ontario.........(Meteorite Identification)

KATHLEEN HOUSTON, Saskatoon, Saskatchewan............................(Astronomical Sketching)

RICHARD HUZIAK, Saskatoon, Saskatchewan ....(Carbon Stars)

PETER JEDICKE, Fanshawe College, London, Ontario .... (Star Clusters)

LEE JOHNSON, Vancouver, B.C. .... (Magnification and Contrast in Deep-Sky Observing)

STELLA KAFKA (AAVSO†), Cambridge, Massachusetts ....(Variable Stars)

*International Occultation Timing Association............†American Association of Variable Star Observers

TOOMAS KARMO, Richmond Hill, Ontario............ (The Brightest Stars, Spectroscopy of Stars)

PATRICK KELLY, Falmouth, Nova Scotia .... (Magnitudes of Naked-eye Planets, RAs of the Sun and Planets, The Sky Month by Month (events), Ephemeris of the Sun, Phenomena of Jupiter's Satellites)

ROBERT KERR, Bloomington, Minnesota .... (Astronomical League Programs)

DAVE LANE, Saint Mary's University, Halifax, Nova Scotia .... (Nebular Filter Transmission Chart, The Sky Month by Month (tables))

DAVID H. LEVY, Vail, Arizona .... (Deep-Sky Gems, Observing Comets)

ALISTER LING, Edmonton, Alberta .... (Deep-Sky Challenge Objects, The Sky Month by Month (lunar graphics))

BLAIR MacDONALD, Bedford, Nova Scotia .... (Polar Alignment)

BARRY F. MADORE, Caltech, Pasadena, California .... (Galaxies: Brightest and Nearest, Galaxies with Proper Names)

PAUL D. MALEY, Cave Creek, Arizona....................................... (Observing Artificial Satellites)

PAUL MARKOV, Toronto, Ontario... (The Observing Logbook)

BRIAN D. MASON, U.S. Naval Observatory, Washington, D.C. .... (Double and Multiple Stars)

PHILIP McCAUSLAND, Western University, London, Ontario.................................... (Fireballs)

BRUCE McCURDY, Edmonton, Alberta.......... (The Sky Month by Month text, Lunar Observing)

ANTHONY MOFFAT, Université de Montréal, Montréal, Québec......................... (Star Clusters)

SYUICHI NAKANO, Sumoto, Japan .... (Comets in 2018)

PHILIP D. NICHOLSON, Cornell University, Ithaca, New York....(Natural Satellites of the Planets)

RON OSTROMECKI, Erie, Pennsylvania .... (Carbon Stars)

MURRAY PAULSON, St. Albert, Alberta .... (The Planets in 2018)

JOSHUA PEPPER, Lehigh University, Bethlehem, Pennsylvania........................... (Variable Stars)

HUGH PETT, Kelowna, British Columbia......................... (Radio Astronomy and Radio Sources)

DOUGLAS PITCAIRN, Dartmouth, Nova Scotia .... (Limiting Magnitudes)

STEVE PRESTON (IOTA*), Medina, Washington .... (Planetary Occultations)

ALLAN RAHILL, Canadian Meteorological Centre, Dorval, Québec... (Weather Resources on the Internet)

EBERHARD RIEDEL (IOTA*), München, Germany................ (Grazing Occultation Predictions)

WILLIAM ROBERTS, Vancouver, B.C. .... (Magnification and Contrast in Deep-Sky Observing)

JOSEPH E. RODRIGUEZ, Harvard-Smithsonian CfA, Cambridge, Massachusetts (Variable Stars)

RANDALL ROSENFELD, Toronto, Ontario.. (Feature Star Field)

JOSHUA ROTH, Amateur Telescope Makers of Boston, Arlington, Massachusetts........................ (Night Myopia and Stargazing Glasses)

JOHN SPRAY, University of New Brunswick, Fredericton, New Brunswick................................. (Meteorite Impact Craters of North America)

KEIVAN STASSUN, Vanderbilt and Fisk Universities, Nashville, Tennessee.........(Variable Stars)

IAN STEER, Toronto, Ontario .... (Galaxies: Brightest and Nearest)

KEN TAPPING, Dominion Radio Astrophysical Observatory, Penticton, British Columbia............ (Radio Astronomy and Radio Sources, Solar Activity)

HEATHER THEIJSMEIJER, Kagawong, Ontario.......... (Teaching and the *Observer's Handbook*)

TENHO TUOMI, Lucky Lake, Saskatchewan .... (Digital Astrophotography)

DAVID TURNER, Dartmouth, Nova Scotia .... (Astronomical Precession)

ELIZABETH O. WAAGEN (AAVSO†), Cambridge, Massachusetts .... (Variable Stars)

ALAN WHITMAN, Penticton, British Columbia.................... (Southern Hemisphere Splendours)

*International Occultation Timing Association.............†American Association of Variable Star Observers

THE *OBSERVER'S HANDBOOK*

The *Observer's Handbook* is one of Canada's oldest scientific publications. Created by C.A. Chant, Professor of Astronomy at the University of Toronto, it first appeared over a century ago as *The Canadian Astronomical Handbook for 1907*, a small (13 × 17 cm), 108-page publication. A second edition covered the year 1908, but for the following two years most of the information that would have appeared was published instead in installments in the *Journal of the RASC*. The Council of the Society decided to return to a separate publication for 1911 with a new name—the *Observer's Handbook*—and it has been published annually ever since.

Each year, some 9000 copies of the Handbook are distributed to many countries throughout the world, to amateur and professional astronomers, to educators at school and university levels, and to many observatories, planetaria, and libraries. The Handbook is the main source of income for The Royal Astronomical Society of Canada. Since the first edition in 1907, the editorial team (see p. 8) and contributors (see p. 6) have voluntarily given their time and expertise every year to produce this unique book.

EDITORS OF THE *OBSERVER'S HANDBOOK*

		Position	Editions	RASC President
C.A. Chant	(1865–1956)	Editor	1907–1957	1903–1907
Frank S. Hogg	(1904–1951)	*Ass't Editor*	1939–1951	1940–1942
Ruth J. Northcott	(1913–1969)	*Ass't Editor*	1952–1957	1962–1964
		Editor	1958–1970	
John R. Percy	(1941–	Editor	1971–1981	1978–1980
Roy L. Bishop	(1939–	Editor	1982–2000	1984–1986
Rajiv Gupta	(1958–	Editor	2001–2006	2002–2004
Patrick Kelly	(1958–	Editor	2007–2011	
David M.F. Chapman	(1953–	Editor	2012–2016	
James S. Edgar	(1946–	*Ass't Editor*	2012–2016	2014–2016
		Editor	2017–	

The *Observer's Handbook* is intended to be "a companion which the observer would wish always to have in his pocket or on the table before him."

C.A. Chant, Toronto, 1906

"We believe that the *Observer's Handbook* is a truly significant contribution that Canadian astronomy in general and our Society in particular has been making to the dissemination of astronomical knowledge for half a century. I trust that it will still occupy the same position of respect after the first hundred years."

Ruth Northcott, Ottawa, 1964

"The more one knows, the more one can benefit from the Handbook. It inspires all who leaf through its pages to learn and question what the tables, graphs and data mean, perhaps to speculate on the mysteries of the Universe, and above all, to get out and look beyond our world. You have in your hands a key to the Universe—a key which will fit many doors. Please use it well and treasure it."

Peter Broughton, Toronto, 1992
Author of *Looking Up, A History of the RASC*

"The *Observer's Handbook* is the single most useful publication for the observational astronomer. Its combination of authoritative data, informative diagrams, and concise text is unique. Anyone interested in astronomy, beginner or expert, amateur or professional, student or teacher, will find the *Observer's Handbook* indispensable. Its international reputation for quality is a credit both to its many contributors and to Canadian astronomy."

Roy Bishop, Halifax, 2000

THE ROYAL ASTRONOMICAL SOCIETY OF CANADA

The beginnings of The Royal Astronomical Society of Canada go back to 1868. Then, in 1890, the Society was incorporated within the province of Ontario, received its Royal appellation from King Edward VII in 1903, and was federally incorporated in 1968. The Society Office (containing the business office and historical archives) is located at 203–4920 Dundas Street West, Toronto ON M9A 1B7; telephone: 416-924-7973 or 888-924-7272 from within Canada; email: nationaloffice@rasc.ca; website: www.rasc.ca.

The RASC has over 5000 members, who are from many countries and all walks of life. Members receive this *Observer's Handbook* (published every fall for the next calendar year) and electronic access to the bimonthly *Journal of the RASC*, which contains review articles, research papers on historical and contemporary topics, education notes, general notes of astronomical interest, book reviews, news items concerning the Society and its Centres, informal articles, and letters. (A print version of the *Journal* is available at a modest extra cost.) Also included in membership is *SkyNews*, Canada's popular bimonthly astronomy magazine, published by the RASC.

Membership fees are $75 per year, with a reduced rate for persons under 21 years of age (under 25, if enrolled in postsecondary education). For members outside of Canada, these figures are to be read as U.S. dollars, and there is an additional fee ($18 for U.S. addresses; $48 for international addresses) to cover higher mailing costs. An applicant may affiliate with one of the Centres of the Society across Canada or join the Society directly as an Unattached Member. Membership in some Centres may require a higher fee.

The Society currently has 29 Centres located in Canada's major cities. Most Centres hold monthly meetings at which prospective members are welcome. For contact information and details on activities, please visit www.rasc.ca/locations-across-canada for the appropriate Centre website URL.

REPORTING OF ASTRONOMICAL DISCOVERIES

Historically, the worldwide center for reporting transient astronomical discoveries (including new comets, novae, unusual variable stars, interesting meteor activity, interesting planetary features, new planetary satellites, etc.) has been the Central Bureau for Astronomical Telegrams; since 1965, it has been located on the Harvard University campus. You can e-mail discovery reports to the CBAT at cbatiau@eps.harvard.edu or cbat@iau.org, and the CBAT's Transient Objects Confirmation Page is where observers can post observations of non–Solar System transient variables and get preliminary designations (see www.cbat.eps.harvard.edu/unconf/tocp.html). Starting in early 2016, supernovae discoveries were moved to the "Transient Name Server" (see wis-tns.weizmann.ac.il//user/register).

All discovery reports should include your name, contact details, observation method (visual, CCD, etc.), a description of the instruments used, exposure details (if nonvisual), and the observation site. If new to reporting discoveries, you should provide background information on your observing experience. Inexperienced observers should have their observation checked before contacting CBAT.

Regarding the object itself, report the date and time (UT) of observation, RA and Dec (with equinox) of the object, its estimated magnitude (with bandpass noted), and details of its physical appearance, depending on the type of object. Incomplete discovery reports may be ignored as not being truly serious. Please review the detailed instructions at www.cbat.eps.harvard.edu/DiscoveryInfo.html.

To avoid false alarms, before emailing CBAT, it is highly recommended to make one or more additional observations of the object over a time period of hours or a day. Such observations may be contributed by a privately notified independent observer.

Possible new **minor planets** should be reported to the IAU Minor Planet Center (www.minorplanetcenter.net/iau/info/TechInfo.html).

To report a **fireball** (a meteor brighter than magnitude –5), see p. 255.

EDITOR'S COMMENTS

With each new edition, we get new contributors and some drop away. We thank those people who give so willingly of their time to make this Handbook a great success. While we bid adieu to Michèle Arenburg, Scott Donnell, Edwin Goffin, Ulisse Munari, and James Stamm, at the same time, we welcome these new contributors and assistants, Pierre Paquette is back as a Proofreader, and we have three new names added to the Variable Stars Section: Joseph E. Rodriguez, Joshua Pepper, and Keivan Stassun.

Early in 2017, the RASC Publications Committee (myself included) decided to create, for the first time, a USA Edition of the Handbook. Much new material is added to replace some of the more Canada-centric examples and tables. Joining with us in this enterprise is the Astronomical League, whose president and members contributed or suggested ways to improve the Handbook for the American audience. I think those changes will make for an interesting symbiosis. We look forward to more such collaborations in the future!

It may not look like the tables and data change year to year, but much hard work by many people working in the background goes into ensuring we have the most up-to-date information available for the observers who will use this Handbook. There are many minor, but important, changes within these pages.

This year, the RASC celebrates 150 years of astronomy education and outreach. Let's all join in to make this a banner year!

Lastly, thanks to the willing astrophotographers who so freely gave permission to use their work: Stephen Bedingfield, Alan Dyer, David Levy, Paul Luckas, and Damien Peach.

James S. Edgar
handbookeditor@rasc.ca
Melville, Saskatchewan
2017 Sep. 14

THE *OBSERVER'S HANDBOOK* EDITORIAL TEAM

EDITOR	**COPY EDITOR**
James S. Edgar	Betty Robinson
EDITORIAL CONSULTANT	**PROOFREADERS**
Roy Bishop	Chris Malicki
	Bruce McCurdy
GRAPHICS CONSULTANT	Pierre Paquette
Michael Gatto	

Several other individuals and organizations played a role in the production of this Handbook: Some of the data come from the publications *Astronomical Phenomena for the Year 2018* and *The Astronomical Almanac for the Year 2018*, both prepared jointly by the U.S. Naval Observatory's Nautical Almanac Office and Her Majesty's Nautical Almanac Office. Corrections or suggestions for improvement that were incorporated in this edition were provided by Jeff MacKinnon, John O'Hanley, and Grant Tomchuk.

Front cover: The Rho Ophiuchi reflection and emission nebula with Antares and M4 globular cluster. The image was taken by Lynn Hilborn, 2014 February 04, in Arikok National Park, Aruba, with a modified Canon 6D and Canon 135-mm f/2 lens @ f/2.8; 20 exposures × 60 sec each at ISO 800. Object tracked with an iOptron ZEQ25 mount.

Back Cover: A composite of the 2017 August 21 total solar eclipse, with a range of exposures from 1/1000 s to 0.4, to retain the corona while bringing out faint streamers. The blue sky contains several stars, including mag. 1 Regulus, a rare sight at any eclipse. A bit of Earthshine is faintly visible. Taken from the Teton Valley, north of Driggs, Idaho.

The images, taken with a Canon 6D Mark II, at ISO 100, on a polar-aligned equatorial tracking mount, were shot through a 106-mm Astro-Physics refractor with a 0.85× Reducer/ Flattener for an effective focal ratio of f/5 and focal length of 500 mm. North is to the left.

GUEST EDITORIAL:
LOOK AT TODAY'S ASTRONOMICAL LEAGUE
BY JOHN J. GOSS

Sometimes it all begins just by perusing a star atlas. You see something that intrigues you, that jogs your memory. Perhaps you're carefully examining the page depicting the beautiful region between Betelgeuse and Procyon in northern Monoceros. The Christmas Tree Cluster, the Cone Nebula, Hubble's Variable Nebula, NGC 2251, and the Rosette Nebula are all in this compact area. You've read about them, and you've seen fantastic images of them. Now you want to see each of them with your own eyes.

Wouldn't it be advantageous to be part of a group that understands your desire to personally experience the wonder, beauty, and mystery of this incredible Universe, such as all those deep-sky objects in northern Monoceros? Wouldn't it be wonderful if you were a member of a respected national organization dedicated to accompanying people on their journeys exploring the celestial realm?

That organization is the Astronomical League, the largest federation of amateur astronomers in the United States. For 70 years the League has grown and evolved, constantly striving to improve time spent under the starry dome. Why not take a closer look at today's Astronomical League?

• Do you appreciate spending time under the stars, contemplating what lies above? The Astronomical League is best known for its many observing programs, now numbering well over 50. Some are meant for beginners, many others are best suited for intermediates, and a few have been developed strictly for advanced observers. No other organization in the world offers anything like this extensive array of observing activities.

• Do you want to keep abreast of the state of our amazing avocation? Every Astronomical League member receives *Reflector*, a full-color quarterly magazine published by and for amateur astronomers.

• Do you know someone who makes astronomy happen, perhaps a dedicated webmaster, an energetic newsletter editor, or an accomplished observer? Why not nominate that person for one of the Astronomical League's recognition awards?

• Do you want to encourage youth in astronomy? Then look to the 10 paths to receive a youth award, whether it is for club and community involvement, imaging what lies above, writing about our Universe, or for conducting science-based research. These avenues open young minds to contemplate what their futures may hold, open young hearts to a lifelong love of the night sky, and open young intellects to discover the Universe around them.

• Have you heard about the amazing Library Telescope Program? The League donates up to 11 telescopes each year so library patrons can check them out as they would books. This is the perfect outreach project, one that positively affects the community and reaches youths.

• Are you interested in recording the celestial wonders you spy through the eyepiece? Why not try for the Astronomics Sketching Award or enter the imaging awards competition sponsored by Oceanside Photo and Telescope?

There is much, much more:

AstroNotes and Outreach Downloads help with improving club operations and connecting with the public; affordable liability insurance is available for League clubs; the Celestial Savings program allows members to enjoy product discounts from participating vendors; the Astronomy Day Awards program recognizes those League clubs that bring astronomy to the public; the discount Book Service program offers savings on books and other printed materials; light-pollution advocacy helps fight obtrusive sky glow; and ALCons, the Astronomical League's national conventions, bring people together. The next ALCon will be hosted by the Minneapolis Astronomical Society 2018 Jul. 11–14.

The Astronomical League is a member-directed, member-supported, and nationally respected organization dedicated to enhancing your personal observing experience and making the most of your time spent under the stars. If you or your club is not a member yet, why not join today?

John Jardine Goss is president of the Astronomical League, the largest federation of amateur astronomers in the United States with 17,000 members. He and his wife, Genevieve, live in Fincastle, Virginia.

RECOMMENDED READING, ATLASES, AND SOFTWARE

Astronomy, a non-technical monthly magazine for amateur astronomers (Canada and U.S.: 800-533-6644; www.astronomy.com).

The Backyard Astronomer's Guide (3rd ed.), by Terence Dickinson and Alan Dyer. Firefly Books (Canada: 800-387-6192, United States: 800-387-5085; www.fireflybooks.ca), 2010. The best guide to equipment and techniques for amateur astronomers, by two experienced observers.

Catalog of the Astronomical Society of the Pacific, an excellent source of astronomical educational resources (415-337-1100; www.astrosociety.org).

Catalog of Sky Publishing, a good source of a variety of astronomical materials, including items listed on this page. (617-864-7360; www.shopatsky.com).

Exploring the Night Sky, by Terence Dickinson. Firefly Books (see above), 1987. A guide to stargazing, recommended for children.

A Field Guide to the Stars and Planets, by Jay M. Pasachoff. Houghton Mifflin Company, New York, 2015. In the Peterson Field Guides series, this classic work (also available as an e-book) is packed with star maps and accessible information.

Nightwatch (4th ed.), by Terence Dickinson. Firefly Books (see above), 2006. An excellent introductory observing guide.

Sky & Telescope, a monthly magazine widely read by both amateur and professional astronomers (617-864-7360; www.skyandtelescope.com).

SkyNews, the Canadian magazine of astronomy and stargazing, published bimonthly by the RASC (866-759-0005; www.skynews.ca).

Publications of the Astronomical Society of the Pacific, an online service for journal content (iopscience.iop.org).

The Reflector, a quarterly publication of the Astronomical League giving pertinent news in amateur astronomy (www.astroleague.org/reflector).

Millennium Star Atlas, by Roger Sinnott and Michael Perryman. A comprehensive atlas based on data from the *HIPPARCOS* satellite. Three volumes, each covering 8 hours in RA. Contains more than 1 000 000 stars to mag. 11 and more than 10 000 clusters, nebulae, and galaxies on 1548 charts (out of print).

Sky & Telescope's **Pocket Sky Atlas,** by Roger W. Sinnott, 2007. Introductory atlas containing 30 796 stars to mag. 7.6, many double stars, and the brighter deep-sky objects, on 80 charts. Spiral-bound, folds flat, great for a small telescope.

Sky Atlas 2000.0 (2nd ed.), by Wil Tirion and Roger Sinnott, 1998. Large format and well done. Contains 81 000 stars to mag. 8.5 and 2700 clusters, nebulae, and galaxies on 26 charts; laminated version available.

Uranometria 2000.0 Deep Sky Atlas, by Wil Tirion, Barry Rappaport, and Will Remaklus, 2001. A second edition of the popular atlas, with stellar data from the *HIPPARCOS* satellite. Contains more than 280 000 stars to mag. 9.75 and 30 000 clusters, nebulae, and galaxies on 220 double-page charts.

Computer-based Planetarium Programs: Available for a variety of platforms, e.g. *Coelix, ECU V6.0 (Earth Centered Universe), MegaStar5, Redshift 7, Starry Night, TheSkyX, Stellarium* (freeware), and *SkySafari*. For more information, see the catalogs listed above or do an Internet search at, for example, www.google.com.

Applications for Mobile Devices: There is a rapidly expanding universe of convenient "apps" for smart phones and tablets: star charting, lunar phase, observing logs, telescope controllers, and so on. See: Apple iTunes (www.apple.com/itunes); BlackBerry App World (appworld.blackberry.com); Windows Store (www.microsoft.com/en-us/windows/windows-10-apps); and Android Market (market.android.com). Also see Andrew Fraknoi's article at tinyurl.com/c63hk4a.

SELECTED OBSERVATORIES, *STAR PARTIES*, AND PLANETARIA

Observatories and *star parties* are ordered by longitude, planetaria are ordered alphabetically by city. Some *star party* dates are listed on p. <?>.

Location	Lat.	Long.	Alt. (m/ft.)
Anglo-Australian Observatory—Siding Spring, Australia www.aao.gov.au	31°17′S	149°04′E	1164/3819
Mount Stromlo Observatory—Canberra, Australia rsaa.anu.edu.au/observatories	35°19′S	149°00′E	767/2516
Perth Observatory—Bickley, Australia www.wa.gov.au/perthobs	32°00′S	116°08′E	380/1247
Effelsberg Radio Telescope—Effelsberg, Germany www.mpifr-bonn.mpg.de/effelsberg	50°31′N	6°53′E	319/1046
Greenwich Observatory—Greenwich, England www.rog.nmm.ac.uk	51°29′N	0°00′	31/102
Lovell Radio Telescope—Jodrell Bank, England www.jb.man.ac.uk	53°14′N	2°18′W	89/292
Armagh Observatory—Armagh, Northern Ireland www.arm.ac.uk/home.html	54°21′N	6°39′W	43/144
"Leviathan" Great Telescope—Birr, Ireland birrcastle.com/telescope-astronomy	53°05′N	7°54′W	59/194
Isaac Newton Telescope—La Palma, Canary Islands www.ing.iac.es/Astronomy/telescopes/int	28°45′N	17°53′W	2336/7664
Butterpot Star Party—Butter Pot Prov. Park, Newfoundland www.stjohnsrasc.ca/star-party.shtml	47°23′N	53°04′W	164/538
Burke-Gaffney Observatory—Halifax, Nova Scotia www.smu.ca/academic/science/ap/bgo.shtml	44°38′N	63°35′W	93/300
Nova East—Smileys Provincial Park, Nova Scotia halifax.rasc.ca/ne/home.html	45°01′N	63°58′W	150/492
St. Croix Observatory—St. Croix, Nova Scotia halifax.rasc.ca/sco.html	44°57′N	64°02′W	65/213
Acadia Night Sky Festival—Bar Harbor, Maine www.acadianightskyfestival.com	44°23′N	68°12′W	30/96
Arecibo Observatory—Arecibo, Puerto Rico www.naic.edu/general	18°21′N	66°45′W	307/1007
Paranal Observatory (ESO)—Cerro Paranal, Chile www.eso.org/paranal/site/paranal.html	24°38′S	70°24′W	2635/8645
Las Campanas Observatory—Cerro Las Campanas, Chile www.lco.cl	29°00′S	70°42′W	2282/7486
Gemini South Observatory—Cerro Pachon, Chile www.gemini.edu	30°14′S	70°44′W	2722/8930
La Silla Observatory (ESO)—Cerro La Silla, Chile www.eso.org/sci/facilities/lasilla.html	29°15′S	70°44′W	2400/7980
Cerro Tololo Inter-American Observatory—Cerro Tololo, Chile www.ctio.noao.edu	30°10′S	70°49′W	2200/7220
Mont Mégantic Observatory—Mont Mégantic, Québec omm.craq-astro.ca	45°27′N	71°09′W	1114/3654
Stellafane—Springfield, Vermont www.stellafane.com	43°16′N	72°31′W	393/1290
Franklin Institute Bloom Observatory—Philadelphia, Pennsylvania www.fi.edu/exhibit/observatory	39°58′N	75°10′W	76/250
Harrisburg Star Party—Harrisburg, Pennsylvania www.astrohbg.org/ASH/index.php	40°15′N	76°53′W	701/2300

Location	Lat.	Long.	Alt. (m/ft.)
Cherry Springs Star Party—Cherry Springs S.P., Coudersport, PA www.cherrysprings.org	41°40′N	77°49′W	704/2310
Staunton River Star Party—Halifax County, Virginia www.chaosastro.com/starparty	36°42′N	78°41′W	107/350
Almost Heaven Star Party—Spruce Knob, West Virginia www.ahsp.org	38°40′N	79°34′W	1201/3942
Green Bank Star Quest—Green Bank, West Virginia www.greenbankstarquest.org	38°26′N	79°50′W	803/2634
Green Bank Telescope—Green Bank, West Virginia science.nrao.edu/facilities/gbt	38°26′N	79°50′W	803/2634
Allegheny Observatory—Pittsburgh, Pennsylvania www.pitt.edu/~aobsvtry	40°29′N	80°01′W	380/1247
Starfest—Mount Forest, Ontario www.nyaa.ca/starfest.htm	44°04′N	80°50′W	400/1312
Winter Star Party—Camp Wesumkee, Florida www.scas.org/winter-star-party	24°39′N	81°19′W	1/4
Apollo Rendezvous—John Bryan State Park, Ohio www.mvas.org/node/5372	39°48′N	83°51′W	319/1049
Yerkes Observatory—Williams Bay, Wisconsin astro.uchicago.edu/Yerkes	42°34′N	88°33′W	314/1030
Midsouth Star Gaze—French Camp, Mississippi www.rainwaterobservatory.org/rainwater	33°17′N	89°23′W	146/479
Illinois Dark Sky Star Party—Jim Edgar Panther Creek FWA sas-sky.org	39°59′N	90°04′W	187/615
Heart of America Star Party—Butler, Missouri www.hoasp.askc.org	38°15′N	94°19′W	252/828
Nebraska Star Party—Valentine, Nebraska www.nebraskastarparty.org	42°36′N	100°53′W	909/2982
Okie-Tex Star Party—Camp Billy Joe, Oklahoma www.okie-tex.com	36°54′N	102°57′W	353/4439
Texas Star Party—Fort Davis, Texas texasstarparty.org	30°36′N	103°57′W	1542/5057
McDonald Observatory—Fort Davis, Texas www.as.utexas.edu/mcdonald/mcdonald.html	30°40′N	104°01′W	2065/6773
Rocky Mountain Star Stare—Gardner, Colorado www.rmss	37°50′N	105°11′W	2320/7612
Very Large Array—Socorro, New Mexico www.vla.nrao.edu	34°05′N	107°37′W	2123/6965
Enchanted Skies Star Party—Magdalena, New Mexico www.enchantedskies.org	34°05′N	107°18′W	2123/6965
Steward Observatory—Tucson, Arizona skycenter.arizona.edu	32°26′N	110°47′W	2510/8230
Fred Lawrence Whipple Observatory—Amado, Arizona www.sao.arizona.edu/FLWO/whipple.html	31°41′N	110°53′W	2554/8379
Kitt Peak National Observatory—Tucson, Arizona www.noao.edu/kpno	31°57′N	111°36′W	2078/6816
Lowell Observatory—Flagstaff, Arizona www.lowell.edu	35°12′N	111°40′W	2206/7236

Location	Lat.	Long.	Alt. (m/ft.)
U.S. Naval Observatory—Flagstaff, Arizona www.nofs.navy.mil	35°11'N	111°44'W	2262/7421
Craters of the Moon Star Party—Craters of the Moon SP www.ifastro.org/home/calendar-of-events-events/observatory	43°27'N	113°32'W	1755/5759
Wilson Coulee Observatory—Okotoks, Alberta calgary.rasc.ca/tourrequest.htm	50°46'N	114°02'W	1127/3697
Idaho Star Party—Bruneau Dunes State Park, Idaho isp.boiseastro.org	42°53'N	115°43'W	771/2530
Riverside Telescope Makers Conference—Camp Oakes, Calif. www.rtmcastronomyexpo.org	34°14'N	116°45'W	2316/7600
Palomar Observatory—San Diego, California www.astro.caltech.edu/palomar	33°21'N	116°52'W	1706/5597
Death Valley Star Party—Death Valley, California www.oasisatdeathvalley.com/activities/stargazing	36°27'N	116°51'W	9/28
Mt. Wilson Observatory—Pasadena, California www.mtwilson.edu	34°13'N	118°03'W	1740/5700
Dominion Radio Astrophysical Observatory—Penticton, B.C. www.nrc-cnrc.gc.ca/eng/solutions/facilities/drao.html	49°19'N	119°37'W	545/1788
Mount Kobau Star Party—Osoyoos, British Columbia www.mksp.ca	49°07'N	119°40'W	1860/6102
Oregon Star Party—Ochoco National Forest, Oregon www.oregonstarparty.org	44°18'N	120°08'W	1499/4918
Table Mountain Star Party—Ellensburg, Washington www.tmspa.com	47°15'N	120°35'W	1937/6357
Goldendale Observatory—Goldendale, Washington parks.state.wa.us/512/Goldendale-Observatory	45°51'N	120°47'W	640/2100
Pine Mountain Observatory—Pine Mountain, Oregon pmo-sun.uoregon.edu	43°47'N	120°57'W	1905/6250
Lick Observatory—San Jose, California mthamilton.ucolick.org	37°20'N	121°39'W	1290/4232
Golden State Star Party—Bieber, California goldenstatestarparty.org	40°08'N	120°59'W	1315/4314
Gordon Southam Observatory—Vancouver, B.C. www.spacecentre.ca/gms	49°16'N	123°09'W	6/21
Dominion Astrophysical Observatory—Victoria, B.C. www.nrc-cnrc.gc.ca/eng/solutions/facilities/dao.html	48°31'N	123°25'W	238/780
RASCals Star Party—Malahat, British Columbia victoria.rasc.ca/events/rascals-star-party-2017	48°33'N	123°34'W	345/1132
James Clerk Maxwell Telescope—Mauna Kea, Hawaii www.eaobservatory.org/jcmt	19°49'N	155°28'W	4092/13 426
Canada-France-Hawaii Telescope—Mauna Kea, Hawaii www.cfht.hawaii.edu	19°49'N	155°28'W	4204/13 793
Gemini North—Mauna Kea, Hawaii www.gemini.edu/public	19°49'N	155°28'W	4213/13 824

Planetarium	Notes
Fiske Planetarium—Boulder fiske.colorado.eduZ/beta 303-492-5001	Evening shows and weekend matinees; observatory available following shows for stargazing; school groups welcome
Morehead Planetarium—Chapel Hill moreheadplanetarium.org 919-918-1155	Regular programming and special events for youth, teens, and adults; science summer camps, skywatching, and starry nights
Adler Planetarium—Chicago www.adlerplanetarium.org 312-922-7827	Historic, first in Western Hemisphere; large collection of historic instruments; Doane Observatory on-site

Planetarium	Notes
McAuliffe-Shepard Discovery Center—Concord www.starhop.com/plan-your-visit 603-271-7827	Dedicated to first "Teacher In Space" who tragically died in shuttle *Challenger* disaster 1986 Jan. 28
Denver Museum of Nature and Science—Denver www.dmns.org 303-370-6000	Planetarium; IMAX theater; exhibit galleries; event planning and venue for large groups; programs for kids of all ages.
Halifax Planetarium—Halifax www.astronomynovascotia.ca 902-494-2314	Features a historic Spitz Model A-1 projector; great venue for small groups; teachers, group leaders, and individuals welcome
W.J. McCallion Planetarium—Hamilton, Ontario www.physics.mcmaster.ca/planetarium 905-525-9140	Shows are especially geared toward a younger audience and their family members; programs include solar and nighttime viewing
Burke Baker Planetarium—Houston www.hmns.org/see_do/planetarium.asp 713-639-4629	One of the Challenger Centers; dome is used for training astronauts to identify star fields; SkyScan digital stars; theatre seats 232
Samuel Oschin Planetarium—Los Angeles griffithobservatory.org/programs/soplanetarium.html 213-473-0800	Completely renovated with state-of-the-art technology; 300-seat theatre; Zeiss Mark IX star projector; and Digistar 3-laser system
Frost Museum of Science—Miami www.frostscience.org 305-434-9600	Frost Planetarium, with 250 seats, uses 16-million-color 8K projection; on-site food; retail store; easy access from city center.
Planétarium de Montréal—Montréal espacepourlavie.ca/en/access/rio-tinto-alcan-planetarium 514-868-3000	The Rio Tinto Alcan Planetarium offers an original and innovative approach to astronomy, with two theaters resembling telescopes
Mystic Seaport Planetarium—Mystic www.mysticseaport.org/visit/explore/planetarium 860-572-5315	Celestial navigation workshops; 30-foot dome; specialized group programs; history of navigation exhibit; GPS workshop
Hayden Planetarium—New York www.amnh.org/our-research/hayden-planetarium 212-769-5100	At American Museum of Natural History; programs, courses, and lectures; Zeiss Mark IX Universarium Star Projector
Harry C. Kendall Planetarium—Portland www.omsi.edu/planetarium 503-797-4610	Fifty-two-foot domed theater with Digistar 3 projection; presentations on astronomy, space science, and lasers; school programs
James S. McDonnell Planetarium—St. Louis www.slsc.org 314-289-4400	The 80-foot dome houses a Zeiss Model IX; includes exhibits about living and working in space; camp-ins for the whole family
Clark Planetarium—Salt Lake City slco.org/clark-planetarium 385-468-7827	Salt Lake City's go-to destination for visitors of all ages who want to discover and learn about space and science.
Ontario Science Centre—Toronto www.ontariosciencecentre.ca/tour/live-planetarium-show 416-696-1000	In central Toronto; OMNIMax theater; kids' sleepovers; summer day camps; home of the RASC Toronto Centre
MacMillan Planetarium—Vancouver www.spacecentre.ca 604-738-7827	Close to downtown Vancouver; special laser shows in summer; numerous programs for school groups of all ages; teacher packages
Albert Einstein Planetarium—Washington airandspace.si.edu/visit/mall/things-to-do/planetarium.cfm 202-633-1000	At National Air and Space Museum; café; IMAX theatre; planetarium upgraded to include Sky Vision™ dual digital projection
Northern Lights—Watson Lake, Yukon www.northernlightscentre.ca 867-536-7827	All-dome video planetarium; daily shows; programs concentrate on aurora borealis and northern experience
Aldrin Planetarium—West Palm Beach www.sfsciencecenter.org/planetarium-shows 561-832-1988	Laser shows; telescopes; exhibits; science camps; teachers' programs; birthday party programs
Manitoba Planetarium—Winnipeg manitobamuseum.ca/main/visit/planetarium/ 204-956-2830	In central Winnipeg; science center, museum, and planetarium in one site; school programs; new Digistar 5 All-Dome projector

SELECTED INTERNET RESOURCES

The World Wide Web is an important source of astronomical information. A selection of websites together with a reference to a page number in this Handbook (if any) is given below. A listing of all websites mentioned in this Handbook, with URL links to the various sites, is available at **www.rasc.ca/web-links.**

URL	Description
www.aavso.org	American Association of Variable Star Observers (p. 298)
www.alpo-astronomy.org	Association of Lunar and Planetary Observers (p. 221)
www.astrosociety.org	Astronomical Society of the Pacific (p. 18)
www.astronomy.com	*Astronomy* magazine (p. 10)
www.cleardarksky.com/csk	Clear Sky Chart, by Attilla Danko (p. 78)
www.badastronomy.com/index.html	Phil Plaitt's "Bad Astronomy" blog
www.rasc.ca/david-h-levy-logbooks	David H. Levy Logbooks (p. 324)
www.MrEclipse.com	Eclipse photography and safety (p. 142)
heritage.stsci.edu	Hubble Heritage Site, access to HST images
space.com	News about spaceflight, science, and astronomy
www.cbat.eps.harvard.edu/index.html	International Astronomical Union Central Bureau for Astronomical Telegrams (p. 7)
www.worldwidetelescope.org	Use your computer as a personal telescope
www.google.com/mars	Explore the surface of Mars right from home
www.darksky.org	International Dark-Sky Association (p. 79)
www.imo.net	International Meteor Organization (p. 254)
www.lunar-occultations.com/iota	International Occultation Timing Association (p. 162)
www.jpl.nasa.gov	Jet Propulsion Laboratory, activities for adults and kids
miac.uqac.ca	Meteorites and Impacts Advisory Committee, Canadian Space Agency (p. 255)
cdsads.u-strasbg.fr	NASA Astrophysics Data System (ADS); bibliographic database, access to millions of articles
www.cloudynights.com	Member forum; items for sale; astronomy tips and tricks
eclipse.gsfc.nasa.gov	NASA eclipse site (p. 142)
nedwww.ipac.caltech.edu	NASA/IPAC Extragalactic Database (p. 334)
spaceflight.nasa.gov	NASA space flight site giving current information on *ISS* activities and human space flight
planetary.org	Planetary Society—contains over 2000 pages of information about space exploration
www.saguaroastro.org	Saguaro Astronomy Club, includes observing list database (p. 87)
www.heavens-above.com	Satellite tracking information, including *International Space Station*
simbad.u-strasbg.fr/simbad	SIMBAD astronomical database
www.skyandtelescope.com	*Sky & Telescope* and Sky Publishing (p. 10)
www.skynews.ca	*SkyNews*—Canada's astronomy magazine, published by the RASC (p. 10)
www.stsci.edu	Space Telescope Science Institute; access to Digitized Sky Survey
seds.org	Students for the Exploration and Development of Space
vizier.hia.nrc.ca/viz-bin/VizieR	VizieR service; access to most astronomical catalogs

TEACHING AND THE *OBSERVER'S HANDBOOK*
BY HEATHER THEIJSMEIJER

You are holding in your hand a valuable resource for teaching astronomy. Every user of this Handbook, whether amateur or professional astronomer, or teacher in any setting, at any level, can contribute to education in astronomy; see *JRASC, 96* (October 2002), p. 196, for information on how you can, too.

The RASC, in partnership with the Canadian Astronomical Society and other organizations, has recently embarked on several major education and public outreach initiatives. These include www.rasc.ca/education-public-outreach (the RASC astronomy education website), and the RASC publication *Skyways*, by Mary Lou Whitehorne, an excellent astronomy guide for teachers. A French version, *Explorons l'astronomie*, is also available.

Countering Misconceptions
Surveys show that many basic astronomical concepts are misunderstood by most people. Examples of common misconceptions include the relative sizes and distances within the Solar System, the "reason for the seasons," and the cause of lunar phases. Poor understanding of these physical systems is often based on false logic (e.g. it is warmer in the summer because the Earth is closer to the Sun) and misleading diagrams (with a poorly chosen, or no existing scale) in common reference books. There is an excellent review and explanation of these and other misconceptions at the Private Universe Project: www.learner.org/teacherslab/pup—certainly worth checking out.

Many of these concepts are so basic that it is worth taking the time to teach them correctly. During learning activities, students' preconceptions can be monitored through conversations and observations. As teachers, we can make sure that these concepts are understood, and that the students can explain them from personal understanding—not just from memorization. This section of the Handbook is designed to do just that.

Igniting Creativity
Nearly every topic in astronomy fires up the imagination and engages a student's creativity. At first glance, while you may be uncertain how a handbook of historical facts and observing data could help you teach space science, the wealth of information found here can easily serve as a jumping-off point for delving into the curriculum. Each topic below is divided into two sections: **Minds-on** will show you where to get information and background pertaining to the specific topic for the classroom, and how it relates to teaching; **Hands-on** will suggest teaching activities to reinforce the concepts discussed in Minds-on, along with other resources.

The Sun
Minds-on: Students are often amazed to learn that the surface of the Sun is quite turbulent and always changing. The SOLAR OBSERVING section (p. 186) describes in detail the types of "blemishes" that can be seen on the surface of the Sun, as well as safe methods of observing the Sun. The SOLAR ACTIVITY section (p. 189) explains the effects that an unstable solar atmosphere can have on the Earth, while Roy Bishop's section on rainbows, halos, etc. (p. 194) examines some of the more common visual phenomena caused by the interaction of sunlight with water droplets and ice crystals in our own atmosphere.

Hands-on: Students can track the motion of the Sun throughout the course of the day, or the position of the Sun at the same time of day throughout the year. Likewise, sunrise and sunset times can be charted to try to find patterns (the times can be found on p. 205), and senior students can apply concepts of periodic motion. Building a sundial (see www.sundials.co.uk/projects.htm) can give students a sense of how the Sun is linked to our 24-hour clock. Viewing the Sun by projection is an easy way to search for sunspots in a classroom setting. See the link above or the Handbook section VIEWING A SOLAR ECLIPSE–A WARNING (p. 145) for a description of these methods. However, **NEVER** observe the Sun directly, especially by looking through binoculars or a telescope; permanent eye damage could result. Daily images of the Sun are available at **sohowww.nascom.nasa.gov.**

The Moon

Minds-on: Four hundred years ago, the Moon was one of Galileo's first telescopic targets. It is one of the easiest objects to observe as a class, and can often be found in the daytime sky! A detailed map of the Moon can be found on p. 148, with historical and geographical details. The sections on TIMES OF MOONRISE AND MOONSET (p. 150) and LUNAR OBSERVING (p. 158) can be used to help determine when the Moon can best be seen. The sections ECLIPSES IN 2018 (p. 126) and THE SKY MONTH BY MONTH (p. 98) can be consulted to learn if there are any special celestial events involving the Moon. Finally, the section TIDES AND THE EARTH-MOON SYSTEM (p. 179) gives an excellent review of the Moon's effects on Earth, to which many Canadian students can relate.

Hands-on: As for the Sun during the day, the appearance of the Moon can be sketched from night to night throughout the lunar month. Using the maps in this Handbook, students can learn to identify the prominent lunar features they saw and drew. With a light source to act as the Sun, a scale model of the Moon can be used to explain eclipses and the phases of the Moon (**www.exploratorium.edu/ronh/solar_system**). Pairing-up widely separated groups of students (**education.skype.com**), when a lunar eclipse is visible to one group but not the other, connects youth globally and provides an opportunity to share experiences of celestial events. Extending the modelling to the entire Solar System allows comparison of the size of the Moon with that of the satellites of other planets (p. 24) and even the planets and dwarf planets themselves (p. 22). Earth's satellite is one of the largest!

The Night Sky

Minds-on: In a sense, astronomy is the easiest strand of science to practice—simply go outside at night and look up! Star charts may be found in many books and magazines (see p. 10), as well as in the MAPS OF THE NIGHT SKY section (p. 339). Aside from finding the Moon, many people can identify constellations, a listing of which can be found on p. 270, and with images at **www.dibonsmith.com/constel.htm.** THE SKY MONTH BY MONTH (p. 98) will also give you a concise overview of what's up in the night sky during a particular time of the year.

Hands-on: Have the students create a planisphere, which they can use to locate objects in the sky ((National Research Council of Canada has a good one—see p. 5 of http://goo.gl/xl50hj). This can also be used to teach the proper way to read a star chart. Students can practice the science of observation by drawing what they see in the night sky, including the horizon and compass points, and by keeping an observing logbook (p. 86). Even the study of light pollution (p. 79) can be an educational experience, relating astronomy to the environment; see *JRASC, 96* (February 2002), p. 24, and the Astronomical Society of the Pacific (**tinyurl.com/4ygwrgu**).

The Solar System, Including Comets, Dwarf Planets, and Minor Planets

Minds-on: The Solar System is our celestial neighborhood. Our planetary neighbors are introduced below, but who else resides in the 'hood? The PRINCIPAL ELEMENTS OF THE SOLAR SYSTEM (p. 22) and the VOYAGES IN THE SOLAR SYSTEM (p. 36) are an excellent introduction to the history of exploration of the Solar System, as well as what types of objects are believed to be typical in stellar systems. THE DWARF PLANETS (p. 241) and THE BRIGHTEST MINOR PLANETS (p. 244) can be helpful in finding those bodies in the night sky (most only need binoculars), while a table of brightness, sizes, and distances from the Sun can be found on p. 23. The section on METEORITE IMPACT CRATERS OF NORTH AMERICA (p. 260) brings the idea of meteorite impacts a little closer to home for students.

Hands-on: The "Toilet-paper Solar System" (**www.nthelp.com/eer/HOAtpss.html**) and the "Earth as a Peppercorn" model (Guy Ottewell, see **tinyurl.com/2ooch5**) are both excellent, hands-on activities for modelling the vast distances in the

Solar System. Likewise, students can design their own scale model using www.exploratorium.edu/ronh/solar_system. Students can simulate meteoric impacts in the class with the "craters-in-the-classroom" activity (see http://goo.gl/RIVAMx) and can even build a comet out of dry ice, sand, and other organic materials, with instructions found at www.noao.edu/education/crecipe.html.

The Planets
Minds-on: Learning about "another world" in the classroom and then seeing that planet in the night sky serves to stimulate student interest and fire up their imaginations. THE SKY MONTH BY MONTH (p. 98) tells us when the various planets are visible, and these are sure to be the highlight of any outdoor observing session with students. THE PLANETS FOR 2018 (p. 211) gives more information about each planet, as does the tabular data starting on p. 22. A history of the theories pertaining to the motion of the planets is provided in the ORBITAL MOTION section (p. 27).
Hands-on: Using the information summarized from THE PLANETS IN 2018 (p. 211), students can "design an alien" that could live on a particular planet, given the surface temperature, atmospheric composition, surface features, etc. This could also be adapted for older students by having them design a human colony on another planet. It is certainly true that a picture can be worth a thousand words—many of the resources listed on p. 10 and p. 15 help bring these other worlds into the classroom. Finally, Exploratorium has calculators for one's age and weight on other planets at www.exploratorium.edu/ronh, as well as other activities.

Is a Telescope Necessary?
Binoculars and telescopes can be useful but are not essential; much interesting astronomy can be done with the unaided eye. However, binoculars are often available and should be used when helpful. See the section BINOCULARS (p. 60) for a guide to their selection and use. The inexpensive, make-it-yourself *Project STAR* telescopes and *Galileoscopes* (www.galileoscope.org) are highly recommended. See TELESCOPE PARAMETERS (p. 49) and the pages following for more on observing with telescopes.

Resources
In addition to the list of reading material below, and the RASC's *Skyways*, you may be able to make use of the following:
(1) See the SELECTED OBSERVATORIES, *STAR PARTIES*, AND PLANETARIA section in this Handbook (p. 11). Take your students to visit one of these.
(2) The Astronomical League offers a wide variety of activities that might be interesting to you and your students. For example, a member might be willing to visit your class and demonstrate a telescope (see pp. 9 and 82). The Astronomical Society of the Pacific's *Project ASTRO How-To Manual* can facilitate such visits. See www.astrosociety.org/edu/astro/astropubs/how_to.html.

Astronomical Society of the Pacific, 390 Ashton Ave, San Francisco CA 94112, USA; 415-337-1100. In addition to their excellent educational material, the ASP publishes a free quarterly teachers' newsletter; download current and back issues from www.astrosociety.org/publications/universe-in-the-classroom.

Project STAR Hands-on Science Materials, Science First/STARLAB, 86475 Gene Lasserre Blvd, Yulee FL 32097, USA; 800-537-8703; www.starlab.com. Unique, high-quality, low-cost materials for introducing students (and teachers) to astronomy.

SkyNews, 203–4920 Dundas Street W, Toronto ON M9A 1B7; 866-759-0005; www.skynews.ca, published bimonthly by the RASC and included as a membership benefit. General astronomy from a Canadian perspective.

The Universe at Your Fingertips, and *More Universe at Your Fingertips*, edited by Andrew Fraknoi et al., Astronomical Society of the Pacific, 390 Ashton Ave, San Francisco CA 94112, USA. Another excellent collection of teaching activities and resources for grades 3–12. See also www.astrosociety.org/education/activities/astroacts.html.

BASIC DATA

TERMINOLOGY AND SYMBOLS

COORDINATE SYSTEMS

Astronomical positions are usually measured in a system based on the *celestial poles* and *celestial equator*, the intersections of Earth's rotation axis and equatorial plane, respectively, and the infinite sphere of the sky. *Right ascension* (RA or α) is measured in hours (h), minutes (m), and seconds (s) of time, eastward along the celestial equator from the vernal equinox (see below). *Declination* (Dec or δ) is measured in degrees (°), minutes ('), and seconds (") of arc, northward (N or +) or southward (S or −) from the celestial equator toward the north or south celestial pole.

Positions can also be measured in a system based on the *ecliptic*, the intersection of Earth's orbital plane and the infinite sphere of the sky. The Sun appears to move eastward along the ecliptic during the year. *Longitude* is measured eastward along the ecliptic from the vernal equinox; *latitude* is measured at right angles to the ecliptic, northward or southward toward the north or south ecliptic pole. The *vernal equinox* is one of the two intersections of the ecliptic and the celestial equator; it is the one at which the Sun crosses the celestial equator moving from south to north.

An object is *in conjunction with the Sun* if it has the same longitude as the Sun and *at opposition* if its longitude differs from that of the Sun by 180°. Mercury and Venus are in *superior* conjunction when they are more distant than the Sun and in *inferior* conjunction when they are nearer than the Sun (see the diagram on the next page). An object is *stationary* when it reaches an extreme longitude.

Two *nonsolar* objects are in conjunction if they have the same RA. Generally, but not always, close mutual approaches correspond to conjunctions; following Jean Meeus, we use the term *quasi-conjunction* to denote close (< 5°) nonconjunctional approaches.

If an object crosses the ecliptic moving northward, it is at the *ascending node* of its orbit; if it crosses the ecliptic moving southward, it is at the *descending node*.

Elongation is the geocentric angle between an object and the Sun, or between a satellite and its primary, measured in the plane formed by Earth and the other two bodies.

SYMBOLS

Solar System Objects

☉	Sun	♀	Venus	♃	Jupiter	♆	Neptune
☾	Moon	⊕	Earth	♄	Saturn	♇	Pluto
☿	Mercury	♂	Mars	⛢	Uranus		

Signs of the Zodiac

♈	Aries	0°	♌	Leo	120°	♐	Sagittarius	240°
♉	Taurus	30°	♍	Virgo	150°	♑	Capricornus	270°
♊	Gemini	60°	♎	Libra	180°	♒	Aquarius	300°
♋	Cancer	90°	♏	Scorpius	210°	♓	Pisces	330°

The Greek Alphabet

A, α.....alpha *(alfa)**	H, η........eta	N, ν...... nu *(niu)*	T, τ....... tau
B, β .....beta	Θ, θ, ϑ....theta *(teta)*	Ξ, ξ ...... xi *(ksi)*	Y, υ...... upsilon
Γ, γ......gamma	I, ι..........iota	O, o...... omicron	Φ, φ...... phi
Δ, δ .....delta	K, κ........kappa	Π, π...... pi	X, χ...... chi *(khi)*
E, ε......epsilon *(eps)*	Λ, λ........lambda	P, ρ....... rho	Ψ, ψ ..... psi
Z, ζ......zeta	M, μ ....mu *(miu)*	Σ, σ ...... sigma	Ω, ω ..... omega

*Variant spellings are used in some online search databases (see www.aavso.org/greek-letters).

SOLAR SYSTEM GEOMETRY

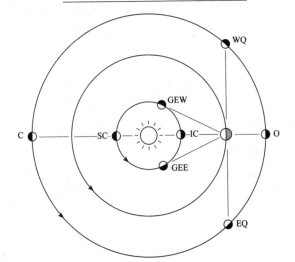

The diagram is a simplified view of the Solar System, from the north side. Earth is shown (middle orbit) together with an inferior planet (i.e. Mercury or Venus) and a superior planet (e.g. Mars). Four special geometrical configurations of the inferior planet relative to Earth are shown; in counterclockwise chronological sequence they are inferior conjunction (IC), greatest elongation west (GEW), superior conjunction (SC), and greatest elongation east (GEE). Four special configurations of the superior planet relative to Earth are also shown; in clockwise chronological sequence they are opposition (O), eastern quadrature (EQ), conjunction with the Sun (C), and western quadrature (WQ).

HANDY SKY MEASURES

Angular measure in the sky can be quickly estimated using the fingers of an outstretched arm, or by comparing with the star separations in the Big Dipper.

(Adapted from *Nightwatch* by Terence Dickinson, see Handbook p. 10.)

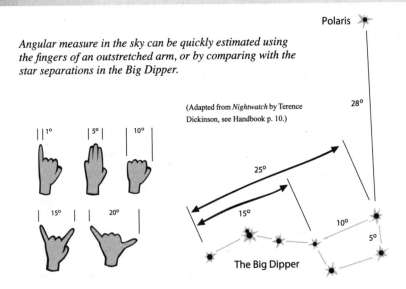

ASTRONOMICAL PRECESSION
BY DAVID TURNER AND ROY BISHOP

Physical causes of precession: In addition to causing oceanic tides, the Moon and (to a lesser extent) the Sun exert a tidal torque on Earth's equatorial bulge, tending to align Earth's equatorial plane with the Moon and Sun. The axis of the spinning Earth responds, not by tilting to achieve that alignment, but by slowly moving in a conical path, a motion called *precession*. The precession of a rotating body, be it a toy top or planet Earth, appears strange or counterintuitive only because we naively tend to assume that the body should behave in the same way that it would if it were not spinning. Once the spin is acknowledged, it becomes apparent that the various parts of the body are moving as expected, according to Newton's second law of motion. The off-center support force on a tilted, spinning, toy top on a table applies a torque tending to increase the tilt, and the resulting precession is in the same rotational sense as the spin. The tidal torque on Earth tends to decrease the tilt, so Earth's precession is opposite to its spin. Although the other planets have an almost negligible tidal effect on Earth, they do cause the plane of Earth's orbit, the ecliptic, to wobble a small amount (see **Earth's rotation relative to the equinox,** p. 40). As a result of the combined precession of the equator and precession of the ecliptic, the equinoxes (the intersection points of the celestial equator and the ecliptic) drift westward (retrograde) about 50.29″ per year (a period of approximately 25 800 years).

Coordinates of celestial objects: As a consequence of precession, the locations of the celestial poles continually move along circles of radius 23.4° around the north and south ecliptic poles; consequently, the RA and Dec coordinates of even a "fixed" celestial body continually change, and must be referred to the *epoch* (i.e. Julian year date) of the equatorial grid used. Most of the positions in this Handbook are referred to J2000.0 for compatability with current star charts and atlases. In the event that a conversion of coordinates is required from one epoch to another, use the precession formulae found in ANGULAR RELATIONS, p. 32. To the accuracy that amateur computer-controlled or Go To telescopes are capable of pointing, precession may not be a significant factor, although it is always advisable to keep software and firmware up to date.

Precession and the constellations: The vernal equinox was located in the constellation Gemini 7500 years ago, in Taurus 4500 years ago, and in Aries 3000 years ago. It moved into Pisces from the "first point of Aries" around the beginning of the Christian era 2000 years ago, at roughly the same time as Hipparchus discovered precession of the equinoxes.

Precession causes stars to apparently move almost parallel to the ecliptic, relative to the vernal equinox, but our civil calendar (since the inception of the Gregorian calendar) is regularly adjusted so that the annual seasons are synchronized with the months. Consequently, *where* and *when* the constellations appear in the sky slowly change over the years. The faint stars in the 105-degree-long constellation of Hydra, the Water Snake, lay along the celestial equator 4600 years ago, but are inclined more than 30° away from the celestial equator today. With so few stars of any significance, it could only have originated as a navigational aid, helping ancient sailors steer an east-west course. In 12 000 years, the "summer" constellation Sagittarius will appear high in Northern Hemisphere winter skies, while Orion will barely rise in the summer sky.

The *shape* of a constellation is affected mainly by the relative proper motions of its member stars in the sky, and this effect on sky lore can be more interesting. The bright stars of Ursa Major, for example, bore a resemblance to the outline of a bear's head 125 000 years ago; and 4000 years ago, the bright star Arcturus was located near the center of Boötes rather than at its southern tip.

PRINCIPAL ELEMENTS OF THE SOLAR SYSTEM

PHYSICAL ELEMENTS

Object (Pronun.)	Equatorial Diameter km	Oblate- ness	Mass Earth=1*	Den- sity t/m³	Grav- ity† Earth=1	Escape Speed† km/s	Rotation Period d	Inclina- tion‡ °	Albedo
Sun	1 392 530	0	332 946.0	1.41	27.9	617.5	25–35††		
Mercury (mûr'kū–rē)	4 879	0	0.055 274	5.43	0.38	4.2	58.6462	0.0	0.11
Venus (vē'nŭs)	12 104	0	0.815 01	5.24	0.90	10.4	–243.0185	2.6	0.65
Earth (ûrth)	12 756	1/298	1	5.513	1.00	11.2	0.99727	23.4	0.37
Moon	3 475	0	0.012 300	3.34	0.17	2.4	27.32166	6.7	0.12
Mars (màrz)	6 792	1/170	0.107 45	3.93	0.38	5.0	1.02596	25.2	0.15
Ceres^A (cē'rēz)	952	1/15	0.000 157	2.08	0.028	0.5	0.3781	10.6	0.07
Jupiter (jōō'pĭ–tēr)	142 984 ‡‡	1/15	317.83	1.33	2.53	59.5	0.4135†††	3.1	0.52
Saturn (sát'ûrn)	120 536 ‡‡	1/10	95.161	0.69	1.06	35.5	0.44401	26.7	0.47
Uranus^B (yûr'à–nŭs)	51 118 ‡‡	1/49	14.536	1.27	0.90	21.3	–0.71833	82.2	0.51
Neptune^C (nĕp'tyōōn)	49 528 ‡‡	1/59	17.148	1.64	1.14	23.5	0.67125	28.3	0.41
Pluto^A (plōō'tō)	2 390	0?	0.002 184	1.82	0.067	1.3	–6.3872	60.4	0.30
Eris^A (ĕr'ĭs)	2 400	0?	0.002 795	2.52	0.08	1.4	1.0800	44.0	0.86

*5.972 × 10²⁴ kg †At the equator ‡ Inclination of equator to orbital plane †† Depending on latitude ‡‡ At 1 atmosphere (101.325 kPa) ††† For the most rapidly rotating part, the equatorial region

^A Dwarf planet (see 2006 IAU Resolution B5). *Ceres* discovered by Giuseppe Piazzi, 1801 Jan. 1; *Pluto* discovered by Clyde Tombaugh, 1930 Feb. 18; *Eris* discovered by M. Brown et al., 2005 Jan. 5
^B Discovered by William Herschel, 1781 Mar. 13
^C Position predicted by Le Verrier (independently by Adams) and located by Johann G. Galle, 1846 Sep. 23
Pronunciation guide: à gàgà; ē wē; ĕ mĕt; ē makēr; ī bĭt; ō gō; ōō mōōn; û ûnite; ŭ sŭn; û ûrn

OSCULATING ORBITAL ELEMENTS FOR 2018

The tables at the right give the orbital elements of the planets, three dwarf planets, and the 25 brightest minor planets, from the *Astronomical Almanac*. At any given time or "epoch," six basic quantities determine each body's elliptical orbit, for example:

(1) the mean distance from the Sun, a, equal to the semimajor axis of the ellipse;
(2) the eccentricity e of the ellipse;
(3) the inclination i of the orbital plane to the ecliptic;
(4) the longitude Ω of the ascending node of the orbital plane on the ecliptic;
(5) the longitude $\tilde{\omega}$ of perihelion;
(6) the body's mean longitude L at the given epoch.

The date of the ecliptic and equinox used to measure the last four quantities must also be specified, and may be different from the given epoch. Other, equivalent, parameters may be substituted: the distance q of perihelion in place of a; the argument of perihelion, $\omega = \tilde{\omega} - \Omega$, in place of $\tilde{\omega}$; or the mean anomaly, $M = L - \tilde{\omega}$, or time T of perihelion in place of L. Once six fundamental quantities are known, all other attributes of the orbit of the body, such as the sidereal period P and synodic period S, can be derived.

If the body followed a perfectly elliptical orbit as predicted by classical orbital mechanics, then for a fixed ecliptic and equinox the first five quantities above would be constant over time. However, because of perturbations caused by the gravitational influence of other bodies, the orbits are not perfectly elliptical; hence the orbital elements depend on the epoch. The given *osculating* elements can be used to determine an elliptical orbit that is a close approximation to the actual path of the body for times near the given epoch. Elements for two epochs are provided for each planet, 240 days (roughly 8 months) apart; the elements can be linearly interpolated to other epochs in 2018 for precision of a few arcseconds (typically 1″ or 2″), noting that multiples of 360° must be added to the second value of L if the planet completes one (or more) orbits between those dates. For selected *dwarf planets* and minor planets, elements for one epoch (2018 Oct. 9) are given, with resulting precision of about 1′ (for more information, see ssd.jpl.nasa.gov).

HELIOCENTRIC OSCULATING ORBITAL ELEMENTS FOR 2018
REFERRED TO THE MEAN ECLIPTIC AND EQUINOX OF J2000.0

Planet	Epoch Julian Date 245...	Mean Distance* a au	Eccen-tricity e	Incli-nation i °	Long. of Asc. Node Ω °	Long. of Perihelion ω̃ °	Long. at Epoch L °	Sidereal Period P y	Synodic Period† S d
For Julian Date 245 8160.5 (2018 Feb. 11.0) and Julian Date 245 8400.5 (2018 Oct. 9.0)									
Mercury	8160.5	0.3870985	0.205638	7.0040	48.3083	77.4829	325.1175	0.2408	115.9
	8400.5	0.3870981	0.205648	7.0039	48.3078	77.4866	227.2770	0.2408	
Venus	8160.5	0.723331	0.006746	3.3944	76.6331	131.6533	124.1110	0.6156	584.9
	8400.5	0.723328	0.006786	3.3945	76.6285	131.3854	148.6197	0.6155	
Earth‡	8160.5	0.999977	0.016666	0.0024	174.4	102.8838	140.7619	1	—
	8400.5	0.999996	0.016713	0.0025	174.8	103.0051	17.3079	1	
Mars	8160.5	1.523768	0.093389	1.8483	49.5084	336.1114	222.1895	1.8847	778
	8400.5	1.523682	0.093352	1.8482	49.5040	336.1921	347.9575	1.8774	
Jupiter	8160.5	5.202290	0.048875	1.3037	100.5136	14.2211	224.0822	11.8549	398.9
	8400.5	5.202523	0.048847	1.3037	100.5150	14.1765	244.0281	11.8822	
Saturn	8160.5	9.566847	0.052140	2.4868	113.5915	93.5317	271.2526	29.5709	378
	8400.5	9.570015	0.051808	2.4864	113.5941	93.0898	279.2962	29.6009	
Uranus	8160.5	19.111070	0.050169	0.7714	74.0250	174.3084	30.7632	82.8938	369.7
	8400.5	19.120760	0.049374	0.7711	74.0494	174.5012	33.5243	83.0896	
Neptune	8160.5	30.015980	0.006027	1.7719	131.8116	50.456	344.2054	161.7864	367.5
	8400.5	30.061640	0.006575	1.7714	131.8008	37.338	345.6128	162.1269	

*1 au = 1.496 × 10^{11} m † Synodic period = (product of Ps of two planets) ÷ (difference of the Ps)
Tabular values are relative to Earth ‡ Values are actually for the Earth–Moon barycenter

Dwarf Planet or Minor Planet	Absolute Mag.*	Diam. km	Mean Distance a au	Eccen-tricity e	Incli-nation i °	Long. of Asc. Node Ω °	Long. of Perihelion ω̃ °	Long. at Epoch L °	Sidereal Period P y
For epoch Julian Date 245 8400.5 (2018 Oct. 9.0)									
Eris	−1.20	2 400	67.781	0.440	44.176	35.890	151.690	114.767	557.4
Pluto	−0.40	2 390	39.519	0.252	17.110	110.297	114.498	242.194	252.7
4 Vesta	3.20	512	**2.3614**	**0.0888**	**7.142**	**103.812**	**254.515**	**296.071**	**3.6289**
1 Ceres	3.34	952	2.768	0.075	10.594	80.308	73.219	23.267	4.603
2 Pallas	4.13	524	**2.7723**	**0.2304**	**34.838**	**173.081**	**123.098**	**140.114**	**4.6162**
15 Eunomia	5.28	320	**2.6457**	**0.1860**	**11.745**	**292.952**	**31.234**	**269.020**	**4.3036**
3 Juno	5.33	274	2.6693	0.2570	12.989	169.857	58.011	47.722	4.3615
10 Hygiea	5.43	444	3.1410	0.1126	3.832	283.210	235.436	352.302	5.5667
7 Iris	5.51	211	**2.3852**	**0.2313**	**5.524**	**259.563**	**44.831**	**131.725**	**3.6840**
6 Hebe	5.71	190	2.4254	0.2030	14.737	138.643	18.484	52.462	3.7774
16 Psyche	5.90	239	**2.9262**	**0.1336**	**3.095**	**150.088**	**18.504**	**267.830**	**5.0058**
9 Metis	6.28	209	**2.3859**	**0.1230**	**5.577**	**68.910**	**75.298**	**298.684**	**3.6855**
14 Irene	6.30	180	2.5854	0.1667	9.122	86.124	183.992	301.492	4.1573
22 Kalliope	6.45	181	2.9131	0.0983	13.719	66.053	61.604	219.186	4.9720
8 Flora	6.49	138	**2.2010**	**0.1569**	**5.887**	**110.899**	**36.157**	**170.705**	**3.2656**
20 Massalia	6.50	145	2.4087	0.1422	0.709	206.108	102.701	167.866	3.7385
18 Melpomene	6.51	138	2.2963	0.2181	10.129	150.440	18.314	228.999	3.4799
11 Parthenope	6.55	153	2.4522	0.1006	4.630	125.558	321.311	188.705	3.8401
13 Egeria	6.74	208	2.5770	0.0847	16.537	43.231	123.856	263.589	4.1369
5 Astraea	6.85	120	2.5739	0.1912	5.367	141.581	140.299	14.905	4.1296
23 Thalia	6.95	108	2.6257	0.2351	10.114	66.847	127.496	56.983	4.2549
24 Themis	7.08	175	3.1369	0.1249	0.752	35.936	142.860	102.609	5.5561
19 Fortuna	7.13	225	2.4417	0.1585	1.574	211.144	33.199	178.895	3.8155
12 Victoria	7.24	113	2.3343	0.2201	8.373	235.411	305.046	23.129	3.5667
21 Lutetia	7.35	98	2.4359	0.1637	3.064	80.866	330.723	263.227	3.8019
26 Proserpina	7.50	95	2.6543	0.0902	3.563	45.778	239.204	299.358	4.3245
17 Thetis	7.76	90	2.4704	0.1329	5.591	125.552	261.752	154.346	3.8829
25 Phocaea	7.83	75	2.4004	0.2545	21.605	214.135	304.396	64.266	3.7193

*Ordered by absolute magnitude, which is the hypothetical magnitude at zero phase angle with both Earth and Sun at 1 au distance. At opposition, the body will appear dimmer than this value by 2–20 mag., depending on the actual distance. Note that the largest are not always the brightest. **Bold** = opposition in or near 2018 at mag. 10.5 or brighter (see p. 245 for the ephemerides of these and some others).

NATURAL SATELLITES OF THE PLANETS
BY PHILIP D. NICHOLSON

Of the 175 known natural satellites of the 8 Solar System planets, all but 3 orbit the giant planets. At latest count, Jupiter has 69, Saturn has 62 (though one reported in 2009 may be no more than a temporary dust cloud in the rings), Uranus has 27, and Neptune has 14. With a few exceptions, these moons may be divided into three groups, which presumably reflect their different origins. Closest to the planets are small ring moons, less than 200 km in diameter and with strong evolutionary and dynamical connections to the planetary ring systems. Many of these objects were discovered during the Voyager flybys of 1979–1989, and all are very difficult to observe from Earth. They include the Saturnian shepherd satellites Prometheus and Pandora, and the co-orbital satellites Janus and Epimetheus, all of which have been photographed from Earth (or by the *Hubble Space Telescope*) when the rings turn edge-on.

Next come the larger "regular" satellites in near-circular orbits in or near their planets' equatorial planes, thought to have been formed in situ via accretion in circumplanetary disks at the dawn of the Solar System. This group extends out to Callisto, Iapetus, Oberon, and Proteus, but does not include Triton, which is now thought to have been captured. There are numerous orbital resonances among the regular satellites, for example, Io:Europa:Ganymede (1:2:4), Mimas:Tethys (1:2), Enceladus:Dione (1:2), and Titan:Hyperion (3:4); the origin of these resonances is generally ascribed to orbital expansion driven by tidal interactions with Jupiter or Saturn. Temporary capture in similar resonances in the past may have been responsible for the anomalously large inclinations of Miranda and (perhaps) Naiad. Tidal-energy dissipation within Io is responsible for this moon's spectacular volcanic activity, and similar heating at a lower level may still occur within Europa and Enceladus.

The third and outermost group—and the group whose numbers have increased so much in recent years—comprises the "irregular"satellites. These generally small bodies (2–200 km in diameter, except for 340-km Nereid) move in quite eccentric orbits at large inclinations. Their orbits are not random; rather, they fall into several more-or-less tight clusters in semimajor axis and inclination: three or four at Jupiter (all but one retrograde), and three at Saturn (one retrograde). These clusters are believed to be due to collisional disruptions of a smaller number of original objects captured from heliocentric orbits. The situation at Uranus and Neptune remains unclear, although there are now nine Uranian irregulars (all but one retrograde) and six Neptunians (three retrograde). The orbits of the irregular satellites, along with that of Earth's Moon, are subject to strong solar gravitational perturbations, and thus maintain approximately fixed inclinations to their respective planet's orbital planes rather than to their equators.

Of the five officially recognized dwarf planets, three have satellites, for a total of eight: Pluto has five, Haumea has two, and Eris has one.

The *New Horizons* spacecraft flew by the Pluto system in July 2015 and continues to transmit data acquired during the rapid flyby. The current diameter estimates of Pluto (2380 ±2 km) and its satellites are Charon (1210 km), Hydra and Nix (55 & 50 km in longest direction, respectively), Kerberos and Styx (19 & 16 km in longest direction, respectively). In late 2015, *New Horizons* was directed toward Kuiper belt object 2014 MU69, with an anticipated flyby date of 2019 Jan. 1.

The following table OBSERVABLE SATELLITES OF THE PLANETS (updated by Chris Malicki for 2018) contains only those satellites considered to be visually observable using typical amateur telescopes. The level of difficulty ranges from "easy" to "very challenging." For up-to-date orbital and physical elements of all the planetary satellites, see ssd.jpl.nasa.gov/?satellites.

OBSERVABLE SATELLITES OF THE PLANETS

Name (pronunciation)[1]	Mean Diameter km	GM[2] km³/s²	Density gm/cm³	Visual Mag.[3]	Albedo	Mean Dist. from Planet 10³ km	Orbital Period d	Eccentricity	Orbital Incl.[4] °	Discovery
Satellite of Earth										
Moon (mo͞on)	3475	4902.801 (1)	3.34	−12.7	0.12	384.4	27.322	0.055	5.16	—
Satellites of Mars[5]										
I Phobos (fō′bŏs)	22	0.000711 (1)	1.9	11.4	0.07	9.38	0.319	0.0151	1.08	A. Hall, 1877
II Deimos (dī′mōs)	12	0.000099 (2)	1.5	12.5	0.07	23.46	1.262	0.0002	1.79	A. Hall, 1877
Satellites of Jupiter										
V Amalthea[6] (ăm″l-thē′á)	167	0.14 (3)	0.85	14.1	0.09	181.4	0.498	0.0032	0.38	E. Barnard, 1892
I Io[7] (ī′ō)	3643	5959.92 (1)	3.53	5.0	0.63	421.8	1.769	0.0041	0.04	Galileo, 1610
II Europa[7] (ū-rō′pá)	3122	3202.74 (1)	3.01	5.3	0.67	671.1	3.551	0.0094	0.47	Galileo, 1610
III Ganymede[7] (găn′ē-mēd′)	5262	9887.83 (2)	1.94	4.6	0.43	1070.4	7.155	0.0013	0.18	Galileo, 1610
IV Callisto (ká-lĭs′tō)	4821	7179.29 (1)	1.83	5.7	0.17	1882.7	16.689	0.0074	0.19	Galileo, 1610
VI Himalia[8] (hĭm′á-lĭ-á)	170	0.45	2.6	14.2	0.04	11 460.0	250.6	0.159	28.6	C. Perrine, 1904

[1] Pronunciation guide: ă tăp; â câre; ä däte; à gägà; ē wē; ĕ mĕt; ī īce; ĭ bĭt; ō gō; ŏ hŏt; ô ôrb; ŏŏ mo͞on; ŭ ŭp; ū cūte; û ûrn
For some background on the names of the satellites, visit planetarynames.wr.usgs.gov/Page/Planets.

[2] The satellite's *standard gravitational constant*. Divide by G for mass in kg. The numbers in parentheses are uncertainties in the last digit.

[3] Visual magnitude at mean opposition distance.

[4] Inclinations are relative to the *Laplace Plane*, which for inner satellites (those closer than 100 planetary radii) is close to the planet's *equator*, but for most outer satellites (such as Himalia) is close to the planet's *orbital plane*. For our Moon, the inclination relative to Earth's orbital plane is 5°; relative to Earth's equator it varies between 18° and 29° in an 18.61-year cycle.

[5] The Martian satellites are so close to the primary, the use of an *occulting bar eyepiece* is recommended. For instructions on how to modify an eyepiece in this way, see www.skyandtelescope.com/observing/the-martian-moons-in-200708.

[6] Amalthea, the last satellite to be discovered visually, is but one example of a *very challenging* visual object, owing to its proximity to Jupiter. Amateurs using large professional telescopes have observed Amalthea and other challenging natural satellites not shown in this table.

[7] The revolutions of this trio of Jovian satellites form a *Laplace resonance*; longitudes satisfy $L(\text{Io}) − 3L(\text{Europa}) + 2L(\text{Ganymede}) ≈ 180°$. Also, the mean motions are such that the three periods are nearly 1:2:4.

[8] Himalia is an *irregular satellite* with a highly inclined and highly eccentric orbit that carries it well out of Jupiter's equatorial plane.

OBSERVABLE SATELLITES OF THE PLANETS (continued)

Name (pronunciation)	Mean Diameter km	GM km³/s²	Density gm/cm³	Visual Mag.	Albedo	Mean Dist. from Planet 10³ km	Orbital Period d	Eccentricity	Orbital Incl. °	Discovery
Satellites of Saturn										
I Mimas[9],[10] (mī′mǎs)	396	2.5026 (6)	1.15	12.8	0.6	185.5	0.942	0.0196	1.57	W. Herschel, 1789
II Enceladus[10] (ĕn-sĕl′ȧ-dŭs)	504	7.20 (1)	1.61	11.8	1.0	238.0	1.370	0.0000	0.00	W. Herschel, 1789
III Tethys[10] (tē′thĭs)	1066	41.207 (4)	0.97	10.3	0.8	294.7	1.888	0.0001	1.09	J. Cassini, 1684
IV Dione[10] (dī-ō′nē)	1123	73.115 (2)	1.48	10.4	0.6	377.4	2.737	0.0022	0.03	J. Cassini, 1684
V Rhea (rē′à)	1529	153.943 (4)	1.23	9.7	0.6	527.1	4.518	0.0002	0.33	J. Cassini, 1672
VI Titan (tī′t'n)	5149[11]	8978.138 (2)	1.88	8.4	0.2	1221.8	15.945	0.0288	0.31	C. Huygens, 1655
VII Hyperion (hī-pēr′ĭ-ŏn)	270	0.37 (1)	0.54	14.4	0.3	1500.9	21.277	0.0232	0.62	Bond et al.[12], 1848
VIII Iapetus[13] (ī-ăp′ĕ-tŭs)	1471	120.504 (8)	1.08	11.0v	0.05–0.5	3560.9	79.330	0.0293	8.30	J. Cassini, 1671
Satellites of Uranus[14]										
I Ariel (âr′ē-ĕl)	1158	86. (5)	1.59	13.7	0.39	190.9	2.520	0.0012	0.04	W. Lassell, 1851
II Umbriel (ŭm′brē-ĕl′)	1169	82. (5)	1.46	14.5	0.21	266.0	4.144	0.0039	0.13	W. Lassell, 1851
III Titania (tī′tä′nē-à)	1578	228. (5)	1.66	13.5	0.27	436.3	8.706	0.0011	0.08	W. Herschel, 1787
IV Oberon (ō′bà-rŏn)	1523	192. (7)	1.56	13.7	0.23	583.5	13.463	0.0014	0.07	W. Herschel, 1787
Satellites of Neptune										
I Triton (trī′t'n)	2707	1428. (2)	2.06	13.5	0.72	354.8	5.877	0.0000	156.9	W. Lassell, 1846

[9] Mimas is another *very challenging* object, best observed when Saturn's rings are edge-on, so their glare is reduced.
[10] The orbital periods of the pair Mimas:Tethys show a near-1:2 resonance, as do Enceladus:Dione.
[11] As seen in the eyepiece, Titan's cloud-top diameter is 5550 km.
[12] W. Bond, G. Bond, and W. Lassell
[13] The highly variable magnitude of Iapetus is due to its dark and bright hemispheres, tidally locked to Saturn (see p. 237).
[14] Best within 6 weeks of opposition. An occulting-bar eyepiece is recommended for Ariel and Umbriel.

ORBITAL MOTION
BY ROY BISHOP

Whether you are observing a distant galaxy, the stars in a globular cluster, the waltz of Jupiter's Galilean satellites, the drift of the Moon during an occultation, or merely uttering an expletive as an artificial satellite passes through the field of your camera, an understanding of orbital motion is central to an appreciation of the heavens.

Among early cosmologies were those of **Aristotle** (340 BC) and **Ptolemy** (published as the *Almagest*, c. 150 CE), and the superior heliocentric model proposed 1_2^3 by **Copernicus** (*De revolutionibus*, 1543). These attempts at modelling the heavens used complex systems of circles upon circles, of eccentric deferents and epicycles. John Milton, a contemporary of Galileo, wrote the following lines in his epic poem "Paradise Lost" (1674), possibly expressing his discontent with the Ptolemaic and Copernican systems of compounded circles:

> *From Man or Angel the great Architect*
> *Did wisely to conceal, and not divulge*
> *His secrets to be scann'd by them who ought*
> *Rather admire; or if they list to try*
> *Conjecture, he his Fabric of the Heav'ns*
> *Hath left to thir disputes, perhaps to move*
> *His laughter at thir quaint Opinions wide*
> *Hereafter, when they come to model Heav'n*
> *And calculate the Stars, how they will wield*
> *The mighty frame, how build, unbuild, contrive*
> *To save appearances, how gird the Sphere*
> *With Centric and Eccentric scribbl'd o'er,*
> *Cycle and Epicycle, Orb in Orb.*

Kepler, using observations accumulated by Tycho Brahe, broke with the 2000-year preoccupation with circles when he discovered that the planets move in an elegantly simple way along elliptical paths (*Astronomia nova*, 1609). Although he had discovered *how* the planets move, Kepler was unable to explain quantitatively *why* they move in this way.

Galileo strongly supported the Copernican heliocentric Universe (*Dialogue on the Two Chief World Systems*, 1632) and achieved brilliant insights concerning the motion of objects (*Two New Sciences*, 1638); however, he ignored Kepler's ellipses and did not apply his mechanics to the sky.

Newton united the heavens and Earth by showing that the laws governing motions on Earth also apply to the heavens. In his *Principia* (1687), the greatest book in the physical sciences, Newton presented his three laws of motion and the first ever physical force law, his law of gravitation. He used these to explain the motions not only of bodies on Earth, but also of the planets, comets, stars, equinoxes, tides, etc. Newton was the first to realize that the Moon is falling toward Earth just as freely as does an apple, and that the elliptical orbit of the center of mass of the Earth–Moon system is the path that results (as he described it) as these two bodies free-fall under the action of the Sun's gravitational force.

In popular-level explanations of phenomena involving rotary motion, such as spinning wheels, automobiles on corners, tides, and orbital motion, "centrifugal force" is usually invoked. That is unfortunate because centrifugal force is a fiction, and its use in a popular description of motion obscures understanding.[*]

---

[*]Brief descriptions of tides in the Newtonian context (without invoking the obfuscating centrifugal force!) and in the context of the general theory of relativity appear on p. 179 and p. 183, respectively.

In the case of orbits, the common misconception is that the inward gravitational force is balanced by an outward "centrifugal force." Newton's view is simpler: There is only one force, the inward pull of gravity. There is *no physical agent* to cause an outward force. (Note that forces cause accelerations, not vice versa.) Also, if there *were* an outward supporting force, the two forces would cancel and, as Galileo realized, the body would then move along a straight line. If you choose a rotating reference frame and then ignore the rotation (mistake no. 1), you have to pretend there is a "centrifugal force" (mistake no. 2) in order to make sense of motions occurring within this frame. The two mistakes effectively cancel, but the description has been made needlessly complicated, and if you do not realize what you have done, you do not understand the motion.

Einstein's general theory of relativity (GTR) of 1915 superseded Newton's description of gravity. The arbiter of which is a good theory and which theory is wrong is nature. Newton's laws are accurate enough for most of NASA's calculations, but they do not work exactly. For example, if the computer programs used in the Global Positioning System (GPS) were based on Newton's gravitation, the system would be a multibillion-dollar boondoggle. Einstein's conception of gravitation is essential to the operation of this satellite-based navigation system. In the case of strong gravitation and/or speeds approaching the speed of light, Newton's laws fail dramatically. The GTR may be wrong too, but so far it has passed all experimental tests. Science does not hie after ultimate explanations or "truth"; its goal is a rational, coherent description of the measurable physical world, a description that has beauty in its simplicity, a description that makes sense. In the courtroom of nature, any aspect of science is falsifiable. Modern technology is making possible increasingly precise tests of general relativity (for instance, see einstein.stanford.edu, and also *Sky & Telescope*, July 2004, p. 22, and August 2010, p. 29).

According to Einstein's GTR, gravitation is not a mysterious force that one mass exerts upon a distant mass; gravitation is the geometry (non-Euclidean) of the 4-dimensional spacetime within which we and the stars exist. Golf balls (if air friction is ignored), satellites, planets, stars, and light follow *geodesics*, the straightest possible, force-free paths through a spacetime whose geometry is shaped by mass–energy. The difficulty in intellectually grasping a non-Euclidean spacetime originates with us. Common sense is inadequate. That is not surprising, given that our common sense is based on the Euclidean, three-dimensional geometry of straight lines, rectangles, and spheres we learned in the crib by age two. The underlying cause of our delusion is that our senses and thought processes are constrained by the speed of neuron signals. Compared to light, neuron signals ooze along at a very slow rate, about one ten-millionth the speed of light. Consequently, to us a second of time is brief, light looks instantaneous, relativistic effects seem foreign, and time appears to be independent of space.

Gravitation is geometry. That is why no one has ever felt a force of gravity. Like the centrifugal force, it never did exist. A force of gravity was the glue Newton invented to make his naïve, Euclidean, space-plus-time model of the Universe approximate reality. Newton himself was well aware of the unsatisfactory nature of several of his assumptions, far more so than most people who came after him.

When you release a coin from your hand, you see the coin "fall" because the contact force of the ground on your feet (the *only* force you feel) accelerates you the other way. An orbiting astronaut experiences no such force, so he or she remains beside a released coin. Orbital motion could not be simpler—*no* forces are involved.

What would Milton have written had he been familiar with the conjectures of Newton and Einstein?

SOME ASTRONOMICAL AND PHYSICAL DATA
BY ROY BISHOP

Many of the numbers listed below are based on measurement. Exceptions include defined quantities (indicated by ≡), quantities calculated from defined quantities (e.g. m/ly, au/pc), and numbers of mathematical origin such as π and conversion factors in angular measure. Of those based on measurement, some are known to only approximate precision and the equal sign is reduced to ≈. Many others are known to quite high precision (the uncertainties occur after the last digit given), and several are from "the 2014 CODATA recommended values of the fundamental physical constants" (see physics.nist.gov/cuu/Constants). The units (Système International (SI) where possible), symbols, and nomenclature are based on recommendations of the International Astronomical Union and the International Union of Pure and Applied Physics.

LENGTH

1 metre (m) ≡ the distance traveled by light in a vacuum in $(299\,792\,458)^{-1}$ s
1 astronomical unit (au) ≡ $1.495\,978\,707 \times 10^{11}$ m = 499.004 783 8 light-s
1 light-year (ly)　　　= $9.460\,730 \times 10^{15}$ m (based on average Julian year)
　　　　　　　　　　= 63 241 au (63 360 inches = 1 mile)
1 parsec (pc)　　　　= $3.085\,678 \times 10^{16}$ m = 206 264.8 au = 3.261 564 ly
1 mile*　　　　　　　≡ 1.609 344 km
1 micron*　　　　　　≡ 1 μm　　　　　　　*Indicates deprecated unit;
1 angstrom*　　　　　≡ 0.1 nm　　　　　　unit on right is preferred

TIME

1 second (s) ≡　9 192 631 770 periods of the radiation involved in the transition between the two hyperfine levels of the ground state of the ^{133}Cs atom at mean sea level

Day:	Mean sidereal (equinox to equinox)	= 86 164.0921 s
	Mean rotation (fixed star to fixed star)	= 86 164.1005 s
	Day (d)	≡ 86 400. s
	Mean solar	= 86 400.0016 s
Month:	Draconic (node to node)	= 27.212 221 d
	Tropical (equinox to equinox)	= 27.321 582 d
	Sidereal (fixed star to fixed star)	= 27.321 662 d
	Anomalistic (perigee to perigee)	= 27.554 550 d
	Synodic (new Moon to new Moon)	= 29.530 589 d
Year:	Eclipse (lunar node to lunar node)	= 346.620 075 d
	Tropical (equinox to equinox) (y)	= 365.242 190 d
	Average Gregorian	≡ 365.242 5 d
	Average Julian	≡ 365.25 d
	Sidereal (fixed star to fixed star)	= 365.256 363 d
	Anomalistic (perihelion to perihelion)	= 365.259 635 d

EARTH

Mass, $M_E = 5.972 \times 10^{24}$ kg　Age ≈ 4.6 Gy　Central T ≈ 5000 K to 6000 K
Geocentric gravitational constant, $GM_E = 3.986\,004\,42 \times 10^{14}$ m³/s²
Radius:　Equatorial, a = 6378.14 km　　　Polar, b = 6356.75 km
　　　　　Mean = $(a^2 b)^{1/3}$ = 6371.00 km　Of metallic core = 3475 km
Solar parallax = 8.794 143″ (Earth equatorial radius ÷ 1 au)
1° of latitude = 111.132 95 − 0.559 82 cos 2φ + 0.001 17 cos 4φ km (at latitude φ)
1° of longitude = 111.412 88 cos φ − 0.093 50 cos 3φ + 0.000 12 cos 5φ km

1 knot = 1 nautical mile ($\approx$ 1$'$ of latitude) per hour $\equiv$ 1.852 km/h = 0.51444 m/s
Distance of sea horizon for eye h metres above sea level
  (allowing for refraction) $\approx$ 3.9$h^{1/2}$ km $\approx$ 2.1$h^{1/2}$ nautical miles
Atmospheric pressure: 1 atm $\equiv$ 101.325 kPa (There is $\approx$ 1 kg of air above 1 cm^2.)
Density of air at sea level (1 atm, 20 °C) = 1.2 kg/m^3
Values of atmospheric refraction for various elevations (assuming 1 atm, 10 °C):
  90°: 0$'$; 44°: 1$'$; 26°: 2$'$; 18°: 3$'$; 11°: 5$'$; 6°: 8$'$; 4°: 12$'$; 2°: 18$'$; 0°: 34$'$
Speed of sound in standard atmosphere = 331 m/s $\approx$ 1 km/3 s $\approx$ 10^{-6} c
Magnetic field at surface $\approx$ 5 $\times$ 10^{-5} T (**B** field comes out of a N-seeking pole)
Magnetic dip poles: 86°N, 181°E; 64°S, 136°E (as of 2018)
Standard acceleration of gravity $\equiv$ 9.806 65 m/s^2
Meteoritic flux $\approx$ 1 $\times$ 10^{-15} kg/(m^{2}s) $\approx$ 10^4 t/y over entire Earth
Obliquity of ecliptic = 23.4369° (2018.0)   Constant of aberration = 20.495 52$''$
Annual general precession = −50.29$''$ (2000.0); Precession period $\approx$ 25 800 y
Escape speed from Earth = 11.2 km/s   Mean orbital speed = 29.786 km/s
Escape speed at 1 au from Sun = 42.1 km/s (= $\sqrt{2}$ $\times$ orbital speed)

SUN

Mass = 1.9891 $\times$ 10^{30} kg   Radius = 695 660 km   Eff. temp. $\approx$ 5770 K
Output: Power = 3.83 $\times$ 10^{26} W, M_{bol} = 4.74
       Luminous intensity = 2.84 $\times$ 10^{27} cd, M_v = 4.82
At 1 au outside Earth's atmosphere:
    Energy flux = 1.36 kW/m^2, m_{bol} = −26.83
    Illuminance = 1.27 $\times$ 10^5 lx, m_v = −26.75
Inclination of the solar equator on the ecliptic of date = 7.25°
Longitude of ascending node of the solar equator on the ecliptic of date = 76°
Period of rotation at equator $\equiv$ 25.38 d (sidereal), 27.2753 d (mean synodic)
Solar wind speed near Earth $\approx$ 450 km/s (travel time, Sun to Earth $\approx$ 4 d)
Solar velocity = 19.4 km/s toward α = 18.07h, δ = +30° (solar apex)
Location in Milky Way Galaxy: $\approx$ 27 kly from center, $\approx$ 50 ly N of galactic
  plane, on the inner edge of the Orion arm

MILKY WAY GALAXY

Mass $\approx$ 10^{12} solar masses   Diameter $\approx$ 300 kly (including the galactic halo)
Center: α = 17h 45.7m, δ = −29°00$'$; N pole: α = 12h 51m, δ = 27°08$'$ (2000.0)
Rotation speed at Sun $\approx$ 230 km/s, period $\approx$ 200 My
Velocity relative to 3 K background radiation $\approx$ 400 km/s toward $\alpha \approx$ 14h, $\delta \approx$ −30°

CONSTANTS

Speed of light, c $\equiv$ 299 792 458 m/s (This, in effect, defines the metre.)
Planck's constant, h = 6.626 070 $\times$ 10^{-34} J·s = 4.135 668 $\times$ 10^{-15} eV·s
Gravitational constant, G = 6.674 $\times$ 10^{-11} N·m^2/kg^2
Elementary charge, e = 1.602 177 $\times$ 10^{-19} C
Constant in Coulomb's law $\equiv$ 10^{-7} c^2 (SI units) (This defines the coulomb.)
Avogadro constant, N_A = 6.022 141 $\times$ 10^{26} kmol^{-1}
Boltzmann constant, k = 1.380 65 $\times$ 10^{-23} J/K = 8.6173 $\times$ 10^{-5} eV/K $\approx$ 1 eV/10^{4}K
Stefan–Boltzmann constant, σ = 5.6704 $\times$ 10^{-8} W/(m^{2}K^4)
Wien's Law: $\lambda_m T$ = 2.897 77 $\times$ 10^{-3} m·K (per dλ)
Hubble constant, H = 68 $\pm$ 1 km/(s·Mpc)   Age of Universe = 13.80 $\pm$ 0.04 Gy
−273.15 °C (degree Celsius) = 0 K (kelvin) (lowest thermodynamic temperature)
Volume of ideal gas at 0 °C, 101.325 kPa = 22.4140 m^3/kmol
Water: fusion at 0 °C: 0.333 MJ/kg   vapourization at 100 °C: 2.26 MJ/kg
      thermal capacity and density (near 20 °C): 4.18 kJ/(kg·C°) and 1.00 t/m^3
      surface tension (near 20 °C): 0.073 N/m

MASS AND ENERGY

Mass is a measure of sluggishness of response to a net force. (SI unit: kg)
Weight ($\neq$ mass) is the magnitude of the force required to support a body. (SI unit: N)
  (1 pound-mass* = 0.453 59 kg) (1 pound-force* = 4.4482 N)

1 kilogram (kg) $\equiv$ mass of a platinum-iridium cylinder stored in Paris, France
1 atomic mass unit (u) $\equiv$ 1/12 of the mass of an atom of ^{12}C
$\qquad = 1.660\,539 \times 10^{-27}$ kg $= N_A^{-1} = 931.4941$ MeV
1 joule (J) $\equiv$ work done by a force of 1 N acting through a distance of 1 m
  $\approx$ the kinetic energy gained by this Handbook in falling freely 0.3 m
1 electron-volt (eV) $\equiv$ the kinetic energy gained by a particle carrying one unit
    of elementary electrical charge *(e)* in falling through an
    electrical potential difference of one volt (V)
    $= 1.602\,177 \times 10^{-19}$ J

Electron mass = $9.109\,38 \times 10^{-31}$ kg = 548.579 909 μu = 0.510 998 9 MeV
Proton mass = $1.672\,622 \times 10^{-27}$ kg = 1.007 276 467 u = 938.2721 MeV
Neutron mass = $1.674\,927 \times 10^{-27}$ kg = 1.008 664 916 u = 939.5654 MeV

Some atomic masses: ^{1}H (1.007 825 u) ^{2}H (2.014 102 u) ^{4}He (4.002 603 u)

Thermochemical calorie* (cal) = 4.184 J
1 erg*/s = 10^{-7} J/s = 10^{-7} W
1 BTU*/h = 1054.35 J/h = 0.292 88 W   *Indicates deprecated unit;
1 horsepower* = 745.7 W   unit on right is preferred.
1 eV per event = 23 060 cal/mol
$C + O_2 \rightarrow CO_2 + 4.1$ eV   4 ^{1}H $\rightarrow$ ^{4}He + 26.73 MeV

Highest cosmic-ray energy (carried by protons) $\approx 10^{20}$ eV
Power output (average) of an adult human $\approx$ 100 W
1 kg of TNT or milkshake releases 4.2 MJ $\approx$ 1000 kcal $\approx$ 1 kWh
Fuel oil: 6.36 GJ/barrel (1 barrel $\equiv$ 42 U.S. gallons = 35.0 Imp. gallons = 159 L)

Relation between rest mass *(m)*, linear momentum *(p)*, total energy *(E)*, kinetic
  energy *(KE)*, and $\gamma \equiv (1 - v^2/c^2)^{-0.5}$, where *c* is the speed of light and *v* is the
  speed of the object: $E = \gamma mc^2 = mc^2 + KE = [(mc^2)^2 + (pc)^2]^{0.5}$

MAGNITUDE RELATIONS (See also p. 49 and p. 54.)

Log of light intensity ratio $\equiv$ 0.4 times magnitude difference
Distance modulus *(D)* $\equiv$ apparent magnitude *(m)* – absolute magnitude *(M)*
Log of distance in ly = 0.2 *D* + 1.513 435 (neglecting absorption)
Magnitude of sum of magnitudes m_i is equal to $-2.5 \log \Sigma_i\, 10^{-0.4 m_i}$

Moon's apparent visual magnitude at phase angle *P* degrees (0° = full Moon)
  when at its average distance from Earth: $-12.7 + 0.026\,|P| + (4 \times 10^{-9})P^4$

A light source of apparent visual magnitude *m* provides an illuminance
  E (lux) where $E = 10^{-0.4\,(m + 13.99)}$ or $m = -13.99 - 2.5 \log E$
A diffuse (matte) surface with albedo *A* subject to illuminance *E* (lux) will have
  luminance *L* (visual surface brightness): $L = AE \div \pi$ (cd/m^2)
To convert luminance *S* (magnitude/arcsecond^2) to luminance *L* (cd/m^2):
  $L = 10^{0.4(12.59-S)}$ or $S = 12.59 - 2.5 \log L$

DOPPLER RELATIONS FOR LIGHT

$\alpha \equiv$ angle between velocity of source and line from source to observer
$\beta \equiv v/c$ $\gamma \equiv (1 - \beta^2)^{-0.5}$
Frequency: $f = f_0\,\gamma^{-1}(1 - \beta \cos \alpha)^{-1}$ $z \equiv (\lambda - \lambda_0)/\lambda_0 = \gamma\,(1 - \beta \cos \alpha) - 1$
For $\alpha = \pi$ radians: $z = (1 + \beta)^{0.5}(1 - \beta)^{-0.5} - 1$ ($\approx \beta$ if $\beta << 1$)
    $\beta = [(1 + z)^2 - 1][(1 + z)^2 + 1]^{-1}$

OPTICAL WAVELENGTH DATA

Bright-adapted (photopic) visible range $\approx 400 - 750$ nm ($L \approx 0.005 - 10^5$ cd/m^2)
Dark-adapted (scotopic) visible range $\approx 400 - 620$ nm ($L \approx 1 - 5000$ μcd/m^2)
Wavelength of peak sensitivity of eye: ≈ 555 nm (photopic), 507 nm (scotopic)
Mechanical equivalent of light: 1 lm $\equiv 1/683$ W at 540 THz ($\lambda \approx 555$ nm)
  i.e. 1.46 W/klm (A 60-W incandescent light bulb emits about 1 klm = 1000 lm.
    Compared to an optimum light source that delivers all its energy as light
    at 540 THz, a 60-W incandescent light bulb is 1.46/60 $\approx 2.4\%$ efficient.)
Colors (representative wavelength, nm):
  violet (420), blue (470), green (530), yellow (580), orange (610), red (660)

Some useful wavelengths (element, spectral designation or color and/or
(Fraunhofer line)):

H Lyman α	121.6 nm	N_2^+ blue†	465.2	Hg yellow	577.0
Ca (K solar)	393.4	Hβ (F solar)*	486.1	Hg yellow	579.1
Ca (H solar)	396.8	O^{++} green*	495.9	Na (D$_2$ solar)	589.0
Hg violet	404.7	O^{++} green*	500.7	Na (D$_1$ solar)	589.6
Hδ (h solar)	410.2	Green laser	532.	O red†	630.0
Hγ (g solar)	434.0	Hg green	546.1	O red†	636.4
Hg deep blue	435.8	O yel.-green†	557.7	Hα (C solar)	656.3

* Strong contributor to the visual light of gaseous nebulae   † Strong auroral lines

ANGULAR RELATIONS

2π radians $= 360°$ $\pi = 3.141\,592\,653\,589\,793\,2... \approx (113 \div 355)^{-1}$
Number of square degrees on a sphere $= 41\,253$

For $360° = 24$ h, $15° = 1$ h, $15' = 1$ min, $15'' = 1$ s (Earth turns 360° in 86 164.1 s)

Relations between sidereal time t, right ascension α, hour angle h, declination δ,
azimuth A (measured east of north), altitude a, and latitude ϕ:

$h = t - \alpha$
$\sin a = \sin \delta \sin \phi + \cos h \cos \delta \cos \phi$
$\cos \delta \sin h = -\cos a \sin A$
$\sin \delta = \sin a \sin \phi + \cos a \cos A \cos \phi$

Annual precession in α (in seconds) $\approx 3.0748 + 1.3361 \sin \alpha \tan \delta$
Annual precession in δ (in seconds of arc) $\approx 20.042 \cos \alpha$
(Convert α to degrees for the trigonometric functions above.)
e.g. for RA 4h 20m, Dec +40°, the annual change is $\Delta\alpha = 4.091$ s and $\Delta\delta = 8.470''$

SOME SI SYMBOLS AND PREFIXES

m	metre	N	newton (kg·m/s^2)	a	atto	10^{-18}
kg	kilogram	J	joule (N·m)	f	femto	10^{-15}
t	tonne (10^3 kg)	W	watt (J/s)	p	pico	10^{-12}
s	second	Pa	pascal (N/m^2)	n	nano	10^{-9}
min	minute	A	ampere	μ	micro	10^{-6}
h	hour	C	coulomb (A·s)	m	milli	10^{-3}
d	day	V	volt (J/C)	c	centi	10^{-2}
y	year (tropical) (*not SI*)	Ω	ohm (V/A)	h	hecto	10^2
Hz	hertz (s^{-1})	F	farad (C/V)	k	kilo	10^3
rad	radian	Wb	weber (V·s)	M	mega	10^6
sr	steradian	T	tesla (Wb/m^2)	G	giga	10^9
K	kelvin (temperature)	lm	lumen	T	tera	10^{12}
L	litre (10^{-3} m^3)	cd	candela (lm/sr)	P	peta	10^{15}
ha	hectare (10^4 m^2)	lx	lux (lm/m^2)	E	exa	10^{18}

THE ELECTROMAGNETIC SPECTRUM
BY ROY BISHOP

The Scottish physicist James Clerk Maxwell (1831–1879) was the first to understand the nature of light. In 1865, with elegant mathematics, Maxwell predicted that light is a self-sustaining electromagnetic wave, a quivering linkage of electric and magnetic fields in which a changing electric field generates a magnetic field, and vice versa, sustaining each other as they travel at a prodigious speed.

Four decades later Albert Einstein (1879–1955) revealed three more remarkable properties of light: (1) unlike water waves and sound waves, electromagnetic waves require no medium whatsoever in which to travel; (2) the speed of electromagnetic waves is the same for all observers, irrespective of any motion of the source of the waves; (3) when electromagnetic waves interact with matter, they do so as if composed of discrete particles, photons, whose individual energy E is proportional to the frequency f of the wave: $E = hf$, where h is Planck's constant (see p. 30).

The product of wavelength λ and wave frequency is the speed of a wave: $\lambda f = c$, where c is the usual symbol for the speed of an electromagnetic wave. The frequency (or photon energy, or wavelength) range of electromagnetic waves is unlimited, but our eyes see only a very narrow slice of this spectrum. Vision has a range of less than an octave, $\lambda \sim 400$ to 750 nm (see p. 32). We are almost blind! Nevertheless, once the physics was understood, the technologies to generate and detect all parts of the electromagnetic spectrum were soon developed. The first step in this direction occurred prior to Maxwell's work, in 1800 when astronomer William Herschel (1738–1822) discovered *infrared* radiation beyond the red end of the visible spectrum.

The diagram at the end of this article summarizes the electromagnetic spectrum. The various named parts of the spectrum overlap to some extent. One part is defined by the source of the radiation rather than by wavelength or photon energy: *gamma rays* refer to electromagnetic radiation emitted by radioactive atomic nuclei. *X-rays* overlap with gamma rays but are produced by sources other than atomic nuclei—an arbitrary distinction based on the historical origins of these two terms. A detector defines another part of the spectrum: *light* is usually restricted to human vision, although occasionally this term is extended to include the adjacent *ultraviolet* portion of the spectrum.

The importance of the particle aspect at high frequencies and of the wave aspect at low frequencies is implied by the names; for instance, gamma **rays** and radio **waves**. Photon energy, not wavelength, dominates the behaviour of gamma rays. At the other end of the spectrum, the energy of individual photons is very small, obscuring the granular nature of the radiation, and frequency is usually the measured characteristic of the radiation. Vision operates between these two extremes where *both* particle and wave properties play significant roles. Events in the retina are triggered by individual photons, and wave diffraction is relevant for minimum eye pupil size and the spacing of retinal photoreceptors. For the infrared and microwave regions, wavelength has a convenient range and is usually cited. The transition across the spectrum from photon through wavelength to frequency domination is indicated in the diagram by the range of the units on the left side of each of the three scales.

Photon energy determines how electromagnetic radiation interacts with matter. Chemistry and biology involve changes in atomic and molecular structure, the energies involved being typically a few *electron-volts* (eV) per reaction (see p. 31). Retinal photochemistry operates over a very limited energy range, and thereby determines the narrow visual window on the electromagnetic spectrum. For $\lambda > 750$ nm, the photon energy is insufficient (<1.6 eV) to alter the structure of light-sensing protein molecules in the retina, so we cannot see the infrared. For $\lambda < 400$ nm, the photon energy is high enough (>3.1 eV) to damage these delicate molecules; however, the cornea and lens of the eye absorb that radiation before it can reach the retina. Thus, we cannot see the ultraviolet.

Although the energy of an infrared photon is too weak to stimulate vision, infrared photons are readily absorbed by many types of molecules, such as water, causing the molecules to move more rapidly, thereby increasing the temperature of the substance. In this manner, infrared radiation from the Sun, a fire, or a hot stove warms us. Hence infrared is often called heat radiation, although it is *not* heat that is being radiated. The heating is a secondary effect, generated in our bodies subsequent to the absorption of the photons.

Confusion of sensation with electromagnetic radiation also occurs with visible light. For instance, almost invariably we speak of colors as if they were a property of light, or of the bodies emitting the light, rather than being indescribable hue sensations arising in the brain. As Sir Isaac Newton cautioned us three centuries ago: "The rays, to speak properly, are not colored." The light reflected by a leaf is not green, and neither is the leaf; green exists only in the neuron-based representation of the leaf in the observer's consciousness, and then only if the light is not too dim. The electromagnetic radiation from a leaf is characterized by a particular spatial and spectral distribution of radiant power. A CCD or CMOS chip finds only photons. It is we who create the color and the brightness. The distinction between our internal visual world and the external physical world is profound but rarely appreciated. It is the distinction between how the world *looks* to us, and how it *is*.

Visual perception aside, what *is* light, a wave or a particle? Light travels like a wave (Maxwell was right) and interacts like a particle (Einstein was right). A detector finds photons, but *where* the detector finds photons is determined by a wave. When a typical backyard telescope is aimed at an average star in the night sky, at any instant there is seldom more than one photon from that star in transit through the telescope. Yet the distribution of light in the star's image at the focal plane is determined by an aperture-filling wave. In the case of a Newtonian telescope with a four-vane spider support for the secondary mirror, in some real sense, each photon passes through all four quadrants of the spider. But it is not that the spider quarters the hapless photon like a cleaver quarters a steak in a butcher shop; whole photons, not quartered photons arrive at the detector. The message of physics revealed during the first half of the last century is that it is simply *wrong* to speak of the path of a photon while in transit to a detector. Light is queerer than we can imagine. Matter is equally queer, for it too displays a wave-particle duality, a duality that is particularly obvious on the subatomic scale. Just as it is wrong to speak of the path of a photon, it is wrong to speak of the path of an electron in an atom—as if, for example, it were in orbit about the nucleus. The wave-particle puzzle is of our own making, for we try to apply naïve concepts abstracted from crude sensory experiences on the macroscopic scale of everyday life to the subatomic world. Pure waves or pure particles never did exist. Reality is more subtle.

Despite the strange behaviour of electromagnetic radiation, we know how to describe its interaction with matter quantitatively and with astounding accuracy. The theory encompasses the work of Maxwell and Einstein, and was completed in the mid-20th century by Richard Feynman (1918–1988) and Julian Schwinger (1918–1994) of the United States, and Sin-Itiro Tomonaga (1906–1979) of Japan, for which they shared the Nobel Prize in Physics in 1965. The theory is called quantum electrodynamics. With the exception of gravitation and things that go on inside atomic nuclei, quantum electrodynamics appears to describe all phenomena in the physical world—in principle, if not in actuality, in the case of complex systems because of the complexity.

THE ELECTROMAGNETIC SPECTRUM

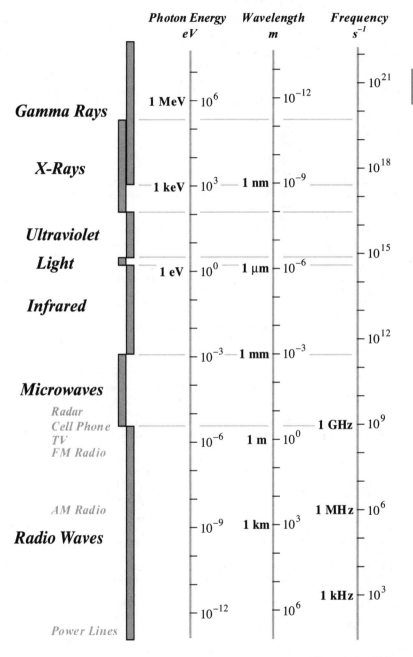

Diagram by Roy Bishop

VOYAGES IN THE SOLAR SYSTEM
BY J. RANDY ATTWOOD

During the second half of the 20th century, humankind began its reconnaissance of the Solar System. Although people have traveled only as far as the Moon, robotic space probes have been sent to all the major planets plus a few minor planets and comets. Our understanding of the solar neighborhood is increasing at a tremendous pace as a result of the improving sophistication of these spacecraft.

The following is a list of some of the important firsts in the short history of the exploration of the Solar System. Note that all space missions are not recorded, not even all the space firsts. A short list of upcoming missions to watch for is also included.

Year	Name	Significance
1957	*Sputnik 1*	First artificial satellite of Earth (Oct. 4); USSR
1957	*Sputnik 2*	First living being in Earth orbit (a dog named Laika); USSR
1959	*Luna 1*	First to escape Earth's gravity; USSR
1959	*Luna 2*	First to impact on the Moon; USSR
1959	*Luna 3*	First to image the far side of the Moon; USSR
1961	*Vostok 1*	First human in Earth orbit (Yuri Gagarin, Apr. 12); USSR
1961	*Freedom 7*	First American in space (Alan Shepard, May 5); USA
1962	*Friendship 7*	First American in Earth orbit (John Glenn, Feb. 20); USA
1962	*Mariner 2*	First to fly by another planet, Venus; USA
1962	*Alouette 1*	First Canadian satellite placed in Earth orbit
1963	*Vostok 6*	First woman to fly in space (Valentina Tereshkova, Jun. 16); USSR
1965	*Voshkod 2*	First astronaut to take a spacewalk (Alexei Leonov, Mar. 18); USSR
1965	*Mariner 4*	First to fly by Mars and take pictures; USA
1966	*Luna 9*	First soft landing on the Moon; USSR
1966	*Venera 3*	First to impact on another planet, Venus; USSR
1966	*Luna 10*	First to orbit the Moon; USSR
1967	*Apollo 1*	Astronauts perish in a fire during a launch-pad test (Grissom, White, and Chaffee, Jan. 27); USA
1967	*Soyuz 1*	First astronaut to die during spaceflight (Vladimir Komarov, Apr. 24); USSR
1968	*Apollo 8*	First human voyage to the Moon (orbit without landing); USA (Frank Borman, James Lovell, and William Anders, Dec. 24)
1969	*Apollo 11*	First humans to land and walk on the Moon; USA (Neil Armstrong and Edwin Aldrin, Jul. 20)
1970	*Apollo 13*	Moon mission cancelled after onboard explosion (Apr. 14); USA
1970	*Venera 7*	First soft landing on another planet, Venus; USSR
1971	*Mariner 9*	First to orbit another planet, Mars; USA
1971	*Mariner 9*	First close views of outer satellites Phobos, Deimos; USA
1972	*Anik A1*	First Canadian communications satellite placed in Earth orbit
1972	*Apollo 17*	Last two of 12 men to walk on the Moon; USA
1973	*Pioneer 10*	First to fly by Jupiter, reach solar escape speed; USA
1974	*Mariner 10*	First to fly by and study Mercury; USA
1975	*Venera 9*	First to return surface pictures of Venus; USSR
1976	*Viking 1*	First to softly land on Mars, return pictures; USA
1979	*Voyager 1*	First close-up study of Jupiter and its moons; USA
1979	*Pioneer 11*	First to fly by Saturn; USA
1980	*Voyager 1*	First close-up study of Saturn and its moons; USA
1981	STS 1	First launch of the reuseable *Space Transportation System* (Space Shuttle); USA
1983	STS 7	First American woman to fly in space (Sally Ride, Jun. 18); USA
1984	*Soyuz T–7*	First woman to walk in space (Svetlana Savitskaya, Jul. 25); USSR
1984	STS 41G	First Canadian to fly in space (Marc Garneau, Oct. 5); Canada
	"	First American woman to walk in space (Kathy Sullivan); USA
	"	First time two women in space at the same time (Kathy Sullivan, Sally Ride); USA

Year	Name	Significance
1985	ICE	*(International Cometary Explorer)* First to study a comet; USA
1986	*Voyager 2*	First close-up study of Uranus and its moons; USA
1986	*Challenger*	First American astronauts to die during spaceflight (Jan. 28); USA
1986	*Giotto*	First images taken of a comet nucleus, Halley; ESA
1989	*Voyager 2*	First close-up study of Neptune and its moons; USA
1989	*Magellan*	First radar maps made of Venus from orbit; USA
1989	COBE	First precise data on cosmic microwave background radiation; USA
1990	*Hubble*	Launch of the *Hubble Space Telescope*
1991	*Galileo*	First flyby, closeup photos of a minor planet, 951 Gaspra; USA
1992	STS 42	First Canadian woman in space (Roberta Bondar, Jan. 22); Canada
1994	*Clementine*	First images of perma-shadowed areas at the Moon's south pole; USA
1994	*Hubble, Galileo*	Images of comet fragments of Shoemaker–Levy 9 impacting Jupiter
1994–5	*Mir*	Longest single spaceflight: 437 days in Earth orbit (V. Polyakov); USSR
1995	*Ulysses*	First flyby above the Sun's south/north poles; ESA
1995	*Galileo*	First to orbit Jupiter and 1st to send probe into Jupiter's atmosphere; USA
1996	*Pathfinder*	First rover on Mars (Sojourner); USA
1998	*Deep Space 1*	First test of ion propulsion; navigates to Comet Borelly (2001); USA
1999	*Chandra*	Launch of the *Chandra X-Ray Observatory*; USA
2001	*Soyuz TM-32*	First private citizen to pay for a spaceflight (Dennis Tito)
2001	NEAR *Shoemaker*	First to orbit and land softly on a minor planet, 433 Eros; USA
2001	*Genesis*	First solar-wind sample return; USA
2003	*Columbia*	Second Space Shuttle disaster; crew of 7 lost (Feb. 1)
2003	MOST	First Canadian space telescope launched into Earth orbit
2003	*Shenzhou V*	First Chinese taikonaut to orbit Earth (Yang Liwei)
2004	*Mars Rovers*	First long-range surface exploration of Mars; USA
2004	*Stardust*	First collection and return of cometary material, Wild 2; USA
2004	*Cassini*	First to orbit Saturn; USA
2004	*Gravity Probe B*	First test of Einstein's general theory of relativity in space; USA
2005	*Huygens*	First to land on Titan; USA/ESA
2005	*Deep Impact*	First to impact and study the interior of a comet, Tempel 1; USA
2008	*Mars Phoenix*	First to examine Martian arctic soil; discovered water ice; USA
2009	ISS	Most people (13) together in one spacecraft: (Expedition 20/21 and STS 127), including two Canadians (Robert Thirsk, Julie Payette)
2009	*Kepler*	First to verify Earth-sized planets at nearby stars; USA
2010	*Hayabusa*	First minor-planet-sample return mission(rendezvous in 2005); Japan
2010	ISS	Four women in space at one time: Expedition 23, STS 131
2011	*Messenger*	First spacecraft to orbit and study Mercury; USA
2011	*Atlantis*	135th and last Space Shuttle flight
2011	*Dawn*	First to orbit a minor planet (4 Vesta) and a dwarf planet (1 Ceres), in 2015; USA
2011	*Juno*	First mission to study Jupiter from a polar orbit (July 2016); USA
2012	*Mars Science Laboratory*	
		Carrying Curiosity, the first nuclear-powered rover on Mars; USA
2012	*NEOSSat*	First to look for objects on a potential Earth-collision course; Canada
2014	*Rosetta/Philae*	First to soft land on a comet (67P/Churyumov–Gerasimenko); ESA
2014	*Enterprise*	SS2 class, lost in test flight, with fatality; Virgin Galactic, UK
2015	*New Horizons*	First to fly by and closely image the Pluto system; USA
2016	OSIRIS-*Rex*	First NASA/CSA mission to sample an asteroid (101955 Bennu)

As of August 2017, a total of 553 people have traveled into space.

Upcoming Missions

2018+	JWST*	Launch of the *James Webb Space Telescope*: USA/ESA
2019+	*New Horizons*	First to fly by Kuiper Belt Objects; USA
2020	*Euclid**	First mission to map the Dark Universe; ESA
2022	JUICE*	First mission to primarily study JUpiter's ICEy moons; ESA

*Mission not yet launched

OBSERVING ARTIFICIAL SATELLITES
BY PAUL D. MALEY

Spotting satellites is now easier with Android and iPhone apps that can be downloaded either for free or with a small fee. These apps have evolved from general stargazing assistants to software that makes satellite viewing possible from anywhere on Earth. If you are interested in seeing some of the brighter satellites, you might wish to consider checking out the reviews for such apps as *Sky Safari 5*, *Night Sky 4*, *Sky Guide*, *SpyMeSat*, *GoSatWatch*, *Stellarium*, *Satellite Tracker ProStat*, *SkyView*, *Satellite Explorer Pro*, *Satellite Watcher*, and others that might help give you this all-sky perspective on any given evening regardless of your location. An app called *ISS Spotter* is one of the more downloaded apps since the *International Space Station* is the biggest dynamic satellite target these days. The aforementioned apps are similar, yet different, as some have unique features that you might really want or need. It would be good to do a thorough online investigation before jumping into one of those apps to be sure it suits your personal needs.

For school-night demonstrations, having a phone app makes it easy to come up with ideas on satellites to watch in real time, especially if weather causes delays or cancellation of evening sky-watching sessions for astro educators. There is no need for preplanning since you can do it as the weather changes. If someone has forgotten to bring a telescope to an outreach session, then you can use unaided-eye satellite viewing as an alternate education tool. Most sky-watching sessions done for public education and outreach generally rely on bright objects to show first-time sky viewers, such as the Moon and easily seen planets. School programs might consider the use of such apps to stimulate interest from student, since it delegates downward the ability of specific students who might be charged up by the sight of their first artificial Earth satellite. That way, they can take this newfound energy and watch at home, thus building up their knowledge and interest in this exciting offshoot.

My first amazing experience was in 1960 when I saw the Echo I balloon satellite in the postsunset sky moving slowly from north to south in my eastern sky from San Antonio, Texas, with only the naked eye. It was to me a transformative experience. Here I was more than 1600 km away from this 30-metre-diameter satellite and saw it gliding at mag. 0 through the starry background. This was before smart phones, before apps, and before the internet. Back then, predictions were made by hand using things like a table of times when a satellite crossed the equator on its ascending node. Now, one need not have any background in celestial mechanics or even knowledge of astronomy to be able to use a smartphone app to make such visibility calculations on a host of spacecraft candidates.

There are still other applications that will let you track satellites in real time, such as at N2YO.com. Now, if you hear about a brand-new satellite launch and want to go out to watch a payload fly over, consider some things. Satellite creators get more bang for the buck by launching groups of satellites together. Cubesats are an example of efficient design. They are small structures only 10×10×10 cm across, and are inexpensive to build and fly. Don't expect to actually see them, as they will not be visible without magnification. Even if you had binoculars or a telescope, it is unlikely you might come across one of those tiny objects flying through your field of view. But do not despair, as the sky is literally filled with satellites that can be spotted accidentally or intentionally.

If you live in a highly lighted urban environment, use www.heavens-above.com, and use their magnitude feature to look for satellites brighter than mag. 3.0. That way, you will not waste your time looking for fainter objects that are masked by light pollution in major cities. Where I live in Arizona, I can spot satellites to mag. 4 or 5 on a nightly basis. If you should spot an accidental satellite at night, you can even use Heavens-Above.com to potentially identify which one it was, after the fact.

Make it a point to access a satellite visibility program, either on your desktop or smartphone. Then go outdoors tonight and start looking up!

TIME

TIME AND TIME SCALES
BY ROY BISHOP

Time has been said to be nature's way of keeping everything from happening at once. In 1687, Sir Isaac Newton (1642–1727) perceived time as being separate from and more fundamental than the spinning of changeable planets or the oily mechanisms of clocks: "Absolute, true, and mathematical time, of itself, and from its own nature flows equably without regard to anything external." That is the common sense or intuitive view most people have of time.

Albert Einstein (1879–1955) was the first to understand that time is but an abstraction that does not exist independently of clocks. In his special theory of relativity (1905), Einstein predicted that clocks moving relative to an observer run slower, a phenomenon called time dilation or the second-order Doppler effect. For example, relative to a clock fixed beside a road, the wristwatch of a person driving past at a speed of 100 km/h loses 0.26 ps per minute (ps = picosecond = 10^{-12} s; see p. 32). A decade later, in his theory of gravitation, the general theory of relativity, Einstein predicted that clocks lower or higher than the observer in a gravitational field run slower or faster, respectively, than the observer's clock. In the case of a lower clock, it is called the gravitational redshift. For example, an alarm clock on the floor a metre below your bed loses 3.1 ps per 8-h night relative to a watch on your wrist. These counterintuitive effects are not only real, but in recent years they have found their way into the consumer marketplace in the form of GPS (Global Positioning System) receivers. These handheld units receive signals from orbiting atomic clocks and rely on programs that allow for time dilation and gravitational redshift (see *Physics Today*, May 2002, p. 41). In astronomy, the general theory of relativity was mostly ignored until the last few decades of the 20th century, when increasing precision of clocks and advances in theoretical astrophysics and cosmology demanded its use.

As to understanding time, Lord Kelvin (1824–1907) said that you know a physical quantity if you can measure it. Time can indeed be measured, with mind-boggling precision. For those who feel compelled to state "We still don't know what time actually is," perhaps the mystery resides merely in the meaning of this statement.

The essence of time is that isolated material changes occur in invariant ratios one with respect to another. That is, as Sir Hermann Bondi (1919–2005) put it: "Time is that which is manufactured by clocks." Thus, to deal with time, clocks must be devised and units and time scales established. Readers who wish to pursue this topic beyond the brief overview presented here should consult *The Measurement of Time*, by C. Audoin and B. Guinot, Cambridge University Press, 2001, and the *Explanatory Supplement to the Astronomical Almanac, 3rd ed.*, by S.E. Urban and P.K. Seidelmann (eds.), University Science Books, 2013. For less-technical descriptions of many aspects of time see *A Matter of Time*, a special edition of *Scientific American* (vol. 21, no. 1, 2012).

Periodic Time Intervals and Clocks

There are three obvious, natural, periodic time intervals on Earth: the seasonal cycle (year), the cycle of lunar phases (month), and the day–night cycle (day). The cycle of the seasons is called the *tropical year* and contains 365.242 190 days. The cycle of lunar phases is known as the *synodic month* and equals 29.530 589 days. The average day–night (diurnal) cycle is the *mean solar day* and presently contains approximately

86 400.0016 s. Other types of year, month, and day have been defined and are listed along with brief definitions and durations on p. 29.

The problem of accurately subdividing these natural intervals to make time locally available at any moment (i.e. timekeeping) was satisfactorily solved in 1657 by Christiaan Huygens, who invented the first practical pendulum clock. Through successive refinements, the pendulum clock reigned supreme for nearly three centuries, until it was surpassed in precision by the quartz oscillator in the 1940s. Within another 20 years the quartz clock was, in turn, superseded by the cesium atomic clock, which by the year 2000 reached a precision of about 1 part in 10^{15}. Today, clocks based on single ions of other elements are approaching a short-term stability of one part in 10^{17} (one second in 3 billion years), and optical-lattice clocks are exceeding that figure (see *Physics Today*, March 2014, p. 12).

Earth's Rotation and Time Scales

Of the three obvious, natural, periodic time intervals on Earth (year, month, and day), the day dominates our lives and determines the various time scales we have created. The day is caused primarily by Earth's rotation on its axis. To count rotations, a reference or fiducial point is required. Four such points are of interest, and three of these are the basis of five time scales:

(1) Earth's rotation relative to the distant stars: Although the distant stars (or better, extragalactic sources) provide a reference frame to determine the "true" period of Earth's rotation (presently about 86 164.1005 s), because of Earth's orbital motion and its rotational precession, this true period is not that of either the solar day or the RA/Dec coordinate grid used to specify astronomical positions. Hence no time scales are based on Earth's true rotational period.

(2) Earth's rotation relative to the equinox: The equator and poles of the RA/Dec celestial coordinate grid are aligned with Earth's mean equator and poles. ("Mean" denotes that small, periodic variations caused by the nutation of Earth's axis have been averaged out. Nutation involves the true pole moving relative to the mean pole with an amplitude of about $9''$ and a variety of short periods up to 18.6 years.) Hence the RA/Dec grid slowly shifts relative to the distant stars as Earth's rotation axis and equator precess, a motion caused primarily by the torques exerted by the Moon and Sun on Earth's equatorial bulge (see p. 21). The other planets make a smaller contribution to this *precession of the equator* and also cause a *precession of the ecliptic*. The sum of these two precessions is called *general precession*. General precession causes the zero point of right ascension (the "Greenwich of the skies," the vernal equinox, or "first point of Aries") to drift westward (retrograde) along the ecliptic about $50''$ per year. As a result, Earth's rotation period relative to the equinox (called the *mean sidereal day*, currently 86 164.0921 s) is 8.4 ms shorter than the time for one rotation (see p. 29). At any longitude on Earth, the RA of a star on the meridian (corrected for nutation) is the *Local Mean Sidereal Time* (**LMST**) at that instant. At the Greenwich meridian ($0°$ longitude), this is called *Greenwich Mean Sidereal Time* (**GMST**). LMST may be used to set a telescope on an object of known right ascension. The hour angle of the object equals the sidereal time less the RA. LMST may be available from a sidereal clock, or it can be calculated as explained in the middle of p. 47. Because Earth makes one more rotation with respect to the other stars than it does with respect to the Sun during a year, sidereal time gains relative to time scales linked to the Sun (see below) by about 3 min 56 s per day, or 2 h per month.

(3) Earth's rotation relative to the real Sun: A common misconception is that the Sun is highest in the sky and lies on the local north–south meridian at 12:00 noon. However, time based on the position of the Sun in the sky, known as local *apparent solar* *time* or *sundial time*, can differ by up to an hour or more from civil time (the time that we normally use). There are two reasons for this discrepancy. One reason is that the Sun's eastward annual apparent motion around the sky is far from uniform, both because of Earth's elliptical orbit and because of the inclination of the celestial equator to the ecliptic. Thus apparent solar time does not have a uniform rate (see the next paragraph). The second reason for the difference between sundial time and civil time is the use of standard time zones (see the penultimate paragraph of this article).

(4) Earth's rotation relative to the mean Sun: If the Sun is replaced by a fictitious mean sun moving uniformly along the celestial equator, Earth's rotation relative to this mean sun defines *Local Mean (solar) Time* (**LMT**). Apparent solar time can differ by up to 16 min from LMT, depending upon the time of year (see the diagram on p. 185). Small, periodic shifts of Earth's crust relative to the axis of rotation *(polar motion)* affect astronomical time determinations through the resulting east–west shift in the meridian at latitudes away from the equator. LMT at the Greenwich meridian (0° longitude), when corrected for this polar motion, is called *Universal Time* (**UT1**, or often simply **UT**). UT1 is determined using very-long-baseline interferometry, satellite laser-ranging data, lunar laser-ranging data, and GPS data (via the International GPS Service).

All the above mean time scales (LMST, GMST, LMT, and UT1), being based upon Earth's rotation, are only as uniform as that rotation. By the mid-19th century, discrepancies between theory and the observed motion of the Moon indicated that, over the long term, Earth's rotation is slowing down. However, not until clocks became better timekeepers than the spinning Earth (c. 1940, when crystal-controlled clocks exceeded precisions of 1 in 10^{10}) was it realized how complex is the variable rotation of our planet. There are (i) long-, (ii) medium-, and (iii) short-term accelerations:

(i) Over many centuries, there is a *secular* slowing caused by tidal friction of about 8 parts in 10^{13} per day (i.e. the day becomes one second longer about every 40 000 years).

(ii) Over a few decades, there are *random* accelerations (positive and negative), apparently caused by core–mantle interactions and possibly by changes in ocean currents. These are about 10 times larger than the tidal deceleration, and thus completely obscure the latter effect over time intervals of less than a century or so.

(iii) The largest accelerations in Earth's rotation rate are short-term ones: *periodic components* are associated mainly with lunar-induced tides (over two-week and monthly intervals) and seasonal meteorological factors (over semiannual and annual intervals); *nonperiodic* (chaotic) high-frequency variations are associated mainly with the global atmospheric wind and pressure distributions. These short-term accelerations are typically one or two orders of magnitude larger again than the random, decadal fluctuations on which they are superimposed (see the article by John Wahr in the June 1986 issue of *Sky & Telescope*, p. 545).

Uniform Time Scales

(1) Based on orbital motion: Although Earth's axial rotation is not sufficiently predictable to serve as a precise clock, the orbital motions of our Moon, Earth, and the other planets are predictable to high accuracy. Through the dynamical equations describing these motions plus extended astronomical observations, a uniform dynamical time scale can be derived. Such a scale, known as *Ephemeris Time* (ET), was for several years (1952–1984) the basis of astronomical ephemerides. The ephemeris second, defined in 1955 as a certain fraction of the tropical year 1900.0, was the fundamental unit of time. Early in the 20th century, the UT1 and ET scales coincided, but because Earth's rotation rate has been generally slower than the ET rate, by 1984 UT1 was 54 s behind ET and was losing about half a second per year. Between 1984 and 2017, Earth's rotation rate has varied (part of the random decadal fluctuations), losing between 0.2 and 0.8 s per year relative to ET (actually TT, see below).

(2) Based on atomic transition frequency: The quantum nature of matter gives atoms a permanence and stability that macroscopic objects such as quartz crystals, planets, and pendulums do not possess. The idea of an atomic clock was proposed by the Austrian–American physicist Isidor Rabi in 1945. In 1967, the second was given an atomic definition: 9 192 631 770 periods of the radiation involved in the transition between the two hyperfine levels of the ground state of the cesium 133 atom (the only stable isotope of cesium, an element that has a single valence electron). This is known as the SI (for Système International) second (abbreviation s, *not* sec). The number 9 192 631 770 was chosen so that on the rotating geoid (i.e. for clocks fixed on Earth at mean sea level), the SI second is identical to the older ET second to within the precision of measurement.

The previous sentence implies that clocks on the geoid run at the same rate. What about Earth's rotation? Clocks nearer the equator move faster, so does time dilation not make them run slower relative to clocks at higher latitudes? Ignoring the Moon and Sun, if Earth did not rotate and had an isotropic density distribution, its geoid (mean sea-level surface) would be spherical, and clocks fixed on this geoid would, by symmetry, all run at the same rate (they would all be at rest and have similar positions in Earth's gravitational field). For a rotating Earth, the equatorial bulge is such that clocks away from the poles are just enough higher in Earth's gravitational field that the resulting gravitational blueshift exactly cancels the time dilation associated with their rotational speed. This simple, elegant, and convenient result is a consequence of Einstein's principle of equivalence: A body at rest in a gravitational field is equivalent to a body being accelerated in a field-free space. As described by general relativity, gravitation is geometry, not a force, which is why no one has ever felt a force of gravity. The only force acting on Earth-based clocks, or on any stationary Earth-based objects, is the electromagnetic contact force supporting them. Any two nearby clocks located on the same surface perpendicular to the direction of this contact force (the plumb-bob direction) will have identical rates. Thus *all* clocks on the geoid run at the same rate. Whether or not the planet beneath is rotating is immaterial.

Five SI-second-based time scales are in use today. One of these (UTC) merely differs an integral number of seconds from one of the other four and is described in the last section. The fundamental time scale for unambiguously dating events within the Solar System and beyond (e.g. planet and interplanetary spacecraft motions, and pulsar signals) is **Barycentric Coordinate Time (TCB)**. TCB is the time base of a nonrotating coordinate system with its origin located at the center of mass of the Solar System, and it is not influenced by the gravitational fields of any bodies in the Solar System. It is as if the Solar System were not present.

The fundamental time scale for unambiguously dating events in the vicinity of Earth (e.g. motions of Earth-orbiting satellites) is **Geocentric Coordinate Time (TCG)**. TCG is the time base of a nonrotating coordinate system with its origin located at the center of mass of Earth, and it is not influenced by the gravitational field of Earth. It is as if all bodies of the Solar System except Earth were present.

TCG runs at a slower (and slightly variable) rate relative to TCB because of both time dilation associated with Earth's orbital motion and gravitational redshift associated with Earth's location within the Sun's gravitational well, and (to a much lesser extent) the gravitational wells of all the other bodies in the Solar System (except Earth). Relative to TCB, TCG loses about 467 ms per year.

One might expect that TCG would be the time scale of choice for Earth-based observers (e.g. for dealing with apparent geocentric ephemerides); however, cesium atomic clocks at Earth's surface are deep within Earth's gravitational well and lose about 22 ms per year relative to TCG. To avoid this inconvenience, a second geocentric coordinate time scale has been devised, **Terrestrial Time (TT)**. TT is defined as having a rate exactly $1 - 6.969290134 \times 10^{-10}$ as large as the TCG rate so that the unit of the TT scale is very close to the SI second on the rotating geoid, matching the rate of Earth-based atomic clocks. Thus TT is an idealized atomic time scale on the geoid, and is a derived scale, not fundamental. The TT rate definition is based upon TCG and not the geoid because of uncertainties surrounding the realization of the geoid (the geoid would coincide with Earth's sea surface *if* the waters of the oceans were homogeneous and at rest). TT loses about $22 + 467 = 489$ ms (nearly half a second) per year relative to TCB.

TCB, TCG, and TT are theoretical, ideal time scales. Real clocks are needed for measurements. To this end in 1972, *International Atomic Time* (**TAI** = Temps Atomique International) was introduced. TAI is based on a weighted average of more than 200 atomic clocks in more than 30 countries and presently is the most precise *achievable* time scale. Not even atomic clocks are perfect time keepers (they drift randomly one with respect to another), so TAI shifts unpredictably relative to the ideal TT rate by about 0.1 μs/year (a few parts in 10^{15}). The TAI scale was set to agree with UT1 on 1958 Jan. 1, which led to the definition that TT be exactly 32.184 s ahead of TAI on 1977 Jan. 1.0 (TAI) to ensure continuity of TT with ET, TT's predecessor for geocentric ephemerides.

TCB, TCG, and TT are defined to have had the same reading on 1977 Jan. 1.0 (TAI) at Earth's center of mass, all three being exactly 32.184 s ahead of TAI at that point in spacetime. At the beginning of 2018, TT is about 0.9 s behind TCG, and 20 seconds behind TCB. TCB, TCG, and TT are realized via TAI.

Three time scales no longer in use are associated with the SI second: ET, TDT, and TDB. ET and TDT have been abandoned, and TDB is deprecated. Unfortunately they still appear in some publications so they must be mentioned. *Ephemeris Time* (ET), introduced in section (1) above, was defined and adopted by the International Astronomical Union in 1952. The transition from ET to the modern TT took place in three steps: (i) Because of several difficulties surrounding both the original concept of ET and its determination (the most serious being that it ignored relativity), and because atomic clocks had become readily available, in 1984 ET was abandoned in favor of *Terrestrial Dynamical Time* (TDT). The unit of TDT was the SI second on the rotating geoid, and its scale was chosen to agree with the 1984 ET scale; (ii) In 1991, the general theory of relativity was explicitly adopted as the theoretical background for spacetime reference systems. To emphasize that TDT was no longer derived from observations of the dynamical aspects of Solar System bodies, TDT was renamed simply Terrestrial Time (TT); (iii) Because of uncertainties surrounding the realization of the geoid (mentioned above), TT was redefined in terms of TCG in 2000.

In 1976, *Barycentric Dynamical Time* (TDB) was introduced when it became necessary to acknowledge relativistic effects, but before the general theory of relativity was accepted by astronomers. It was similar to TCB, except its scale unit was adjusted to approximate ET (currently TT). TDB was needlessly complex and confusing; however, it was used extensively by the Jet Propulsion Laboratory for ephemerides in planetary exploration, so was not completely abandoned when TCB was introduced in 1991. This unsatisfactory situation was resolved in 2006 when TDB was redefined by a simple linear relation in terms of TCB. Although redundant and deprecated, TDB is now an alternative way to express TCB, with the minor convenience that it keeps nearly in step with TT at Earth's center.

(3) Based on pulsars: Millisecond radio pulsars (old, rapidly spinning neutron stars) display extraordinary stability in their rotation. Their stability, after allowing for spin-down, is almost as good as the best atomic clocks. However, uncertainties in

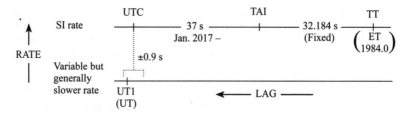

This diagram displays the rate and scale relations between Earth-based time scales that run at or near the SI rate at sea level and that are not longitude-dependent.

predicting the spin-down rate of a pulsar and in Earth's motion relative to a pulsar, the elaborate equipment needed to observe a pulsar, and the complex data analysis required all make it unlikely that a pulsar will ever replace cesium clocks as the basis for a uniform time scale. Like quartz crystals, planets, and pendulums, pulsars do not possess the permanence and stability of atoms.

Uniform Time Scales with Steps (to track the mean Sun)

Closely related to UT1 (which follows Earth's variable rotation relative to the mean Sun) is *Coordinated Universal Time* (**UTC**), introduced in its present form in 1972. UTC, the basis of the world system of civil time, runs at the TAI rate and is offset an integral number of seconds from TAI so that it approximates UT1. When required (usually on Jun. 30 or Dec. 31), "leap seconds" are inserted into (or, if necessary, deleted from) UTC so that the difference UT1 − UTC = ΔUT1 does not exceed ±0.9 s. The most recent insertion of a leap second occurred at the beginning of 2017, making the difference TAI − UTC = ΔAT = 37 s. Hence TT − UTC = 37 s + 32.184 s = 69.184 s exactly (see the diagram above). When the next leap second may be required will depend upon Earth's rate of rotation during the coming months. For announcements of leap seconds see ftp://hpiers.obspm.fr/iers/bul/bulc/bulletinc.dat. UTC is readily available via radio time signals and GPS receivers. (Note: The term *Greenwich Mean Time* (GMT) over the years has had three different meanings: the same as UT1, UTC, and mean solar time at the Greenwich meridian with 0 h corresponding to noon. To avoid confusion, the term *Greenwich Mean Time* should not be used.)

The websites maia.usno.navy.mil and toshi.nofs.navy.mil provide Earth-orientation data, including the cumulative number of leap seconds, values of UT1–UTC during recent years, and a link to values of (TT–UT1) = "ΔT" at monthly intervals since 1973. A graph of ΔT versus time reveals how Earth's rotation has been varying during the past few decades. The present value of UT1–UTC is also coded in radio time signals (see p. 47).

Local Mean (solar) Time (LMT) would suffice for the inhabitants of an isolated village, but with the advent in the 19th century of rapid travel and communication (railways, steamships, and the telegraph), it became essential that clocks over a range of longitudes indicate the same time. To keep these clocks reasonably in phase with the day–night cycle and yet avoid the inconvenience to travellers of a local time that varies continuously with longitude, in 1884, Earth was divided into 24 *Standard Time* zones, adjacent zones generally differing by one hour and each ideally 15° wide (see the time-zone map on p. 46). All clocks within the same zone read the same time. The Canadian railway surveyor and construction engineer Sir Sandford Fleming (1827–1915) was instrumental in establishing this system of standard time zones. The zero zone is centered on the Greenwich meridian (longitude 0°), and, since 1972, standard time in that zone is UTC. Thus the world system of civil time is based on UTC and includes the "leap seconds," which keep UTC near UT1. Depending upon an observer's location within his or her standard time zone, standard time may differ by up to an hour or so from LMT (see the third paragraph on p. 205). That is the second reason why the Sun seldom, if ever, is on the observer's meridian at 12:00 noon, standard time.

Humans generally have an awake/asleep cycle that is delayed by a few hours relative to the day/night cycle. Consequently, in higher latitudes during the spring and summer, when the Sun rises before humans do, more energy is needed for lighting in the evening than would be the case if the two cycles coincided. To shift the lifestyles of their citizens more in phase with the day/night cycle, many countries adopt *Daylight Saving Time*, advancing clocks by one hour during the spring and summer (a better term would be *Energy Saving Time* because it is energy that is being saved, not daylight). For most of Canada and the United States[1], clocks are advanced by one hour at 02:00 local time on the second Sunday in March, and return to standard time at 02:00 local time on the first Sunday in November: *spring ahead, fall back.*

---

[1] Some regions, such as northwestern Ontario, Saskatchewan, northeastern and southeastern British Columbia, Hawaii, and most of Arizona, do not observe Daylight Saving Time. For more information see webexhibits.org/daylightsaving.

STANDARD TIME ZONES

The map on the following page shows the world system of standard time zones. It was prepared and provided by Her Majesty's Nautical Almanac Office. Over the open oceans, the time zones are uniformly spaced and are bounded by lines of longitude 15° apart. In populated regions, political and other considerations have considerably modified the ideal geometry.

The standard time zones are generally designated by letters of the alphabet. The zero time zone, centered on the longitude 0° meridian passing through the Airy Transit Circle at the Old Royal Observatory in Greenwich, England, is denoted Z. Standard time within this zone is Coordinated Universal Time (UTC). Zones A, B, C,…, M (J excluded), increase eastward at one-hour intervals to the International Date Line (where, continuing eastward, the day of the week jumps discontinuously back by one day), while zones N, O, P,…, Y decrease westward at one-hour intervals to the same boundary (where, continuing westward, the day of the week jumps discontinuously ahead by one day). Zones M and Y are only one-half hour wide. Also, as indicated on the map, there are several partial zones that are one-half hour different from the adjacent main zones.

In Canada and the USA, there is one partial zone and seven standard time zones. In terms of their name (and letter designation, hours behind the Greenwich zone, and the west longitude of the reference or standard meridian), these are:

(1)	Newfoundland	(P*,	3 h 30 min, 52.5°)
(2)	Atlantic	(Q,	4 h, 60°)
(3)	Eastern	(R,	5 h, 75°)
(4)	Central	(S,	6 h, 90°)
(5)	Mountain	(T,	7 h, 105°)
(6)	Pacific	(U,	8 h, 120°)
(7)	Alaska	(V,	9 h, 135°)
(8)	Hawaii	(W,	10 h, 150°)

Note: Caution is advised when relying on the time-zone information given in this map. The zones are drawn based on the best information available as of August 2017 and are subject to change. Also, local jurisdictions, especially those near depicted zone boundaries, often adopt a different time. For current official Canadian and U.S. time zones visit www.nrc-cnrc.gc.ca/eng/services/inms/time-services.html and www.time.gov, respectively.

WORLD MAP OF TIME ZONES

TIME SIGNALS

National time services distribute Coordinated Universal Time (UTC). UTC is coordinated through the Bureau International des Poids et Mesures (BIPM) in Sèvres, France, so that most time services are synchronized to a tenth of a millisecond. Radio time signals available in North America include:

CHU Ottawa, Ontario, Canada 3.330, 7.850, 14.670 MHz
WWV Fort Collins, Colorado, USA 2.5, 5, 10, 15, 20 MHz

For CHU, each minute starts at the *beginning* of the tone following the voice announcement, the tone for the 29th second is omitted, and the tones for seconds 31 through 39 have a different sound from the others.

The difference ΔUT1 = UT1 – UTC to the nearest tenth of a second is coded in the signals. If UT1 is ahead of UTC, second markers beginning at the 1-second mark of each minute are doubled, the number of doubled markers indicating the number of tenths of a second UT1 is ahead of UTC. If UT1 is behind UTC, the doubled markers begin at the 9-second point.

Time signals are also available by telephone from the National Research Council in Ottawa. Call 613-745-1576 for English, and 613-745-9426 for French; the call may be routed via one or two communications satellite hops, being delayed by 0.25 seconds per hop. Internet time services can be found at time5.nrc.ca and www.nist.gov/pml/div688/grp40/its.cfm.

MEAN SIDEREAL TIME, 2018

The following is the Greenwich Mean Sidereal Time (GMST) in hours on day 0 at 0h UT of each month ("day 0" is the last day of the previous month):

Jan. 6.6409	Apr. 12.5548	Jul. 18.5344	Oct. 0.5797
Feb. 8.6779	May 14.5261	Aug. ...20.5714	Nov. 2.6167
Mar. 10.5178	Jun. 16.5631	Sep. 22.6084	Dec. 4.5880

GMST (in hours) at hour t UT on day d of the month =
GMST at 0h UT on day 0 + 0.065710d + 1.002738t

LMST (Local Mean Sidereal Time) = GMST – west longitude (or + east longitude)

LMST computed by this method is accurate to ±0.2 s provided t is stated to ±0.1 s or better and the observer's longitude is known to ±1″. Note that t must be expressed in decimal hours UT and longitude in hours, not degrees. Also, to achieve ±0.1 s accuracy in t, the correction ΔUT1 must be applied to UTC. See TIME SIGNALS above.

JULIAN DATE (JD), 2018

The Julian Date (JD) is commonly used by astronomers to refer to the time of astronomical events, because it avoids some of the annoying complexities of the civil calendar. Julian Date 0.0 was the instant of Greenwich mean noon on 4713 Jan. 1 BCE (see "The Origin of the Julian Day System" by G. Moyer, *Sky & Telescope*, April 1981, and en.wikipedia.org/wiki/Julian_day#Julian_Date).

The Julian day **commences at noon** (12h) UT. To find the JD at any time during 2018, determine the day of the month and time at the Greenwich meridian, convert this to a decimal day, and add it to one of the following numbers according to the month (these numbers are the JD for 0h UT on the 0th day of each month):

Jan. ...245 8118.5	Apr. ... 245 8208.5	Jul. 245 8299.5	Oct. 245 8391.5
Feb. ...245 8149.5	May ... 245 8238.5	Aug. ..245 8330.5	Nov. ...245 8422.5
Mar. ..245 8177.5	Jun. ... 245 8269.5	Sep. ...245 8361.5	Dec. ...245 8452.5

For example, 21:36 EDT on May 18 = 1:36 UT on May 19 = May 19.07 UT = 245 8238.5 + 19.07 = JD 245 8257.57.

The JD for 0h UT Jan. 0 for the five proximate years are 245 0000.5 plus: 7022 (2015), and 7387 (2016), and 7753 (2017), and 8483 (2019), and 8848 (2020).

ASTRONOMICAL TWILIGHT AND SIDEREAL TIME
by RANDALL BROOKS

The diagram gives for any day of the year: (1) the LMT of the end and beginning of astronomical twilight at seven specified latitudes (curved lines); (2) the (LMST = right ascension at the observer's meridian) as a function of LMT (diagonal lines). Months and right ascensions shown in **boldface** are for observers in the Northern Hemisphere, those in italics are for observers in the Southern Hemisphere.

OPTICS AND OBSERVING

TELESCOPE PARAMETERS
BY ROY BISHOP

Equations

Objective: f_o = focal length
D = diameter
FR = focal ratio

Eyepiece: f_e = focal length
d_f = diameter of field stop
θ_p = apparent angular field

Whole Instrument: M = angular magnification
d_p = diameter of exit pupil
θ_c = actual angular field

$$M \equiv \tan(\theta_p/2)/\tan(\theta_c/2) = f_o/f_e = D/d_p \approx \theta_p/\theta_c \quad FR = f_o/D$$

$$d_f = 2f_o \tan(\theta_c/2) = 2f_e \tan(\theta_p/2) \approx f_o\theta_c^* \approx f_e\theta_p^*$$

$^*(\theta_c$ and θ_p must be expressed in radians.)

Performance

D is assumed to be expressed in millimetres.

Light Grasp (LG) is the ratio of the light flux intercepted by a telescope's objective lens or mirror to that intercepted by a human eye having a 7-mm-diameter entrance pupil.

Limiting Visual Magnitude $m \approx 2.7 + 5 \log D$, assuming transparent, dark-sky conditions and magnification $M \geq 1D$ (see *Sky & Telescope*, *45*, 401, 1973; *77*, 332, 1989; *78*, 522, 1989).

Smallest Resolvable Angle $\alpha \approx 116/D$ seconds of arc (Dawes's limit). However, atmospheric conditions seldom permit values less than 0.5″.

Useful Magnification Range $\approx 0.2D$ to $2D$. The lower limit ($0.2D$) guarantees that, for most observers, all the light exiting a telescope can reach the retina. (The reciprocal of the coefficient to D is the diameter (in mm) of the telescope's exit pupil. Also, see the next section concerning exit pupils and magnification.) The upper limit ($2D$) is determined by the wave nature of light and the optical limitations of the eye, although atmospheric turbulence usually limits the maximum magnification to 400× or less. For examination of double stars, detection of faint stars, and studying structure in bright nebulae, magnifications of up to $3D$ are sometimes useful.

Chapman's Magnification Rule: For any telescope, an eyepiece of focal length FR mm provides $M = D$ and a 1-mm exit pupil.

Values for some common apertures

D (mm):	60	100	125	150	200	250	330	444
LG:	73	200	320	460	820	1300	2200	4000
m:	11.6	12.7	13.2	13.6	14.2	14.7	15.3	15.9
α:	1.93″	1.16″	0.93″	0.77″	0.58″	0.46″	0.35″	0.26″
$0.2D$:	12×	20×	25×	30×	40×	50×	66×	89×
$2D$:	120×	200×	250×	300×	400×	500×	660×	890×

TELESCOPE EXIT PUPILS
BY ROY BISHOP

The performance of a visual telescope is constrained by Earth's atmosphere, the wave aspect of light, the design of the telescope and imperfections in its optical system, and the properties of the human visual system. Telescope and eye meet at the *exit pupil* of the telescope, which is the image of the telescope's objective lens or mirror formed by its eyepiece. When a telescope is pointed at a bright area, such as the daytime sky, the exit pupil appears as a small disk of light hovering in the space just behind the eyepiece. (Insert a small piece of paper in this vicinity to prove that this disk of light *really is* located behind the eyepiece.) Since the exit pupil is the narrowest point in the beam of light emerging from the telescope, it is here that the observer's eye must be located to make optimum use of the light passing through the telescope.

The diagram on p. 52 may be used to display the relation between the diameter of the exit pupil (d_p) of a telescope and the focal lengths (f_e) of various eyepieces. Both d_p and f_e are expressed in millimetres. The numbered scale around the upper right-hand corner of the diagram indicates the focal ratio (FR) of the objective lens or mirror of the telescope. (The FR equals the focal length of the objective divided by its diameter; see p. 49.) To prepare the diagram for a particular telescope, locate the FR of the telescope's objective on the FR scale, and draw a straight diagonal line from there to the origin (the lower left-hand corner). The diagram provides a visual display of the standard relation $d_p = f_e/\text{FR}$. One can see at a glance what range of eyepiece focal lengths is suitable for a particular telescope. Concerning the "AGE" scale on the diagram, see the section Very Low (RFT) Magnifications below.

To determine, for example, the eyepiece focal length required to produce a 3-mm exit pupil on a certain telescope, locate $d_p = 3$ on the ordinate, run horizontally across to the diagonal line corresponding to the FR of that telescope, and from there drop vertically downward to the abscissa to find f_e. This procedure may, of course, be reversed: for a given f_e, find the corresponding d_p.

Magnification Ranges

The ranges H, M, L, and RFT blocked off along the ordinate of the diagram break the d_p scale into four sections, starting at 0.5 mm and increasing by factors of 2. Although this sectioning is somewhat arbitrary, it does correspond closely to what are usually considered to be the high (H), medium (M), low (L), and "richest-field telescope" (RFT) magnification ranges of any visual telescope—and the associated d_p ranges are easy to remember. Note that these magnification ranges are defined by d_p, not by the numerical value of the magnification; for example, a magnification of 100× is "high" for a telescope of aperture $D = 70$ mm, "medium" for $D = 150$ mm, "low" for $D = 300$ mm, "very low (RFT)" for $D = 600$ mm, and "ultra-low" for D larger than 0.8 m.

High Magnifications: In the case of the Moon, the planets, and all but the dimmest stars, the highest useful magnification is the point at which blurring due to diffraction (caused by the wave nature of light) becomes noticeable. That corresponds approximately to $d_p = 0.5$ mm, assuming good optics and negligible atmospheric turbulence (i.e. excellent "seeing"). Higher magnifications will not reveal any more detail in these images and will cause reductions in four desirable features: sharpness, brightness, field of view, and eye relief (the space between the eye and eyepiece). However, for double stars and for some objects requiring the use of averted vision (e.g. faint stars) very high magnifications ($d_p < 0.5$ mm) can sometimes be used to advantage.

Medium Magnifications: A problem with high magnifications is that exit-pupil diameters of about 1 mm and smaller cause "floaters" (mobile debris in the vitreous humour of the eye in front of the retina) to interfere with vision. That problem increases with the age of the observer and with decreasing d_p. To avoid the distraction of floaters, an observer might choose to keep exit-pupil diameters no smaller than 1.5 mm (i.e. in the "medium" magnification range). For this lower limit the diagram indicates a minimum eyepiece focal length of, for example, 7 mm for a FR = 4.5 telescope, 15 mm for a FR = 10 telescope, and 24 mm for a FR = 16 telescope. With this restriction, to achieve a magnification of 250× for observing planets, a telescope would need an aperture of at least $D = M \times d_p = 250 \times 1.5 = 375$ mm. Hence, in addition to providing more light and greater resolution, a large-aperture telescope makes floaters less noticeable and magnifications in the "high" range less necessary.

With magnifications greater than very low (RFT) magnifications and also possibly greater than low magnifications, structure in dim, extended objects, such as galaxies and bright and dark nebulae, will be more easily seen. To see such objects, observers use averted vision, which places the image on the peripheral retina, which is composed primarily of the very sensitive "rod" photoreceptor cells. However, the number of rod cells far exceeds the number of nerve axons available to carry the signals to the visual centers in the brain. To accommodate this limitation and to cope with spontaneous thermal noise in the rod cells, the cells are grouped into detector units of various sizes (analogous to binning of pixels in a CCD chip). Because of the thermal noise, only those signals triggered by almost simultaneous photon hits in several rod cells are allowed to produce a conscious sensation. Thus in very dim light only large retinal detector units receive enough photon hits to respond. As a consequence, our ability to see detail is greatly reduced in dim light. Hence extra magnification helps to reveal structure in galaxies and nebulae.

Low Magnifications: Low magnifications have several advantages over certain other magnification ranges:

(1) For most observers an exit-pupil diameter between 2 mm and 4 mm results in the sharpest optical image because the combined influence of optical aberrations in the eye of the observer (which increase with increasing d_p) and blurring due to diffraction (which decreases with increasing d_p) is at a minimum. Assuming, for example, that the optimum d_p for a "typical observer" is 2.5 mm, then to realize this and achieve a magnification of 250× for observing planets, a telescope needs an aperture of $D = M \times d_p = 250 \times 2.5 = 625$ mm. Once again, the superiority of a large telescope (by amateur standards) is apparent. Another example: the reason for the crisp images provided by Canon's image-stabilized binoculars is that their d_p is in the "low magnification" range, and their optical quality is up to the challenge.

(2) Low magnifications provide greater luminance than high or medium magnifications, enabling the eye to discern contrast variations over a wider range of spatial frequencies.

(3) Viewing is more comfortable than with very low (RFT) magnifications, since the observer can move a bit (move the head and/or scan the field) without cutting into the light beam and dimming the image. As mentioned below, ultra-low magnifications have the same advantage, but light is wasted.

(4) Light entering near the edge of the pupil of the dark-adapted eye is not as effective in stimulating the rod cells in the retina—the "scotopic Stiles–Crawford effect" (see VanLoo and Enoch, *Vision Research, 15* (1975), p. 1005). Thus low magnifications make more effective use of the light than very low (RFT) magnifications.

(5) Low magnifications provide a darker sky background than very low (RFT) magnifications, producing views that some observers consider to be aesthetically more pleasing.

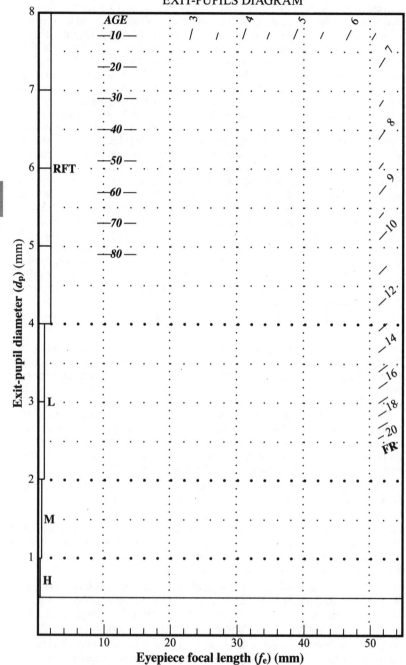

EXIT-PUPILS DIAGRAM

Diagram by Roy Bishop

Very Low (RFT) Magnifications: Magnifications in the RFT range are useful because they yield wide fields of view, the brightest (greatest luminance) images of extended objects, and for common telescope apertures, the most stars visible in one view (hence the term *richest field*). The lowest magnification that still makes use of the full aperture of a telescope is determined by the point at which the diameter of the telescope's exit pupil matches the diameter of the *entrance pupil* of the observer's eye.

For the dark-adapted eye, the entrance-pupil diameter seldom equals the often-quoted figure of 7 mm, but depends, among other things, upon the age of the observer as indicated by the scale in the upper-left portion of the diagram (see Kadlecová et al., *Nature, 182* (1958), p. 1520; *Sky & Telescope*, May 1992, p. 502). Note that this scale indicates *average* values; the maximum diameter of the entrance pupil of the eye of any *one* individual may differ by up to a millimetre from these values. A horizontal line should be drawn across the diagram corresponding to the maximum diameter of one's own entrance pupil. This line will be an upper bound on d_p in the same sense that the line at $d_p = 0.5$ mm is a lower bound. Note that in daylight, the entrance pupil of the eye has a diameter in the range of 2 mm to 4 mm. Thus for daylight use of telescopes, the upper bound on d_p will be correspondingly reduced.

Ultra-Low Magnifications: If a d_p value larger than the entrance pupil of the eye is used, the iris of the observer's eye will cut off some of the light passing through the telescope to the retina; that is, the iris will have become the light-limiting aperture *(aperture stop)* of the system rather than the edge of the telescope's objective. In this case, the cornea of the eye together with the lenses of the telescope's eyepiece form an image of the observer's iris at the objective of the telescope; to the incoming starlight, a highly magnified image of the iris hovers as an annular skirt covering the outer region of the objective of the telescope! A telescope can be used at such "ultra-low" magnifications, but obviously a telescope of smaller aperture would perform as well. However, ultra-low magnifications have two advantages:

(1) A wider actual field of view, assuming the field stop of the eyepiece will permit this (an eyepiece having a 2-in. barrel diameter is usually necessary).

(2) Ease of alignment of the entrance pupil of the eye with the exit pupil of the telescope, an aspect of viewing that is usually troublesome when these two pupils are nearly the same size. An oversize exit pupil provides "slop," making alignment less critical. That is particularly helpful when using binoculars during activities involving motion, such as boating or bird watching, and is one advantage of using 7 × 50 (= M × D) binoculars rather than 7 × 35 binoculars for daytime activities, although less than half of the light entering the larger binoculars can reach the observer's retinas.

Some examples using the diagram:

(1) Consider the common 8-in. Schmidt–Cassegrain telescopes. These have $D = 200$ mm and (usually) FR = 10. The diagram indicates that eyepieces with focal lengths from 5 mm to 55 mm are usable for most observers. With a 32-mm eyepiece, the diagram gives $d_p = 3.2$ mm, in the L magnification range, and the magnification $M = D/d_p = 200/3.2 = 62×$.

(2) If an observer wishes to use the full aperture of an FR = 4.5 telescope, a 40-mm eyepiece is ruled out. Similarly, a 70-year-old observer should probably not use even a 27-mm eyepiece on such a telescope and should not bother with 7 × 50 or 11 × 80 binoculars, unless ease of eye/exit-pupil alignment is the main consideration.

(3) There is no point in using extremely short focal length eyepieces, especially when combined with Barlow lenses, on telescopes having large FRs. That is a common fault (among many others!) with camera/department store "junk telescopes."

MAGNIFICATION AND CONTRAST
IN DEEP-SKY OBSERVING
BY LEE JOHNSON AND WILLIAM ROBERTS

For visual observation of point sources (stars), magnitude limits of common telescope apertures are given in TELESCOPE PARAMETERS (see p. 49). Additional challenges attend the observation of faint, extended, deep-sky objects. This article explores methods to determine the visibility of diffuse objects such as galaxies, dense star clusters, and gaseous nebulae. The main variables governing the visibility of such an object are its average luminance ("surface brightness" in older sources), its angular dimensions, the sky luminance, the telescope aperture, and the magnification used (or, equivalently, the exit pupil of the telescope). Additional factors include the effects of filters, atmospheric extinction, and the limitations of monocular vision. Addressing all these factors, this article builds on seminal research on visual contrast thresholds (Blackwell, 1946), and concludes by linking to an online **Magnification and Contrast Calculator** for estimating the visibility of deep-sky objects. (For an alternative treatment of the same research, especially in relation to the structure of the eye, see Clark, 1990.)

Luminance and Exit Pupils

Table 1 shows the magnitude, size, and luminance of two representative deep-sky objects, with luminance expressed in units of magnitude per square arcsecond (mag/arcsec^2). (For more details on these two objects, see the referenced pages in this Handbook.) When these luminance values are compared to those of skies corresponding to mountain-top observatories (22), dark country sites (21), sites with 5th-mag. stars visible (19.5), and a suburban setting with 4th-mag. stars visible (18.5), it is clear that an object can be dimmer than the sky background; that is, the contrast between the object and the sky is very low. A Sky Quality Meter (unihedron.com) provides a baseline luminance measurement for such a comparison.

TABLE 1—MAGNITUDE, SIZE, AND LUMINANCE

Object	Type	m_v	Size (arcmin)	Luminance (mag/arcsec^2)	OH Page Ref.
NGC 7317	galaxy	13.6	0.5×0.5	20.7	p. 337
Jones 1	planetary nebula	12.1	5.5×5.5	24.4	p. 323

Size, magnitude, and luminance (surface brightness) of deep-sky objects can be found in *The Deep Sky Field Guide to Uranometria 2000.0* and (for a few objects) in A DEEP-SKY SELECTION (see p. 309). In addition, most tables in THE DEEP SKY (see p. 307) include magnitudes and sizes of objects. For any extended deep-sky object, the luminance, S, in mag/arcsec^2, can be estimated from size and magnitude by

$$S = m_v + 2.5\log(2827ab),$$

where a and b are, respectively, the object's major and minor diameters in arcminutes, assuming an elliptical shape. (Subtract 8.9 to convert units to mag/arcmin^2.)

The exit pupil of a telescope (objective diameter divided by magnification) determines the luminance of the image of both the object and the sky as viewed through the eyepiece (see TELESCOPE EXIT PUPILS, p. 50). When an extended object is magnified to the extent that the telescope exit pupil becomes smaller than the entrance pupil of the eye—nominally 7 mm—its luminance decreases relative to the naked-eye view. The decrease is the same for both the object and the sky; in other words, **magnification does not alter contrast**. Table 2 gives the reduction in luminance of both object and sky as the exit pupil decreases.

TABLE 2—DIMMING WITH RESPECT TO A 7-MM EXIT PUPIL

Exit Pupil (mm)	7	6	5	4	3	2	1	0.5
Dimming (mag)	0.0	0.3	0.7	1.2	1.8	2.7	4.2	5.7

Human binocular vision has a lower luminance limit of approximately 1 μcd/m^2, which, when adjusted for monocular vision, is about 27 mag/arcsec^2. When the dimming due to reduced exit pupils (from Table 2) is combined with the sky luminance, it is apparent that the luminance of a magnified dark sky may approach the detection limit of the eye; for example, a 1-mm exit pupil in a 22.0 mag/arcsec^2 sky reduces the apparent sky luminance to 26.2 mag/arcsec^2, which is near the limit of the eye.

The Relation Between Size and Threshold Luminance

Blackwell (1946), in a massive World War II study that is still the only one of its kind, analysed approximately 450 000 observations of threshold contrast over a wide range of background illumination. Table 3, derived from Blackwell's data, gives the minimum detectable luminance of an object for various combinations of object size and background luminance. The values are corrected for monocular vision and assume a 50% probability of detection; for 90% probability, subtract 0.5 from the entries in the table.

TABLE 3—THRESHOLD LUMINANCE OF EXTENDED OBJECTS

Object Size (')	Background Luminance (mag/arcsec^2)							
	26	25	24	23	22	21	20	19
360	26.3	26.0	25.6	25.0	24.4	23.7	23.0	22.3
240	26.1	25.8	25.4	24.8	24.2	23.5	22.8	22.2
120	25.5	25.3	24.9	24.4	23.7	23.1	22.4	21.8
60	24.7	24.5	24.2	23.7	23.1	22.5	21.9	21.3
30	23.8	23.8	23.3	22.8	22.3	21.7	21.1	20.6
15	22.5	22.3	22.0	21.6	21.1	20.6	20.1	19.7

The table confirms that low-luminance objects of a given size are more easily seen against darker backgrounds. For a given background luminance, large objects are more easily detected than small ones of equal luminance. Applied to the case of an object viewed through a telescope, as magnification increases, one moves up in the table (larger apparent size) and also to the left (smaller exit pupil = darker sky). Hence, detectability benefits from higher magnifications, in agreement with observing experience. However, note that this benefit is smaller toward the upper-left corner of the table. As magnification increases, a point may be reached where the decreasing exit pupil reduces the object luminance faster than the increasing size raises the threshold luminance. Thus the object would become more difficult to detect, but the increased magnification might make it easier to identify bright detail within the object.

It is important to note that the table values are guidelines only. If Table 3 suggests that the detection of an object is marginal, do not be discouraged; try anyway. Other factors that affect object detection are: atmospheric extinction, light loss in the telescope optics, the difference between the nighttime and daytime response of the eye (see FILTERS, 64), and the observer's visual acuity. Typically, the cumulative effect of these factors is between −0.5 and +0.5 mag.; see Schaefer (1990) for further details.

An example using Table 3: Consider the galaxy NGC 7317 in a 21.0 mag/arcsec^2 sky. A magnification of 148× with a 445-mm telescope gives an apparent object size of 74′ with a telescope exit pupil of 3 mm. From Table 2, a 3-mm exit pupil dims both object and sky by 1.8 mag., resulting in luminance values of 22.5 (object) and 22.8 (sky). The entry in Table 3 for background luminance 23 and object size 60′ gives a threshold luminance of 23.7. That is more than one magnitude dimmer than the image of NGC 7317, which should therefore be clearly visible under the specified conditions. On the other hand, a smaller, 130-mm telescope with a magnification of 43× gives a reduced object size of 22′ with a 3-mm exit pupil, hence the values of object and sky luminance are the same as before. Again from the fourth column of Table 3, the interpolated threshold luminance of this smaller image is 22.2, so the object will likely not be visible in this smaller instrument at this magnification. Alternatively, finding the object luminance in that column, we see that the minimum apparent size is almost 30′, and since 22′ is less than this, the object is unlikely to be seen.

The Relation between Minimum Detectable Size and Contrast

Figure 1 shows another way of interpreting Blackwell's data, a graphical representation of Table 3, whose columns are now a set of curves (odd-valued sky luminance values are shown with dashed lines for clarity). The vertical axis represents the minimum detectable size of an object, and the horizontal axis is the object–sky magnitude contrast, that is, the magnitude difference between object luminance and sky luminance. Whereas Table 3 emphasizes detectability as a function of object luminance and size, Figure 1 emphasizes detectability as a function of the object–sky magnitude contrast and size.

FIGURE 1—MINIMUM DETECTABLE SIZE VS. CONTRAST

An example using Figure 1: Emission and planetary nebulae are special cases, as contrast can be improved using filters (see FILTERS, 64). Bandpass filters such as the UHC, OIII, and Hβ improve contrast by passing light near the emission wavelengths and rejecting broad-spectrum light from light pollution and natural skyglow at other wavelengths, effectively reducing the sky luminance by about 1.6 mag. through the UHC filter and about 2.6 mag. through the OIII and Hβ filters. The visible light from emission nebulae is mainly in the OIII and Hβ wavelengths, which lie close to the peak response of the dark-adapted eye. Filters such as the UHC pass all the light from these lines and do not significantly dim the nebulae. These filters therefore do not require an increase in exit pupil in order to maintain the object luminance. On the other hand, OIII filters—and especially Hβ filters—may pass only a portion of the light from an emission nebula, hence dimming the nebula. Here, restoring the object's luminance requires an increase in exit pupil and thus a decrease in magnification. The OIII filter passes most of the light from a typical planetary nebula and thus does not require an increase in exit pupil; it is therefore the filter of choice for these objects. The situation for other emission nebulae is not so clear.

Consider viewing Jones 1, a dim planetary nebula of luminance 24.4 mag/arcsec^2, in a sky of luminance 21.0, a magnitude contrast of +3.4. An exit pupil of 2 mm or smaller would reduce the object luminance below the eye's absolute threshold of 27. In a 250-mm aperture, a magnification of 50× gives an exit pupil of 5 mm, which results in a sky luminance of 21.7 and an object size of 275′. Figure 1 shows the minimum detectable size at a contrast of 3.4 to be greater than 360′, so Jones 1 would not be visible under these conditions. An OIII filter would reduce the sky luminance by 2.6 mag. without dimming Jones 1 appreciably and results in a sky luminance of 24.3. The magnitude contrast would be +0.8 mag., and the minimum apparent size is approximately 40′. The planetary nebula should be visible when viewed in that telescope with the filter.

Magnification and Contrast Calculator

Table 3 has been incorporated into a **Magnification and Contrast Calculator** spreadsheet, available online at www.rasc.ca/handbook/supplements. When data for an object, the sky, the telescope, and possible filters are entered, the spreadsheet calculates the observed image parameters and makes a detection prediction of YES, NO, or MAYBE.

Summary

Generally, experienced deep-sky observers select eyepieces that produce exit pupils in the range 2–3 mm when viewing a faint deep-sky object. This range of exit pupils corresponds to the middle of both Table 3 and Figure 1. Larger exit pupils correspond to the lower right of the table, where small, faint objects may fall below the threshold of visibility; and smaller exit pupils to the upper left, where excessive magnification may dim the object to invisibility. At any fixed apparent size, moving from right to left across the table results in a decrease in threshold brightness, which shows the benefit of observing in increasingly dark skies or with the aid of a filter.

References and Resources

- Blackwell, H.R., "Contrast thresholds of the human eye," *J. Opt. Soc. Am. 36*, 624–643 (1946).
- Clark, Roger N., *Visual Astronomy of the Deep Sky*, Sky Publishing Corp., Cambridge, Mass., 1990, p. 13 *ff*. Also see www.clarkvision.com/visastro
- Schaefer, Bradley "Telescopic Limiting Magnitudes," *Publ. Astron. Soc. Pac. 102*, 213–215 (February, 1990).
- Mel Bartels' internet page *Visual Astronomy*: www.bbastrodesigns.com/visual.html

NIGHT MYOPIA AND STARGAZING EYEGLASSES
BY JOSHUA ROTH

For most of human history, visual astronomy relied on one and only one optical instrument: the human eye. For the past four centuries, though, we have taken to scrutinizing the heavens with optical aid, and the telescope—once a rarity—is attainable by nearly everyone in the developed world who wishes to own one. With its ability to provide more light and magnify the rings of Saturn, gaseous nebulae, and Milky Way beyond what our own eyes can do, telescopic viewing understandably has displaced naked-eye observing as the *modus operandi* of the modern visual astronomer. Nevertheless, there are many observations, some purely aesthetic, others of scientific value, that are best made with the unaided eye.

Unaided, that is, except for eyeglasses or contact lenses; and then only when warranted. But when exactly is such "unit-magnification" optical aid warranted? Most of us get glasses or contacts only when an eyecare professional diagnoses a vision defect. However, even those who were born with decent daytime vision may need eyeglasses or contact lenses to best see the stars by night; and those who *do* use eyeglasses or contact lenses by day may need a different prescription for stargazing. Are you one of those people? In what follows, I will tell you how to find out, but first, a little background on the eye as an optical instrument.

Using its varied layers and components, the eye functions like a converging lens. This means that it brings numerous light rays from a star—or any other point in the field of view—to focus at a single point in space. In practice, of course, not all of the rays that enter the eye from one point can be brought to a single focus: various aberrations conspire against this. Still, at its best the eye brings much of the light from a star to focus at a single point.

Unfortunately, in many cases that point fails to land on the retina: the pad of light-sensitive cells that functions as the eye's "CCD." In many cases, the light is focused in front of the retina, and it spreads out anew before reaching our rods and cones. We call this condition *myopia*, or nearsightedness, because a person so afflicted can see nearby objects well, even though distant ones are blurred, sometimes beyond recognition.

Needless to say, those of us who suffer from myopia typically wear our eyeglasses or contact lenses when looking at the constellations or watching for meteors. If we are purely near- or farsighted, we can do without them at the telescope, since a twist of the focus knob can correct for these visual defects. Astigmatism, on the other hand, requires us to keep using our eyeglasses or contacts at the eyepiece.

Still, many of us have been less than satisfied with our "unit-magnification" views of the night sky, straining to see 6th-magnitude stars or large, diffuse objects like the Beehive Cluster. In many cases, this is because our eyes are not bringing starlight to a focus on our retinae *even if our daytime vision is essentially perfect (be it with or without glasses or contacts)*. Rather, in many cases (though by no means all), humans become more nearsighted as their pupils dilate. This *night myopia* requires correction—above and beyond any correction that may already be in use for daylight hours—if we are to use our eyes to the fullest at night.

Eyecare professionals have debated the causes of night myopia for decades. One theory attributes the effect to the notion that humans tend to focus on their immediate surroundings when startled, frightened, or deprived of adequate visual stimulus. In recent years, it has become possible to measure the human eye's optical figure precisely. In doing so, researchers have found that many peoples' eyes evince significant amounts of spherical aberration when their pupils are dilated.[1]

As a practical matter, one quick way to probe any night myopia you may have would be to borrow eyeglasses from a friend who is more myopic than you, but a better probe—and one that will quantify the effect—is to use a set of optometrists' "flippers": a pair of mounted lenses that can be held in front of your eyes (or your eyeglasses) and quickly flipped in and out of position.[2] Do-it-yourselfers can use biconcave or plano-concave lenses with focal lengths of one metre or greater (corresponding to powers of one diopter and below). Alternatively, an astronomy club could split the (admittedly modest) cost of a set of flippers.

Once you have your flippers in hand, how will you use them to establish whether or not you suffer from night myopia (and, if so, to what degree)? Ideally, lie out for at least half an hour in a setting free of light pollution, and periodically assess your night myopia as you become increasingly dark adapted. Targets such as Ursa Minor and the Pleiades, with their well-established sequences of apparent magnitudes, are ideal, but any star field you are familiar with will do. View the field through your existing eyeglasses or contact lenses (if any), then insert the various flipper lens pairs between your eyes and the night sky and take careful note of any change in limiting magnitude or image quality. Consider allowing for the possibility that each eye may have a different amount of night myopia.

If indeed you find that a particular flipper lens pair best shows you the stars, you may find that looking at the stars through your flipper is all you need to enhance your experience of the night sky. (Certainly it would suffice for a quick look through a reflex sight (e.g. *Telrad*) or to determine limiting magnitude for one's observing log.) On the other hand, you may find that you prefer to obtain a set of eyeglasses dedicated to "naked-eye" stargazing, so that you can gaze heavenward with your arms at rest. These stargazing glasses should be made of a material that separates different colors of light as little as possible (above all, do not use polycarbonate, which is very impact-resistant but also "prisms" points of light into little rainbows, especially near the edges of one's field of view). Many aficionados recommend antireflection coatings.

Anecdotal reports on internet discussion boards suggest that correcting for night myopia has enabled many visual observers to gain a half magnitude or more in their ability to see faint stars. Such reports also suggest that the typical observer who does order a pair of stargazing eyeglasses finds him/herself correcting for ½ to ¾ diopter of night myopia (above and beyond any daytime nearsightedness that they already may be correcting with glasses or contacts). My own stargazing eyeglasses (one extra diopter) enabled me to spot Uranus "naked-eye" and a dozen or so NGC star clusters for the first time. More importantly, they improved the definition of dark nebulae and lanes in the Milky Way. I now consider them by far my most important piece of optical equipment. Systematic research on this topic by active observers among the RASC membership would be a valuable addition to the literature of visual astronomy.

References:

[1] See "Spectacles for Spectacular Skies" p. 30 in the September 2005 issue of *Sky & Telescope* for details and illustrations. As of this writing it is available free of charge in PDF at **www.skyandtelescope.com/howto/visualobserving**.

[2] Ontario-based Optego Vision Inc. (**optego.com**) sell two affordable sets of Night Myopia Diagnostic Flippers (one with ¼ and ½ diopter of myopia correction, and another with ¾ and 1 diopter). Between these two sets, you can correct for night myopia as strong as 1½ diopters, as the flippers can be stacked. Optego also offer flippers with other diopter settings. 341 Deloraine Ave., Toronto ON M5M 2B7. Tel: 416-780-1289 or toll free 800-678-3464

BINOCULARS
BY ROY BISHOP

For an experienced observer, binoculars are indispensable. For a beginning observer, binoculars are preferable to an astronomical telescope. For a beginner unfamiliar with the large-scale features of the sky, who cannot yet identify a dozen constellations on any clear night, a telescope's narrow field of view, confusing image orientations, and unfamiliar controls will quickly cause more frustration than fun. The beginner is at a double disadvantage because he or she also does not know enough about astronomical telescopes to distinguish those that are worthy of the name from the common camera/department-store "junk telescopes"—the $299 wonders with poor optics and wobbly mounts. How many such telescopes are gathering dust in closets, their young owners turned off astronomy and their parents a few hundred dollars poorer? Far better had the same investment been made in a good pair of binoculars. With their ease of use, wide field of view, and unreversed, upright images, binoculars are a great help in finding one's way around the sky, and provide many unique views of the heavens.

Binoculars magnifying 6 to 10 times are ideal for locating planets in the twilight, scanning the constellations, studying the larger dark nebulae and star fields of our galaxy, and viewing bright comets. Binoculars magnifying 10 to 20 times provide the best views of objects spanning a few degrees, such as the Hyades, the Pleiades, the North America Nebula, and the Andromeda Galaxy; they also give the finest view of the slender crescent Moon, or of the full Moon with broken clouds blowing by.

Binoculars permit us to view the Universe with both eyes, thereby providing more advantages: an improved sense of reality and depth (although parallax is negligible when viewing the heavens); more relaxed viewing; a complete view in the sense that the blind areas of one eye (associated with blood vessels and the region where the optic nerve attaches to the retina) are compensated by the field provided by the other eye; and dim objects appear brighter when viewed with two eyes.

Sizes: Binocular sizes are specified by numbers, for example, 7 × 50 and 8 × 30. The first number, including the "×," is the angular magnification or "power"; the second number is the diameter of the front (objective) lenses in millimetres. That is, in the notation on p. 49: $M \times D$. Thus the exit-pupil diameter is easily calculated from $D \div M$ (e.g. 7 × 35 binoculars have exit pupils of $35 \div 7 = 5$ mm). Another important parameter is field of view. Binoculars have apparent angular field diameters of about 50° when equipped with standard eyepieces, to near 70° with wide-angle eyepieces. The actual field of view on the sky (typically 3° to 10°) equals approximately the apparent field divided by the magnification. Thus the area of sky visible decreases rapidly with higher magnifications, making aiming binoculars at an object of interest more difficult.

What is the best binocular size for astronomical use? There is no simple answer. Almost *any* pair of binoculars will show far more than can be seen with the unaided eyes; however, for astronomical use the objective lenses should be at least 30 mm in diameter. Also, small binoculars of high quality are more enjoyable to use than a large pair of low quality.

Caveat emptor! Low-quality binoculars (and telescopes) are common. Images seen through low-quality binoculars are slightly fuzzy (usually not apparent to the inexperienced observer), one's eyes will be strained in trying to compensate for imperfectly aligned optics, and the focusing mechanism is usually flexible and crackling with an excess of grease used to mask poor workmanship. Avoid both zoom (variable magnification) binoculars and binoculars that do not have an adjustable focus—invariably these are of low quality.

Considering that binoculars contain at least 14 pieces of glass with 36 optical surfaces, antireflection coatings on (hopefully) all air-to-glass surfaces, plus two focusing mechanisms and an interpupillary adjustment, it is not surprising that top-quality instruments cost about $1000 or more. Such prices buy crisp, high-contrast images, accurately aligned optics, precise, rugged, dust- and moisture-proof construction, and pleasurable service for a lifetime. Nevertheless, there is a big market for $99 binoculars and $299 telescopes, and manufacturers are happy to satisfy the demand. When it comes to optical equipment, quality usually matches price.

Stability: One aspect of binocular use not often appreciated is how much more can be seen if the binoculars are mounted on a stable support, such as a camera tripod. That eliminates the constant jiggling associated with hand-holding and also supports the weight of the instrument. Adapters for attaching binoculars to a tripod are available, although usually it is not difficult to make your own. A recent major advance in binocular design is "image stabilization," an active optical system built into binoculars that compensates for the tremor associated with hand-holding. For example, the Canon company has introduced microprocessor-controlled binocular image stabilization that gives almost tripod-like stability with the convenience of hand-holding (see *SkyNews*, July/August 1998, p. 12; and *Sky & Telescope*, July 2000, p. 59). The Canon 10 × 42L model in particular, with its superb optics, convenient 6.5° diameter actual field, and close focusing ability, is the single best, hand-held set of binoculars ever created for both general daytime use and astronomy. It accepts 52-mm camera UV filters to protect the objective lenses.

Rating Binoculars

A frequently cited figure for binocular performance is "Relative Brightness," which equals the square of the diameter (in millimetres) of the instrument's exit pupils. For example, for 7 × 50 binoculars this figure is $(50 \div 7)^2 \approx 51$. Although this is a measure of the surface brightness *(luminance)* of an extended object seen through the binoculars under nighttime conditions, it is a totally inadequate measure of binocular performance on the night sky. For instance, using this figure of merit, large 14 × 100 binoculars have practically the same rating as the unaided eyes (which, when young and in dim light, are effectively 1 × 7 binoculars)!

Since seeing depends upon light, and the amount of light passing through a pair of binoculars depends primarily upon the *area* of the objective lenses (diameter D), a D^2 dependence appears reasonable. However, although the amount of light going into the point images of stars increases as D^2, assuming constant magnification the increase in the luminance of the background sky as D increases leads to a somewhat slower improvement in the visibility of these stars. A similar muted improvement occurs for dim extended images, resulting in an approximately D^1 dependence, rather than D^2.

Also, for constant D the detail that can be seen in the night sky increases with the magnification M. The resulting lower luminance of the background sky allows fainter stars to be seen, and the visibility of structure in extended images improves as M increases because the image is larger and of fixed contrast relative to the sky background.

The simplest figure of merit for the performance of binoculars in low-light conditions that combines both variables is the mathematical product $M \times D$ (which happens to look the same as the binocular size specification). In the case of two pairs of binoculars, one having twice the M and twice the D of the other, $M \times D$ indicates that "four times as much" should be visible in the larger instrument (e.g. 16 × 60 versus 8 × 30 binoculars). That is to be expected, since in the larger instrument stars will be four times brighter and extended images will have four times the area from which the eyes can glean information, with luminances being the same in both instruments.

For many decades the venerable Carl Zeiss optical company has cited $\sqrt{(M \times D)}$ as a "Twilight Performance Factor" for binoculars, its value said to be proportional to the distance at which various binoculars will show the same detail. That is equivalent to $M \times D$ being proportional to *the amount of detail that can be seen at the same distance*. The latter situation is relevant for astronomy since, unlike a bird or other object on Earth, a star or a galaxy is always at essentially the *same distance* from the observer. $M \times D$ could be called the *visibility factor*.

Binocular Performance Diagram

The diagram on the following page enables one to quickly compare binoculars in terms of their ability to reveal detail in the night sky. The vertical axis is magnification M; the horizontal axis is aperture D. The uniform grid of small dots is a guide to reading the diagram. The five straight lines indicate constant exit-pupil diameters of 3, 4, 5, 6, and 7 mm, as indicated both by numbers and by circles of these diameters near the top ends of the lines. The five curved arcs indicate constant values of $M \times D$ (the visibility factor), increasing by successive powers of 2 toward the upper right (100, 200, 400, 800, and 1600). Each large dot represents a common size of binoculars. The arrows in the lower-right corner indicate the directions on the diagram in which various quantities increase most rapidly.

Each straight line (constant exit-pupil diameter) also corresponds to constant luminance of extended areas, such as the Orion Nebula or the background sky glow, with the luminance being proportional to the square of the exit-pupil diameter (provided the entrance pupils of the observer's eyes are large enough to accommodate the exit pupils of the binoculars). However, exit pupils of 3 to 5 mm ensure that (i) all the light transmitted by the binoculars can enter the dark-adapted eyes no matter what the observer's age; (ii) alignment of exit pupils with dark-adapted eye pupils is relatively easy to achieve; (iii) the background sky glow will be subdued; and (iv) star images will be less distorted by aberrations in the observer's eyes (see TELESCOPE EXIT PUPILS, p. 50).

Examples (see the diagram): for viewing the night sky 10×50 binoculars will show about twice as much detail as 7×35s; 11×80 and 15×60 binoculars are equally capable, as are 8×30s and 6×42s (assuming one's eye pupils can accommodate the exit pupils of the instrument with the larger D); 10×50 binoculars are appreciably better than 7×50s for visibility (although, assuming equal apparent angular fields, 7×50s will show about twice as much sky area as will 10×50s). Canon's image-stabilized 15×45 binoculars are nearly equivalent to tripod-mounted 10×70s, with the *triple* advantage of smaller size, accommodating observers whose pupils will not open to 7 mm, and not requiring a tripod!

The visibility factor *($M \times D$)* is applicable to the usual range of binocular sizes (exit pupils between about 2 mm and 7 mm), but should not be extrapolated indefinitely. For instance, as the magnification is increased on a telescope and the exit pupil approaches 1 mm or less, a point will be reached (dependent upon the darkness of the sky) where the background sky glow is imperceptible. Also, stars will begin to show either seeing disks or diffraction disks. A further increase in M will not cause a noticeable improvement in the visibility of stars, and the perceived contrast between an extended object and the sky will decrease. In addition, the angular size of an extended object must be kept in mind. Once M is increased to the point at which the object fills the field of view of the instrument, the object may not be visible at all! For example, a large, dim comet coma may be visible in 15×60 binoculars ($M \times D = 900$) but *invisible* in a 45×200 telescope ($M \times D = 9000$).

BINOCULAR PERFORMANCE DIAGRAM

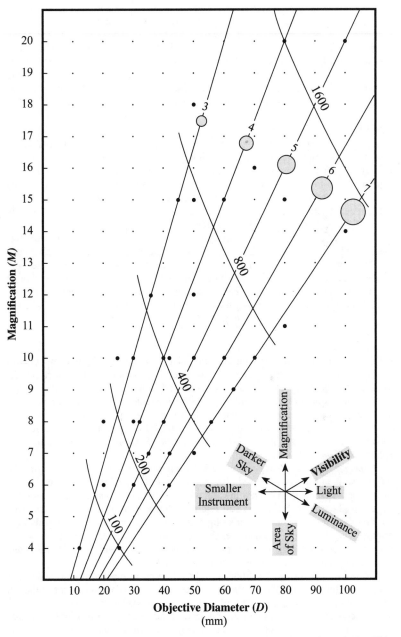

Diagram by Roy Bishop

FILTERS
BY ROY BISHOP

Optical filters reflect and absorb some portion of the incident light. *Neutral-density filters* reflect and absorb light more or less uniformly across the visible spectrum. *Colored (dye) filters* typically pass only one or two moderately broad portions of the spectrum. *Interference filters* are more selective and typically pass only one or two well-defined, narrow segments of the spectrum. All three types of filter are invaluable in astronomy.

In addition to categorization by physical type, filters may be categorized according to their intended use: lunar and planetary (neutral-density and dye filters), solar (neutral-density and interference filters), and nebular (interference filters).

Lunar and Planetary Filters

As viewed in a telescope, the Moon and the planets Venus, Mars, and Jupiter are often uncomfortably bright. A neutral-density filter, which passes only 13%–25% of the light, solves this problem while avoiding the loss in resolution that would accompany stopping down the aperture of the telescope to decrease the brightness to the same level. With a less-glaring image, light scattering in the observer's eye is reduced and fine details are easier to see. A neutral-density filter is typically about 26 mm in diameter and is attached to the forward-facing end of an eyepiece.

Dye filters can enhance the visibility of various planetary features. For instance, a red or yellow filter will absorb bluish light scattered by the Martian atmosphere and thereby improve the contrast of features on the surface of Mars. A green filter will increase the visibility of pale red and blue areas in the atmosphere of Jupiter (although the entire image will then appear green). Also, since they absorb an appreciable fraction of the light, dye filters or polarizing filters have the same advantage as a weak neutral-density filter when viewing bright objects.

Solar Filters

A filter is essential when observing the Sun. Solar filters must be designed not only to reduce the brightness of the solar surface to a comfortable level, but to block out the invisible but damaging infrared and ultraviolet radiation. Just because a filter makes the Sun dim enough to view comfortably is no guarantee that it is not transmitting damaging amounts of invisible radiation! This is no place to experiment with do-it-yourself filter designs—use only a proper solar filter from a reputable manufacturer. *Failure to use a proper filter when observing the Sun can cause immediate and irreversible damage to vision.*

A special warning: Heavy atmospheric haze near sunrise or sunset often dims the Sun so that it appears as a dull red disk, not uncomfortably bright to the eye. At such times resist the temptation to view the Sun with a telescope without using a solar filter. The atmosphere at such times is still relatively transparent in the invisible infrared portion of the spectrum, and the great light grasp of a telescope can result in thermal retinal damage! With the unaided eyes the retinal solar image, although just as bright, is much smaller and the eye can better dissipate the heat. Also, with unaided vision, one is less apt to fixate on the Sun for a prolonged period.

For white-light views of the Sun a dark, broad-spectrum, neutral-density solar filter is needed. Aluminized Mylar and metal-coated glass are common designs, although they usually do not attenuate light uniformly across the visible spectrum (i.e. they are not perfect neutral-density filters). Aluminized Mylar gives a bluish color to the solar image, while metal-coated glass filters usually give an orange color.

The filter should be 50 mm or more in diameter and must be positioned to cover the *front* of the telescope. Ensure that the filter is *securely attached* so that a gust of wind or a bump cannot dislodge it. (Some small telescopes are sold with a "Sun filter" designed to attach to the eyepiece, just before the observer's eye. Sunlight concentrated by the telescope can overheat and shatter a filter of this design. Such filters should be thrown in the garbage!)

For direct viewing of the Sun (not using binoculars or a telescope) shade #14 (no other shade) rectangular welder's glass may be used; this is available for a few dollars at welding supplies shops. These filters are not suitable for attaching to the front of binoculars or a telescope simply because their poor optical quality results in a fuzzy image.

Red, flame-like prominences at the Sun's limb and much structure in its chromosphere across the solar disk can be seen in hydrogen-alpha (Hα) light, a strong spectral line emitted by atomic hydrogen. This light is totally overwhelmed by the rest of the solar spectrum, so a neutral-density filter will not work. Advances in vacuum thin-film technology have made possible interference filters, filters that operate on the same principle as Fabry–Perot interferometers, involving the interference of multiply reflected beams of light. These filters can be constructed so they are transparent only to light having an extremely narrow range of wavelengths, typically 0.15 to 0.05 nm for solar viewing, although band-passes of up to 1 nm are used in solar-prominence viewers designed to occult the solar disk. If this band-pass is centered on the Hα wavelength (656.3 nm), nearly all the Sun's light will be blocked, leaving an image in Hα light.

Hα filters are expensive, particularly for band-passes near 0.05 nm that are needed for high-contrast images of the solar disk. These filters may be located either in front of the objective of a telescope or between the objective and the eyepiece. In the latter case, because the wavelength of the center of the narrow band-pass varies with the angle at which light rays enter the filter (a characteristic of interference filters), the focal ratio of the imaging telescope must be near $f/20$ for 0.15-nm band-pass filters and $f/30$ or higher for filters with narrower band-passes. Temperature control is usually required to keep the band-pass centered on the Hα wavelength, although some Hα filters are designed to be tilted in order to tune them to the Hα wavelength (the wavelength of peak transmittance is shifted toward shorter wavelengths when the filter is tilted away from 90° incidence).

Hα filters require a broadband "energy-rejection prefilter," located at the front of the telescope. The prefilter has a band-pass of about 100 nm in the red part of the spectrum and blocks essentially all the infrared, ultraviolet, and much of the visible part of the solar radiation from entering the telescope.

Nebular Filters

From the surface of Earth, the night sky is not completely dark. Even in the absence of light pollution (human-made and lunar), the air itself emits a feeble light called airglow. In higher latitudes, aurorae can also contribute to the glow of the atmosphere. Two other components of the light of the night sky are the zodiacal light and background starlight. The diffuse glow from all four sources reduces the contrast of celestial objects and, in the case of dim comets, galaxies, and nebulae, the object may be completely obscured by the brightness of the sky.

Filters transmit only a fraction of the incident light. Thus employing them to see faint objects may seem counterproductive. However, there are objects in the heavens that emit light only at certain wavelengths. This behaviour is characteristic of plasmas—excited gases, matter composed of separate atoms energized either by ultraviolet radiation from nearby hot stars or by collisions such as occur in supernova explosion shock fronts. Such regions are called emission nebulae and include star-forming regions, planetary nebulae, and some supernova remnants. A filter that selectively blocks most of the background sky glow but is transparent to the wavelengths at which such objects emit most of their visible light will darken the sky background without appreciably dimming the object of interest. With narrow-band-pass interference-type filters the effect can be dramatic, improving contrast and revealing details that otherwise are completely invisible. It is the next best thing to observing these objects from above Earth's atmosphere!

Dark-adapted (scotopic) human vision responds to light having wavelengths from approximately 400 to 620 nm. In bright light (photopic vision) the spectral range extends to somewhat longer wavelengths, about 750 nm. For both types of vision the response curve (sensitivity vs. wavelength) is "bell-shaped," the wavelength of maximum sensitivity being in the middle of the visible range—near 507 nm for scotopic vision and 555 nm for photopic vision (see the figure "Nebular Filter Transmission" on the following page). The photopic sensation produced by 555-nm light is green; for scotopic vision color is not produced, but at photopic levels 507-nm light appears blue-green.

Hydrogen is the predominant element in the Universe. Atomic hydrogen, when excited by ultraviolet radiation from a nearby hot star, emits light in the visible spectrum at only four discrete wavelengths: 656, 486, 434, and 410 nm (designated as Hα, Hβ, Hγ, and Hδ, respectively, part of the *Balmer spectrum* of hydrogen). Scotopic vision is blind to 656-nm (Hα) light and relatively insensitive to the less intense 434- and 410-nm light. However, 486 nm (Hβ) lies near the 507-nm peak sensitivity of scotopic vision, and an Hβ ("H-beta") filter having a narrow band-pass at this wavelength will greatly reduce the surrounding sky brightness and reveal Hβ-emitting nebulae.

The classic example is the Horsehead Nebula, a dark, silhouetted column of dust just southeast of the east end of Orion's belt. The surrounding hydrogen gas, excited probably by the nearby hot star ζ Orionis, fluoresces dimly with Hβ light. If the obscuring airglow is blocked by an Hβ filter, the dark Horsehead can distinctly be seen in a telescope having an aperture of 400 mm or greater and an eyepiece giving an exit pupil near 5 mm (see pp. 50–53). However, the number of objects that can be viewed advantageously with an Hβ filter is very limited, apparently because few nebulae emit strongly in Hβ light.

Two other strong nebular emission lines lie at 496 and 501 nm, nearly at the peak sensitivity of scotopic vision. Originally detected in 1864 by the British astronomer William Huggins, the origin of these lines was unknown at that time, and they were attributed to a hypothetical new element, "nebulium." In 1927, the American astrophysicist Ira Bowen identified the lines as due to doubly ionized oxygen (O^{++} or OIII), which glows brightly when very low-density nebular gas is strongly excited (high temperature). A filter that has a narrow band-pass spanning these two wavelengths gives striking views of highly excited nebulae. A good example is the Veil Nebula, a supernova remnant in eastern Cygnus. Through an OIII filter on a dark, transparent night, the direct view of the Veil in a large amateur telescope is more spectacular than any photograph or CCD image. Planetary nebulae (fluorescing, low-density shells of gas surrounding hot central stars) also show up well with an OIII filter; examples include the Helix Nebula, the Owl Nebula (M97), the Dumbbell Nebula (M27), and the Ring Nebula (M57).

Because of their narrow band-passes, Hβ and OIII filters are sometimes called *line filters*, although their band-passes are much wider than that of an Hα filter. Filters encompassing both the Hβ and OIII lines, such as the Lumicon Ultra High Contrast (UHC) filter, are termed *narrowband filters*. These filters also enhance views of many emission nebulae, although with the wider band-pass the sky background is brighter. With a large telescope under dark skies, I find that the single most useful filter is the

NEBULAR FILTER TRANSMISSION

The dotted, dashed, and continuous curves show the transmission versus wavelength* characteristic of four interference filters (in descending order in the legend): two line filters, a narrowband filter, and a broadband filter. The bell-shaped curves composed of small open and solid circles show the relative response of bright-adapted (photopic) vision and dark-adapted (scotopic) vision. In ascending sequence above the curves are spectral colors, nebula emission lines, and light-pollution lines (M = mercury, S = high-pressure sodium, and LPS = low-pressure sodium). High-pressure sodium light sources emit an additional broad continuum spectrum that is not shown. The two unlabelled light-pollution lines are strong airglow/auroral lines produced by atomic oxygen. (Dave Lane used a "Varian Model Cary 50 Conc UV-Visible Spectrophotometer" owned by the Chemistry Department at Saint Mary's University to obtain the filter curves; he also prepared the diagram.)

OIII line filter. With smaller apertures (less than about 200 mm), the narrowband Lumicon UHC filter (or equivalent filter from other manufacturers) may be preferable since it dims the stars less.

Some other nebulae that are greatly enhanced by OIII and narrowband filters include the Omega or Loon Nebula (M17), the Trifid Nebula (M20), the Lagoon Nebula (M8), the Rosette Nebula, the Eagle Nebula (M16), the North America Nebula, and the Carina Nebula (NGC 3372).

Stars emit light across the entire visible spectrum. Thus line filters and narrowband filters impair views of single stars, reflection nebulae, star clusters, and galaxies. Filters with wide band-passes extending from about 450 to 530 nm are called *broadband filters*. Examples are the Lumicon Deep Sky filter, the Orion SkyGlow filter, and the Meade Broadband filter. These decrease the airglow somewhat and block several of the brighter wavelengths emitted by sodium- and mercury-vapour streetlights, without dimming stars and galaxies too much. Thus they provide a modest improvement in the visibility of some objects from light-polluted sites. Because of their wide band-pass and high transmission at the Hα line, they are also useful for photography of emission nebulae. However, under dark skies an unfiltered view is preferable to that through a broadband filter.

(See p. 32 for basic information on optical wavelength and color.)

LIMITING MAGNITUDES
BY DOUGLAS PITCAIRN

Limiting Visual Magnitude

One of the many difficulties with visual observing from the surface of our planet is the variability of the atmosphere. In any record of observations it is important to note the condition of the sky. Parameters such as brightness and contrast are greatly affected by the transparency of the sky and the presence of light pollution or aurorae.

One of the simplest ways to quantify local sky conditions is to note the magnitude of the faintest star visible with the unaided eye: the *limiting visual magnitude* (LVM). (See **www.rasc.ca/lpa/sky-quality-measurement-project** for an alternative method using an electronic *sky quality meter* that measures sky brightness in units of *magnitude per square arcsecond*.) Although individuals differ in their ability to detect faint stars, these differences are generally small, and for any one observer such observations provide a consistent measure of sky quality. The chart at the left shows a 9° field in the vicinity of Polaris (the brightest star on the chart) and is useful for observers at latitude 20°N or higher. For orientation, the solid lines mark the beginning of the handle of the Little Dipper (see MAPS OF THE NIGHT SKY, p. 339). Several stars have their visual magnitudes indicated (with decimal points omitted). Using this field to determine your LVM has several advantages: it is always above the horizon in mid-northern latitudes; its altitude does not change with the time of night or year, so the variation of atmospheric extinction with altitude is not a consideration; there are no bright stars or planets in the field to dazzle the eye; the faint stars are quite well spaced and therefore easy to identify; and being a simple field, it can be memorized. Especially note the dashed spiral of descending magnitudes labelled "A" through "F."

Limiting Telescopic Magnitude

Aperture, telescope design, eyepiece design, magnification, and the quality of optical surfaces are a few of the many variables that will determine the faintest stars visible through a given telescope and eyepiece. By determining an instrument's limiting magnitude—the *limiting telescopic magnitude* (LTM)—you can effectively assess the effect of these variables. The quality of the night sky will also affect the LTM. Therefore, changes in the LVM should be taken into account when determining the LTM. (The relationship between LTM and LVM is complex; readers may explore it using the excellent web-based calculator at **www.bogan.ca/astro/optics/maglimit.html**.) The LTM is a useful guide when attempting faint targets (Pluto in a 150-mm scope?), comparing the performance of different instruments, or determining whether a mirror or lens needs cleaning (many people clean their optics too often, assuming that dust degrades optical performance more than it actually does). For a study on sky brightness, telescope magnification, and contrast in deep-sky observing, see p. 54.

To help determine the LTM of your instrument, use the charts on the next page, which show an 8′-wide section of the northwest quadrant of M67 centered at RA 8 h 50.1 m and Dec +11° 53′. This old open cluster lies 8° south-southeast of M44, Cancer's famous Beehive Cluster. The accompanying table lists the visual magnitudes

M67 Limiting Telescopic Magnitude Chart

STAR	VISUAL	B – V
A	10.60	1.10
B	11.19	0.43
C	11.59	0.42
D	12.01	0.57
E	12.26	0.68
F	12.57	0.59
G	13.04	0.85
H	13.35	0.59
I	13.61	0.59
J	13.96	0.62
K	14.34	0.56
L	14.66	0.67
M	14.96	0.69
N	15.30	0.79
O	15.58	0.84
P	16.06	0.74
Q	16.31	0.99
R	16.62	0.81
S	17.05	1.26
T	17.38	1.17
U	17.64	1.31
V	18.04	1.27
W	18.38	0.76
X	18.69	1.17
Y	19.07	1.56
Z	19.29	0.61
a	19.42	1.34
b	20.10	0.00
c	20.35	0.83
d	20.61	1.55
e	21.03	0.32

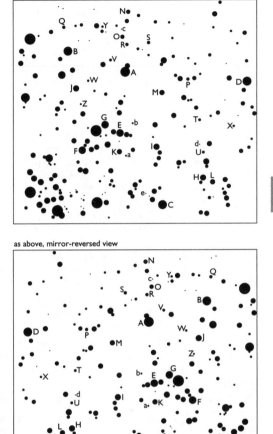

as above, mirror-reversed view

The upper chart is for telescopes with an even number of reflecting surfaces (e.g. Newtonian reflectors) and the "mirror-reversed" chart is for telescopes with an odd number of reflecting surfaces (e.g. a refractor with a diagonal). North is at top in both of these charts.

and the *B – V* color indices of the labeled stars. The diagram was constructed from a photograph taken by René Racine of the Université de Montréal, who exposed a 103a-D plate at the *f*/3.67 focus of the Hale Reflector. The magnitudes are based on work by Racine and Ronald Gilliland of the Space Telescope Science Institute.

Correction for Atmospheric Extinction

Atmospheric extinction varies with altitude above the horizon. To normalize observations to the zenith (altitude 90°), the following values should be added to estimates of faintest visible magnitude obtained using the charts. The format is: (altitude range) **correction:**

(18°–20°) **0.5** (20°–24°) **0.4** (24°–29°) **0.3** (29°–36°) **0.2** (36°–52°) **0.1** (52°–90°) **0.0**

These corrections are for near sea level and would be reduced at higher elevations. Also, excellent sky conditions are assumed; under less-than-ideal conditions, the corrections are generally larger and can be quite uncertain, especially when the target area is closer to the horizon.

POLAR ALIGNMENT
BY BLAIR MACDONALD

Beginning observers are often confused by the concept of telescope mount alignment. With the advent of Go To mounts, this confusion is compounded by the fact that the *computer* of such a mount must also be oriented to the sky. Polar alignment applies only to equatorial mounts; it is an independent physical alignment of the polar axis of the mount with the north celestial pole (NCP) or the south celestial pole (SCP).

Ideally, the polar axis is parallel to Earth's rotational axis and therefore must point at a celestial pole. The required alignment accuracy depends on the observing goals. For casual visual observing, it is usually sufficient to align the polar axis of an equatorial mount with Polaris (in the Northern Hemisphere) or σ Octantis (in the Southern Hemisphere). The charts on the facing page show the location of the NCP and SCP in their surrounding star fields, and the caption describes the alignment procedure.

For long-exposure astrophotography or for an automated observing program, significantly more accurate polar alignment is necessary. A dedicated polar axis telescope with a Polaris-offset reticle on a German equatorial mount, makes it simple to achieve polar alignment. However, any equatorial mount can be polar aligned by the straightforward *drift alignment* method. As outlined below, the drift alignment method uses a reticle eyepiece and the viewing of two stars on the celestial equator, one near the meridian and the other near the eastern horizon. The method also works in the Southern Hemisphere: simply interchange north and south, clockwise and counterclockwise.

1. Roughly level the mount and point the polar axis at Polaris. A simple eyeball alignment is sufficient, but the closer you get now, the fewer drifting iterations you will have to make later. The rough alignment described above is usually good enough.

2. Install a reticle eyepiece with the lines aligned to the right ascension (RA) and declination (Dec) axes directions as follows: First, center a star on one of the lines. Then move the telescope slightly in RA and rotate the eyepiece until the star moves parallel to the line.

3. Point the telescope at a star on the celestial equator in the south near the meridian.

4. With the drive engaged, center the star on a reticle line aligned with the RA direction. Ignoring RA drift, note the Dec drift of the star over several minutes.

5. If you must move the telescope north to recenter the star, then adjust the mount clockwise in azimuth as seen from above. If you must move the telescope south to recenter the star, then adjust the mount counterclockwise in azimuth.

6. Repeat Steps 4 and 5 until there is no visible drift over several minutes.

7. Now point the telescope at a star near the eastern horizon on the celestial equator.

8. Center the star on a reticle line aligned with the RA axis as in Step 4. Ignoring RA drift, note the Dec drift of the star over several minutes.

9. If you must move the telescope north to recenter the star, then tilt the polar axis downward. If you must move the telescope south to recenter the star, then tilt the polar axis upward.

10. Repeat Steps 8 and 9 until there is no visible drift over several minutes.

Repeat Steps 3–10 for improved accuracy, because adjusting the elevation often requires further adjustment in azimuth and vice versa. The longer it takes to detect Dec drift, the more accurate the polar alignment. For a star near the equator, a Dec drift of d arcseconds over time t minutes indicates a polar axis misalignment of $p \approx 3.8 \, d \,/\, t$

arcminutes. For example, a 10″ drift over 1 min indicates a polar axis misalignment of 38′, while a 5″ drift over 5 min indicates a polar axis misalignment of only 3.8′.

The drift method produces very accurate alignment even when the optical tube is not exactly aligned with the mount.

See **www.backyardastronomy.com/Backyard_Astronomy/Downloads.html** for a comprehensive treatment of polar alignment.

FINDER CHARTS FOR THE NORTH AND SOUTH CELESTIAL POLES

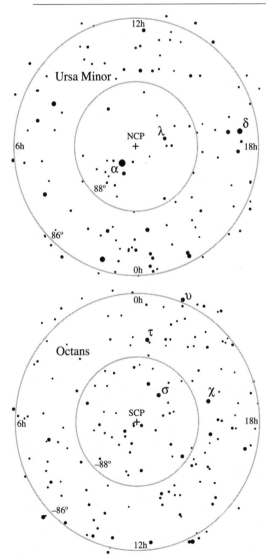

The finder charts depict mirror-correct fields of view with circles of diameter 4° and 8° centered on the celestial poles (Dec is indicated on the circles). Stars are shown to magnitude 9. δ UMi is the penultimate "handle" star in Ursa Minor.

For casual visual observing, it is sufficient to align the polar axis of an equatorial mount to Polaris (α UMi, magnitude 2.0), near the NCP, or to σ Oct (magnitude 5.5), near the SCP, as follows:

Roughly level the mount and orient the RA axis to true north (south) in azimuth. Set the RA axis elevation to the observing latitude. Lock the Dec axis to +90° (–90°). While viewing through the finder or telescope at low magnification, adjust the azimuth and elevation to center the pole star. For finer alignment, align to the estimated position of the NCP (SCP) relative to the star field.

For accurate polar alignment, the drift alignment method (described on the facing page) is recommended and works for all equatorial mounts.

(Finder charts were derived from sky charts generated with Voyager III, a product of Carina Software.)

Diagram by Dave Chapman

FREQUENCY OF NIGHTTIME CLOUD COVER
BY JAY ANDERSON

FEBRUARY–MAY MEAN NIGHTTIME CLOUD COVER IN PERCENT

The maps on these pages are constructed from observations taken from 16 years of satellite observations ending in 2009. These sensors detect emitted and reflected radiation in several wavelengths and use a statistical, climatological, model-based algorithm to determine the amount of cloud in 1-degree longitude by 1-degree latitude bins. The Patmos-x dataset used in these maps is one of the best of several approaches to cloud measurement.

The months chosen give a good year-round depiction of annual cloud climatology, while avoiding June and July. Several notable trends are shown: the clearer skies over western Canada that come with frigid winter temperatures, the heavy winter cloudiness around the Great Lakes, the sunny Prairie summers, the higher cloud amounts in mountainous terrain, and the onset and decay of the mid-summer Southwest Monsoon of Arizona and New Mexico.

February cloud amounts follow a quasi-latitudinal pattern across Canada, interrupted by the very high cloudiness across the Great Lakes. The situation in the U.S. is more complex, with more cloud over the northern Rockies, Appalachians, and the northeast U.S, where the influence of the Great Lakes and east-coast storms dominates. The southwest states have the least cloudiness, mostly because their low latitude takes them out of the path of the major winter storms, along with the shelter provided by the mountain chains in the area. That protective topography has an influence farther north, creating a zone of low cloud that extends northward along the Front Range of the Rockies as far north as the Canadian border.

AUGUST–NOVEMBER MEAN NIGHTTIME CLOUD COVER IN PERCENT

In May, the cold air retreats northward and much of Canada returns to a cloudier climatology. The protection provided by the Rockies fades away, leaving a broad band of moderate cloudiness across the Great Plains. The Appalachians north of Georgia retain their reputation for high cloudiness, but in the American Southwest May is the sunniest month, sandwiched between the winter months with their occasional low-latitude snows and the summer's onset of convective thunderstorms.

In August, the Southwest becomes one of the cloudiest regions, as Gulf of California moisture spreads north. Noteworthy is the very low cloud amount in central California. The plains retain a modest amount of cloud—it's still thunderstorm season, but the protection of the Rockies is still evident in the arc of below-50% contours from southern Saskatchewan and Alberta to Texas. The Appalachian states still hold onto high cloud frequencies, but eroded from earlier maximums.

November brings a hint of winter, though the low cloud amounts that come with freeze-up are still limited to the Northwest Territories. The monsoon season is long gone over the southwest, the Great Lakes have begun their role as winter cloud-makers, but winter has not reached the south; the Appalachians enjoy their sunniest season of the year. Rocky Mountain cloudiness has increased over British Columbia as the first of the fall storms arrive onshore, and the Prairies are gradually losing their sunny disposition.

Additional maps of global cloudiness may be found on the author's website at **www.eclipsophile.com**. Data source: Patmos-x/CIMMS/SSEC.

WEATHER RESOURCES ON THE INTERNET
BY ALLAN RAHILL

Despite public skepticism, weather forecasts are in fact quite accurate, provided they are from informed sources. Specialized weather services—usually involving a fee—are available for aviation, agriculture, forestry, and marine applications. Previously, there was no such service for astronomy, likely because there was no directly related economy. However, the Canada-France-Hawaii Observatory at Mauna Kea has been using a seeing and transparency forecast for more than eight years to "queue schedule" observing activities. Currently, professional observatories are making the best use of weather conditions and are able to effectively manage activities accordingly.

Similar information has been freely available to amateur and professional astronomers worldwide on the internet for many years. With light pollution becoming more and more pervasive, amateur astronomers must drive long distances to get to dark skies. They can avoid frustration by using the information and URLs below to plan their observing sessions.

Satellite Images

Many astronomers rely on satellite images to predict nighttime cloud cover. Real-time images are available from GOES satellites for the eastern and western Americas; other satellites such as Meteosat give the same service for Europe and Africa. These satellites give three main types of images: visible, infrared (IR), and water vapour. Visible images are easy to interpret, but they are available only during the day; for nighttime tracking of clouds, IR images are available. Water-vapour images do not track clouds; they indicate the total moisture in the air mass. Usually the darkest areas in those images have good correlation with the best sky transparency.

Particularly useful for short-term forecasting are IR satellite loops, which are available at many websites. IR images show the radiance emission from Earth and indicate the temperature of the ground and/or clouds. During cold seasons, the ground can be as cold as, if not colder than, the air mass, and single IR satellite images are not very helpful in identifying low-level clouds such as stratocumulus. One way to separate clouds from the ground in these situations is to use a time-lapse loop and look for motion: the ground doesn't move, but clouds do. People in northern latitudes from late fall to early spring should keep this trick in mind.

There are many IR image enhancements available at various websites, and you should be aware that many of them do not display *any* low clouds, even with the trick mentioned above. One way to familiarize yourself with low-cloud detection is to compare visible GOES images to IR enhancements in the early morning, when the ground is still cold. In some situations, you may be surprised by the amount of low cloud not displayed in the IR satellite images. By comparing IR and visible images, you can select a website that you feel gives accurate images and one that you are comfortable with. I recommend the following website for IR satellite images because it provides the ability to zoom into your region, to choose different satellite-image enhancements, and to do animation easily **weather.unisys.com/satellite/infrared.php**.

To make the best use of weather-satellite images, you also should be aware of the behaviour of certain types of cloud. Low-level clouds such as stratus usually develop locally and generally move much more slowly than high clouds. These clouds appear during the night and usually get burned off by the Sun during the day. Coastal regions will usually see the low clouds moving inland in the evening and out to sea in the morning.

In addition, cumulus, towering cumulus, and cumulonimbus clouds arise with daytime convective heating if the air mass is unstable. The depth or height of the cloud structure is related to the level of instability and can reach up to 20 000 m for severe thunderstorms. On satellite loops, these clouds appear as clear areas that are gradually filled with clouds during the day and that slowly vanish in the evening. In the summer, some of the most unstable cumulonimbus clouds will survive at night. Even though thunderstorms, associated with cumulonimbus clouds, can be far from your location, cirrus blowoff from these cells may reach you quite quickly, depending on the upper wind direction, and thus ruin your observing session. Satellite and radar loops are good ways to keep track of these thunderstorm lines.

Radar

Remote-controlled observatories, where the operator is not physically present, and star parties, where telescopes are often left set up and exposed, are becoming more popular. When the sky conditions are variable, there is one common worry: is there a fast-moving precipitation band approaching the observing site? The best way to track precipitation in the short term is with radar. The radar network is extensive across the United States; it also covers populated regions of Canada.

Radar images require careful interpretation. During the night, the air cools near the ground and creates a temperature inversion. On some nights with strong inversions, radar signals are refracted, or bent, toward the ground and scattered back to the radar, thus appearing as precipitation on the graphical displays. Similar situations occur in mountainous areas, where higher terrain interrupts the radar signal. A radar loop will help you distinguish these areas: sometimes they are nearly motionless; at other times they shift around in a chaotic jumble. Precipitation moves in a smoother fashion, at times linearly. The best websites for access to radar loops for Canada and the United States, respectively, are **weather.gc.ca/radar** and **www.intellicast.com** (click on "radar").

Weather Forecasts for Astronomy

Cloud Forecasts: Local media and television "experts" cannot always be relied upon when conditions are uncertain. Usually their forecasts cover a large area, and the weather can be quite different within the region. Also, for most people, including many local weather forecasters, skies are considered clear despite thin, high cloudiness that may interfere with observing.

The best forecasts for clouds are from the direct output of numerical models. Weather models are not perfect, but they are surprisingly good at capturing local effects and predicting cloud formation and dissipation. The biggest problem with numerical forecasting is convection (thunderstorms): it is like trying to predict the next bubble in boiling water. Complex thunderstorm cells can be forecast much farther away than they actually appear, leading to poor cloud progression forecasts for regions hundreds of kilometres ahead.

Some weather channels and websites use animated forecasts to show cloud progression for the next day, but these animations generally have low resolution and are not very useful for astronomy. The only North American high-resolution cloud forecast I still know of is produced at the Canadian Meteorological Centre (CMC) and is at **weather.gc.ca/astro/clds_vis_e.html**.

Occasionally, especially in the fall when low clouds (stratocumulus) are omnipresent, a weather balloon can be launched into a cloud hole, and the resulting cloud forecast may be too optimistic for the surrounding regions. To avoid a bad forecast, always compare the cloud-cover forecast with the latest satellite picture. In these situations, an old forecast may be a better choice. This is why the most recent old forecast, in addition to the current forecast, is available at this website; hourly forecasts are now available.

Sky Transparency Forecasts: For deep-sky observing, sky transparency is critical because it largely determines how dark the sky will be. Aerosols—particles suspended in the atmosphere—and moisture reduce sky transparency and brighten the sky by diffusing the light in the sky. Aerosols include volcanic ash, pollen, sea salts, and smoke from forest fires. Spectacular examples of events that introduced aerosols into the atmosphere are the Mount St. Helens volcanic eruption, which spread roughly 540 million tonnes of ash into the atmosphere in 1980, and the more recent large forest fires: in summer 2003 over British Columbia, which spread smoke over large areas, and in 2002 in northern Québec, which spread smoke over all of northeastern North America. Specialized weather numerical models handle aerosol phenomena; websites that track aerosol envelopes with up to five-day forecasts across the world are ozoneaq.gsfc.nasa.gov and www.nrlmry.navy.mil/aerosol/#currentaerosolmodeling.

Moisture is the only weather element affecting sky transparency that can be forecast with confidence. For many northern-latitude residents, moisture is the most important contributor to reduced sky transparency; despite clear skies, very often, high-level ice crystals (extremely thin clouds) are present and can be seen only at sunset and sunrise. In addition, moisture from open waters, vegetation (evapotranspiration), or moist soil can keep the low-level atmosphere humid.

Over the years, I have compared water-vapour satellite images to various observers' estimates of background sky brightness. The resulting hourly sky transparency forecasts can be found at weather.gc.ca/astro/transparence_e.html.

There is a good correlation between the darkest areas in water-vapour images and the darkest observed sky conditions. There are some cases where the sky background is brighter than expected due to moisture trapped by a temperature inversion. Based on this observation and others, the forecasts in the above website emphasize humidity near the surface and also near the tropopause (cirrus heights).

Seeing Forecasts: Seeing conditions determine the steadiness of images through a telescope and are relevant for planetary as well as deep-sky observing. When highest resolution is necessary for planetary imaging or visual observing, seeing should be at its best.

Conditions are favorable when the atmosphere is turbulence-free all across the path of the light. The best weather pattern is weak wind circulation at all levels. These conditions occur more frequently over the southeastern United States than any other region of North America, with Atlantic Canada generally having the worst conditions among populated North American regions. Canadian and U.S. central prairies often experience blocking weather systems that give weak upper wind circulation and excellent seeing conditions.

Another pattern for excellent seeing takes place when moderate winds blow from the same direction at all levels, that is, when horizontal and vertical wind shear are weak at all levels. In other words, no jet stream (strong winds reaching 200 km/h–400 km/h at an altitude of 10 km–12 km) or sudden shifts or increase in wind speed with height are present.

At locations downwind from mountains when winds are moderate, it is best to be far away from the mountains, since "gravity waves"—vertical air-mass oscillations caused by the mountains—can downgrade seeing. In general, topography is quite important because rough terrain increases the wind shear in the low-level atmosphere, due to friction and gravity waves.

Temperature variation at the surface also plays a role in seeing conditions. Nights of excellent wind conditions as described above may nevertheless have marginal seeing. On such nights, temperatures quickly and steadily fall, and large telescopes have trouble cooling at the same rate as the surrounding air. This creates what is called "local seeing": thermal heat released from the optics (despite good ventilation) ruins the seeing despite the excellent weather pattern. The opposite is also true: the best planetary observations with a large telescope often take place just before thick clouds roll in or when looking through thin cirrostratus cloud. Under these conditions, the temperature usually rises a few degrees before the clouds appear. Thin cirrostratus clouds usually keep the temperature steady, eliminating any negative local seeing effects. Thin clouds also play the role of a neutral-density filter, increasing fine detail and contrast on bright planets. Ground fog can also be associated with excellent seeing conditions (until the fog thickens), if you can keep your optics dry.

Predicting favorable seeing conditions requires the ability to interpret weather charts, something that is difficult for most observers to do. The Canadian weather service has a seeing forecast, available at their astro-weather website, which attempts to simulate wind shears, topography, and temperature effects; it is at weather.gc.ca/astro/seeing_e.html.

Some Tips to Get the Most Out of Your Telescope: "Local seeing" is the term used to describe the effects of heat radiating from the components of a telescope (e.g. its optics) or from the immediate surroundings (e.g. observatory walls and floor, trees, flowing water, neighboring houses). If the local seeing is bad, the telescopic viewing will be significantly deteriorated. However, in contrast to atmospheric seeing, the effects of local seeing can be controlled.

Tube currents in particular will dramatically deteriorate telescopic images. Mirror-type instruments are more sensitive to such currents than refractors. Large mirrors can take hours to cool down during the night and in fact may never reach full thermal equilibrium. However, the amateur astronomer can accelerate the cooling of the primary mirror by installing one or more battery-type fans behind it. Their use will cool down the mirror to near the ambient temperature in one or two hours. Another approach is to use a high-quality but thin primary mirror. Many manufacturers offer mirror blanks of thickness 2.5 cm for mirror diameters up to 400 mm, in addition to the traditional mirrors of thickness 5–8 cm. The thinner mirrors will reach thermal equilibrium 2–3 times faster[*] than the thicker ones. Many amateurs also ventilate the front of their primary mirror with two fans placed on either side of the mirror, separated by 180°. One fan pulls air into the tube while the other pushes it out. Such ventilation has two benefits: it breaks up the thermal boundary layer near the mirror surface (and therefore reduces convective-type turbulence) and it cools the mirror up to 50% more quickly than without the fans[*].

The popular Schmidt–Cassegrain telescopes do not come with cooling fans and they are known to suffer from internal turbulence, especially at large apertures. Only a few advanced amateur astronomers will have the courage to add fans to those telescopes. Any telescope, and particularly the Schmidt–Cassegrain type, should always be brought outside to cool it down at least two hours before the observing session. Better yet is to keep a telescope permanently outside in a backyard observatory.

To minimize the occurrence of poor local seeing, one must avoid all potential sources of heat in the surroundings. For example, concrete structures and buildings or houses have the capacity to retain daytime heat and then release it during the night. Even trees during the growing season can release heat at night, and so deteriorate the local seeing for astronomical objects found just above their canopy. Ideally, the amateur should choose an environment free from all these elements. If you are lucky enough to have an observatory, then remember that all the outside walls must be white, since even pale colors will allow the walls to heat up during the day and then create local seeing problems when they release the heat at night.

The local geography can also be used to one's advantage: observing can be better at the top of a hill than at its base. It appears that the local seeing is improved at the top of a hill, due to nighttime katabatic winds that drain air down the slope of the hill

[*]*Sky & Telescope*, June 2004, p. 122 (Improving the Thermal Properties of Newtonian Reflectors—Part 2)

to its base. This means that air above the hill must also move downward to replace the air that moved away. This descent creates a dry subsidence inversion that, combined with the cool surface temperature at the top of the hill, stabilizes the air locally. This results in good seeing. Many of my best planetary observations took place on hill tops.

One final tip: near dusk and dawn, if you can spot planets, then there will often be a 20–60-min window during which the seeing will be one or two notches better than during the night. This seems to be related to large-scale tidal motions in the atmosphere that create more-stable conditions at those times, but the effect is not well understood. Give it a try in the early morning and the early evening.

The Clear Sky Chart

The Canadian Meteorological Centre's numerical weather forecasts, given in the URLs above, are unique because they are specifically designed for astronomers. They can be found on the "Weather forecast for astronomy" page of the Environment Canada website at **weather.gc.ca/astro**. There are several products for the astronomy community, including hourly forecast images of cloud cover, sky transparency, seeing, and near-ground weather. However, they include 842 forecast images per day, covering all of North America, so it can be a chore to find the precise one you need. All the above astronomical weather forecasts can be viewed at a glance for any particular observing site in North America using Attilla Danko's excellent Clear Sky Chart at **www.cleardarksky.com/csk**.

Editor's Note: Attilla Danko, a member of the Ottawa Centre of The Royal Astronomical Society of Canada, received the Ken Chilton Prize from the Society in 2005 for his creation of the Clear Sky Chart, which uses the Canadian Meteorological Centre's forecasts for astronomers created by Allan Rahill. Most popular observing locations in North America now have an associated chart, and many amateur astronomers rely on these forecasts to plan their observing sessions. Several websites give useful information similar to the Clear Sky Chart. The spatial resolution of these sites is quite low compared to the Canadian Meteorological Centre's products.

For the UK: www.weatherweb.net/wxwebastronomy.php
For Australia: www.philhart.com/content/cloud-forecasts-astronomers
For the U.S.:   www.accuweather.com (Click the + sign and choose "Astronomy.")

Sagittarius and the Milky Way in a clear, dark sky, free of light pollution. (photo: Dave Chapman)

LIGHT POLLUTION
BY DAVID L. CRAWFORD

A Lost Heritage: Most people on Earth have now lost the spectacular view of the Universe that our ancestors enjoyed on clear, dark nights. The development of electrical lighting in the last century and the increase in urban population have caused a rapid increase in sky glow above towns and cities. As a result, fewer and fewer members of the general public have ever seen a prime dark sky; our children and grandchildren may never. It seems that the night now exists for watching television and for discos, not for nature. For urban dwellers, star-studded nights are limited to planetaria. Even in rural areas, poorly designed yard lights often obscure the splendour of the night sky. As Leslie Peltier, one of the most famous amateur astronomers of the 20th century, stated eloquently in his autobiography *Starlight Nights:*

> *The Moon and the stars no longer come to the farm. The farmer has exchanged his birthright in them for the wattage of his all-night sun. His children will never know the blessed dark of night.*

The increased sky glow that adversely affects the environment is a major part of what is called *light pollution*. Light pollution originates from excess light that does nothing to increase useful night-time illumination. It is light that sprays horizontally and upward into the sky from ill-conceived lighting fixtures. It is light that glares into the eyes of motorists and homeowners, compromising visibility, safety, and security. It is light that depresses property values by

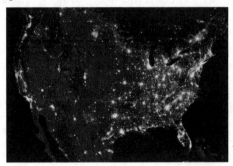

A nighttime satellite view of central North America

reducing the aesthetic quality of a neighborhood. It is light that can seriously affect the circadian rhythm of all living things, including humans, as well as creating other hazards for many species (birds, sea turtles, etc.). In the United States and Canada, billions of dollars (plus large amounts of energy) are lost annually in generating this wasted light. It makes for increased air pollution and CO_2 emissions. Any night lighting that causes such light pollution is neither effective nor efficient. Unfortunately, such adverse lighting is still in a growth stage, even with the increasing emphasis on improved, energy-efficient night lighting. There is a great lack of awareness by users of lighting.

A Threat to Astronomy: Light pollution poses special perils to astronomy. Many observations, including most of those of cosmological interest, can be made only from prime observing sites, far removed from centers of population. Some older observatories, such as the David Dunlap in Ontario and Mount Wilson in California, are severely affected by light pollution from nearby urban centers. Newer observatories usually are located at remote sites, and amateur astronomers routinely drive long distances to escape the glare of towns and cities. The argument that all astronomy can be done from space is incorrect because it does not make sense to do in space, at much higher costs, what can be done from the ground. There are observations that can only be done from space, but the recent decades of space astronomy have greatly increased the need for ground-based observatories.

Solutions: There are solutions to the problem of light pollution. Outdoor lighting ordinances or policies have been instituted in many locales by governmental agencies,

Inefficient street lighting

particularly near large observatories, such as: near Tucson, Arizona; San Diego, California; and in Hawaii. The solutions involve several methods to control light output. The first is the use of lighting fixtures that direct the light output only where it is needed, well below the horizontal, not upward and sideways, hence less overall output than older generation fixtures use and less power is required.

The type of light source also makes a difference: it should be an energy-efficient lamp. Worldwide, quite a few cities are realizing substantial savings each year through extensive use of efficient outdoor lighting, including the use of LED and low-pressure sodium (LPS) street lighting. For example, replacing a 175-W mercury-vapour lighting fixture with a fully-shielded, 35-W LPS fixture produces the same amount of useful light with none of the glare and light trespass. The energy saving is remarkable. In addition to providing illumination at the lowest cost, LPS lights are nearly monochromatic, with the result that most of their light can be filtered out by astronomers. Low-pressure-sodium lights are especially good for street lighting, parking-lot lighting, security lighting, and any application where color rendering is not important. A number of cities are converting their street lighting to either LED or induction lamps, also rather energy efficient, especially when used at lower wattages than existing facilities. It is essential to reduce the wattage to realize power savings, and not to confuse power consumption (watts) with actual light output. **It is critical to avoid the use of bluish-looking LED or induction lamps, sold often in the name of energy efficiency.** Such night lighting can badly affect the circadian rhythms of humans, other fauna, and flora, compromising the health of our bodies and of the ecosystem. It also scatters more in the atmosphere and hence adds much to the artificial sky glow.

Common Types of Outdoor Lights
(in increasing order of efficiency)

Type	Power (W/klm)
incandescent	50
mercury vapour	20
compact fluorescent	15
metal halide	13
LED and induction	13
high-pressure sodium (orange-gold)	12
low-pressure sodium (yellow)	8

A full-cutoff, efficient light fixture

It is essential to use no more light than is required, and local ordinances usually regulate the maximum amount of light that can be used for different tasks. Too much light (and poorly shielded luminaires) will create glare and ruin adaptation to night lighting, blinding us just when we need to see. When we go from too-bright to too-dark environments, or vice versa, "transient adaptation" is impaired, and we suffer poor visibility for a while. Do not exceed lighting levels recommended by the Illuminating Engineering Society of North America (IESNA, see www.iesna.org). Overkill never helps; it usually just adds glare, and it always wastes energy. In addition, lights should be used only when necessary (timers are useful for controlling lights). Curfews are usually included in lighting ordinances.

Another common inclusion in lighting ordinances is the use of lighting zones.

Different areas have different requirements for lighting; downtown Toronto is not the same as rural Ontario. In addition, some locales have officially been declared Dark-Sky Preserves or Urban Sky Parks, regions where lighting is strictly controlled or prohibited. A number of these are located in Canada, and the RASC has been instrumental in helping establish these. (See LIGHT-POLLUTION ABATEMENT IN CANADA, overleaf.)

Lighting Myths: Increased lighting levels are generally perceived to provide higher security, yet there is no statistically significant evidence that increased lighting leads to reduced crime. Criminals need light, and they are more likely to be up and about at 3 a.m. than the property owner. Furthermore, security lights may draw attention to a house or business that would otherwise go unnoticed, and mask any unusual light that criminals may need to do their work. Our cities and towns are more brightly lit than ever, yet there has been little or no reduction in the crime rate. Security can best be provided by shielded, motion-activated luminaires that light up only when triggered by nearby movement. These serve to startle criminals, alert others that there is a potential problem, and provide glare-free visibility (when properly installed); they also use insignificant amounts of energy. The *Myth of the More the Better* is just that: a myth.

Lack of Awareness: The biggest problem in controlling light pollution is lack of awareness rather than resistance. After all, it costs money to pollute with light. Unlike the case with many other forms of pollution, simple solutions are available; moreover, *everyone benefits* in applying these solutions. Most people are not yet aware of the expense, the waste, and the harm associated with excess lighting. They put up with distant lights that shine directly into their eyes, not realizing that not only does this do *nothing* to illuminate the area near the light but that it also produces a veiling glare. The pollution usually involves not only the light itself but also other forms of environmental pollution associated with the production of the wasted light: the extraction, transportation, and burning of coal and oil. This general lack of awareness has been summarized nicely by Doug Pitcairn, an astronomy teacher in Nova Scotia:

> *"It surprises me how someone who would never think of leaving a plastic bottle on the ground at a picnic site will pay extra money each month to illuminate half the neighborhood with unnecessary, distracting light."*

Education: Educating the public, government officials, lighting professionals, and astronomers is a major thrust of current programs. These efforts have helped. Most committees in the IESNA and the International Commission on Illumination (CIE) have been addressing these issues, and Recommended Practices and other documents reflect these concerns. As they are issued, one will see them implemented, albeit on a slow time schedule. Astronomers and environmentalists should do all they can to both learn from these documents and to help publicize them and thereby get them into existing practices in our communities. The International Dark-Sky Association (IDA) is another source of good information (see www.darksky.org). Members receive a regular newsletter, have access to members-only material on the website, and may join one of several local Sections worldwide. For effective visual images that celebrate the night sky, also see The World at Night (www.twanight.org) and APOD (apod.nasa.gov).

In summary: Educate everyone you can, everywhere you can, by any means you can about the value of both dark skies and quality night-time lighting. There are solutions to control the light output: use light only where needed (shine it down), only when needed (turn it off), only the level needed (more is not better), and use energy-efficient (but not blue-white) light sources. It can be done, and it must be done if we are to improve the value of our night environment, for ourselves and for everyone, everywhere.

Get involved!

ASTRONOMICAL LEAGUE PROGRAMS
BY ROBERT KERR

For most of us, the excitement of our hobby is the time we spend under the stars, but because amateur astronomers comprise a diverse community, our observing circumstances vary considerably. We have different sizes of telescopes or binoculars and varying levels of experience. We may prefer visual observing, imaging, or sketching. Some of us belong to clubs and others don't. There are those who can observe under dark skies from home, while many must tolerate annoying levels of light pollution or pack up and drive miles to suitably dark skies.

The Astronomical League has its members covered with a menu of over 50 observing programs that specifically address the variability in what members want or need. The programs provide ample opportunities for experienced observers, newcomers, owners of all kinds of instruments, those with less familiarity with the sky (including youngsters), and observers constrained by varying degrees of light pollution. There's even a suite of programs for the Southern Hemisphere. So, when you find yourself thinking, "I feel like getting the scope out tonight. I wonder what is there to see," the League has you covered so you can turn your observing uncertainty into observing enjoyment.

The observing programs include customized lists of the best celestial targets visible under virtually any sky condition. In fact, the Urban Program is especially for observers who can't see the Milky Way at all. The numerous benefits of these programs have been widely recognized and acknowledged over the years, but the most often cited benefit is that they provide an incentive to go out and use your telescope.

"The programs are meant to encourage our members to get out and experience the wonder, beauty, and mystery of the night sky," says Astronomical League President John Goss. He emphasizes the League's core mission: to promote the science of astronomy by fostering astronomical education and by providing incentives for observation and research. This is done by assisting communication among the League's 298 affiliated astronomy clubs, as well as a community of over 17,000 members-at-large, patron members, and supporting members. Goss points out that "The League's highly successful roster of observing programs, along with award certificates and pins upon completion, is a core benefit of membership."

The League's inventory of programs has been evolving through the years since the introduction of the Messier Club in 1967. It has been the League's most popular program ever since, with over 2,700 awards presented to members. Launched in 1980, the Herschel 400 Club was the League's second program, and its award certificate is one of the most highly prized. However, the Binocular Messier Club, launched in 1991, is second highest in overall member participation. Following the success of these three clubs (now called programs), there followed a succession of offerings that have also become favorites among League observers: Lunar, Double Star, Binocular Deep Sky, Caldwell, and Globular Cluster programs.

Sue French, popular astronomy writer and "Deep-Sky Wonders" columnist for *Sky & Telescope*, reflects on her own early experiences with the League's observing programs: "A few years after beginning my first tentative explorations of the night sky, I joined a local astronomy club and learned about the Astronomical League. The League's Messier Observing Program led me to find and describe all the Messier objects in the League's booklet, which was very useful for a novice like me. I had a lot of fun and proudly received my certificate in 1980. I next tackled the Herschel 400 Program, which I can honestly say taught me how to observe. But you don't need to be just a deep-sky enthusiast to enjoy the League's programs."

Coauthors of the well-respected *Night Sky Observer's Guide,* George R. Kepple and Glen Sanner are long-time Astronomical League members and active program participants.

According to Kepple, "These programs give you a sense of purpose and a list of objects you might not have observed before." Sanner hadn't undertaken a program until a fellow Huachuca Astronomy Club member suggested he give it a try. "I soon jumped in with both feet," he recalls. "Any of the League programs are a way to discover the great variety of objects to be enjoyed at the eyepiece."

In 2001, to recognize those highly skilled members with broad interests, the League introduced the Master Observer Award. This prestigious award requires a breadth of observing experience while also permitting members to pursue special interests. To qualify, at least 10 programs must be completed, including a suite of 5 core programs, of which the Herschel 400 is one. Currently, the League has 175 members who proudly bear the distinction of Master Observer. Recently, the League announced a major enhancement under the new title of Master Observer Progression. This is largely in response to the substantial growth in the number of League programs introduced since 2001, as well as the continuing mastery of astronomy by League members seeking new challenges. The Progression includes six levels ranging from the Observer Award to Master Observer Platinum Award. The existing Master Observer Program remains the same, but is now one of the steps in the Progression.

National Observing Program directors Aaron Clevenson and Cliff Mygatt stay busy keeping all these programs on track and ensuring that the League's "celestial machinery" is properly oiled and running. According to Clevenson, "The goal is to provide observing subjects of interest to everyone, with differing levels of complexity and varying equipment requirements. The programs are structured not only to provide a list of things to see, but also to provide the opportunity for the observer to learn about those objects and astronomy in general." There are also more than 30 Observing Program coordinators assisting with the administration of the programs.

Details about all the programs can be found on the Astronomical League website www.astroleague.org.

Mygatt says the listing is a handy resource for observers to begin "shopping" for programs of interest. However, these are only guidelines, leaving ample room for individuality based on a member's own experience, preferences, and sense of exploration. "In the end, we just want people to be successful and to enjoy themselves."

Observers may work on multiple programs at the same time and take as much time as they require for completion. The programs generally follow a similar format: an introduction or overview; documentation on the nature of the objects to be observed; the object list and number of objects to be observed; a requirements section, which includes specifics on maintaining an observing log and other materials; and how to submit observations to the program's coordinator for an award.

Members may choose to submit their observations for award certificates and pins, or they may use the program lists purely to add variety to their observing sessions.

To assist beginners working the programs, Clevenson maintains handy observing tools on the League website called "What's Up, Doc?" and "What's Up Tonight, Doc?" These resources help members know which objects from various observing lists can be viewed during the current month or evening, removing some of the guesswork involved in preparing for a night under the stars.

The numbered award certificates and pins may be mailed directly to the member or to the member's club coordinator for presentation at a local club meeting. Member names, certificate numbers, and League affiliations are published quarterly in *Reflector* under "Observing Awards." Members can also check the status of their awards in a database maintained on the League's website.

Involving young people in the science of astronomy has been a long-standing priority of the Astronomical League at both the national and local levels. As local clubs explore inventive forms of youth outreach, the League continues its 23-year support for these efforts with award programs directed at encouraging and recognizing outstanding youth accomplishments. Astronomical League Vice-President Bill Bogardus oversees these programs: "Youth awards are given to encourage, celebrate, and honor those students who pursue the area of astronomy in their educational learning experience." The premier recognition is the National Young Astronomer Award (NYAA), presented annually at Astronomical League conventions.

Youth interest is best nurtured at the local club level with the commitment of adult members willing to share their time and expertise. For example, League programs have helped one teenager discover astronomy and bolster much-needed self-esteem. As a youngster, Ethan Maitra was diagnosed with Asperger's syndrome and found it challenging to find activities where he felt socially comfortable with others. Thomas Pennino, of the Astronomical Society of Long Island, has been mentoring Ethan. The young observer has derived a great sense of accomplishment through club membership, as well as pride in receiving awards for the Sunspotter and Binocular Double Star Programs. Pennino says, "Ethan reminds us what we felt when we began observing the many wonders of the heavens."

League observers eagerly anticipate the annual introduction of new observing programs. Where do these programs come from? They're created by fellow members with a passion for a particular aspect of observing they wish to share. Cindy Krach of the Haleakala Amateur Astronomers was the lead author, assisted by club members, on the Sketching Program. She had read how sketching would help hone her observing skills. Trying it, she realized much more detail revealed itself when she spent time capturing what she observed as accurately as possible. When looking at very faint fuzzies in particular, it really hit home what a valuable tool sketching becomes in the observing process: "The Sketching Program helps people increase their powers of observation when they slow down long enough to faithfully record what they observe. And you absolutely don't have to be an artist!"

Another new program has presented challenges and rewards even for the League's most seasoned observers—the Active Galactic Nuclei Program, authored by Master Observer Al Lamperti of the Delaware Valley Amateur Astronomers, joins programs such as Galaxy Groups and Clusters, Flat Galaxy, and Herschel II, which benefit from observer experience, larger apertures, and dark skies.

According to Lamperti, the purpose of his program is to provide the opportunity to find and detect elusive active galactic nuclei, including quasars, BL Lacertae objects, and Seyfert galaxies. He says his most satisfying personal experience has been splitting lensed quasar QSO B0957+561 in Ursa Major: "Neat to see a dot whose light left seven billion years ago. Quite humbling."

President John Goss has an enthusiastic outlook on the future of amateur astronomy, as well as the personal benefits that result from the social aspects of astronomy clubs. He thinks that even though we may have spectacular images at our fingertips, amateur astronomers will always want to see things in real time with their own eyes and personally experience the beauty and mystery of the incredible Universe: "More people will desire what I call the 'authentic observing experience,' that is, that special relationship of telescope, observer, and sky. The Astronomical League observing programs are an excellent place to find that."

DEEP-SKY OBSERVING HINTS
BY ALAN DYER

In the 1960s and 1970s, few observers owned telescopes larger than 200-mm aperture. Today, 250-mm to 600-mm Dobsonian-mounted reflectors are commonplace. Using computerized telescopes, observers can now find thousands of objects at the push of a button. As a result, deep-sky observing has soared in popularity.

However, owners of less-sophisticated, small-aperture instruments shouldn't think they are shut out of deep-sky viewing. In a dark sky, an 80-mm to 100-mm telescope will show all the Messier objects and reveal hundreds of brighter NGC (New General Catalogue) objects. In fact, many large objects are best seen in fast (*f*/4 to *f*/6), small-aperture telescopes or in giant 70-mm and 80-mm binoculars. Contrary to popular belief, even slow f-ratio instruments (*f*/11 to *f*/16) are useful; their only disadvantage is the difficulty of achieving a low-power wide field. No matter what telescope you use, follow these techniques to get the most out of a night's deep-sky viewing:

- Always plan each night's observing: Prepare a list of a dozen or so objects for the night. Hunt them down on star charts or with computer programs first during the day to become familiar with their location.
- Seek out dark skies; a black sky improves contrast and makes up for lack of aperture.
- To preserve night vision, always use a dim red flashlight for reading charts.
- Avoid prolonged exposure to bright sunlight earlier in the day (such as a day at the beach); it will reduce your ability to dark adapt and make for tired eyes at night.
- Use averted vision; looking to one side of an object places it on a more sensitive part of the retina.
- Another technique for picking out faint objects is to jiggle the telescope (and the image) slightly.
- Don't be afraid to use high power; it often brings out small, faint objects such as planetary nebulae and galaxies, and resolves detail in globulars, in small, rich open clusters, and in bright galaxies.
- Use a nebular filter on emission and planetary nebulae (see FILTERS on p. 64); even in a dark sky, filters can dramatically enhance the view of these kinds of objects, often making obvious an otherwise elusive nebula.
- Be comfortable; sit down while at the eyepiece and be sure to dress warmly.
- Collimate and clean your optics; a poorly maintained telescope will produce distorted star images, reduce image contrast, and make it more difficult to see faint stars and other threshold objects.
- Don't expect to use analog setting circles; in a portable telescope "dial-type" circles will rarely be accurate.
- Digital setting circles and Go To telescopes can find objects precisely. While they are wonderful observing aids, they can overwhelm observers with thousands of targets, often supplying scant information about each one. When making a list for a night's viewing, books such as the three-volume *Burnham's Celestial Handbook* and the two-volume *Night Sky Observer's Guide* by Kepple and Sanner are still the best guides.
- Don't be in a rush to check off targets; take time to examine each object, and take notes or make drawings. Both will help train your eye to see subtle detail; you'll learn to see the most through your telescope.
- Consider keeping a logbook or journal of your nightly tours of the sky; including eyepiece impressions and drawings provides a record of your improving observing skills that is fun to look back upon in future years. See the section THE OBSERVING LOGBOOK (immediately following) for suggestions on organizing a journal.

THE OBSERVING LOGBOOK
BY PAUL MARKOV

There are many good reasons for maintaining an observing logbook: A logbook is useful for recalling the details of previous observations and comparing past observations with current ones; maintaining one will make your observing organized and methodical; and having to describe an object forces you to *look* for more details, thus sharpening your observing skills. Finally, if you are planning to apply for one of the several RASC observing certificates (see note on p. 308), then a logbook with your observations may be required when submitting your application.

Logbooks can be chronological or sectional. In a chronological logbook, all observations are listed sequentially by date, regardless of object type. In a sectional logbook, observations are grouped by object type, such as open clusters and galaxies. With either format, you may want to keep a master index of objects for cross-referencing to the correct page in your logbook.

What about the book itself? Typical choices are the simple three-ring binder with standard lined paper, spiral-bound notebooks, and hardcover record/accounting books. In my opinion, the most practical is the three-ring binder because it allows you to insert auxiliary materials into your logbook with the help of a three-hole punch. With this choice, entering observations out of sequence is never an issue because you can easily rearrange the sheets. Also, should you wish to make a "soft" copy of your logbook using a scanner that generates Adobe Acrobat PDF files, it is much easier with loose sheets.

For recording observations, using a preprinted observing form offers these advantages: the fill-in-the-blank fields remind you to record the relevant data; many of these forms have a space for making a drawing of the observed object; and they give your book a neat and organized look. An example of an observing form can be found at www.rasc.ca/handbook/obsform.pdf; you may prefer to design your own observing form by using the fields suggested below. However, I prefer to use plain, lined paper as there is less repetition when writing observing session details, and I do not have to worry about using different forms for different objects or running out of forms.

There are two choices for recording your observations: using full sentences and using acronyms and abbreviations. Using full sentences is the preferred method if you enjoy re-reading your observations from past years, or if you want others to be able to easily read your logbook. But if your intent is to keep a data book for reference purposes only, then acronyms and abbreviations are the recommended choices.

It is useful to record the following information for each observing session: date; time of arrival and departure (if you have traveled somewhere to observe); location; names of other people at the observing site; sky transparency (i.e. clarity of the atmosphere, which is generally noted by faintest visible stellar magnitude; see LIMITING MAGNITUDES, p. 68); seeing (i.e. the steadiness of the atmosphere: if stars and planets appear to shimmer, that indicates poor seeing; if they appear sharp and steady, that indicates good seeing), and environmental conditions (e.g. temperature, dew, wind, sources of light pollution, snow cover, and the presence of insects). You can also number each observing session sequentially for easy referencing within your logbook.

Be sure to standardize your time/date format. For recording time, choose either the military time or a.m./p.m. format. In addition, use alpha characters to specify the month rather than numbers. For example, use 2018 Aug. 5 instead of 8/5/18; this will avoid ambiguity in reading the date.

For each object observed, record the following information as a minimum: date and time of observation, object name or designation, type of object, constellation, telescope and magnification used, type of filter (if any), and visual description. Making drawings is highly recommended and adds substantially to the value of your logbook. It is also important to record failed observations because these entries will remind you to try again in your next observing session. Remember to update the observing notes if the sky conditions change, if you have equipment trouble, if you take extended "coffee breaks," or if you see something unusual like a fireball or aurora.

If you are able to write neatly while observing, it is best to enter observations directly into your logbook. However, if this proves too difficult given the environmental circumstances, you can record your observations in a temporary notebook and transcribe them into your logbook the next day. An audio recorder can also be used if you are careful to ensure its mechanical integrity while in the field and if you are diligent enough to transcribe the recorded observations into your observing logbook regularly. Below are some suggestions on what to look for when observing deep-sky objects.

All Object Types: What is the shape of the object? What is its size (based on the field of view of your eyepiece)? Is averted vision required to see the object? Does averted vision allow you to see more detail? (If yes, describe the extra detail.) Is the object near (or in the same field of view as) other deep-sky objects or bright stars? What magnification gives the best view of the object? Does a filter improve the view? (See FILTERS, p. 64.)

Open Cluster: Is there a greater concentration of stars in a specific part of the cluster? Is it fully resolved into its component stars, or are there any unresolved stars causing the cluster to appear nebulous? How many stars can you see (only if reasonable to count them)? Are there any bright stars within the cluster? Are there any colored stars? (If so, describe their tints and locations within the cluster.) Does the cluster stand out from the background star field?

Globular Cluster: What is the degree of star concentration (high, medium, low)? How much can be resolved to component stars (none, outer edges, middle, to the core)?

Galaxy: Is it uniform in brightness, or does it have a brighter nucleus? Is it diffuse or stellar? Can any detail or mottling be seen in the arms? Are any stars visible within the arms?

Emission or Reflection Nebula: Is the brightness even, or are there brighter/darker areas? Are the edges of the nebula well defined? Are there any stars within the nebula? Is there a hint of any color?

Planetary Nebula: Is it stellar in appearance, or can a disk be seen? Are the edges well defined or diffuse? Are there any brighter/darker areas? Can a central star be seen? Is there a hint of any color? Can it be "blinked" with a filter or averted vision?

Dark Nebula: Is it easy or difficult to discern the dark nebula from the background sky? Are there any stars within the nebula?

Logbooks and Databases

If you enjoy using computers, an electronic database can be a helpful complement to an observing logbook. You can obtain commercially available deep-sky databases that allow you to enter your own observations for any object. These databases are also useful for creating observing lists and planning observing sessions. A highly recommended database, which also happens to be freeware, is the Saguaro Astronomy Club (SAC) deep-sky database, available at **www.saguaroastro.org**. With minimal tweaking, the SAC database can be formatted to accept your own observations.

You can transcribe complete observations from your logbook into the database or simply enter four valuable pieces of information for each observed object: seen (Y/N), date, telescope used, and location. With these fields filled in, in a matter of seconds you can determine which and how many objects you have observed, and the date field for any object will direct you to the correct page in your observing logbook. You can also determine interesting facts such as from which observing location you observed the most objects or which telescope produced the most observations.

ASTRONOMICAL SKETCHING
BY KATHLEEN HOUSTON

Drawing creates a tangible connection between the observer and the sky. The visual recording of celestial wonders is part of a long-standing tradition, e.g. the Chaco Culture petroglyphs in New Mexico (c. 1000), Galileo's sketches of Jupiter's moons (1610), William Parsons' drawing of the Whirlpool Galaxy (1845), David Levy's drawings of the impact sites of Comet Shoemaker–Levy 9 on Jupiter (1994). Pencil-to-paper is an active, energy-shifting experience that allows one to see more, to go beyond the casual ten-second glance through a telescope at a public star party. Sketching is an expression of curiosity, to experience the sky on a personal, scientific, and spiritual level. For those new to sketching, you are supported by your innate skills of visual perception. Connect with other sketchers in your Center, share images, swap stories, and learn from each other. Pose your burning questions to the RASC Astrosketchers Group (www.rasc.ca/astrosketchers-group) and sample the diverse collective of experience and ideas. Host sketching workshops at star parties and observing sessions to move this solitary activity into the realm of a group learning experience.

Drawing Toolkit: Start with a small kit of drawing supplies and build on it. The materials can be found at craft stores (e.g. *Michaels*) or art supply stores (e.g. *DeSerres*). Make up a set of wooden pencils having a range of hardness: an HB pencil makes a light grey color, and is excellent for the mapping-out stage; for a darker black that stands out, try 2B, 4B, or 6B; some sketchers include very light pencils in the 2H range. I prefer woodless graphite pencils, because I can use the side of the pencil to create large areas of soft grey to deep black, and the coating on the pencil keeps my hands clean. A retractable eraser stick is perfect to delicately remove fine detail; a bullet pencil sharpener keeps pencil tips fine, and takes little room. Include a blending stump (rolled paper) for smudging and blending grey levels. Sure, throw in a ballpoint pen!

Experiment with your toolkit: In daylight, take your toolkit for a spin on plain paper. Draw a comet such as Hale–Bopp: create a dark dot with the side of your pencil, and extend the shape outwards. Smudge it with your finger to make the tail, and refine the shape, length, and width of the tail (work from a photograph, if you wish). Try pivoting your pencil to create stars in clusters. The hardness range of your pencils helps you to portray star magnitudes. Make a nebulous shape with the side of your pencil, smooth it with your finger, and use an adjustable eraser to carve out detail. You can modify with the blending stump to control and feather the smudge shape. Add and subtract your sketch, making marks at will. The key is to maintain a level of comfort, to be open, to learn how the hand and eye transform your experience and view to the paper surface.

Illumination: To preserve night vision, use a red-filtered book light or headlamp, with the intensity adjusted to the lowest practical setting. Cover the light while viewing at the eyepiece, to open your eyes to the darkroom of the telescope; uncover the light when drawing, enough to see the details of the pencil marks on the paper.

White paper (drawing in the negative, black stars on white background): For typical projects, use medium-weight paper with medium-tooth finish. Consider using a template on a clipboard, with pre-drawn circles and text lines to write comments and notes.

Grey paper (drawing in the positive, white & black on grey): Sketching on grey paper can be a novel experience, because on white paper one is usually focused on bright things; grey paper allows the exploration of dark dust lanes within nebulosity. Try light-to medium-grey paper, such as Canson's "Mi-Teintes" series. On this, try HB, 2B, 4B, and 6B pencils, white china marker, and white conté pencil. The white china marker is good for stars. The conté is smudgable and erasable and is excellent to build up highlights in nebulosity. (I like drawing the dark dust-lane areas with 4B–9B pencils.)

Principal Drawing Steps
- Orient yourself: select a star field from an atlas or choose a favorite subject. Frame the subject in your optics. Note guide stars in your finder, and star patterns at the eyepiece. Wander through the field, get to know the neighborhood, and pick out details that catch your interest.
- Draw the field stars and the general shape of the subject itself. Use your natural spatial awareness to estimate separations of stars from one another. Use imaginary horizontal and vertical lines to help with angles. Draw two stars, and build up from there to form triangles, polygons, or sprays of stars.
- Either work from object to periphery, or from the outer edge in toward the object. One method may be more natural to you than the other. Experiment!
- Use averted vision, jiggle the scope. Breathe deeply, put a cover over your head to block outside light. Stay at the eyepiece to allow your eye and brain to open up.
- Vary magnification, from low to medium, to high, and back. Stack information and detail in wide, medium, and narrow fields. (Take a break at this stage, if you like.)
- Once the field becomes familiar and you have sketched out an overall map, make a second sweep. Use a clock dial to divide the field into quadrants: 12, 3, 6, and 9. Define edges, carve out highlights and texture, and capture more detail.
- Mark west (the direction of drift) and north, especially if the view is mirror-reversed.
- Finish in the warm-up shelter. Adjust tones, make field notes, tidy up.
- Share your drawings and your story. Prepare a list of subjects for your next session.

Drawing in color: Color is an adventure on its own, and presents a special challenge. The light level required to see color at night closes up your dark-adapted eyes. One solution is to create a black & white drawing and to write in color descriptors, for finishing later in the warm-up shelter, or at home. To record a lunar eclipse, create templates in advance, so you can concentrate on the shifting shadow and deepening orange color, especially where the Earth's atmosphere bends the light.

OBSERVING SKILLS AND SKETCHING STRATEGIES

Subject	Observing Skills	Sketching Strategy
Stars and star clusters	Look for triangles and hockey sticks, stars that define a specific shape or pattern, curve, etc.	Pivot HB pencil point for small stars, 4B (softer) for larger stars.
Galaxies	Explore at high magnification to define edges and luminance details of galaxy structure.	Use the side of a 2B or 4B pencil to define the overall shape, then the fingertip to diffuse the edge and a blending stump to feather out shape and detail.
Nebulae and comets	Locate two or three field stars to orient and frame the general shape and size of the diffuse subject.	As for galaxies. Use a second sweep around the clock quadrants to detect edges and fainter stars.
Moon	Work at the the terminator for high contrast. Observe the shape of the crater, like a shadow on an inverted apple, and how the shadow defines the cavity.	Work from the crater rim, and draw the shapes of the shadow and subtle grays. Note details of surface texture. Dark adaptation of the eye is not important.

Guidelines To Facilitate Drawing

- Create a comfort zone with your binoculars or telescope. Stand or sit, as you wish, or use an adjustable chair to make yourself comfortable at the eyepiece during sustained drawing. On cool nights, take breaks to keep warm.
- Become dark adapted at the eyepiece. Take a really good long look at your subject, and let your eyes open up. Minimize exposure to your drawing light. Sketch what you see in the finder scope, to map how to get there.
- Sketching and drawing. Sketching is generally a quick observation on one sheet of paper, taking 5–10 minutes. A drawing is a sustained effort with more attention to detail and contrast, taking 30–60 minutes, or perhaps multiple sessions.

The Looking and Drawing Experience: Frederick Franck describes the experience of looking and drawing as mini-moments: **The Three Nens** (*The Awakened Eye*, Vintage, 1979). The *1st Nen* is the simple act of seeing and sketching in short, quick glances. Draw what you see using speed as a friend, and use your natural spatial awareness. The *2nd Nen* follows rapidly to build on 1st Nen ingenuity, expanding on the texture, fully mapping the field, and moving naturally from eye to hand to paper. The *3rd Nen* engages the thinking mind to redraw or improve subject distances, refine contrast, define edges, name and judge what you are looking at. You can choose to extend the sitting, or decide to look for more information. Once you notice the freedom of drawing in the 1st and 2nd Nen, you see that it is a fluid, uninterrupted, and focused energy. Use your 3rd Nen to synthesize the work, finish up, and write notes.

During the **First Sitting**, minimize eye travel between eyepiece and paper. Stay between the moments of 1st and 2nd Nen. Explore the texture variations: where is the nebula or galaxy edge? Draw everything you see, include fleeting detail. During the **Second Sitting** with the same subject/drawing, when you are familiar with the subject, the inner eye accumulates the experience, and you observe more.

Favorites, challenges, and want-to-try objects: summer and winter Milky Way, naked-eye; zodiacal light; a night landscape; a binocular field mosaic in Sagittarius; a fireball, with a collaborating observer; ashen light on Venus; objects in the Isabel Williamson Lunar Observing Program; extreme lunar libration objects; the natural bridge on the Moon; cloud belts of Jupiter; Jovian moon activities, including shadow transits; sunspots, prominences, filaments, light bridges, and transits; globular clusters (finding shapes in the complexity); meteor showers; the complete Veil Nebula; Barnard's Dark Nebulae (including B86, The Ink Spot); The Coalsack; Arp Galaxies; and (finally) anything beautiful and in color: for the next cover of the *Observer's Handbook!*

Astronomical Sketching Publications

- Bratton, Mark, "Become a Better Observer: Sketch!" *SkyNews*, July/August 2009.
- Houston, Kathleen, "Drawing at the Eyepiece," *JRASC*, December 2010, pp. 237–240.
- French, Sue, *Celestial Sampler, 60 Small-Scope Tours for Starlit Nights* (*Sky & Telescope* Stargazing Series), Sky Publishing, 2005.
- O'Meara, Stephen James, *Deep-Sky Companions: The Messier Objects*, Cambridge University Press, 1998.
- Richard Handy et al., *Astronomical Sketching, a Step-by-Step Introduction* (Patrick Moore's Practical Astronomy Series), Springer–Verlag, 2007.

Astronomical Sketching Webpages

- Sketching techniques, tutorials, templates: tinyurl.com/27rz2ax
- Carol Lakomiak's tutorials: www.rasc.ca/lakomiak-lunar and www.rasc.ca/lakomiak-sundso
- Astronomy Sketch of the day (ASOD): www.asod.info (archive)
- *Cloudy Nights* Sketching Forums: tinyurl.com/puf2gz7

DIGITAL ASTROPHOTOGRAPHY: A PRIMER
BY TENHO TUOMI

In 1610, when Galileo turned his telescope to the heavens, he observed detail that he could not see with his eyes alone. The camera was the next step (c. 1850), capturing more detail than the eye and telescope together. Along with sketching, photography became an archiving tool for recording astronomical views and events. For many, the camera has become an artistic tool to produce beautiful pictures of astronomical objects. The recent digital camera revolution makes it possible for anyone to enjoy this endeavor. The second part of the revolution has been the rapid development of computer software for enhancing astronomical photographs. The following primer on astronomical photography is only the starting point: consult the books, websites, and user forums listed below for more information and guidance.

Field of view: The angular span of an astrophoto is determined by the focal length (f) of the image-forming optics and a linear dimension (d) of the sensor (width, height, or diagonal, accordingly). The field of view (FOV) is given by

FOV = $2 \arctan(d/2f)$ ($\approx 57.3\ d/f$ degrees when f is much larger than d).

For example, the 36×24-mm sensor of a professional "full-frame" camera on a telescope with $f = 1000$ mm has a FOV of $2.1° \times 1.4°$. The smaller 22.2×14.8-mm APS-C sensor (used in many prosumer cameras) gives a smaller $1.3° \times 0.9°$ FOV on the same telescope, a good size to frame the Orion Nebula. At the other extreme, a 50-mm lens on a camera with an APS-C sensor gives a FOV of $25° \times 17°$, large enough to capture most of the constellation Orion itself.

Camera-and-tripod astrophotography: Many good astrophotos can be taken with an ordinary camera using the supplied lens, mounted on a solid tripod. Typical subjects include: aurorae, conjunctions of planets (or of the planets with the Moon), solar eclipses, lunar eclipses, and wide-field views of constellations and the Milky Way. Exposures are typically longer than for daytime photography, requiring a tripod (or some other way of holding the camera steady). For best results, turn off image stabilization (if the lens has it) and use the self-timer or a remote shutter control to reduce camera shake. Some cameras have automatic settings for nighttime photos, but manual settings are recommended. Initially set the camera sensitivity (ISO number) as high as it will go and the f/stop one or two stops higher than wide open (for sharp stars). Set the focus to infinity (which may have to be verified visually with most modern lenses). Set the shutter speed long enough to register the background sky, up to about 30 s. (For cameras with exposure histograms, the peak levels would be in the 20–30% range.) Too long an exposure time will show elongated or streaked stars. To estimate the maximum exposure time t in seconds for a lens of focal length f mm, use the formula $t = 500/f$. If the camera does not have a "full-frame" sensor, use the "35-mm equivalent focal length" (check the camera manual). Experiment with different settings to find what works best for your camera, lens, and sky conditions.

Wide-field astrophotography with cameras on equatorial mounts: If your camera has a "bulb" setting, you can capture fainter objects without stars streaking by "piggy-backing" the camera on a telescope with an equatorial (EQ) mount, or by using a specialized commercial camera mount or homemade "barn-door" tracker aligned equatorially. The EQ mount can be driven manually, mechanically, or electrically to follow the motion of the heavens. For example, a tracked exposure of several minutes with a lens focal ratio (FR) of $f/3.5$ and sensor sensitivity of ISO 1600 will produce acceptable photos of the Milky Way or the zodiacal light. Any EQ mount that is used for long-exposure photography with standard camera lenses should be at least approximately polar-aligned (see POLAR ALIGNMENT, p. 70).

Afocal astrophotography of Solar System objects at the telescope eyepiece: It is possible to take an astrophoto simply by placing the camera and lens at the eyepiece of a telescope. For best results, use a mechanical adapter that aligns the lens to the eyepiece and clamps them together. This afocal technique works well with older cameras and lenses, but many modern cameras with zoom lenses suffer from bad vignetting with afocal photography, showing a black border around a small image in the middle. However, one can still take very pleasing astrophotos of bright subjects such as the filtered Sun, the Moon, Saturn, and Jupiter with its moons, using simple cameras (even cell phones!), just by using the viewscreen to align the picture.

Prime-focus astrophotography: High-quality deep-sky astrophotos usually require a Digital Single-Lens Reflex (DSLR) camera at prime focus with the camera lens replaced by the telescope objective lens or mirror, which—in effect—becomes a long telephoto lens. Adapters are available for attaching the camera to the telescope. In this case, the EQ mount must be carefully polar-aligned and the drive should be guided to follow the stars exactly. Most drives have irregularities that limit unguided exposure to times as short as 15 s. Good astrophotos may result from such short exposures if the telescope optics are "fast," i.e. $f/6$ or less. Longer exposures require guiding the photographic telescope on a star using the finder or another comounted telescope, either manually or with special automatic guiding electronics. Even better astrophotos can be obtained with a camera having a modified infrared filter over the sensor (such as the Canon 60Da), and from dedicated astronomical CCD cameras. With an acceptable image (or images) as a starting point, computer software can help tease out the interesting details in images and enhance the overall appearance of the composition.

The best deep-sky astrophotos result from taking multiple short exposures, often called "subframes," and combining them in software to create a master frame. The total exposure time may range from tens of minutes to hours. The following table suggests minimum *subframe* exposure times for various objects, using an $f/5$ telescope with a camera sensitivity of ISO 1600. For other configurations, multiply the suggested times by the factor $64\,FR^2/ISO$ (where FR denotes the focal ratio). For example, if the FR of the telescope is 10 instead of 5, multiply the time by 4; if the ISO is 800 instead of 1600, multiply the time by 2, and so on.

Deep-Sky Object	Exposure time for $f/5$ and ISO 1600
Star clusters, bright comets	30 s
Small planetary nebulae (M57, M76)	30 s
Larger planetary nebulae (M27, M97)	120 s (2 min)
Galaxies, faint comets	120 s (2 min)
Reflection and emission nebulae	120–300 s (2–5 min)
Dim nebulae (Veil Nebula)	300 s (5 min)

Some objects have large dynamic range, like M42 (the Orion Nebula), requiring different sub-frame exposure times for different parts. The nebula center and the Trapezium stars show best with a few seconds exposure. To show the entire nebula requires a several-minute exposure, but that overexposes the center. Computer software can be used to combine short and long exposures to show all parts of the nebula. M45 (the Pleiades) is another example where a short exposure shows the stars sharply, but a long exposure is required to show the nebulosity around the stars.

Long-focus and eyepiece projection astrophotography: The Sun, Moon, and planets are bright and can benefit from slower telescopes (larger FR) and lower ISO settings. To increase the apparent size of the planets or details of the Sun and Moon, use a Barlow lens or eyepiece (in a special adaptor) to project a magnified image to the sensor. This increases the effective telescope focal ratio (FR). The following suggested exposure times, using an $f/10$ telescope with a camera sensitivity of ISO 400, can be adjusted for other configurations by multiplying by the factor $4\,FR^2/ISO$.

Sun, Moon, and Planets	Exposure time for $f/10$ and ISO 400
Filtered Sun	1/2000 s
Moon	1/1000 s – 1/25 s
Planets	1/800 s – 1/50 s

Webcam astrophotography: Excellent astrophotos of the lunar detail and the brighter planets have been obtained with computer webcams, such as the *Logitech QuickCam Pro*, by removing the lens and making an adaptor to attach to the telescope focuser. Capture a video of 100 to 1000 frames, and combine the best frames (those uncorrupted by atmospheric turbulence) with computer software, such as *RegiStax*. For planets, a Barlow lens can be used to increase the image size.

Postprocessing of astrophotos: Many methods can be used to reduce noise, graininess, and uneven illumination in astrophotos, most of which require specialized computer software. Steps relevant to the image data-collection stage include:
• Take multiple exposures and stack them using *RegiStax* or *DeepSkyStacker*.
• Expose "dark frames," stack them, and subtract them from the stacked "light frames." (With care, in-camera noise reduction may be used.)
• Use "flat frames" to adjust uneven exposure across the field.

   Almost all astrophotos require some computer enhancement to obtain the best results. Usually the first aim is to stretch the image, that is, to darken the background and to brighten the faint detail of nebulae or galaxies without overbrightening the stars or galaxy cores. Another priority is to reduce the noise in the image without losing desirable low-level detail. No two astrophotographers enhance pictures the same way, for it is usually a matter of taste and compromise. Computer software supplied with cameras usually has some capabilities to enhance pictures. Good results can be obtained with freeware image-processing programs like *IrfanView* (www.irfanview.com) or *GIMP* (www.gimp.org), using the gamma and contrast adjustments in their menus. Best results usually require commercial image-processing software such as *Adobe PhotoShop* (www.adobe.com) or astronomy-specific software like *MaxIm DL* (www.cyanogen.com).

Suggested astrophotography resources
• Dickinson, T. and Dyer, A., "Digital Astrophotography," *The Backyard Astronomer's Guide*, Firefly Books, Ltd., 2010, Chapter 13.
• Dyer, A., *How to Photograph and Process Nightscapes and Timelapses* (interactive eBook, 2014) www.amazingsky.com/nightscapesbook.html
• RASC astrophotography online forum: tech.groups.yahoo.com/group/RASCAG
• *Cloudy Nights* (several online imaging forums): www.cloudynights.com
• *RegiStax* (image-stacking and processing freeware): www.astronomie.be/registax
• *DeepSkyStacker* (image-stacking and registration freeware): deepskystacker.free.fr
• Lodriguss, Jerry, *Catching the Light*, astrophotography page: www.astropix.com
• *Tenho Tuomi Observatory*: www.lex.sk.ca/astro/index.htm

Editor's note: The author has completely photographed the Handbook lists THE MESSIER CATALOGUE, THE FINEST NGC OBJECTS, *and* DEEP-SKY GEMS.

THE SKY MONTH BY MONTH

BY BRUCE MCCURDY (TEXT), LARRY BOGAN (JUPITER'S SATELLITES), PATRICK KELLY (EVENTS), DAVE LANE (TABLES), AND ALISTER LING (LUNAR IMAGES)

INTRODUCTION

In the descriptions on the left-hand monthly pages (pp. 98–120), the right ascension (**RA**), declination (**Dec**) (both for equinox J2000.0), distance from Earth's center in astronomical units (**Dist**), visual magnitude (**Mag**), and equatorial angular diameter (**Size**) are tabulated for seven planets for 0h UT on the 1st, 11th, and 21st day of each month. The RA, Dec, distance, and diameter of the Sun are also given. **In the text below the tables, the meridian transit times at Greenwich (in UT) may be read as Standard Time at an observer's standard meridian (the error is no more than a minute or two). If the observer is west (east) of the standard meridian, the Standard Time of transit will be later (earlier) by 4 min per degree of longitude difference from the standard meridian. Remember to add one hour for Daylight Saving Time, if applicable.**

Sun

Data concerning the position, transit, orientation, rotation, and activity of the Sun plus times of sunrise and sunset appear on pp. 184–187, 189–193, and 205–207. For detailed information on this year's solar eclipses, see ECLIPSES IN 2018 on p. 126.

Moon

Conjunctions of the Moon with the naked-eye planets and the bright Messier objects that lie near the ecliptic—the Beehive Cluster (M44), M35, and the Pleiades Cluster (M45)—are given in the right-hand monthly tables (pp. 94–121). Only events for which the elongation of the Moon is at least 14° are included, and only selected such events involving the Messier objects are listed. See p. 19 for the definition of conjunction and elongation.

The Moon's phases, perigees, and apogees (computed with *Multiyear Interactive Computer Almanac 1800–2050*, Willmann–Bell, 2005) are also given in the right-hand tables. The phases new Moon, first quarter, full Moon, and last quarter correspond, respectively, to the Moon having a longitude 0°, 90°, 180°, and 270° east of the Sun. The age of the Moon is the time since the new phase; first-quarter, full, and last-quarter phases correspond approximately to 7.4, 14.8, and 22.1 days, respectively. For times of moonrise and moonset, see pp. 150–94.

The Sun's selenographic colongitude (SSC), given on the left-hand monthly pages, indicates the position of the sunrise terminator as it moves across the face of the Moon and provides a method of ascertaining the angle of illumination of features on the Moon's surface. The SSC is the angle of the sunrise terminator measured toward the observer's east (i.e. westward on the Moon) starting from the lunar meridian that passes through the mean center of the apparent disk. Its value increases by nearly 12.2° per day, or about 0.5° per hour, and is approximately 0°, 90°, 180°, and 270° at the first-quarter, full, last-quarter, and new phases, respectively. Values of the SSC are given on pp. 98–120 for the 0th day of each month.

Selenographic longitude (λ) is measured toward the observer's west (i.e. eastward on the Moon) from the mean central lunar meridian. Thus sunrise will occur at a given point on the Moon when SSC = 360° − λ; values of 360° − λ for several lunar features are listed in the MAP OF THE MOON on p. 148. The longitude of the sunset terminator differs by 180° from that of the sunrise terminator.

Libration, also given on the left-hand pages, is the apparent rocking motion of the Moon as it orbits Earth. As a consequence, over time, about 59% of the lunar surface can be viewed from Earth (see *Sky & Telescope*, July 1987, p. 60). Libration in longitude (±8°) results from the nearly uniform axial rotation of the Moon combined with its varying orbital speed along its elliptical orbit, while libration in latitude (±7°) is caused by the tilt of the Moon's equator to its orbital plane. A smaller contribution (up to ±1°), called *diurnal libration*, is associated with the shifting of the observer due to Earth's rotation.

When the libration in longitude is positive, more of the Moon's east limb, the limb near Mare Crisium, is exposed to view (in reference to the lunar limbs, *east* and *west* are used in this lunar sense; see also the "E" and "W" labels on the MAP OF THE MOON, p. 148). When the libration in latitude is positive, more of the Moon's north limb is exposed to view. The monthly dates of the greatest positive and negative values of the libration in longitude and latitude and the dates of greatest northern and southern declination are given on the left-hand pages.

The lunar graphics on the right-hand pages give the geocentric appearance of the Moon at 0h UT on odd-numbered days of the month. They depict the Moon's phase, size, and libration. A small dot of size proportional to the amount of libration appears near the limb that is exposed. The graphics were prepared by Alister Ling with the aid of his *Lunar Calculator* software (lunarcal.shawwebspace.ca), jointly processed with the *JPL HORIZONS* ephemerides (ssd.jpl.nasa.gov/?horizons) to ensure accuracy.

The Moon's orbit is inclined 5° 09′ to the ecliptic. The gravitational influences of Earth and the Sun cause (i) the orbital plane to wobble, and (ii) the major axis of the orbit to precess: (i) The wobble shifts the line of nodes (see p. 122) westward (retrograde) along the ecliptic with a period of 18.60 years (18.61 years relative to the vernal equinox). During 2018, the ascending node regresses from longitude 136.9° to 117.6° across Cancer to Gemini. The Moon's declination reaches a northern extreme of +21.48° on Nov. 26 and a southern extreme of –21.43° on Dec. 9. In 2015, around the September equinox, the Moon's declination range had minimum extremes of ±18.1° (a minor standstill); from then on, the extreme range of the Moon's declination continually increases, reaching a peak of ±29° in 2025; (ii) The precession shifts the perigee point eastward (prograde) with a period of 8.85 years, although the positions of successive perigees fluctuate considerably from the mean motion. The Moon's mean equatorial plane, its mean orbital plane, and the plane of the ecliptic intersect along a common line of nodes, the equator being inclined at 1°32′ to the ecliptic and at 1°32′ + 5°09′ = 6°41′ to the orbit (i.e. the ascending node of the equator on the ecliptic coincides with the descending node of the orbit).

Jupiter's Satellites

The configurations of Jupiter's Galilean satellites, provided by Larry Bogan, are given on the right-hand monthly pages. In these diagrams, the vertical double line represents the equatorial diameter of the disk of Jupiter. Time is shown on the vertical scale, successive horizontal lines indicating 0h UT on the various days of the month. The relative positions of the four satellites with respect to the disk of Jupiter are given by the four curves, where I = Io, II = Europa (dashed curve), III = Ganymede, and IV = Callisto. Note the "West–East" orientation given at the top of each diagram; these directions are those of the observer's sky, not Jupiter's limbs. Double-shadow transits of Jupiter's Galilean satellites that are not within 1.5 months of Jupiter's conjunction with the Sun are listed. Double-satellite transits that are not accompanied by a double-shadow event are generally also listed. For more information about the various transits, occultations, and eclipses of Jupiter's Galilean satellites, see PHENOMENA OF THE GALILEAN SATELLITES (p. 230).

Lunar Occultations of Bright Stars and Planetary Bodies

Occultations by the Moon of the bright stars that lie near the ecliptic (Aldebaran, Antares, Regulus, and Spica) are given in the right-hand tables along with those of the seven planets, the dwarf planet Ceres, and some bright minor planets (Pallas, Juno, and Vesta). If the elongation of the Moon is less than 14°, the event is not listed. Footnotes give areas of visibility; for more details on occultations visible in North America, including several involving members of the Pleiades (M45), see LUNAR OCCULTATIONS (p. 162) and PLANETARY OCCULTATIONS (p. 247).

Minima of Algol

Estimated predicted times of mid-eclipse are based on the formula heliocentric minimum = $2\,440\,953.5087 + 2.867\,3075E$ *(courtesy of AAVSO, 2015)* and are expressed as geocentric times for comparison with observations. The first number is the Julian Date for the minimum of 1971 Jan. 2.01, and the second is the period of Algol in days; E is an integer. The presence of a third stellar component introduces variations in these times, and careful timings by observers are encouraged (see VARIABLE STARS, p. 298).

Planets

Conjunctions of the planets with each other and the bright ecliptic stars and Messier objects are listed in the right-hand tables. Only events for which the elongation of the inner planet is greater than 11° are included, and not all events involving the Messier objects are listed. Also included are oppositions, conjunctions with the Sun, greatest elongations, and stationary times. See p. 19 for definitions of these terms, and TABLE OF CONTENTS or the INDEX for the location of more information on each of the planets. The following diagrams give an overview of the circumstances of the planets in 2018.

Miscellaneous Entries

The lunation number is the number of times the Moon has circled the Earth since January 1923, based on a series described by Ernest W. Brown in *Planetary Theory*, 1933. Peaks of major meteor showers (see also p. 254), equinoxes and solstices, heliocentric phenomena of the planets, phenomena of the bright dwarf planets and minor planets, and a few other events and occasional notes are given in the right-hand tables.

MAGNITUDES OF NAKED-EYE PLANETS IN 2018

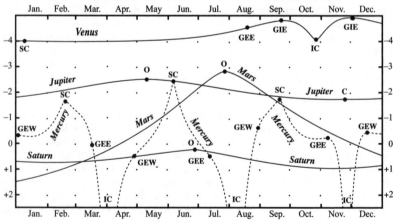

The visual magnitudes of the five classical (naked-eye) planets during 2018 are given. Oppositions (O), conjunctions (C), inferior and superior conjunctions (IC, SC), and greatest elongations east and west (GEE, GEW) are indicated. A diagram explaining these terms is on p. 20. Greatest illuminated extent (GIE), if shown, occurs when the illuminated area of Venus, as viewed from Earth, covers the most square degrees. (Chart provided by Patrick Kelly.)

RIGHT ASCENSIONS OF THE SUN AND PLANETS IN 2018

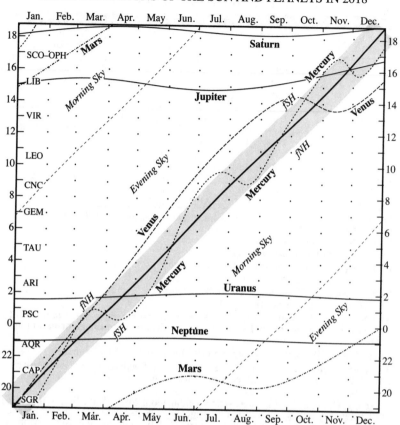

This diagram shows the variation during the year in the right ascension (vertical axis) of the Sun and planets. The slightly curved, heavy diagonal line represents the Sun; the shaded regions approximately indicate parts of the night sky affected by twilight. The two thin, dashed diagonal lines at the upper left and lower right represent the boundary between the evening sky and the morning sky.

The diagram may be used to determine in what part of the sky a planet may be found (including in which constellation—note the abbreviations along the vertical axis), when a superior planet is in conjunction with the Sun or at opposition (opposition is approximately where its curve intersects the dashed diagonal lines, and note that, due to retrograde motion, this point is also where the planet's curve has its maximum negative slope), when Mercury and Venus have their various greatest elongations and conjunctions, and when there are conjunctions of planets—that is, when the curves for planets intersect. For example, note the oppositions of Jupiter (early May) and Saturn (late Jun.). In early March, Mercury and Venus come together in the evening sky. They meet again in the evening in mid-October. Later that month, Mercury moves to join Jupiter. Mars appears close to Neptune in early December.

For observers in mid-latitudes, at certain times of the year the ecliptic stands steeply to the horizon in the western evening sky or the eastern morning sky, making apparitions of planets in these parts of the sky favorable from the Northern Hemisphere ("fNH" on the diagram) or favorable from the Southern Hemisphere ("fSH").

For more information on all these events, see the following 24 monthly pages and THE PLANETS FOR 2018 (p. 211). (Chart provided by Patrick Kelly.)

THE SKY FOR JANUARY

		Mercury	Venus	Mars	Jupiter	Saturn	Uranus	Neptune	Sun
RA	1	17h 07m	18h 36m	14h 47m	14h 58m	18h 05m	1h 31m	22h 54m	18h 45m
	11	17h 58m	19h 31m	15h 12m	15h 05m	18h 10m	1h 31m	22h 55m	19h 28m
	21	18h 59m	20h 24m	15h 37m	15h 10m	18h 15m	1h 31m	22h 56m	20h 11m
Dec	1	−20° 52′	−23° 39′	−15° 09′	−15° 49′	−22° 32′	+8° 54′	−8° 02′	−23° 02′
	11	−22° 53′	−22° 38′	−16° 59′	−16° 15′	−22° 32′	+8° 55′	−7° 56′	−21° 53′
	21	−23° 28′	−20° 28′	−18° 36′	−16° 37′	−22° 31′	+8° 58′	−7° 50′	−20° 01′
Dist	1	1	1.71	1.96	5.96	11.03	19.64	30.4	0.983
	11	1.18	1.71	1.87	5.82	10.99	19.81	30.55	0.983
	21	1.3	1.71	1.77	5.67	10.93	19.98	30.67	0.984
Mag	1	−0.3	−4	1.5	−1.8	0.5	5.8	7.9	
	11	−0.3		1.4	−1.9	0.5	5.8	7.9	
	21	−0.3	−4	1.3	−1.9	0.5	5.8	7.9	
Size	1	6.7″	9.8″	4.8″	33.1″	15.1″	3.6″	2.2″	32′ 32″
	11	5.7″	9.7″	5.0″	33.9″	15.1″	3.5″	2.2″	32′ 32″
	21	5.2″	9.8″	5.3″	34.8″	15.2″	3.5″	2.2″	32′ 30″

Moon: On January 0 at 0h UT*, Sun's selenographic colongitude is 63.93° and increases by 12.2° each day thereafter.
Greatest N declination on the 2nd (+20.0°).
Greatest S declination on the 16th (–20.0°).
Libration in longitude: E limb most exposed on the 8th (+7.6°),
  W limb most exposed on the 24th (–7.3°).
Libration in latitude: N limb most exposed on the 26th (+6.8°),
  S limb most exposed on the 11th (–6.8°).

The Moon occults Aldebaran somewhere in the world each lunar month until September, and Regulus each lunar month until April. See the right-hand pages for details.

Large tides in the days following the full Moons of Jan. 2 and Jan. 31.

Total lunar eclipse on Jan. 31, visible from western South America, North America, Asia, Australia, the Middle East, eastern Africa, eastern Europe, the Pacific Ocean and the Indian Ocean.

Mercury: Opens 2018 at greatest western elongation, 23° from the Sun. Will remain in the dawn sky throughout the month, brightening as its phase angle increases, even as the planet itself is receding. Saturn passes just 0.6° to the north of Mercury on the 13th, while the waning crescent Moon will make it a wider trio on the 14–15. This apparition of Mercury is best seen by more southerly observers.

Venus: In superior conjunction with the Sun on Jan. 09. Too close to the Sun to be seen throughout the month.

Mars: As the year begins Mars is passing just 0.7° north of the fine binocular double star Zubenelgenubi in the morning sky, with Jupiter just to the east in the same binocular field. Mars will pass just 0.2° south of Jupiter on the 7th in a splendid dawn conjunction. The waning crescent Moon passes 5° to the north on the 11th.

Jupiter: Situated in central Libra where it is joined by Mars for the first part of the month. The pair will be separated by just 0.2° on the 7th, and will form a wide trio with the waning crescent Moon on the 11th.

Saturn: Emerging from its late-December conjunction with the Sun into the morning sky. Might be seen with difficulty late in the month, very low in the SE in morning twilight. Has a close conjunction just 0.6° from Mercury on the morning of the 13th, where both objects will be visible in a low-power telescope field, gibbous Mercury about twice as bright as ringed Saturn.

Uranus: Well placed in the evening sky in eastern Pisces, surrounded by 4th and 5th mag. stars. Uranus itself is at mag. 5.8, theoretically visible to the naked eye from a dark site. Meridian transit times at Greenwich on the 1st, 11th, 21st – 18:46, 18:07, 17:28 UT*.

Neptune: Begins 2018 just 0.5° south of mag. –3.7 lambda Aquarii. It will spend the year tracking between lambda and mag. –4.2 phi Aquarii, 5° to the east.

*See p. 94, the bold-faced sentences of the first paragraph.

Time (UT) d h m	JANUARY EVENTS	Jupiter's Satellites West East
Mon. 1 16 13	Algol at minimum	
20	**Mercury greatest elongation W (23°)**	1.0
22	Moon at perigee (356565 km) **Large tides**	2.0
Tue. 2 2 24	**Full Moon** (largest in 2018)	
21	Uranus stationary	3.0
Wed. 3 6	Earth at perihelion (147097233 km)	4.0
21	Quadrantid meteors peak	
Thu. 4 13 02	Algol at minimum	5.0
Fri. 5 2 34	**Double shadow transit on Jupiter**	6.0
8	**Regulus 0.9° S of Moon, occultation†**	
Sat. 6		7.0
Sun. 7 4	**Mars 0.2° S of Jupiter**	
9 51	Algol at minimum	8.0
Mon. 8 22 25	**Last quarter**	9.0
Tue. 9 7	Venus in superior conjunction	
Wed. 10 6 40	Algol at minimum	10.0
Thu. 11 6	Jupiter 4° S of Moon	11.0
10	Mars 5° S of Moon	
Fri. 12 4	**Vesta 0.4° N of Moon, occultation‡**	12.0
5 45	**Double shadow transit on Jupiter**	13.0
Sat. 13 3 29	Algol at minimum	
7	**Mercury 0.6° S of Saturn**	14.0
Sun. 14		15.0
Mon. 15	Mercury at descending node	
2	Saturn 3° S of Moon	16.0
2	Moon at apogee (406464 km)	17.0
7	Mercury 3° S of Moon	
Tue. 16 0 18	Algol at minimum	18.0
Wed. 17 2 17	**New Moon** (lunation 1176)	19.0
Thu. 18 21 07	Algol at minimum	20.0
Fri. 19 9 43	**Double shadow transit on Jupiter**	
Sat. 20		21.0
Sun. 21 17 55	Algol at minimum	22.0
Mon. 22		
Tue. 23	Venus at aphelion	23.0
Wed. 24 14 44	Algol at minimum	
22 20	**First quarter**	24.0
Thu. 25	Mercury at aphelion	25.0
Fri. 26		
Sat. 27 11 33	Algol at minimum	26.0
11	**Aldebaran 0.7° S of Moon, occultation††**	27.0
Sun. 28		
Mon. 29		28.0
Tue. 30 8 22	Algol at minimum	29.0
10	Moon at perigee (358994 km) **Large tides**	
Wed. 31 13	Ceres at opposition	30.0
13 27	**Full Moon**	31.0
	Total Lunar Eclipse (p. 126)	

† Alaska, E tip of Russia, northern Canada, Greenland, Svalbard, Iceland, most of Europe, NW Africa
‡ Southern Africa, Madagascar, French Southern and Antarctic Lands, SW Australia, Tasmania
†† Most of India, central Asia, most of China, Mongolia, most of Russia, Alaska, NW N. America

THE SKY FOR FEBRUARY

		Mercury	Venus	Mars	Jupiter	Saturn	Uranus	Neptune	Sun
RA	1	20h 12m	21h 21m	16h 05m	15h 16m	18h 20m	1h 32m	22h 57m	20h 57m
	11	21h 21m	22h 10m	16h 30m	15h 19m	18h 24m	1h 33m	22h 58m	21h 37m
	21	22h 30m	22h 57m	16h 56m	15h 22m	18h 28m	1h 35m	23h 00m	22h 16m
Dec	1	−21° 44′	−16° 57′	−20° 09′	−16° 56′	−22° 29′	+9° 03′	−7° 42′	−17° 15′
	11	−17° 44′	−12° 54′	−21° 18′	−17° 09′	−22° 27′	+9° 10′	−7° 34′	−14° 11′
	21	−11° 21′	−8° 17′	−22° 13′	−17° 17′	−22° 24′	+9° 18′	−7° 25′	−10° 45′
Dist	1	1.38	1.7	1.67	5.5	10.83	20.17	30.79	0.985
	11	1.4	1.69	1.58	5.33	10.72	20.33	30.86	0.987
	21	1.36	1.68	1.48	5.17	10.59	20.47	30.91	0.989
Mag	1	−0.6	−3.9	1.2	−2	0.6	5.8	8	
	11	−1.2	−3.9	1.1	−2	0.6	5.9	8	
	21	−1.6	−3.9	0.9	−2.1	0.6	5.9	8	
Size	1	4.9″	9.8″	5.6″	35.9″	15.4″	3.5″	2.2″	32′ 28″
	11	4.8″	9.9″	5.9″	36.9″	15.5″	3.4″	2.2″	32′ 25″
	21	4.9″	9.9″	6.3″	38.1″	15.7″	3.4″	2.2″	32′ 21″

Moon: On February 0 at 0h UT*, Sun's selenographic colongitude is 80.81° and increases by 12.2° each day thereafter.
Greatest N declination on the 26th (+20.0°).
Greatest S declination on the 12th (−20.0°).
Libration in longitude: E limb most exposed on the 5th (+7.0°),
  W limb most exposed on the 20th (−6.0°).
Libration in latitude: N limb most exposed on the 22nd (+6.8°),
  S limb most exposed on the 7th (−6.8°).

Partial solar eclipse on Feb. 15, visible from South America, Antarctica, the South Pacific Ocean, and the South Atlantic Ocean.

Mercury: In superior conjunction on the 17th and unfavorably placed for Northern Hemisphere observers throughout the month. Observable with difficulty in the dawn sky early in the month from the Southern Hemisphere.

Venus: Slowly pulls away from the Sun in the evening sky and may be observable with difficulty late in the month.

Mars: Begins the month near Graffias in the crown of the Scorpion, then proceeds eastward into Ophiuchus for most of the month. The waning crescent Moon passes 4° to the north on the 9th. By month-end, Mars rises around 3 a.m. local time.

Jupiter: In central Libra where it will spend the majority of 2018. Will have a wide conjunction with the third quarter Moon on the 7–8. Meridian transit times at Greenwich on the 1st, 11th, 21st – 06:31, 05:55, 05:18 UT*.

Saturn: Situated in central Sagittarius, as it will be throughout 2018. Now within 45° of Jupiter, as the two giant planets continue to close towards their next conjunction in 2020. At present Mars is sandwiched between the two, making for a naked-eye sweep of the three brightest outer planets in the dawn sky.

Uranus: In the evening sky throughout the month among the stars of Pisces.

Neptune: Begins the month 30° from the Sun and closing fast towards its Mar. 4 conjunction. Telescopically visible early in the month, but will be a much better target in the late summer and autumn.

*See p. 94, the bold-faced sentences of the first paragraph.

Time (UT) d h m	FEBRUARY EVENTS	Jupiter's Satellites West East
Thu. 1 19	Regulus 1.0° S of Moon, occultation†	
Fri. 2	**Zodiacal light vis. in N lat. in W after**	
	evening twilight for next two weeks	
5 11	Algol at minimum	
Sat. 3		
Sun. 4		
Mon. 5 2 00	Algol at minimum	
Tue. 6		
Wed. 7 15 54	**Last quarter**	
20	Jupiter 4° S of Moon	
22 49	Algol at minimum	
Thu. 8		
Fri. 9 5	Mars 4° S of Moon	
13	**Vesta 0.9° N of Moon, occultation‡**	
Sat. 10 19 38	Algol at minimum	
Sun. 11 14	Moon at apogee (405 700 km)	
15	Saturn 2° S of Moon	
Mon. 12		
Tue. 13 16 27	Algol at minimum	
Wed. 14	Mercury at greatest heliocentric lat. S	
	Venus at greatest heliocentric lat. S	
11	Juno in conjunction with the Sun	
Thu. 15 21 05	**New Moon (lunation 1177)**	
	Partial Solar Eclipse (p. 129)	
Fri. 16 13 16	Algol at minimum	
Sat. 17 12	Mercury in superior conjunction	
Sun. 18		
Mon. 19 10 05	Algol at minimum	
Tue. 20		
Wed. 21		
Thu. 22 6 54	Algol at minimum	
Fri. 23 8 09	**First quarter**	
18	**Aldebaran 0.7° S of Moon, occultation††**	
Sat. 24		
Sun. 25 3 43	Algol at minimum	
Mon. 26		
Tue. 27 15	Moon at perigee (363 932 km)	
Wed. 28 0 32	Algol at minimum	

† Scandinavia, N Greenland, Svalbard, N and E Russia, NE China, NW Alaska, most of Japan
‡ Chatham Island, most of Antarctica   †† Bermuda, NE North America, Greenland,
  most of Europe, Svalbard, most of Russia, Kazakhstan, W Mongolia, NW China

THE SKY FOR MARCH

		Mercury	Venus	Mars	Jupiter	Saturn	Uranus	Neptune	Sun
RA	1	23h 25m	23h 34m	17h 17m	15h 23m	18h 31m	1h 36m	23h 01m	22h 47m
	11	0h 25m	0h 19m	17h 42m	15h 24m	18h 33m	1h 38m	23h 02m	23h 24m
	21	0h 56m	1h 05m	18h 07m	15h 23m	18h 36m	1h 40m	23h 04m	0h 00m
Dec	1	−4° 45′	−4° 19′	−22° 47′	−17° 21′	−22° 22′	+9° 25′	−7° 18′	−7° 47′
	11	+3° 56′	+0° 48′	−23° 16′	−17° 21′	−22° 20′	+9° 36′	−7° 09′	−3° 55′
	21	+9° 17′	+5° 55′	−23° 31′	−17° 16′	−22° 18′	+9° 47′	−7° 01′	+0° 02′
Dist	1	1.26	1.66	1.4	5.05	10.48	20.58	30.93	0.991
	11	1.04	1.64	1.31	4.9	10.32	20.69	30.93	0.993
	21	0.77	1.61	1.21	4.76	10.16	20.78	30.9	0.996
Mag	1	−1.3	−3.9	0.8	−2.2	0.6	5.9	8	
	11	−0.9	−3.9	0.7	−2.2	0.6	5.9	8	
	21	0.8	−3.9	−2.3	−2.2	0.6	5.9	8	
Size	1	5.3″	10.0″	6.7″	39.1″	15.9″	3.4″	2.2″	32′ 17″
	11	6.5″	10.2″	7.2″	40.3″	16.1″	3.4″	2.2″	32′ 12″
	21	8.7″	10.3″	7.7″	41.4″	16.4″	3.4″	2.2″	32′ 07″

Moon: On March 0 at 0h UT*, Sun's selenographic colongitude is 61.5° and increases by 12.2° each day thereafter.
Greatest N declination on the 25th (+20.3°).
Greatest S declination on the 11th (−20.0°).
Libration in longitude: E limb most exposed on the 5th (+5.9°),
    W limb most exposed on the 18th (−5.3°).
Libration in latitude: N limb most exposed on the 21st (+6.7°),
    S limb most exposed on the 6th (−6.7°).

Mercury: Emerges in the evening sky early in the month to begin the best evening apparition of the year for observers at mid-northern latitudes, all the easier to follow due to the proximity of brilliant Venus. The two are just over a degree apart from the 2nd through the 5th, when both bright objects will nonetheless be a challenge to spot in early evening twilight. The two inner planets have a second, wider conjunction on the 18th when Mercury reaches its stationary point while Venus overtakes it. The pair will remain with 5° of each other (within a standard binocular field of view) for the first three weeks of March. At perihelion on the 10th, meaning Mercury is physically close to the Sun but intrinsically brighter as a result. At greatest elongation 18° east of the Sun just three days later. Fades throughout the month as it approaches its inferior conjunction on Apr. 01.

Venus: Gradually emerging into the evening sky where it will enjoy a fine apparition right into early autumn. In conjunction with Mercury on the 5th and again on the 18th, on which date the waxing crescent Moon will also pass to the south, briefly forming a straight line of inner Solar System objects some 8° long. Has an extremely close conjunction with Uranus on the evening of the 28th, when the two will be separated by <10 arc seconds on the sky, but by a factor of 10,000 in brightness.

Mars: Passes from Scorpius into Sagittarius on the 11th and gradually closes the gap on Saturn for the remained of March. The two are within 1.5° by the 31st.

Jupiter: Reaches its first stationary point on the 9th and begins its retrograde motion among the stars of Libra. The waning gibbous Moon passes 4° to the north on the morning of the 7th. Meridian transit times at Greenwich on the 1st, 11th, 21st – 04:48, 04:09, 03:29 UT*.

Saturn: Remains in the deep south constellation of Sagittarius and can be seen low in the SE in morning twilight. The thick waning crescent Moon passes to the north on the 10th and 11th.

Uranus: Can be found in the early evening sky with increasing difficulty as it approaches its April conjunction.

Neptune: In conjunction with the Sun on the 4th and remains too close to the Sun to be seen all month.

*See p. 94, the bold-faced sentences of the first paragraph.

Time (UT)			MARCH EVENTS	Jupiter's Satellites	
d	h	m		West	East

	d	h	m	Event
Thu.	1	6		Regulus 0.9° S of Moon, occultation†
Fri.	2	0	51	**Full Moon**
		21	21	Algol at minimum
Sat.	3			
Sun.	4	14		Neptune in conjunction with the Sun
Mon.	5			Mercury at ascending node
				Zodiacal light vis. in N lat. in W after
				evening twilight for next two weeks
		18		**Mercury 1.4° N of Venus**
		18	10	Algol at minimum
Tue.	6			
Wed.	7	7		Jupiter 4° S of Moon
Thu.	8	14	59	Algol at minimum
Fri.	9	10		Jupiter stationary
		11	20	**Last quarter**
Sat.	10			Mercury at perihelion
		1		Mars 4° S of Moon
Sun.	11			**DAYLIGHT SAVING TIME BEGINS**
		2		Saturn 2° S of Moon
		9		Moon at apogee (404 678 km)
		11	48	Algol at minimum
Mon.	12			
Tue.	13			
Wed.	14	8	37	Algol at minimum
Thu.	15	15		**Mercury greatest elongation E (18°)**
Fri.	16			Mars at descending node
Sat.	17	5	26	Algol at minimum
		13	12	**New Moon (lunation 1178)**
Sun.	18	19		**Venus 4° N of Moon**
Mon.	19			
Tue.	20			Mercury at greatest heliocentric lat. N
		2	15	Algol at minimum
		16	15	**Equinox**
		21		Ceres stationary
Wed.	21			
Thu.	22	17		Mercury stationary
		23		**Aldebaran 0.9° S of Moon, occultation‡**
		23	04	Algol at minimum
Fri.	23			
Sat.	24	15	35	**First quarter**
		21	22	**Double shadow transit on Jupiter**
Sun.	25	19	53	Algol at minimum
Mon.	26	17		Moon at perigee (369 106 km)
Tue.	27			
Wed.	28	14		Regulus 1.0° S of Moon, occultation††
		16	42	Algol at minimum
Thu.	29	0		**Venus 0.07° S of Uranus**
Fri.	30			
Sat.	31	12	37	**Full Moon**
		13	31	Algol at minimum

† NE tip of Russia, N. North America, Greenland, Svalbard, W edge of Europe, Azores
‡ NE Russia, NW North America, Greenland, Svalbard, most of Scandinavia, Great Britain, Ireland
†† Most of Scandinavia, N and E Russia, Svalbard, N Greenland, NW N. America, Aleutian Is.

THE SKY FOR APRIL

		Mercury	Venus	Mars	Jupiter	Saturn	Uranus	Neptune	Sun
RA	1	0h 41m	1h 55m	18h 34m	15h 20m	18h 37m	1h 42m	23h 05m	0h 40m
	11	0h 19m	2h 42m	18h 58m	15h 17m	18h 38m	1h 44m	23h 06m	1h 17m
	21	0h 24m	3h 31m	19h 20m	15h 13m	18h 38m	1h 46m	23h 07m	1h 54m
Dec	1	+7° 36′	+11° 17′	–23° 33′	–17° 06′	–22° 16′	+10° 00′	–6° 52′	+4° 20′
	11	+2° 39′	+15° 42′	–23° 24′	–16° 52′	–22° 16′	+10° 12′	–6° 44′	+8° 07′
	21	+0° 43′	+19° 28′	–23° 07′	–16° 36′	–22° 15′	+10° 24′	–6° 38′	+11° 41′
Dist	1	0.6	1.58	1.11	4.63	9.98	20.85	30.84	0.999
	11	0.61	1.54	1.02	4.53	9.81	20.89	30.75	1.002
	21	0.71	1.5	0.93	4.46	9.65	20.89	30.64	1.005
Mag	1		–3.9	0.3	–2.4	0.5	5.9	8	
	11	2.6	–3.9	0.1	–2.4	0.5	5.9	8	
	21	0.9	–3.9	–0.1	–2.5	0.4	5.9	7.9	
Size	1	11.2″	10.6″	8.4″	42.6″	16.7″	3.4″	2.2″	32′ 01″
	11	11.0″	10.8″	9.2″	43.5″	17.0″	3.4″	2.2″	31′ 55″
	21	9.4″	11.1″	10.1″	44.2″	17.2″	3.4″	2.2″	31′ 50″

Moon: On April 0 at 0 h UT*, Sun's selenographic colongitude is 79.06° and increases by 12.2° each day thereafter.
Greatest N declination on the 21st (+20.4°).
Greatest S declination on the 8th (–20.3°).
Libration in longitude: E limb most exposed on the 2nd (+4.9°).
  W limb most exposed on the 14th (–5.7°).
Libration in latitude: N limb most exposed on the 17th (+6.6°),
  S limb most exposed on the 3rd (–6.6°) & 30th (–6.5°).

Mercury: In inferior conjunction on the 1st, and spends the remainder of April emerging in the morning sky, reaching maximum western elongation (27°) on the 29th at which point it will have brightened to mag.+0.4.

Venus: Becomes much more prominent in evening twilight for Northern Hemisphere observers as it climbs the steepest section of the ecliptic while gaining separation from the Sun throughout the month. The waxing crescent Moon passes 5° to its south on the 17th. Within 5° of the Pleiades from the 22–28, achieving minimum separation of 3.5° on the 25th

Mars: Begins April in close proximity to Saturn, achieving conjunction on the 2nd when the two are separated by 1.3°. The waning crescent Moon will join the group on the 7th, when the three will be visible in a standard binocular field just above the Teapot of Sagittarius low in the SE in morning twilight. Meridian transit times at Greenwich on the 1st, 11th, 21st – 05:58, 05:42, 05:25 UT*.

Jupiter: In retrograde through central Libra throughout the month as it approaches its May 9 opposition. The waning gibbous Moon passes 4° to its north on the 3rd and again on the 30th when the Moon is just past Full. Meridian transit times at Greenwich on the 1st, 11th, 21st – 02:44, 02:01, 01:17 UT*.

Saturn: Remains in the southern zodiacal constellation of Sagittarius, where it will achieve conjunction with Mars on the 2nd. Reaches its first stationary point on the 18th and begins its retrograde (westward) motion thereafter. Meridian transit times at Greenwich on the 1st, 11th, 21st – 06:00, 05:22, 0:443 UT*.

Uranus: Too close to the Sun to be seen. In conjunction on the 18th.

Neptune: Gradually emerging in morning twilight for telescopic observers.

*See p. 94, the bold-faced sentences of the first paragraph.

| Time (UT) | | | APRIL EVENTS | Jupiter's Satellites | |
| d | h | m | | West | East |

Sun.	1	18		Mercury in inferior conjunction
Mon.	2	12		**Mars 1.3° S of Saturn**
Tue.	3	10	20	Algol at minimum
		14		Jupiter 4° S of Moon
Wed.	4			
Thu.	5			
Fri.	6	7	09	Algol at minimum
Sat.	7	13		**Saturn 1.9° S of Moon**
		18		Mars 3° S of Moon
Sun.	8	6		Moon at apogee (404 144 km)
		7	18	**Last quarter**
Mon.	9	3	58	Algol at minimum
Tue.	10			
Wed.	11			
Thu.	12			Venus at ascending node
		0	47	Algol at minimum
Fri.	13			Mercury at descending node
Sat.	14	4		Mercury stationary
		9		Mercury 4° N of Moon
		21	36	Algol at minimum
Sun.	15			
Mon.	16	1	57	**New Moon** (lunation 1179)
Tue.	17			Saturn at aphelion
		18	25	Algol at minimum
		19		**Venus 5° N of Moon**
Wed.	18	2		Saturn stationary
		14		Uranus in conjunction with the Sun
Thu.	19	5		**Aldebaran 1.1° S of Moon, occultation**†
Fri.	20	15		Moon at perigee (368 714 km)
		15	14	Algol at minimum
Sat.	21			
Sun.	22	18		Lyrid meteors peak
		21	46	**First quarter**
Mon.	23			Mercury at aphelion
		7		**Moon 1.9° S of Beehive (M44)**
		12	03	Algol at minimum
Tue.	24	20		**Regulus 1.2° S of Moon, occultation**‡
Wed.	25			
Thu.	26	8	52	Algol at minimum
Fri.	27			
Sat.	28			
Sun.	29	5	41	Algol at minimum
		18		**Mercury greatest elongation W (27°)**
Mon.	30	0	58	**Full Moon**
		17		Jupiter 4° S of Moon

† Most of Uzbekistan and Kazakhstan, C and N Russia, N and E Scandinavia, N Greenland, N Canada
‡ Central Russia, NE tip of Kazakhstan

THE SKY FOR MAY

		Mercury	Venus	Mars	Jupiter	Saturn	Uranus	Neptune	Sun
RA	1	0h 54m	4h 22m	19h 41m	15h 08m	18h 38m	1h 48m	23h 08m	2h 32m
	11	1h 41m	5h 14m	20h 00m	15h 03m	18h 37m	1h 50m	23h 09m	3h 10m
	21	2h 42m	6h 07m	20h 17m	14h 58m	18h 35m	1h 53m	23h 10m	3h 50m
Dec	1	+2° 41′	+22° 23′	−22° 44′	−16° 16′	−22° 16′	+10° 37′	−6° 32′	+14° 55′
	11	+7° 21′	+24° 17′	−22° 20′	−15° 56′	−22° 17′	+10° 48′	−6° 27′	+17° 45′
	21	+13° 39′	+25° 03′	−22° 00′	−15° 36′	−22° 19′	+10° 59′	−6° 23′	+20° 05′
Dist	1	0.86	1.45	0.85	4.41	9.5	20.88	30.51	1.007
	11	1.02	1.4	0.76	4.4	9.37	20.83	30.37	1.01
	21	1.18	1.34	0.69	4.42	9.25	20.76	30.21	1.012
Mag	1	0.3	−3.9	−0.4	−2.5	0.4	5.9	7.9	
	11	−0.1	−3.9	−0.6	−2.5	0.3	5.9	7.9	
	21	−0.6	−3.9	−0.9	−2.5	0.2	5.9	7.9	
Size	1	7.8″	11.5″	11.1″	44.7″	17.5″	3.4″	2.2″	31′ 45″
	11	6.6″	11.9″	12.2″	44.8″	17.8″	3.4″	2.2″	31′ 40″
	21	5.7″	12.4″	13.6″	44.6″	18.0″	3.4″	2.2″	31′ 36″

Moon: On May 0 at 0 h UT*, Sun's selenographic colongitude is 84.94° and increases by 12.2° each day thereafter.

Greatest N declination on the 19th (+20.5°).

Greatest S declination on the 5th (−20.5°).

Libration in longitude: E limb most exposed on the 25th (+5.5°),
  W limb most exposed on the 12th (−6.6°).

Libration in latitude: N limb most exposed on the 15th (+6.5°),
  S limb most exposed on the 27th (−6.6°).

Mercury: Begins the month on the Cetus–Pisces border and gradually advances eastward through Pisces, Aries and into Taurus over the course of the month. It brightens throughout May as its phase angle increases, achieving mag. 0.0 on the 12th when it is still nearly 25° ahead of the Sun in morning twilight. An excellent apparition for southern observers, less so in the Northern Hemisphere.

Venus: Near Aldebaran and the Hyades to open the month. Venus continues to climb the ecliptic, its declination topping out at +25° late in the month when depending on location it sets near or after midnight local daylight time at mid-northern latitudes. The waxing crescent Moon makes a wide pass 5° to its south on the 17th.

Mars: Continues its prograde path, crossing from Sagittarius into Capricornus in mid-month. Doubles in brightness over the course of the month from mag.-0.4 to -1.2 as Earth on its inside track draws ever nearer the Red Planet. The waning gibbous Moon passes 3° to its north on the 6th. Meridian transit times at Greenwich on the 1st, 11th, 21st – 05:06. 04:46, 04:23 UT*.

Jupiter: Reaches opposition on the 9th, when it is 37 light-minutes (4.40 au) from Earth, mag. −2.5 with a 43.8″ disk, and 16° S. of the celestial equator. At this time, its four large (Galilean) satellites are also at their brightest with their widest apparent separation. The waxing gibbous Moon passes 4° to its north on the 27th. Meridian transit times at Greenwich on the 1st, 11th, 21st – 00:34, 23:44, 23:00 UT*.

Saturn: Situated in the southerly zodiacal constellation of Sagittarius, its subtle retrograde (westerly) motion gains momentum throughout the month in advance of its late June opposition. The waning gibbous Moon will make a wide pair on the 4th and 5th. Meridian transit times at Greenwich on the 1st, 11th, 21st – 04:03, 03:22, 02:41 UT*.

Uranus: Returns to the dawn sky around mid-month in the Southern Hemisphere, later in the Northern Hemisphere.

Neptune: In the morning sky among the late-rising stars of Aquarius.

*See p. 94, the bold-faced sentences of the first paragraph.

Time (UT) d h m	MAY EVENTS	Jupiter's Satellites West East
Tue. 1		
Wed. 2 2 30	Algol at minimum	1.0 — I
Thu. 3		2.0 — II
Fri. 4 20	**Saturn 1.7° S of Moon**	3.0 —
23 19	Algol at minimum	4.0 —
Sat. 5 7	η-Aquariid meteors peak	III
Sun. 6 1	Moon at apogee (404 457 km)	5.0 —
7	Mars 3° S of Moon	6.0 —
Mon. 7 20 08	Algol at minimum	7.0 —
Tue. 8 2 09	**Last quarter**	IV
10	Vesta stationary	8.0 —
Wed. 9 1	**Jupiter at opposition**	9.0 —
Thu. 10 16 57	Algol at minimum	10.0 —
Fri. 11		
Sat. 12 21	Mercury 2° S of Uranus	11.0 —
Sun. 13	Mercury at greatest heliocentric lat. S	12.0 —
13 46	Algol at minimum	
17	Mercury 2° N of Moon	13.0 —
Mon. 14		14.0 —
Tue. 15 11 48	**New Moon** (lunation 1180)	15.0 —
Wed. 16	Venus at perihelion	
10 35	Algol at minimum	16.0 —
13	**Aldebaran 1.2° S of Moon, occultation†**	17.0 —
Thu. 17 18	**Venus 5° N of Moon**	18.0 —
21	Moon at perigee (363 776 km)	19.0 —
Fri. 18		
Sat. 19 7 24	Algol at minimum	20.0 —
Sun. 20 12	Moon 1.7° S of Beehive (M44)	21.0 —
Mon. 21 10	Venus 0.7° N of M35	22.0 —
Tue. 22 1	**Regulus 1.5° S of Moon**	
3 49	**First quarter**	23.0 —
4 13	Algol at minimum	24.0 —
Wed. 23		25.0 —
Thu. 24		
Fri. 25 1 02	Algol at minimum	26.0 —
Sat. 26		27.0 —
Sun. 27 18	Jupiter 4° S of Moon	28.0 —
21 51	Algol at minimum	
Mon. 28		29.0 —
Tue. 29 14 20	**Full Moon**	30.0 —
Wed. 30 18 40	Algol at minimum	31.0 —
Thu. 31		

† Central and northern Canada, northwest Greenland, northernmost central Russia

THE SKY FOR JUNE

		Mercury	Venus	Mars	Jupiter	Saturn	Uranus	Neptune	Sun
RA	1	4h 08m	7h 04m	20h 33m	14h 53m	18h 32m	1h 55m	23h 11m	4h 34m
	11	5h 42m	7h 55m	20h 43m	14h 49m	18h 29m	1h 56m	23h 11m	5h 16m
	21	7h 10m	8h 44m	20h 50m	14h 46m	18h 26m	1h 58m	23h 11m	5h 57m
Dec	1	+20° 49′	+24° 31′	−21° 47′	−15° 16′	−22° 21′	+11° 11′	−6° 20′	+21° 59′
	11	+24° 48′	+22° 51′	−21° 49′	−15° 01′	−22° 24′	+11° 20′	−6° 19′	+23° 03′
	21	+24° 27′	+20° 11′	−22° 11′	−14° 51′	−22° 26′	+11° 28′	−6° 19′	+23° 26′
Dist	1	1.3	1.27	0.61	4.47	9.15	20.66	30.03	1.014
	11	1.3	1.2	0.55	4.54	9.09	20.54	29.86	1.015
	21	1.19	1.13	0.49	4.64	9.06	20.4	29.69	1.016
Mag	1	−1.7	−3.9	−1.2	−2.5	0.2	5.9	7.9	
	11	−1.7	−4	−1.5	−2.4	0.1	5.9	7.9	
	21	−0.7	−4	−1.8	−2.4	0.1	5.9	7.9	
Size	1	5.1″	13.1″	15.3″	44.1″	18.2″	3.4″	2.2″	31′ 33″
	11	5.2″	13.8″	17.0″	43.4″	18.3″	3.4″	2.2″	31′ 30″
	21	5.7″	14.7″	18.9″	42.5″	18.4″	3.4″	2.3″	31′ 29″

Moon: On June 0 at 0 h UT*, Sun's selenographic colongitude is 103.44° and increases by 12.2° each day thereafter.

Greatest N declination on the 15th (+20.7°).

Greatest S declination on the 1st (−20.7°).

Libration in longitude: E limb most exposed on the 21st (+6.7°),

  W limb most exposed on the 9th (−7.4°).

Libration in latitude: N limb most exposed on the 11th (+6.7°),

  S limb most exposed on the 23rd (−6.7°).

Mercury: After passing through superior conjunction on the 6th, emerges into the evening sky in mid-month when it briefly achieves a declination of +25° while still around mag. −1.0, albeit just 12–14° from the Sun. By month-end, its magnitude has dropped to 0.0 but its elongation has extended to 24°, still a good chance to spy it low in the northwest in evening twilight.

Venus: Remains prominent in evening twilight throughout the month, even as the angle of the evening ecliptic becomes less favorable for Northern Hemisphere observers. The Moon passes 2° to its south on the 16th.

Mars: Continues to dive ever south of the ecliptic in western Capricornus throughout the month as Earth continues to overtake it. Achieves its first stationary point on the 28th, then begins its retrograde loop over the subsequent two months. The waning gibbous Moon passes 3° to its north on the 3rd. Meridian transit times at Greenwich on the 1st, 11th, 21st – 03:56, 03:27, 02:54 UT*.

Jupiter: Moderately well-placed for observation throughout the evening hours as it moves in retrograde in western Libra. The waxing gibbous Moon passes 4° to the north on the 23rd. Meridian transit times at Greenwich on the 1st, 11th, 21st – 22:12, 21:29, 20:47 UT*.

Saturn: Reaches opposition on the 27th, just 6 days after the summer solstice. This places Saturn not far from the winter solstice point, very low in the southern sky for observers in the Northern Hemisphere, 22.5° S of the celestial equator. At opposition, Saturn is 75 light-minutes (9.05 au) from Earth, mag. 0.0 the northern side of the ring plane tilted near its maximum extent (26.7°). The rings span nearly 42 seconds of arc, the disk of the planet some 18.4″. At opposition, the full Moon will be in conjunction, passing 2° to the north of the ringed planet on the night of the 27–28. Meridian transit times at Greenwich on the 1st, 11th, 21st – 01:55, 01:13, 00:31 UT*.

Uranus: Visible in the morning sky among the stars of Pisces.

Neptune: Reaches its first stationary point on the 19th, still among the stars of Aquarius. The distant giant's retrograde motion is the subtlest and the slowest of any major planet in the Solar System, lasting 159 days in 2018.

*See p. 94, the bold-faced sentences of the first paragraph.

Time (UT) d h m	JUNE EVENTS	Jupiter's Satellites West East
Fri. 1	Mercury at ascending node	
1	**Saturn 1.6° S of Moon**	1.0
Sat. 2 15 29	Algol at minimum	2.0
17	Moon at apogee (405 317 km)	III
Sun. 3 12	Mars 3° S of Moon	3.0
Mon. 4		IV 4.0
Tue. 5 12 18	Algol at minimum	5.0
Wed. 6	Mercury at perihelion	
	Venus at greatest heliocentric lat. N	6.0
2	Mercury in superior conjunction	7.0 II
18 32	**Last quarter**	
Thu. 7		8.0
Fri. 8 9 07	Algol at minimum	9.0
Sat. 9		I
Sun. 10		10.0
Mon. 11 5 56	Algol at minimum	11.0
Tue. 12		
Wed. 13 19 43	**New Moon** (lunation 1181)	12.0
Thu. 14 2 45	Algol at minimum	13.0
Fri. 15 0	Moon at perigee (359 503 km)	14.0
Sat. 16	Mercury at greatest heliocentric lat. N	
13	**Venus 2° N of Moon**	15.0
20	Moon 1.5° S of Beehive (M44)	16.0
23 34	Algol at minimum	
Sun. 17		17.0
Mon. 18 8	**Regulus 1.7° S of Moon**	18.0
Tue. 19 12	Neptune stationary	19.0
20	Vesta at opposition	
20 23	Algol at minimum	20.0
Wed. 20 5	Venus 0.4° N of Beehive (M44)	21.0
10 51	**First quarter**	
Thu. 21 10 07	**Solstice**	22.0
Fri. 22 17 12	Algol at minimum	23.0
Sat. 23 19	Jupiter 4° S of Moon	
Sun. 24		24.0
Mon. 25 14 01	Algol at minimum	25.0
Tue. 26		26.0
Wed. 27 9	Vesta 0.3° S of Moon, occultation†	
13	**Saturn at opposition**	27.0
Thu. 28 4	Saturn 1.8° S of Moon	28.0
4 53	**Full Moon**	
10 50	Algol at minimum	29.0
14	Mars stationary	30.0
Fri. 29		31.0
Sat. 30 3	Moon at apogee (406 061 km)	

†Micronesia, Kiribati, northern French Polynesia, southern Mexico, Central America, Galapagos Is.

THE SKY FOR JULY

		Mercury	Venus	Mars	Jupiter	Saturn	Uranus	Neptune	Sun
RA	1	8h 20m	9h 30m	20h 51m	14h 44m	18h 23m	1h 59m	23h 11m	6h 39m
	11	9h 09m	10h 13m	20h 47m	14h 44m	18h 20m	2h 00m	23h 10m	7h 20m
	21	9h 35m	10h 54m	20h 38m	14h 44m	18h 17m	2h 01m	23h 10m	8h 00m
Dec	1	+20° 57′	+16° 41′	−22° 52′	−14° 45′	−22° 29′	+11° 35′	−6° 20′	+23° 08′
	11	+16° 13′	+12° 32′	−23° 51′	−14° 45′	−22° 32′	+11° 40′	−6° 23′	+22° 10′
	21	+11° 56′	+7° 57′	−24° 56′	−14° 51′	−22° 34′	+11° 43′	−6° 26′	+20° 34′
Dist	1	1.02	1.06	0.45	4.76	9.05	20.26	29.53	1.017
	11	0.86	0.98	0.41	4.89	9.07	20.1	29.39	1.017
	21	0.72	0.91	0.39	5.04	9.13	19.93	29.25	1.016
Mag	1	−0.1	−4.1	−2.2	−2.3	0	5.8	7.9	
	11	0.3	−4.1	−2.5	−2.2	0.1	5.8	7.9	
	21	1	−4.2	−2.7	−2.2	0.1	5.8	7.8	
Size	1	6.6″	15.7″	20.9″	41.4″	18.4″	3.5″	2.3″	31′ 28″
	11	7.8″	16.9″	22.6″	40.3″	18.3″	3.5″	2.3″	31′ 28″
	21	9.4″	18.4″	23.8″	39.1″	18.2″	3.5″	2.3″	31′ 29″

Moon: On July 0 at 0 h UT*, Sun's selenographic colongitude is 110.05° and increases by 12.2° each day thereafter.
Greatest N declination on the 12th (+20.6°).
Greatest S declination on the 26th (−20.7°).
Libration in longitude: E limb most exposed on the 20th (+7.5°),
  W limb most exposed on the 7th (−7.6°).
Libration in latitude: N limb most exposed on the 8th (+6.8°),
  S limb most exposed on the 20th (−6.8°).
Large tides in the days following New Moon (Jul. 13).
Partial solar eclipse on Jul 13, visible from extreme southern Australia, the south Pacific Ocean, and the south Indian Ocean.
Total lunar eclipse on Jul 27, visible from Australia, Antarctica, Asia, Africa, the Middle East, Europe, South America, the south Pacific Ocean, the Indian Ocean and the Atlantic Ocean.
Mercury: Continues to stretch its separation from the Sun until achieving a maximum eastern elongation of 26° on the 12th, but is both fading and dropping in declination making it a more difficult observation from the Northern Hemisphere than last month. Southern Hemisphere observers are favored, and can look for a close pass of the Beehive Cluster on the 4th.
Venus: Remains well-placed in evening twilight even as it dives some 14° in declination over the course of the month, bringing it ever lower to the horizon even as it is technically increasing in elongation from the Sun. Passes near Regulus on the 9th, and will have a fine conjunction with the three-day-old crescent Moon in the evening hours of the 15th as seen from North America.
Mars: In retrograde (westward) motion throughout the month as Earth overtakes it, achieving opposition on the 27th and closest approach to Earth on the 31st. At opposition Mars is 3.2 light-minutes (0.39 au) from Earth, mag. −2.8 with a 24.3″ disk, and 25.5° S. of the celestial equator. On that same date, the totally eclipsed Full Moon will pass some 6° to its north, with the Eastern Hemisphere favored to see the remarkable duo. At month-end, Mars will achieve its closest approach to Earth since the exceptional perigean opposition of 2003, and will not again be as close until 2035. Meridian transit times at Greenwich on the 1st, 11th, 21st – 02:16, 01:32, 00:44 UT*.
Jupiter: In the evening sky throughout the month. It reaches its second stationary point near Zubenelgenubi in western Libra on the 11th, after which it gradually resumes eastward motion. The waxing gibbous Moon passes 4° to its north on 20th. Meridian transit times at Greenwich on the 1st, 11th, 21st – 20:06, 19:26, 18:48 UT*.
Saturn: Now in the evening sky, post-opposition Saturn remains in the constellation Sagittarius and low for Northern Hemisphere observers. The waxing gibbous Moon passes 2° to Saturn's north on the night of the 24–25 in the Americas. Meridian transit times at Greenwich on the 1st, 11th, 21st – 23:44, 23:02, 22:19 UT*.
Uranus: Visible in the morning sky among the stars of Pisces.
Neptune: Visible in the overnight and morning hours in Aquarius. Meridian transit times at Greenwich on the 1st, 11th, 21st – 04:35, 03:55, 03:15 UT*.

*See p. 94, the bold-faced sentences of the first paragraph.

Time (UT)			JULY EVENTS	Jupiter's Satellites	
d	h	m		West	East

	d	h m	JULY EVENTS	
Sun.	1	2	Mars 5° S of Moon	
		7 39	Algol at minimum	
Mon.	2			
Tue.	3			
Wed.	4	4 28	Algol at minimum	
		15	Mercury 0.7° S of Beehive (M44)	
Thu.	5			
Fri.	6	7 51	**Last quarter**	
		17	Earth at aphelion (152 095 566 km)	
Sat.	7	1 17	Algol at minimum	
Sun.	8			
Mon.	9	20	**Venus 1.1° N of Regulus**	
		22 06	Algol at minimum	
Tue.	10		Mercury at descending node	
		10	**Aldebaran 1.1° S of Moon, occultation†**	
Wed.	11	4	Jupiter stationary	
Thu.	12	5	**Mercury greatest elongation E (26°)**	
		10	Pluto at opposition	
		18 55	Algol at minimum	
Fri.	13	2 48	**New Moon (lunation 1182)**	
			Partial Solar Eclipse (see p. 131)	
		8	Moon at perigee (357 431 km) **Large tides**	
Sat.	14	6	Moon 1.4° S of Beehive (M44)	
		22	Mercury 2° S of Moon	
Sun.	15	15 44	Algol at minimum	
		17	**Regulus 1.8° S of Moon**	
Mon.	16	4	**Venus 1.6° S of Moon**	
Tue.	17			
Wed.	18	12 33	Algol at minimum	
Thu.	19	19 52	**First quarter**	
Fri.	20		Mercury at aphelion	
Sat.	21	0	Jupiter 4° S of Moon	
		9 22	Algol at minimum	
Sun.	22			
Mon.	23			
Tue.	24	6 11	Algol at minimum	
Wed.	25	6	Saturn 2° S of Moon	
		7	Mercury stationary	
Thu.	26			
Fri.	27	3 00	Algol at minimum	
		5	**Mars at opposition**	
		6	Moon at apogee (406 223 km)	
		20 20	**Full Moon (smallest in 2018)**	
			Total Lunar Eclipse (see p. 131)	
Sat.	28	9	S. δ-Aquariid meteors peak	
Sun.	29	23 49	Algol at minimum	
Mon.	30	7 21	**Double shadow transit on Jupiter**	
Tue.	31	8	**Mars at closest approach**	

†Central and northern North America, most of Greenland, north-central Russia

THE SKY FOR AUGUST

		Mercury	Venus	Mars	Jupiter	Saturn	Uranus	Neptune	Sun
RA	1	9h 31m	11h 36m	20h 26m	14h 46m	18h 14m	2h 01m	23h 09m	8h 44m
	11	9h 03m	12h 13m	20h 16m	14h 49m	18h 12m	2h 01m	23h 08m	9h 22m
	21	8h 53m	12h 47m	20h 09m	14h 53m	18h 11m	2h 01m	23h 07m	9h 59m
Dec	1	+9° 56'	+2° 37'	−25° 58'	−15° 03'	−22° 36'	+11° 45'	−6° 31'	+18° 09'
	11	+12° 01'	−2° 18'	−26° 29'	−15° 18'	−22° 38'	+11° 45'	−6° 37'	+15° 25'
	21	+15° 16'	−7° 05'	−26° 30'	−15° 38'	−22° 40'	+11° 44'	−6° 43'	+12° 17'
Dist	1	0.61	0.82	0.38	5.2	9.22	19.74	29.13	1.015
	11	0.62	0.74	0.39	5.35	9.32	19.58	29.04	1.014
	21	0.77	0.66	0.41	5.51	9.45	19.42	28.98	1.012
Mag	1	2.9	−4.3	−2.8	−2.1	0.2	5.8	7.8	
	11	5	−4.4	−2.6	−2	0.3	5.8	7.8	
	21	1.1	−4.5	−2.4	−2	0.3	5.8	7.8	
Size	1	11.0"	20.4"	24.3"	37.9"	18.0"	3.5"	2.3"	31' 31"
	11	10.9"	22.6"	23.8"	36.8"	17.8"	3.6"	2.3"	31' 33"
	21	8.7"	25.3"	22.6"	35.8"	17.6"	3.6"	2.3"	31' 37"

Moon: On August 0 at 0h UT*, Sun's selenographic colongitude is 128.90° and increases by 12.2° each day thereafter.

Greatest N declination on the 9th (+20.7°).

Greatest S declination on the 22nd (−20.7°).

Libration in longitude: E limb most exposed on the 17th (+7.6°),

 W limb most exposed on the 3rd (−7.0°).

Libration in latitude: N limb most exposed on the 5th (+6.8°),

 S limb most exposed on the 17th (−6.8°).

Large tides in the days following New Moon (Aug 11)

Partial solar eclipse on Aug 11, visible from extreme North America, northern Europe, Asia, and the north Atlantic Ocean.

Mercury: Too close to the Sun to be seen for much of the month, Mercury emerges into the morning sky late in the month, achieving maximum western elongation of 18° on the 26th. The innermost planet will continue to brighten in the days that follow, and its favorable geometry relative the ecliptic makes it the best morning apparition of the year for Northern Hemisphere observers.

Venus: Reaches maximum eastern elongation on the 17th, when it is 46° to the east of the Sun but also some 18° more southerly in declination. The unfavorable geometry will make for relatively poor visibility of the second planet throughout the most interesting part of its cycle, which this month will see its phase change from gibbous to crescent.

Mars: Continues its retrograde motion in western Capricornus and gradually begins to lose its lustre, fading from mag. −2.8 to −2.1 over the course of the month. With a declination of some −26° throughout the month, it will be very low in the sky for Northern Hemisphere observers. Reaches its second stationary point on the 28th, exactly two months after its first having traveled some 10° to the west to a point along the Capricornus–Sagittarius border. Meridian transit times at Greenwich on the 1st, 11th, 21st – 23:44, 22:54, 22:09 UT*.

Jupiter: Low in the evening sky throughout the month, it undergoes a series of double shadow transits for telescopic observers as detailed in the events calendar at right. The not-quite-first-quarter Moon passes 5° to its north on the 17th. Meridian transit times at Greenwich on the 1st, 11th, 21st – 18:06, 17:30, 16:55 UT*.

Saturn: Visible in the south in the evening hours. The waxing gibbous Moon passes 2° to the north on the 21st. Meridian transit times at Greenwich on the 1st, 11th, 21st – 21:33, 20:52, 20:11 UT*.

Uranus: Reaches its first stationary point on the 7th in southwestern Aries and begins its subtle retrograde motion thereafter. Visible to the naked eye in a dark sky, binoculars required in an urban location. Meridian transit times at Greenwich on the 1st, 11th, 21st – 05:23, 04:44, 04:04 UT*.

Neptune: Rises in mid-evening, in retrograde motion in Aquarius. Meridian transit times at Greenwich on the 1st, 11th, 21st – 02:31, 01:51, 01:11 UT*.

*See p. 94, the bold-faced sentences of the first paragraph.

Time (UT) d h m	AUGUST EVENTS	Jupiter's Satellites West East
Wed. 1	Venus at descending node	1.0 — I
20 38	Algol at minimum	
23	Vesta stationary	2.0 — III
Thu. 2 20 18	**Double shadow transit on Jupiter**	
Fri. 3		3.0 —
Sat. 4 17 27	Algol at minimum	IV
18 18	**Last quarter**	4.0 — II
23	**Juno 1.2° S of Moon, occultation†**	
Sun. 5		5.0 —
Mon. 6 9 16	**Double shadow transit on Jupiter**	6.0 —
19	**Aldebaran 1.1° S of Moon, occultation‡**	
Tue. 7 13	Pallas in conjunction with the Sun	7.0 —
14 16	Algol at minimum	
21	Uranus stationary	8.0 —
Wed. 8		9.0 —
Thu. 9	Mercury at greatest heliocentric lat. S	
2	Mercury in inferior conjunction	10.0 —
22 13	**Double shadow transit on Jupiter**	
Fri. 10 11 05	Algol at minimum	11.0 —
18	Moon at perigee (358078 km) **Large tides**	12.0 —
Sat. 11 9 58	**New Moon (lunation 1183)**	
	Partial Solar Eclipse (see p. 133)	13.0 —
Sun. 12		
Mon. 13 1	**Perseid meteors peak**	14.0 —
7 54	Algol at minimum	15.0 —
11 10	**Double shadow transit on Jupiter**	
Tue. 14 14	Venus 6° S of Moon	16.0 —
Wed. 15 5 39	**Double shadow transit on Jupiter**	
Thu. 16 4 43	Algol at minimum	17.0 —
Fri. 17 0 08	**Double shadow transit on Jupiter**	18.0 —
11	Jupiter 5° S of Moon	
17	**Venus greatest elongation E (46°)**	19.0 —
Sat. 18 7 49	**First quarter**	20.0 —
12	Mercury stationary	
Sun. 19 1 32	Algol at minimum	21.0 —
Mon. 20 13 16	**Double shadow transit on Jupiter**	
Tue. 21	Mars at greatest heliocentric lat. S	22.0 —
10	Saturn 2° S of Moon	
22 21	Algol at minimum	23.0 —
Wed. 22 8 50	**Double shadow transit on Jupiter**	24.0 —
Thu. 23 11	Moon at apogee (405 746 km)	
Fri. 24 2 35	**Double shadow transit on Jupiter**	25.0 —
19 10	Algol at minimum	
Sat. 25		26.0 —
Sun. 26 11 56	**Full Moon**	27.0 —
21	**Mercury greatest elongation W (18°)**	
Mon. 27 15 54	**Double shadow transit on Jupiter**	28.0 —
15 59	Algol at minimum	
Tue. 28	Mercury at ascending node	29.0 —
10	Mars stationary	30.0 —
Wed. 29		
Thu. 30 12 48	Algol at minimum	31.0 —
Fri. 31 5 12	**Double shadow transit on Jupiter**	

† Eastern Europe, W Russia, Scandinavia, northeastern Greenland, extreme northern Canada
‡ Mongolia, central Russia, Svalbard, most of Greenland, northernmost Canada

THE SKY FOR SEPTEMBER

		Mercury	Venus	Mars	Jupiter	Saturn	Uranus	Neptune	Sun
RA	1	9h 36m	13h 21m	20h 07m	14h 59m	18h 10m	2h 00m	23h 06m	10h 40m
	11	10h 44m	13h 49m	20h 12m	15h 05m	18h 10m	1h 59m	23h 05m	11h 16m
	21	11h 54m	14h 10m	20h 22m	15h 11m	18h 11m	1h 58m	23h 04m	11h 52m
Dec	1	+15° 04′	−12° 01′	−26° 00′	−16° 04′	−22° 42′	+11° 40′	−6° 50′	+8° 28′
	11	+9° 55′	−15° 58′	−25° 10′	−16° 31′	−22° 43′	+11° 35′	−6° 56′	+4° 45′
	21	+2° 19′	−19° 11′	−24° 01′	−16° 59′	−22° 45′	+11° 29′	−7° 03′	+0° 55′
Dist	1	1.06	0.57	0.45	5.67	9.61	19.26	28.94	1.009
	11	1.28	0.5	0.49	5.81	9.77	19.14	28.94	1.007
	21	1.39	0.42	0.54	5.93	9.93	19.03	28.96	1.004
Mag	1	−0.8	−4.6	−2.1	−1.9	0.4	5.7	7.8	
	11	−1.4	−4.7	−1.8	−1.9	0.4	5.7	7.8	
	21	−1.8	−4.8	−1.6	−1.8	0.5	5.7	7.8	
Size	1	6.4″	29.1″	20.9″	34.8″	17.3″	3.6″	2.3″	31′ 42″
	11	5.3″	33.6″	19.1″	33.9″	17.0″	3.7″	2.3″	31′ 46″
	21	4.8″	39.3″	17.4″	33.2″	16.7″	3.7″	2.3″	31′ 51″

Moon: On September 0 at 0h UT*, Sun's selenographic colongitude is 147.55° and increases by 12.2° each day thereafter.

Greatest N declination on the 5th (+20.7°).

Greatest S declination on the 18th (−20.8°).

Libration in longitude: E limb most exposed on the 14th (+7.0°),

  W limb most exposed on the 1st (−6.2°).

Libration in latitude: N limb most exposed on the 11th (+6.7°) & 28th (+6.6°),

  S limb most exposed on the 13h (−6.7°).

Mercury: Visible in the first few days in evening twilight for Northern Hobservers, but being reined in by the Sun for its Sep 21 superior conjunction and invisible to all but (careful) daytime observation by telescopic observers for most of the month.

Venus: Its unfavorable placement for Northern Hemisphere observation is encapsulated by its monthly conjunction with the Moon, which passes fully 10° to its north on the 12th. Achieves its greatest illuminated extent on the 21st, when it is at −19° Dec while the Sun is still north of the celestial equator. Despite its brilliance (mag. −4.8) the prospective observer would be advised to find an unobstructed southwestern horizon to spy it in early evening twilight.

Mars: Now in the evening sky, Mars has resumed prograde (eastward) motion and gradually begins to pick up (apparent) speed in western Capricornus. The still-gleaming Red Planet will see its brightness cut in half over the course of September, from mag. −2.1 to −1.3. The waxing gibbous Moon passes 5° to its north on the evening of the 19–20 in North America. Meridian transit times at Greenwich on the 1st, 11th, 21st – 21:25, 20:51, 20:22 UT*.

Jupiter: Low in the early evening sky throughout the month. The waxing crescent Moon passes 4° to its north on the evening of the 13th for observers in the Americas.

Saturn: Reaches its second stationary point among the stars of Sagittarius on the 10th, and resumes prograde motion thereafter. Low in the southwestern sky in the evening hours, setting before midnight local daylight time before month-end. Meridian transit times at Greenwich on the 1st, 11th, 21st – 19:27, 18:48, 18:10 UT*.

Uranus: Now rising before midnight as it approaches its late October opposition. Meridian transit times at Greenwich on the 1st, 11th, 21st – 03:20, 02:40, 02:00 UT*.

Neptune: Visible all night in Aquarius. At opposition on the 7th, mag. +7.8, 4.0 light-hours (28.9 au). Meridian transit times at Greenwich on the 1st, 11th, 21st – 00:26, 23:42, 23:02 UT*.

*See p. 94, the bold-faced sentences of the first paragraph.

Time (UT)			SEPTEMBER EVENTS	Jupiter's Satellites	
d	h	m		West	East

Sat.	1			
Sun.	2		Mercury at perihelion	
		9	**Venus 1.4° S of Spica**	
		9 37	Algol at minimum	
Mon.	3	2	**Aldebaran 1.2° S of Moon, occultation†**	
		2 37	**Last quarter**	
		18 31	**Double shadow transit on Jupiter**	
Tue.	4			
Wed.	5		Venus at aphelion	
			Zodiacal light vis. in N lat. in E before morning twilight for next two weeks	
		6 26	Algol at minimum	
		23	**Mercury 1.0° N of Regulus**	
Thu.	6	10	Saturn stationary	
Fri.	7	3	**Moon 1.4° S of Beehive (M44)**	
		7 50	**Double shadow transit on Jupiter**	
		18	**Neptune at opposition**	
Sat.	8	1	Moon at perigee (361 351 km)	
		3 15	Algol at minimum	
Sun.	9	18 01	**New Moon (lunation 1184)**	
Mon.	10			
Tue.	11	0 04	Algol at minimum	
Wed.	12		Mercury at greatest heliocentric lat. N	
Thu.	13	20 53	Algol at minimum	
Fri.	14	2	Jupiter 4° S of Moon	
Sat.	15			
Sun.	16		Mars at perihelion	
		17 42	Algol at minimum	
		23 15	**First quarter**	
Mon.	17	16	Saturn 2° S of Moon	
Tue.	18			
Wed.	19	14 31	Algol at minimum	
Thu.	20	1	Moon at apogee (404 876 km)	
		7	Mars 5° S of Moon	
Fri.	21	2	Mercury in superior conjunction	
		10	**Venus greatest illuminated extent**	
Sat.	22	11 20	Algol at minimum	
Sun.	23	1 54	**Equinox**	
Mon.	24			
Tue.	25	2 52	**Full Moon**	
		8 09	Algol at minimum	
Wed.	26			
Thu.	27		Venus at greatest heliocentric lat. S	
Fri.	28	4 58	Algol at minimum	
Sat.	29			
Sun.	30	8	Aldebaran 1.4° S of Moon	

† Greenland, northernmost Canada

THE SKY FOR OCTOBER

		Mercury	Venus	Mars	Jupiter	Saturn	Uranus	Neptune	Sun
RA	1	12h 57m	14h 22m	20h 36m	15h 18m	18h 12m	1h 57m	23h 03m	12h 28m
	11	13h 56m	14h 21m	20h 54m	15h 26m	18h 14m	1h 56m	23h 02m	13h 04m
	21	14h 52m	14h 05m	21h 13m	15h 35m	18h 17m	1h 54m	23h 02m	13h 41m
Dec	1	–5° 27′	–21° 19′	–22° 37′	–17° 29′	–22° 46′	+11° 22′	–7° 08′	–2° 59′
	11	–12° 27′	–21° 52′	–20° 57′	–18° 00′	–22° 47′	+11° 14′	–7° 14′	–6° 49′
	21	–18° 16′	–20° 13′	–19° 03′	–18° 30′	–22° 47′	+11° 06′	–7° 18′	–10° 30′
Dist	1	1.41	0.36	0.59	6.05	10.1	18.95	29.02	1.001
	11	1.36	0.31	0.65	6.14	10.26	18.9	29.1	0.998
	21	1.28	0.28	0.71	6.22	10.42	18.88	29.21	0.996
Mag	1	–0.9	–4.8	–1.3	–1.8	0.5	5.7	7.8	
	11	–0.4	–4.6	–1.1	–1.8	0.5	5.7	7.8	
	21	–0.2	–4.2	–0.8	–1.8	0.6	5.7	7.8	
Size	1	4.8″	46.2″	15.8″	32.6″	16.5″	3.7″	2.3″	31′ 57″
	11	4.9″	53.9″	14.4″	32.1″	16.2″	3.7″	2.3″	32′ 02″
	21	5.3″	59.9″	13.1″	31.7″	16.0″	3.7″	2.3″	32′ 08″

Moon: On October 0 at 0h UT*, Sun's selenographic colongitude is 153.60° and increases by 12.2° each day thereafter.

Greatest N declination on the 30 (+21.3°).

Greatest S declination on the 15th (–20.9°).

Libration in longitude: E limb most exposed on the 12th (+6.1°),
   W limb most exposed on the 24th (–4.8°).

Libration in latitude: N limb most exposed on the 25th (+6.6°),
   S limb most exposed on the 10th (–6.5°).

Mercury: Re-emerges in the evening sky early in the month in what will be a lengthy and excellent apparition for Southern Hemisphere observers.

Venus: Reaches its stationary point on the 5th and retrogrades rapidly toward the Sun thereafter. Achieves inferior conjunction on the 26th when it passes 6° 15′ south of the Sun and will be visible as an exquisitely slender crescent in daytime hours to an advanced telescopic observer (who must exercise great caution to avoid the Sun).

Mars: Now in full retreat, Mars fades from mag. –1.3 to –0.6 over the course of the month as it moves eastward against the stars of Capricornus. The first quarter Moon is nearby on the 18th and 19th. Meridian transit times at Greenwich on the 1st, 11th, 21st – 19:57, 19:35, 19:15 UT*.

Jupiter: Low in the southwest in evening twilight, Jupiter's observing window is now closing rapidly. The young crescent Moon makes a wide pair with Jupiter on the 10th and 11th.

Saturn: Low in the southwestern sky in the early evening hours. The thick waxing crescent Moon passes 2° to its north in the evening hours of the 14th in the Americas.

Uranus: Located along the Pisces–Aries border. Reaches opposition on the 24th, mag. +5.7, with a 3.7″ disk. At 11° north of the celestial equator, its first opposition north of declination +10.0° since that of 1963. For Northern Hemisphere observers that aspect will continue to improve each subsequent year as the gas giant continues its slow rise to the top of ecliptic in 2032. For the third time in 2018, a Full Moon is in the vicinity of an opposed planet, this time to the south. Meridian transit times at Greenwich on the 1st, 11th, 21st – 01:19, 00:38, 23:53 UT*.

Neptune: Visible most of the night, just past opposition and well-placed in the mid-evening sky. Meridian transit times at Greenwich on the 1st, 11th, 21st – 22:22, 21:42, 21:02 UT*.

*See p. 94, the bold-faced sentences of the first paragraph.

Time (UT) d h m	OCTOBER EVENTS	Jupiter's Satellites West East
Mon. 1 1 47	Algol at minimum	
Tue. 2 9 45	**Last quarter**	
Wed. 3 22 36	Algol at minimum	
Thu. 4 10	**Moon 1.2° S of Beehive (M44)**	
Fri. 5 4	Venus stationary	
18	Mercury 2° N of Spica	
22	**Regulus 1.9° S of Moon**	
22	Moon at perigee (366 392 km)	
Sat. 6	Mercury at descending node	
19 25	Algol at minimum	
Sun. 7 10	Ceres in conjunction with the Sun	
Mon. 8 15	Draconid meteors peak	
Tue. 9 3 47	**New Moon** (lunation 1185)	
16 14	Algol at minimum	
Wed. 10		
Thu. 11 21	Jupiter 4° S of Moon	
Fri. 12 13 03	Algol at minimum	
Sat. 13	**Zodiacal light vis. in N lat. in E before morning twilight for next two weeks**	
Sun. 14		
Mon. 15 3	**Saturn 1.8° S of Moon**	
9 52	Algol at minimum	
Tue. 16	Mercury at aphelion	
18	Juno stationary	
18 02	**First quarter**	
Wed. 17 19	Moon at apogee (404 227 km)	
Thu. 18 6 41	Algol at minimum	
13	**Mars 1.9° S of Moon**	
Fri. 19		
Sat. 20		
Sun. 21 3 30	Algol at minimum	
18	Orionid meteors peak	
Mon. 22		
Tue. 23		
Wed. 24 0 19	Algol at minimum	
1	**Uranus at opposition**	
16 45	**Full Moon**	
Thu. 25		
Fri. 26 14	**Venus in inferior conjunction**	
21 08	Algol at minimum	
Sat. 27 14	Aldebaran 1.6° S of Moon	
Sun. 28		
Mon. 29 17 57	Algol at minimum	
Tue. 30 4	Mercury 3° S of Jupiter	
Wed. 31 16	Moon 1.0° S of Beehive (M44)	
16 40	**Last quarter**	
20	Moon at perigee (370 204 km)	

THE SKY FOR NOVEMBER

		Mercury	Venus	Mars	Jupiter	Saturn	Uranus	Neptune	Sun
RA	1	15h 52m	13h 43m	21h 36m	15h 44m	18h 20m	1h 52m	23h 01m	14h 24m
	11	16h 35m	13h 31m	21h 59m	15h 53m	18h 24m	1h 51m	23h 01m	15h 03m
	21	16h 41m	13h 34m	22h 22m	16h 02m	18h 28m	1h 49m	23h 00m	15h 44m
Dec	1	−22° 51′	−16° 09′	−16° 42′	−19° 04′	−22° 47′	+10° 56′	−7° 22′	−14° 15′
	11	−24° 45′	−12° 22′	−14° 22′	−19° 33′	−22° 46′	+10° 48′	−7° 24′	−17° 16′
	21	−23° 22′	−10° 10′	−11° 51′	−20° 00′	−22° 44′	+10° 40′	−7° 25′	−19° 48′
Dist	1	1.12	0.28	0.79	6.29	10.58	18.89	29.35	0.993
	11	0.93	0.3	0.86	6.33	10.71	18.93	29.5	0.99
	21	0.73	0.35	0.93	6.35	10.82	19	29.67	0.988
Mag	1	−0.2	−4.2	−0.6	−1.7	0.6	5.7	7.8	
	11	−0.2	−4.6	−0.4	−1.7	0.6	5.7	7.9	
	21	1.5	−4.8	−0.2	−1.7	0.6	5.7	7.9	
Size	1	6.0″	60.6″	11.9″	31.3″	15.7″	3.7″	2.3″	32′ 13″
	11	7.2″	55.3″	10.9″	31.1″	15.5″	3.7″	2.3″	32′ 18″
	21	9.2″	47.8″	10.0″	31.1″	15.4″	3.7″	2.3″	32′ 23″

Moon: On November 0 at 0h UT*, Sun's selenographic colongitude is 171.31° and increases by 12.2° each day thereafter.
Greatest N declination on the 26th (+21.5°).
Greatest S declination on the 12th (−21.4°).
Libration in longitude: E limb most exposed on the 8th (+5.3°),
 W limb most exposed on the 21st (−5.5°).
Libration in latitude: N limb most exposed on the 21st (+6.6°),
 S limb most exposed on the 6th (−6.5°).

Mercury: Continues its fine evening apparition for Southern Hemisphere observers, reaching maximum eastern elongation of 23° on the 6th. Very low in the sky and at unfavorable geometry for Northern Hemisphere observation. Returns to inferior conjunction on the 27th

Venus: Now in "Morning Star" mode, it emerges in morning twilight in the second half of the month.

Mars: The Red Planet finally gains a more favorable altitude to the horizon for Northern Hemisphere observers as it speeds from Capricornus into Aquarius, but continues to fade in the evening sky, reaching mag. 0.0 by month-end. The first quarter Moon makes a close pass on the evening of the 15–16.
Meridian transit times at Greenwich on the 1st, 11th, 21st – 18:55, 18:38, 18:21 UT*.

Jupiter: Might be glimpsed with difficulty in early evening twilight at the beginning of the month, but rapidly disappearing into the sunset. In conjunction with the Sun on the 26th.

Saturn: Visible with increasing difficulty in evening twilight, low in the southwest. The four-day-old Moon passes nearby on the 11th.

Uranus: Now in the evening sky, the +5.7–mag. gas giant is well-placed fairly high in the sky for viewing with the naked eye from a dark site. Meridian transit times at Greenwich on the 1st, 11th, 21st – 23:08, 22:28, 21:47 UT*.

Neptune: Well-placed in the early evening sky. Reaches its second stationary point on the 25th, thereafter resuming direct eastward motion, albeit at a near imperceptible rate at first. Meridian transit times at Greenwich on the 1st, 11th, 21st – 20:18, 19:38, 18:58 UT*.

*See p. 94, the bold-faced sentences of the first paragraph.

Time (UT) d h m	NOVEMBER EVENTS	Jupiter's Satellites West East
Thu. 1 14 46	Algol at minimum	
Fri. 2		
Sat. 3		
Sun. 4	**DAYLIGHT SAVING TIME ENDS**	
11 35	Algol at minimum	
Mon. 5	Mercury at greatest heliocentric lat. S	
18	S. Taurid meteors peak	
Tue. 6 15	**Mercury greatest elongation E (23°)**	
Wed. 7 8 24	Algol at minimum	
16 02	**New Moon** (lunation 1186)	
Thu. 8		
Fri. 9 6	**Mercury 1.8° N of Antares**	
Sat. 10 5 13	Algol at minimum	
Sun. 11 16	**Saturn 1.5° S of Moon**	
Mon. 12 17	N. Taurid meteors peak	
18	**Pluto 0.9° S of Moon, occultation†**	
Tue. 13 2 02	Algol at minimum	
Wed. 14 3	Venus stationary	
16	Moon at apogee (404 339 km)	
Thu. 15 14 54	**First quarter**	
22 51	Algol at minimum	
Fri. 16 4	**Mars 1.0° N of Moon, occultation‡**	
Sat. 17 5	Mercury stationary	
22	**Juno at opposition**	
Sun. 18 0	Leonid meteors peak	
19 40	Algol at minimum	
Mon. 19		
Tue. 20		
Wed. 21 16 29	Algol at minimum	
Thu. 22	Venus at ascending node	
Fri. 23 5 39	**Full Moon**	
22	Aldebaran 1.7° S of Moon	
Sat. 24	Mercury at ascending node	
13 18	Algol at minimum	
Sun. 25 8	Neptune stationary	
Mon. 26 7	Jupiter in conjunction with the Sun	
12	Moon at perigee (366 620 km)	
Tue. 27 9	Mercury in inferior conjunction	
10 07	Algol at minimum	
21	**Moon 0.7° S of Beehive (M44)**	
Wed. 28		
Thu. 29	Mercury at perihelion	
Fri. 30 0 19	**Last quarter**	
6 56	Algol at minimum	

† Northeastern North America, southern Greenland, Iceland, Azores, most of western Europe
‡ Most of Antarctica, Falkland Islands, southern South America

THE SKY FOR DECEMBER

		Mercury	Venus	Mars	Jupiter	Saturn	Uranus	Neptune	Sun
RA	1	15h 54m	13h 49m	22h 45m	16h 12m	18h 33m	1h 48m	23h 00m	16h 27m
	11	15h 47m	14h 14m	23h 09m	16h 21m	18h 38m	1h 47m	23h 01m	17h 11m
	21	16h 28m	14h 46m	23h 33m	16h 30m	18h 43m	1h 47m	23h 01m	17h 55m
Dec	1	−18° 17′	−9° 48′	−9° 11′	−20° 26′	−22° 42′	+10° 34′	−7° 25′	−21° 43′
	11	−17° 13′	−10° 50′	−6° 25′	−20° 50′	−22° 39′	+10° 29′	−7° 23′	−22° 57′
	21	−20° 09′	−12° 44′	−3° 34′	−21° 12′	−22° 35′	+10° 25′	−7° 20′	−23° 26′
Dist	1	0.7	0.41	1.01	6.34	10.91	19.1	29.84	0.986
	11	0.91	0.48	1.09	6.32	10.98	19.22	30.01	0.985
	21	1.13	0.55	1.17	6.27	11.02	19.36	30.18	0.984
Mag	1	3	−4.9	0	−1.7	0.6	5.7	7.9	
	11	−0.3	−4.8	0.1	−1.7	0.5	5.7	7.9	
	21	−0.5	−4.7	0.3	−1.8	0.5	5.7	7.9	
Size	1	9.6″	40.7″	9.3″	31.1″	15.2″	3.7″	2.2″	32′ 26″
	11	7.4″	34.8″	8.6″	31.2″	15.1″	3.6″	2.2″	32′ 29″
	21	6.0″	30.2″	8.0″	31.4″	15.1″	3.6″	2.2″	32′ 31″

Moon: On December 0 at 0h UT*, Sun's selenographic colongitude is 176.39° and increases by 12.2° each day thereafter.

Greatest N declination on the 23rd (+21.4°).

Greatest S declination on the 9th (−21.5°).

Libration in longitude: E limb most exposed on the 5th (+5.4°) & 31st (+6.5°),
  W limb most exposed on the 19th (−6.7°).

Libration in latitude: N limb most exposed on the 18th (+6.8°),
  S limb most exposed on the 3rd (−6.6°).

Mercury: Return to the morning sky where it has a modestly favorable apparition for Northern Hemisphere observers, achieving greatest western elongation of 21° on the 15th. On the 21st it will be in conjunction with Jupiter, with the two objects potentially visible in the same low-power telescopic field. Jupiter will be the brighter object at mag. −1.8 to Mercury's −0.5, but the tiny inner planet at under 20% Jupiter's apparent diameter will have much greater surface brightness, making for an odd couple to greet the December solstice later that same day.

Venus: Visible in bright morning twilight, crescent Venus remains relatively close to Earth, reaching its greatest illuminated extent on the 2nd. The waning crescent Moon passes 4° to its north on the third.

Mars: Makes an exceptionally close pass just 0.04° from Neptune on 7th. Passes from Aquarius into Pisces later in the month, ending the year as a mag. +0.5 gibbous (87% illuminated) disk, just 7.4″ in diameter across its long axis and setting the stage for a fairly desultory showing in 2019.

Jupiter: Re-emerges into morning twilight late in the month, low in the southeastern sky.

Saturn: Too close to the Sun to be easily seen and headed for solar conjunction on 2019 Jan 02.

Uranus: In the evening sky among the stars along the Pisces–Aries border. Meridian transit times at Greenwich on the 1st, 11th, 21st – 21:06, 20:26, 19:46 UT*.

Neptune: In the western evening sky in Aquarius, setting in the late evening. The angle of the ecliptic favors northern observers..

*See p. 94, the bold-faced sentences of the first paragraph.

Time (UT)			DECEMBER EVENTS	Jupiter's Satellites	
d	h	m		West	East
Sat. 1					
Sun. 2	0		**Venus greatest illuminated extent**		
Mon. 3	3	45	Algol at minimum		
	19		**Venus 4° S of Moon**		
Tue. 4					
Wed. 5	21		**Mercury 1.9° S of Moon**		
Thu. 6	0	34	Algol at minimum		
	20		Mercury stationary		
Fri. 7	7	20	**New Moon (lunation 1187)**		
	15		**Mars 0.04° N of Neptune**		
Sat. 8	21	23	Algol at minimum		
Sun. 9			Mercury at greatest heliocentric lat. N		
	5		**Saturn 1.1° S of Moon, occultation†**		
Mon. 10	4		**Pluto 0.7° S of Moon, occultation‡**		
Tue. 11	18	12	Algol at minimum		
Wed. 12	12		Moon at apogee (405 177 km)		
Thu. 13					
Fri. 14	13		**Geminid meteors peak**		
	15	01	Algol at minimum		
	23		Mars 4° N of Moon		
Sat. 15	11	49	**First quarter**		
	12		**Mercury greatest elongation W (21°)**		
Sun. 16					
Mon. 17	11	50	Algol at minimum		
Tue. 18					
Wed. 19					
Thu. 20	8	39	Algol at minimum		
Fri. 21	8		**Aldebaran 1.7° S of Moon**		
	15		**Mercury 0.9° N of Jupiter**		
	22	23	**Solstice**		
Sat. 22	17	49	**Full Moon**		
	21		Ursid meteors peak		
Sun. 23	5	28	Algol at minimum		
Mon. 24	10		Moon at perigee (361 062 km)		
Tue. 25	5		Moon 0.6° S of Beehive (M44)		
Wed. 26			Venus at perihelion		
	2	17	Algol at minimum		
Thu. 27	15		Juno stationary		
Fri. 28	23	06	Algol at minimum		
Sat. 29	9	34	**Last quarter**		
Sun. 30					
Mon. 31	19	55	Algol at minimum		

† Southeastern Russia, northern tip of China
‡ Northeastern China, E Mongolia, Japan, E and SE Russia, N Micronesia, Aleutian Islands

ECLIPSES

ECLIPSE PATTERNS
BY ROY BISHOP

Eclipse Seasons

The plane of the Moon's orbit is tilted about 5° to the plane of Earth's orbit, the ecliptic. Since 5° is considerably larger than both the north–south range of lunar parallax for various localities on Earth (≈1.9°) and the angular radii of the Sun and Moon (each ≈0.25°), solar eclipses can occur only when the Sun is near (within about

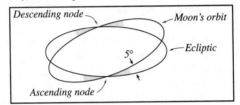

±15° to ±18°) one of the two points at which the Moon's orbit crosses the ecliptic (nodes). Lunar eclipses have a comparable restriction. The *ascending* node is the one at which the Moon crosses to the *north* side of the ecliptic.

The Sun moves eastward along the ecliptic about 1° per day; thus the interval during which an eclipse can occur is at most about (2 × 18°) ÷ 1°/d = 36 d, an *eclipse season*. The interval between new moons (29.5 days) is somewhat less, thus one or two solar eclipses will occur in each eclipse season. Six months later, when the Sun is near the other node, another eclipse season occurs. However, the plane of the Moon's orbit wobbles, making the nodes regress slowly westward along the ecliptic with a period of 18.60 years (see p. 95); thus the two eclipse seasons drift backward through the year, occurring about 19 days earlier each year. *The eclipse seasons of 2018 occur in January–February and July–August.*

In a calendar year,
- there can be as many as seven eclipses (solar and lunar combined, as last occurred in 1982) and as few as four (the usual number);
- there can be as many as five solar or lunar eclipses and as few as two;
- the number of total or annular solar eclipses can range from zero to two, the number of total lunar eclipses from zero to three.

In 2018, there are five eclipses: three solar (all partial) and two lunar (both total).

The Saros

Eclipses of the Sun and Moon recur with various periodicities that are more or less approximate. These periodicities are interesting both as numerical curiosities and because they may be used to predict eclipses. The most famous periodicity, the *Saros*, has been known since ancient times. It is a consequence of a remarkable commensurability between three lunar average periods:

Synodic month *(S)* (new to new)   = 29.530 589 d, 223*S* = 6585.3213 d
Draconic month *(N)* (node to node)   = 27.212 221 d, 242*N* = 6585.3575 d
Anomalistic month *(P)* (perigee to perigee) = 27.554 550 d, 239*P* = 6585.5375 d

Several aspects of this arithmetic are relevant to the pattern of eclipses (for brevity, the following comments are restricted primarily to the case of solar eclipses):

(1) An integer number of Ss (223) ensures a new Moon and hence the possibility of a second solar eclipse.

(2) $242N \approx 223S$ means that the new Moon will be at almost the same position relative to a node, ensuring that an eclipse *will* occur again and that it will occur on Earth's globe about the same distance north or south of the ecliptic plane as did the first eclipse.

(3) The Saros $(223S) = 6585.3213$ d $= 18$ years $+$ *only* 10.3213 d or 11.3213 d (depending on the number of intervening leap years). Thus one Saros later Earth will be at almost the same point in its elliptical orbit and hence at nearly the same distance from the Sun. Moreover, the inclination of Earth toward the Sun (season) will be nearly the same; thus the same latitude region of Earth will be exposed to the eclipse.

(text continues on next page)

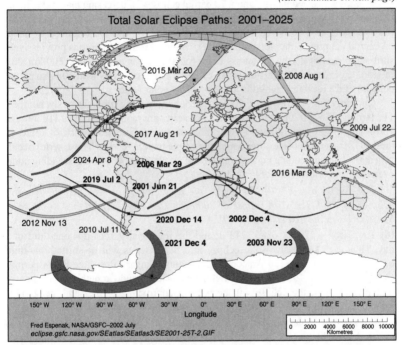

The figure shows the paths of all total solar eclipses, excluding hybrid annular/total eclipses, occurring during the years 2001–2025. There are 15 eclipses, one in each of the years 2001, 2002, 2003, 2006, 2008, 2009, 2010, 2012, 2015, 2016, 2017, 2019, 2020, 2021, and 2024. Because the 25-year period covered by the figure is somewhat longer than the 18-year Saros interval, the first four and last four eclipses, drawn with heavy shading and with labels in bold type, make up four Saros pairs, with Saros numbers 127, 142, 152, and 139, respectively. Note that the members of each pair are both total eclipses, are separated in time by one Saros, have similar path shapes, and occur at similar latitudes; note also that the later member is shifted 120° westward in longitude (see items (2) through (6) of the text explaining these features). The figure was produced by Fred Espenak and is presented here with his permission. For figures showing total solar eclipses, annular eclipses, and hybrid annular/total eclipses for the period –1999 to +3000 (2000 BCE to 3000 CE), see eclipse.gsfc.nasa.gov/SEatlas/SEatlas.html.

(4) $239P \approx 223S$ means that one Saros later the new Moon will be at almost the same point in its elliptical orbit and thus at the same distance from Earth. With the same lunar and solar distances, the type of eclipse (total or annular) will be the same. Since the eclipse will occur near the same geographic latitude (see **(2)** and **(3)**), the duration of totality or annularity, or the magnitude of partial eclipse if the eclipse is not central, will be almost the same as it was one Saros earlier.

(5) $242N - 223S = 0.0361$ d $= 0.87$ h. This, together with the $0.55°$/h eastward speed of the Moon in its orbit, means that after one Saros the Moon will be about $0.5°$ west of its former position relative to its node. Thus a Saros series does not last forever; there will be about $36°/0.5° \approx 72$ eclipses in a Saros series (the number ranges from 69 to 87). Furthermore, any one Saros series will last for about $72 \times 18 \approx 1300$ years (the range is 1226 to 1551 years).

A Saros series begins with about 10 partial eclipses of increasing magnitude in the north or south polar region, depending upon whether the eclipses are occurring near the ascending or descending lunar node, respectively. These are followed by about 50 central eclipses (either total or annular), which over many centuries progressively shift southward or northward across Earth (on average an approximate 300-km shift in latitude occurs with each successive eclipse). The series ends with 10 or so partial eclipses of decreasing magnitude in the opposite polar region.

Currently, for solar eclipses, 40 Saros series are running simultaneously, numbers 117 through 156 (for lunar eclipses, 41 Saros series are running, numbers 110 through 150). That is, in any 18-year 11-day interval, one eclipse from each of these 40 (and 41) series takes place, after which the whole pattern repeats. Those series occurring at the lunar ascending node are given odd numbers; those at the descending node, even numbers (vice versa for lunar eclipses).

The five eclipses of 2018 belong to the same five Saros series as the first five eclipses of 2000. The sixth eclipse of 2000 (on December 25) belongs to the same Saros series as the first eclipse of 2019.

(6) The Saros $= 223S = 6585.3213$ d, and the fractional 0.3213 d $\approx$ one-third of a day. Thus each successive solar eclipse in a Saros series will be shifted one-third of the way westward ($120°$ in longitude) around Earth. After three Saros periods (3×6585.3213 d $\approx 19\,756$ d, or approximately 54 years and 1 month), a cycle known as the *Exeligmos*, the eclipse will be back at approximately the same geographic longitude, although shifted about 1000 km in latitude. Two examples follow:

(a) The total solar eclipse of 2017 Aug. 21 that swept across the contiguous United States (see the map on the previous page) was number 22 of Saros 145. Number 21 of that Saros was the total solar eclipse of 1999 Aug. 11 that began near Nova Scotia and crossed Europe and southwestern Asia.

(b) The total solar eclipse of 2024 Apr. 8 (no. 30 of Saros 139), which sweeps northeastward across eastern North America, will be geographically similar to that of 1970 Mar. 7 (no. 27 of Saros 139), which followed the eastern seaboard of North America one Exeligmos earlier. Also, one Saros earlier we had the similar total solar eclipse of 2006 Mar. 29 (no. 29 of Saros 139), which occurred about $120°$ to the east, across Africa and the Mediterranean (see the figure on the previous page). You, the reader, should now be able to figure out the date, the shape of the path of totality, and the geographic location of solar eclipse no. 28 of Saros 139!

The Metonic Cycle

The sequence of lunar phases and the year repeat their relative pattern at 19-year intervals, a cycle known to astronomers in ancient Babylon and that was discovered independently around 430 BCE by Meton, a Greek astronomer. We have $235S = 235 \times 29.530\,589 = 6939.6884$ d;

19 years = 6939 d or 6940 d (depending on leap years).

Moreover, $255N$ is also very close to 19 years,

$255N = 255 \times 27.212\,221 = 6939.1164$ d.

Thus solar and lunar eclipses also repeat on a 19-year "Metonic" cycle. Since $255N$ is less than $235S$, the Moon does not reach the same phase (new or full for an eclipse) until it has moved eastward relative to the node by

$(235S - 255N) \times 24$ h $\times 0.55°/h = 7.5°$.

Thus a Metonic eclipse series will have only

eclipse season width on the ecliptic $(36°) \div 7.5° \approx 4$ or 5 eclipses;

and the geographic latitude of successive solar eclipses in a series will change substantially (north or south, depending upon whether the Moon is at its ascending node or descending node, respectively).

What about the Moon's position in its orbit relative to its perigee? Using the anomalistic month P (the Moon returns to perigee on average every 27.554 550 d),

$235S \div P = 251.85$, which is *not* near an integer.

Thus in a Metonic series the Moon's distance is not the same from one eclipse to another. Hence the type of solar eclipse (total or annular) will vary within the series.

With only about four eclipses in a series, a mix of eclipse types, and scattered geographic occurrence, a Metonic eclipse series is not as elegant or useful as a Saros series. The main feature of a Metonic eclipse series is that, like lunar phases, the successive eclipses occur on (almost) the *same day* of the year.

Examples of the Metonic cycle for a lunar phase, lunar eclipses, and a Western Hemisphere total solar eclipse are given below. The numbers in parentheses are Saros numbers.

Full Moon	Lunar Eclipses	Solar Eclipses
1961 Dec. 22	1980 Jan. 31 (no eclipse)	1967 Apr. 9 (no eclipse)
1980 Dec. 21	1999 Jan. 31 Penumbral (114)	1986 Apr. 9 Partial (119)
1999 Dec. 22	**2018** Jan. 31 Total (124)	2005 Apr. 8 Ann/Tot (129)
2018 Dec. 22	2037 Jan. 31 Total (134)	**2024** Apr. 8 Total (139)
2037 Dec. 22	2056 Feb. 1 Penumbral (144)	2043 Apr. 9 Total (149)
2056 Dec. 22	2075 Jan. 31 (no eclipse)	2062 Apr. 9 (no eclipse)

Canons of Eclipses

Anyone with an interest in eclipses will be impressed by the *Five Millennium Canon of Solar Eclipses* (2006) and the *Five Millennium Canon of Lunar Eclipses* (2009) and their accompanying catalogs (four books in all), by Fred Espenak and Jean Meeus, and published by NASA. These monumental works give maps and tabular data for all 23 962 eclipses (11 898 solar and 12 064 lunar) occurring during the period –1999 to +3000 (2000 BCE to 3000 CE). The books are available from: NASA Center for AeroSpace Information, 7115 Standard Drive, Hanover MD 21076-1320, USA.

Three decades ago NASA published Fred Espenak's *Fifty Year Canon of Solar Eclipses* and *Fifty Year Canon of Lunar Eclipses*. Included are maps and data for all eclipses during the two centuries, 1901–2100, plus diagrams and maps (larger scale than in the *Five Millennium* canons) for eclipses during the 50-year period 1986–2035.

ECLIPSES IN 2018
BY FRED ESPENAK

In 2018, there are three partial solar eclipses and two total lunar eclipses:

Jan. 31:	Total Lunar Eclipse
Feb. 15:	Partial Solar Eclipse
Jul. 13:	Partial Solar Eclipse
Jul. 27:	Total Lunar Eclipse
Aug. 11:	Partial Solar Eclipse

Predictions for the eclipses are summarized in Figures 1 through 5. World maps show the regions of visibility for each eclipse. The lunar eclipse diagrams also include the path of the Moon through Earth's shadow. Contact times for each principal phase are tabulated along with the magnitudes and geocentric coordinates of the Sun and Moon at greatest eclipse. All times are given in terms of UT1[1].

Total Lunar Eclipse of January 31

The first lunar eclipse of the year occurs at the lunar orbit's ascending node in Cancer. The apparent diameter of the Moon is larger than average since the eclipse occurs 1.2 days after perigee (Jan. 30 at 09:54 UT). This is the first of three consecutive total lunar eclipses in 2018 and 2019, each one separated by six months.

The Moon's orbital trajectory takes it through the southern half of Earth's umbral shadow. In this particular case, the Moon passes deeply into the umbral shadow leading to a relatively long total eclipse lasting 1 h 16 min.

The Moon's path through Earth's shadow as well as a map illustrating worldwide visibility of the event are shown in Figure 1 (p. 128). The times of the major eclipse phases are listed as follows.

Penumbral Eclipse Begins:	10:51:13 UT1
Partial Eclipse Begins:	11:48:28 UT1
Total Eclipse Begins:	12:51:49 UT1
Greatest Eclipse:	13:29:51 UT1
Total Eclipse Ends:	14:07:53 UT1
Partial Eclipse Ends:	15:11:14 UT1
Penumbral Eclipse Ends:	16:08:32 UT1

At the instant of greatest eclipse (13:29:51 UT1)[2], the Moon lies at the zenith for a point in the South Pacific about 2900 km west of the Hawaiian Islands. The umbral eclipse magnitude[3] peaks at 1.3155 as the Moon's northern limb passes 1.8′ south of the umbra's central axis.

In contrast, the Moon's southern limb lies 10.5′ from the edge of the shadow. As a result, the northern half of the Moon will appear much darker than the southern half because the Moon samples a large range of umbral depths during the total phase. The exact brightness distribution in the umbra is difficult to predict, so observers are encouraged to estimate the Danjon value at mid-totality (see Danjon Scale of Lunar Eclipse Brightness). It may also be necessary to assign different Danjon values to different portions of the Moon (e.g. north vs. south).

---

[1] *Universal Time* (UT1) is within 0.9 s of Coordinated Universal Time (UTC). See p.44.
[2] The instant of greatest eclipse for lunar eclipses occurs when the distance between the Moon's shadow axis and Earth's geocenter reaches a minimum.
[3] Umbral eclipse magnitude is defined as the fraction of the Moon's diameter occulted by Earth's umbral shadow.

During totality, the winter/spring constellations are well placed for viewing, so a number of bright stars can be used for magnitude comparisons. Procyon (mag. +0.40) is 21° to the southwest of the eclipsed Moon, while Pollux (mag. +1.40) and Castor (mag. +1.58) are 19° and 23°, respectively, northwest, and Regulus (mag. +1.40) is 19° southeast.

The entire event is visible from the western Pacific Ocean, Alaska, western Canada, Hawaii, Australia, New Zealand, Indonesia, the Philippines, China, Japan, and eastern Siberia. Much of the eclipse will be seen from North America, but eastern observers will miss the later stages of the eclipse because they occur after moonset. Likewise parts of Eastern Europe and central Asia experience moonrise after the eclipse begins. None of the eclipse is visible from Western Europe or Africa., nor most of South America. *(continued on p. 129)*

TOTAL SOLAR ECLIPSE OF 2017 AUGUST 21

The total solar eclipse of 2017 Aug. 21 captured at the moment of third contact with the dazzling Diamond Ring, thus ending totality. Asymmetrical coronal streamers appear at the 2, 7, 9, and 12 o'clock positions, and polar brushes project from the north and south solar poles at 11 and 5 o'clock, respectively.

Photograph by Stephen Bedingfield taken near Casper, Wyoming, under clear skies. He used a Canon 7D, a 100-400-mm lens at 400 mm, ISO 800, f/8.0, and a 1/60-s exposure; some minor adjustments were made to the image.

FIGURE 1—TOTAL LUNAR ECLIPSE OF 2018 JANUARY 31

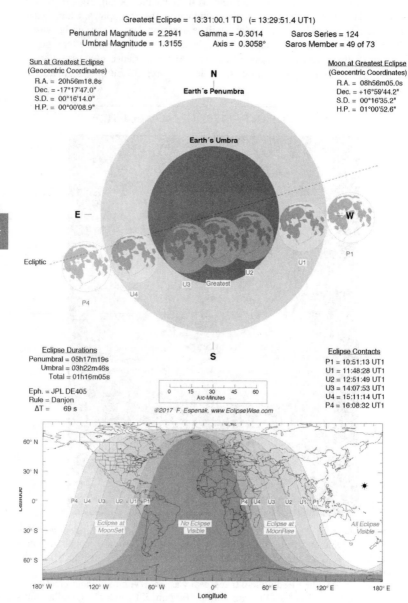

Greatest Eclipse = 13:31:00.1 TD (= 13:29:51.4 UT1)

Penumbral Magnitude = 2.2941   Gamma = -0.3014   Saros Series = 124
Umbral Magnitude = 1.3155   Axis = 0.3058°   Saros Member = 49 of 73

Sun at Greatest Eclipse
(Geocentric Coordinates)
R.A. = 20h56m18.8s
Dec. = -17°17'47.0"
S.D. = 00°16'14.0"
H.P. = 00°00'08.9"

Moon at Greatest Eclipse
(Geocentric Coordinates)
R.A. = 08h56m05.0s
Dec. = +16°59'44.2"
S.D. = 00°16'35.2"
H.P. = 01°00'52.6"

N
Earth's Penumbra

Earth's Umbra

E —   — W

Ecliptic   P1

U2
U3   Greatest   U1

U4

P4

S

Eclipse Durations
Penumbral = 05h17m19s
Umbral = 03h22m46s
Total = 01h16m05s

Eph. = JPL DE405
Rule = Danjon
ΔT = 69 s

0   15   30   45   60
Arc-Minutes

©2017 F. Espenak, www.EclipseWise.com

Eclipse Contacts
P1 = 10:51:13 UT1
U1 = 11:48:28 UT1
U2 = 12:51:49 UT1
U3 = 14:07:53 UT1
U4 = 15:11:14 UT1
P4 = 16:08:32 UT1

See p. 138 for an explanation of this figure.

Table 1 (below) lists predicted umbral immersion and emersion times for 25 well-defined lunar craters. The timing of craters is useful in determining the atmospheric enlargement of Earth's shadow (see Crater Timings During Lunar Eclipses).

The Jan. 31 eclipse is the 49th eclipse of Saros 124. This series began on 1152 Aug. 17 and is composed of 73 lunar eclipses in the following sequence: 20 penumbral, 8 partial, 28 total, 8 partial, and 9 penumbral eclipses (Espenak and Meeus, 2009a). In this context, the Jan. 31 eclipse is the 21st total eclipse in the series. The last total eclipse is on 2144 Apr. 18 and the final eclipse of the series is on 2450 Oct. 21.

For more information about the Jan. 31 total lunar eclipse, see www.EclipseWise.com/lunar/LEprime/2001-2100/LE2018Jan31Tprime.html.

TABLE 1—TOTAL LUNAR ECLIPSE OF 2018 JANUARY 31 CRATER IMMERSION AND EMERSION TIMES

UT of Immersion	Crater Name	UT of Emersion	Crater Name
11:54	Riccioli	14:12	Riccioli
11:54	Aristarchus	14:12	Grimaldi
11:55	Grimaldi	14:15	Billy
11:59	Kepler	14:22	Campanus
12:03	Billy	14:23	Aristarchus
12:04	Pytheas	14:23	Kepler
12:06	Copernicus	14:26	Tycho
12:06	Timocharis	14:32	Copernicus
12:06	Plato	14:33	Pytheas
12:11	Autolycus	14:37	Timocharis
12:14	Aristoteles	14:41	Plato
12:15	Eudoxus	14:44	Autolycus
12:16	Campanus	14:47	Manilius
12:18	Manilius	14:49	Aristoteles
12:20	Menelaus	14:49	Dionysius
12:23	Endymion	14:50	Eudoxus
12:24	Plinius	14:50	Menelaus
12:24	Dionysius	14:54	Plinius
12:29	Tycho	14:56	Censorinus
12:32	Censorinus	14:58	Endymion
12:33	Proclus	15:00	Goclenius
12:36	Taruntius	15:02	Messier
12:38	Messier	15:03	Taruntius
12:39	Goclenius	15:03	Proclus
12:43	Langrenus	15:05	Langrenus

Predictions include a ~1% enlargement of the umbral shadow due to Earth's atmosphere.

FIGURE 2—PARTIAL SOLAR ECLIPSE OF 2018 FEBRUARY 15

Greatest Eclipse = 20:52:33.3 TD (= 20:51:24.3 UT1)

Eclipse Magnitude = 0.5991   Saros Series = 150
Gamma = -1.2116   Saros Member = 17 of 71

Sun at Greatest Eclipse
(Geocentric Coordinates)
R.A. = 21h57m18.8s
Dec. = -12°28'07.3"
S.D. = 00°16'11.4"
H.P. = 00°00'08.9"

Moon at Greatest Eclipse
(Geocentric Coordinates)
R.A. = 21h58m26.9s
Dec. = -13°32'29.9"
S.D. = 00°14'59.4"
H.P. = 00°55'00.9"

External/Internal
Contacts of Penumbra
P1 = 18:55:50.5 UT1
P4 = 22:47:10.3 UT1

ΔT = 69.0 s   Eph. = JPL DE405

Circumstances at Greatest Eclipse: 20:51:24.3 UT1
Lat. = 71°01.6'S   Sun Alt. = 0.0°
Long. = 000°38.5'E   Sun Azm. = 228.4°

©2016 F. Espenak
www.EclipseWise.com

0   1000   2000   3000   4000   5000
Kilometres

Courtesy of the *"21st Century Canon of Solar Eclipses,"* Fred Espenak, AstroPixels Publishing, 2016
Courtesy of the *"21st Century Canon of Solar Eclipses,"* Fred Espenak, AstroPixels Publishing, 2016

See p. 138 for an explanation of this figure.

Partial Solar Eclipse of February 15

The first solar eclipse of 2018 occurs in Capricornus at the Moon's descending node. This Southern Hemisphere event is visible from a wedge-shaped region in the Antarctic Ocean that includes 2/3 of Antarctica and southern South America (Figure 2, at left). At greatest eclipse (20:51:24 UT1), the magnitude is 0.5991.

Local circumstances and eclipse times for a number of cities in South America are listed in Table 2 (below). The Sun's altitude and azimuth, the eclipse magnitude and eclipse obscuration are all given at the instant of maximum eclipse. When the eclipse is in progress at sunset, this information is indicated by "— s".

The 2018 Feb. 15 Solar Eclipse Calculator (www.EclipseWise.com/solar/SEcirc/2001-2100/SE2018Feb15Pcirc.html) is an interactive webpage that can quickly calculate the local circumstances for the eclipse from any geographic location not included in Table 2.

This event is the 17th eclipse of Saros 150. The family will produce 22 partial eclipses, followed by 40 annular eclipses, and ending with 9 more partials. The entire series of 69 eclipses spans the years 1729 through 2991.

For additional information about this partial solar eclipse, see

www.EclipseWise.com/eclipse.html#yr2018

TABLE 2—LOCAL CIRCUMSTANCES FOR THE PARTIAL SOLAR ECLIPSE OF 2018 FEBRUARY 15

Geographic Location		Eclipse Begins h:m	Max. Eclipse h:m	Eclipse Ends h:m	Sun Alt. °	Sun Azm. °	Ecl. Mag.	Ecl. Obsc.
Antarctica	South Pole	19:25	20:23	21:21	13	238	0.508	0.390
	McMurdo	19:07	20:00	20:54	15	80	0.366	0.246
	Palmer	20:13	21:15	22:13	19	282	0.474	0.355
Argentina	Buenos Aires	21:37	22:13	— s	6	259	0.165	0.077
	Cordoba	21:53	22:19	22:44	9	261	0.080	0.026
	Rosario	21:44	22:16	22:47	7	260	0.126	0.052
	San Justo	21:36	22:13	— s	6	259	0.166	0.078
Brazil	Porto Alegre	21:48	22:11s	— s	0	255	0.112	0.043
Chile	Santiago	21:49	22:16	22:42	15	265	0.076	0.024
Uruguay	Montevideo	21:34	22:12	— s	5	258	0.181	0.088

All times are Universal Time (UT1).
'r' indicates an eclipse in progress at sunrise.
's' indicates an eclipse in progress at sunset.

FIGURE 3—PARTIAL SOLAR ECLIPSE OF 2018 JULY 13

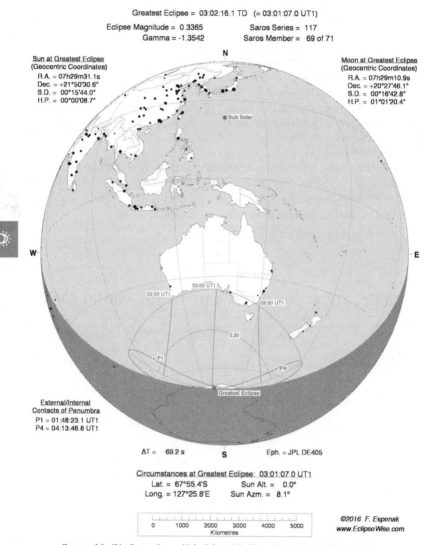

Greatest Eclipse = 03:02:16.1 TD   (= 03:01:07.0 UT1)

Eclipse Magnitude = 0.3365   Saros Series = 117
           Gamma = -1.3542   Saros Member = 69 of 71

Sun at Greatest Eclipse
(Geocentric Coordinates)
R.A. = 07h29m31.1s
Dec. = +21°50'30.6"
S.D. = 00°15'44.0"
H.P. = 00°00'08.7"

Moon at Greatest Eclipse
(Geocentric Coordinates)
R.A. = 07h29m10.9s
Dec. = +20°27'46.1"
S.D. = 00°16'42.8"
H.P. = 01°01'20.4"

External/Internal
Contacts of Penumbra
P1 = 01:48:23.1 UT1
P4 = 04:13:46.8 UT1

ΔT =   69.2 s   S   Eph. = JPL DE405

Circumstances at Greatest Eclipse: 03:01:07.0 UT1
Lat. = 67°55.4'S   Sun Alt. =   0.0°
Long. = 127°25.8'E   Sun Azm. = 8.1°

0   1000   2000   3000   4000   5000
               Kilometres

©2016 F. Espenak
www.EclipseWise.com

Courtesy of the *"21st Century Canon of Solar Eclipses,"* Fred Espenak, AstroPixels Publishing, 2016

See p. 138 for an explanation of this figure.

TABLE 3—LOCAL CIRCUMSTANCES FOR THE PARTIAL SOLAR ECLIPSE OF 2018 JULY 13

COUNTRY	CITY	Eclipse Begins h:m	Maximum Eclipse h:m	Eclipse Ends h:m	Sun Altitude h:m	Sun Azm. °	Eclipse Mag. %	Eclipse Obs. %
Australia	Geelong, VC	03:01	03:20	03:40	29	346	0.032	0.007
	Hobart, TS	02:52	03:25	03:56	23	343	0.095	0.035
	Launceston, TS	02:56	03:25	03:53	25	343	0.072	0.024
	Melbourne, VC	03:05	03:21	03:38	29	345	0.023	0.004

Partial Solar Eclipse of July 13

The next solar eclipse of 2018 occurs in Gemini at the Moon's ascending node. It is also a Southern Hemisphere event and is visible from southeastern Australia and the Antarctic Ocean (Figure 3, at left). At greatest eclipse (03:01:07 UT1), the magnitude is 0.3365.

Local circumstances and eclipse times for a number of cities in Australia appear in Table 3 (above). This is a very minor eclipse from Australia with eclipse magnitudes no greater than 0.10.

This event is the 69th eclipse of Saros 71. The entire series of 71 eclipses spans the years 792 through 2054.

For additional information about this partial solar eclipse, see

www.EclipseWise.com/eclipse.html#yr2018

Total Lunar Eclipse of July 27

The second total lunar eclipse of 2018 occurs at the Moon's descending node in Capricornus. It takes place just 0.6 days after the Moon reaches apogee (Jul. 27 05:44 UT1) so the Moon's apparent size (14′ 43″) is near its minimum.

This total lunar eclipse is even deeper than the first one with the Moon passing through the middle of the umbral shadow. At greatest eclipse, the center of the Moon passes 6.3′ from the axis of the shadow. This corresponds to an umbral eclipse magnitude of 1.6087. Depending on the transparency of Earth's atmosphere, this could be a very dark eclipse.

The times of the major eclipse phases are as follows.

Penumbral Eclipse Begins:	17:14:48 UT1
Partial Eclipse Begins:	18:24:28 UT1
Total Eclipse Begins:	19:30:17 UT1
Greatest Eclipse:	20:21:45 UT1
Total Eclipse Ends:	21:13:14 UT1
Partial Eclipse Ends:	22:19:03 UT1
Penumbral Eclipse Ends:	23:28:42 UT1

At the instant of greatest eclipse (20:21:45 UT1), the Moon lies near the zenith from a location in the Indian Ocean just east of Madagascar. The event is well placed for observers in Europe, Africa, Asia, and Australia. None of the eclipse will be

FIGURE 4—TOTAL LUNAR ECLIPSE OF 2018 JULY 27

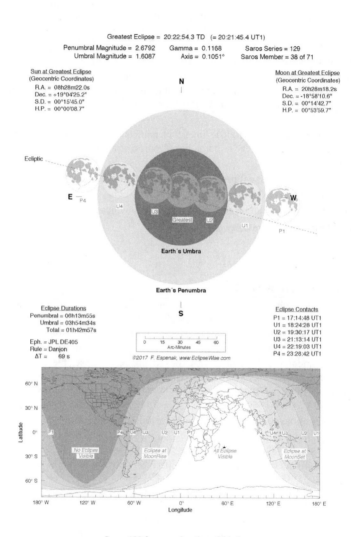

Greatest Eclipse = 20:22:54.3 TD   (= 20:21:45.4 UT1)

Penumbral Magnitude = 2.6792   Gamma = 0.1168   Saros Series = 129
Umbral Magnitude = 1.6087   Axis = 0.1051°   Saros Member = 38 of 71

Sun at Greatest Eclipse
(Geocentric Coordinates)
R.A. = 08h28m22.0s
Dec. = +19°04'25.2"
S.D. = 00°15'45.0"
H.P. = 00°00'08.7"

Moon at Greatest Eclipse
(Geocentric Coordinates)
R.A. = 20h28m18.2s
Dec. = -18°58'10.6"
S.D. = 00°14'42.7"
H.P. = 00°53'59.7"

Ecliptic

Earth's Umbra

Earth's Penumbra

Eclipse Durations
Penumbral = 06h13m55s
Umbral = 03h54m34s
Total = 01h42m57s

Eph. = JPL DE405
Rule = Danjon
ΔT =   69 s

Eclipse Contacts
P1 = 17:14:48 UT1
U1 = 18:24:28 UT1
U2 = 19:30:17 UT1
U3 = 21:13:14 UT1
U4 = 22:19:03 UT1
P4 = 23:28:42 UT1

©2017 F. Espenak, www.EclipseWise.com

See p. 138 for an explanation of this figure.

TABLE 4—TOTAL LUNAR ECLIPSE OF 2018 JULY 27
CRATER IMMERSION AND EMERSION TIMES

UT of Immersion	Crater Name	UT of Emersion	Crater Name
18:26	Riccioli	21:15	Riccioli
18:27	Grimaldi	21:16	Grimaldi
18:32	Billy	21:23	Billy
18:39	Kepler	21:23	Aristarchus
18:41	Campanus	21:26	Kepler
18:41	Aristarchus	21:33	Campanus
18:48	Copernicus	21:35	Pytheas
18:49	Tycho	21:36	Copernicus
18:51	Pytheas	21:38	Plato
18:56	Timocharis	21:38	Timocharis
19:04	Autolycus	21:40	Tycho
19:04	Manilius	21:45	Autolycus
19:05	Plato	21:48	Aristoteles
19:07	Dionysius	21:50	Eudoxus
19:08	Menelaus	21:51	Manilius
19:12	Plinius	21:55	Menelaus
19:13	Eudoxus	21:57	Dionysius
19:14	Aristoteles	21:58	Endymion
19:14	Censorinus	21:59	Plinius
19:18	Goclenius	22:05	Censorinus
19:20	Messier	22:09	Proclus
19:21	Taruntius	22:10	Goclenius
19:22	Proclus	22:10	Taruntius
19:23	Langrenus	22:11	Messier
19:24	Endymion	22:15	Langrenus

Predictions include a ~1% enlargement of the umbral shadow due to Earth's atmosphere.

visible from North America. South America will see some of the late stages of the eclipse as the Moon rises.

Table 4 (above) lists predicted umbral immersion and emersion times for 25 well-defined lunar craters. The timing of craters is useful in determining the atmospheric enlargement of Earth's shadow (see Crater Timings During Lunar Eclipses).

The July 27 eclipse is the 38th eclipse of Saros 129. This series began on 1351 Jun. 10 and is composed of 71 lunar eclipses in the following sequence: 10 penumbral, 21 partial, 11 total, 21 partial, and 8 penumbral eclipses (Espenak and Meeus, 2009a). The last total eclipse is on 2090 Sep. 08 and the final eclipse of the series is on 2613 Jul. 24.

For more information about the Jul. 27 total lunar eclipse, see

www.eclipsewise.com/lunar/LEprime/2001-2100/LE2018Jul27Tprime.html

FIGURE 5—PARTIAL SOLAR ECLIPSE OF 2018 AUGUST 11

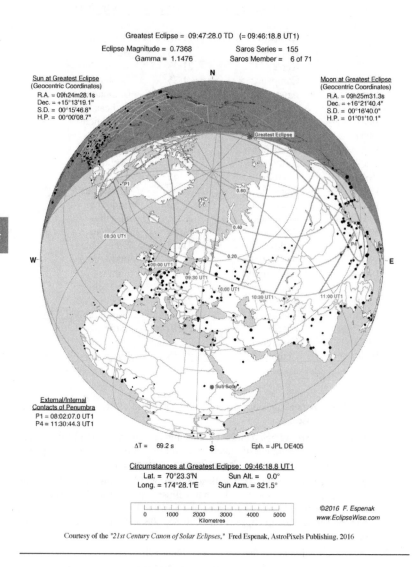

Greatest Eclipse = 09:47:28.0 TD (= 09:46:18.8 UT1)

Eclipse Magnitude = 0.7368   Saros Series = 155
Gamma = 1.1476   Saros Member = 6 of 71

Sun at Greatest Eclipse
(Geocentric Coordinates)
R.A. = 09h24m28.1s
Dec. = +15°13'19.1"
S.D. = 00°15'46.8"
H.P. = 00°00'08.7"

Moon at Greatest Eclipse
(Geocentric Coordinates)
R.A. = 09h25m31.3s
Dec. = +16°21'40.4"
S.D. = 00°16'40.0"
H.P. = 01°01'10.1"

External/Internal
Contacts of Penumbra
P1 = 08:02:07.0 UT1
P4 = 11:30:44.3 UT1

ΔT = 69.2 s   Eph. = JPL DE405

Circumstances at Greatest Eclipse: 09:46:18.8 UT1
Lat. = 70°23.3'N   Sun Alt. = 0.0°
Long. = 174°28.1'E   Sun Azm. = 321.5°

0   1000   2000   3000   4000   5000
Kilometres

©2016 F. Espenak
www.EclipseWise.com

Courtesy of the *"21st Century Canon of Solar Eclipses,"* Fred Espenak, AstroPixels Publishing, 2016

See p. 138 for an explanation of this figure.

TABLE 5 — LOCAL CIRCUMSTANCES FOR THE PARTIAL SOLAR ECLIPSE OF 2018 AUGUST 11

COUNTRY	CITY	Eclipse Begins h:m	Maximum Eclipse h:m	Eclipse Ends h:m	Sun Altitude h:m	Sun Azm. °	Eclipse Mag. %	Eclipse Obs. %
Arctic	North Pole	08:35	09:25	10:15	15	140	0.625	0.543
China	Beijing	10:12	10:51	- s	4	287	0.341	0.230
	Chengdu	10:46	11:07	11:28	8	283	0.085	0.030
	Chongqin	10:47	11:08	11:28	6	284	0.080	0.027
	Harbin	09:56	10:39	- s	1	291	0.480	0.375
	Nanjing	10:30	10:52s	- s	0	288	0.189	0.097
	Shanghai	10:30	10:40s	- s	0	288	0.105	0.041
	Shenyang	10:06	10:46	- s	1	290	0.407	0.297
	Tianjin	10:14	10:52	- s	3	287	0.332	0.221
	Wuhan	10:37	11:04	- s	1	288	0.152	0.070
	Xi'an	10:30	11:01	11:31	6	284	0.192	0.099
	Zibo	10:19	10:55	- s	1	288	0.295	0.186
Finland	Helsinki	08:51	09:18	09:45	43	157	0.079	0.027
Iceland	Reykjav√≠k	08:10	08:44	09:20	21	99	0.198	0.104
Kazakhstan	Alma-Ata	10:15	10:41	11:07	35	257	0.090	0.033
Korea, South	Seoul	10:13	10:29s	- s	0	290	0.217	0.119
Mongolia	Ulaanbaatar	09:56	10:41	11:23	14	277	0.409	0.298
Norway	Oslo	08:41	09:01	09:22	39	135	0.049	0.013
Russia	Chelyabinsk	09:28	10:07	10:44	43	224	0.174	0.086
	Gorki	09:18	09:44	10:11	48	193	0.073	0.024
	Kazan	09:22	09:52	10:21	48	203	0.095	0.035
	Moscow	09:22	09:36	09:51	49	180	0.021	0.004
	Novosibirsk	09:36	10:23	11:07	31	251	0.339	0.229
	Omsk	09:33	10:17	11:00	37	241	0.266	0.161
	Perm	09:17	09:57	10:36	44	213	0.191	0.099
	St. Petersburg	08:56	09:24	09:53	45	166	0.091	0.033
	Ufa	09:28	10:01	10:34	46	216	0.123	0.051
Svalbard & Jan Mayen Is.	Svalbard	08:30	09:19	10:09	26	157	0.456	0.349
Sweden	Stockholm	08:50	09:09	09:29	42	145	0.042	0.010

Partial Solar Eclipse of August 11

The last eclipse of the year is the third partial solar eclipse. It occurs in Leo at the Moon's ascending node. This time the event is visible from the Northern Hemisphere and includes northeastern Canada, Greenland, Iceland, Northern Europe, north and eastern Asia (Figure 5, at left). At greatest eclipse (09:46:19 UT1), the magnitude is 0.7368.

Local circumstances and eclipse times for a number of cities in Europe and Asia are listed in Table 5 above. The Sun's altitude and azimuth, the eclipse magnitude and eclipse obscuration are all given at the instant of maximum eclipse. When the eclipse is in progress at sunset, this information is indicated by "– s".

The 2018 Aug 11 Solar Eclipse Calculator (www.EclipseWise.com/solar/SEcirc/2001-2100/SE2018Aug11Pcirc.html) is an interactive web page that can quickly calculate the local circumstances for the eclipse

For additional information about this partial solar eclipse, see www.EclipseWise.com/eclipse.html#yr2018

Explanation of Solar Eclipse Figures

For each solar eclipse, an orthographic projection map of Earth shows the path of penumbral (partial) eclipse. North is to the top in all cases and the daylight terminator is plotted for the instant of greatest eclipse. An asterisk (*) indicates the sub-solar point on Earth.

Current political borders are plotted for easy reference. The black dots represent major cities, where the size of the dot is an indication of the population size.

The limits of the Moon's penumbral shadow delineate the region of visibility of the partial solar eclipse. This irregular or saddle shaped region often covers more than half of the daylight hemisphere of Earth and consists of several distinct zones or limits. At the northern and/or southern boundaries lie the limits of the penumbra's path. Partial eclipses have only one of these limits, as do central eclipses when the Moon's shadow axis falls no closer than about 0.45 radii from Earth's center.

Great loops at the western and eastern extremes of the penumbra's path identify the areas where the eclipse begins/ends at sunrise and sunset, respectively. If the penumbra has both a northern and southern limit, the rising and setting curves form two separate, closed loops. Otherwise, the curves are connected in a distorted figure eight. Bisecting the "eclipse begins/ends at sunrise and sunset" loops is the curve of maximum eclipse at sunrise (western loop) and sunset (eastern loop. The points P1 and P4 mark the coordinates where the penumbral shadow first contacts (partial eclipse begins) and last contacts (partial eclipse ends) Earth's surface. If the penumbral path has both a northern and southern limit, then points P2 and P3 are also plotted. These correspond to the coordinates where the penumbral shadow cone is internally tangent to Earth's disk.

A curve of maximum eclipse is the locus of all points where the eclipse is at maximum at a given time. Curves of maximum eclipse are plotted at each half-hour Universal Time (UT1) and are labelled with the time. They generally run between the penumbral limits in the north/south direction, or from the maximum eclipse at sunrise and sunset curves to one of the limits.

The curves of constant eclipse magnitude delineate the locus of all points where the magnitude at maximum eclipse is constant. These curves run between the curves of maximum eclipse at sunrise and sunset. They are roughly parallel to the northern/southern penumbral limits. In fact, the northern and southern limits of the penumbra are curves of constant magnitude of 0.0. The adjacent curves are for magnitudes of 0.2, 0.4, 0.6 and 0.8 and are labeled as such.

Greatest eclipse is defined as the instant when the axis of the Moon's shadow passes closest to Earth's center. An asterisk (*) marks the point on Earth's surface intersected by the lunar shadow axis at greatest eclipse. For partial eclipses, the shadow axis misses Earth entirely, so the point of greatest eclipse lies on the day/night terminator and the Sun appears on the horizon.

Data pertinent to the eclipse appear with each map. At the top is listed the instant of greatest eclipse, expressed in both Terrestrial Dynamical Time and Universal Time. The eclipse magnitude is defined as the fraction of the Sun's diameter obscured by the Moon at greatest eclipse. For central eclipses, the magnitude listed is actually the geocentric ratio of diameters of the Moon and the Sun. Gamma is the minimum distance (in Earth radii) of the Moon's shadow axis from Earth's center at greatest eclipse. The Saros series of the eclipse is listed, followed by the member position. The first number

---

[4]   The sub-solar point is the geographic location where the Sun appears directly overhead (zenith).

identifies the sequence position of the eclipse in the Saros, while the second number is the number of eclipses in the entire series.

In the upper left and right corners are the geocentric coordinates of the Sun and the Moon, respectively, at the instant of greatest eclipse. They are:

RA   Right Ascension
Dec Declination
S.D. Apparent Semi-Diameter
H.P. Horizontal Parallax

To the lower left are exterior/interior contact times of the Moon's penumbra with Earth, which are defined:

P1   Instant of first exterior tangency of penumbra with Earth's limb
      (partial eclipse begins)
P4   Instant of last exterior tangency of penumbra with Earth's limb.
      (partial eclipse ends)

At the bottom are the geographic coordinates of the position of greatest eclipse along with the local circumstances at that location (i.e., Sun altitude, Sun azimuth).

The solar eclipse figures are courtesy of *21st Century Year Canon of Solar Eclipses* (Espenak, 2016).

Lunar Eclipse Figures

Each lunar eclipse has two diagrams associated with it along with data pertinent to the eclipse. The top figure shows the path of the Moon through Earth's penumbral and umbral shadows. Above this figure are listed the instant of ecliptic conjunction of the Moon with the point 180° from the Sun (i.e., Full Moon) and the instant of greatest eclipse, expressed in Terrestrial Dynamical Time and Universal Time. The penumbral and umbral magnitudes are defined as the fraction of the Moon's diameter immersed in the two shadows at greatest eclipse. Gamma is the minimum distance in Earth radii of the Moon's center from Earth's shadow axis at greatest eclipse, and Axis is the same parameter expressed in degrees. The Saros series of the eclipse is listed, followed by a pair of numbers. The first number identifies the sequence position of the eclipse in the Saros; the second is the total number of eclipses in the series.

In the upper left and right corners are the geocentric coordinates of the Sun and the Moon, respectively, at the instant of greatest eclipse. They are:

RA Right Ascension
Dec Declination
S.D. Apparent Semi-Diameter
H.P. Horizontal Parallax

To the lower left are the semi-durations (half-durations) of the penumbral, umbral (partial), and total eclipses. Below them are the extrapolated value of ΔT (the difference between Terrestrial Dynamical Time and Universal Time) and the Sun/Moon ephemerides used in the predictions. To the lower right are the contact times of the Moon with Earth's penumbral and umbral shadows, defined as follows:

P1   Instant of first exterior tangency of Moon with penumbra
        (penumbral eclipse begins)
U1   Instant of first exterior tangency of Moon with umbra
        (partial umbral eclipse begins)
U2   Instant of first interior tangency of Moon with umbra
        (T\total umbral eclipse begins)
U3   Instant of last interior tangency of Moon with umbra
        (total umbral eclipse ends)
U4   Instant of last exterior tangency of Moon with umbra
        (partial umbral eclipse ends)
P4   Instant of last exterior tangency of Moon with penumbra
        (penumbral eclipse ends)

The bottom figure is a cylindrical equidistant projection map of Earth that shows the regions of visibility for each stage of the eclipse. In particular, the moonrise/moonset terminator is plotted for each contact and is labelled accordingly. An asterisk indicates the point where the Moon is at the zenith at greatest eclipse. The region that is unshaded will observe the entire eclipse, while the darkly shaded area will witness no eclipse. The remaining lightly shaded areas will experience moonrise or moonset while the eclipse is in progress. The lightly shaded zones east of the asterisk (*) will witness moonset before the eclipse ends, and the lightly shaded zones west will witness moonrise after the eclipse has begun.

The lunar eclipse figures are updates of versions originally published in *Fifty Year Canon of Lunar Eclipses: 1986–2035* (Espenak, 1989).

Danjon Scale of Lunar Eclipse Brightness

The Moon's appearance during a total lunar eclipse can vary enormously from one eclipse to the next. Obviously, the geometry of the Moon's path through the umbra plays an important role. Not as apparent is the effect that Earth's atmosphere has on total eclipses. Although the physical mass of Earth blocks all direct sunlight from the umbra, the planet's atmosphere refracts some of the Sun's rays into the shadow. Earth's atmosphere contains varying amounts of water (clouds, mist, precipitation) and solid particles (meteoric dust, organic debris, volcanic ash). This material significantly filters and attenuates the sunlight before it is refracted into the umbra. For instance, very dark, red eclipses often follow large or frequent volcanic eruptions, which dump huge quantities of ash into the atmosphere for several years. Extensive cloud cover along Earth's limb also tends to darken the eclipse by blocking sunlight. The French astronomer André-Louis Danjon proposed a useful five-point scale for evaluating the visual appearance and brightness of the Moon during total lunar eclipses. L values for various luminosities are defined as follows:

L=0 Very dark eclipse.
        (Moon almost invisible, especially at mid-totality)
L=1 Dark eclipse, grey or brownish in coloration.
        (details distinguishable only with difficulty)
L=2 Deep red or rust-colored eclipse.
        (very dark central shadow, while outer umbra is relatively bright)

L=3 Brick-red eclipse.
(umbral shadow usually has a bright or yellow rim)
L=4 Very bright copper-red or orange eclipse.
(umbral shadow has a bluish, very bright rim)

The assignment of an L value to lunar eclipses is best done with the naked eye, binoculars, or a small telescope near the time of mid-totality. It is also useful to examine the Moon's appearance just after the beginning and just before the end of totality. The Moon is then near the edge of the shadow, providing an opportunity to assign an L value to the outer umbra. In making any evaluations, the instrumentation used and the time should both be recorded. Also note any variations in color and brightness in different parts of the umbra, as well as the apparent sharpness of the shadow's edge. Pay attention to the visibility of lunar features within the umbra. Notes and sketches made during the eclipse are often invaluable in recalling important details, events, and impressions.

Crater Timings During Lunar Eclipses

In 1702, Pierre de La Hire made a curious observation about Earth's umbra. In order to accurately predict the duration of a lunar eclipse, he found it necessary to increase the radius of the shadow about 1% more than is warranted by geometric considerations. Although the effect is clearly related to Earth's atmosphere, it is not completely understood, since the shadow enlargement seems to vary from one eclipse to the next. The enlargement can be measured through careful timings of lunar craters as they enter and exit the umbra.

Such observations are best made using a low-power telescope and a clock or watch synchronized with radio time signals. Timings should be made to a precision of about 5 seconds. Record the instant when the most abrupt gradient at the umbra's edge crosses the apparent center of the crater. In the case of large craters like Tycho and Copernicus, record the times when the shadow touches the two opposite edges of the crater. The average of these times is equal to the instant of crater bisection.

As a planning guide, Tables 1 and 4 list a number of well-defined craters with predicted umbral immersion and emersion times during the two lunar eclipses of 2018. You should be thoroughly familiar with these features before viewing an eclipse in order to prevent confusion and misidentification. The four umbral contacts with the Moon's limb can also be used in determining the shadow's enlargement. However, these events are less distinct and therefore difficult to time accurately. Observers are encouraged to make crater timings and to send their results to Sky & Telescope (Sky & Telescope, 90 Sherman Street, Cambridge MA 02140-3264, USA) for analysis.

All predictions presented here use Danjon's rule of shadow enlargement (see: Shadow Diameters and Lunar Eclipses). In particular, the diameter of the umbral shadow has been calculated assuming an enlargement of Earth's radius of 1/85 to account for the opacity of the terrestrial atmosphere. The effects of Earth's oblateness have also been included.

Shadow Diameters and Lunar Eclipses

To compensate for Earth's atmosphere when calculating the circumstances for lunar eclipses, Chauvenet [1891] introduced an empirical enlargement of 1/50 to the diameters of the umbral and penumbral shadows. This rule has been employed by many of the national institutes in their official eclipse predictions (including the author's work at NASA). However, Danjon [1951] pointed out a flaw in this method because it applies the same relative correction to the umbra and penumbra instead of using the same absolute correction. From eclipse observations, Danjon proposed to enlarge Earth's diameter by 1/85 to compensate for the atmosphere. The umbral and penumbral shadow diameters are then calculated based on this modified geometry. The French almanac *Connaissance des Temps* has used the Danjon rule in its eclipse predictions since 1951. The resulting umbral and penumbral eclipse magnitudes are smaller by approximately 0.005 and 0.026, respectively, as compared to predictions using the traditional 1/50 rule.

In Eclipses During 2018, the Danjon rule is used in calculating lunar eclipse circumstances and magnitudes.

Eclipse Altitudes and Azimuths

The altitude a and azimuth A of the Sun or Moon during an eclipse depends on the time and the observer's geographic coordinates. They are calculated as follows:

h $\quad = 15\,(GST + UT - \alpha) + \lambda,$
a $\quad = \arcsin [\, \sin \delta \sin \varphi + \cos \delta \cos h \cos \varphi \,],$ and
A $\quad = \arctan [\, -(\cos \delta \sin h) / (\sin \delta \cos \varphi - \cos \delta \cos h \sin \varphi) \,],$

in which:

h $\quad$ = Hour Angle of Sun or Moon,
a $\quad$ = Altitude,
A $\quad$ = Azimuth,
GST = Greenwich Sidereal Time at 0:00 UT,
UT $\quad$ = Universal Time,
α $\quad$ = RA of Sun or Moon,
δ $\quad$ = Dec of Sun or Moon,
λ $\quad$ = Observer's Longitude (East +, West −), and
φ $\quad$ = Observer's Latitude (North +, South −).

During the eclipses of 2018, the values for GST and the geocentric Right Ascension and Declination of the Sun or the Moon (at greatest eclipse) are as follows:

Eclipse	Date	GST	α	δ
Total Lunar	Jan. 31	8.715	8.935	16.996
Partial Solar	Feb. 15	9.721	21.955	−12.469
Partial Solar	Jul. 13	19.397	7.492	21.842
Total Lunar	Jul. 27	20.364	20.472	−18.970
Partial Solar	Aug. 11	21.321	9.408	15.222

Two web-based tools can also be used to calculate the local circumstances for all solar and lunar eclipses visible from any location. They are the Javascript Solar

Eclipse Explorer and the JavaScript Lunar Eclipse Explorer. The URLs for these two tools are

www.eclipsewise.com/solar/JSEX/JSEX-index.html, and
www.eclipsewise.com/lunar/JLEX/JLEX-index.html

In 2019, there are three solar eclipses and two lunar eclipses:

Jan. 06:	Partial Solar Eclipse
Jan. 21:	Total Lunar Eclipse
Jul. 02:	Total Solar Eclipse
Jul. 16:	Partial Lunar Eclipse
Dec. 26:	Annular Solar Eclipse

A full report on these eclipses will be published in the *Observer's Handbook 2019*.
Additional information may be found at www.EclipseWise.com/eclipse.html#yr2019

Eclipse Websites

EclipseWise.com is a website dedicated to predictions and information on eclipses of the Sun and Moon. It offers a graphically intuitive interface and contains maps, diagrams, tables, and information about every solar and lunar eclipse from 2000 BCE to 3000 CE. This period includes 11 898 solar eclipses and 12 064 lunar eclipses.

Much of EclipseWise is based on the newly published *Thousand Year Canon of Solar Eclipses: 1501 to 2500* (Espenak 2014a) and the *Thousand Year Canon of Lunar Eclipses: 1501 to 2500* (Espenak 2014b). These eclipse predictions use the Jet Propulsion Lab's DE406—a computer ephemeris used for calculating high-precision coordinates of the Sun and Moon for thousands of years into the past and future.

Although still available, the older NASA website (eclipse.gsfc.nasa.gov/eclipse.html) has been retired as an archival reference source for eclipse predictions prior to 2015. Predictions for future eclipses will be posted on the newer EclipseWise.com website.

Detailed information on solar and lunar eclipse photography, and tips on eclipse observing and eye safety may be found at www.mreclipse.com/MrEclipse.html.

Acknowledgments

All eclipse predictions were generated on a Macintosh G4 PowerPC using algorithms developed from the *Explanatory Supplement...* [1974] with additional algorithms from Meeus, Grosjean, and Vanderleen [1966]. The solar and lunar coordinates used in the eclipse predictions are based on the JPL DE405. For lunar eclipses, the diameter of the umbral and penumbral shadows was calculated using Danjon's rule of enlarging Earth's radius by 1/85 to compensate for the opacity of the terrestrial atmosphere; corrections for the effects of oblateness have also been included.

All calculations, diagrams, tables, and opinions presented in this paper are those of the author, and he assumes full responsibility for their accuracy. This publication is available electronically at www.EclipseWise.com/oh/ec2018.html with additional information and updates.

References and Bibliography

Chauvenet, W., *Manual of Spherical and Practical Astronomy,* Vol.1, 1891 (Dover edition 1961).

Danjon, A., "Les éclipses de Lune par la pénombre en 1951," *L'Astronomie, 65*, 51-53 (Feb. 1951).

Espenak, F. and Meeus, J., *Five Millennium Canon of Solar Eclipses: −2000 to +3000 (2000 BCE to 3000 CE),* NASA TP–2006-214141, Goddard Space Flight Center, Greenbelt, MD (2006).

Espenak, F. and Meeus, J., *Five Millennium Canon of Lunar Eclipses: −2000 to +3000 (2000 BCE to 3000 CE),* NASA TP–2009-214172, Goddard Space Flight Center, Greenbelt, MD (2009a).

Espenak, F., *Thousand Year Canon of Solar Eclipses: 1501 to 2500,* Astropixels Publishing, Portal, AZ (2014a).

Espenak, F., *Thousand Year Canon of Lunar Eclipses: 1501 to 2500,* Astropixels Publishing, Portal, AZ (2014b).

Espenak, F., *21st Century Canon of Solar Eclipses,* Astropixels Publishing, Portal, AZ (2016).

Explanatory Supplement to the Astronomical Ephemeris and the American Ephemeris and Nautical Almanac, Her Majesty's Nautical Almanac Office, London, 1974.

VIEWING A SOLAR ECLIPSE—A WARNING

Solar eclipses are among the most widely publicized and observed celestial events. It is essential to be aware of the visual danger associated with a solar eclipse. The safety rule is simple but not widely appreciated: **Never look at the surface of the Sun, either directly with the unaided eyes or through binoculars or a telescope.** To do so one risks permanent partial blindness, and this can occur almost instantly in the case of telescopic viewing. Viewing our Sun is just as dangerous on any clear day, but at the time of an eclipse people have a reason to want to look at it—and often resort to dangerous methods.

A direct view of the Sun is safe only if a suitable filter is used in a proper manner. In the case of binoculars or a telescope, the filter must be one that attaches *securely* to the *front* end of the instrument, never one that attaches to the eyepiece end (the heat developed near the eyepiece can shatter such a filter).

Filters specifically designed for solar viewing include aluminized Mylar and glass filters plated with a slightly transparent, metallic film. Such filters may be purchased at telescope supply stores. Shade #14 (no other shade) rectangular welder's glass may be used; however, since these filters are of low optical quality, they are useful only for views not involving binoculars or a telescope. All of these are commercial items and cannot be replaced with ordinary household items. For example, layers of photographic color film, colored glass, stacked sunglasses, crossed polarizers, smoked glass, or photographic neutral-density filters must never be used. Although one may devise a combination that dims the *visible* sunlight to a comfortable level, the makeshift filter may be quite transparent in the infrared part of the solar spectrum, and this invisible radiation will damage the retina of the observer's eye. For the same reason, one must never rely on clouds or heavy atmospheric haze to dim the solar image when using a telescope. Two layers of fully exposed and developed, silver-based, black and white photographic film provides adequate protection, but many modern films, including all color films, are based on dyes that do not provide protection in the infrared. Thus it is best to avoid using filters made of photographic film.

One of the simplest, safest, and least known ways to observe the partial phases of a solar eclipse is *pinhole mirror projection*. Take a small pocket mirror and, with masking tape, cover all but a small section of the mirror's surface. The shape and size of the small opening are not critical, but a square about 6 mm on a side works well. Prop the mirror up on a sunny windowsill and orient the mirror so the reflected sunlight shines on the ceiling or a wall of the room—but not directly into anyone's eyes! The spot of light on the viewing surface will be a *pinhole image* of the solar disk. The mirror has a great advantage over the usual "pinhole-in-a-box arrangement" in that the image can be aimed across a substantial distance to a convenient viewing screen. The greater the projection distance, the larger, but dimmer, the Sun's image. The size of the mirror aperture should be adjusted for the best compromise between image brightness and image sharpness. With this simple device the progress of a solar eclipse can be viewed in complete safety by a group of children in a darkened room.

A sharper and brighter image of the solar disk may be projected onto a white viewing screen placed 30 or 40 cm behind the eyepiece of binoculars or a small telescope (the telescope aperture should be stopped down to about 50 mm in order to limit the intensity of sunlight passing through the instrument, and the viewing screen should be shielded from direct sunlight). However, one must *not* look through the instrument when aiming it, and, especially if children are present, a physical barrier should be used to prevent anyone from attempting to look into the eyepiece. If the telescope has a finderscope, it should be either covered or removed.

ECLIPSE HISTORY
BY JAMES EDGAR

Eclipses have been recorded in history for as long as there have been records. Ancient Greeks used the term *ekleipsis*, meaning "the abandonment" or "the darkening of a heavenly body," from which we derive the current term. Experiencing a total solar eclipse is unforgettable, and such events created great fear in early observers.

Even though early astrologers (for it was they who kept track of heavenly events) were familiar with the apparent movements in the Solar System, measurements weren't precise enough and their Earth-centered model inadequate to establish that the Sun is at the center of the Solar System. Nor did they know at first what caused the Sun to suddenly darken for part of a day.

A standing-stone monument inscribed with petroglyphs at the Loughcrew Cairn L in Ireland is believed to record the solar eclipse of 3340 Nov. 30 BCE. Another record from China likely marks the day when "the Sun and Moon did not meet harmoniously" on 2134 Oct. 22 BCE. Fear that the Sun may not come back was quite real at that time. According to Chinese tradition, loud noises, banging drums and pots, and even shouting scared away the "dragon" that was eating the Sun.

Later scribes in Babylon kept careful records of celestial events on clay tablets, some of which exist to this day. We know from one of these records that on 1063 Jul. 31 BCE, a total solar eclipse "turned day into night." Assyrian observers in Nineveh wrote of the eclipse of 763 Jun. 15 BCE. These careful records led to the discovery of the Saros cycle (see p. 122). By about 610 BCE, Thales of Miletus was able to predict a solar eclipse, but his method does not survive. Ptolemy's writings in the *Almagest* around 150 CE show that he had a method for predicting both lunar and solar eclipses. The findings of Meton were widely known around the Mediterranean by then, as well (see p. 124).

For many, an eclipse was no longer something to be feared, but an interesting celestial regularity, something to anticipate with joy and excitement, much like today.

Science enters the picture

Many discoveries have occurred in the years since Ptolemy: solar prominences were first reported in 334 CE; a comet was observed during an eclipse in 418; Johannes Kepler wrote an accurate description of a total solar eclipse in 1605; Edmund Halley made an extremely accurate prediction of the solar eclipse of 1715 May 3, only missing the mark by 4 min and 30 km. The solar corona puzzled many observers, but by 1724, the proposal that it was part of the Sun met with acceptance. Francis Baily, in 1836, noted the "beads" of light that now bear his name—rays of light streaming through the mountain passes on the lunar limb as the eclipse is about to begin and then end. Helium was discovered as an element from a solar spectral line during a total solar eclipse in 1868, and a new element, "coronium," caused a brief flurry of excitement in 1869, until it was finally confirmed in 1941 to be ionized iron.

Sir Arthur Eddington is famously known for confirming Albert Einstein's prediction in his general theory of relativity that an object's mass "warps" spacetime, such that light travelling from a distant star curves past the edge of the Sun. The first proposal to measure the amount of bend came in the middle of WW I, but was postponed until after the war's end. Eddington chose the island of Principe off Africa's western coast to observe and photograph the eclipse of 1919 May 29, where the Moon's shadow, having crossed

South America and the southern Atlantic Ocean, would pass right over his vantage point.

Fortuitously, in late May, the Sun is set against the bright stars of the Hyades star cluster, which, of course, would be obscured by the Sun's glare except during an eclipse. Even though the images Eddington recorded were of poor quality, the measurements derived from them showed that light does indeed bend near the edge of the Sun, and by the amount predicted by Einstein. This effect has been measured to exquisite accuracy, even with stars occulted by Jupiter. Gravitational lensing is a similar effect, and observations of such events are now used routinely to study the nature of very distant stars and galaxies.

Lunar Eclipses

Although not as spectacular as total solar eclipses, lunar eclipses also have been equally studied since ancient times, contributing to myths in many cultures. Was it a sow eating the Moon, as the Egyptians thought? Did a jaguar eat the Mayan Moon? Did a three-legged toad in China swallow the Moon whole? Many cultures—many myths. Careful study, though, especially by the ancient Greeks, led to discoveries such as the Saros and Metonic cycles. The early Greeks even declared that Earth is round like a globe, because the shadow cast on the Moon during an eclipse is always round.

Columbus is remembered for his "discovery" of the Americas, but he also famously used lunar eclipse predictions, stating that he could make the Moon disappear and then reappear to frighten the natives in Jamaica who were rebelling against the Spaniards eating all their food. He pulled off the stunt. The next day the natives continued to supply food.

Superstition has generally given way to scientific study and accurate measurement of events. As explained by Fred Espenak in the preceding pages, measuring crater timings—the moment when Earth's umbral shadow encroaches on a crater's central point—gives valuable information about the size of the shadow. A better way to measure is to accurately note the time when the shadow touches the crater rims, then divide the difference by 2 to get the average central time. It's known that Earth's shadow will be slightly larger than geometry requires, but what is still not well understood is why the enlargement varies from one eclipse to another, or what it is about Earth's atmosphere that causes such variation.

Eclipsophiles

When Eddington traveled to Principe to observe and measure during the 1919 eclipse, it was a big deal. Travel wasn't easy, and he traveled with a lot of baggage. These days, with easy travel arrangements, eclipsophiles can go anywhere in the world to bask in the glory of the Moon's shadow. And they do. There are at least two solar eclipses per year, and often one of them proves to be total. Many are the photos from people who travel to wherever the eclipse track takes them—the Australian Outback, Africa, onboard a ship, and even flying in a specially chartered aircraft to chase the shadow!

People continue to talk about the Great Eclipse of 2009, during which totality lasted over 6 minutes. This included travel to East Asia to see it. How about the one over northeast Australia in 2012? Or Svalbard in 2015? Many were the astronomers who visited those countries to see the Sun blotted out by the Moon. The hobby is more than a passion to some, who will continue to calculate, plan, and seek out places to get a fleeting glimpse of nature's amazing wonder—a total solar eclipse.

THE MOON

MAP OF THE MOON
BY ROY BISHOP

Maria	
LS	Lacus Somniorum (Lake of Dreams) (330°)
MC	Mare Crisium (Sea of Crises) (300°)
MFe	Mare Fecunditatis (Sea of Fertility) (310°)
MFr	Mare Frigoris (Sea of Cold) (0°)
MH	Mare Humorum (Sea of Moisture) (40°)
MI	Mare Imbrium (Sea of Rains) (20°)
MNe	Mare Nectaris (Sea of Nectar) (325°)
MNu	Mare Nubium (Sea of Clouds) (15°)
MS	Mare Serenitatis (Sea of Serenity) (340°)
MT	Mare Tranquillitatis (Sea of Tranquillity) (330°)
MV	Mare Vaporum (Sea of Vapours) (355°)
OP	Oceanus Procellarum (Ocean of Storms) (50°)
SA	Sinus Aestuum (Seething Bay) (8°)
SI	Sinus Iridum (Bay of Rainbows) (32°)
SM	Sinus Medii (Central Bay) (0°)
SR	Sinus Roris (Bay of Dew) (60°)

Lunar Probes

2 *Luna 2*, First to reach Moon (1959-9-13) (0°)
7 *Ranger 7*, First close pictures (1964-7-31) (21°)
9 *Luna 9*, First soft landing (1966-2-3) (64°)
11 *Apollo 11*, First men on Moon (1969-7-20) (337°)
12 *Apollo 12* (1969-11-19) (23°)
14 *Apollo 14* (1971-2-5) (17°)
15 *Apollo 15* (1971-7-30) (356°)
16 *Apollo 16* (1972-4-21) (344°)
17 *Apollo 17* (1972-12-11) (329°)

Angles in parentheses equal 360°– λ, where λ is the selenographic longitude of the center of the feature. 0° marks the mean center of the lunar disk and the angles increase toward the observer's east (i.e. westward on the Moon). These angles facilitate locating the feature on the accompanying map, and may be correlated with the Sun's selenographic colongitude (see THE SKY MONTH BY MONTH (p. 98) to determine the optimum times for viewing the feature.

Mountains

A	Alpine Valley (356°)	H	Caucasus Mountains (352°)	V	Spitzbergen (5°)
B	Alps Mountains (359°)	K	Haemus Mountains (349°)	W	Straight Range (20°)
E	Altai Scarp (336°)	M	Jura Mountains (34°)	X	Straight Wall (8°)
F	Apennine Mountains (2°)	N	Pyrenees Mountains (319°)	Y	Taurus Mountains (319°)
G	Carpathian Mountains (24°)	R	Rheita Valley (312°)	Z	Teneriffe Mountains (13°)
		S	Riphaeus Mountains (27°)		

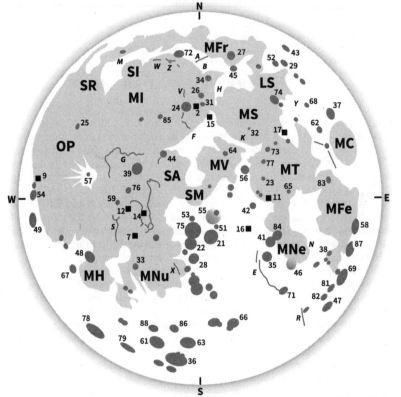

chart by Roy Bishop and Michael Gatto

Craters

21 Albategnius (356°)	37 Cleomedes (304°)	55 Hipparchus (354°)	73 Plinius (336°)
22 Alphonsus (3°)	38 Cook (311°)	56 Julius Caesar (345°)	74 Posidonius (330°)
23 Arago (338°)	39 Copernicus (20°)	57 Kepler (38°)	75 Ptolemaeus (2°)
24 Archimedes (4°)	41 Cyrillus (336°)	58 Langrenus (299°)	76 Reinhold (23°)
25 Aristarchus (47°)	42 Delambre (342°)	59 Lansberg (27°)	77 Ross (338°)
26 Aristillus (358°)	43 Endymion (305°)	61 Longomontanus (21°)	78 Schickard (55°)
27 Aristoteles (342°)	44 Eratosthenes (11°)	62 Macrobius (314°)	79 Schiller (40°)
28 Arzachel (2°)	45 Eudoxus (343°)	63 Maginus (6°)	81 Snellius (304°)
29 Atlas (315°)	46 Fracastorius (326°)	64 Manilius (351°)	82 Stevinus (305°)
31 Autolycus (358°)	47 Furnerius (299°)	65 Maskelyne (330°)	83 Taruntius (313°)
32 Bessel (342°)	48 Gassendi (40°)	66 Maurolycus (345°)	84 Theophilus (333°)
33 Bullialdus (22°)	49 Grimaldi (68°)	67 Mersenius (49°)	85 Timocharis (13°)
34 Cassini (355°)	51 Halley (354°)	68 Newcomb (316°)	86 Tycho (11°)
35 Catharina (336°)	52 Hercules (321°)	69 Petavius (298°)	87 Vendelinus (298°)
36 Clavius (15°)	53 Herschel (2°)	71 Piccolomini (327°)	88 Wilhelm (20°)
	54 Hevelius (66°)	72 Plato (10°)	

For expanded photographic views of the lunar surface see the-moon.wikispaces.com/Rükl+Index+Map (based on the Rükl zones) and wms.LROC.asu.edu/LROC (a *Lunar Reconnaissance Orbiter* Camera mosaic).

UNIVERSAL TIME OF NEW-MOON DATES

2018				2019			
Jan.	17.1	May 15.5	Sep. 9.8	Jan. 6.1	May 4.9	Sep. 28.8
Feb.	15.9	Jun. 13.8	Oct. 9.2	Feb. 4.9	Jun. 3.4	Oct. 28.2
Mar.	17.6	Jul. 13.1	Nov. 7.7	Mar. 6.7	Jul. 2.8	Nov. 26.6
Apr.	16.1	Aug. 11.4	Dec. 7.3	Apr. 5.4	Aug. 1.1	Dec. 26.2
					Aug. 30.4	

These dates will be useful for planning observing sessions, determining favorable dates for observing very thin lunar crescents, and setting Moon dials on clocks. The dates are indicated to lower precision in the 2018 calendar on the inside back cover.

TIMES OF MOONRISE AND MOONSET

The table on pp. 152–157 gives the times of moonrise and moonset for locations ranging from 20°N to 60°N latitude. Dates of new Moon and full Moon are given in **bold** and *italic* respectively. The table may be interpolated linearly for nontabular latitudes and can be extrapolated beyond the 20° and 60° limits a few degrees without significant loss of accuracy. "Rise" and "Set" correspond to the upper limb of the Moon appearing at the horizon for an observer at sea level. The times are local mean time (LMT) for the Greenwich meridian (i.e. UT at 0° longitude). Because of the relatively rapid eastward motion of the Moon, unlike the sunrise and sunset table, for observers not near 0° longitude, the times cannot be read directly as LMT; the table must be interpolated according to the observer's longitude. Also, to convert from the observer's LMT to standard time, the observer's longitude correction relative to his or her standard meridian must be applied. After it is prepared for a given location, the chart at the right enables the sum of these two corrections to be determined in one step.

To prepare the **Moonrise/Moonset Correction Diagram**, first mark your longitude on the *West or East Longitude* scale. Draw a diagonal line from this mark to the (0,0) point. Next, the *Correction in minutes* axis (which is subdivided at two-minute intervals) must be labelled. As a guide, the first three divisions have been tentatively labelled 0, ±2, ±4 *(use + if you are west of the prime meridian in Greenwich, England, – if east)*; but, to these numbers must be added your longitude correction relative to your standard meridian (see the third paragraph on p. 205). As an aid both for labelling and for reading the chart, the vertical lines at 10-min intervals are wider. **Examples:** For Edmonton, which is 8.5° W of its standard meridian of 105°W, the longitude correction is +34 min, so an observer in Edmonton would label the Correction axis 34, 36, 38,...; an observer in Boston (longitude correction –16) would label the axis –16, –14, –12,...; an observer in Hong Kong (east longitude, longitude correction +24) would label the axis 24, 22, 20,...; an observer in Vienna (longitude correction –6) would label the axis –6, –8, –10,....

The chart is now ready for use on any day from your position. Interpolating for nontabular latitudes, from the table obtain today's time for the event (moonrise, or moonset) and tomorrow's time if you are west of Greenwich, yesterday's time if east, enter the difference on the *Tabular Delay* axis, and run horizontally across to meet the diagonal line. The correction, to the nearest minute, can then be read directly below off the Correction axis. This correction is applied to the tabular "today's time" and results in the standard time of the event for your position. **Example:** The longitude of Billings, Montana, is 108°W, and latitude is 46°N. Interpolating the 45°N and 50°N entries, the table gives for 46°N a moonrise time of 14:12 on Jul. 21 and 15:15 on Jul. 22. The Correction corresponding to a 14-min Tabular Delay, when the chart is prepared for Billings as described above, is +33 min; hence the time of moonrise is 14:12 + 33 min = 14:45 MST or 15:45 MDT Jul. 21.

MOONRISE/MOONSET CORRECTION DIAGRAM

Note: Due to a difference in elevation between the observer and the actual horizon, the observed time may differ by several minutes from the predicted time.

The correction in minutes can also be calculated from the formula:

$$(L/360) \times (\text{Tabular Delay}) + 4(L - L_s)$$

in which L = longitude of the observer from Greenwich, and L_s = longitude of the observer's time-zone standard meridian (L and L_s are in degrees, and are negative if east of Greenwich). The term $4(L - L_s)$ is tabulated for several North American cities on p. 205.

Alternatively, see p. 10 for computer-based planetarium programs or applications for mobile devices. A browser-based online rise/set calculator can be found at aa.usno.navy.mil/data/docs/RS_OneYear.php (United States Naval Observatory).

MOONRISE AND MOONSET, JANUARY AND FEBRUARY 2018
UNIVERSAL TIME AT GREENWICH MERIDIAN

Latitude:	+20°		+30°		+35°		+40°		+45°		+50°		+55°		+60°	
Event:	RISE	SET	RISE	SET	RISE	SET	RISE	SET	RISE	SET	RISE	SET	RISE	SET	RISE	SET
Jan. 1	17:10	5:39	16:51	5:57	16:40	6:08	16:27	6:20	16:13	6:35	15:55	6:53	15:32	7:15	15:00	7:47
2	*18:14*	*6:43*	*17:56*	*7:02*	*17:45*	*7:13*	*17:33*	*7:26*	*17:18*	*7:40*	*17:00*	*7:58*	*16:38*	*8:21*	*16:06*	*8:53*
3	19:19	7:45	19:03	8:02	18:53	8:12	18:42	8:24	18:29	8:37	18:14	8:54	17:54	9:14	17:26	9:43
4	20:23	8:41	20:10	8:55	20:02	9:04	19:54	9:14	19:43	9:25	19:31	9:38	19:15	9:56	18:54	10:18
5	21:25	9:32	21:15	9:43	21:10	9:49	21:03	9:56	20:56	10:05	20:47	10:15	20:36	10:27	20:22	10:44
6	22:22	10:18	22:17	10:25	22:14	10:29	22:11	10:34	22:07	10:39	22:02	10:45	21:56	10:53	21:48	11:03
7	23:18	11:00	23:16	11:03	23:16	11:05	23:15	11:07	23:14	11:09	23:13	11:12	23:12	11:15	23:10	11:20
8		11:40		11:39		11:39		11:38		11:38		11:37		11:36		11:34
9	0:11	12:19	0:13	12:14	0:15	12:12	0:17	12:08	0:19	12:05	0:22	12:01	0:26	11:55	0:30	11:49
10	1:02	12:58	1:09	12:49	1:13	12:44	1:17	12:39	1:22	12:33	1:29	12:25	1:37	12:16	1:47	12:03
11	1:53	13:37	2:03	13:25	2:09	13:19	2:16	13:11	2:24	13:02	2:34	12:51	2:46	12:38	3:01	12:20
12	2:43	14:18	2:57	14:03	3:04	13:55	3:13	13:45	3:24	13:34	3:36	13:20	3:52	13:03	4:14	12:41
13	3:33	15:01	3:49	14:44	3:59	14:34	4:09	14:23	4:22	14:10	4:37	13:54	4:57	13:34	5:23	13:06
14	4:23	15:45	4:41	15:27	4:51	15:17	5:03	15:04	5:17	14:50	5:34	14:33	5:56	14:10	6:27	13:39
15	5:12	16:32	5:31	16:14	5:42	16:03	5:54	15:50	6:09	15:35	6:27	15:17	6:50	14:54	7:23	14:21
16	6:00	17:21	6:19	17:03	6:30	16:52	6:42	16:40	6:57	16:26	7:15	16:08	7:38	15:45	8:09	15:13
17	**6:46**	**18:11**	**7:04**	**17:54**	**7:14**	**17:45**	**7:26**	**17:33**	**7:39**	**17:20**	**7:56**	**17:04**	**8:18**	**16:43**	**8:47**	**16:15**
18	7:31	19:02	7:46	18:48	7:55	18:39	8:06	18:29	8:18	18:18	8:32	18:04	8:51	17:46	9:16	17:23
19	8:13	19:53	8:26	19:41	8:33	19:35	8:42	19:27	8:52	19:18	9:04	19:07	9:19	18:53	9:38	18:35
20	8:53	20:44	9:03	20:36	9:09	20:31	9:15	20:26	9:22	20:19	9:31	20:12	9:42	20:02	9:57	19:50
21	9:32	21:36	9:39	21:31	9:42	21:29	9:46	21:26	9:51	21:22	9:57	21:18	10:04	21:13	10:12	21:06
22	10:11	22:28	10:14	22:27	10:15	22:27	10:17	22:27	10:18	22:26	10:21	22:26	10:23	22:25	10:27	22:24
23	10:50	23:21	10:49	23:25	10:48	23:27	10:47	23:29	10:46	23:32	10:45	23:35	10:43	23:39	10:41	23:44
24	11:31		11:25		11:22		11:19		11:14		11:10		11:04		10:56	
25	12:14	0:17	12:04	0:24	11:59	0:29	11:53	0:34	11:46	0:40	11:37	0:47	11:27	0:55	11:13	1:07
26	13:01	1:14	12:48	1:26	12:40	1:33	12:32	1:40	12:22	1:49	12:10	2:00	11:55	2:14	11:35	2:31
27	13:52	2:15	13:36	2:30	13:27	2:39	13:16	2:49	13:04	3:00	12:49	3:14	12:30	3:32	12:04	3:57
28	14:49	3:18	14:31	3:35	14:20	3:45	14:08	3:57	13:54	4:11	13:37	4:28	13:15	4:49	12:44	5:19
29	15:50	4:21	15:32	4:40	15:21	4:51	15:08	5:03	14:53	5:18	14:35	5:36	14:12	5:59	13:40	6:31
30	16:55	5:23	16:37	5:41	16:27	5:52	16:15	6:04	16:01	6:19	15:44	6:36	15:22	6:59	14:52	7:29
31	*18:00*	*6:22*	*17:45*	*6:38*	*17:36*	*6:48*	*17:26*	*6:59*	*17:14*	*7:11*	*17:00*	*7:27*	*16:41*	*7:46*	*16:17*	*8:12*
Feb. 1	19:04	7:16	18:52	7:30	18:46	7:37	18:38	7:46	18:29	7:56	18:18	8:08	18:05	8:23	17:47	8:43
2	20:05	8:06	19:58	8:15	19:54	8:21	19:49	8:27	19:43	8:34	19:36	8:42	19:28	8:53	19:16	9:06
3	21:04	8:52	21:01	8:57	20:59	9:00	20:57	9:03	20:54	9:07	20:52	9:12	20:48	9:17	20:44	9:24
4	22:00	9:34	22:01	9:35	22:01	9:36	22:02	9:37	22:03	9:37	22:04	9:38	22:06	9:39	22:07	9:40
5	22:53	10:15	22:59	10:12	23:02	10:10	23:05	10:08	23:09	10:06	23:14	10:03	23:20	10:00	23:28	9:55
6	23:46	10:55	23:55	10:48		10:44		10:39		10:34		10:28		10:20		10:10
7		11:35		11:24	0:00	11:18	0:06	11:11	0:13	11:03	0:21	10:54	0:32	10:42	0:45	10:27
8	0:37	12:16	0:49	12:02	0:57	11:54	1:05	11:45	1:14	11:35	1:26	11:22	1:41	11:07	2:00	10:46
9	1:28	12:58	1:43	12:42	1:52	12:32	2:02	12:22	2:14	12:09	2:28	11:54	2:46	11:35	3:11	11:09
10	2:18	13:42	2:35	13:24	2:45	13:14	2:57	13:02	3:10	12:48	3:27	12:31	3:48	12:09	4:17	11:40
11	3:07	14:28	3:26	14:09	3:37	13:59	3:49	13:46	4:04	13:31	4:21	13:13	4:44	12:50	5:16	12:18
12	3:56	15:16	4:15	14:58	4:25	14:47	4:38	14:34	4:53	14:20	5:11	14:02	5:34	13:39	6:06	13:07
13	4:43	16:06	5:01	15:49	5:11	15:38	5:23	15:27	5:37	15:13	5:55	14:56	6:17	14:34	6:47	14:05
14	5:28	16:57	5:44	16:41	5:54	16:32	6:04	16:22	6:17	16:10	6:33	15:55	6:52	15:36	7:19	15:11
15	**6:11**	**17:48**	**6:25**	**17:36**	**6:33**	**17:28**	**6:42**	**17:20**	**6:53**	**17:10**	**7:06**	**16:58**	**7:22**	**16:43**	**7:44**	**16:23**
16	6:52	18:40	7:03	18:31	7:10	18:25	7:17	18:19	7:25	18:12	7:35	18:03	7:47	17:52	8:03	17:38
17	7:32	19:32	7:40	19:26	7:44	19:23	7:49	19:19	7:55	19:15	8:01	19:10	8:10	19:03	8:20	18:55
18	8:12	20:24	8:15	20:23	8:17	20:22	8:20	20:21	8:23	20:19	8:26	20:18	8:30	20:16	8:35	20:13
19	8:51	21:18	8:51	21:20	8:50	21:21	8:50	21:23	8:50	21:25	8:50	21:27	8:50	21:29	8:49	21:33
20	9:31	22:12	9:27	22:19	9:24	22:22	9:21	22:26	9:18	22:31	9:14	22:37	9:10	22:45	9:04	22:54
21	10:13	23:08	10:04	23:19	10:00	23:25	9:54	23:31	9:48	23:39	9:41	23:49	9:32		9:20	
22	10:57		10:45		10:38		10:31		10:22		10:11		9:57	0:01	9:40	0:17
23	11:46	0:06	11:30	0:20	11:22	0:28	11:12	0:38	11:00	0:48	10:46	1:01	10:28	1:18	10:05	1:40
24	12:38	1:06	12:21	1:23	12:11	1:33	11:59	1:44	11:45	1:57	11:29	2:13	11:08	2:33	10:39	3:01
25	13:36	2:07	13:17	2:26	13:06	2:36	12:53	2:49	12:39	3:03	12:21	3:21	11:58	3:44	11:26	4:15
26	14:37	3:08	14:18	3:26	14:07	3:37	13:55	3:50	13:41	4:04	13:23	4:22	13:00	4:46	12:28	5:17
27	15:40	4:06	15:23	4:24	15:13	4:34	15:02	4:45	14:49	4:59	14:33	5:15	14:13	5:37	13:45	6:05
28	16:43	5:01	16:29	5:16	16:22	5:25	16:13	5:35	16:02	5:46	15:49	6:00	15:33	6:17	15:12	6:40

Bold = new Moon, *italic* = full Moon. A gap in a column indicates the event will take place early the next day.

MOONRISE AND MOONSET, MARCH AND APRIL 2018
UNIVERSAL TIME AT GREENWICH MERIDIAN

Latitude:	+20°		+30°		+35°		+40°		+45°		+50°		+55°		+60°	
Event:	RISE	SET	RISE	SET	RISE	SET	RISE	SET	RISE	SET	RISE	SET	RISE	SET	RISE	SET
Mar. 1	17:45	5:52	17:36	6:04	17:30	6:10	17:24	6:18	17:16	6:26	17:07	6:37	16:56	6:50	16:41	7:06
2	18:46	6:40	18:40	6:47	18:37	6:52	18:33	6:56	18:29	7:02	18:24	7:08	18:18	7:16	18:10	7:27
3	19:44	7:24	19:43	7:27	19:42	7:29	19:41	7:31	19:41	7:34	19:40	7:36	19:39	7:40	19:37	7:44
4	20:40	8:07	20:43	8:06	20:45	8:05	20:47	8:04	20:50	8:03	20:53	8:02	20:56	8:01	21:01	7:59
5	21:34	8:48	21:41	8:43	21:46	8:40	21:50	8:36	21:56	8:32	22:03	8:28	22:11	8:22	22:23	8:14
6	22:27	9:29	22:38	9:20	22:45	9:14	22:52	9:09	23:00	9:02	23:11	8:54	23:24	8:43	23:41	8:30
7	23:19	10:10	23:33	9:58	23:42	9:50	23:51	9:42		9:33		9:21		9:07		8:49
8		10:52		10:37		10:28		10:18	0:02	10:07	0:15	9:52	0:32	9:34	0:55	9:11
9	0:11	11:36	0:27	11:19	0:37	11:09	0:48	10:58	1:01	10:44	1:17	10:28	1:37	10:07	2:05	9:38
10	1:01	12:22	1:19	12:04	1:30	11:53	1:42	11:40	1:56	11:26	2:14	11:08	2:36	10:45	3:07	10:13
11	1:50	13:10	2:09	12:51	2:20	12:40	2:32	12:27	2:47	12:12	3:05	11:54	3:29	11:31	4:01	10:58
12	2:37	13:59	2:56	13:41	3:06	13:30	3:19	13:18	3:33	13:04	3:51	12:46	4:14	12:24	4:45	11:53
13	3:23	14:49	3:40	14:33	3:50	14:23	4:01	14:12	4:15	13:59	4:31	13:44	4:52	13:24	5:20	12:56
14	4:07	15:40	4:22	15:27	4:30	15:18	4:40	15:09	4:52	14:58	5:06	14:45	5:24	14:28	5:47	14:06
15	4:49	16:32	5:01	16:22	5:08	16:15	5:16	16:08	5:25	16:00	5:37	15:50	5:50	15:37	6:09	15:21
16	5:30	17:25	5:38	17:18	5:44	17:14	5:49	17:09	5:56	17:03	6:04	16:57	6:14	16:49	6:26	16:38
17	6:10	18:18	6:15	18:15	6:18	18:13	6:21	18:11	6:25	18:08	6:29	18:05	6:35	18:02	6:42	17:57
18	6:49	19:12	6:50	19:13	6:51	19:13	6:52	19:14	6:53	19:15	6:53	19:16	6:55	19:17	6:56	19:18
19	7:30	20:07	7:27	20:12	7:25	20:15	7:23	20:18	7:21	20:22	7:18	20:27	7:15	20:33	7:11	20:41
20	8:11	21:03	8:04	21:13	8:00	21:18	7:56	21:24	7:50	21:31	7:44	21:40	7:36	21:51	7:26	22:05
21	8:56	22:01	8:45	22:15	8:38	22:22	8:31	22:31	8:23	22:41	8:13	22:53	8:01	23:08	7:45	23:29
22	9:43	23:01	9:29	23:17	9:20	23:27	9:11	23:37	9:00	23:50	8:46		8:30		8:08	
23	10:34		10:17		10:07		9:56		9:43		9:26	0:05	9:06	0:25	8:38	0:52
24	11:29	0:01	11:11	0:19	11:00	0:30	10:47	0:42	10:33	0:57	10:15	1:14	9:52	1:37	9:20	2:08
25	12:28	1:01	12:09	1:20	11:58	1:31	11:45	1:43	11:30	1:58	11:12	2:17	10:49	2:40	10:16	3:13
26	13:28	1:58	13:11	2:17	13:01	2:27	12:49	2:39	12:35	2:54	12:18	3:11	11:57	3:33	11:27	4:03
27	14:30	2:53	14:15	3:09	14:06	3:18	13:56	3:29	13:44	3:42	13:30	3:57	13:12	4:16	12:48	4:41
28	15:31	3:44	15:19	3:57	15:13	4:04	15:05	4:13	14:56	4:23	14:45	4:35	14:32	4:50	14:14	5:09
29	16:30	4:31	16:23	4:41	16:19	4:46	16:14	4:52	16:08	4:59	16:01	5:07	15:53	5:17	15:42	5:31
30	17:28	5:16	17:25	5:21	17:24	5:24	17:22	5:27	17:19	5:31	17:17	5:36	17:13	5:41	17:09	5:48
31	18:25	5:59	18:26	5:59	18:27	6:00	18:28	6:00	18:29	6:01	18:30	6:02	18:32	6:03	18:34	6:04
Apr. 1	19:20	6:40	19:26	6:37	19:29	6:35	19:33	6:32	19:37	6:30	19:42	6:27	19:49	6:23	19:57	6:18
2	20:15	7:21	20:24	7:14	20:30	7:09	20:36	7:05	20:43	6:59	20:52	6:52	21:03	6:44	21:18	6:34
3	21:08	8:03	21:21	7:52	21:29	7:45	21:37	7:38	21:47	7:29	22:00	7:19	22:15	7:07	22:36	6:51
4	22:01	8:45	22:16	8:31	22:26	8:23	22:36	8:13	22:49	8:02	23:04	7:49	23:23	7:33	23:49	7:11
5	22:52	9:29	23:10	9:12	23:20	9:03	23:32	8:52	23:46	8:39		8:23		8:03		7:36
6	23:42	10:15		9:56		9:46		9:33		9:19	0:04	9:01	0:26	8:39	0:56	8:08
7		11:02	0:01	10:43	0:12	10:32	0:25	10:19	0:40	10:04	0:58	9:45	1:22	9:22	1:55	8:49
8	0:31	11:51	0:50	11:32	1:01	11:21	1:13	11:08	1:28	10:54	1:47	10:35	2:10	10:12	2:43	9:39
9	1:17	12:40	1:35	12:23	1:46	12:13	1:58	12:01	2:12	11:47	2:29	11:31	2:51	11:09	3:21	10:40
10	2:01	13:31	2:18	13:16	2:27	13:07	2:38	12:57	2:50	12:45	3:05	12:30	3:25	12:12	3:51	11:47
11	2:44	14:22	2:57	14:10	3:05	14:03	3:14	13:55	3:25	13:45	3:37	13:34	3:53	13:19	4:14	13:00
12	3:25	15:14	3:35	15:05	3:41	15:00	3:48	14:55	3:56	14:48	4:05	14:40	4:17	14:29	4:32	14:16
13	4:05	16:07	4:12	16:02	4:15	15:59	4:20	15:56	4:25	15:52	4:31	15:48	4:39	15:42	4:48	15:35
14	4:45	17:01	4:47	17:00	4:49	17:00	4:51	16:59	4:53	16:59	4:56	16:58	4:59	16:57	5:03	16:56
15	5:25	17:56	5:24	18:00	5:23	18:02	5:22	18:04	5:21	18:07	5:20	18:10	5:18	18:14	5:17	18:19
16	6:07	18:53	6:01	19:01	5:58	19:06	5:54	19:11	5:50	19:17	5:45	19:24	5:39	19:33	5:32	19:45
17	6:51	19:53	6:41	20:04	6:36	20:11	6:29	20:19	6:22	20:28	6:13	20:39	6:03	20:53	5:49	21:12
18	7:38	20:53	7:25	21:09	7:17	21:18	7:08	21:28	6:58	21:40	6:46	21:55	6:30	22:13	6:10	22:38
19	8:29	21:55	8:13	22:13	8:03	22:23	7:52	22:35	7:39	22:49	7:24	23:07	7:04	23:29	6:38	23:59
20	9:24	22:56	9:05	23:15	8:55	23:26	8:42	23:39	8:28	23:54	8:10		7:47		7:16	
21	10:22	23:55	10:03		9:52		9:39		9:24		9:05	0:13	8:42	0:37	8:08	1:10
22	11:23		11:04	0:14	10:54	0:25	10:41	0:37	10:27	0:52	10:09	1:10	9:46	1:33	9:15	2:05
23	12:23	0:50	12:07	1:07	11:58	1:17	11:47	1:29	11:35	1:42	11:19	1:58	11:00	2:18	10:33	2:46
24	13:24	1:41	13:11	1:56	13:03	2:04	12:55	2:13	12:45	2:24	12:33	2:38	12:17	2:54	11:57	3:16
25	14:22	2:29	14:13	2:40	14:08	2:46	14:02	2:53	13:55	3:01	13:47	3:11	13:37	3:23	13:23	3:38
26	15:19	3:13	15:15	3:20	15:12	3:24	15:09	3:28	15:05	3:33	15:01	3:39	14:55	3:46	14:48	3:56
27	16:15	3:55	16:15	3:58	16:14	3:59	16:14	4:01	16:14	4:03	16:13	4:05	16:13	4:07	16:12	4:11
28	17:10	4:36	17:14	4:34	17:16	4:33	17:18	4:32	17:21	4:31	17:25	4:29	17:29	4:27	17:35	4:25
29	18:04	5:16	18:12	5:10	18:16	5:07	18:22	5:03	18:28	4:59	18:35	4:54	18:44	4:47	18:56	4:39
30	18:58	5:57	19:09	5:47	19:16	5:42	19:24	5:35	19:33	5:28	19:44	5:19	19:57	5:09	20:16	4:55

MOONRISE AND MOONSET, MAY AND JUNE 2018
UNIVERSAL TIME AT GREENWICH MERIDIAN

Latitude:	+20°		+30°		+35°		+40°		+45°		+50°		+55°		+60°	
Event:	RISE	SET	RISE	SET	RISE	SET	RISE	SET	RISE	SET	RISE	SET	RISE	SET	RISE	SET
May 1	19:51	6:39	20:06	6:26	20:14	6:18	20:24	6:09	20:36	5:59	20:50	5:47	21:08	5:32	21:32	5:13
2	20:43	7:22	21:00	7:06	21:11	6:57	21:22	6:46	21:36	6:34	21:52	6:19	22:14	6:00	22:43	5:35
3	21:34	8:07	21:53	7:49	22:04	7:39	22:17	7:27	22:32	7:13	22:50	6:56	23:14	6:34	23:46	6:03
4	22:24	8:54	22:43	8:35	22:55	8:24	23:07	8:11	23:23	7:56	23:42	7:37		7:14		6:40
5	23:11	9:43	23:30	9:23	23:41	9:12	23:54	8:59		8:44		8:25	0:06	8:01	0:40	7:27
6	23:56	10:32		10:14		10:03		9:51	0:08	9:36	0:27	9:18	0:50	8:56	1:22	8:24
7		11:22	0:14	11:06	0:24	10:56	0:35	10:45	0:49	10:32	1:05	10:16	1:26	9:56	1:54	9:29
8	0:39	12:13	0:54	11:59	1:03	11:51	1:13	11:42	1:24	11:31	1:38	11:18	1:56	11:01	2:19	10:39
9	1:20	13:04	1:32	12:53	1:39	12:47	1:47	12:40	1:56	12:32	2:07	12:22	2:21	12:10	2:39	11:53
10	2:00	13:55	2:09	13:49	2:13	13:45	2:19	13:40	2:26	13:35	2:33	13:28	2:43	13:20	2:55	13:10
11	2:39	14:48	2:44	14:45	2:47	14:44	2:50	14:42	2:53	14:39	2:58	14:37	3:03	14:33	3:10	14:29
12	3:18	15:42	3:19	15:44	3:20	15:44	3:20	15:45	3:21	15:46	3:21	15:48	3:22	15:49	3:23	15:51
13	3:59	16:39	3:56	16:44	3:54	16:48	3:51	16:51	3:49	16:56	3:46	17:01	3:42	17:08	3:37	17:16
14	4:42	17:37	4:34	17:47	4:30	17:53	4:25	18:00	4:19	18:08	4:12	18:17	4:04	18:29	3:53	18:44
15	**5:28**	**18:39**	**5:16**	**18:53**	**5:10**	**19:01**	**5:02**	**19:10**	**4:53**	**19:21**	**4:42**	**19:34**	**4:29**	**19:51**	**4:12**	**20:13**
16	6:19	19:42	6:03	19:59	5:54	20:09	5:44	20:20	5:32	20:34	5:18	20:50	5:00	21:12	4:36	21:40
17	7:14	20:45	6:56	21:04	6:45	21:16	6:33	21:28	6:19	21:43	6:02	22:02	5:40	22:26	5:10	22:59
18	8:13	21:47	7:53	22:07	7:42	22:18	7:29	22:31	7:14	22:46	6:55	23:05	6:31	23:29	5:58	
19	9:14	22:46	8:55	23:04	8:44	23:14	8:31	23:26	8:16	23:40	7:58	23:58	7:34		7:01	0:02
20	10:17	23:39	9:59	23:55	9:49		9:38		9:24		9:08		8:47	0:19	8:18	0:49
21	11:18		11:04		10:56	0:04	10:46	0:14	10:35	0:26	10:22	0:40	10:05	0:59	9:42	1:23
22	12:18	0:28	12:07	0:41	12:01	0:48	11:54	0:55	11:46	1:05	11:37	1:15	11:25	1:29	11:09	1:47
23	13:15	1:14	13:09	1:22	13:05	1:26	13:01	1:32	12:56	1:38	12:51	1:45	12:43	1:54	12:34	2:05
24	14:10	1:56	14:08	2:00	14:07	2:02	14:06	2:05	14:05	2:07	14:03	2:11	14:01	2:15	13:58	2:21
25	15:04	2:36	15:07	2:36	15:08	2:36	15:10	2:35	15:11	2:35	15:14	2:35	15:16	2:35	15:20	2:34
26	15:58	3:15	16:04	3:11	16:08	3:09	16:12	3:06	16:17	3:03	16:23	2:59	16:31	2:54	16:40	2:48
27	16:51	3:55	17:01	3:47	17:07	3:42	17:14	3:37	17:22	3:30	17:31	3:23	17:44	3:14	17:59	3:02
28	17:43	4:36	17:57	4:24	18:05	4:17	18:14	4:09	18:25	4:00	18:38	3:49	18:54	3:36	19:16	3:18
29	*18:36*	*5:18*	*18:52*	*5:03*	*19:02*	*4:54*	*19:13*	*4:44*	*19:26*	*4:33*	*19:42*	*4:19*	*20:02*	*4:01*	*20:30*	*3:38*
30	19:28	6:02	19:46	5:45	19:57	5:35	20:09	5:23	20:24	5:09	20:42	4:53	21:05	4:32	21:37	4:03
31	20:18	6:48	20:37	6:29	20:49	6:18	21:02	6:06	21:17	5:51	21:36	5:32	22:01	5:09	22:35	4:36
Jun. 1	21:06	7:36	21:26	7:17	21:37	7:05	21:50	6:52	22:05	6:37	22:24	6:18	22:48	5:53	23:22	5:19
2	21:53	8:25	22:11	8:06	22:21	7:55	22:33	7:43	22:48	7:28	23:05	7:09	23:27	6:45	23:58	6:12
3	22:36	9:15	22:52	8:58	23:02	8:48	23:13	8:36	23:25	8:22	23:40	8:05	23:59	7:44		7:14
4	23:17	10:06	23:31	9:50	23:39	9:42	23:48	9:31	23:58	9:20		9:05		8:47	0:25	8:22
5	23:57	10:56		10:44		10:37		10:29		10:19	0:10	10:08	0:26	9:53	0:46	9:34
6		11:46	0:07	11:38	0:13	11:33	0:20	11:27	0:28	11:20	0:37	11:12	0:48	11:02	1:03	10:49
7	0:35	12:37	0:42	12:33	0:46	12:30	0:50	12:27	0:55	12:23	1:01	12:18	1:08	12:13	1:18	12:06
8	1:14	13:30	1:16	13:29	1:18	13:28	1:20	13:28	1:22	13:27	1:24	13:27	1:27	13:26	1:31	13:25
9	1:52	14:24	1:51	14:27	1:50	14:29	1:49	14:31	1:48	14:34	1:47	14:37	1:46	14:41	1:44	14:47
10	2:33	15:20	2:28	15:28	2:24	15:33	2:21	15:38	2:17	15:44	2:12	15:51	2:06	16:00	1:58	16:12
11	3:17	16:20	3:07	16:32	3:02	16:39	2:55	16:47	2:48	16:56	2:39	17:07	2:28	17:21	2:14	17:40
12	4:05	17:22	3:51	17:38	3:43	17:47	3:35	17:58	3:24	18:10	3:12	18:25	2:56	18:44	2:35	19:10
13	**4:58**	**18:27**	**4:41**	**18:45**	**4:31**	**18:56**	**4:20**	**19:08**	**4:07**	**19:23**	**3:51**	**19:40**	**3:31**	**20:03**	**3:04**	**20:35**
14	5:56	19:31	5:37	19:51	5:26	20:02	5:13	20:15	4:59	20:31	4:40	20:50	4:17	21:14	3:45	21:48
15	6:59	20:34	6:39	20:53	6:28	21:04	6:15	21:16	5:59	21:31	5:40	21:49	5:16	22:13	4:42	22:45
16	8:03	21:31	7:45	21:48	7:34	21:58	7:22	22:09	7:07	22:22	6:50	22:38	6:27	22:58	5:55	23:25
17	9:07	22:24	8:52	22:38	8:43	22:46	8:32	22:54	8:20	23:05	8:05	23:17	7:46	23:33	7:20	23:53
18	10:10	23:12	9:58	23:22	9:51	23:27	9:43	23:33	9:34	23:41	9:22	23:49	9:08		8:50	
19	11:09	23:56	11:01		10:57		10:52		10:46		10:39		10:30	0:00	10:18	0:14
20	12:06		12:03	0:01	12:01	0:04	11:58	0:08	11:56	0:12	11:53	0:17	11:49	0:23	11:44	0:30
21	13:01	0:37	13:02	0:38	13:02	0:39	13:03	0:40	13:04	0:41	13:05	0:42	13:06	0:43	13:07	0:45
22	13:54	1:17	13:59	1:14	14:02	1:12	14:06	1:09	14:10	1:08	14:14	1:05	14:20	1:02	14:28	0:58
23	14:47	1:56	14:56	1:49	15:01	1:45	15:07	1:40	15:14	1:35	15:23	1:29	15:33	1:21	15:47	1:11
24	15:39	2:36	15:52	2:25	15:59	2:19	16:07	2:12	16:17	2:04	16:29	1:54	16:44	1:42	17:04	1:26
25	16:33	3:17	16:47	3:03	16:56	2:55	17:06	2:46	17:18	2:35	17:33	2:22	17:52	2:06	18:18	1:44
26	17:23	4:00	17:41	3:43	17:51	3:33	18:03	3:22	18:17	3:09	18:34	2:54	18:57	2:34	19:27	2:07
27	18:13	4:45	18:33	4:26	18:44	4:15	18:57	4:03	19:12	3:49	19:31	3:31	19:55	3:08	20:29	2:37
28	*19:03*	*5:32*	*19:22*	*5:12*	*19:33*	*5:01*	*19:47*	*4:48*	*20:02*	*4:33*	*20:21*	*4:14*	*20:46*	*3:49*	*21:20*	*3:15*
29	19:50	6:21	20:08	6:01	20:19	5:50	20:32	5:37	20:47	5:22	21:05	5:03	21:28	4:38	22:00	4:04
30	20:34	7:10	20:51	6:52	21:01	6:42	21:12	6:29	21:26	6:15	21:42	5:57	22:02	5:35	22:30	5:03

Bold = new Moon, *italic* = full Moon. A gap in a column indicates the event will take place early the next day.

MOONRISE AND MOONSET, JULY AND AUGUST 2018
UNIVERSAL TIME AT GREENWICH MERIDIAN

Latitude:	+20°		+30°		+35°		+40°		+45°		+50°		+55°		+60°	
Event:	RISE	SET	RISE	SET	RISE	SET	RISE	SET	RISE	SET	RISE	SET	RISE	SET	RISE	SET
Jul. 1	21:16	8:01	21:31	7:44	21:39	7:35	21:49	7:24	22:00	7:12	22:14	6:56	22:31	6:36	22:53	6:09
2	21:56	8:51	22:08	8:37	22:14	8:30	22:22	8:21	22:31	8:10	22:41	7:58	22:54	7:42	23:11	7:20
3	22:34	9:41	22:42	9:31	22:47	9:25	22:52	9:18	22:59	9:10	23:06	9:01	23:15	8:49	23:26	8:34
4	23:12	10:31	23:16	10:24	23:19	10:21	23:22	10:17	23:25	10:12	23:29	10:06	23:33	9:58	23:40	9:49
5	23:49	11:21	23:50	11:19	23:50	11:19	23:50	11:16	23:51	11:14	23:51	11:12	23:51	11:09	23:52	11:05
6		12:13		12:15		12:16		12:17		12:18		12:20		12:21		12:24
7	0:28	13:07	0:24	13:13	0:22	13:16	0:20	13:20	0:17	13:24	0:14	13:30	0:10	13:37	0:05	13:45
8	1:09	14:03	1:01	14:13	0:57	14:19	0:52	14:26	0:46	14:33	0:39	14:43	0:30	14:54	0:20	15:10
9	1:54	15:03	1:42	15:17	1:35	15:25	1:27	15:34	1:18	15:45	1:08	15:58	0:55	16:15	0:37	16:37
10	2:43	16:05	2:27	16:23	2:19	16:32	2:08	16:44	1:57	16:57	1:43	17:14	1:25	17:35	1:01	18:04
11	3:37	17:10	3:19	17:29	3:09	17:40	2:57	17:53	2:43	18:08	2:26	18:27	2:04	18:50	1:34	19:24
12	4:38	18:14	4:18	18:33	4:07	18:45	3:54	18:58	3:38	19:13	3:20	19:32	2:55	19:56	2:22	20:30
13	5:42	19:15	5:23	19:33	5:12	19:44	4:59	19:56	4:44	20:10	4:25	20:27	4:01	20:49	3:28	21:19
14	6:48	20:12	6:31	20:27	6:21	20:36	6:09	20:46	5:56	20:58	5:40	21:12	5:18	21:30	4:49	21:54
15	7:54	21:04	7:40	21:15	7:32	21:22	7:23	21:30	7:12	21:38	6:59	21:49	6:42	22:02	6:20	22:18
16	8:57	21:51	8:47	21:58	8:41	22:02	8:35	22:07	8:28	22:13	8:19	22:19	8:07	22:27	7:53	22:37
17	9:57	22:35	9:52	22:37	9:49	22:39	9:45	22:41	9:41	22:43	9:36	22:46	9:30	22:49	9:23	22:53
18	10:54	23:16	10:53	23:14	10:53	23:14	10:52	23:13	10:52	23:11	10:51	23:10	10:51	23:09	10:50	23:06
19	11:49	23:56	11:53	23:50	11:55	23:47	11:57	23:43	12:00	23:39	12:03	23:34	12:08	23:28	12:13	23:20
20	12:43		12:50		12:55		13:00		13:06		13:13	23:59	13:22	23:48	13:33	23:35
21	13:35	0:36	13:47	0:26	13:53	0:21	14:01	0:15	14:10	0:08	14:21		14:34		14:52	23:52
22	14:27	1:16	14:42	1:04	14:51	0:56	15:00	0:48	15:12	0:38	15:26	0:26	15:44	0:11	16:07	
23	15:19	1:59	15:36	1:43	15:46	1:34	15:58	1:23	16:11	1:11	16:28	0:56	16:49	0:38	17:18	0:13
24	16:10	2:43	16:29	2:25	16:40	2:14	16:52	2:03	17:07	1:48	17:26	1:31	17:49	1:09	18:22	0:39
25	16:59	3:29	17:19	3:10	17:30	2:59	17:43	2:46	17:59	2:31	18:18	2:12	18:42	1:48	19:17	1:15
26	17:47	4:17	18:06	3:58	18:17	3:46	18:30	3:33	18:45	3:18	19:03	2:59	19:27	2:34	20:00	2:00
27	*18:32*	*5:07*	*18:50*	*4:48*	*19:00*	*4:37*	*19:12*	*4:24*	*19:26*	*4:10*	*19:43*	*3:52*	*20:04*	*3:28*	*20:34*	*2:56*
28	19:15	5:57	19:31	5:40	19:40	5:30	19:50	5:19	20:02	5:05	20:16	4:49	20:35	4:28	20:59	4:00
29	19:56	6:47	20:09	6:33	20:16	6:24	20:24	6:15	20:34	6:04	20:45	5:50	21:00	5:33	21:19	5:09
30	20:35	7:37	20:44	7:26	20:49	7:20	20:56	7:12	21:02	7:03	21:11	6:53	21:21	6:40	21:35	6:22
31	21:12	8:27	21:18	8:20	21:21	8:15	21:25	8:10	21:29	8:04	21:34	7:57	21:40	7:48	21:48	7:37
Aug. 1	21:49	9:17	21:51	9:14	21:52	9:11	21:53	9:09	21:55	9:06	21:56	9:02	21:58	8:58	22:01	8:53
2	22:27	10:08	22:25	10:08	22:23	10:08	22:22	10:09	22:20	10:09	22:18	10:09	22:16	10:09	22:13	10:09
3	23:06	11:00	23:00	11:04	22:56	11:07	22:52	11:10	22:48	11:13	22:42	11:17	22:35	11:22	22:26	11:28
4	23:48	11:54	23:37	12:02	23:32	12:07	23:25	12:12	23:17	12:19	23:08	12:27	22:57	12:36	22:42	12:49
5		12:50		13:02		13:09		13:18	23:52	13:27	23:39	13:39	23:23	13:53	23:02	14:12
6	0:33	13:49	0:19	14:05	0:11	14:14	0:02	14:25		14:37		14:52	23:56	15:11	23:29	15:37
7	1:23	14:51	1:07	15:09	0:57	15:20	0:46	15:32	0:32	15:47	0:17	16:04		16:27		16:27
8	2:19	15:54	2:00	16:13	1:49	16:24	1:37	16:38	1:22	16:53	1:04	17:12	0:40	17:36	0:08	18:10
9	3:20	16:56	3:01	17:15	2:49	17:26	2:36	17:38	2:21	17:53	2:02	18:12	1:37	18:35	1:03	19:07
10	4:25	17:55	4:07	18:12	3:56	18:21	3:44	18:33	3:29	18:46	3:11	19:02	2:48	19:22	2:17	19:49
11	5:31	18:49	5:16	19:03	5:06	19:11	4:56	19:20	4:44	19:30	4:29	19:43	4:10	19:58	3:44	20:18
12	6:37	19:40	6:25	19:49	6:18	19:55	6:10	20:01	6:01	20:08	5:50	20:16	5:36	20:27	5:17	20:40
13	7:40	20:26	7:32	20:31	7:28	20:34	7:23	20:37	7:18	20:41	7:11	20:45	7:02	20:51	6:51	20:58
14	8:40	21:10	8:38	21:10	8:36	21:11	8:34	21:11	8:32	21:11	8:30	21:11	8:27	21:12	8:23	21:12
15	9:38	21:52	9:40	21:48	9:41	21:46	9:42	21:43	9:44	21:40	9:45	21:36	9:48	21:32	9:50	21:27
16	10:34	22:33	10:40	22:25	10:44	22:20	10:48	22:15	10:53	22:09	10:58	22:02	11:06	21:53	11:15	21:41
17	11:28	23:14	11:39	23:02	11:45	22:56	11:51	22:48	11:59	22:39	12:09	22:28	12:21	22:15	12:36	21:57
18	12:23	23:56	12:35	23:42	12:43	23:33	12:52	23:23	13:03	23:12	13:16	22:58	13:32	22:40	13:52	22:17
19	13:14		13:31		13:40		13:51		14:04	23:48	14:20	23:31	14:40	23:10	15:08	22:42
20	14:06	0:40	14:24	0:23	14:35	0:13	14:47	0:01	15:02		15:20		15:43	23:47	16:15	23:14
21	14:56	1:26	15:15	1:07	15:26	0:56	15:39	0:43	15:55	0:28	16:14	0:10	16:38		17:13	23:56
22	15:44	2:13	16:03	1:54	16:14	1:43	16:27	1:29	16:43	1:14	17:02	0:55	17:26	0:30	18:00	
23	16:30	3:02	16:48	2:43	16:59	2:32	17:11	2:19	17:25	2:04	17:43	1:46	18:05	1:22	18:36	0:48
24	17:14	3:52	17:30	3:35	17:40	3:25	17:50	3:13	18:03	2:59	18:18	2:42	18:38	2:20	19:04	1:50
25	17:55	4:43	18:09	4:28	18:17	4:19	18:26	4:08	18:36	3:57	18:49	3:42	19:04	3:23	19:25	2:58
26	*18:35*	*5:33*	*18:45*	*5:21*	*18:51*	*5:14*	*18:58*	*5:06*	*19:06*	*4:56*	*19:15*	*4:45*	*19:27*	*4:30*	*19:42*	*4:11*
27	19:13	6:24	19:20	6:15	19:24	6:10	19:28	6:04	19:33	5:57	19:39	5:49	19:47	5:39	19:56	5:26
28	19:50	7:14	19:53	7:09	19:55	7:06	19:57	7:03	19:59	6:59	20:02	6:55	20:05	6:49	20:09	6:42
29	20:28	8:05	20:27	8:04	20:26	8:03	20:25	8:03	20:25	8:02	20:24	8:01	20:23	8:00	20:21	7:58
30	21:06	8:56	21:01	9:00	20:58	9:01	20:55	9:03	20:51	9:06	20:47	9:09	20:41	9:12	20:34	9:17
31	21:46	9:49	21:37	9:56	21:32	10:01	21:26	10:05	21:19	10:11	21:11	10:18	21:01	10:26	20:49	10:37

MOONRISE AND MOONSET, SEPTEMBER AND OCTOBER 2018
UNIVERSAL TIME AT GREENWICH MERIDIAN

Latitude:	+20°		+30°		+35°		+40°		+45°		+50°		+55°		+60°	
Event:	RISE	SET	RISE	SET	RISE	SET	RISE	SET	RISE	SET	RISE	SET	RISE	SET	RISE	SET
Sep. 1	22:29	10:44	22:17	10:55	22:09	11:02	22:01	11:09	21:51	11:18	21:40	11:28	21:25	11:41	21:06	11:58
2	23:17	11:41	23:01	11:56	22:52	12:04	22:41	12:14	22:29	12:25	22:14	12:39	21:55	12:57	21:30	13:21
3		12:40	23:50	12:57	23:40	13:08	23:27	13:19	23:13	13:33	22:56	13:50	22:33	14:12	22:03	14:41
4	0:09	13:40		13:59		14:11		14:24		14:39	23:47	14:58	23:23	15:22	22:49	15:55
5	1:06	14:40	0:46	15:00	0:35	15:11	0:22	15:24	0:06	15:40		15:59		16:23	23:52	16:57
6	2:07	15:39	1:48	15:57	1:36	16:08	1:24	16:20	1:08	16:34	0:50	16:51	0:26	17:13		17:43
7	3:11	16:35	2:54	16:50	2:44	16:59	2:32	17:09	2:18	17:21	2:02	17:35	1:41	17:53	1:12	18:17
8	4:16	17:26	4:02	17:38	3:54	17:45	3:44	17:52	3:33	18:01	3:20	18:12	3:04	18:25	2:41	18:42
9	**5:19**	**18:15**	**5:10**	**18:22**	**5:04**	**18:26**	**4:58**	**18:31**	**4:50**	**18:36**	**4:41**	**18:43**	**4:30**	**18:50**	**4:15**	**19:01**
10	6:22	19:00	6:16	19:02	6:14	19:04	6:10	19:06	6:06	19:08	6:02	19:10	5:56	19:13	5:48	19:16
11	7:22	19:43	7:21	19:41	7:21	19:40	7:21	19:39	7:21	19:37	7:20	19:36	7:20	19:34	7:19	19:31
12	8:20	20:25	8:24	20:19	8:26	20:16	8:29	20:11	8:33	20:07	8:37	20:01	8:41	19:54	8:48	19:45
13	9:16	21:08	9:25	20:57	9:30	20:51	9:36	20:45	9:42	20:37	9:50	20:28	10:00	20:16	10:13	20:01
14	10:12	21:51	10:24	21:37	10:31	21:29	10:40	21:20	10:49	21:09	11:01	20:56	11:16	20:40	11:35	20:19
15	11:06	22:35	11:21	22:18	11:30	22:09	11:41	21:58	11:53	21:45	12:08	21:29	12:27	21:09	12:53	20:42
16	11:59	23:21	12:17	23:02	12:27	22:51	12:39	22:39	12:53	22:24	13:11	22:06	13:33	21:43	14:04	21:12
17	12:50		13:09	23:48	13:20	23:37	13:33	23:24	13:49	23:08	14:08	22:49	14:32	22:25	15:06	21:50
18	13:39	0:08	13:59		14:10		14:23		14:39	23:57	14:58	23:38	15:23	23:14	15:58	22:39
19	14:26	0:57	14:45	0:37	14:56	0:26	15:09	0:13	15:24		15:42		16:05		16:38	23:38
20	15:11	1:46	15:28	1:28	15:38	1:17	15:49	1:05	16:03	0:51	16:19	0:33	16:40	0:10	17:08	
21	15:53	2:37	16:08	2:21	16:16	2:11	16:26	2:00	16:37	1:47	16:51	1:32	17:08	1:12	17:31	0:44
22	16:33	3:27	16:45	3:14	16:52	3:06	16:59	2:57	17:08	2:47	17:19	2:34	17:32	2:18	17:49	1:56
23	17:12	4:18	17:20	4:08	17:25	4:02	17:30	3:55	17:36	3:48	17:43	3:38	17:52	3:26	18:04	3:11
24	17:50	5:09	17:54	5:03	17:57	4:59	17:59	4:55	18:03	4:50	18:06	4:44	18:11	4:37	18:17	4:27
25	*18:28*	*6:00*	*18:28*	*5:58*	*18:28*	*5:56*	*18:28*	*5:55*	*18:28*	*5:53*	*18:29*	*5:51*	*18:29*	*5:48*	*18:29*	*5:45*
26	19:06	6:52	19:02	6:54	19:00	6:55	18:57	6:56	18:55	6:58	18:51	6:59	18:47	7:01	18:42	7:04
27	19:46	7:45	19:38	7:51	19:33	7:55	19:28	7:59	19:22	8:03	19:15	8:09	19:07	8:16	18:55	8:25
28	20:28	8:40	20:17	8:50	20:10	8:56	20:02	9:02	19:53	9:10	19:42	9:20	19:29	9:31	19:12	9:47
29	21:14	9:36	20:59	9:50	20:50	9:58	20:40	10:07	20:28	10:18	20:14	10:31	19:57	10:48	19:33	11:10
30	22:04	10:35	21:46	10:52	21:36	11:01	21:24	11:13	21:10	11:26	20:53	11:42	20:31	12:03	20:02	12:32
Oct. 1	22:59	11:34	22:39	11:53	22:28	12:04	22:15	12:17	21:59	12:32	21:40	12:51	21:16	13:14	20:42	13:48
2	23:57	12:33	23:37	12:53	23:26	13:04	23:13	13:18	22:57	13:33	22:38	13:53	22:13	14:17	21:38	14:52
3		13:31		13:50		14:01		14:13		14:28	23:45	14:47	23:22	15:10	22:50	15:42
4	0:58	14:25	0:40	14:42	0:29	14:52	0:17	15:03	0:02	15:16		15:32		15:52		16:19
5	2:01	15:17	1:45	15:30	1:36	15:38	1:26	15:47	1:14	15:57	0:59	16:09	0:40	16:25	0:14	16:45
6	3:03	16:05	2:51	16:14	2:45	16:20	2:37	16:26	2:28	16:33	2:17	16:41	2:03	16:52	1:44	17:05
7	4:04	16:50	3:57	16:55	3:53	16:58	3:48	17:01	3:42	17:05	3:36	17:09	3:27	17:14	3:16	17:21
8	5:05	17:34	5:02	17:34	5:00	17:34	4:59	17:35	4:57	17:35	4:54	17:35	4:51	17:35	4:47	17:35
9	**6:03**	**18:16**	**6:05**	**18:12**	**6:07**	**18:10**	**6:08**	**18:07**	**6:10**	**18:04**	**6:11**	**18:00**	**6:14**	**17:55**	**6:17**	**17:49**
10	7:01	18:59	7:08	18:50	7:11	18:45	7:16	18:40	7:21	18:33	7:27	18:26	7:35	18:16	7:45	18:04
11	7:58	19:42	8:08	19:30	8:15	19:22	8:22	19:14	8:30	19:05	8:40	18:53	8:53	18:39	9:10	18:21
12	8:53	20:27	9:08	20:11	9:16	20:02	9:26	19:51	9:37	19:39	9:51	19:25	10:08	19:06	10:32	18:41
13	9:48	21:12	10:05	20:54	10:15	20:44	10:27	20:32	10:41	20:17	10:57	20:00	11:19	19:38	11:48	19:08
14	10:41	22:00	11:00	21:40	11:11	21:29	11:24	21:16	11:40	21:00	11:58	20:41	12:23	20:17	12:56	19:43
15	11:32	22:49	11:52	22:29	12:04	22:17	12:17	22:04	12:33	21:48	12:52	21:29	13:18	21:03	13:53	20:28
16	12:21	23:39	12:40	23:19	12:52	23:08	13:05	22:55	13:20	22:40	13:39	22:21	14:04	21:57	14:38	21:23
17	13:06		13:24		13:35		13:47	23:50	14:02	23:36	14:19	23:19	14:41	22:57	15:12	22:28
18	13:49	0:29	14:05	0:11	14:15	0:01	14:25		14:38		14:53		15:12		15:37	23:38
19	14:30	1:19	14:43	1:05	14:51	0:56	14:59	0:46	15:09	0:34	15:21	0:20	15:36	0:02	15:56	
20	15:09	2:10	15:19	1:58	15:24	1:51	15:31	1:44	15:38	1:35	15:47	1:24	15:58	1:10	16:12	0:52
21	15:47	3:00	15:53	2:52	15:56	2:48	16:00	2:43	16:05	2:36	16:10	2:29	16:17	2:20	16:25	2:07
22	16:25	3:52	16:27	3:48	16:28	3:45	16:29	3:43	16:30	3:39	16:32	3:36	16:34	3:31	16:37	3:25
23	17:03	4:43	17:01	4:44	16:59	4:44	16:58	4:44	16:56	4:44	16:54	4:44	16:52	4:44	16:49	4:44
24	*17:43*	*5:37*	*17:36*	*5:41*	*17:33*	*5:44*	*17:28*	*5:47*	*17:24*	*5:50*	*17:18*	*5:54*	*17:11*	*5:59*	*17:02*	*6:06*
25	18:25	6:32	18:14	6:41	18:08	6:46	18:01	6:51	17:54	6:58	17:44	7:06	17:32	7:16	17:17	7:30
26	19:11	7:29	18:56	7:42	18:48	7:49	18:39	7:58	18:28	8:08	18:14	8:20	17:58	8:35	17:36	8:55
27	20:00	8:28	19:43	8:45	19:33	8:54	19:21	9:05	19:08	9:18	18:51	9:33	18:30	9:53	18:02	10:20
28	20:54	9:28	20:35	9:47	20:23	9:58	20:10	10:11	19:55	10:26	19:36	10:44	19:12	11:08	18:39	11:40
29	21:52	10:29	21:32	10:49	21:20	11:00	21:06	11:14	20:50	11:30	20:31	11:49	20:06	12:14	19:30	12:50
30	22:52	11:27	22:33	11:47	22:22	11:58	22:09	12:11	21:54	12:27	21:35	12:46	21:11	13:10	20:37	13:44
31	23:53	12:22	23:37	12:40	23:27	12:50	23:16	13:02	23:02	13:16	22:46	13:33	22:26	13:55	21:57	14:24

Bold = new Moon, *italic* = full Moon. A gap in a column indicates the event will take place early the next day.

MOONRISE AND MOONSET, NOVEMBER AND DECEMBER 2018
UNIVERSAL TIME AT GREENWICH MERIDIAN

Event	+20° RISE	+20° SET	+30° RISE	+30° SET	+35° RISE	+35° SET	+40° RISE	+40° SET	+45° RISE	+45° SET	+50° RISE	+50° SET	+55° RISE	+55° SET	+60° RISE	+60° SET
Nov. 1		13:14		13:29		13:37		13:47		13:58		14:12	23:46	14:29	23:25	14:52
2	0:54	14:01	0:41	14:13	0:33	14:19	0:25	14:26	0:14	14:34	0:02	14:44		14:57		15:13
3	1:55	14:46	1:45	14:53	1:40	14:57	1:34	15:01	1:27	15:06	1:18	15:12	1:08	15:20	0:54	15:29
4	2:53	15:29	2:49	15:31	2:46	15:32	2:43	15:34	2:39	15:36	2:35	15:37	2:30	15:40	2:23	15:43
5	3:51	16:10	3:51	16:08	3:51	16:07	3:51	16:05	3:51	16:04	3:51	16:02	3:51	15:59	3:51	15:56
6	4:48	16:52	4:52	16:45	4:55	16:41	4:58	16:37	5:02	16:32	5:06	16:26	5:11	16:19	5:18	16:09
7	**5:44**	**17:34**	**5:53**	**17:23**	**5:58**	**17:17**	**6:04**	**17:10**	**6:11**	**17:02**	**6:20**	**16:52**	**6:30**	**16:40**	**6:44**	**16:24**
8	6:40	18:18	6:53	18:03	7:01	17:55	7:09	17:46	7:19	17:35	7:32	17:21	7:47	17:04	8:08	16:42
9	7:36	19:03	7:52	18:46	8:02	18:36	8:12	18:24	8:25	18:11	8:41	17:55	9:01	17:34	9:28	17:05
10	8:30	19:51	8:49	19:31	9:00	19:20	9:12	19:07	9:27	18:52	9:45	18:33	10:09	18:09	10:42	17:36
11	9:23	20:40	9:43	20:19	9:55	20:08	10:08	19:54	10:24	19:38	10:44	19:18	11:09	18:53	11:45	18:17
12	10:13	21:30	10:33	21:10	10:45	20:58	10:59	20:45	11:15	20:29	11:34	20:09	12:00	19:44	12:36	19:08
13	11:00	22:20	11:20	22:02	11:31	21:51	11:44	21:38	11:59	21:24	12:17	21:06	12:41	20:42	13:14	20:10
14	11:45	23:11	12:02	22:54	12:12	22:45	12:24	22:34	12:37	22:21	12:53	22:05	13:14	21:46	13:43	21:18
15	12:26		12:41	23:47	12:49	23:40	12:59	23:31	13:10	23:20	13:24	23:08	13:41	22:52	14:04	22:31
16	13:06	0:01	13:17		13:24		13:31		13:40		13:50		14:03		14:20	23:45
17	13:43	0:51	13:51	0:41	13:56	0:35	14:01	0:29	14:07	0:21	14:14	0:12	14:22	0:01	14:33	
18	14:21	1:41	14:24	1:35	14:27	1:32	14:29	1:28	14:32	1:23	14:36	1:17	14:40	1:11	14:45	1:02
19	14:58	2:32	14:58	2:30	14:58	2:29	14:57	2:28	14:57	2:26	14:57	2:25	14:57	2:22	14:57	2:20
20	15:37	3:24	15:32	3:27	15:30	3:28	15:27	3:30	15:23	3:31	15:20	3:34	15:15	3:36	15:09	3:40
21	16:18	4:19	16:09	4:25	16:04	4:29	15:58	4:34	15:52	4:39	15:44	4:45	15:35	4:53	15:22	5:03
22	17:02	5:15	16:49	5:26	16:42	5:33	16:34	5:40	16:24	5:49	16:12	5:59	15:58	6:12	15:39	6:29
23	*17:51*	*6:15*	*17:35*	*6:30*	*17:25*	*6:39*	*17:15*	*6:49*	*17:02*	*7:00*	*16:47*	*7:14*	*16:28*	*7:32*	*16:02*	*7:57*
24	18:45	7:17	18:26	7:35	18:15	7:45	18:02	7:57	17:47	8:12	17:29	8:29	17:06	8:52	16:34	9:23
25	19:43	8:19	19:23	8:39	19:11	8:51	18:57	9:04	18:41	9:20	18:21	9:39	17:56	10:05	17:20	10:40
26	20:44	9:20	20:24	9:40	20:13	9:52	19:59	10:06	19:44	10:22	19:24	10:41	18:59	11:07	18:24	11:43
27	21:47	10:18	21:29	10:37	21:18	10:48	21:06	11:01	20:52	11:15	20:35	11:33	20:13	11:56	19:42	12:28
28	22:49	11:12	22:34	11:28	22:26	11:37	22:16	11:48	22:04	12:00	21:51	12:15	21:33	12:34	21:09	13:00
29	23:49	12:01	23:39	12:14	23:33	12:21	23:26	12:29	23:17	12:38	23:07	12:50	22:55	13:04	22:39	13:22
30		12:46		12:55		12:59		13:05		13:11		13:18		13:27		13:39
Dec. 1	0:48	13:29	0:42	13:33	0:38	13:35	0:34	13:37	0:29	13:40	0:24	13:44	0:17	13:48	0:07	13:53
2	1:45	14:10	1:43	14:09	1:42	14:09	1:41	14:08	1:40	14:08	1:39	14:07	1:37	14:06	1:34	14:05
3	2:41	14:50	2:44	14:45	2:45	14:42	2:47	14:39	2:49	14:35	2:52	14:30	2:56	14:25	3:00	14:18
4	3:36	15:31	3:43	15:21	3:47	15:16	3:52	15:10	3:58	15:03	4:05	14:55	4:13	14:45	4:24	14:31
5	4:31	16:13	4:42	16:00	4:49	15:52	4:57	15:44	5:05	15:34	5:16	15:22	5:30	15:07	5:48	14:47
6	5:26	16:57	5:41	16:41	5:50	16:31	6:00	16:20	6:11	16:08	6:26	15:53	6:44	15:33	7:09	15:07
7	**6:20**	**17:43**	**6:38**	**17:24**	**6:49**	**17:13**	**7:01**	**17:01**	**7:15**	**16:46**	**7:32**	**16:28**	**7:54**	**16:05**	**8:25**	**15:34**
8	7:14	18:31	7:34	18:11	7:45	18:00	7:58	17:46	8:14	17:30	8:33	17:10	8:58	16:45	9:34	16:09
9	8:05	19:21	8:26	19:01	8:38	18:49	8:51	18:35	9:08	18:19	9:28	17:59	9:54	17:33	10:30	16:56
10	8:54	20:12	9:14	19:52	9:26	19:41	9:39	19:28	9:55	19:13	10:14	18:54	10:39	18:29	11:14	17:54
11	9:40	21:02	9:58	20:45	10:09	20:35	10:21	20:23	10:36	20:09	10:53	19:52	11:16	19:31	11:47	19:01
12	10:23	21:53	10:39	21:38	10:48	21:29	10:59	21:20	11:11	21:08	11:26	20:54	11:45	20:36	12:10	20:12
13	11:03	22:43	11:16	22:31	11:23	22:24	11:32	22:17	11:42	22:08	11:53	21:57	12:08	21:43	12:28	21:25
14	11:41	23:32	11:50	23:24	11:56	23:20	12:02	23:14	12:09	23:08	12:18	23:01	12:28	22:52	12:42	22:40
15	12:17		12:23		12:26		12:30		12:34		12:40		12:46		12:54	23:56
16	12:54	0:22	12:55	0:18	12:56	0:15	12:58	0:13	12:59	0:10	13:01	0:06	13:02	0:02	13:05	
17	13:31	1:12	13:28	1:12	13:27	1:12	13:25	1:13	13:24	1:13	13:22	1:13	13:19	1:13	13:16	1:13
18	14:09	2:04	14:03	2:09	13:59	2:11	13:55	2:14	13:50	2:18	13:44	2:22	13:37	2:27	13:28	2:33
19	14:51	2:59	14:41	3:07	14:35	3:13	14:28	3:20	14:20	3:25	14:10	3:33	13:58	3:43	13:43	3:57
20	15:38	3:56	15:23	4:09	15:15	4:17	15:05	4:25	14:54	4:35	14:41	4:48	14:24	5:03	14:02	5:23
21	16:29	4:57	16:11	5:14	16:01	5:23	15:49	5:34	15:35	5:47	15:19	6:03	14:57	6:24	14:28	6:51
22	*17:26*	*6:00*	*17:06*	*6:19*	*16:55*	*6:31*	*16:41*	*6:44*	*16:26*	*6:59*	*16:06*	*7:17*	*15:42*	*7:42*	*15:07*	*8:16*
23	18:28	7:04	18:08	7:24	17:56	7:36	17:42	7:50	17:26	8:06	17:06	8:26	16:40	8:52	16:04	9:28
24	19:33	8:06	19:14	8:25	19:02	8:37	18:50	8:50	18:34	9:06	18:16	9:25	17:52	9:49	17:19	10:23
25	20:38	9:03	20:21	9:21	20:12	9:31	20:01	9:43	19:48	9:56	19:33	10:13	19:13	10:34	18:46	11:02
26	21:41	9:56	21:29	10:13	21:22	10:19	21:13	10:28	21:04	10:38	20:52	10:51	20:38	11:07	20:19	11:28
27	22:42	10:45	22:34	10:54	22:30	11:00	22:24	11:06	22:18	11:14	22:11	11:23	22:02	11:34	21:51	11:48
28	23:40	11:29	23:37	11:34	23:35	11:37	23:33	11:41	23:31	11:45	23:28	11:50	23:24	11:55	23:20	12:03
29		12:11		12:11		12:12		12:12		12:13		12:14		12:15		12:16
30	0:37	12:51	0:38	12:47	0:39	12:45	0:40	12:43	0:41	12:40	0:43	12:37	0:44	12:33	0:46	12:28
31	1:32	13:31	1:38	13:23	1:41	13:19	1:45	13:14	1:50	13:08	1:55	13:01	2:02	12:52	2:11	12:41

LUNAR OBSERVING
BY BRUCE MCCURDY

I feel quite sure that I first viewed the moon in my small scope with just as much incredible delight as Galileo did in his. It is true that I had seen photographs of the moon and therefore had some vague idea of what its appearance would be like, but I was still wholly unprepared for all the wonders which I found on that first night as I explored the lunar surface. No photograph has yet been made which is not cold and flat and dead when compared with the scenes that meet one's eyes when the moon is viewed through even a small telescope.

Leslie Peltier, *Starlight Nights*

The Moon is the first astronomical object to grab anyone's eye in the night sky, and has provided "first light" for countless telescopes in the four centuries from Galileo's time to the present. Galileo himself was beaten to the punch by the underappreciated Englishman, Thomas Harriot, who was likely the first telescopic visual observer of Earth's satellite, and certainly the first to sketch an eyepiece view, on 1609 Jul. 26. This was some four months before Galileo did the same.

While the invention of the telescope may be considered the birth of modern astronomy, the Moon has been an object of fascination and mystique since the earliest annals of history, and presumably long before that. Early scientists in ancient observatories carefully tracked lunar cycles and recorded the extremes of its rising and setting points along the horizon. Some 23 centuries ago, the enterprising Aristarchus of Samos carefully observed a total lunar eclipse and derived impressively accurate measurements of the Moon's diameter ($^1/_3$ that of Earth; the actual percentage is 27.2) and distance (30 Earth diameters, similar to the modern accepted mean value).

One hardly needs a telescope to enjoy the Moon. If observed even briefly on a regular basis, Earth's only natural satellite has much to offer the modern-day naked-eye observer. Noteworthy phenomena include its wandering path through the constellations of the zodiac, the inexorable progression of phases, frequent conjunctions with planets and bright stars, occasional eclipses, libration, earthshine, and atmospheric effects.

Many of the cycles that fascinated the ancients can be observed directly. Understanding these cycles is interesting in its own right. It is also of value to telescopic lunar observers who can benefit when the Moon is favorably placed in the sky, as well as to dark-sky enthusiasts who may be more interested in knowing when it is below the horizon.

Every child learns that the Moon, like the Sun, rises in the east and sets in the west. Relative to a terrestrial landmark (or when viewed through an unpowered telescope!) the Moon appears to move its own diameter (~0.5°) westward in about 2 min. When measured against the background stars, however, it moves about its own diameter *eastward* in an hour, the same direction that Earth rotates. The 30:1 ratio between these rates nicely squares with the time periods involved: one day for Earth to rotate, one sidereal month (about 27.3 d) for the Moon to complete an orbit.

If one observes the Moon at about the same time from night to night, its eastward motion against the background stars becomes apparent. The Moon transits the meridian about 50 min later from one day to the next, a period that rules the tides (see TIDES AND THE EARTH–MOON SYSTEM, p. 179). However, rise and set times vary much more as the Moon's eastward motion also contains a significant northward or southward component, causing moonrise times to bunch together for part of each month, and moonset times to similarly cluster two weeks later. This is famously manifest in the Harvest Moon, an observation of interest to almost everyone. Every two weeks, a rise or set event occurs just after midnight, explaining why one day has no moonrise and another no moonset; over the course of a synodic month (new Moon to new Moon), Luna transits the meridian one fewer time than does the Sun (see TIMES OF MOONRISE AND MOONSET, p. 150).

Note the Moon's phase during a conjunction with a bright star, and again the following month when it returns: the phase is 2 d less (see the table). The extra couple of days it needs to get back to the same phase means travelling almost an additional 30°. This is due to the Sun's own apparent motion across the sky, also about 30° per month. If one tracks its position among the stars from, for example, one full Moon to the next, it is easy to see that the full Moon appears to be shifted eastward by about one zodiacal constellation each lunar month.

No two months are the same: the lunar orbit is significantly out of round (e = 0.0549) and its path ever-changing.

2018 passages of the Moon through 6 h RA (highest declination, in northern Orion)		
Date	Age (d)	Phase
Jan. 01	14	one day before full Moon
Jan. 28	12	high-phase waxing gibbous
Feb. 24	9	moderate waxing gibbous
Mar. 24	7	first quarter
Apr. 20	5	thick waxing crescent
May 17	3	moderate waxing crescent
Jun. 14	<1	new Moon
Jul. 11	28	thin waning crescent
Aug. 07	26	moderate waning crescent
Sep. 04	23	thick waning crescent
Oct. 01	21	last quarter
Oct. 28	19	moderate waning gibbous
Nov. 25	17	high-phase waning gibbous
Dec. 22	15	full Moon

While mean distances and periods are known to high accuracy, the Moon's distance from Earth is not constant, rather it is constrained between 356 000 and 407 000 km. Each month, the Moon's perigee (closest approach to Earth) ranges from 35 000 to 50 000 km closer than its apogee, depending on the orientation of these orbital positions relative to the Sun. Thus the Moon varies in size from about 30′ to 34′. Nor is its speed constant; the Moon near perigee and apogee can be travelling as much as 5% faster and slower, respectively, than its mean orbital speed of 1.023 km/s. Our perception of the Moon's ever-changing path is further enhanced through the effects of parallax.

Among the major satellites of the Solar System, only the Moon and Neptune's Triton do not orbit in the plane of the equator of its planet. The Moon roughly orbits in the plane of the ecliptic, causing it to ride high or low at different points in the month, and at different phases throughout the calendar year. For example, a first-quarter Moon always cruises high in the sky around the time of the spring equinox but low around the autumn equinox; a full Moon is high around the time of the winter solstice but low around the summer solstice. The same statements apply to both Northern and Southern Hemispheres; however, the seasons themselves are six months out of phase.

Moreover, the Moon's orbit is tilted some 5° 09′ to the ecliptic, with the nodes (crossing points) of its orbit regressing rapidly, completing a full cycle (the regression of the nodes) in just 18.61 years. The combination of these two tilts can be constructive or destructive, exaggerating or muting the seasonal effects noted above. The extremes of azimuth for rise and set points, and of altitude for meridian transits, are likewise modulated. In 2018, this effect is mostly destructive, with the Moon having a declination range of ~19.0° in January, increasing to ~20° in December (see THE SKY MONTH BY MONTH, p. 98 and p. 120). Occultation series for stars near the ecliptic, the brightest of which are listed in the Zodiacal Catalog, also follow the 18.61-year cycle (see LUNAR OCCULTATIONS p. 162).

A period quite similar to the 18.61 year period of "lunar nodes regression" is the 6585⅓ day (or 18.03 year) period of the Saros. Used for many centuries to explain and predict solar and lunar eclipses, the Saros also explains near-repetitions of the lunar librations and such phenomena as extreme perigees and apogees. Remarkably, the major lunar and solar cycles (draconic, sidereal, anomalistic, and synodic month, eclipse year, and calendar year) all have near-integer values during this important cycle, with the result that all three bodies return to very nearly their starting positions (see ECLIPSE PATTERNS, p. 122 and SOME ASTRONOMICAL AND PHYSICAL DATA, p. 29).

At the eyepiece, the closest astronomical target offers the greatest wealth of detail available to any given telescope, binocular, or camera, regardless of its size or quality. Of the countless recognizable features on the lunar nearside, over 1000—virtually all of them within reach of a moderate amateur telescope—have been formally named by the International Astronomical Union. Many of the greatest names in astronomy, exploration, and discovery are so commemorated. Observation of the Moon can be a lesson in the history of science. Seven Canadians have been immortalized by having observable lunar craters named after them: Ostwald Avery (1877–1955), Frederick Banting (1891–1941), Carlyle Beals (1899–1979), Reginald Daly (1871–1957), Simon Newcomb (1835–1909), John S. Plaskett (1865–1941), and Joshua Slocum (1844–1909). Remarkably, three of the seven—Avery, Beals, and Newcomb—were born in Nova Scotia. Both Newcomb and Plaskett have been commemorated with RASC awards.

The face of the Moon is itself a history lesson of the early bombardment period of the inner Solar System. On a world devoid of erosion processes like wind, water, weather, glaciation, volcanism, plate tectonics, sedimentation, and life itself that have modified Earth, most of the Moon's features were sculpted billions of years ago. The largest of the ancient impact basins were subsequently filled with lava flows from its then-molten interior that hardened into basaltic rock and formed the distinctively dark, primarily circular regions wrongly but permanently identified as lunar maria, or seas. The brighter white areas, highlands that surround the maria and dominate the southern portion of the Earth-facing hemisphere, feature innumerable smaller but similarly ancient impact craters. With bombardment slowed to a relative trickle and the Moon remaining geologically inert since those ancient lava flows, Luna's appearance has changed but little over the past three billion years. Today, only the cosmic sandblasting of micrometeorites serves to gradually soften her features.

Observation of the Moon is nonetheless a very dynamic activity, due to the ever-changing angles of illumination. The terminator (the sunrise/sunset line) shifts westward across lunar features at ~0.5° per hour, a consequence of its 360° rotation in one month, about 12° per 24 hours. (Note that lunar east and west are reversed to celestial east and west, having been changed to the terrestrial standard during the early days of lunar exploration so as not to confuse the astronauts.) This slow but inexorable progression is particularly dramatic near the lunar terminator, where oblique sunlight reveals "in-depth" details of lunar features.

During the Moon's waxing phases (from new Moon to full), the sunrise terminator advances across new ground, exposing the most elevated features first. It can be a fascinating experience to look a little beyond the terminator for little points of light that might be mountain peaks or raised crater rims, and over the course of a single observing session, watch these features gradually expand under the oblique illumination of the rising Sun. It may take a few hours or even days before all the features on the crater floors are completely lighted. It is well worth revisiting an area of interest night after night to observe its changing appearance, even as the advancing Sun is revealing new wonders by the hour. Or, as the eloquent Peltier put it, "the geography of a whole new world…turning page by nightly page."

Under magnification, the darker areas, including the maria and the floors of large craters called "walled plains," are primarily flat and smooth. Occasional shift features such as scarps, wrinkle ridges, rilles, and rounded domes catch the eye, especially under low angles of illumination. Relatively few craters dot the landscape, proof positive of the greatly reduced rate of bombardment since those lava plains were formed. Frequently, they are surrounded by circular mountain ranges that represent the vestiges of the outer rings of the ancient impact structures. At low Sun angles, these cast long and impressive shadows whose jagged forms give a false impression of the rounded mountain tops. Long shadows yield interesting information about the topography under careful measurement, yet they often obscure features of interest in the lower terrain beyond. Hadley Rille of *Apollo 15* fame is theoretically well placed near the terminator at first quarter, but is lost in the shadows of towering Mount Hadley and the Apennine Mountains, which take days to recede. A return to this area just before last quarter will reveal the same scene lit from the opposite direction, the western faces of the mountains bathed in sunlight and the rille nicely illuminated.

At times of high angles of illumination around full Moon, a different aspect of the Moon is revealed. The three-dimensional context created in the brain from the pattern of light and dark is lost when the shadows are cast directly behind the features. Depth perception is problematic except right along the terminator, which now effectively encircles the Moon. Although the surface looks flat, a huge range of tonality is gained. Relatively young craters and their splash effects, such as ray systems and ejecta blankets, appear especially bright. Many small and otherwise unremarkable features stand out as brilliant points of light.

Full Moon is also the best time to observe the lunar libration zones. For line-of-sight reasons, explained on p. 95, the Moon displays a gentle rocking motion, revealing, over time, about 59% of its total surface area to the Earth-bound observer. Librations of longitude are zero when the Moon is at perigee or apogee; librations of latitude are zero when the Moon crosses the ecliptic at its ascending or descending node. Therefore, these librations follow the anomalistic month and draconic month, respectively, and thus gradually change with respect to each other, to bring different quadrants into favorable position. Libration has a more general effect on every lunar observing session, as even accessible nearside features can become more or less favorably situated to the line of sight, offering a more vertical or horizontal aspect from one viewing to the next. Details on current librations can be found in THE SKY MONTH BY MONTH, p. 98 and following.

The RASC's Isabel Williamson Lunar Observing Program is a detailed guide containing key information about the lunar surface and how to observe it. The program booklet lists 135 specific observing objectives (with sub-objectives) and optional activities such as Libration Challenge Features, lunar surface drawings, imaging, Observable Craters with Canadian Connections, and more. It also provides a detailed overview of the history of the Moon and the various geological eras that have shaped its surface, explaining each type of lunar feature and providing tips for observing each of them. See www.rasc.ca/observing/williamson-lunar-observing-certificate (open to all to download, but RASC membership is required to earn the pin and certificate).

From Aristarchus to Galileo, from Peltier to the 21st-century amateur astronomer, the Moon has remained among the most reliable and rewarding celestial targets for observers of all experience levels.

Recommended Reading:

- Brunier, S. and Legault, T., *New Atlas of the Moon*, Firefly Books Ltd., 2006.
- Peltier, L., *Starlight Nights: The Adventures of a Sky-Gazer*, Sky Publishing, 2007.
- Rükl, A., *Atlas of the Moon*, Sky Publishing, 2004.
- Sheehan, W. and Dobbins, T., *Epic Moon: A History of Lunar Exploration in the Age of the Telescope*, Willmann–Bell Inc., 2001.
- Westfall, J., *Atlas of the Lunar Terminator*, Cambridge University Press, 2000.
- Wood, C., *The Modern Moon: A Personal View*, Sky Publishing, 2003.
- Lunar Picture of the Day: lpod.wikispaces.com

LUNAR OCCULTATIONS
BY DAVID W. DUNHAM

The Moon often passes between Earth and a star, an event called an *occultation*. During an occultation, a star suddenly disappears as the advancing limb of the Moon crosses the line between the star and the observer. The star reappears from behind the following limb some time later. Because the Moon moves through an angle about equal to its own diameter every hour, the longest time for an occultation is about an hour; the time is shorter if the occultation is not central. Solar eclipses are actually occultations: the star being occulted by the Moon is the Sun.

Since observing occultations is rather easy, amateur astronomers should try this activity. The slow, majestic drift of the Moon in its orbit is interesting, with the disappearance or reappearance of a star at the Moon's limb a remarkable sight, particularly when it occurs as a graze near the Moon's northern or southern limb. During a graze, a star may disappear and reappear several times in succession as mountains and valleys in the Moon's polar regions drift by it. On rarer occasions, the Moon occults a planet, but no such events will be observable from North America in 2018.

A series of occultations of 0.9-mag. α Tauri (Aldebaran) ends in 2018, six of them visible from different parts of our continent. One on Apr. 19 is not in our tables, as it will only be visible from Yukon, Northwest Territories, and northwesternmost Saskatchewan. It will be a spectacular southern-limit graze by the 12%-sunlit Moon, accessible under good conditions from roads near Wrigley and Ft. Providence, NT. The series of occultations of 1.4-mag. α Leo (Regulus) ends on Apr. 24, with information for two events (on Jan. 5 and Mar. 1) given, and with another visible only from Alaska under good conditions on Mar. 28 around 15h UT. Other bright stars (magnitudes 2.9 to 3.9) occulted during 2018 are the Hyades stars γ and δ¹ Tauri; γ Librae; μ, o, and π Sagittarii; and γ and δ Capricorni. There will be occultations of relatively faint stars during the total lunar eclipse of Jan. 31 visible best from western North America, including three grazing occultations.

Lunar-occultation and graze observations refine our knowledge of the shape of the lunar profile and the fundamental star-coordinate system. These observations complement those made by other techniques, such as *Kaguya* and *Lunar Reconnaissance Orbiter* laser ranging and photographs. Improved knowledge of the lunar profile is useful in determinations of the Sun's diameter from solar-eclipse records. Occultation observations are also useful for detecting double stars and measuring their separations. Binaries with separations as small as 0.02″ have been discovered visually during grazes. Doubles with separations in this range are useful for filling the gap between doubles that can be directly resolved and those whose duplicity has been discovered spectroscopically. Now that the *Kepler* spacecraft is observing stars for exoplanet transits in the zodiac, that project is interested in the occultation of close double stars since stellar duplicity complicates their analysis.

Observations

The **International Occultation Timing Association (IOTA)** analyzes lunar-occultation observations and is the world clearinghouse for such observations. Anyone interested in pursuing a systematic program of lunar-occultation observations should consult the lunar- and grazing-occultation sections of *Chasing the Shadow: The IOTA Occultation Observer's Manual*, available as a free Adobe PDF download at www.poyntsource.com/IOTAmanual/Preview.htm. Readers without access to the internet may download the file at any public library, or write to IOTA's North American coordinator of lunar-occultation observations: Derek Breit, 17370 B Hawkins Lane, Morgan Hill, CA 95037 (e-mail breit_ideas@poyntsource.com). For general information, write to IOTA at PO Box 7152, Kent, WA 98042, USA (email business@occultations.org). IOTA provides predictions and coordination services for occultation observers—detailed graze predictions are available ($1.50 USD each; free by email); observing instructions are also available ($5 USD or see the IOTA manual). Annual IOTA membership is $40 USD in North America ($45 USD overseas). Online electronic-only membership is just $15 USD for all and is strongly encouraged. Membership includes free graze predictions, descriptive materials, and a subscription to *Journal for Occultation Astronomy*. IOTA's administrative website is www.occultations.org; www.lunar-occultations.com/iota is the site for predictions, updates, observations, and other technical information, including more predictions than can be given here. For observers in the southwestern Pacific (New Zealand, Australia, Papua New Guinea, and nearby areas), the Royal Astronomical Society of New Zealand (RASNZ) provides occultation data (total lunar, lunar grazing, planetary, and Jupiter's satellites), plus comprehensive instructions for new observers, at www.occultations.org.nz.

The main information required in a lunar-occultation observation is the time of the event and the observer's location. Supplementary data include the seeing conditions, telescope size, timing method, estimate of the observer's reaction time and the accuracy of the timing, and whether or not the reaction-time correction has been applied. The timing should be accurate to 0.5 s or better (a short-wave radio time signal and audio recorder provide a simple, permanent time record, but a video record provides higher accuracy). The observer's longitude, latitude, and altitude should be reported to the nearest tenth of an arcsecond and 10 m, respectively, and should be accurate to at least 0.5″ or 16 m. These can be determined from either GPS measurements (10 min of position averaging and an unobstructed view of the sky above about 15° altitude are needed) or a suitable topographical map. For the United States (except Alaska), write to US Geological Survey, Map Sales, PO Box 25286, Denver CO 80225, asking for an index to topographical maps in the desired state, or call 800-USA-MAPS. For Alaska, write to US Geological Survey, Map Sales, 4230 University Dr, Room 101, Anchorage AK 99508-4664, or phone 907-786-7011. Parts of USGS maps can be viewed and printed at nationalmap.gov/ustopo—enter a location or click on the USA map to zoom in and click on the "Topo map" tab. Detailed imagery is also available from Google Earth and other websites. IOTA is using these resources for predictions; they are usually (especially for North America) accurate enough for reporting lunar-occultation observations.

Observers are encouraged to learn how to video-record occultations in order to obtain reliable and accurate timings. Inexpensive yet sensitive video cameras are available. Visual timings must be accurate to ±0.2 s to be good enough for further improvement of the lunar profile and other parameters, except for grazes, where ±0.5 s is adequate. Information about video-recording occultations is on IOTA's technical website and in the IOTA manual mentioned previously. Check IOTA's technical website for report forms and reporting procedures. If you have questions, correspond with the North American coordinator specified on the previous page.

Tables of total-occultation predictions start on p. 165, and a table and maps of northern or southern limits for grazing occultations start on p. 174.

1. TOTAL LUNAR-OCCULTATION PREDICTIONS
BY DAVID HERALD AND DAVID W. DUNHAM

The total lunar-occultation predictions listed in the tables on pp. 165–170 are for the 18 standard stations identified on the map on the next page; the longitudes and latitudes of these stations are given in the table headings. The predictions were computed for IOTA by David Herald in Murrumbateman, Australia.

The predictions include all stars brighter than mag. 6.0. The first five columns give for each occultation the **Date**, the Zodiacal Catalog (**ZC**) number of the star, its magnitude (**mag.**), the phenomenon (**PH**), and the sunlit % of the Moon (**%sl**), with "+" for waxing and "−" for waning phases. Under each station are the event time (**UT**), time factors **A** and **B** (see below), and the cusp angle **CA** (measured around the Moon's limb from the North or South cusp, positive on the dark side, negative on the sunlit side, to the point of occurrence of the phenomenon); if the occultation occurs during a lunar eclipse, "E" is used and the value is the percent of the Moon's disk not in the umbral shadow. If no data appear for a given station, it is because there is no occultation, the star is below the horizon, or it is daytime there. If A or B have values larger than 5 min/degree, as can happen in the case of near-grazes, they will not give a reliable prediction for other places.

The terms A and B are for determining corrections to the times of the events for stations within 300 km of the standard stations. If Lo* and La* represent the longitude and latitude of the standard station, and Lo and La those of the observer, then for the observer,

UT of event = UT of event at the standard station + A(Lo − Lo*) + B(La − La*),

where Lo, etc. are expressed in degrees, and A and B are in minutes of time per degree. Longitude measured west of Greenwich is assumed to be *negative* (which is now the IAU convention and that used by IOTA's *Occult* software). Due regard must be paid to the algebraic signs of the terms. To convert UT to the standard time of the observer, see the section STANDARD TIME ZONES on p. 45.

As an example, consider the occultation of 5.4-mag. ZC 1733 (7 Vir) on 2018 Jan. 7 as seen from Boulder, Colorado. For Boulder, Lo = −105.3° and La = 40.0°. The nearest standard station is Denver, for which Lo* = −105.0° and La* = 39.8°. Therefore, the UT of the reappearance at the dark limb (RD) is 9:18.9 + 1.1 × (−105.3° +105.0°) min − 0.8 × (40.0° − 39.8°) min = 9:18.4. The % illumination of the Moon is 65−, showing the Moon is gibbous, about a day before last quarter. The cusp angle of reappearance is approximately 65° from the northern cusp on the Moon's dark limb. At Boulder, northwest of Denver, the cusp angle should be about the same. The local time is 2:18 a.m. MST of Jan. 7, since Mountain Standard Time is 7h behind UT (that is, MST = UT −7 hours).

The number of events observable from any location increases *rapidly* as predictions are extended to fainter stars. Observers who wish to pursue such work should email (preferred) **webmaster@lunar-occultations.com** to request software or more extensive lists, or write to Walter Robinson, 515 W Kump, Bonner Springs KS 66012–1439, USA—please provide accurate geographical coordinates, your largest telescope aperture, and a long, self-addressed envelope (with postage). Alternatively, you can generate your own predictions with IOTA's free *Occult 4* software available at **www.lunar-occultations.com/iota/occult4.htm**.

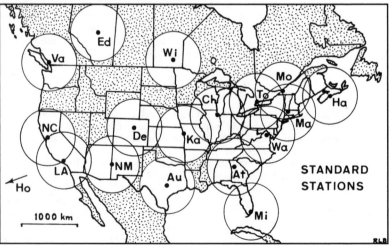

TOTAL LUNAR OCCULTATIONS FOR 2018

Date	ZC	mag.	PH	%sl	HALIFAX 44.6°N, 63.6°W UT	A m/deg	B m/deg	CA °	MONTRÉAL 45.5°N, 73.6°W UT	A m/deg	B m/deg	CA °	TORONTO 43.7°N, 79.4°W UT	A m/deg	B m/deg	CA °
Jan. 9	1950	5.7	RD	45–	08:40.5	+1.8	+1.1	66S	08:24.7	+1.6	+1.9	56S				
25	364	4.3	DD	52+					04:30.0	+0.1	–2.4	46S	04:33.7	+0.3	–3.1	36S
28	947	5.2	DD	91+					23:59.3	+2.0	–1.7	33S	23:50.9	+1.9	–1.6	33S
Feb. 11	2638	5.3	RD	17–	09:32.0	+1.4	+2.2	61S								
23	692*	0.9	RB	55+	16:48.1	+0.1	+1.2	–78N								
Mar. 1	1487†	1.4	DD	99+	06:13.1	–0.1	–3.9	30S								
1	1487†	1.4	RB	99+	06:45.8	+2.0	+0.5	–27S								
20	405	4.3	DD	13+	23:28.6	+0.6	–1.0	89S	23:19.7	+1.0	–0.8	88N				
28	1434	5.4	DD	86+	03:46.1	+1.5	–0.9	71N	03:29.9	+1.6	–0.9	81N	03:22.4	+1.6	–1.1	88S
Apr. 19	650	5.6	DD	11+									01:12.4	+1.7	+5.0	10N
22	1259	5.9	DD	51+	23:47.5	+1.9	+0.0	62N								
May 4	2633	3.8	RD	82–									09:47.1	+2.2	–1.8	40N
5	2759	3.5	RD	76–	05:08.4	+0.5	–0.3	30N								
18	913	5.1	DD	9+	00:14.6	+0.0	–1.5	83S								
24	1733	5.4	DD	72+									05:00.4	+1.8	+0.4	23N
Jul. 2	3190	2.9	RD	86–	05:15.5	+1.5	+2.3	49S	05:03.5	+1.3	+2.4	52S	04:51.2	+1.3	+2.8	47S
9	508	4.1	RD	20–	06:09.1	–0.3	+1.5	82S								
22	2223	3.9	DD	72+	00:56.2	+2.6	+0.8	37N	00:30.4	+2.6	+0.9	49N				
26	2779	3.8	DD	98+					05:03.5	+2.5	–2.6	33S	04:53.2	+2.5	–2.3	33S
Aug. 8	940	5.8	RD	13–	08:18.1	+0.1	+1.8	67S	08:19.0	+0.0	+1.5	79S	08:16.7	–0.1	+1.4	80S
Sep. 4	888	6	RD	35–					09:06.7	+1.4	+0.6	72N	08:57.9	+1.2	+0.6	71N
4	895	5.9	RD	35–									10:13.1	+1.1	+2.0	58S
21	3190	2.9	DD	91+	23:20.3	+1.5	+1.0	59S	23:08.8	+1.0	+1.3	60S				
28	405	4.3	DD	90–	06:09.2	+1.7	+1.0	78S	05:53.1	+1.7	+0.9	88N	05:41.6	+1.7	+1.0	84N
Oct. 2	995	4.1	RD	52–	05:16.1	–0.1	+2.6	38S	05:18.8	–0.1	+2.0	52S	05:16.1	–0.2	+1.9	54S
16	2779	3.8	DD	43+					02:30.8	+0.5	–1.0	78N	02:28.8	+0.7	–0.8	76N
21	3419	4.2	DD	87+					06:07.8	+0.7	–0.8	82S	06:04.5	+0.9	–0.7	83S
28	764	4.9	RD	86–	01:49.4	+0.0	+1.8	60S	01:51.0	–0.1	+1.6	70S				
30	1113	5.1	RD	65–	08:26.4	+1.8	+8.5	10S	08:16.9	+1.3	+4.6	22S	08:01.4	+0.7	+6.1	13S
Nov. 10	2547	4.9	DD	11+	21:37.6	+2.7	–5.1	15S								
25	894	4.4	RD	95–	04:44.5	+1.0	+3.5	23S	04:37.2	+1.0	+2.5	37S	04:27.5	+0.8	+2.6	37S
Dec. 15	3428	5	DD	45+	00:07.6	+4.6	–6.8	22S	23:34.4	+2.5	–1.2	53S	23:21.3	+2.6	–0.5	58S
18	364	4.3	DD	82+	22:56.4	+1.6	–1.0	71S	22:44.1	+1.1	+1.6	85S	22:35.4	+0.9	+1.7	88S
27	1576	5.3	RD	71–	11:00.8	+1.6	–0.9	64S	10:42.1	+2.1	+0.1	51S	10:25.1	+3.4	+2.6	30S

DB/DD = Disappearance at Bright/Dark limb; RB/RD = Reappearance at Bright/Dark limb

See p. 163 for additional explanation of these tables.

*ZC 692 = Aldebaran †ZC 1487 = Regulus

Figure 1—Jupiter is about to be occulted by the Moon's dark limb in this image taken by the Australian astronomer Paul Luckas in 2013.

TOTAL LUNAR OCCULTATIONS FOR 2018 (continued)

					WINNIPEG 49.9°N , 97.2°W				EDMONTON 53.6°N , 113.4°W				VANCOUVER 49.2°N , 123.1°W			
						A	B	CA		A	B	PA		A	B	CA
Date	ZC	mag.	PH	%sl	UT	m/deg	m/deg	°	UT	m/deg	m/deg	°	UT	m/deg	m/deg	°
Jan. 20	3268	5.3	DD	7+	00:46.1	+0.4	−0.3	67N	00:40.8	+0.2	+0.8	38N				
25	364	4.3	DD	52+	04:07.6	+0.9	−1.7	63S	03:45.1	+1.2	−0.6	82S	03:33.9	+1.6	−0.4	75S
26	508	4.1	DD	65+					08:05.1	+0.2	−1.8	65S	08:12.1	+0.3	−2.5	45S
27	635	3.7	DD	74+					03:43.0	+1.8	−1.9	41S	03:33.0	+2.6	−3.1	29S
27	667	5	DD	75+	08:14.7	+0.3	−0.6	70N	08:05.3	+0.6	−0.5	69N	08:01.5	+0.8	−0.8	86N
27	677	4.8	DD	76+					08:57.2	+0.1	−1.9	61S	09:05.5	+0.1	−2.7	40S
27	692*	0.9	DD	77+					11:04.6	−0.2	−0.9	83N	11:11.3	−0.2	−1.2	81S
28	832	4.3	DD	85+	09:23.7	+0.2	−0.8	70N	09:14.5	+0.5	−0.8	73N	09:12.7	+0.7	−1.1	89S
30	1175	4.9	DD	98+					11:44.6	+0.1	−1.8	68S	11:51.8	+0.1	−2.1	50S
Feb. 1	1434	5.4	RD	99−					09:09.9	+0.9	−2.0	52N	09:06.1	+1.3	−1.1	73N
11	2666	4.9	RD	16−									14:23.0	+0.3	−0.8	24N
22	462	6	DD	37+									05:21.1	+0.7	−0.6	78N
Mar. 7	2223	3.9	RD	68−					13:29.3	+1.2	−1.3	56N	13:21.0	+1.5	−0.9	68N
11	2759	3.5	RD	30−					13:55.1	+1.6	+1.3	57S	13:29.1	+2.0	+2.8	41S
22	692*	0.9	DD	31+					22:06.0	+1.8	−0.7	45S	21:50.9	+1.8	−0.5	43S
22	692*	0.9	RB	31+					22:46.7	+0.5	+3.4	−25S	22:27.6	+0.1	+3.8	−21S
28	1434	5.4	DD	86+	02:50.7	+1.4	−0.1	88N	02:31.1	+1.1	+0.7	83N				
Apr. 19	667	5	DD	11+	03:06.3	+9.9	+9.9	11S								
May 4	2633	3.8	RD	82−	09:06.6	+1.3	−0.8	30N	08:48.9	+0.8	+0.1	36N	08:39.7	+0.8	+0.6	53N
10	3419	4.2	RD	27−									11:21.6	+0.5	+2.1	76S
18	940	5.8	DD	9+	03:24.4	−0.1	−1.1	75N								
20	1259	5.9	DD	29+									06:20.7	+0.4	−0.8	47N
24	1733	5.4	DD	72+	04:25.4	+2.1	−0.1	37N								
Jul. 10	692*	0.9	RD	11−	09:02.6	−0.6	+2.1	40S								
22	2247	5.4	DD	73+									05:03.9	+1.5	−1.1	72S
26	2779	3.8	DD	98+	04:12.2	+1.5	−0.2	47S								
29	3171	3.7	RD	98−					08:00.0	+0.6	+2.3	17S	07:40.0	+1.0	+3.5	15S
31	3419	4.2	RD	89−	09:36.3	+2.5	−1.2	48N								
31	3425	4.4	RD	89−	10:50.1	+0.9	+0.7	53S	10:33.7	+1.3	+0.4	78S	10:16.8	+1.5	+0.9	81S
Aug. 4	364	4.3	RD	54−	10:17.6	+1.7	+0.6	61N	09:49.3	+2.4	−0.9	22N	09:30.7	+3.5	−3.9	13N
8	940	5.8	RD	13−	08:27.1	−0.2	+1.0	74N								
Sep. 4	895	5.9	RD	35−	10:05.2	+0.9	+1.3	89N	09:57.8	+0.6	+1.0	66N				
28	405	4.3	RD	90−	05:17.0	+1.7	+0.1	42N								
Oct. 2	995	4.1	RD	51−	05:29.7	−0.2	+1.3	81S								
4	1310	3.9	RD	26−	11:50.8	+1.2	+0.1	78N	11:34.5	+0.9	−0.1	59N	11:26.3	+0.7	+0.3	69N
13	2361	4.2	DD	17+	01:32.1	+0.8	−1.7	83S	01:11.2	+1.1	−1.3	88N				
15	2635	5.5	DD	34+					02:32.8	+1.1	−0.8	67N	02:22.9	+1.5	−0.4	68N
16	2779	3.8	DD	43+	02:12.7	+0.8	+0.1	43N	02:05.4	+0.1	+3.2	13N	01:44.3	+1.5	+2.8	22N
19	3171	3.7	DD	72+	05:23.7	+1.9	−3.1	35S	04:50.3	+1.5	−0.9	67S	04:36.3	+1.9	−0.3	70S
21	3419	4.2	DD	87+	05:49.5	+0.7	+0.7	60N	05:50.9	−1.0	+4.0	19N	05:45.0	+9.9	+9.9	6N
21	3425	4.4	DD	88+	06:53.8	+1.5	−2.3	43S	06:26.2	+1.3	−0.5	73S	06:12.8	+1.7	+0.0	75S
30	1113	5.1	RD	65−	08:05.5	+0.8	+2.0	56S	08:02.1	+0.5	+1.5	78S	07:51.9	+0.2	+1.5	75S
Nov. 12	2725	5.4	DD	19+					02:01.9	+1.4	−2.1	47S	01:55.9	+1.7	−1.9	48S
15	3113	5.4	DD	45+	02:07.8	+1.0	−0.1	68N	03:57.7	+0.9	+0.9	44N	01:38.8	+1.1	+1.6	41N
25	894	4.4	RD	95−	04:26.4	+0.6	+1.6	72S	04:22.9	+0.4	+1.3	86N	04:14.5	+0.2	+1.2	85N
Dec. 14	3428	5	DD	45+	22:49.7	+1.5	+1.2	89N								
18	364	4.3	DD	82+	22:38.2	+0.2	+2.1	68N								
19	405	4.3	DD	85+	08:34.1	+0.3	−1.3	73S	08:21.6	+0.7	−1.0	84S	08:18.2	+1.0	−1.2	71S
27	1576	5.3	RD	72−	09:51.0	+2.7	+4.3	25S	09:33.5	+1.5	+3.9	28S				
30	1950	5.7	RD	37−					15:00.0	+3.0	+1.9	26S				

DB/DD = Disappearance at Bright/Dark limb; RB/RD = Reappearance at Bright/Dark limb

See p. 163 for additional explanation of these tables.
*ZC 692 = Aldebaran

"Since observing occultations is rather easy, amateur astronomers should try this activity. The slow, majestic drift of the Moon in its orbit is interesting, with the disappearance or reappearance of a star at the Moon's limb a remarkable sight, particularly when it occurs as a graze near the Moon's northern or southern limb."

TOTAL LUNAR OCCULTATIONS FOR 2018 (continued)

Date	ZC	mag.	PH	%sl	MASSACHUSETTS 42.5°N, 72.5°W UT	A m/deg	B m/deg	CA °	WASHINGTON, D.C. 38.9°N, 77.0°W UT	A m/deg	B m/deg	CA °	CHICAGO 41.9°N, 87.7°W UT	A m/deg	B m/deg	CA °
Jan. 7	1733	5.4	RD	66–					09:47.9	+0.2	–4.0	26N	09:32.6	+0.7	–2.8	35N
9	1950	5.7	RD	45–	08:20.1	+2.0	+2.6	45S								
0	3268	5.3	DD	7+									00:56.0	+0.5	–1.1	80S
25	364	4.3	DD	52+	04:38.2	+0.0	–3.2	32S					04:37.4	+0.5	–5.0	22S
28	947	5.2	DD	91+									23:38.7	+1.5	–0.7	39S
Mar. 3	1733	5.4	RD	98–									05:46.9	+0.9	–2.0	36N
20	405	4.3	DD	13+	23:23.8	+1.0	–1.2	82S	23:23.8	+1.2	–1.6	69S				
28	1434	5.4	DD	86+	03:34.7	+1.6	–1.2	87N	03:32.5	+1.6	–1.6	78S	03:11.2	+1.6	–1.3	74S
Apr. 19	650	5.6	DD	11+					01:05.8	+0.7	+0.8	38N				
May 4	2633	3.8	RD	82–					10:01.3	+2.3	–1.7	52N	09:32.2	+2.1	–1.4	43N
5	2759	3.5	RD	76–	05:04.1	+0.5	+0.3	46N	04:59.9	+0.5	+0.7	61N				
24	1733	5.4	DD	72+					05:04.1	+1.3	–0.3	36N	04:46.3	+1.8	–0.5	42N
Jul. 2	3190	2.9	RD	86–	04:57.2	+1.4	+2.8	46S	04:39.0	+1.5	+3.9	34S	04:35.3	+1.2	+3.6	37S
22	2223	3.9	DD	72+	00:31.0	+2.6	+0.7	55N								
26	2779	3.8	DD	98+	05:17.7	+3.9	–5.8	18S					04:36.7	+2.3	–2.0	32S
31	3419	4.2	RD	89–									10:02.7	+1.8	–0.3	84N
Aug. 4	364	4.3	RD	53–									10:27.2	+1.7	+1.2	88S
8	940	5.8	RD	13–	08:14.3	–0.1	+1.6	71S	08:09.4	–0.2	+1.5	67S	08:16.1	–0.3	+1.2	83S
Sep. 4	888	6	RD	35–	09:06.1	+1.4	+0.8	82N	08:56.7	+1.2	+1.0	88N	08:47.3	+1.0	+0.6	66N
4	895	5.9	RD	35–					10:03.7	+0.9	+3.1	38S	10:01.0	+0.9	+2.0	61S
21	3190	2.9	DD	91+	23:06.4	+1.1	+1.1	55S								
28	405	4.3	RD	90–	05:51.9	+1.7	+1.2	84S	05:39.8	+1.6	+1.4	82S	05:26.4	+1.5	+1.0	77N
Oct. 2	995	4.1	RD	52–	05:12.3	–0.2	+2.2	43S	05:05.6	–0.4	+2.3	38S	05:15.2	–0.3	+1.7	58S
16	2779	3.8	DD	43+	02:34.5	+0.6	–1.1	86N	02:35.2	+0.8	–1.1	90N	02:23.0	+1.0	–0.5	71N
21	3419	4.2	DD	87+	06:11.4	+0.8	–1.1	72S	06:11.5	+1.1	–1.2	64S	05:57.0	+1.1	–0.3	87S
27	653	4.8	RD	92–					09:43.3	+1.5	–3.8	44N				
30	1113	5.1	RD	65–									07:47.2	+0.1	+6.1	11S
Nov. 15	3113	5.4	DD	45+									02:22.6	+1.3	–0.9	82S
25	894	4.4	RD	95–	04:29.3	+0.7	+3.4	24S	04:13.3	+0.2	+4.4	14S	04:17.3	+0.6	+2.4	42S
Dec. 13	3190	2.9	DD	27+	01:24.5	–0.6	+2.2	26N	01:19.3	–0.2	+1.6	36N				
14	3428	5	DD	45+	23:42.7	+3.3	–2.4	40S	23:35.2	+4.1	–2.7	36S	23:00.9	+2.4	+0.3	67S
18	364	4.3	DD	82+	22:40.8	+1.3	+1.4	78S	22:30.2	+1.1	+1.4	76S	22:26.1	+0.6	+1.8	87N
21	653	4.8	DD	96+					02:52.1	–0.1	+6.1	22N				
27	1576	5.3	RD	71–	10:43.8	+2.6	+0.6	42S								

DB/DD = Disappearance at Bright/Dark limb; RB/RD = Reappearance at Bright/Dark limb

See p. 163 for additional explanation of these tables.

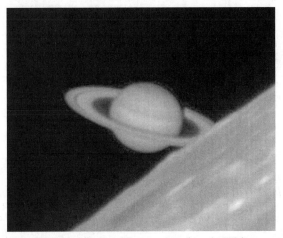

Figure 2—An occultation of Saturn as seen from the UK in March 2007. (Source: Damian Peach)

TOTAL LUNAR OCCULTATIONS FOR 2018 (continued)

					MIAMI 25.8°N, 80.3°W				ATLANTA 33.8°N, 84.3°W				AUSTIN 30.2°N, 97.8°W			
						A	B	CA		A	B	CA		A	B	CA
Date	ZC	mag.	PH	%sl	UT	m/deg	m/deg	°	UT	m/deg	m/deg	°	UT	m/deg	m/deg	°
Jan. 7	1733	5.4	RD	65–	10:15.9	+2.1	–1.6	76N	09:54.8	+1.5	–1.9	59N	09:35.3	+1.9	–0.4	89N
20	3268	5.3	DD	7+									01:06.5	+1.4	–2.5	46S
Feb. 1	1434	5.4	RD	99–									10:07.3	+1.5	–1.2	85S
7	2133	5.5	RD	53–	08:06.2	+0.4	–2.1	39N								
25	913	5.1	DD	71+	05:58.9	+1.1	+0.8	50N					05:37.6	+1.7	+0.7	56N
Mar. 3	1733	5.4	RD	98–	06:22.4	+2.2	–1.1	75N	06:04.7	+1.6	–1.4	57N	05:43.4	+1.9	+0.0	87N
28	1434	5.4	DD	86+	04:05.6	–0.1	–5.4	24S	03:32.2	+1.3	–2.7	51S				
Apr. 4	2291	5.5	RD	84–									10:28.4	+3.1	+0.7	60S
10	3079	4.1	RD	30–	10:53.1	+2.2	–2.0	27N					10:23.4	+0.3	–2.0	17N
19	650	5.6	DD	14+	01:05.0	+0.4	–0.7	89N	00:59.3	+0.7	–0.1	65N				
21	995	4.1	DD	30+	03:22.6	+0.6	+0.1	56N	03:24.4	+1.4	+1.8	27N	03:07.1	+1.2	–0.2	65N
23	1275	5.3	DD	52+	04:09.7	+1.1	–0.3	60N	04:04.6	+1.7	+0.6	38N	03:43.2	+1.7	–0.7	74N
May 1	2223	3.9	RD	98–	06:50.3	+2.0	–2.3	34N	06:24.5	+1.1	–2.6	17N	06:10.9	+1.7	–0.9	49N
4	2633	3.8	RD	82–	10:09.4	+2.7	–0.7	82N	09:50.8	+2.6	–1.2	61N	09:17.8	+2.6	–0.2	72N
5	2759	3.5	RD	76–	04:43.7	+0.9	+1.6	78S								
5	2797	2.9	RD	74–									12:45.0	+2.6	–1.6	61N
10	3419	4.2	RD	27–									10:47.0	+0.8	+5.5	25S
18	915	4.6	DD	9+	00:40.9	+0.6	–0.4	72N								
24	1733	5.4	DD	72+	05:10.8	+1.1	–1.2	73N	04:57.5	+1.4	–0.9	58N	04:40.2	+1.7	–1.4	85N
Jun. 4	3126	4.3	RD	72–									11:05.4	+9.9	+9.9	10N
Jul. 8	405	4.3	RD	28–	09:59.0	+2.1	+0.0	52N								
22	2223	3.9	DD	72+	00:12.7	+2.2	–1.0	73S								
25	2633	3.8	DD	94+	05:09.0	+2.2	+0.8	55N	05:13.5	+1.6	+2.9	24N	04:29.8	+3.2	+2.8	37N
26	2797	2.9	DD	98+	08:23.7	+0.4	+0.5	53N								
31	3419	4.2	DD	89–	09:59.0	+0.6	+2.7	36S	10:07.0	+1.5	+0.8	69S	09:38.6	+2.3	+0.9	82S
Aug. 4	364	4.3	RD	54–	10:02.0	+0.6	+4.0	29S	10:20.1	+1.5	+2.1	63S	09:52.5	+1.4	+1.9	75S
9	1113	5.1	RD	6–	10:16.2	+0.9	–0.6	54N								
25	3126	4.3	DD	98+	06:07.6	–0.1	+4.2	30N								
Sep. 4	888	6	RD	35–	08:34.6	+0.6	+1.9	58S	08:43.4	+0.9	+1.2	87S	08:30.6	+0.5	+0.9	86N
4	894	4.4	RD	35–	09:39.4	+2.4	–0.8	58N								
4	895	5.9	RD	35–					09:41.9	+0.3	+3.7	27S	09:27.8	+0.1	+2.8	36S
6	1193	5.4	RD	15–	08:17.1	+0.5	–0.6	57N								
28	405	4.3	RD	90–	05:11.3	+1.1	+2.3	55S	05:21.0	+1.4	+1.5	80S	04:59.3	+1.0	+1.3	90N
Oct. 4	1310	3.9	RD	27–									11:22.4	+1.1	+3.9	26S
13	2361	4.2	DD	17+									02:13.6	+1.4	–3.4	36S
16	2779	3.8	DD	43+	02:50.6	+1.7	–2.2	55S	02:33.0	+1.3	–1.0	86S	02:14.3	+2.0	–0.5	87N
21	3419	4.2	DD	87+					06:08.5	+1.7	–1.5	55S	05:45.4	+2.3	–0.6	66S
27	648	3.8	RD	92–	09:11.8	+2.4	–2.0	63N								
27	653	4.8	RD	91–	09:58.6	+1.9	–0.2	81S	09:43.9	+1.9	–1.7	69N	09:17.3	+2.6	–0.9	77N
Nov. 15	3113	5.4	DD	45+					02:39.6	+2.0	–2.2	51S	02:15.2	+2.5	–1.1	65S
24	730	5.1	RD	99–	03:15.5	+3.2	–2.1	59N								
25	894	4.4	RD	95–									03:43.2	–0.5	+3.5	15S
Dec. 13	3190	2.9	DD	27+	01:07.3	+0.9	+0.3	76N	01:11.4	+0.2	+1.5	43N	01:01.3	+0.0	+3.1	27N
13	3190	2.9	RB	27+									01:50.6	+2.7	–2.8	–45N
14	3425	4.4	DD	45+	23:01.2	+1.1	+3.2	40N								
14	3428	5	DD	45+					23:16.0	+4.7	–2.4	36S				
21	653	4.8	DD	96+	02:07.1	+1.5	+2.0	70N	02:25.8	+0.4	+4.1	34N				

DB/DD = Disappearance at Bright/Dark limb; RB/RD = Reappearance at Bright/Dark limb

See p. 163 for additional explanation of these tables.

"The Moon often passes between Earth and a star, an event called an occultation. During an occultation, a star suddenly disappears as the advancing limb of the Moon crosses the line between the star and the observer. The star reappears from behind the following limb some time later. Because the Moon moves through an angle about equal to its own diameter every hour, the longest time for an occultation is about an hour. The time is shorter if the occultation is not central. Solar eclipses are actually occultations: the star being occulted by the Moon is the Sun."

TOTAL LUNAR OCCULTATIONS FOR 2018 (continued)

Date	ZC	mag.	PH	%sl	KANSAS CITY 39.0°N, 94.5°W UT	A m/deg	B m/deg	CA °	DENVER 39.8°N, 105.0°W UT	A m/deg	B m/deg	CA °	NEW MEX., ARIZ. 34.0°N, 109.0°W UT	A m/deg	B m/deg	CA °
Jan. 7	1733	5.4	RD	65–	09:32.2	+1.2	–1.5	56N	09:18.9	+1.1	–0.8	65N	09:16.2	+1.4	+0.0	88N
20	3268	5.3	DD	7+	00:55.3	+0.7	–1.1	77S	00:45.5	+1.0	–0.6	88N				
27	667	5	DD	75+					08:21.9	+0.2	–1.3	75S	08:30.0	+0.1	–1.9	53S
28	832	4.3	DD	85+					09:32.4	+0.1	–1.3	77S	09:40.6	+0.0	–1.7	56S
Feb. 1	1434	5.4	RD	99–	09:56.9	+0.9	–2.0	69N	09:43.7	+1.3	–1.6	80N	09:44.3	+1.9	–0.8	79S
9	2399	4.9	RD	32–									11:51.3	–1.4	–5.3	8N
25	913	5.1	DD	71+									05:19.7	+2.1	+1.2	51N
Mar. 3	1733	5.4	RD	98–	05:43.8	+1.2	–1.1	54N								
28	1434	5.4	DD	86+	03:05.2	+1.5	–2.0	58S	02:48.0	+1.4	–2.0	52S				
Apr. 4	2291	5.5	RD	84–	10:36.4	+2.2	–0.6	83S	10:11.7	+2.4	+0.2	76S	09:55.8	+3.4	+1.6	55S
10	3079	4.1	RD	30–									10:16.7	–0.4	–2.0	13N
21	995	4.1	DD	30+	03:18.8	+2.5	+4.1	17N	02:59.9	+1.8	+1.3	36N	02:50.7	+1.6	–0.1	65N
23	1275	5.3	DD	53+	03:48.2	+2.2	+0.8	37N	03:26.3	+2.1	+0.2	52N	03:19.6	+2.0	–0.7	77N
May 1	2223	3.9	RD	98–	06:03.5	+0.8	–1.8	19N	05:53.6	+0.9	–0.8	34N	05:52.0	+1.3	–0.2	56N
4	2633	3.8	RD	82–	09:20.8	+2.1	–0.8	51N	08:59.9	+1.8	–0.2	56N	08:52.1	+2.0	+0.3	72N
5	2797	2.9	RD	74–					12:00.5	+3.2	–4.0	20N	12:04.8	+3.0	–2.2	39N
10	3419	4.2	RD	27–					11:12.5	+0.9	+2.5	59S	10:52.7	+0.8	+3.3	44S
17	764	4.9	DD	4+									02:52.6	+0.2	–0.2	55N
18	940	5.8	DD	9+					03:38.4	–0.2	–1.5	75N	03:49.6	–0.4	–2.0	53S
24	1733	5.4	DD	72+	04:36.1	+1.8	–0.8	59N	04:15.2	+2.0	–0.9	73N	04:14.3	+1.1	–1.4	87S
Jul. 22	2247	5.4	DD	73+									05:55.1	+1.6	–2.8	49S
25	2633	3.8	DD	94+									04:04.1	+3.6	+3.9	33N
26	2779	3.8	DD	98+	04:28.9	+2.0	–3.1	21S	04:11.7	+0.8	–3.4	14S				
31	3419	4.2	RD	89–	09:49.5	+2.2	–0.1	81N	09:23.1	+2.8	–0.2	62N	09:11.8	+2.8	+0.3	70N
31	3425	4.4	RD	89–					10:29.3	+0.8	+2.2	37S	10:10.8	+0.5	+3.4	26S
Aug. 4	364	4.3	RD	53–	10:11.8	+1.7	+1.3	89N	09:55.6	+1.6	+1.1	73N	09:42.7	+1.3	+1.3	80N
14	1733	5.4	DD	10+					03:13.0	+0.1	–1.6	86S	03:22.1	+0.1	–1.7	74S
Sep. 4	888	6	RD	35–	08:39.3	+0.8	+0.6	66N								
4	895	5.9	RD	35–	09:49.7	+0.7	+2.0	60S	09:45.0	+0.5	+1.6	74S	09:33.8	+0.2	+1.7	64S
28	405	4.3	RD	90–	05:13.6	+1.3	+1.0	74N	05:01.7	+1.1	+0.7	58N	04:53.5	+0.8	+0.8	68N
Oct. 4	1310	3.9	RD	27–	11:47.4	+1.5	+1.3	65S	11:34.6	+1.1	+1.2	71S	11:21.5	+0.8	+1.9	52S
13	2361	4.2	DD	17+	01:54.5	+0.9	–2.1	61S	01:42.0	+1.2	–1.8	70S	01:48.1	+1.5	–2.2	58S
15	2635	5.5	DD	34+					02:56.4	+1.3	–1.3	84S	02:58.4	+1.7	–1.5	74S
16	2779	3.8	DD	43+	02:16.4	+1.3	–0.3	70N	02:00.9	+1.6	+0.4	58N	01:51.0	+2.2	+0.4	68N
21	3419	4.2	DD	87+	05:48.8	+1.4	–0.1	87S	05:33.9	+1.4	+0.8	76N	05:22.4	+1.9	+0.9	84N
27	653	4.8	RD	92–	09:04.1	+3.4	–6.9	33N					08:35.7	+4.2	–4.4	40N
30	1113	5.1	RD	65–					07:36.1	+0.0	+3.2	28S				
Nov. 15	3113	5.4	DD	45+	02:14.7	+1.7	–0.6	84S	01:56.6	+1.7	+0.2	80N	01:47.1	+2.3	+0.3	87N
25	894	4.4	RD	95–	04:07.3	+0.4	+2.3	42S	04:05.5	+0.3	+1.8	57S	03:54.2	+0.0	+1.9	46S
Dec. 19	405	4.3	DD	85+	08:54.9	–0.1	–2.8	33S	08:51.4	+0.3	–3.2	31S				

DB/DD = Disappearance at Bright/Dark limb; RB/RD = Reappearance at Bright/Dark limb

See p. 163 for additional explanation of these tables.

TOTAL LUNAR OCCULTATIONS FOR 2018 (continued)

					LOS ANGELES 34.1°N, 118.3°W				N. CALIFORNIA 38.0°N, 122.0°W				HONOLULU 21.3°N, 157.9°W			
						A	B	CA		A	B	CA		A	B	CA
Date	ZC	mag.	PH	%sl	UT	m/deg	m/deg	°	UT	m/deg	m/deg	°	UT	m/deg	m/deg	°
Jan. 1	913	5.1	DD	99+	10:35.9	+1.8	+1.6	60N					09:07.3	+2.6	−0.3	60S
7	1733	5.4	RD	65−	09:04.9	+1.1	+0.4	85S	09:02.4	+0.8	+0.1	83N				
25	364	4.3	DD	52+					03:57.9	+3.9	−7.4	22S				
27	667	5	DD	75+	08:27.4	+0.4	−2.4	45S	08:17.2	+0.7	−1.9	58S				
28	832	4.3	DD	85+	09:39.5	+0.2	−2.2	46S	09:30.3	+0.4	−2.0	56S				
Feb. 1	1434	5.4	RD	99−	09:24.1	+2.4	+0.1	67S	09:15.6	+2.1	−0.2	75S				
9	2399	4.9	RD	32−	11:54.1	+0.1	−1.6	32N	11:47.5	−0.5	−2.3	22N				
11	2666	4.9	RD	16−					14:27.6	+1.2	+0.0	54N				
24	764	4.9	DD	60+									06:53.1	+2.4	+3.5	37N
25	913	5.1	DD	71+	05:00.0	+2.2	+1.3	56N	04:59.3	+2.1	+2.7	38N				
25	940	5.8	DD	72+									08:40.0	+1.9	−0.9	81S
Mar. 7	2223	3.9	RD	68−	13:45.3	+2.3	−0.9	89S	13:33.4	+2.2	−0.9	86N				
11	2757	5	RD	31−	13:16.1	+1.5	−0.2	52N	13:10.3	+1.1	−0.2	45N				
24	888	6	DD	45+									06:51.4	+2.3	+1.3	54N
24	895	5.9	DD	46+									08:08.9	+1.3	−0.2	76N
Apr. 21	995	4.1	DD	30+	02:34.4	+1.9	−0.2	73N								
23	1275	5.3	DD	52+	03:00.1	+2.1	−0.8	87N								
May 1	2223	3.9	RD	98−	05:40.6	+1.1	+0.4	69N	05:38.5	+0.8	+0.4	63N				
4	2633	3.8	RD	82−	08:35.4	+1.6	+0.8	82N	08:33.3	+1.3	+0.8	76N				
5	2797	2.9	RD	74−	11:38.4	+2.5	−1.8	35N	11:22.8	+1.9	−2.2	23N	10:24.2	+1.3	+1.8	72S
10	3419	4.2	RD	27−	10:46.5	+0.6	+3.4	42S	10:56.0	+0.5	+2.7	54S				
18	940	5.8	DD	9+	03:53.6	−0.5	−2.8	40S								
20	1259	5.9	DD	29+					06:31.2	+0.1	−1.0	70N				
23	1625	5.8	DD	62+									06:39.9	+2.5	−1.0	81N
24	1733	5.4	DD	72+	03:57.4	+1.7	−1.7	73S	03:45.5	+1.7	−1.3	77S				
Jun. 1	2759	3.5	RD	92−									13:44.7	+4.2	−5.4	23N
Jul. 22	2247	5.4	DD	73+	05:38.9	+1.8	−2.7	47S	05:23.0	+1.7	−2.1	54S				
25	2633	3.8	DD	94+	03:34.8	+2.7	+2.7	49N	03:36.5	+2.8	+3.4	40N				
26	2797	2.9	DD	98+									05:29.5	+2.0	+2.9	51N
31	3419	4.2	RD	89−	08:46.0	+2.7	+0.1	56N	08:35.6	+2.6	−0.5	39N				
31	3425	4.4	RD	89−	10:01.6	+1.4	+2.4	45S	10:04.0	+1.6	+1.8	60S	08:33.5	+0.9	+3.2	42S
Aug. 4	364	4.3	RD	53−	09:31.7	+1.1	+1.1	68N	09:31.5	+1.0	+0.8	55N				
8	995	4.1	RD	11−									14:18.6	−0.2	+1.6	53S
9	1127	5.9	RD	5−	12:07.4	+0.9	−1.3	37N								
18	2223	3.9	DD	50+									08:43.4	+1.0	−1.1	85N
Sep. 3	764	4.9	RD	44−									14:34.4	+0.8	+3.3	35S
4	915	4.6	RD	33−									13:00.0	+0.4	+1.3	70S
5	1077	4	RD	23−	13:03.2	+1.5	+0.4	82N	12:58.2	+1.5	−0.2	64N	12:27.2	+0.1	+0.1	75N
15	2291	5.3	DD	52+	04:24.4	+0.8	−0.7	64N	04:19.0	+0.9	−0.4	52N				
28	405	4.3	DD	90−	04:47.9	+0.5	+0.5	58N	04:47.2	+0.5	+0.0	42N				
Oct. 4	1310	3.9	RD	27−	11:15.4	+0.5	+1.6	60S	11:18.7	+0.5	+1.1	76S				
6	1576	5.3	RD	8−									14:30.1	+0.0	+1.3	46S
13	2361	4.2	DD	17+	01:32.6	+1.8	−1.9	62S								
15	2635	5.5	DD	34+	02:40.7	+2.1	−1.0	82S	02:30.0	+2.0	−0.6	87N				
16	2779	3.8	DD	43+	01:29.3	+2.5	+1.1	63N	01:25.2	+2.4	+1.5	54N				
19	3171	3.7	DD	72+					04:48.3	+3.3	−1.8	42S				
21	3419	3.9	DD	87+	05:06.0	+1.7	+1.7	68N	05:08.3	+1.2	+2.2	53N				
21	3425	4.4	DD	88+					06:20.9	+3.1	−1.4	45S	04:40.4	+1.9	+0.4	53S
30	1113	5.1	RD	65−	07:21.5	−0.5	+3.1	24S	07:32.3	−0.2	+2.1	44S				
Nov. 15	3113	5.1	RD	45−	01:26.1	+2.3	+1.1	76N	01:23.4	+2.0	+1.5	64N				
25	894	4.4	RD	95−	03:54.9	−0.1	+1.5	58S	04:00.7	+0.0	+1.3	71S				
29	1504	5.4	RD	55−									12:33.0	+1.3	+0.0	86S
Dec. 10	2838	5.6	DD	8+									05:12.7	+1.1	−1.3	67S
19	405	4.3	DD	85+					08:47.6	+1.3	−6.7	16S				

DB/DD = Disappearance at Bright/Dark limb; RB/RD = Reappearance at Bright/Dark limb

See p. 163 for additional explanation of these tables.

"Lunar occultation and graze observations refine our knowledge of the shape of the lunar profile and the fundamental star coordinate system. These observations complement those made by other techniques, such as Kaguya and Lunar Reconnaissance Orbiter laser ranging and photographs."

NAMES OF STARS OCCULTED IN 2018

ZC	Name	ZC	Name	ZC	Name
364	ξ² Cet	1077	ζ Gem (Mekbuda)	2223	γ Lib (Zuben-el-Akrab)
405	μ Cet	1113	56 Gem	2247	η Lib
626	48 Tau	1127	61 Gem	2291	49 Lib
635	γ Tau (Hyadum I)	1171	79 Gem	2361	χ Oph
636	55 Tau	1193	85 Gem	2633	μ Sgr
648	δ¹ Tau (Hyadum II)	1259	20 Cnc	2635	14 Sgr
653	δ² Tau	1275	θ Cnc	2725	28 Sgr
667	75 Tau	1362	78 Cnc	2759	ξ² Sgr
692	α Tau (Aldebaran)	1370	80 Cnc	2779	o Sgr
764	104 Tau	1415	7 Leo	2797	π Sgr (Al Baldah)
832	119 Tau	1418	8 Leo	2838	50 Sgr
836	120 Tau	1420	11 Leo	3069	20 Cap
863	127 Tau	1434	ψ Leo	3113	30 Cap
894	χ¹ Ori	1487	α Leo (Regulus)	3126	ι Cap (Tae)
913	64 Or	1493	34 Leo	3171	γ Cap (Nashira)
915	χ² Ori	1576	53 Leo	3190	δ Cap (Deneb Algedi)
940	68 Ori	1702	ν Vir	3268	42 Aqr
947	71 Ori	1733	7 Vir	3288	50 Aqr
991	16 Gem	1950	80 Vir	3356	74 Aqr
995	ν Gem	1978	88 Vir	3419	ψ¹ Aqr
1006	22 Gem	2128	ξ¹ Lib	3428	ψ³ Aqr

Names of occulted stars

The stars that are occulted by the Moon are stars that lie along the zodiac; hence they are known by their number in the ZC compiled by James Robertson and published in the *Astronomical Papers Prepared for the Use of the American Ephemeris and Nautical Almanac, Vol. 10*, Part 2 (U.S. Government Printing Office, Washington, 1940). Robertson's ZC has been out of print for several years. In 1986, Isao Sato, a member of the Lunar Occultation Observers Group in Japan, republished the ZC. This new edition is based on the epoch J2000 and includes much new data, particularly on double stars. Since stars are not usually recognized by their ZC numbers, the equivalent Bayer designations or Flamsteed numbers of the stars occulted during the year are given in the table above. The ZC and XZ (now version XZ80Q) catalogs, updated in 2005 by D. Herald using *HIPPARCOS*, Tycho–2, and UCAC–2 data, are available through IOTA's website.

2. GRAZING OCCULTATIONS: PREDICTIONS AND STAR DATA
BY EBERHARD RIEDEL AND DAVID W. DUNHAM

Grazing occultation predictions

The table on pp. 174–175 lists grazing lunar-occultation predictions for much of North America for 2018. The events are limited to stars of mag. 7.0 or brighter that will graze the limb of the Moon when it is at a favorable elongation from the Sun and at least as high above the horizon in degrees as the star's magnitude (e.g. a 3rd-mag. star is included only if its altitude is at least 3°). The star's USNO reference number is the ZC number, unless the number is prefixed with an X, which are not in the ZC; their numbers are from the XZ catalog, a more extensive zodiacal catalog first prepared at the U.S. Naval Observatory but now updated by D. Herald of Australia.

The maps on pp. 176–178 show the predicted graze tracks. The maps are "false" projections, since the lat/long scales are both linear. This makes it much easier for measuring coordinates or plotting locations with known coordinates than is possible with any other type of projection. The longitude scale is compressed by a factor of cos 50°. The maps are not detailed enough for locating oneself in the zone 2–3 km wide where multiple disappearances of a star may occur. To obtain detailed predictions of any observable graze, the GRAZPREP software can be downloaded via **www.grazprep.com** (password "IOTA/ES"). The software gives complete worldwide information needed for a successful observation for any location in relation to the projected lunar profile and corrected for elevation. For many grazes, IOTA overlays the predicted limit line on the very detailed maps and imagery of maps.google.com, available at **www.iota.timerson.net**, but further corrections are needed based on the predicted lunar profile and the observer's elevation above sea level.

Each track is keyed to the sequential number in the table. The computer-drawn number appears at the east and west ends of the track and is aligned parallel to it. Some overlapping numbers have been omitted for legibility; in these cases, check the other end of the track for the number. Conditions are represented by three different types of lines:

solid line = dark limb (night)

dashed line = bright limb (night)

dotted line = dark or bright limb (day)

Thicker lines are drawn for 1st-mag. stars and planets. Many tracks begin and/or end with the letter A, B, or S: A denotes that the Moon is at a low altitude, B that the bright limb interferes, and S that sunlight or twilight interferes. The tick marks along the tracks indicate multiples of 10 min of every hour. For example, if the time for the west end of the track is 3:16.2, the tick marks proceeding eastward correspond to 3:20; 3:30; etc. Time always increases from west to east along the path. *The time ticks, track numbers, and the A, B, and S letters are on the side of the limit with an occultation*, that is, north of southern limits and south of northern limits. Asterisks on the graze maps indicate the locations of the North American standard stations for lunar total-occultation predictions (see p. 164).

Occulted stars known to be double

In the table on the next page are data on double stars for which graze predictions are given. This information is from DSFILE, a comprehensive file of zodiacal double-star data compiled by Don Stockbauer, Henk Bulder, Mitsuru Sôma, David Herald, and David Dunham; most of the data for the ZC stars are in the Sato ZC catalog. The successive columns give the **USNO** reference number of the star, the **Graze #**, the double star code (**d**), the **magnitude** of the brighter (**A**) and dimmer (**B**) components, the separation (**Sep.**) in arcseconds, and the position angle (**PA**) of B from A measured eastward from north. If the star is triple, the third component's magnitude is given under **C**, and its separation and PA from A are given in the last columns. XZ numbers are given for the last three non-ZC stars.

The parameters are given for the epoch of the occultation, computed from orbital elements when available or from extrapolations from a long series of observations. If there is little change in the available observations, the last-observed separation and PA are used. Most components fainter than magnitude 12.0 are not listed, and some very close doubles whose parameters are not known, generally with separations less than 0.2″, are also not listed. The latter include spectroscopic binaries (code J, U, or sometimes V) and visual occultation doubles (most codes K and X, and many Vs).

STARS OCCULTED IN 2018 AND KNOWN TO BE DOUBLE

USNO	Graze #	d	magnitude A	B	Sep. "	PA °	C	Sep. "	PA °
210	120	A	6.6	8.6	6.0	328			
608	89	V	6.1	8.8	3.8	222			
618	112	V	7.3	10.0	0.1	77			
636	114	O	7.4	8.0	0.6	10			
648	161	B	3.9	9.5	0.1	190	13.0		
684	163	V	6.9	7.0	3.1	97			
764	74	O	5.6	5.6	0.09	96			
940	78	Y	6.5	6.5	0.1	62	9.2	91.0	205
947	16	A	5.2	11.2	7.8	202	10.5	64.3	279
995	17, 60	B	4.3	6.0	0.2	139	8.6	112.5	329
1077	79, 127	Y	4.5	4.5	0.1	90	11.7	99.0	348
1113	62, 115	A	5.2	12.2	13.3	195			
1123	116	S	7.2	8.3	6.4	44			
1415	47	Y	7.0	7.0	0.1	90	10.0	41.2	80
1487	1, 34	B	1.4	12.0	0.06		7.6	174.0	308
1493	181	O	6.8	7.6	0.2	285			
1625	183	Y	6.7	6.7	0.1	90	11.4	21.5	238
2035	131	V	7.4	8.6	0.51	92			
2223	104	Y	4.7	4.9	0.1	128	11.2	41.7	153
2436	169	D	6.3	8.3	4.7	231			
2463	37	M	7.2	8.7	0.17	106			
2633	106	T	4.1	7.0	0.01		11.5	16.9	258
2797	25, 70	C	3.8	3.8	0.1	150			
3356	174	V	6.4	6.9	0.08	109			
3419	72, 108, 160	A	4.5	8.5	49.6	312			
3428	198	A	5.2	11.2	1.8	134			
X13546	18	M	8.8	9.4	1.2	171			
X15714	168	M	7.7	8.8	0.1	45			
X15876	148	C	7.6	9.0	56.3	338			

The codes have the following meanings:

A   Double listed by Aitken and/or Burnham (ADS, BDS)
B   Close double with 3rd star nearby with separate XZ number
C   Double listed by Innes, Couteau, or other visual observers
D   Primary of wide pair; secondary has separate catalog entry
E   Secondary star of wide pair
J   Single-line spectroscopic binary
K   Possible double from occultation
M   Mean position (center of light) of a close pair is used by the ZC and/or XZ catalog
N   Northern component of nearly equal double star
O   Orbital elements available and used to calculate the separation and PA
S   Southern component of nearly equal double star
T   Visual triple star
U   Double, separation 0.05 " or less, usually a 2-line spectroscopic binary
V   Close double discovered by occultation or by interferometry
X   Probable double from occultation
Y   Triple, K or X (visual A component) and A or C (C component)

Some close pairs have rapid orbital motion so the current PA is unknown.

GRAZING LUNAR OCCULTATIONS FOR 2018

This table lists lunar grazing occultation predictions for much of North America (p. 171). Graze tracks are shown in the 6 maps on pp. 176–178. For each graze, the table provides:

No. .... a chronological sequential number used on the maps
Date .... the date
USNO d ... the star's USNO (U.S. Naval Observatory) reference number and its double-star code (in the "**d**" column)—(see the bottom of the facing page)
m .... its visual magnitude
%sl .... the percent of the Moon sunlit (+ for waxing, − for waning, E for lunar eclipses)
L .... whether the track is a northern (N) or southern (S) limit
W.U.T. ..... the Universal Time at the west end of the track
Lo., La. .... the longitude and latitude of the west end of the track

No.	Date	USNO d		m	%sl	L	W.U.T.	Lo.	La.	No.	Date	USNO d		m	%sl	L	W.U.T.	Lo.	La.
1	Jan. 5	1487†	B	1.4	86–	S	7:36.8	–86	55	47	Mar. 27	1415	Y	6.3	85+	S	23:32.6	–76	43
2	7	1728		6.7	67–	S	8:13.8	–94	36	48	28	1420		6.6	85+	S	0:22.3	–88	37
3	7	1733		5.4	66–	N	8:37.9	–130	53	49	28	1434		5.4	86+	S	2:43.1	–124	36
4	9	1950		5.7	46–	S	7:40.6	–98	44	50	Apr. 4	2291	V	5.5	85–	S	8:54.3	–130	40
5	9	1976		7.0	43–	S	14:58.7	–130	43	51	7	2704	K	5.9	58–	S	11:51.4	–130	51
6	10	2072		6.6	35–	S	10:43.1	–121	51	52	9	X28263		6.9	39–	S	12:12.9	–130	35
7	11	2200		7.5	25–	S	15:37.1	–130	55	53	12	3339		6.7	14–	S	10:52.4	–101	20
8	20	3268		5.3	7+	S	1:16.8	–111	21	54	18	491		6.0	4+	S	0:05.3	–68	55
9	21	X31275	X	7.1	13+	S	1:05.2	–127	55	55	19	667	V	5.0	11+	S	2:58.3	–117	54
10	23	106		6.6	32+	S	5:44.2	–130	48	56	20	X6886		7.3	19+	S	1:18.5	–93	44
11	24	X02150		7.4	40+	S	1:19.4	–114	31	57	20	832		4.3	20+	S	4:47.0	–112	55
12	25	364		4.3	52+	S	3:52.3	–130	35	58	21	971	K	7.3	28+	S	0:14.3	–81	30
13	25	X03361		7.0	52+	N	5:30.6	–113	48	59	21	991		6.2	29+	N	2:38.8	–118	30
14	27	626		6.3	73+	S	1:25.5	–121	41	60	21	995	B	4.1	29+	N	2:54.4	–120	47
15	27	635	K	3.6	73+	S	3:34.1	–130	45	61	21	1006	V	7.1	31+	S	5:31.1	–104	55
16	28	947	A	5.2	90+	S	23:43.2	–94	36	62	21	1113	A	5.1	39+	N	23:34.1	–77	21
17	29	995	B	4.1	92+	N	6:44.3	–114	24	63	22	1127	V	5.9	40+	N	1:32.6	–104	27
18	31	X13546	M	8.3	100E	N	14:28.2	–130	41	64	22	1135		6.7	40+	N	3:02.5	–74	55
19	31	X13436		10.3	100E	N	12:48.8	–130	33	65	22	1138		7.1	40+	N	3:04.0	–112	49
20	31	X13469		9.3	100E	S	13:22.6	–127	47	66	22	1151		6.8	42+	S	6:24.9	–116	55
21	Feb. 7	2128		5.8	54–	S	6:55.9	–87	47	67	23	1259		5.9	50+	N	0:10.5	–62	55
22	8	2245		6.3	44–	S	6:59.1	–80	34	68	23	1275	X	5.3	52+	N	3:20.4	–120	52
23	9	2390		6.7	33–	S	10:33.4	–104	50	69	May 4	2618		6.4	84–	S	6:17.2	–70	55
24	9	X22561		7.5	33–	S	13:34.5	–130	53	70	5	2797	C	2.9	75–	N	10:47.9	–130	45
25	12	2797	C	2.9	11–	S	11:32.5	–64	55	71	9	3303		6.4	37–	S	11:57.4	–130	48
26	19	66		7.1	10+	S	2:08.8	–124	39	72	10	3419	A	4.2	28–	S	10:22.9	–116	30
27	20	208		7.0	18+	S	4:36.1	–130	52	73	16	692*		0.9	2+	S	12:20.5	–97	50
28	21	X03132		6.8	27+	N	6:22.8	–127	46	74	17	764	O	4.9	4+	N	3:03.2	–113	47
29	22	X03962		7.5	34+	S	0:03.9	–95	55	75	17	X08084		7.5	8+	S	23:45.0	–58	48
30	22	444		5.9	35+	S	0:26.2	–99	43	76	18	913	L	5.1	8+	S	0:49.6	–85	35
31	22	453	X	7.1	36+	S	3:19.4	–130	22	77	18	915	L	4.6	8+	N	0:51.5	–83	41
32	22	453	X	7.1	36+	N	3:56.4	–71	55	78	18	940	Y	5.8	10+	S	4:08.5	–130	34
33	25	913	L	5.1	70+	N	5:08.8	–130	42	79	18	1077	Y	4.0	16+	N	23:26.5	–87	35
34	Mar. 1	1487†	B	1.4	99+	S	5:36.7	–96	55	80	19	1084		7.3	17+	S	1:39.2	–76	55
35	5	1978	V	6.6	87–	S	8:31.1	–112	55	81	19	1109		7.2	19+	S	6:10.3	–130	42
36	6	2072		6.6	80–	S	3:15.6	–65	48	82	19	1733		5.4	71+	N	4:41.9	–93	55
37	9	2463	M	6.9	51–	S	9:27.9	–114	42	83	Jun. 1	2704	K	5.9	94–	S	2:15.4	–77	24
38	10	2599		6.8	41–	S	10:33.9	–115	43	84	2	2851		6.1	89–	S	3:32.4	–75	39
39	11	2759		3.5	31–	S	12:58.6	–130	47	85	4	3126		4.3	73–	N	10:22.5	–109	26
40	14	3126		4.3	10–	S	9:56.6	–67	45	86	5	3240		6.7	64–	S	7:44.3	–115	23
41	20	405	V	4.3	12+	S	23:48.7	–84	30	87	8	60		6.9	35–	S	8:06.7	–88	50
42	22	692*		0.9	30+	S	21:51.0	–130	42	88	8	66		7.1	34–	N	9:09.4	–87	21
43	23	832		4.3	41+	S	22:17.0	–60	48	89	12	608	V	6.0	3–	S	10:49.5	–96	38
44	23	836		5.7	41+	S	22:50.8	–65	54	90	17	X13516		7.2	15+	N	2:29.0	–102	38
45	24	863		6.7	43+	S	2:39.2	–123	40	91	19	X16224		7.4	34+	N	2:05.8	–91	43
46	26	1186		6.0	68+	N	6:32.5	–130	34	92	Jul. 2	3190	J	2.9	87–	S	4:11.2	–90	39

*ZC 692 = Aldebaran †ZC 1487 = Regulus

No.	Date	USNO d	m	%sl	L	W.U.T.	Lo.	La.	No.	Date	USNO d	m	%sl	L	W.U.T.	Lo.	La.
93	Jul. 3	3339	6.7	77−	N	11:47.8	−124	20	151	Oct. 15	2618	6.4	33+	N	0:06.5	−98	40
94	5	X00375	6.9	59−	N	11:57.7	−130	24	152	15	2635	5.5	34+	S	3:45.3	−109	20
95	8	405 V	4.3	29−	N	9:10.4	−112	20	153	16	2779	3.8	43+	N	1:45.0	−130	51
96	9	526	6.7	19−	N	9:21.8	−106	39	154	16	2779	3.8	43+	S	3:20.9	−79	20
97	10	677 X	4.8	11−	S	6:34.9	−62	50	155	18	3035	6.8	62+	S	3:47.8	−108	20
98	10	X05894	7.2	11−	N	8:31.7	−86	47	156	18	3055	6.8	64+	S	6:47.4	−130	37
99	10	692*	0.9	11−	S	8:36.2	−91	43	157	19	3171 V	3.7	72+	S	4:52.9	−130	28
100	11	832	4.3	5−	S	6:46.0	−55	49	158	20	3288	5.8	79+	S	3:00.7	−97	20
101	11	862	7.3	4−	S	10:27.2	−98	40	159	20	3303	6.4	80+	S	6:49.9	−119	20
102	11	863	6.7	4−	S	10:38.2	−102	42	160	21	3419 A	4.2	87+	S	6:14.4	−98	20
103	20	2005	7.0	52+	N	1:51.3	−98	32	161	27	648 B	3.8	92−	N	7:23.8	−112	20
104	22	2223 Y	3.9	71+	N	1:00.2	−70	55	162	27	653 X	4.8	92−	N	7:34.7	−130	25
105	22	2247	5.4	73+	S	6:08.5	−125	26	163	27	684 V	6.2	91−	N	13:30.3	−130	36
106	25	2633 T	3.8	93+	N	3:54.4	−130	46	164	28	796	6.7	85−	N	6:41.5	−130	37
107	26	2759	3.5	97+	N	0:10.3	−89	35	165	28	798 K	6.2	85−	N	6:45.5	−130	22
108	31	3419 A	4.2	90−	N	8:05.5	−130	41	166	29	935	6.8	77−	N	2:59.6	−82	23
109	Aug. 2	106	6.6	74−	N	8:20.5	−120	20	167	Nov. 1	1395	6.3	42−	N	9:13.9	−130	43
110	4	364	4.3	55−	N	9:18.8	−130	46	168	2	X15714 M	7.3	30−	N	13:15.3	−103	50
111	4	X03361	7.0	54−	N	10:02.6	−111	20	169	10	2436 D	6.6	6+	N	1:01.8	−115	27
112	6	618 V	7.2	33−	N	7:11.0	−91	28	170	12	2725 A	5.4	19+	S	2:26.4	−130	36
113	6	627	6.6	32−	N	9:44.5	−130	33	171	12	2838 K	5.6	24+	N	20:22.2	−59	51
114	6	636 O	7.0	32−	N	11:03.2	−130	28	172	13	2964	6.8	33+	S	21:17.1	−65	41
115	9	1113 A	5.1	6−	N	9:57.6	−92	27	173	15	3113 K	5.4	44+	S	2:44.9	−99	20
116	9	1123 S	7.3	6−	N	11:15.8	−106	22	174	17	3356 V	5.8	63+	S	1:21.9	−120	22
117	9	1127 V	5.9	6−	N	11:56.3	−123	35	175	21	405 V	4.3	98+	N	20:46.0	−68	50
118	13	1603	7.2	4+	N	2:44.8	−118	29	176	26	1086	6.4	87−	N	9:38.8	−130	48
119	17	2089	6.7	39+	N	5:33.9	−130	38	177	27	X12132	7.0	80−	N	5:31.7	−124	32
120	30	210 A	6.6	86−	N	9:35.0	−124	20	178	28	1340	6.6	70−	N	3:18.6	−78	36
121	31	X03132	6.8	78−	N	11:33.3	−130	31	179	28	1343	6.3	70−	N	3:49.4	−90	44
122	Sep. 4	888 V	6.0	36−	N	8:15.7	−119	39	180	28	1370 V	6.9	69−	N	8:45.8	−124	20
123	4	892	6.7	36−	N	8:27.2	−92	20	181	29	1493 O	6.5	57−	S	10:56.5	−103	46
124	4	894	4.4	36−	N	8:48.8	−105	20	182	29	1506 V	7.0	55−	S	14:34.6	−119	55
125	4	X08159	6.9	35−	N	12:41.9	−130	22	183	30	1625 Y	5.8	44−	S	15:12.1	−116	55
126	5	X10116	7.4	25−	N	9:26.6	−83	20	184	Dec. 1	1741	7.1	33−	S	13:35.0	−130	50
127	5	1077 Y	4.0	24−	N	12:32.0	−130	44	185	3	1965 V	6.5	15−	S	11:51.6	−118	51
128	6	1193	5.4	16−	N	8:02.3	−83	30	186	3	X19687	7.2	15−	S	12:35.6	−123	40
129	6	1205	6.3	15−	N	9:58.2	−109	27	187	4	2089	6.7	8−	N	14:16.6	−130	51
130	7	1362 X	7.2	7−	N	12:19.8	−116	20	188	9	2806	7.0	6+	N	23:02.0	−107	55
131	13	2035 V	7.2	14+	N	2:28.8	−122	30	189	9	2806	7.0	6+	S	23:59.0	−78	20
132	14	2158	7.5	23+	N	3:03.7	−128	45	190	10	2929 K	7.1	12+	S	23:08.7	−86	26
133	15	2291 V	5.5	32+	N	4:20.6	−130	49	191	12	3069	6.3	19+	S	1:51.5	−97	20
134	16	X22561	7.5	40+	N	0:28.4	−93	22	192	12	X29213	7.0	20+	S	2:47.8	−130	42
135	16	2408	6.6	40+	S	1:59.9	−87	24	193	12	3171 V	3.7	25+	N	19:48.4	−90	21
136	19	2851	6.1	71+	S	7:39.1	−130	23	194	12	X29967	7.2	26+	S	21:33.2	−76	47
137	21	3190 J	2.9	91+	S	23:04.8	−90	30	195	13	3190 J	2.9	27+	N	0:31.1	−120	20
138	28	405 V	4.3	90−	N	4:37.3	−129	40	196	14	X30841	7.5	36+	S	2:21.1	−114	20
139	29	516 K	6.9	83−	N	2:51.9	−90	38	197	14	X30915	7.4	38+	S	5:44.2	−130	40
140	Oct. 2	991	6.2	52−	N	4:39.2	−89	48	198	14	3428 A	5.0	44+	S	23:13.1	−90	27
141	3	1127 V	5.9	41−	N	4:14.7	−74	54	199	18	364	4.3	82+	S	22:31.7	−77	21
142	3	X11213	7.5	40−	N	5:28.4	−78	37	200	19	398 V	6.5	84+	N	8:10.4	−100	30
143	3	1150 X	6.7	40−	N	8:09.2	−126	50	201	26	1418 K	5.7	84−	N	2:16.1	−80	35
144	3	X11479 V	7.3	39−	N	8:59.7	−130	50	202	27	1576	5.3	72−	S	9:02.1	−130	52
145	3	X11613	7.3	38−	N	10:56.3	−130	47	203	28	1702	4.0	61−	N	9:15.0	−130	29
146	3	1171	6.5	38−	N	11:11.0	−130	39	204	28	1709	6.5	60−	S	12:03.5	−130	52
147	4	1312	6.8	28−	N	11:17.1	−94	20	205	30	1950	5.7	37−	S	14:39.5	−119	55
148	6	X15876 C	7.2	10−	N	8:42.5	−79	45	206	31	2043 K	6.5	29−	S	9:20.7	−99	44
149	13	2361	4.2	17+	S	2:20.0	−121	20	207	31	2047	6.6	29−	S	9:45.3	−102	49
150	14	2614	6.2	33+	N	23:23.6	−89	42									

*ZC 692 = Aldebaran

GRAZING OCCULTATION MAPS

JANUARY 1 – FEBRUARY 28

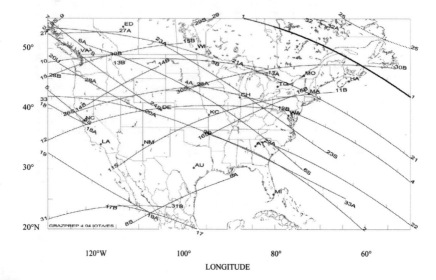

LONGITUDE

MARCH 1 – APRIL 30

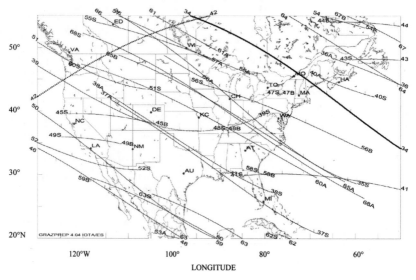

LONGITUDE

GRAZING OCCULTATION MAPS (continued)

MAY 1 – JULY 15

JULY 16 – SEPTEMBER 30

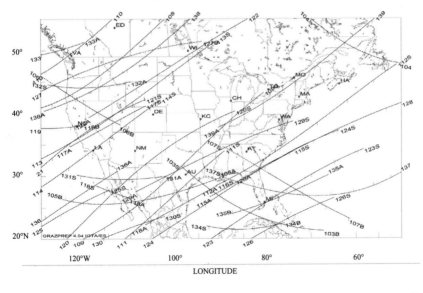

GRAZING OCCULTATION MAPS (continued)

OCTOBER 1 – NOVEMBER 15

LONGITUDE

NOVEMBER 16 – DECEMBER 31

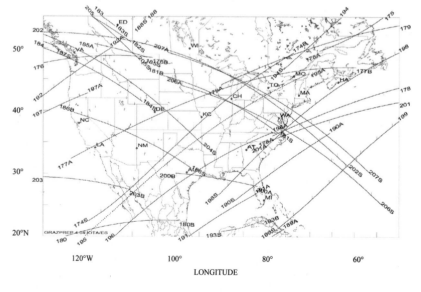

LONGITUDE

TIDES AND THE EARTH–MOON SYSTEM
BY ROY BISHOP

The tidal aspect of gravitation produces some of the most interesting phenomena in the Universe, from the structure of interacting galaxies, such as M51, to the volcanoes of Io, the fragmentation of Comet Shoemaker–Levy 9 by Jupiter in 1992, the synchronous rotation of our Moon, and the pulse of the seas on our planet. Because they occur at our feet, the tides of the oceans are often overlooked when considering the heavens; yet the pulse of the tides is the heartbeat of a greater Universe beyond Earth.

Newtonian Tides

Tides have been known for millennia, but an understanding of their origin came just over three centuries ago with the publication of Newton's *Principia* (1687). In the Newtonian context, the decrease of the force of gravity with distance causes the tides. The Moon exerts a force on Earth, and Earth responds by accelerating toward the Moon; however, the waters on the hemisphere facing the Moon, being closer to the Moon, accelerate more and fall ahead of Earth. Similarly, Earth itself accelerates more than the waters on the other hemisphere and falls ahead of those waters; the Moon is yanking Earth out from under the waters on the more distant hemisphere, leaving those waters behind. Thus two tidal bulges are produced, one on the side of Earth facing the Moon and one on the side facing away from the Moon. Because the Moon is quite far from Earth (about 60 Earth radii), the two tidal bulges are essentially equal in size.

Note that the waters directly under the Moon and the waters farthest from the Moon do not rise up because of the slightly larger and smaller, respectively, lunar gravity at these two locations; all that results from the Moon's action on the waters at these two points is a slight decrease in the pressure on the floor of the sea. The two tidal bulges form because the variation in the Moon's gravity causes the *surrounding* waters on each hemisphere to flow horizontally across Earth's surface into these regions:

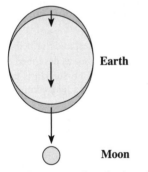

Earth

Moon

In order of decreasing length, the arrows indicate the force per unit mass (acceleration) produced by the Moon's gravity on the near side, center, and far side of Earth. It is the resulting horizontal flow of the water across Earth's surface toward the two points nearest and farthest from the Moon that produces the two tidal bulges (indicated by heavy shading).

As Earth rotates on its axis, the orientation of the two bulges relative to the Moon remains fixed; hence the rise and fall of the oceans on Earth. The solid Earth is not perfectly rigid. It too responds to the tidal influences of Moon and Sun, resulting in an elastic *body tide* (vertical range ~0.4 m). Lesser, more-localized deformations of the solid Earth are caused indirectly by *ocean tide loading*.

Because of the Moon's orbital motion, it transits on average 50.47 min later each day. Thus on successive days, high tides recur about 50 min later; or for the many regions experiencing two high tides daily, these tides recur at intervals of 12 h 25 min.

The Sun exerts a gravitational force 180 times stronger than that exerted by the Moon on Earth; however, because the Moon is so much closer, the *variation* in the Moon's force across Earth's diameter is about 2.2 times larger than the variation in the Sun's force. As described above, it is this variation that produces tides; thus the pair of bulges raised by the Moon is considerably larger than the pair raised by the Sun. As the Moon goes through its monthly cycle of phases, the two pairs of tidal bulges get in and out of step, combining in step to produce *spring tides* (no connection with the season) when the Moon is new or full (syzygy) and out of step to produce *neap tides* when the Moon is at first or last quarter (quadrature).

Another factor having a substantial influence on tidal ranges is the elliptical shape of the Moon's orbit. The Moon is only 9% to 12% closer at perigee than at apogee; however, because the *variation* in its gravitational force varies inversely as the cube of its distance (the force itself varies inversely as the square of the distance), the Moon's tidal influence is 31% to 49% greater at perigee than at apogee. Because the Sun tidally influences the shape of the Moon's orbit, exceptionally close perigees coincide with full or new Moon, and the resulting extreme tides are known as *perigean spring tides*. If the lunar orbit were fixed in orientation, such tides would recur at half-year intervals, alternately with new and full Moon; however, the major axis of the lunar orbit rotates prograde with a period of 8.85 years, making the average interval between perigean spring tides about 23 days longer than half a year (205.9 days).

The extreme range of a spring tide, or of a perigean spring tide, occurs a day or two after the astronomical influences peak. The variation in the range of the tides at a given locality is determined both by the energy being put into the tides and by the energy being lost through friction with the seabed. As long as the input is greater than the loss, the tide range will increase even though the input may have peaked and already be decreasing. Hence the tide range is greatest not when the astronomical factors are greatest, but a day or two later when the decreasing input equals the increasing loss. At that point the energy in the tides is at a maximum.

Influences on the Tides

Five, basic, astronomical periods impact the tides. In increasing length these are: Earth's mean rotation day, the draconic, sidereal, and anomalistic months, and the sidereal year (see p. 29). The resulting periods that show up in the tides include (in ascending order):

(1) semidiurnal, 12 h 00 min (two solar-induced tidal bulges, as described above);

(2) semidiurnal, 12 h 25 min (two lunar-induced tidal bulges, as described above);

(3) diurnal, 24 h 00 min (the usual nonzero declination of the Sun shifts the pair of solar tidal bulges out of Earth's equatorial plane, resulting in a tidal component with a one-day period);

(4) diurnal, 24 h 50 min (the usual nonzero declination of the Moon shifts the pair of lunar tidal bulges out of Earth's equatorial plane, resulting in a tidal component with a one-day period; that is the dominant tide in some areas, such as parts of the southern coast of Canada's Gulf of St. Lawrence);

(5) semimonthly, 13.66 days (variation in the Moon's declination);

(6) semimonthly, 14.77 days (spring–neap cycle, described above);

(7) monthly, 27.55 days (perigee–apogee cycle, described above);

(8) semiannual, 182.63 days (variation in the Sun's declination);

(9) semiannual, 205.9 days (perigean spring cycle, described above);

(10) annual, 365.26 days (perihelion–aphelion cycle);

(11) 4.43 years (perigean-spring tides near an equinox recur at half the prograde precession period of the major axis of the lunar orbit); and

(12) 18.61 years (retrograde precession of the nodes of the lunar orbit).

In addition to astronomical factors, the tides on Earth are strongly influenced by the sizes, boundaries, and depths of ocean basins and inlets and by Earth's rotation, winds, and barometric pressure fluctuations. Using Newton's gravitation and laws of motion, the French physicist Pierre-Simon Laplace (1749–1827) developed the dynamical theory of the tides on the rotating Earth (*Mécanique Céleste*, 1799), but because of the complexity of the tides the full application of his theory was not possible until the advent of the digital computer in the last third of the 20th century.

Tides typically have ranges (vertical high to low) of a metre or two, but there are regions in the oceans where the various influences conspire to produce virtually no tides at all (called amphidromic points) and others where the tides are greatly amplified. Among the latter regions are the Sea of Okhotsk, the Gulf of Alaska, the northwest coast of Australia, the English Channel, and in Canada, Ungava Bay in northern Québec, and the Bay of Fundy between New Brunswick and Nova Scotia. The tidal ranges in these regions are of the order of 10 m.

Fundy Tides

Only two localities on Earth sometimes have a vertical tide range exceeding 16 m (52 ft.), and both are in Canada: Minas Basin, the eastern extremity of the Bay of Fundy in Nova Scotia, and Leaf Basin, a remote inlet on the southwestern side of Ungava Bay in northern Québec. The current best data give Minas Basin a slight edge; however, several years of tide gauge data continuing through a peak in the 18.61-year tide cycle are needed to determine which site, if either (to the precision that measurements can be made), has the greater tide range.

The primary cause of the immense tides of Fundy is a resonance of the Bay of Fundy/Gulf of Maine system. The system is effectively bounded at its outer end by the edge of the continental shelf with its approximately 40:1 increase in depth. The system has a natural period of approximately 13 hours, a Q-value[*] of about 5, and is driven near resonance, not directly by the Moon, but by the dominant semidiurnal tides of the Atlantic Ocean. Like a father pushing his daughter on a swing, the gentle Atlantic tidal pulse pushes the waters of the Bay of Fundy/Gulf of Maine basin at nearly the optimum frequency to cause a large oscillation. The seventh Astronomer Royal, Sir G.B. Airy (1801–1892), first developed the theory of the behaviour of tides in restricted arms of the ocean such as the Fundy system.

Fundy tides are unique in that they respond more to the perigee–apogee influence than they do to the spring–neap influence. That is because the lunar tidal period (12.42 hours) is closer to the system's resonant period than is the solar tidal period (12.00 hours). Although the variation in the Moon's distance is not obvious when viewing the Moon directly, near the head of the Bay of Fundy the 3-m to 6-m *increase* in the vertical tidal range makes it obvious when the Moon is near perigee, clear skies or cloudy!

The most dramatic view of the vertical range of Fundy tides is at the Minas Basin Pulp & Power Company wharf in the town of Hantsport, Nova Scotia. That site is practically unknown and, unfortunately, it is not open to the public.

Perhaps the most awesome display of the tides on our planet occurs at Cape Split, Nova Scotia, on the southern side of the entrance to Minas Basin. (Cape Split may be reached by a pleasant two-hour walk along a popular hiking trail from the village of Scots Bay.) Here, at the time of the midpoint of an incoming tide, for a considerable distance the forest on the towering cliffs is filled with a hollow roar produced by

---

[*] The Q-value, or quality-value, of an oscillator indicates its efficiency. A large Q means low energy loss per cycle and a well-defined resonant frequency. A Q of 5 is relatively small, indicative of considerable damping in the Fundy system, yet it is large enough to make these tides among the highest on Earth.

the turbulence of the waters surging over the submarine ridges below. The currents exceed 8 knots (4 m/s), and the flow in the deep, 5-km-wide channel on the north side of Cape Split equals the combined flow of all the streams and rivers on Earth (approximately 1 million tonnes per second, or 4 cubic kilometres per hour). Three hours later the spectacle pauses and then begins flowing in the opposite direction.

The highest of the high tides in the Bay of Fundy occur when a perigean spring high tide coincides with a low-barometric-pressure storm system sweeping northward across New Brunswick, accompanied by hurricane-force southerly winds over the Gulf of Maine and the Bay of Fundy. The close Moon, the in-phase solar tide, the reduced air pressure above the water, and the wind drag pushing more water into the Bay of Fundy (the last two effects are called a storm surge) all contribute to an especially high tide. An additional favorable influence is if all this occurs near an equinox, for then the axis of the tidal bulges of the spring tide is at a right angle to Earth's rotation axis, optimizing the semidiurnal tidal range at all latitudes (see item (11), above). This right-angle-axes enhancement of the tides is strengthened in those years when the declination range of the Moon (±18° to ±29°) is near a minimum, a situation that recurs with the 18.61-year period of the retrograde motion of the nodes of its orbit relative to the equinoxes. (The declination range was at its ±18° minimum in 1959, 1978, 1997, and 2015, and will be again in 2034 and 2052. See p. 95 for the shift in the longitude of the ascending node of the Moon's orbit during 2018.) Furthermore, since perihelion occurs in January, the highest tides of all tend to occur just prior to the March equinox or after the September equinox. The infamous Bay of Fundy "Saxby gale" of 1869 Oct. 5 was a time when all seven of these factors approximately coincided (perigee, spring tide, low pressure, south wind, equinox, minimum declination range, and perihelion enhancement). Weather is unpredictable. Thus, so too is the next major tidal flood in the Bay of Fundy.

Paradoxically, the large tides of Fundy protect its shores from flooding associated with most storm surges, since the normal variation in its high tide levels is already several metres. Only those rare storm surges that happen to coincide with a perigean spring high tide will be a problem. In contrast, shorelines with small tides are much more susceptible to storm surges.

Sea level is slowly increasing in the Bay of Fundy region. That is bringing the resonant period of the Fundy/Gulf of Maine system closer to the lunar tidal period which, in turn, is causing Fundy tides to gradually become even larger (by a few centimetres per decade).

Tidal Friction

Tidal friction, which occurs primarily in shallow seas around the margins of the oceans, transforms Earth's rotational kinetic energy into heat at a rate of about 3.7 TW, comparable to humankind's total rate of energy use. Approximately 1% of this energy transformation occurs in the Bay of Fundy, and, since 1984, a tiny portion of this (20 MW peak) is being turned into commercial electric power at the Annapolis Basin tidal power plant in Nova Scotia. Two larger tidal power plants exist: the Rance in France (240 MW) and the Sihwa Lake in South Korea (254 MW peak), and a third one is nearing completion at Incheon Bay, South Korea (1320 MW).

The aforementioned tidal power plants use turbines located in dams (also called barrages). At a few sites, including the Bay of Fundy, studies presently are underway for using isolated turbines located in tidal currents—effectively underwater windmills. The problem with this approach is that the power available in currents of 8 knots or less is dilute. To generate significant electrical power (100 MW or more), large turbine cross-sections are required, with attendant high capital and maintenance costs.

Tidal friction also transfers angular momentum from Earth to the Moon, lengthening the day and increasing the size of the orbit of the Moon. The day is lengthening by about 1 s every 40 000 years—imperceptible on a human time scale but of profound significance to Earth's rotation over a few billion years. (For example, 900 million years ago, when Earth was already 80% of its present age, there were about 480 18-hour days in a year.) The Moon is receding about 3.8 cm per year, with the result that about one billion years from now total solar eclipses will cease. Presently we are well into the transitional phase: Annular eclipses already outnumber total solar eclipses.

General Relativity and Tides

Einstein's theory of gravitation, general relativity, superseded Newton's theory a century ago, yet descriptions of the tides almost invariably ignore Einstein (as has this article to this point). There are three reasons for using the older, wrong theory: (1) Newton's theory describes the gentle tides on Earth to high accuracy; (2) the mathematics involved is much simpler than that of general relativity; (3) the Newtonian description of the tides is compatible with cultivated common sense. Because of #3, Newton's concepts regarding motion and gravitation form the essential foundation for anyone attempting to understand the tides. One must climb up on Newton's towering shoulders before it is possible to focus clearly on Einstein.

As mentioned in the section ORBITAL MOTION (see p. 27), Newton's Euclidean universe with its force of gravity never did exist. Although Newton's ideas are more than adequate for describing the tides on Earth, for some purposes, such as the Global Positioning System (GPS), Newton's concepts of space, time, and gravitation are inadequate. We inhabit an Einsteinian universe, a universe in which gravitation is a manifestation of the structure of spacetime, the four-dimensional stage of our existence in which space and time are interwoven. The geometry of spacetime is curved by the mass–energy of matter, and the curvature instructs matter how to move. That instruction has an astounding grip. If spacetime were not curved, a mind-boggling 300-km diameter steel cable, stressed to its breaking point, would be required to connect Earth and Moon in order to maintain their mutual orbit.

The Moon's mass alters the structure of spacetime at its location, and this distortion propagates outward, becoming more dilute with the volume encompassed according to the inverse cube of the distance. At Earth, the distortion results in the waters of the oceans following slightly different paths through spacetime than does the rigid planet beneath, producing the characteristic egglike shape of the tidal effect. The tidal heartbeat is that of the very fabric of spacetime. The tides at our feet carry a profound message.

References

For more information, see the superb introduction *The Tides* by E.P. Clancy, Anchor Books, Doubleday and Co., 1969 (now, unfortunately, out of print). For a detailed account of the evolution of our understanding of the tides see *Tides, A Scientific History*, by D.E. Cartwright, Cambridge University Press, 1999. An excellent book covering tides, storm surges, tsunamis, and sea level in general is *Sea-Level Science* by D. Pugh and P. Woodworth, Cambridge University Press, 2014. (Note, however, that none of these four authors mentions general relativity.) For a popular account of general relativity, see *A Journey into Gravity and Spacetime*, by J.A. Wheeler, Scientific American Library, 1990. The major astronomical factors influencing the tides (the phases, perigees, and apogees of the Moon) are tabulated in THE SKY MONTH BY MONTH section (see p. 94) of this Handbook. For information on tides in Canadian waters see www.tides.gc.ca/eng/data/predictions/2018. For tide predictions at many sites worldwide, see tbone.biol.sc.edu/tide/tideshow.cgi.

THE SUN

EPHEMERIS FOR THE SUN
BY PATRICK KELLY

Sundial Correction

The **Greenwich Transit** time in the table opposite may be used to calculate the sundial correction at the observer's position. For example, to find the correction at Washington, D.C. on 2018 Apr. 5, determine the following: At Greenwich, the Sun transits at 12:03:25 on Apr. 3 and at 12:02:15 on Apr. 7. Thus, to the nearest min, on Apr. 5 at both Greenwich and Washington, D.C., the Sun will transit at 12:03 local mean solar time (LMT), or 12:11 Eastern Standard Time (EST) since Washington, D.C. has a longitude correction of +8 min (see the 3rd paragraph on p. 205). Thus a 3-min correction must be added to the reading of a simple sundial to obtain LMT (compare with the horizontal position of the light dot marking Apr. 5 on the analemma, on the bottom right of the facing page), an additional 8 min must be added to obtain EST, and a further 1 hour for Eastern Daylight Time (ADT). Thus solar noon will occur at 1:11 PM EDT.

Even with these corrections, a sundial may still read incorrectly. For the horizontal sundial, the *gnomon* (vertical part) must be aligned to true north with the *dial* (horizontal part) level. The angle of the gnoman and the hour angles on the dial must be appropriate for the latitude. Beware of "consumer" sundials with poorly marked hour angles and crooked styles. (The *style* is the edge of the gnomon that casts the shadow.) Thick gnomons should taper to an edge, otherwise they have two styles, neither casting a shadow in the right place. The 6 a.m and 6 p.m. hour angles should form a straight line perpendicular to the gnomon, meeting where the style meets the dial.

Orientation of the Sun

The table on the next page gives three angles that specify the orientation of the Sun.

P is the position angle of the axis of rotation, measured eastward in the observer's sky from the north point on the disk (i.e. counterclockwise). Note that P varies between +26° (solar north pole tilted eastward) and −26° (tilted westward) during the year. This tilt is associated mainly with the inclination of the ecliptic in the observer's sky, with a smaller contribution from the Sun's 7.2° inclination to the ecliptic (the longitude of the ascending node of the solar equator on the ecliptic is 76°).

B_0 is the heliographic latitude of the center of the disk, and is the result of the Sun's 7.2° inclination to the ecliptic. Note that positive values of B_0 correspond to the solar equator passing south of the center of the disk, with the solar north pole being tipped toward the observer.

L_0 is the heliographic longitude of the center of the disk measured from Carrington's solar prime meridian in the direction of rotation. L_0 decreases about 13° per day. The dates during the year when $L_0 = 0°$ are given in the table below. The rotation period of the Sun depends upon heliographic latitude. The synodic and sidereal periods of rotation at the solar equator are 27.2753 days and 25.38 days, respectively.

Commencement (UT) of Numbered Synodic Solar Rotations

No.*	Commences	No.	Commences	No.	Commences	No.	Commences
2199 '17	Dec. 30.94	2203	Apr. 19.22	2207	Aug. 6.07	2211	Nov. 23.17
2200 '18	Jan. 27.27	2204	May 16.44	2208	Sep. 2.31	2212 '18	Dec. 20.49
2201	Feb. 23.61	2205	Jun. 12.66	2209	Sep. 29.58	2213 '19	Jan. 16.83
2202	Mar. 22.94	2206	Jul. 9.86	2210	Oct. 26.87	2214	Feb. 13.17

*Based on R.C. Carrington's Greenwich photoheliocentric series, in which rotation No. 1 commenced 1853 Nov. 9.

EPHEMERIS FOR THE SUN, 2018

Date 0h UT	Apparent RA (2018) h m	Greenwich Dec ° '	Transit UT	Orientation P	B0	L0	Date 0h UT	Apparent RA (2018) h m	Greenwich Dec ° '	Transit UT	Orientation P	B0	L0
Jan. 1	18 45.7	−23 01	12:03:19	2.1	−3.0	346.0	**Sep. 2**	10 44.2	+8 01	11:59:50	21.3	7.2	4.1
5	19 03.3	−22 38	12:05:10	0.1	−3.5	293.3	6	10 58.7	+6 32	11:58:31	22.2	7.2	311.2
9	19 20.8	−22 08	12:06:53	−1.8	−3.9	240.6	10	11 13.1	+5 02	11:57:09	23.1	7.2	258.4
13	19 38.2	−21 31	12:08:29	−3.7	−4.3	187.9	14	11 27.4	+3 31	11:55:44	23.8	7.2	205.6
17	19 55.4	−20 47	12:09:54	−5.6	−4.7	135.3	18	11 41.8	+1 58	11:54:19	24.5	7.2	152.8
21	20 12.4	−19 57	12:11:09	−7.4	−5.1	82.6	22	11 56.1	+0 25	11:52:53	25.1	7.1	100.0
25	20 29.2	−19 01	12:12:11	−9.2	−5.5	29.9	26	12 10.5	−1 08	11:51:29	25.5	6.9	47.2
29	20 45.8	−18 00	12:13:01	−10.9	−5.8	337.3	30	12 24.9	−2 42	11:50:08	25.8	6.8	354.4
Feb. 2	21 02.2	−16 53	12:13:37	−12.5	−6.1	284.6	**Oct. 4**	12 39.4	−4 14	11:48:51	26.1	6.6	301.6
6	21 18.3	−15 41	12:14:00	−14.1	−6.4	231.9	8	12 54.0	−5 47	11:47:40	26.2	6.4	248.9
10	21 34.3	−14 26	12:14:11	−15.6	−6.6	179.3	12	13 08.7	−7 18	11:46:36	26.3	6.1	196.1
14	21 50.0	−13 07	12:14:09	−17.0	−6.8	126.6	16	13 23.5	−8 47	11:45:40	26.2	5.8	143.3
18	22 05.6	−11 44	12:13:56	−18.3	−6.9	73.9	20	13 38.5	−10 14	11:44:52	25.9	5.5	90.6
22	22 20.9	−10 18	12:13:32	−19.6	−7.1	21.3	24	13 53.6	−11 39	11:44:15	25.6	5.2	37.8
26	22 36.1	−8 49	12:12:57	−20.7	−7.2	328.6	28	14 09.0	−13 01	11:43:48	25.1	4.8	345.0
Mar. 2	22 51.2	−7 18	12:12:13	−21.7	−7.2	275.9	**Nov. 1**	14 24.5	−14 20	11:43:34	24.5	4.4	292.3
6	23 06.1	−5 46	12:11:21	−22.7	−7.2	223.2	5	14 40.3	−15 35	11:43:33	23.8	4.0	239.6
10	23 20.9	−4 13	12:10:23	−23.5	−7.2	170.5	9	14 56.2	−16 46	11:43:46	22.9	3.6	186.8
14	23 35.6	−2 38	12:09:19	−24.2	−7.2	117.8	13	15 12.4	−17 53	11:44:11	22.0	3.1	134.1
18	23 50.2	−1 04	12:08:12	−24.8	−7.1	65.0	17	15 28.9	−18 55	11:44:50	20.9	2.6	81.4
22	0 04.8	+0 31	12:07:01	−25.4	−7.0	12.3	21	15 45.5	−19 51	11:45:43	19.6	2.2	28.6
26	0 19.4	+2 06	12:05:49	−25.8	−6.8	319.6	25	16 02.4	−20 41	11:46:48	18.3	1.7	335.9
30	0 34.0	+3 40	12:04:36	−26.0	−6.7	266.8	29	16 19.4	−21 25	11:48:05	16.9	1.2	283.2
Apr. 3	0 48.5	+5 12	12:03:25	−26.2	−6.4	214.0	**Dec. 3**	16 36.7	−22 03	11:49:33	15.4	0.7	230.5
7	1 03.1	+6 44	12:02:15	−26.3	−6.2	161.3	7	16 54.1	−22 34	11:51:12	13.7	0.2	177.8
11	1 17.8	+8 13	12:01:10	−26.2	−5.9	108.5	11	17 11.6	−22 58	11:52:48	12.0	−0.4	125.0
15	1 32.6	+9 40	12:00:09	−26.0	−5.6	55.7	15	17 29.3	−23 15	11:54:51	10.2	−0.9	72.4
19	1 47.4	+11 05	11:59:13	−25.7	−5.3	2.8	19	17 47.0	−23 24	11:56:48	8.4	−1.4	19.6
23	2 02.4	+12 26	11:58:24	−25.3	−5.0	310.0	23	18 04.7	−23 26	11:58:47	6.5	−1.9	327.0
27	2 17.4	+13 45	11:57:42	−24.8	−4.6	257.2	27	18 22.5	−23 20	12:00:46	4.6	−2.4	274.3
May 1	2 32.6	+15 00	11:57:08	−24.1	−4.2	204.3	31	18 40.2	−23 07	12:02:42	2.7	−2.8	221.6
5	2 48.0	+16 10	11:56:43	−23.4	−3.8	151.4							
9	3 03.5	+17 17	11:56:26	−22.5	−3.4	98.6							
13	3 19.1	+18 19	11:56:19	−21.5	−2.9	45.7							
17	3 34.9	+19 16	11:56:22	−20.4	−2.5	352.8							
21	3 50.9	+20 08	11:56:33	−19.2	−2.0	299.8							
25	4 07.0	+20 54	11:56:52	−17.9	−1.5	246.9							
29	4 23.2	+21 34	11:57:19	−16.6	−1.1	194.0							
Jun. 2	4 39.6	+22 09	11:57:53	−15.1	−0.6	141.1							
6	4 56.1	+22 37	11:58:34	−13.5	−0.1	88.1							
10	5 12.5	+22 59	11:59:19	−11.9	0.4	35.2							
14	5 29.1	+23 15	12:00:09	−10.3	0.9	342.2							
18	5 45.8	+23 24	12:01:01	−8.5	1.4	289.3							
22	6 02.4	+23 26	12:01:53	−6.8	1.8	236.4							
26	6 19.0	+23 22	12:02:44	−5.0	2.3	183.4							
30	6 35.6	+23 11	12:03:33	−3.2	2.7	130.5							
Jul. 4	6 52.1	+22 54	12:04:19	−1.4	3.2	77.5							
8	7 08.6	+22 30	12:04:59	0.4	3.6	24.6							
12	7 24.9	+22 00	12:05:34	2.2	4.0	331.6							
16	7 41.2	+21 24	12:06:01	4.0	4.4	278.7							
20	7 57.3	+20 42	12:06:20	5.8	4.8	225.8							
24	8 13.2	+19 55	12:06:30	7.5	5.1	172.9							
28	8 29.0	+19 02	12:06:30	9.2	5.5	120.0							
Aug. 1	8 44.6	+18 05	12:06:21	10.8	5.8	67.0							
5	9 00.0	+17 02	12:06:02	12.3	6.0	14.1							
9	9 15.3	+15 56	12:05:34	13.8	6.3	321.2							
13	9 30.5	+14 45	12:04:57	15.3	6.5	268.4							
17	9 45.5	+13 30	12:04:10	16.6	6.7	215.5							
21	10 00.3	+12 12	12:03:16	17.9	6.9	162.6							
25	10 15.1	+10 51	12:02:13	19.1	7.0	109.8							
29	10 29.7	+9 27	12:01:04	20.2	7.1	56.9							

The bowling-pin-shaped **analemma** *depicts the drift of apparent solar time or sundial time relative to LMT (horizontal axis) and the changing declination of the Sun (vertical axis) during 2018. For points to the left of the vertical axis ("Sun slow"), the Sun transits after 12:00 LMT. To the right ("Sun fast"), the Sun transits before 12:00 LMT. For each month, a heavy dot marks day 1 with small dots for days 5, 9, 13, 17, 21, 25, and 29. See p. 40 for further details.*

SOLAR OBSERVING
BY KIM HAY

The Sun, our closest star, is a wonderful Solar System object to observe with any type of telescope, if used **SAFELY**. Never look directly at the Sun, and always use a **full-aperture solar filter**. The solar filters that screw into the base of an eyepiece should be **thrown out** and **never used**. The telescope objective concentrates sunlight on such an eyepiece filter, making it very hot, leading to possible breakage, with a high risk of vision loss. The only safe filter is the kind that covers the full aperture of the telescope, at the front, allowing only 1/100 000th of the sunlight through the telescope, thus lowering the heating effect and allowing you to view the Sun safely. Ensure that the filter material is specifically certified as suitable for solar observing.

The preferred solar filters are made of Thousand Oaks glass or Baader film. The Thousand Oaks glass gives the Sun a golden-orange color. The Baader film gives the Sun a natural, white look, which can provide good contrast if there is any plage on the Sun (see below). Other options include lightweight Mylar film (which gives a blue-white tint) and eyepiece projection. Projecting the image from the eyepiece onto white card-stock paper or a wall produces an image that can be safely shared with others.

For safety, the finder must be kept covered. Since your telescope and finder are aligned, look at the shadow of the telescope on the ground and move the telescope until you have the smallest shadow on the ground. The Sun should be in the eyepiece, or close to it. Alternatively, make a small filter for your finder, if you want to use it.

For the amateur, there are alternatives for observing the Sun in various wavelength bands—the simplest method involves a wide spectrum of sunlight, using the solar filters described above. For the enthusiast, narrowband filters, such as the hydrogen-alpha (Hα) red filter (656.3 nm) or the calcium K-line (CaK) violet filter (393.4 nm), can be fitted to existing telescopes (but they also need a broadband pre-filter). Recently, dedicated solar telescopes with built-in narrowband filters have become affordable. An Hα filter shows solar prominences at the solar limb and possibly granulation on the disk. The CaK filter (especially in photographs) enhances granularity and flares.

A Herschel wedge (a type of prism used for white-light observing and photography) can be used, but **with caution**. Only 5% of the light is reflected to the eyepiece. The remaining 95% that is directed out the end of the diagonal is very intense and can burn. Herschel wedges should only be used with refractors or a telescope with an aperture stop to avoid the buildup of heat, which could damage internal components. The cover should only be taken off after the telescope has been set up. You will also need a neutral-density filter (optical density 3.0–4.0, 0.01%–0.001% transmittance). For enhanced viewing comfort, a filter (either green or polarizing) may help, depending on the sky conditions. **A Herschel wedge should only be used by an experienced observer.**

The Sun is best observed at high angular altitude, minimizing the optical effects of the unstable lower 100 m of atmosphere. Try to observe when the Sun is at least 25° above the horizon. Keep in mind that daytime atmospheric seeing conditions are usually very poor, so even a small telescope can be used without loss of detail. Another observing tip is to use a dark hood to cover your head and the eyepiece to block stray light, improving views of fine details.

Observing the morphology of prominences, filaments, flares, sunspots, and other solar phenomena is a great way to witness the dynamics of the Sun. These phenomena result from the strong magnetism within the Sun, which erupts to the surface. An active area can start with plage (white area) and faculae, turn into a pore, and then blossom into a small dark spot. As a pore grows into a sunspot (umbra), a grey area (penumbra) surrounds the sunspot. The umbra is cooler than the surrounding penumbra. Prominences are solar plasma ejections, some of which fall back to the Sun in the form of teardrops or loops; against the Sun's disk, prominences appear as

Nomenclature of phenomena related to sunspots. As the morphology of a sunspot changes, growing into a larger group, it eventually starts to dissipate and show trailing sunspots. Light bridges are formed early and stay with a sunspot over its lifetime. The formation of a light bridge is a slow process taking several days. The light-bridge material generally appears first on the outside of the umbra-penumbra boundary then extends across the umbra. When the light bridge is seen, it can signify the division or final dissolution of the spot. Light bridges have three general features: classic light bridges, islands, and streamers. (Image used with permission from the Solar Astronomy Handbook *and adapted for publication.)*

dark filaments. In a turbulence-free atmosphere, look for white-light flares, which are flash-points produced from sudden discharges of energy. Flares can last from a few moments to several hours, but they are generally measured in minutes. There are also limb flares, flare kernels/hot cores, two-ribbon/two-strand flares, Hyder/impact flares, homologous flares, and Moreton waves, which are shock waves emanating from a white-light flare. An intense solar flare can eject charged particles, which may reach Earth, possibly exciting the upper atmosphere to create aurorae.

Counting sunspots and groups is another interesting activity. For consistency, observing should be done at the same time each day. Start at the limb of the Sun, because this is where you will notice plage and faculae. Then sweep across the disk in a grid pattern to look for disturbances or sunspots. These can be in either hemisphere and at any latitude, depending on the progression of the sunspot cycle. The relative sunspot number (also Wolf number or Zurich number) is $R = 10g + s$, where g is the number of groups (including groups of one) and s is the number of individual spots (including those in groups). Individuals may submit their observations to the Solar Section of the American Association of Variable Star Observers (AAVSO, see below), which compiles monthly averages from all observers. To help locate the latitude and longitude of a sunspot, and to find instructions and a template (called the Stonyhurst disk) to place over your sketch or image, see the weblinks below. See also the EPHEMERIS FOR THE SUN on p. 187, which lists the orientation of the Sun (P, B_0, and L_0) in four-day increments. Solar activity can be mapped as an exercise, using disk templates (Stonyhurst, Porter, or grid) and solar orientation elements (see BAA Solar Section and Atmospheric Optics websites, below).

The Sun takes 25 to 29 days to make a full rotation, with an average of 27 days. The Carrington rotation number, invented by Richard Carrington, counts the number of rotations of the Sun since 1895 Nov. 3. The Solar Section of the Association of Lunar & Planetary Observers (ALPO) uses Carrington rotation numbers for the study and archiving of solar morphology and prominence activity. For an updated Carrington list, visit www.alpo-astronomy.org/solarblog. ALPO accepts sketches and photographs (at all wavelengths) on the Sun Forms that are available on the solar blog webpage. All submissions are stored on the online Solar Gallery. (For instruction on astronomical sketching see ASTRONOMICAL SKETCHING, p. 88; for a primer on astrophotography, see DIGITAL ASTROPHOTOGRAPHY, p. 91.)

A wide range of digital cameras and webcams, combined with various filters, can produce phenomenal images of the Sun. Numerous computer programs allow the combination of multiple images to create an enhanced image or video. Libraries, online chat rooms, and email lists provide a wealth of information on solar photography. The best way to learn is to read and ask questions of experienced solar imagers.

A solar cycle takes 9–14 years (11 years on average) to complete, and we are now on the downward side of Solar Cycle 24. Sunspot counts were waning in the first half of 2016 with 10 days reported having no sunspots. Though the spots are not evident, the Sun is still very active, and is in a very unstable time where activity can spring up at any moment.

Solar Cycle 24 has been the weakest cycle in many years, and it is slowly coming to an end (2008–2019). We will have minimal solar activity for the next while, which may then plateau for a couple more years before starting Solar Cycle 25, possibly starting up in 2019 through to 2030. This is all tantalizingly unpredictable.

If you do not have the proper equipment to observe the Sun, you can always visit the *Solar and Heliospheric Observatory* (SOHO) internet site (see below) and see daily images of the Sun. The following Handbook sections contain related information: FILTERS (p. 64), SOLAR ACTIVITY (p. 189), and VIEWING A SOLAR ECLIPSE—A WARNING (p. 145).

References

ALPO Solar Astronomy Handbook, ALPO Solar Section
Beck, R., Hilbrecht, H., Reinsch, K., and Völker, P., *Solar Astronomy Handbook*, Willmann–Bell, Inc., Richmond, Virginia, 1995.
Bray, R.J. and Loughhead, R.E., *Sunspots*, Dover Publications, 1964.
Broxton, T., *Solar Observer's Handbook*, Authorhouse, 2009.
Jenkins, J.L., *The Sun and How to Observe It*, Springer, 2009.
Rix E., Hay, K., Russell, S., and Handy, R., *Solar Sketching: A Comprehensive Guide to Drawing the Sun*, Springer, 2015.

Websites for Solar Observing and Astrophysics

www.aavso.org/solar (AAVSO)
www.alpo-astronomy.org/solar (ALPO)
www.alpineastro.com/Solar_Observation/Solar_Observation.htm (Alpine Astronomical)
www.atoptics.co.uk/tiltsun.htm (Atmospheric Optics Tilting Sun)
www.oneminuteastronomer.com/999/choose-solar-filter (choosing solar filters)
www.petermeadows.com/html/stonyhurst.html (Stonyhurst disks and instructions)
www.britastro.org/section_front/21 (BAA: Stonyhurst, Porter, and Grid disks)
sdo.gsfc.nasa.gov (NASA *Solar Dynamics Observatory*)
sohowww.nascom.nasa.gov (*Solar and Heliospheric Observatory*)
www.stce.be (STCE: Solar-Terrestrial Centre of Excellence—Belgium)
www.swpc.noaa.gov (NOAA Space Weather Prediction Center)
radiojove.gsfc.nasa.gov (NASA Solar and Planetary Radio Astronomy for Schools)
www.solarham.net (solar page by amateur radio station VE3EN)
www.spaceweatherwoman.com (Dr. Tamitha Skov—Heliosphere Physicist)
halpha.nso.edu (H Alpha Network Monitor)

SOLAR ACTIVITY
BY KEN TAPPING

Cycle 24—the current solar activity cycle—continues to decline, although there have been several small surges of activity over the last year. Some produced auroral displays, at least one of which was quite spectacular. Despite a jump in activity around 2014, the cycle remains the lowest since the start of the F10.7 (10.7-cm solar ratio flux) record. Soon after the maximum of Cycle 23 there was a change in the relationship between F10.7 and the sunspot number index, which is the other most widely used index of solar activity. The sunspot number values became smaller than would be expected on the basis of the F10.7 values, indicating a fall of photospheric activity compared to the level in the corona. This is rather reminiscent of what happened in the Maunder and Dalton Minima, although the current deficit is smaller. At this point, it is impossible to predict whether Cycle 25 will continue to show this trend or whether it will bring a return to a more "normal" pattern of activity.

The 10.7-cm solar radio flux, averaged monthly (see p. 193). This index, which originates in the low solar corona overlying active regions, is a more global index of magnetic activity than sunspot number. The 10–13 year solar activity cycle is clearly visible. The shorter-term spikes are shorter episodes of activity as active regions and clusters of regions form, evolve, and decay. There is some level of activity even during solar minima. The Activity Cycle numbers are shown.

Solar activity is fundamentally a magnetic phenomenon. Deep below the photosphere, differential rotation and convection cause the solar material to move in a complex manner. The density of this material is high enough for its movement to drag the magnetic fields along with it. This generates electric currents, which in turn produce magnetic fields. The result is a complex system of subphotospheric "magnetic flux ropes." The penetration of sections of these flux ropes through the photosphere and into the chromosphere and corona gives rise to the many observed forms of solar activity. Above the photosphere the situation is strikingly different: the density is much lower, and the magnetic fields trap and confine the ionized gas of the solar atmosphere, supporting loops and filaments, and forming the diverse menagerie of photospheric, chromospheric, and coronal structures with which we are familiar, such as sunspots, active regions, complexes of activity, and systems of loops. Changing emissions in the X-ray and ultraviolet wavelengths, and at radio wavelengths, are due to the changing amount of trapped plasma and the strengths of the magnetic fields containing them. The Sun's total energy output is also affected by magnetic activity, fortunately only slightly.

The organization of the subphotospheric magnetic fields gives rise to a consistent pattern in the magnetic configuration of active regions. Each region is magnetically bipolar, with the bipoles arranged east–west on the disk. All bipoles lying in the same hemisphere are arranged with the same magnetic polarity leading (facing in the direction in which the region appears to move as it is carried across the disk by solar

---

*The numbering system for solar activity cycles was started by Rudolph Wolf, who arbitrarily designated the activity maximum of 1750 as that of Cycle 1.

rotation—westward in the observer's sky). In the other hemisphere, the leading and following magnetic polarities are reversed.

Exceptions do occur. Regions are sometimes formed that have a magnetic orientation perpendicular to or even the reverse of the norm for that hemisphere. Such regions usually try to move into the conventional orientation but are impeded by the magnetic linkages formed with their surroundings. These regions tend to produce flares as potential energy builds up in their magnetic structures and is subsequently released catastrophically.

The "conventional" magnetic configurations for active regions reverse on alternate activity cycles. For example, during Cycle 22, active regions in the northern solar hemisphere were oriented with their "negative" (i.e. south-seeking) magnetic polarity ends leading and "positive" (north-seeking) ends following, with the reverse situation in the southern hemisphere. In Cycle 23, this arrangement was reversed. Cycle 24 re-establishes the pattern of Cycle 22. A *magnetic* activity cycle, which is probably a more realistic description of the rhythms of solar activity, is equal to two of Wolf's activity cycles and takes about 22 years to complete.

Active regions are not isolated phenomena; they occur in complexes, comprising several active regions at various stages of development, together with the network of elements remaining from decayed regions. This localization of activity gives rise to a rotational modulation of the 10.7-cm flux as active-region clusters are carried across the disk and disappear around the east limb. To smooth out this modulation in long-term studies of solar activity, the data are averaged over solar rotations rather than by month. Active regions can persist for one or more solar rotations and the complexes for a dozen or so.

The large-scale organization of solar magnetic activity is also apparent in the spatial distribution of active regions during the solar cycle. The first activity of the new cycle is marked by the formation of active regions at high latitudes. As activity builds toward the maximum of the cycle, the number of active regions increases, and they tend to form at lower latitudes. As the activity wanes toward the next minimum, the number of regions decreases, but the average latitude continues to decrease until the last activity of the cycle is located near the equator. Then, as the new cycle starts, new active regions form at high latitudes.

The formation of a new active region begins with the emergence of magnetic loops through the photosphere and into the overlying chromosphere and corona. This is heralded by the appearance of small pores, about 1000 km across, which coalesce and spread into a patch of magnetic flux that may exceed 50000 km in length. The average magnetic-field strength in such patches is of the order of 0.01 T (100 gauss). The emergence of these magnetic fields modifies the spatial and density structure of the chromosphere, giving rise to enhanced emission in the calcium and magnesium II K spectral lines. These bright patches (called plage), which stand out prominently in filtergrams, are the most conspicuous aspect of active regions. In some areas of the new active region, magnetic field strengths reach or exceed 0.1 T. These magnetic fields are strong enough to impede the transfer of energy from within the Sun, leading to these patches being cooler (3000 K) compared with the surrounding photosphere, which has a temperature of about 6000 K. Although actually quite hot and shining quite brightly, in contrast with their hotter surroundings, these flux concentrations appear as dark spots: sunspots. As a region grows, one or more large spots form at the leading end, and a scattering of smaller ones form at the trailing end. Sunspots are a prominent feature of active regions and are the aspect of solar activity that has been longest known.

The growth of the new active region continues through repeated episodes of magnetic flux emergence. In general, the size is directly proportional to the total magnetic flux in the region. Growth stops when the emergence of new magnetic flux ceases. Soon after, the region starts to decay. This proceeds partly by the resubmergence of magnetic flux and partly by fragmentation. The spots disappear, and eventually, all that remains is a large area of magnetic flux arranged in a network pattern, blending in slowly with the remains of other decayed active regions.

Repeated episodes of magnetic-flux emergence, together with motions of the footpoints, which are the photospheric anchors of magnetic loops, lead to the magnetic field overactive regions becoming complex and tangled and storing enormous amounts of energy. The relaxation of these fields is an important aspect of the evolution and dissipation of active regions. In some cases, this can occur noncatastrophically; otherwise, stresses increase until various plasma instabilities allow rapid relaxation and reconnection of the magnetic fields and a rapid release of the stored energy. These energy releases are known as flares.

The Solar Wind and Aurorae

The solar atmosphere is not stable. It is constantly flowing outward as a stream of particles and magnetic fields—the *solar wind*. The flow is strongest where the magnetic loops are very large and impose the least drag on the outwardly flowing particles. Because of their lower coronal densities, these regions produce a lower flux of X-rays and appear in X-ray images as dark patches, known as "coronal holes." The solar wind is not homogeneous or steady; its speed, density, and direction can change according to the positions of coronal holes and the nature of current solar activity.

The solar wind profoundly changes Earth's magnetic field. The wind pressure pushes the field out of its dipole shape into a long teardrop. The magnetic geometry in the tail of the drop makes it the site of many plasma instabilities. The flow of the solar wind over the boundary of Earth's magnetic field (the magnetopause) excites many types of waves, which move along Earth's magnetic field lines and which can be detected on the ground at high magnetic latitudes. Increases in the density or velocity of the solar wind change the pressure equilibrium between the solar wind and the magnetosphere, producing fluctuations in the strength and direction of the magnetic field lines at ground level. If the fluctuations are strong enough, the events are referred to as magnetic storms and substorms. These can disrupt any human activity that involves connected metal networks covering large geographical areas, especially at high magnetic latitudes.

Complex interactions between the solar wind and Earth's magnetic field lead to an accumulation of trapped particles in the magnetosphere. During magnetic storms, instabilities and waves excited in the magnetosphere by the solar wind accelerate some of the trapped particles downward along Earth's magnetic field into increasingly dense atmosphere, where they collide with the atmospheric constituents, exciting them with sufficient energy to produce light. These displays are called aurorae, or the northern and southern lights: *aurora borealis* and *aurora australis*, respectively. Views from space show that aurorae fall in a rough circle (the auroral oval), centered around the magnetic pole, that is, in a definite band of magnetic latitudes. As activity increases, the auroral oval expands, covering lower and lower magnetic latitudes. It also becomes increasingly distorted. During the period of very high activity in March 1989, auroral displays were seen as far south as the Caribbean.

Aurorae occur in many forms and can be steady, moving, or rapidly pulsating, depending upon the nature of the particle streams causing them. Aurorae can appear green or red, although if they are faint, the eye cannot respond in color and they appear grey. The greenish color is due to spectral lines from oxygen (558 nm) and a range of lines from nitrogen covering the band 391 nm to 470 nm. Under highly disturbed conditions, red spectral-line emissions at 630 nm and 636 nm and in a series of bands between 650 nm and 680 nm can also be seen. The green emissions are

AURORAL FORMS

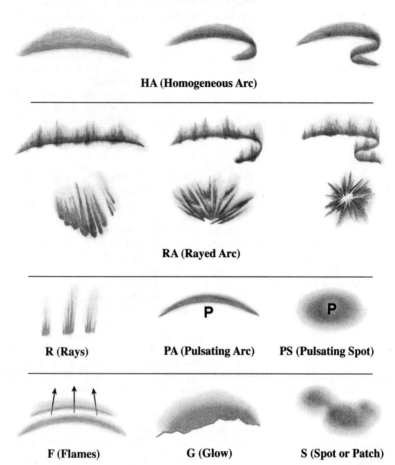

HA (Homogeneous Arc)

RA (Rayed Arc)

R (Rays)   **PA (Pulsating Arc)**   **PS (Pulsating Spot)**

F (Flames)   **G (Glow)**   **S (Spot or Patch)**

The above sketches illustrate standard auroral forms. This simplified classification was devised for visual observers during the International Geophysical Year six decades ago (1957–58). Although there is great variety in auroral patterns, the sketches emphasize fundamental features and minimize variations that depend on the location of the observer. The light of the aurora is emitted by the upper fringes of Earth's atmosphere (heights of 100 to 400 km) as it is bombarded by electrons of the solar wind (solar-wind protons contribute a smaller amount of energy). The modification of the trajectories of these particles by Earth's magnetic field restricts activity to high latitudes, producing the "aurora borealis" in the Northern Hemisphere and the "aurora australis" in the Southern Hemisphere. The wavelengths of four atmospheric molecular and atomic emission lines that can contribute strongly to auroral light are included in the list on p. 32. Whether aurorae appear colored depends on their luminance—light that is too faint will not activate color vision and appears grey. When the luminance is sufficiently great, the relative contributions of blue, green, and red emission lines can result in a variety of auroral hues.

produced at a height of about 110 km; the red, 630-nm and 636-nm emissions, due to atomic oxygen, originate at heights between 200 km and 400 km; the 650-nm to 680-nm emissions are produced at about 90 km.

The Impact and Measurement of Solar Activity

We find evidence of the profound effects of solar activity upon Earth extending as far back in time as we have been able to look. The rhythm of the solar activity cycle is reflected in cores from ocean beds, ice cores, and sediments from lakes that dry up in summer. It is also apparent in the growth rates of trees (determined from the study of tree rings) in recently living timber, wood from medieval buildings, and fossilized trees.

Solar activity can dramatically affect our lives. Magnetic storms due to solar activity induce currents in communications and power-transmission systems having long-distance wires, disrupting their operation for hours. The power blackouts in Québec and Scandinavia produced by a large flare on 1989 Mar. 10 are a particularly outstanding example. Railway signalling systems might also be affected. Increased X-ray emissions from flares cause enhanced ionization of Earth's atmosphere at D-region heights (about 90 km), producing blackouts of shortwave communications.

Solar activity heats the upper atmosphere, causing it to expand further into space, increasing the drag experienced by artificial satellites in low orbits. It is ironic that the lifetime of the *Solar Max* satellite was dramatically shortened in this way. Above the atmosphere, satellites have no protection from high-energy particle fluxes produced by the Sun. Their electronic systems can be damaged, leading to catastrophic failures in some cases, as occurred with two *Anik* communications satellites in January 1994.

The oldest index of solar activity is the sunspot number. A number of techniques, many empirical, have been developed to combine observations from various observatories and observers to form the International Sunspot Number. This is a rather poor index; however, it has given us a database extending back to at least the 17th century.

Probably the best available index of solar activity, at least covering the last six decades or so, is the *10.7-cm flux*, or $F_{10.7}$. This index is an objective measurement of the integrated emission at the 10.7-cm wavelength (a frequency of 2.8 GHz) from all sources present on the solar disk. It has been measured daily by the National Research Council of Canada for over 65 years and is now used worldwide as a primary index of solar activity. In 2003, the program became a joint one with the Canadian Space Agency. $F_{10.7}$ is expressed in solar-flux units (1 sfu = 10^{-22} W·m^{-2}Hz^{-1}). The 10.7-cm flux has the great advantage that it can be measured in all weather conditions and requires no human involvement or "interpretation." When quiet, the Sun produces a $F_{10.7}$ value of 64 sfu, due to free-free thermal emission from the quiet solar corona. Also, $F_{10.7}$ can be used as an objective proxy for other activity-related quantities. The strength of the radio emission constituting $F_{10.7}$ is modulated by the annual variation in the distance between Earth and Sun. When considering solar-driven phenomena at the Earth and in near-Earth space, this is not important, so the "Observed" value of the flux may be applicable. On the other hand, when considering solar activity, this modulation has to be removed from the data. In such instances, the "Adjusted" flux, which is scaled to an Earth–Sun distance of 1 au, should be used.

We are a long way from understanding the nature and the extent of the effects solar activity has upon Earth. Some correlations, like that between the length of miniskirts and solar activity, are probably spurious; others might not be. As we exploit our environment more fully, we become increasingly sensitive to things that might affect it, even slightly.

(See pp. 16, 64, 145, and 186 for safe methods of observing the Sun.)

RAINBOWS AND SOME OTHER
SKY PHENOMENA
BY ROY BISHOP

Sunlight, and more rarely moonlight, interacting with water drops or ice crystals in the sky can result in aerial patterns displaying striking symmetry. This brief account is restricted to the more common sky phenomena. For more extensive treatments, including a dozen relatively rare patterns involving ice crystals, see the book by Greenler in the references and the websites listed there. For comprehensive accounts of the history and physics of the rainbow, see the books by Boyer, and Lee and Fraser.

In order of increasing angular distance from the Sun, ice crystals produce coronae, pillars, halos, sundogs, and circumhorizontal (or circumzenithal) arcs. (Other small particles, including water drops, also produce coronae.) In the half of the sky opposite the Sun, water drops produce rainbows and, surrounding the antisolar point, glories. The heiligenschein is not an atmospheric phenomenon, but like the glory is a bright area in the vicinity of the antisolar point.

Because the rainbow is the most famous, most beautiful, and most complex of these apparitions, I begin with rainbows and devote the greater part of this article to them. Also, if you understand the rainbow, it is easy to understand halos, sundogs, circumhorizontal arcs, circumzenithal arcs, and pillars.

Rainbows

The rainbow has challenged natural philosophers over the centuries, including Aristotle, Roger Bacon, Theodoric of Freiberg, René Descartes, Sir Isaac Newton, Edmund Halley, Thomas Young, Sir George Airy, and Gustav Mie. It was Descartes (1596–1650) who first understood the basic geometry of the rainbow, and it was Newton (1642–1727) who first understood the origin of the colors of the rainbow. In 1803, 1838, and 1908, Young, Airy, and Mie, respectively, gave successively more accurate treatments of the influence of the wave nature of light on the structure of the rainbow. Recently, Alistair Fraser and Raymond Lee, using the power of the computer, provided additional insights concerning the physics of the rainbow. A few poets, including Keats and Goethe, have derided science for analyzing the rainbow, but understanding only deepens one's admiration for the beauty and subtle nature of this phantom.

The Shape of a Raindrop: The shape of a raindrop is relevant for rainbows. Surface tension arising from molecular attraction shrinks raindrops into the shape with the least surface area per unit volume—a sphere. (Raindrops resemble teardrops only after they have crashed against a surface such as a windowpane.) Aerodynamic forces deform large raindrops into a hamburger-bun shape with the short axis vertical, but an average raindrop is essentially spherical.

The Origin of the Rainbow: Sunlight is refracted and reflected by a raindrop (see Figure 1). The *primary* rainbow involves two refractions (where the light ray enters and leaves the drop) and *one* internal reflection. A portion of a ray that enters a drop head-on is deviated through 180° by the internal reflection, but when the ray is shifted off-center, the reflection produces a smaller deviation. When the ray is shifted 86% of the way toward grazing the drop (as in Figure 1), because of the increasing refraction, a *minimum angle of deviation* of approximately 138° is reached. This *stationary* angle concentrates some of the light leaving a raindrop after one reflection near this direction. Dispersion associated with the two refractions makes the minimum angle vary with wavelength, resulting in a spectrum. This interplay of sunlight with single raindrops

Figure 1 *The path of a ray of sunlight interacting with a spherical raindrop is displayed. The ray is shown entering the drop at 86% of the drop radius from head-on entry, causing ray P, exiting after one internal reflection, to be at a minimum angle of deviation of 138° and contributing to the primary rainbow. Ray (S) exiting after two internal reflections is close to but not at the minimum deviation for the secondary rainbow (231°); the ray entering the drop must be shifted closer to grazing incidence (to 95% of the drop radius) before a minimum deviation of*

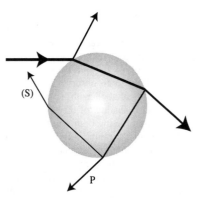

231° is attained. Rays undergoing three or more reflections within the drop are not shown, and neither is chromatic dispersion in the three rays exiting the drop. The widths of the various rays give an approximate indication of their relative intensities.

Figure 2 *Two raindrops are shown, greatly magnified, each with a ray of sunlight striking it such that the exiting ray is at the minimum angle of deviation and heading toward the observer. The drop with one internal reflection is contributing light to the observer's primary rainbow, and the drop with two internal reflections is contributing to the observer's secondary rainbow. Other drops (not shown) located along the rays P and S contribute*

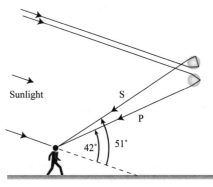

in the same fashion to the two rainbows, and the whole array has rotational symmetry about the dashed line, the extended shadow of the observer's head. The observer, looking from the apices of these conical shells, sees two, circular, colored bands of light.

in the sky is symmetric about an axis extending from the Sun through the eye of the observer; thus the circular arc of a rainbow is centered on that axis. To look at the primary rainbow, the observer's eyes must be turned toward 138° + 180° = 318° or 42° from the antisolar point, the shadow of the observer's head (see Figure 2).

  To Predict Where a Rainbow Might Appear: If the Sun is shining where you are, with the Sun at your back extend your arms together straight out in front of you, splay your fingers and thumbs horizontally, and touch the tips of your thumbs together. Close one eye and align the tip of one little finger with the shadow of your head. As you tilt your hands, the tip of the other little finger will trace out the location of the primary rainbow in the sky. (A double hand-span at arm's length subtends approximately 40°, about the same as the 42° angular radius of the primary rainbow.)

  Rainbows: None, Semicircular, and Circular: Don't expect to see a rainbow in the sky at midday in tropical latitudes, or at midday in spring or summer at higher latitudes. The Sun has to be less than 42° above the horizon for the top of the primary rainbow to be above the horizon (see Figure 2). At sunrise or sunset, the antisolar center of a rainbow is at the horizon, resulting in a semicircular rainbow that meets the horizon at 90°. From an airplane, or by spraying a garden hose, it is possible to see a complete circular rainbow at any time of day, provided there are many water drops and sunlight in the entire region 42° from the antisolar point.

A Rainbow Is Not a Bow: Angle, not distance, determines which raindrops send rainbow light to an observer's eye. Hence, the raindrops contributing to a rainbow lie in a conical shell with its tip at the observer's eye, and its axis coinciding with the extended shadow of the observer's head (see Figure 2). Only those parts of the conical shell having both raindrops and sunlight contribute to the rainbow. Thus, in spatial extent, a rainbow is like an immense, mouse-nibbled, ice-cream cone (sans ice cream). From the perspective of the observer located at the tip of this fragmented conical shell, a rainbow *looks* like a section of a flat circular arc or bow, but the only place a flat bow exists is on the observer's retina. Despite how rainbows are sometimes depicted in art and advertising, a rainbow cannot be viewed obliquely (it always appears circular), and it always has the same immense angular size. (Its 84° diameter spans almost one-quarter of the entire horizon.)

A Filled Cone of Light: Sunlight strikes an entire hemisphere of a raindrop, so in the case of the emerging rays that have undergone one internal reflection, sunlight is deviated over the entire range of possible angles, from 180° to the stationary, minimum, frequency-dependent angle of approximately 138°. Hence the conical shell of enhanced brightness that constitutes the primary rainbow is the outer surface of a filled cone of light (the portion thereof that lies above the observer's horizon) that brightens the disk of sky lying within the primary rainbow. Refractive dispersion occurs at all deviation angles less than 180° down to the approximate 138° minimum, but because of overlap, colors are perceived only near 138° where the overlap is not complete and the frequency-dependent stationary angle enhances the luminance, thereby creating the primary rainbow.

Your Rainbow: A rainbow is located at a particular angle relative to the Sun–observer axis (see Figure 2). When the observer moves, the axis moves, and the rainbow moves. The observer's shadow moves too, but a rainbow is subtler than a shadow; you can see someone else's shadow, but you cannot see their rainbow. Each observer has his or her own private rainbow. Although an observer's eyes image different rainbows, the two rainbows are in the same parallel direction, so when the images fuse, the observer sees one rainbow at infinity. Obviously a rainbow is not an object in the normal sense of the word; it is a pattern of light specific to the observer. Unlike the case of a normal object like a tree, there are as many rainbows as there are observers. If there is no observer, there is no rainbow; only raindrops in the sky, each raindrop independently scattering sunlight symmetrically about its own Sun-raindrop axis.

The Secondary Rainbow: If conditions are favorable (lots of rain and sunlight, and a dark sky background), a secondary rainbow will be visible. The *secondary* rainbow involves *two* internal reflections in each raindrop (see Figure 1). A light ray that enters a drop head-on is deviated through 360° by the two internal reflections, but when the ray is shifted off-center the reflections produce a smaller deviation. When the ray is shifted 95% of the way toward grazing the drop, because of the increasing refraction, a minimum angle of deviation of approximately 231° is reached. This stationary angle concentrates some of the light leaving a raindrop after two reflections near this direction. Dispersion associated with the two refractions makes the minimum angle vary with wavelength, resulting in a spectrum. To look at the secondary rainbow, the observer's eyes must be turned toward 231° + 180° = 411° or 51° from the antisolar point (see Figure 2). Thus the secondary rainbow lies (51° – 42°) = 9° outside of the primary rainbow (9° is about one fist-width at arm's length).

Width of the Secondary Rainbow: A light ray contributing to the secondary rainbow enters a raindrop closer to the edge of the raindrop than does a light ray contributing to the primary rainbow. Consequently, the amount of refraction and associated spectral dispersion are greater. The additional reflection from the curved inner surface of the raindrop further increases the dispersion, making the spectrum of the secondary bow about 60% wider than that of the primary bow (after taking the 0.5° diameter of the Sun into account).

Reversed Spectra: A light ray contributing to the primary rainbow enters the side of a raindrop nearest the convex side of the rainbow, is deviated through 138°, and exits near the opposite side of the drop heading toward the observer (see Figure 2). Long wavelengths are refracted least, emerging at a steeper angle to the rainbow axis, so the convex side of the primary rainbow appears red. A light ray contributing to the secondary rainbow is deviated through 231°. To reach the observer, the ray must rotate through the raindrop in the *opposite* sense to the path followed by the primary rainbow ray. Long wavelengths are refracted least, emerging at a shallower angle to the rainbow axis, so the concave side of the secondary rainbow appears red. Thus the spectral sequences are reversed, with the red of both bows bordering upon the space that is between the bows.

Alexander's Dark Band: The two rays, P and S, shown in Figure 2 undergo minimum deviations of 138° and 231°, the first approaching its minimum counter-clockwise, the other clockwise. Therefore there is a $138° + 231° - 360° = 9°$ gap into which such rays cannot enter. Thus the sky between the bows is darker than elsewhere, a feature called *Alexander's Dark Band* after Alexander of Aphrodisias, a Greek philosopher who drew attention to it c. 200 CE. The "dark" band is only moderately darker than the region beneath the primary rainbow because of three sources of light between the bows: skylight, external reflections off raindrops (see Figure 1), and diffraction of light waves by the raindrops.

The Tertiary Rainbow: Edmund Halley (1656–1742) first calculated that light rays exiting a raindrop after *three* reflections have a minimum angle of deviation of 318°, placing the *tertiary* rainbow only 42° from the Sun. For at least 2000 years, people had been looking for a tertiary rainbow in the vicinity of the primary and secondary rainbows. They had been looking in the wrong part of the sky! The luminance (surface brightness) of the secondary rainbow is less than that of the primary, and the luminance of the tertiary rainbow is less than that of the secondary because of three effects: (1) Light rays contributing to successively higher-order rainbows strike raindrops closer to grazing incidence, causing a greater fraction of the light to reflect without entering the drops; (2) Some light exits the drops at each internal reflection leaving less for higher-order rainbows; (3) Rainbow width increases as the order increases, spreading the light over a greater area. There is little hope of seeing the faint tertiary rainbow because it is almost invariably overwhelmed by two sources of white light in that region of the sky (see Figure 1): (a) *Most* of the sunlight entering raindrops passes through without being internally reflected and illuminates the sunward half of the sky. (The lack of a stationary angle in the deviation of these bright, unreflected rays is why there is no "zero-order" rainbow.); (b) Sunlight externally reflected from raindrops. The quaternary rainbow, fainter again than the tertiary, also occurs in the bright sunward half of the sky, about 44° from the Sun. Higher-order rainbows also occur, but usually only the primary and secondary bows are visible in the sky (see www.atoptics.co.uk/rainbows/ord34.htm).

Banding Beneath: The concave side of a primary rainbow may display two or three narrow bands, called *supernumerary bows* or *supernumerary arcs*. They are caused by the interference of two emerging parallel light rays that have entered a raindrop slightly nearer to and farther from grazing incidence than a ray that undergoes minimum deviation. The two paths have different lengths causing interference. Similar pairs of rays emerging at various angles produce the supernumerary bow pattern. British physicist Thomas Young (1773–1829) was the first to present this explanation, although more accurate descriptions involving diffraction were later provided by British Astronomer Royal, Sir George Airy (1801–1892); German physicist Gustav Mie (1868–1957); and Canadian meteorologist Alistair Fraser (in 1983).

Hamburger Buns and a Pot of Gold: The hamburger-bun distortion of raindrops with increasing drop size has the greatest effect on the top part of a rainbow because light rays in that region traverse a vertical cross section of a raindrop. The distortion has two consequences for the rainbow:

First, the distortion substantially increases the minimum deviation angle such that light from large raindrops of various diameters is spread into a white haze beneath the primary rainbow. Only spherical drops (diameters of about 0.5 mm and smaller) contribute to the upper part of a rainbow, often causing it to be less bright and its colors less vivid than in the lower part of the bow (assuming the Sun is low in the sky so the lower part of the rainbow is at a steep angle to the horizon). In the lower part, drops of all sizes present circular cross sections to light rays that are redirected toward the observer. Thus *all* drops contribute to the lower part of the rainbow, making it the brightest part when there is a heavy rainfall with a wide range of drop sizes. As Lee and Fraser surmise in their book *The Rainbow Bridge*, the bright glow of vivid colors near the end of the rainbow may be the origin of the pot-of-gold myth.

Second, the distortion-induced modification in the shift of the position of supernumerary bows with drop size causes distinct supernumerary bows to occur only for raindrops having diameters in the range of about 0.4 to 0.8 mm, and only in the upper part of a rainbow. The contributions of larger and smaller drops are blurred due to overlap. A bright rainbow *without* supernumerary bows typically involves a heavy rain shower during which there is a wide range of drop diameters. Drops in the 0.4 to 0.8 mm range are present, but the bright area beneath the primary rainbow caused by larger raindrops obscures their otherwise distinct supernumerary bows.

Beware of Sunglasses: The reflection that rainbow light undergoes inside a raindrop occurs very near *Brewster's angle* at which light reflected from a nonmetallic surface becomes 100% polarized (named in honour of Scottish physicist Sir David Brewster (1781–1868), who discovered this phenomenon). Thus the light of a rainbow is almost 100% polarized. The direction of polarization (the direction of the electric field) is tangent to the bow, which for the upper part of a rainbow has the same orientation as that of partially polarized light reflecting from the dash of a car, a highway, or a body of water. Polarizing sunglasses are designed to block polarized light from the latter three sources and will obliterate a rainbow!

Rainbows at Night: Observations of lunar rainbows are rare. The Moon is bright enough to produce a noticeable rainbow only when it is near its full phase. Also, people are usually indoors at night, and when they do step outside it is often into a light-polluted environment, which rules out any chance of seeing a lunar rainbow. Even when conditions are favorable, few people would notice a lunar rainbow because it is usually too dim to activate color vision and therefore appears white.

Not a Good Spectrum: The rainbow is often cited as the paragon of a white-light spectrum. However, five factors make the rainbow spectrum inferior to that produced by a laboratory spectroscope: (1) The minimum property of the stationary angle that produces a rainbow means that light of each wavelength is spread over larger angles, resulting in some overlap of the spectral colors; (2) The Sun is not a point source of light. The 0.5° spread of its rays smears the rainbow spectrum; (3) Sunlight reflected from the front of the raindrops and skylight from behind dilutes the colors making them less saturated; (4) The increase in the minimum angle of deviation associated with aerodynamic drop distortion (significant for drop diameters of 0.5 mm and larger) causes additional spectral smearing in the upper part of a rainbow; (5) Diffraction broadening results in further overlap of the spectral colors, particularly for small raindrops. In the case of fog or cloud (drop diameters in the range 0.01 to 0.1 mm), diffraction broadening causes the various colors to overlap sufficiently to produce a white rainbow, called a *fogbow*. Also known as a *cloudbow*, it may sometimes be seen from an airplane, a large white arc moving along on a cloud layer below the airplane.

Fog and Flashlight: A dark, foggy night provides an opportunity to see the stationary angle that is the key to a primary rainbow. Place a bright, well-collimated flashlight on the ground with its beam directed vertically upward into the fog. Step back a short distance and examine the vertical shaft of light. Look for a bright patch about 40° from the zenith. Fog droplets at that position preferentially redirect the light downward toward your eyes. Diffraction causes the stationary angle to deviate somewhat from the nominal 42° produced by larger drops. Diffraction broadening may make the faint patch of light from the secondary bow undetectable. It will be located about 54° from the zenith, below the fragment of the primary bow.

Rainbow Light on the Moon: The greater part of Earth's albedo is due to clouds. An observer on the Moon would see Earth brighten noticeably for several hours when the Sun–Earth–Moon angle is near 40° and the cloud droplets provide a 2°-diameter fragment of a cloudbow. At this point, the Moon is in its crescent phase, about three days from new, and earthshine will be enhanced. At Sinus Iridum, the Bay of Rainbows, twice each lunar night the plains and surrounding mountains are bathed in the light of a tattered fragment of a white primary rainbow enveloping Earth. Unfortunately, as viewed from Earth at such times, the substantial glare from the fat, sunlit, lunar crescent, plus scattering of moonlight in Earth's atmosphere and in the observer's eyes or camera tends to obscure the enhanced earthshine.

We Are Part of the Rainbow: Although rain and sunlight have been part of Earth's environment for four billion years, colored rainbows occurred quite recently with the appearance of animals possessing color vision. Our visual world with its brightness and colors occurs within our skull. Nevertheless, by some feat of mental projection we think that our visual world coincides spatially with the external world. Thus we confuse the neural rainbow with the external rainbow, and naively attribute the indescribable colors of the former to the latter. Three centuries ago, Sir Isaac Newton, aware of this overpowering illusion, wrote: "The rays to speak properly are not colored. In them there is nothing else than a certain power and disposition to stir up a sensation of this or that color." Yet, even today, most people regard the cone cells of the retina as "color receptors," as if colors existed in the external world. They speak of "the true colors of moonbows and nebulae revealed by time-exposure photographs," unaware that they are attributing a unique property of the neural photograph in their brain to the external photograph in their hands, and subsequently to moonbows and nebulae in the sky. The eye does not detect the colors of the rainbow; the brain creates them. *We* are part of the rainbow, its most beautiful part.

Halos

Under normal conditions of temperature and pressure, the wave and statistical properties of electrons impose hexagonal crystalline structure on water ice. When sunlight interacts with ice crystals in the frosty sky, it translates the atomic architecture into macroscopic aerial patterns of striking symmetry.

Small ice crystals suspended in the air can have a variety of shapes, including multi-crystalline fragments in which the sixfold symmetry is not obvious, rods that resemble pieces of a hexagonal pencil, flat six-sided plates, and snowflakes with their elegant symmetry.

FIGURE 3 *The bottom diagram shows a light ray undergoing a net minimum deviation of 22° when it refracts symmetrically through alternate sides of a hexagonal ice crystal (in effect, a 60° ice prism). The top three diagrams show hexagonal ice crystals having, from left-to-right, increasing length-to-width ratios: a plate, a block, and a pencil. When falling, aerodynamic forces cause the plate and the pencil to orient horizontally, as shown. The block and clusters of crystals can have any orientation. Plates produce sundogs (refraction) and pillars (reflection). Randomly oriented crystals produce halos (refraction). Pencils produce pillars (reflection) and tangent arcs (refraction).*

FIGURE 4 *A schematic diagram of a 22° halo with sundogs, and a corona and pillar adjacent to the Sun low near the horizon in the center. Hexagonal ice crystals are in the sky: plates (refraction/sundogs, reflection/pillar); blocks (refraction/halo); and both types of crystal (diffraction/corona). The absence of an upward-curving tangent arc at the top of the halo indicates that pencil crystals are not present.*

Alternate sides of a hexagonal ice crystal form a 60° prism (see Figure 3). Light passing through this prism is deviated by the two refractions, the angle of deviation being a minimum (about 22°) when the passage is symmetric, with equal refractions at the two surfaces. As in the case of minimum deviation in a water drop, a significant fraction of the light passing through randomly oriented 60° ice prisms is deviated by approximately 22°, enhancing the brightness at that angle.

Adjacent sides of a hexagonal crystal form a 120° prism, but light cannot pass through such a prism; the light undergoes total internal reflection at the second surface. Opposite sides of a hexagonal crystal are parallel and, like a windowpane, provide no net deviation. End faces of the crystal form 90° prisms with the sides; light passing through a 90° ice prism undergoes a minimum deviation of about 46° when the passage is symmetric.

Crystals having lengths about equal to their widths (called "blocks"; see Figure

3) or clusters of two or more single crystals assume random orientations as they fall. Consequently, the refraction of light rays toward an observer by such crystals has symmetry about the Sun–observer axis, and the observer sees a *halo* of light in the sky, centered on the Sun and having an angular radius of 22° (about one hand-span from the Sun at arm's length; see Figure 4). More rarely, refraction in 90° randomly oriented prisms results in an immense but fainter 46° halo, concentric with the 22° halo. Like the rainbow, a halo is not a circular hoop but a fragmented conical structure seen from its apex. Moonlight can also produce halos, particularly if the Moon is bright, near its full phase.

Because the 22° stationary angle of deviation is a minimum, the halo has a relatively sharp inner edge and a diffuse outer edge, the sky being brighter on the convex side of the halo. Because the deviation is least at the red end of the spectrum, the inner edge of a halo may appear reddish; however, ice crystals are not as optically perfect as raindrops, so the spectral colors of halos are not as pronounced as in rainbows.

The first person to understand the geometry of the 22° halo (i.e. minimum deviation in 60° ice prisms) was the French scientist Edme Mariotte (1620–1684). Sir Isaac Newton, apparently independently, arrived at the same explanation when writing his book *Opticks* (1704), but abandoned it in the published editions in favor of an erroneous explanation by the Dutch physicist Christiaan Huygens (1629–1695). Mariotte's theory was largely ignored for more than a century until revived by Thomas Young in 1807.

The ice crystals that produce halos are often in the leading edge of a low-pressure system, so a halo is a fairly reliable sign that within 24 hours the weather will be overcast and possibly stormy.

Sundogs

Like a small twig or leaf falling from a tree, pencil crystals and flat crystals such as snowflakes and plates are dynamically stable when oriented horizontally as they fall, maximizing air resistance (see Figure 3). If ice crystals in the air are predominately plates, only those crystals at the same altitude as the Sun can refract light to the observer (provided the Sun is low in the sky), resulting in two bright spots 22° on either side of the Sun (see Figure 4). Called *sundogs* or *parhelia*, under favorable conditions these spots can be almost too bright to look at. Although sundogs appear as spots in the sky, the contributing 60° ice prisms lie along the arms of a 44° "V" with the observer's eye at its vertex.

Rays passing nonsymmetrically through 60° plate prisms are deviated more than 22°, resulting in tails or smearing of the sundogs away from the Sun (see Figure 4). Also, like the 22° halo, sundogs often display a hazy spectrum with red on their sunward side.

Sundogs (or *moondogs*, if the Moon is the light source) may appear singly or in pairs (plate crystals) and may be accompanied by a 22° halo (randomly oriented crystals in addition to plates). Or only a 22° halo may be present (only randomly oriented crystals, or if plates are also present the Sun is too high in the sky for its rays to access the 60° prisms of these horizontally oriented crystals). If the Sun is moderately high in the sky (altitude ~30°), thick plates can still result in sundogs, but the skew rays involved displace the sundogs somewhat farther than 22° from the Sun.

Circumhorizontal and Circumzenithal Arcs

Closely related to the rare 46° halo, produced by refraction through the 90° faces of randomly oriented crystals, are two uncommon arcs, produced by refraction through the 90° faces of horizontally oriented plates. The 46° minimum deviation corresponds to the incident and exiting light rays making an almost grazing angle of 22° with the crystal faces.

If the incident ray enters a vertical face, the Sun must be at an altitude near 68° and the arc so formed will be only 22° above the horizon—a circumhorizontal arc —bright and rainbow-hued, with its red edge uppermost. Skew rays account for the extent of the arc perpendicular to the vertical plane containing the Sun and observer. Unlike a rainbow, it is not concentric with the observer's shadow, and it is in the same half of the sky as the Sun. If the Sun is much higher or lower, the arc is diffuse and dim, and cannot exist at all if the altitude of the Sun is much less than 60°. Thus the circumhorizontal arc cannot be seen at latitudes more than about 50° from the equator, and at that latitude only at solar noon near the summer solstice.

If the incident ray enters a horizontal face, the Sun must be relatively low in the sky at an altitude near 22°, and the arc so formed will be high in the sky, 68° above the horizon—a circumzenithal arc—bright and rainbow-hued, with its red edge lowermost, resembling an upside-down rainbow. Unlike the circumhorizontal arc, there are no geographical restrictions on a circumzenithal arc; a 22°-altitude Sun can occur anywhere.

Pillars

In cold weather when the Sun or Moon is near or just below the horizon, a vertical column or *pillar* of light sometimes is seen, extending upward from the Sun or Moon (see Figure 4). On winter nights, tall narrow pillars sometimes extend into the sky, the light sources being unshielded streetlights, often not in direct line of sight. Pillars (also known as *snow pillars*) are caused by plate crystals and/or snowflakes with their mirror-like faces oriented horizontally in the air. Reflections from pencil crystals can also produce pillars. *All* these miniature mirrors throughout the sky reflect light, but only those lying near the vertical plane passing through the light source and an observer reflect light toward the observer; hence the observer sees a vertical pillar. The crystals producing the pillar are located between the light source and the observer.

When sundogs accompany a Sun pillar, plate crystals provide at least some of the mirrors causing the pillar. When a short, upward-curving arc tangent to the top of a 22° halo accompanies a Sun pillar, reflections off the sides of pencil crystals contribute to the pillar, the *tangent arc* being due to refraction in the 60° prisms of the horizontally oriented pencils.

Coronae

In the presence of thin high cloud, hazy bright rings may closely surround the Sun or Moon, a pattern called a *corona* (not to be confused with the solar corona, the hot outer atmosphere of the Sun itself). Lying within several diameters of the Sun or Moon (see Figure 4), a corona often displays pale colors, including a reddish outer border—the reverse of the refraction-based reddish *inner* border of halos and sundogs. The red-reversal indicates that the corona is caused not by refraction but by diffraction scattering of light waves.

The scattering bodies are usually cloud droplets, but can be small ice crystals or even pollen grains. The smaller the scattering bodies, the larger the corona; the more uniform their size, the more obvious the ring structure. Thin clouds passing near the Sun or Moon may display a colorful iridescence associated with evaporation-induced variations in drop size, although in the case of the Sun the display may be too bright to view. Very small particles, such as are injected high into the atmosphere by volcanic eruptions, result in a large corona called a *Bishop's Ring*.

When cloud droplets are involved, a corona is caused by light rays that graze the sides of the water drops without entering the drops, and by rays that pass directly through the drops. The theory describing diffraction scattering is complex, and it is not possible to give a simple explanation of the structure and size of the corona. Note that the corona involves scattering of each light ray by only one drop; scattering by multiple drops eliminates the iridescence and structure of the corona.

Glories

The *glory* resembles the corona and is also caused by diffraction scattering of light waves by fog or cloud droplets; however, the glory occurs on the opposite side of the sky, surrounding the antisolar point. Like the corona, the angular size of the glory (seldom more than a few degrees) varies inversely with the size of the scattering drops. Despite the similarity of the corona and the glory, it is easy to remember which is which: the corona is in the same part of the sky as the solar corona (assuming the Sun, not the Moon, to be the light source of the corona).

Usually seen from an airplane on a cloud layer below, the glory appears as a ring-like pattern of hazy colors centered on the observer's position in the shadow of the airplane. If the cloud layer is sufficiently far from the plane, the plane's shadow (then penumbral only) will not be visible. Mountain climbers sometimes see a glory in a cloud (fog) layer below them. If the fog is close, the climber's shadow, distorted by perspective, will appear to the climber as a dark cavity in the fog with its head centered in the glory, a strange apparition called *the spectre of the Brocken* after a mountain in Germany where the phenomenon has often been observed.

In religious art, the rings or disks of light surrounding the heads of saintly figures were likely inspired by observations of the glory, and possibly the heiligenschein (see below). Certainly it flatters an observer to see an aureole surrounding the shadow of one's own head and not those of others!

The glory involves scattering of a light ray by one drop, whereas a white cloud involves scattering of a light ray by more than one drop—which is why clouds are otherwise white. As in the case of the corona, the theory describing the glory is complex, and it is not possible to give a simple explanation of the structure and size of the glory. Light waves moving along the surface of small water drops and reflections within the drops are both involved.

Heiligenschein

Heiligenschein (German for "holy light") refers to a diffuse colorless glow surrounding the shadow of the observer's head when that shadow is projected on a rough surface or on vegetation covered in dewdrops. Unlike the patterns described above, the heiligenschein is not an atmospheric phenomenon; however, like the glory, it surrounds the antisolar point, so it should be mentioned.

A rough surface appears brightest when viewed in the antisolar direction because the shadows associated with the roughness are hidden behind the objects casting the shadows. For example, on a sunny day, a person walking past shrubbery or a field of grass will see a glowing aura surrounding the shadow of his or her head. A forest viewed from an airplane displays a bright patch surrounding the shadow of the airplane. In the case of vegetation covered in dewdrops, the spherical drops redirect the incident light whence it came, enhancing the brightness associated with hidden shadows. Tiny glass spheres imbedded in highway-marker paint or on automobile license plates do the same. If the Moon had a perfectly diffuse matte surface, at full phase it would provide π times more light than at quarter phase when it is half illuminated; however, because of heiligenschein, at full phase the Moon provides more than ten times as much light—the multitude of shadows on the lunar surface are hidden, and impact-produced glass beads littering the lunar surface redirect sunlight toward Earth. When Saturn is near opposition, heiligenschein enhances the brightness of its rings.

Some people call the hidden shadow phenomenon *the opposition effect*, and restrict the term *heiligenschein* to the glow caused by dewdrops, glass spheres, or similar optics. However, etymologically, heiligenschein fits both contributions. Also, in the case of dewdrops, hidden shadows usually contribute too.

Concluding Thoughts

None of these apparitions—rainbows, halos, sundogs, circumhorizontal arcs, circumzenithal arcs, pillars, coronae, glories, and heiligenschein—are objects in the normal sense of the word. They are patterns of light specific to the individual observer. Anyone who understands them will find the world to be a more interesting place.

References

Benn, C.R., "Rainbows, Haloes, and Earthshine," *The Observatory 114*, No. 1120 (1994), p. 115.

Boyer, C.B., *The Rainbow: From Myth to Mathematics*, Princeton University Press, 1987.

Fraser, A.B., "Why Can the Supernumerary Bows Be Seen in a Rain Shower?" *J. Opt. Soc. Am. 73* (1983), p. 1626.

Greenler, R., *Rainbows, Halos, and Glories*, Cambridge University Press, 1980.

Lee, R.L., Jr., "Mie Theory, Airy Theory, and the natural rainbow," *Appl. Opt. 37* (1998), p. 1506.

Lee, R.L., Jr. and Fraser, A.B., *The Rainbow Bridge*, Pennsylvania State University Press, 2001.

Minnaert, M., *Light and Color in the open air*, Bell and Sons, 1940.

Newton, I., *Opticks* (4th ed. 1730), Dover Publications, 1952.

Nussenzveig, H.M., "The Theory of the Rainbow," *Sci. Am. 236* (4) (1977), p. 116.

Shapiro, A.E., "Newton and Huygens' Explanation of the 22° Halo," *Centaurus 24* (1980), p. 273.

Walker, J., "Rainbows in a Water Drop," *Sci. Am.*, July 1977, p. 138.

Walker, J., "Mysteries of Rainbows," *Sci. Am.*, June 1980, p. 174.

Wright, W.D., *The Rays are not Colored*, Adam Hilger Ltd., London, 1967.

Websites:

www.atoptics.co.uk
www.old.meteoros.de/haloe.htm
www.philiplaven.com/index1.html

TIMES OF SUNRISE AND SUNSET

The table on the following two pages gives the times of sunrise and sunset at 4-day intervals for locations ranging from 20° to 60° north latitude. "RISE" and "SET" correspond to the upper limb of the Sun appearing at the horizon for an observer at sea level. The times are local mean time (LMT) for the Greenwich meridian (i.e. UT at 0° longitude), although for North American observers the stated values may be read directly as LMT at the observer's position with an error less than 1 min. The table may be interpolated linearly for both nontabular latitudes and dates, and can be extrapolated beyond the 20° and 60° latitude limits a few degrees without significant loss of accuracy.

It is a common misconception that extreme values for sunrise and sunset times occur on the shortest and the longest days of the year. That is not the case and is due to the tilt of Earth's spin axis to the axis of its orbit, and to Earth's varying speed along its elliptical orbit (as Kepler described in his second law). At mid-northern latitudes, the earliest sunset occurs early in December and the latest sunrise in early January whereas the shortest day (in the sense of hours of daylight) is Dec. 21 or 22. For more information see *Sky & Telescope*, December 1988, p. 674 and July 1972, p. 20, and an article by Terence Hicks in *JRASC, 88*, p. 86, February 1994. Online, see the information on the *Astronomical Applications* page of **www.usno.navy.mil/USNO**.

The standard time of an event at a particular location must take account of the observer's longitude relative to his or her standard meridian (see STANDARD TIME ZONES on p. 45). The table below lists the latitude and the longitude correction (in minutes of time) for a number of cities in the United States. For example, to find the time of sunset in Lansing on 2018 Jun. 16: the latitude is 43°, and from the table the time of sunset at 0° longitude is 19:41 UT (after interpolating for date and latitude). Thus, at Lansing the time of sunset will be approximately 19:41 LMT. Lansing is in the Eastern time zone (E) and is 38 min of time west of the standard meridian for this zone (75° W), plus 1 h to correct for DST. Thus, sunset in Lansing will occur at 21:19 EDT (Eastern Daylight Time).

The longitude correction for any location may be found by converting the difference between the longitude of the place and that of its standard meridian to time (1° = 4 min of time), the correction being + if the place is west of its standard meridian, − if east. **Note**: Due to a difference in elevation between the observer and the actual horizon, the observed time may differ by several minutes from the predicted time.

American Cities								
Albuquerque NM	35°	+7M	Hartford CT	42°	−9E	New Orleans LA	30°	0C
Atlanta GA	34°	+37E	Honolulu HI	21°	+31H	New York NY	41°	−4E
Austin TX	30°	+31C	Huntington WV	38°	+30E	Omaha NE	41°	+24C
Baltimore MD	39°	+6E	Indianapolis IN	40°	+45E	Pittsburgh PA	40°	+20E
Bangor ME	45°	−25E	Jackson MS	32°	+1C	Providence RI	42°	−14E
Billings MT	46°	+14M	Jefferson City MO	39°	+9C	Raleigh NC	36°	+15E
Birmingham AL	34°	+47E	Lansing MI	43°	+38E	Richmond VA	38°	+10E
Bismarck ND	47°	+43C	Laramie WY	41°	+2M	Salem OR	45°	+12P
Boise ID	44°	+45M	Las Vegas NV	36°	−19P	Salt Lake City UT	41°	+28M
Boston MA	42°	−16E	Lexington KY	38°	+38E	San Francisco CA	38°	+10P
Chicago IL	42°	−9C	Little Rock AR	35°	+9C	Seattle WA	48°	+9P
Columbia SC	34°	+24E	Los Angeles CA	34°	−7P	Sioux Falls SD	44°	+27C
Columbus OH	40°	+32E	Madison WI	43°	−2C	Trenton NJ	40°	−1E
Concord NH	43°	−14E	Miami FL	26°	+21E	Tucson AZ	32°	+24M
Denver CO	40°	0M	Minneapolis MN	45°	+13C	Tulsa OK	36°	+24C
Des Moines IA	42°	+14C	Montpelier VT	44°	−10E	Wichita KS	38°	+29C
Fairbanks AK	65°	+51A	Nashville TN	36°	+47E	Wilmington DE	40°	+2E

SUNRISE AND SUNSET, 2018 JANUARY–JUNE
UNIVERSAL TIME AT GREENWICH MERIDIAN

Latitude:	+20°		+30°		+35°		+40°		+45°		+50°		+55°		+60°	
Event:	RISE	SET	RISE	SET	RISE	SET	RISE	SET	RISE	SET	RISE	SET	RISE	SET	RISE	SET
Jan.–2	6:34	17:30	6:55	17:09	7:07	16:57	7:21	16:43	7:38	16:26	7:58	16:06	8:25	15:39	9:03	15:01
2	6:35	17:33	6:56	17:12	7:08	17:00	7:22	16:46	7:38	16:30	7:58	16:10	8:25	15:44	9:02	15:07
6	6:37	17:35	6:57	17:15	7:09	17:03	7:22	16:50	7:38	16:34	7:58	16:14	8:23	15:49	8:59	15:13
10	6:37	17:38	6:57	17:18	7:08	17:07	7:22	16:54	7:37	16:38	7:56	16:19	8:20	15:55	8:55	15:21
14	6:38	17:41	6:57	17:22	7:08	17:11	7:20	16:58	7:35	16:43	7:53	16:25	8:17	16:02	8:49	15:29
18	6:38	17:43	6:56	17:25	7:07	17:14	7:19	17:02	7:33	16:48	7:50	16:31	8:12	16:09	8:43	15:39
22	6:38	17:46	6:55	17:28	7:05	17:18	7:16	17:07	7:30	16:54	7:46	16:37	8:07	16:17	8:35	15:48
26	6:37	17:48	6:53	17:32	7:03	17:22	7:14	17:12	7:26	16:59	7:42	16:44	8:01	16:25	8:27	15:58
30	6:36	17:51	6:51	17:35	7:00	17:27	7:10	17:17	7:22	17:05	7:36	16:51	7:54	16:33	8:19	16:09
Feb. 3	6:35	17:53	6:49	17:39	6:57	17:31	7:07	17:21	7:18	17:11	7:31	16:58	7:47	16:41	8:09	16:19
7	6:33	17:55	6:46	17:42	6:54	17:35	7:03	17:26	7:12	17:16	7:24	17:04	7:40	16:50	7:59	16:30
11	6:31	17:57	6:43	17:45	6:50	17:39	6:58	17:31	7:07	17:22	7:18	17:11	7:31	16:58	7:49	16:40
15	6:29	17:59	6:40	17:49	6:46	17:43	6:53	17:36	7:01	17:28	7:11	17:18	7:23	17:06	7:38	16:51
19	6:27	18:01	6:36	17:52	6:42	17:46	6:48	17:40	6:55	17:33	7:03	17:25	7:14	17:15	7:27	17:01
23	6:24	18:03	6:32	17:55	6:37	17:50	6:42	17:45	6:48	17:39	6:56	17:32	7:05	17:23	7:16	17:12
27	6:21	18:04	6:28	17:58	6:32	17:54	6:37	17:49	6:42	17:44	6:48	17:39	6:55	17:31	7:05	17:22
Mar. 3	6:18	18:06	6:24	18:00	6:27	17:57	6:31	17:54	6:35	17:50	6:39	17:45	6:45	17:40	6:53	17:32
7	6:15	18:07	6:19	18:03	6:22	18:01	6:24	17:58	6:28	17:55	6:31	17:52	6:36	17:48	6:41	17:42
11	6:12	18:08	6:15	18:06	6:16	18:04	6:18	18:02	6:20	18:01	6:23	17:58	6:26	17:56	6:29	17:52
15	6:09	18:10	6:10	18:08	6:11	18:07	6:12	18:07	6:13	18:06	6:14	18:05	6:15	18:04	6:17	18:02
19	6:05	18:11	6:05	18:11	6:05	18:11	6:05	18:11	6:05	18:11	6:05	18:11	6:05	18:11	6:05	18:12
23	6:02	18:12	6:00	18:13	6:00	18:14	5:59	18:15	5:58	18:16	5:57	18:17	5:55	18:19	5:53	18:22
27	5:58	18:13	5:56	18:16	5:54	18:17	5:52	18:19	5:50	18:21	5:48	18:24	5:45	18:27	5:41	18:31
31	5:55	18:14	5:51	18:18	5:49	18:20	5:46	18:23	5:43	18:26	5:39	18:30	5:35	18:35	5:29	18:41
Apr. 4	5:51	18:15	5:46	18:20	5:43	18:24	5:40	18:27	5:36	18:31	5:31	18:36	5:25	18:43	5:17	18:51
8	5:48	18:16	5:41	18:23	5:38	18:27	5:33	18:31	5:28	18:36	5:22	18:43	5:14	18:50	5:05	19:01
12	5:45	18:17	5:37	18:25	5:32	18:30	5:27	18:35	5:21	18:41	5:14	18:49	5:05	18:58	4:53	19:10
16	5:41	18:19	5:32	18:28	5:27	18:33	5:21	18:39	5:14	18:47	5:05	18:55	4:55	19:06	4:41	19:20
20	5:38	18:20	5:28	18:30	5:22	18:36	5:15	18:43	5:07	18:52	4:57	19:01	4:45	19:14	4:29	19:30
24	5:36	18:21	5:24	18:33	5:17	18:40	5:10	18:47	5:01	18:57	4:50	19:08	4:36	19:22	4:18	19:40
28	5:33	18:22	5:20	18:35	5:13	18:43	5:04	18:51	4:54	19:02	4:42	19:14	4:27	19:29	4:07	19:50
May 2	5:30	18:24	5:16	18:38	5:08	18:46	4:59	18:56	4:48	19:07	4:35	19:20	4:18	19:37	3:56	20:00
6	5:28	18:25	5:13	18:41	5:04	18:49	4:54	19:00	4:43	19:11	4:28	19:26	4:10	19:45	3:45	20:10
10	5:26	18:27	5:10	18:43	5:01	18:53	4:50	19:03	4:37	19:16	4:22	19:32	4:02	19:52	3:35	20:20
14	5:24	18:28	5:07	18:46	4:57	18:56	4:46	19:07	4:32	19:21	4:16	19:38	3:54	19:59	3:25	2029
18	5:23	18:30	5:05	18:48	4:54	18:59	4:42	19:11	4:28	19:26	4:10	19:43	3:48	20:06	3:16	20:39
22	5:22	18:32	5:03	18:51	4:52	19:02	4:39	19:15	4:24	19:30	4:05	19:49	3:41	20:13	3:07	20:48
26	5:21	18:33	5:01	18:53	4:50	19:05	4:37	19:18	4:21	19:34	4:01	19:54	3:36	20:19	3:00	20:56
30	5:20	18:35	5:00	18:55	4:48	19:07	4:34	19:21	4:18	19:38	3:58	19:58	3:31	20:25	2:53	21:04
Jun. 3	5:20	18:37	4:59	18:57	4:47	19:10	4:33	19:24	4:16	19:41	3:55	20:02	3:27	20:30	2:47	21:11
7	5:20	18:38	4:59	18:59	4:46	19:12	4:31	19:27	4:14	19:44	3:52	20:06	3:24	20:34	2:42	21:17
11	5:20	18:39	4:58	19:01	4:46	19:14	4:31	19:29	4:13	19:46	3:51	20:09	3:22	20:38	2:38	21:21
15	5:20	18:41	4:59	19:03	4:46	19:15	4:31	19:30	4:13	19:48	3:50	20:11	3:21	20:41	2:36	21:25
19	5:21	18:42	4:59	19:04	4:46	19:17	4:31	19:32	4:13	19:50	3:50	20:12	3:20	20:42	2:36	21:27
23	5:22	18:42	5:00	19:05	4:47	19:18	4:32	19:33	4:14	19:51	3:51	20:13	3:21	20:43	2:36	21:28
27	5:23	18:43	5:01	19:05	4:48	19:18	4:33	19:33	4:15	19:51	3:53	20:13	3:23	20:43	2:39	21:27

Noctilucent clouds: During summer twilight, particularly in the latitude range 53°–60° (in either hemisphere) look for silver-blue, cirrus-like clouds low in the polar sky. These are ice clouds about 80 km high, catching the Sun's light long after it sets (see the newly revised www.rasc.ca/handbook/supplements).
From notes by Mark Zalcik and Mike Boschat.

SUNRISE AND SUNSET, 2018 JULY–DECEMBER
UNIVERSAL TIME AT GREENWICH MERIDIAN

Latitude:	+20°		+30°		+35°		+40°		+45°		+50°		+55°		+60°	
Event:	RISE	SET	RISE	SET	RISE	SET	RISE	SET	RISE	SET	RISE	SET	RISE	SET	RISE	SET
Jul. 1	5:24	18:43	5:02	19:05	4:50	19:18	4:35	19:33	4:17	19:50	3:55	20:12	3:26	20:42	2:42	21:25
5	5:26	18:44	5:04	19:05	4:52	19:17	4:37	19:32	4:20	19:49	3:58	20:11	3:29	20:39	2:47	21:21
9	5:27	18:43	5:06	19:04	4:54	19:17	4:39	19:31	4:22	19:48	4:01	20:09	3:33	20:36	2:53	21:16
13	5:28	18:43	5:08	19:03	4:56	19:15	4:42	19:29	4:26	19:45	4:05	20:06	3:38	20:32	3:00	21:10
17	5:30	18:42	5:10	19:02	4:59	19:13	4:45	19:27	4:29	19:42	4:10	20:02	3:44	20:27	3:07	21:04
21	5:31	18:41	5:12	19:00	5:01	19:11	4:49	19:24	4:33	19:39	4:14	19:58	3:50	20:22	3:16	20:56
25	5:33	18:40	5:15	18:58	5:04	19:08	4:52	19:21	4:37	19:35	4:20	19:53	3:57	20:15	3:24	20:47
29	5:34	18:38	5:17	18:55	5:07	19:05	4:56	19:17	4:42	19:30	4:25	19:47	4:03	20:08	3:33	20:38
Aug. 2	5:36	18:37	5:20	18:53	5:10	19:02	4:59	19:13	4:46	19:25	4:31	19:41	4:10	20:01	3:43	20:28
6	5:37	18:34	5:22	18:49	5:13	18:58	5:03	19:08	4:51	19:20	4:36	19:35	4:18	19:53	3:52	20:18
10	5:38	18:32	5:24	18:46	5:16	18:54	5:07	19:03	4:56	19:14	4:42	19:28	4:25	19:45	4:02	20:07
14	5:40	18:29	5:27	18:42	5:19	18:50	5:10	18:58	5:00	19:08	4:48	19:20	4:32	19:36	4:12	19:56
18	5:41	18:27	5:29	18:38	5:22	18:45	5:14	18:53	5:05	19:02	4:54	19:13	4:40	19:27	4:21	19:45
22	5:42	18:24	5:31	18:34	5:25	18:40	5:18	18:47	5:10	18:55	5:00	19:05	4:47	19:17	4:31	19:33
26	5:43	18:20	5:34	18:30	5:28	18:35	5:22	18:41	5:15	18:48	5:06	18:57	4:55	19:08	4:40	19:22
30	5:44	18:17	5:36	18:25	5:31	18:30	5:26	18:35	5:19	18:41	5:12	18:48	5:02	18:58	4:50	19:10
Sep. 3	5:45	18:14	5:38	18:20	5:34	18:24	5:29	18:29	5:24	18:34	5:18	18:40	5:10	18:48	4:59	18:58
7	5:46	18:10	5:40	18:15	5:37	18:19	5:33	18:22	5:29	18:26	5:24	18:31	5:17	18:38	5:09	18:46
11	5:47	18:06	5:42	18:11	5:40	18:13	5:37	18:16	5:34	18:19	5:30	18:23	5:25	18:27	5:18	18:34
15	5:47	18:03	5:44	18:06	5:43	18:07	5:41	18:09	5:38	18:11	5:36	18:14	5:32	18:17	5:28	18:21
19	5:48	17:59	5:47	18:01	5:46	18:01	5:45	18:02	5:43	18:04	5:42	18:05	5:40	18:07	5:37	18:09
23	5:49	17:55	5:49	17:56	5:49	17:56	5:48	17:56	5:48	17:56	5:48	17:56	5:47	17:57	5:46	17:57
27	5:50	17:52	5:51	17:51	5:52	17:50	5:52	17:49	5:53	17:48	5:54	17:47	5:55	17:46	5:56	17:45
Oct. 1	5:51	17:48	5:53	17:46	5:55	17:44	5:56	17:43	5:58	17:41	6:00	17:39	6:02	17:36	6:05	17:33
5	5:52	17:45	5:56	17:41	5:58	17:39	6:00	17:36	6:03	17:33	6:06	17:30	6:10	17:26	6:15	17:21
9	5:53	17:41	5:58	17:36	6:01	17:33	6:04	17:30	6:08	17:26	6:12	17:22	6:17	17:16	6:24	17:09
13	5:54	17:38	6:00	17:32	6:04	17:28	6:08	17:24	6:13	17:19	6:18	17:13	6:25	17:06	6:34	16:57
17	5:55	17:35	6:03	17:27	6:07	17:23	6:12	17:18	6:18	17:12	6:25	17:05	6:33	16:57	6:44	16:46
21	5:57	17:32	6:06	17:23	6:11	17:18	6:17	17:12	6:23	17:05	6:31	16:57	6:41	16:47	6:54	16:34
25	5:58	17:30	6:09	17:19	6:14	17:13	6:21	17:07	6:29	16:59	6:38	16:50	6:49	16:38	7:04	16:23
29	6:00	17:27	6:11	17:16	6:18	17:09	6:25	17:01	6:34	16:53	6:44	16:42	6:57	16:29	7:14	16:12
Nov. 2	6:02	17:25	6:14	17:12	6:22	17:05	6:30	16:57	6:40	16:47	6:51	16:35	7:05	16:21	7:24	16:02
6	6:04	17:23	6:18	17:09	6:26	17:01	6:35	16:52	6:45	16:42	6:58	16:29	7:14	16:13	7:35	15:51
10	6:06	17:22	6:21	17:07	6:29	16:58	6:39	16:48	6:51	16:37	7:04	16:23	7:22	16:05	7:45	15:42
14	6:08	17:21	6:24	17:04	6:33	16:55	6:44	16:45	6:56	16:32	7:11	16:17	7:30	15:58	7:55	15:32
18	6:10	17:20	6:27	17:03	6:37	16:53	6:48	16:42	7:01	16:28	7:17	16:12	7:38	15:52	8:05	15:25
22	6:13	17:19	6:31	17:01	6:41	16:51	6:53	16:39	7:07	16:25	7:24	16:08	7:45	15:47	8:15	15:17
26	6:15	17:19	6:34	17:00	6:45	16:49	6:57	16:37	7:12	16:22	7:30	16:05	7:52	15:42	8:24	15:10
30	6:18	17:19	6:37	17:00	6:49	16:49	7:01	16:36	7:17	16:20	7:35	16:02	7:59	15:38	8:33	15:04
Dec. 4	6:20	17:20	6:40	17:00	6:52	16:48	7:05	16:35	7:21	16:19	7:40	16:00	8:05	15:35	8:41	14:59
8	6:23	17:21	6:43	17:00	6:55	16:48	7:09	16:35	7:25	16:18	7:45	15:58	8:11	15:33	8:48	14:56
12	6:25	17:22	6:46	17:01	6:58	16:49	7:12	16:35	7:29	16:18	7:49	15:58	8:16	15:32	8:53	14:54
16	6:28	17:23	6:49	17:02	7:01	16:50	7:15	16:36	7:32	16:19	7:53	15:59	8:20	15:32	8:58	14:53
20	6:30	17:25	6:51	17:04	7:03	16:52	7:18	16:37	7:35	16:21	7:55	16:00	8:22	15:33	9:01	14:54
24	6:32	17:27	6:53	17:06	7:05	16:54	7:20	16:40	7:36	16:23	7:57	16:02	8:24	15:35	9:03	14:56
28	6:34	17:30	6:55	17:08	7:07	16:56	7:21	16:42	7:38	16:25	7:58	16:05	8:25	15:38	9:03	15:00
32	6:35	17:32	6:56	17:11	7:08	16:59	7:22	16:45	7:38	16:29	7:59	16:09	8:25	15:42	9:02	15:05

TWILIGHT

Twilight is the interval of time in the morning or evening when the Sun is below the horizon yet perceptibly contributes to sky glow. There are three geometrical definitions for the end of evening twilight or the start of morning twilight: (1) *Civil twilight*—center of the Sun 6° below the horizon, brightest stars and planets visible, marks start and end of night for the purposes of aviation and artificial lighting of ordinary outdoor activities; (2) *Nautical twilight*—center of the Sun 12° below the horizon, horizon indistinct; (3) *Astronomical twilight*—center of the Sun 18° below the horizon, negligible solar component of sky glow. The following table gives the start of morning and the end of evening astronomical twilight in UT at 0° longitude. For observers in North America the times may be handled in the same way as those of sunrise and sunset (see p. 205).

Latitude:	+20°		+30°		+35°		+40°		+45°		+50°		+55°		+60°	
	Morn.	Eve.	Morn.	Eve.	Morn.	Eve.	Morn.	Eve.	Morn.	Eve.	Morn.	Eve.	Morn.	Eve.	Morn.	Eve.
Jan. 0	5:16	18:50	5:30	18:36	5:37	18:29	5:44	18:22	5:52	18:15	6:00	18:07	6:08	17:58	6:18	17:48
10	5:19	18:56	5:32	18:43	5:39	18:36	5:45	18:30	5:52	18:24	5:59	18:17	6:06	18:09	6:15	18:01
20	5:21	19:01	5:32	18:50	5:38	18:45	5:43	18:40	5:48	18:34	5:54	18:29	5:59	18:23	6:06	18:17
30	5:20	19:07	5:29	18:58	5:33	18:54	5:37	18:50	5:41	18:46	5:45	18:43	5:48	18:40	5:51	18:37
Feb. 9	5:18	19:11	5:24	19:05	5:27	19:02	5:29	19:00	5:30	18:59	5:32	18:58	5:32	18:57	5:32	18:58
19	5:13	19:15	5:16	19:12	5:17	19:11	5:17	19:11	5:17	19:12	5:15	19:13	5:13	19:16	5:08	19:21
Mar. 1	5:07	19:18	5:07	19:19	5:06	19:20	5:04	19:22	5:01	19:25	4:56	19:29	4:50	19:36	4:40	19:46
11	4:59	19:21	4:55	19:25	4:52	19:28	4:48	19:33	4:43	19:38	4:35	19:46	4:24	19:58	4:09	20:13
21	4:50	19:25	4:43	19:32	4:38	19:37	4:31	19:44	4:23	19:53	4:11	20:05	3:56	20:21	3:33	20:44
31	4:41	19:28	4:30	19:39	4:23	19:46	4:13	19:56	4:02	20:08	3:46	20:24	3:24	20:46	2:52	21:19
Apr. 10	4:31	19:32	4:17	19:46	4:07	19:56	3:55	20:09	3:40	20:24	3:19	20:45	2:50	21:15	2:03	22:05
20	4:22	19:36	4:04	19:55	3:52	20:07	3:37	20:22	3:17	20:42	2:51	21:09	2:11	21:50	0:44	23:30
30	4:14	19:41	3:52	20:03	3:37	20:18	3:19	20:37	2:55	21:01	2:21	21:36	1:22	22:37	—	—
May 10	4:07	19:46	3:41	20:13	3:24	20:30	3:02	20:52	2:33	21:21	1:49	22:06	—	—	—	—
20	4:01	19:52	3:32	20:22	3:13	20:41	2:48	21:06	2:13	21:42	1:14	22:43	—	—	—	—
30	3:58	19:58	3:26	20:30	3:04	20:51	2:36	21:19	1:56	22:00	0:26	23:38	—	—	—	—
Jun. 9	3:56	20:02	3:23	20:36	3:00	20:59	2:29	21:30	1:44	22:15	—	—	—	—	—	—
19	3:57	20:06	3:22	20:40	2:59	21:04	2:28	21:35	1:40	22:23	—	—	—	—	—	—
29	4:00	20:07	3:25	20:41	3:02	21:05	2:31	21:35	1:44	22:22	—	—	—	—	—	—
Jul. 9	4:04	20:06	3:31	20:39	3:09	21:01	2:40	21:30	1:57	22:13	—	—	—	—	—	—
19	4:09	20:04	3:38	20:34	3:18	20:54	2:51	21:20	2:14	21:57	1:03	23:05	—	—	—	—
29	4:14	19:58	3:47	20:26	3:28	20:44	3:05	21:07	2:33	21:38	1:43	22:27	—	—	—	—
Aug. 8	4:19	19:52	3:55	20:15	3:39	20:31	3:19	20:51	2:53	21:17	2:14	21:54	0:56	23:08	—	—
18	4:24	19:43	4:04	20:03	3:50	20:17	3:34	20:33	3:12	20:54	2:42	21:24	1:54	22:10	—	—
28	4:28	19:34	4:11	19:50	4:01	20:01	3:47	20:14	3:29	20:32	3:06	20:55	2:32	21:28	1:30	22:26
Sep. 7	4:31	19:24	4:19	19:37	4:10	19:45	3:59	19:56	3:46	20:09	3:27	20:27	3:02	20:52	2:23	21:30
17	4:34	19:14	4:25	19:23	4:19	19:29	4:11	19:37	4:01	19:47	3:47	20:01	3:28	20:19	3:01	20:46
27	4:37	19:05	4:31	19:10	4:27	19:14	4:22	19:19	4:14	19:26	4:05	19:36	3:51	19:49	3:32	20:08
Oct. 7	4:39	18:56	4:37	18:58	4:35	19:00	4:32	19:03	4:28	19:07	4:21	19:13	4:12	19:22	4:00	19:34
17	4:42	18:49	4:43	18:47	4:43	18:47	4:42	18:48	4:40	18:50	4:37	18:53	4:32	18:57	4:25	19:04
27	4:45	18:43	4:50	18:38	4:51	18:36	4:52	18:35	4:53	18:34	4:52	18:35	4:51	18:36	4:48	18:38
Nov. 6	4:49	18:39	4:56	18:31	4:59	18:28	5:02	18:24	5:05	18:22	5:07	18:20	5:09	18:18	5:10	18:16
16	4:53	18:36	5:03	18:26	5:08	18:22	5:12	18:17	5:17	18:12	5:21	18:08	5:25	18:04	5:30	17:59
26	4:58	18:36	5:10	18:24	5:16	18:18	5:22	18:13	5:28	18:07	5:34	18:00	5:40	17:54	5:47	17:47
Dec. 6	5:04	18:38	5:17	18:25	5:24	18:18	5:30	18:11	5:37	18:04	5:45	17:57	5:53	17:49	6:02	17:40
16	5:09	18:42	5:23	18:28	5:30	18:21	5:38	18:13	5:45	18:06	5:53	17:58	6:02	17:49	6:12	17:39
26	5:14	18:47	5:28	18:33	5:36	18:26	5:43	18:18	5:50	18:11	5:58	18:03	6:07	17:54	6:18	17:44
Jan. 5	5:18	18:53	5:32	18:39	5:38	18:32	5:45	18:26	5:52	18:19	6:00	18:11	6:08	18:03	6:17	17:54

SKY BRIGHTNESS AT MIDNIGHT
BY ROY BISHOP

Astronomers generally desire dark skies, free of moonlight and man-made light pollution. As mentioned on the previous page, the beginning or end of *astronomical twilight* corresponds to the center of the Sun being 18° below the horizon. At that point the amount of sunlight scattered by the upper layers of Earth's atmosphere is negligible; that is, it is less than the combined illuminance (about 2×10^{-3} lux) from starlight, airglow, and zodiacal light, the three main contributors to the light of the "dark" night sky.

For observers in countries at high latitudes (e.g. the United Kingdom, Norway, southern Argentina and Chile, and most of Canada), around the time of the summer solstice the Sun always lies less than 18° below the horizon, and the sky does not get dark at night. This "midnight twilight" phenomenon can be displayed in a graph as a function of latitude and time of year.

The following diagram indicates the brightness of the sky at local midnight at any time of the year for any latitude north of 45°N or south of 45°S. Below the lower curve the natural sky is dark. Between the two curves twilight prevails. Above the upper curve the Sun is in the sky. Place names in roman type (left-hand side) are in the Northern Hemisphere; place names in *italic* type (right-hand side) are in the *Southern Hemisphere*. On the horizontal axis use the roman-type months for the former, *italic*-type months for the latter. The diagram is simplified slightly in that the months are assumed to be of equal duration, and the seasonal pattern of months and summer solstices for Earth's two hemispheres are assumed to be identical except for a 6-month phase shift.

The latitude of the Arctic and Antarctic Circles (90° subtract the obliquity of the ecliptic = 66°34′) is indicated by the dashed line. This line is *not* tangent to the Midnight Sun curve because at midnight on the summer solstice at either the Arctic or the Antarctic Circle the Sun is above the horizon. Atmospheric refraction raises the apparent Sun about 34′ above the true Sun. Also, rise/set is defined as the top limb of the Sun at a sea-level horizon; thus the 16′ semidiameter of the Sun must also be taken into account. To see the top limb of the Sun on the horizon at local midnight on the summer solstice, an observer must be 34′ + 16′ = 50′ south of the Arctic Circle (or north of the Antarctic Circle), at latitude 65°44′.

By running a horizontal line across the chart at a selected latitude, the reader can determine the approximate dates when midnight twilight and, possibly, midnight Sun begin and end for any locality at north or south latitudes above 48.6°, the lower limit for midnight twilight on the summer solstice. (Remarkably, when rounded to the nearest degree, the latter figure is the latitude of the longest east–west international border: the 2000-km-long 49th parallel between the United States and western Canada.)

Some examples: The diagram shows that Earth's poles are astronomically dark for less than three months of the year. At Grise Fiord, a village on Ellesmere Island and Canada's northern-most community, the sky is never dark from about Mar. 10 until early October, and the midnight Sun lasts from late April until mid-August. Cape Horn at midnight is bathed in dim Antarctic twilight from early November until early February. Even at the latitude of Vancouver there is a period of almost a month each year when the sky never gets astronomically dark. Although the midnight sky should be dark at all latitudes below the lower curve, that is no longer the case in or near populated areas where the natural night sky is immersed in a perpetual twilight: the baleful pall of light pollution (see p. 79). For such areas the TWILIGHT table on the previous page is irrelevant.

SKY BRIGHTNESS AT MIDNIGHT

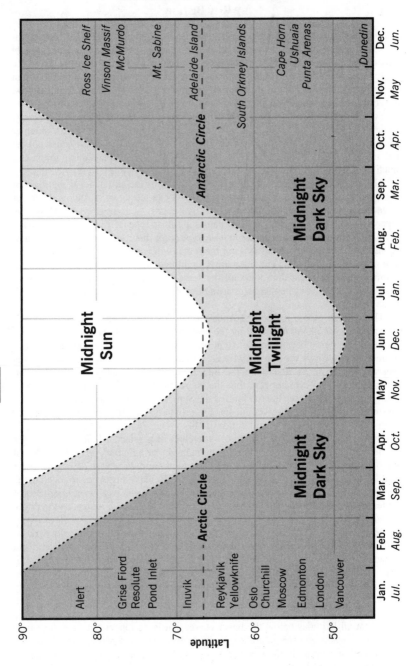

Diagram by Roy Bishop, drawn by Michael Gatto

PLANETS AND SATELLITES

THE PLANETS IN 2018
BY MURRAY PAULSON

INTRODUCTION

You would think that with the internet and today's technology, you would never need a telescope. But nothing replaces that "being there" moment at the eyepiece when, with persistent effort, you see those subtle details obscured by distance and atmosphere revealed for fleeting moments. Seeing the changing face of the planets in real time is something that many of us find alluring. We get to be explorers in that last frontier, and we get to see the beauty of our neighboring planets firsthand. Sometimes we even discover something new and point it out to the rest of the world, like the famous impacts in Jupiter's atmosphere. There is still a role for amateurs to play in discovery.

Optics: When observing the planets, it is important to minimize optical aberrations. To get the most out of your observing sessions, use high magnification with high-quality optics. If you are unable to change the optics, make sure they are clean and well-collimated. If you are considering a change, the best telescopes for the planets are high-quality refractors. The cost of these telescopes may be prohibitive, and "large" refractor apertures are only around 200 mm. The aperture is limited, but quality optics provide for astounding views. There are other high-end optical systems to choose from: Maksutovs, Dall–Kirkhams, and optimized Newtonians work very well.

Also important is resolution. One of the axioms of optics is: The larger the diameter of the telescope, the higher the resolution (see TELESCOPE PARAMETERS, p. 49 and TELESCOPE EXIT PUPILS, p. 50). In the world of amateur planetary imaging, some of the best work is being done with the larger, commercial, Schmidt–Cassegrain telescopes (SCTs) of aperture 300–400 mm. There are some excellent quality, larger SCTs that, when coupled with image-processing software, can do amazing things. Software can produce excellent images by stretching the contrast that central

The apparent minimum and maximum observable size of seven planets.

Jupiter
29.8″– 50.1″

Saturn (disk)
14.9″– 20.7″
Saturn (rings)
33.7″– 46.8″

Mars
3.4″– 25.1″

Uranus
3.3″– 4.0″

Mercury
4.5″– 13.0″

Venus
9.5″– 66.0″

Neptune
2.1″– 2.3″

Illustration by Michael Gatto

obstructions tend to reduce. There are also good-quality Newtonian telescopes and other Cassegrain designs. To evaluate telescope quality for planetary work, H.R. Suiter's book *Star Testing Astronomical Telescopes: A Manual for Optical Evaluation and Adjustment* (Willmann–Bell, Inc., Richmond, 2nd Ed., 2009) provides the appropriate tools.

With a high-quality telescope, you need good eyepieces. The general rule is: The higher the quality and the fewer optical elements, the better. Every surface scatters light, and the features on the planets are subtle. Orthoscopic eyepieces are the benchmark for planetary eyepieces, with Zeiss "orthos" at the top of the scale. These eyepieces produce very clean, high-contrast images. There are other manufacturers that produce Abbe Orthos, notably Takahashi and University Optics, but a few others make a variation on the orthoscopic design that have observers praising them. Try a variety of eyepieces when you can (e.g. at star parties) to see how they work for you. Be critical of what you see, and note the contrast and the color each eyepiece lends to its subject. Then check your wallet! If you are using a nondriven telescope, a wide, flat-field eyepiece like the Tele Vue Nagler or Ethos is indispensable, because the large fields of view of these eyepieces give you ample time to observe at high power before having to reposition the telescope. An alternative is the Nikon NAV SW series, with oculars exhibiting very little distortion or false color. The view in these eyepieces is sharp to the edge of the field. The next step is get a drive for the telescope, which gives the observer uninterrupted time to concentrate on the planetary image and to discern the details. My best view of Mars was with a binoviewer. The use of both eyes gives your eyes and brain the chance to combine the image and ignore "floaters" and other visual defects. It is more expensive to purchase the viewer and the extra eyepieces, but it is effective.

Cleanliness of eyepieces and diagonals is also important. These surfaces are close to the observer, and will contribute the most degradation to image contrast if they are not clean. Do your homework before you clean your eyepieces, and make sure you do not damage them in the cleaning process (see **www.skyandtelescope.com/howto/diy**, for example).

The next factor to consider is the optical tube. If the telescope is warmer than the surrounding air, the warm air rising from the optical surfaces in the tube assembly will mix with the cold ambient air, causing localized turbulence, which degrades the image. Adequate thermal equalization of the telescope is critical for good images. The general rule is: The smaller the thermal mass, the shorter the cooldown period. To avoid long cooldown periods, some amateurs use a cooling fan to flush the heat out of the telescope or to blow cool air onto the mirror. Closed-tube assemblies will limit the mixing of the warm and cool air, and they do not cool quite as fast as an open-tube assembly.

The last of the aberrations is the atmosphere. Local heat sources, such as furnace flues, warm cars, paved parking lots, and even someone standing near the telescope will cause heat plumes that could degrade the seeing. One way of ascertaining whether there are thermal sources affecting the seeing is to defocus your telescope while observing a bright star, and examine the image for any slow-moving anomalous structure. This movement is evidence of a heat plume aberrating the star's image. You may have to move the telescope. Sometimes the atmosphere is just not cooperative, and the jet stream or some other phenomenon will bloat the planet's image to resemble a fuzzy tennis ball. The defocused image will show a river of structure moving in one direction across it. There is not much you can do but try again on another night.

Daytime observing: The inner planets are often very close to the horizon after sunset, and this puts the observer at a disadvantage. Down that low, the shimmering of the atmosphere obscures the fine details on the inner planets. Just finding Mercury is a challenge in the twilight. Daytime observing of the inner planets is possible, but it does take some equipment and planning. The easiest way is to use a Go To telescope. Failing that, use a polar-aligned equatorial mount with setting circles. Both options will get the telescope aimed in the right area of the sky. Note: If the sky is hazy, the task of finding the planet in the daytime becomes significantly more difficult, or next to impossible.

Mars, Jupiter, and Saturn are observable in the daytime hours, so you are not limited to just the inner planets: The outer planets are more challenging, but fun to find. It is especially fun to observe a planetary conjunction in the daytime. My favorites have been Venus and Jupiter, and Mercury and Venus.

It is difficult to locate and acquire focus on planets in the daytime sky, so the recommended procedure is to first set up the telescope with a solar filter and a low-power eyepiece, then focus on the Sun. Once you have a good focus on the Sun, lock the focuser, if possible. (One can also use calibrated or marked focusers, or simply use the same eyepiece/focuser combination from the previous night's observing session.)

Do not remove the solar filter yet. **Do not hunt for planets within 5° of the Sun, because of the hazard that accidental unfiltered exposure to the Sun poses.** Remember that blindness is not a desirable observing attribute! (See VIEWING A SOLAR ECLIPSE—A WARNING, p. 145.) If you are not using a Go To scope, set the coordinates on the mount to the Sun's position, and then move off to the location of the planet you are hunting. With the Go To, just enter the command to go to the planet. **Now it is safe to remove the solar filter.** To make absolutely sure that the Sun is not in the field of view, pass your hand over the eyepiece to see if it is safe, then look.

The resolution of the eye is acute only near the center of vision, so if you are not looking directly at the planet, you probably will not see it, and you will have to scan the field of view to find it. With Venus, this is not a problem, but it is with Mercury and the outer planets. Once the planet is in the field of view, center it and try higher-power eyepieces. Parfocal eyepieces provide easy eyepiece exchange with minimal refocusing. A light-orange filter like the Wratten #21 darkens the light-blue sky and improves the contrast.

If the planet is not in the field, either there is an error in your mount alignment or the planet is very low in contrast. You can scan for the planet, being very careful about sweeping toward the Sun. **Do not sweep too far!** The second choice is to try to improve the mount alignment. Try the drift alignment method (see p. 70) on the Sun or obtain a better north–south reference. The atmosphere heats up throughout the day, so it is most stable in the morning. Objects in the foreground, such as asphalt parking lots, may affect the seeing. If possible, for best stability, observe over grass or water.

Drawing the planets is encouraged (see ASTRONOMICAL SKETCHING, p. 88). I now mostly image the planets, but I am glad for the time I put in to drawing them. Drawing compels the observer to critically observe the planet. This is a worthwhile activity because it gives you multiple opportunities to observe the details that appear in the fleeting moments of good seeing, and this effort teaches your eye and brain how to see the subtle features. You become a much better observer. As a bonus, drawing also provides a record of what you saw during that session, for future reference.

For drawing, use a pair of soft and hard pencils (e.g. an HB and an H), a logbook, and a template (**www.astromax.org/activities/2003/mars2003/sketching.htm**). Mars is typically drawn with a 42-mm circular template, corresponding to the 6792-km (~4200-mile) diameter of Mars. The templates for other planets can be of a convenient size, but do not make them too small. Jupiter and Saturn need an oblate template to make them easier to draw. Draw major features first, then fill in the little details as you see them. Jupiter rotates very rapidly, and the features will visibly shift over a 20-min interval. It is very important that you record the time and date on the drawing, as well as the aperture and eyepiece you are using, filters (if any), the general observing conditions, and your name and location. The Association of Lunar and Planetary Observers is interested in amateur contributions and is happy to receive amateur drawings.

Editor's Note: All dates are UT and some events, as viewed from North America, may occur on the evening of the previous date. Check THE SKY MONTH BY MONTH (p. 98) for exact times, especially for phenomena involving the Moon.

MERCURY

Mercury is a planet of extremes: It is the smallest of the eight planets, it is closest to the Sun and therefore the fastest moving, and it is nearly the hottest planet. Mercury also has the longest solar day, lasting two of its orbital periods, or 176 days. In the peak of its "noonday" heat, Mercury's surface warms to 427 °C, and on the far side the temperature goes down to –163 °C. The coldest place is deep in the shadows of craters near the poles, –183 °C. These extremes give the planet a temperature range of 610 C°.

Mercury has an orbital period of 87.96 days and it rotates on its axis every 58.65 days, locked in a 3:2 resonance with its orbital period around the Sun. This is due to the high eccentricity of its orbit, in which perihelic tidal forces dominate the spin period. Accordingly, every elongation is different, ranging from 18° to 28°. Mercury's orbit has a high inclination of 7.0°, which can place it well above or below the ecliptic during a given apparition. Since Mercury never strays more than 28° from the Sun, it is only visible near the horizon at dusk or dawn.

Most people have never seen Mercury, because the window of opportunity is so narrow near dusk and dawn (they may have seen it, and not realized it!). That fact, coupled with the general poor quality of the atmosphere close to the horizon, makes daytime observation of Mercury the better option, when the planet is higher in the sky and you are looking through less atmosphere. If you can observe early in the day, thermal effects are reduced. (Try observing over a body of water during the

MERCURY—EVENTS FOR 2018

Date	Event	Elong. from Sun °	Ang. Dia. "	Mag.	Date	Event	Elong. from Sun °	Ang. Dia. "	Mag.
Jan. 1	GEW	23 W	6.7	–0.3	Jul. 12	GEE	26 E	8.1	+0.4
Feb. 17	SC	2 S			Aug. 9	IC	5 S		
Mar. 15	GEE	18 E	7.4	–0.4	Aug. 26	GEW	18 W	7.4	–0.2
Apr. 1	IC	3 N			Sep. 21	SC	1 N		
Apr. 29	GEW	27 W	8.0	+0.4	Nov. 6	GEE	23 E	6.6	–0.3
Jun. 5	SC	1 N			Nov. 27	IC	1 N		
					Dec. 15	GEW	21 W		–0.5

GEE = Greatest Elongation East; GEW = Greatest Elongation West; IC = Inferior Conjunction; SC = Superior Conjunction

MERCURY—ELONGATION AND APPARENT SIZE DURING 2018

Elongation is plotted in degrees and angular diameter in arcseconds. The first day of each month is marked on the horizontal axis. Visibility depends not only on the elongation but also on the angle between the ecliptic and the horizon. See the table on the facing page for the most favorable views.

daytime, when the air and water temperatures are not too different, leading to improved seeing.) One difficulty of observing Mercury in twilight is that the high luminance of the planet makes the subtle markings difficult to see. By observing in the daytime, when Mercury is higher than the Sun, the luminance contrast is less, which makes the markings easier to see for Northern Hemisphere observers.

Any telescope equipped with Go To or setting circles can be used to find Mercury (see the daytime observing tips on p. 212). Details on Mercury can be seen in a 130-mm telescope using high magnifications of 1.5× to 3.0× per millimetre of diameter. A red or an orange filter (Wratten #21) can be used to boost the contrast with the blue of the sky. Anecdotally, the best phases to see the subtle details on the planet are between mid-gibbous and a wide crescent, near the greatest elongations. Views of Mercury with 250-mm Maksutovs show surprising detail.

Mercury's mean synodic period (time between successive inferior conjunctions) is 115.88 days, so there are generally three opportunities to see it both after sunset and in the dawn sky every year. The angle of the ecliptic makes fall-evening and spring-morning apparitions at higher latitudes very poor—in both Northern and Southern Hemispheres—because the ecliptic is almost parallel to the horizon, and Mercury sets shortly after the Sun, or rises shortly before the Sun, in bright twilight. One disparity is that the Southern Hemisphere gets the better of the fall-morning and spring-evening elongations, because the inclination of Mercury's orbit to the ecliptic provides a more favorable geometry for Southern Hemisphere observers.

Mercury starts off the year at its greatest elongation west (GEW) 22.7° from the Sun, shining at mag. –0.3. In an eyepiece you would see a 63%-illuminated disk. Dichotomy was on Dec. 28, four days prior to the greatest elongation. On its way back down the ecliptic, it passes close to Saturn on Jan. 12, where the pair rise 75 minutes before the Sun. On the east coast, the pair are separated by 42′ when they rise, and this expands to 49′ separation when the pair rise on the west coast. The closest approach is 38′ and visible around longitude 0. Mercury shines at mag. –0.3 with a 5.5″ gibbous disk, and Saturn with a mag. 0.5, 16.7″ disc. You should be able to resolve both to disks in a medium-power eyepiece. Mercury arrives at its superior conjunction with the Sun on Feb. 17. Mercury joins Venus as it moves up into the evening sky. Closest approach is on Mar. 3, when Venus is 1.1° south of Mercury and they are 13° from the Sun. The mag. –3.9 beacon of Venus should help you find mag. –1.2 Mercury. Venus shows a 10″ disk and Mercury a 5.7″ fat gibbous disk. The two will be visible together as Mercury rises on a very favorable ecliptic in the Northern Hemisphere, until after the Mar. 15 greatest elongation east (GEE), when it will start fading rapidly as it heads back behind the Sun. On Mar. 15, it will show a 42% illuminated 7.5″ mag. –0.3 disk. It is worth putting a scope on it to see dichotomy. With great speed, Mercury returns for the Apr. 1 inferior conjunction as it passes 2.8° above the Sun. Mercury makes a more leisurely climb into the morning sky and comes to its GEW on Apr. 29. The spring morning elongations are on a very shallow ecliptic, not affording a good view of the planets from the Northern Hemisphere, so plan on a daytime viewing. This apparition is one of the best of the year in the Southern Hemisphere, with Mercury sitting 27° from the Sun. It has a 8″ half-illuminated disk and shines at mag. 0.4. Mercury takes its time returning to the next superior conjunction on Jun. 6.

The Jul. 12 GEE is lost in the summer twilight, so you might glimpse it in a daytime session. The speedy planet is moving back between the Earth and the Sun, so its magnitude will drop dramatically as it heads back down the ecliptic. For this reason, Mercury's visibility is better before the elongation. Superior conjunction is on Sep. 21.

The fall evening ecliptic is shallow and so Mercury's visibility is poor in the evening twilight—we will miss the conjunction with Jupiter on Oct. 29. To make things worse, Mercury sits 3° below the ecliptic when at GEE on Nov. 6. From here, it slides down the ecliptic and joins Jupiter in conjunction with the Sun on Nov. 27, but it will be on Earth's side of the Sun.

A little more than a week later, on Dec. 5, Mercury is joined by a thin crescent Moon in the predawn sky. It will sit 5° below the Moon on the east coast, and 3° below on the west coast. Mercury will shine at mag. 0.6, making this conjunction a bit challenging, so use binoculars to search the planet out. That thin crescent Moon will be worth the effort. On Dec. 15, Mercury arrives at GEW, where it shines at mag. –0.5 and will show a 6.6″, 63%-illuminated disk. Mercury rises almost 2 h before the Sun during the best morning apparition of the year. On Dec. 21, Mercury joins Jupiter in the dawn sky, and the mag. –0.5 Mercury passes only 53′ from mag. –1.8 Jupiter. This is a great close conjunction and worth getting up for. The closest approach of 50′ is visible in the west Pacific.

VENUS

Known as both the morning star and the evening star, Venus has impressed us throughout the ages with the brilliance and purity of its light. Ranging in magnitude from –4.9 to –3.8, Venus is bright enough to cast a visible shadow. If you know when and where to look, it is visible to the naked eye in full daylight.

In the prespacecraft era, people thought that our sister planet might bear habit-able zones somewhat like Earth. Nothing could be further from the truth. The surface temperature on Venus is a fairly constant 460 °C, under a runaway greenhouse effect. The dense carbon dioxide atmosphere has a pressure of over 9300 kPa (92 atm) at the surface and a density of 65 kg/m^3, 6.5% the density of water and about 60 times that of Earth's atmosphere. Wind friction would be serious on Venus.

Thick sulphur-dioxide clouds with sulphuric-acid droplets veil the surface of Venus; little light reaches the surface. Occasional detail is seen in the cloud structure in amateur telescopes, but for the most part it appears as a featureless white disk. The subtle structure in the cloud tops is difficult to observe, but too few observers even give it a try. The best times to look are from just between thick crescent and mid-gibbous phases. A violet filter can enhance the visibility of atmospheric structure, and imaging through a UV filter will show cloud details. The Association of Lunar and Planetary Observers is interested in your images of Venus seen this way.

Never far from the Sun, Venus may be found in a telescope during the daytime, when high in the sky, far from the deleterious effects of our thick near-horizon atmosphere. The daytime sky is favorable for viewing the bright disk of Venus, because of the lower luminance contrast. This is a popular daytime activity at star parties (see the discussion on daytime planet viewing in the INTRODUCTION of this section, p. 212).

Venus kicks off 2018 by promptly disappearing into superior conjunction on Jan. 9. It is joined by Pluto on the far side of the Sun, and Pluto is just a bit harder to find. On Feb. 17, a 27-h new Moon sits above Venus in the evening twilight. Use binoculars to find Venus, then look above and to the left for the thin crescent of the Moon. On the east coast, the Moon will be 2.3° above, and 3.6° above on the west coast. In the last days of February, you might notice Mercury as it swings up and joins Venus in the evening twilight. Mercury shines at mag. –1.3 and is fading, as it rises while Venus beams at mag. –3.9. Closest approach is on Mar. 3, when Venus is 1.1° south of Mercury, and they are 13° from the Sun. Venus shows a 10″ disk, and Mercury a 5.7″ fat gibbous disk. The two will be visible together until Mercury fades rapidly as it heads back to the Sun in mid-month. I love close planetary conjunctions and we get a good one on Mar. 29. Venus joins Uranus in the evening sky in a fantastic conjunction. The bright mag. –3.9 beacon of Venus will help you find mag. 5.9 Uranus. This is an extremely close conjunction, with closest approach of 4.1′ visible in eastern North America at 00:51 UT. The pair will spread apart as we move west-ward—5.4′ in Winnipeg, 7.6′ in Alberta, and 9′ on the west coast. You should be able to use some high power on the pair. Venus shows a 10.5″ disk, and Uranus a 3.4″ disk.

Venus has a nice conjunction with a thin crescent moon on Jul. 16, where the pair pass only 20′ apart. The apparition will be visible in the evening twilight and closest approach is visible in the Mid-West of North America. Venus comes to its GEE on Aug. 17 at an elongation of 45.9° from the Sun. It will shine at mag. –4.5, which marks the start of a graceful fall back toward the Sun. Venus will have kept us company in the evening sky for much of the year, but, on Oct. 26, Venus passes 6°

VENUS—ELONGATION AND APPARENT SIZE DURING 2018

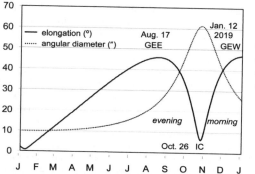

Elongation is plotted in degrees and apparent angular diameter in arcseconds. The first day of each month is marked on the horizontal axis.

below the Sun. This is a view that is truly incredible and a touch dangerous. Again, please pay close heed to Daytime Observing on p. 212, and be very careful. Venus will be at a close inferior conjunction and will show a mag. –4.3, 61.3″ razor-thin crescent.

At this time, you may get a sense that the crescent spans more than 180° of the disk's margin. This is due to Venus's atmosphere refracting some of the sunlight through it. The view is truly breathtaking and I never tire of it. From this point, Venus moves into the morning sky. Observers in the Southern Hemisphere may try their hand at seeing Venus in the evening sky before the conjunction, and again in the morning sky on the following day. I have done this in the Northern Hemisphere, when Venus passed above the Sun. Venus will swing up quickly into the morning sky, and will almost, but not quite, reach GEW by year-end.

MARS

Mars is a planet that inspires us, a place we could anticipate walking on and exploring, a destination where our grandchildren may go. A web of imagined canals has ensnared us, and generations of observers and scientists have devoted their lives to the study of the Red Planet. Despite the unveiling of the mysteries of Mars, with neither Martians nor canals to be found, many of us are still infatuated with the planet.

About every 2 years and 50 days, on average, we renew our acquaintance with Mars, as Earth—on the inside track—overtakes the fourth planet. Over the roughly 15-year cycle between extreme close approaches near perihelion, there are seven oppositions with diverse separations (see OPPOSITIONS OF MARS on p. 220). The Martian day is about 3% longer than our day; this results in us observing the same central meridian of Mars about 38 min later on successive nights. Equivalently, the longitude of the center of the Martian disk reduces by 9.5° per Earth day. Accordingly, near opposition, the same surface features will be visible at the same time of night 41 days later. When the view is near its best, you can expect to enjoy two full rotations of Mars in stroboscopic form.

Mars is accompanied by two small moons, Deimos and Phobos, discovered by Asaph Hall in 1877 with the 66-cm (26-in.) refractor at the U.S. Naval Observatory. These two moons undoubtedly are captured minor planets, given their angular shape and proximity to the asteroid belt. Deimos is the smaller, at 16 × 12 km, and completes one orbit in 30.3 h. Phobos, at 26 × 22 km, orbits Mars in a speedy 7.7 h. Viewed from the Martian surface, Phobos would rise in the west and set in the east. Detecting this pair is a real challenge, because Mars outshines them by 13 to 14 magnitudes, and they never venture very far from the planet. Observe near opposition with an occulting-bar eyepiece to block out the brilliance of the Martian disk (see p. 25), using lots of magnification and a finder chart, so you know where to look.

The year 2018 starts off with a close conjunction between Mars and Jupiter on the morning of Jan. 6. Close approach of 12.1′ is visible from Asia to Eastern Europe. Mars is mag. 1.4 and Jupiter is mag. −1.8. Jupiter will show a 33.5″ disk, while Mars, far from opposition, will only show a 5″ disc. In the east coast of North America, we see them rise 21′ apart, which narrows as we cross the continent, until at the west coast they have narrowed to 16′. The next morning, the east coast will see them as they separate to 15.5′, and the west coast at 21′. We get two chances at this Jupiter/Mars conjunction in North America. On Apr. 2, Mars makes a pass close to M22 and Saturn. Mars rises just after 2:30 a.m. local time, at closest approach passes 21′ from the core of M22, and is 1.3° below Saturn. Mars shines at mag. 0.3 and is 8.5″ in diameter, while Saturn shines at mag. 0.5 and 16.7″ in diameter. They will make for an interesting color contrast.

On Jun. 28, Mars starts retrograde motion at its easternmost stationary point. It now shines at mag. −2.0 and is 20.2″ in diameter. This is prime time for Mars observing, and it will remain larger than 20″ over the summer and into the first week of September. During this time, it loops around in southwestern Capricorn. Mars opposition is on Jul. 27, and we are treated to a mag. −2.8 and a 24.2″ disk. Due to our mutual orbital circumstance, Mars is at its largest size of 24.3″ on Jul. 31. Note that, despite Mars sitting in Capricorn, it is also sitting 6.6° below the ecliptic, marking this as a very southerly opposition with a maximum excursion to −26.5° Dec. On Aug. 28, Mars is at its second stationary point, and it resumes normal motion eastward—prograde. The Red Planet now displays a mag. −2.2, 21.7″ disk.

If you have ever wanted to view the Martian moons, this could be the year to do it. At closest approach, Phobos and Deimos are at mag. 10.5 and 11.6, respectively. They are low in the south, so you definitely need an evening with perfect skies. You also need aperture, clean optics, and an occulting-bar eyepiece to keep that mag. −2.8 Martian glare down. Deimos ventures out to 84″ from Mars, and Phobos only 33″, so it is a tough hunt.

Mars will remain larger than 10″ for the period from Apr. 19 until Nov. 20, so as it lingers in the fall evening sky, we will have plenty of opportunity to watch it as it

MARS—OBSERVING CIRCUMSTANCES IN 2018

Date 0h UT	Distance au	Dec °	Mag.	Equatorial Diam. ″	% Illum.	Rotation Axis PA °	Rotation Axis Incl. °
Jan. 1	1.955	−15.2	1.5	4.8	93	38	16
Feb. 1	1.671	−20.2	1.2	5.6	91	36	8
Mar. 1	1.392	−22.8	0.8	6.7	89	31	1
15	1.248	−23.4	0.6	7.5	88	27	−3
Apr. 1	1.099	−23.5	0.3	8.5	88	22	−7
15	0.964	−23.3	−0.0	9.7	88	18	−10
May 1	0.836	−22.7	−0.4	11.2	88	13	−12
15	0.718	−22.1	−0.8	13.0	89	9	−14
Jun. 1	0.605	−21.7	−1.2	15.5	91	5	−15
15	0.515	−21.9	−1.7	18.2	94	3	−15
Jul. 1	0.444	−22.8	−2.2	21.1	97	3	−14
15	0.399	−24.2	−2.6	23.4	99	4	−13
Aug. 1	0.385	−25.9	−2.8	24.3	100	6	−11
15	0.403	−26.5	−2.5	23.2	98	9	−10
Sep. 1	0.452	−26.0	−2.1	20.7	94	9	−10
15	0.518	−24.7	−1.7	18.1	91	8	−12
Oct. 1	0.598	−22.5	−1.3	15.7	88	5	−15
Nov. 1	0.794	−16.2	−0.6	11.8	86	355	−21
Dec 1	1.016	−9.1	−0.0	9.2	86	344	−25

Data are provided on the first of the month if Mars is >40° from the Sun, plus mid-month if **Equatorial Diam.** ≥10″. *The position angle (**PA**) of the rotation axis is measured counterclockwise from celestial north (clockwise in telescopes having an odd number of reflections); the inclination (**Incl.**) of the rotation axis to the plane of the sky is positive if the north pole is tipped toward Earth.*

slowly climbs the ecliptic. On Dec. 7, Mars gets another chance to pass very close to Neptune, this time at 2.0′ separation at 14:08:08. The closest approach is visible in eastern Europe, and by the time the pair are visible in North America, they are separated by 13′ on the east coast, expanding to 17.7′ when they get to the west coast. Asia–Pacific will see them as they are closing. Since the pair are still at an elongation of almost 90° from the Sun, anywhere between the east coast of China and Eastern Europe will get the closest approach. Mars finishes up the year under the circlet of Pisces.

Observing Mars this apparition: First make note that the rotation of Mars places the morning side of Mars on the following side of the planet, and evening is on the preceding side. The morning side of Mars is where you may see frost patches that often burn off with daytime heating or morning cloud. The Hellas Basin is south of Syrtis Major, and frosts are often seen forming there at this season. I have mistaken Hellas for the south polar cap in poor seeing. We see Mars this apparition as it has passed the autumnal equinox (Mars's northern hemisphere) and is proceeding into spring in the southern hemisphere, as we swing into closest approach on Jul. 27. The southern polar cap should still be significant, and it starts to shrink as Mars recedes after opposition into the fall months. At right is a table of features that will be more or less centered on the disk at 5 UT, which is in the best North American observing window.

The subtle details on Mars can be enhanced by color filters. The one essential filter is the orange Wratten #21, which improves the contrast between the darker maria and the lighter, rust-colored deserts. The #21 is not too dense for smaller aperture telescopes. For 200-mm and larger apertures, a red filter provides the maximum contrast. Yellow and green filters enhance the view of dust-storm activity, and a green filter enhances the view of ground haze and frost. The Hellas, Elysium, and Argyre basins occasionally have frost on their floors and may be quite bright. Blue light does not penetrate the atmosphere of Mars very well, so atmospheric details and clouds are enhanced by blue and violet filters. The surface is not usually visible in deep-blue or violet filters, but occasionally, during the "blue clearing" phenomenon, surface features will be visible through these filters. I do recommend looking at Mars without filters as well. I have noticed white clouds against the salmon pink of the region north of Mare Sirenum–Cimmerium, which I would not have noticed had I used my orange filter. As you spend more time observing Mars, your visual discrimination will get better and subtle details will become more obvious.

MARS FEATURES TO OBSERVE

Jun.21	Tharsis region with Solus Lacus and Mare Erythraeum
28	Niliacus Lacus and Aurorea Sinus
Jul. 5	Meridiani Sinus with Syrtis Major rotating off
12	Syrtis Major front and center
19	Mare Cimmerium with Syrtis Major rotating on
26	Mare Sirenum and Tharsis region with Solus Lacus rotating off
Aug.2	Tharsis region with Solus Lacus, Mare Erythaeum, and Mare Acidalium rotating off
9	Niliacus Lacus and Aurorea Sinus with Meridiani Sinus rotating off
16	Syrtis Major and Sinus Meridiani
23	Syrtis Major Rotating on
30	Mare Cimmerium and Mare Sirenum
Sep. 6	Mare Sirenum and Solus Lacus
13	Mare Erythraeum, Niliacus Lacus, and Aurorea Sinus, Tharsis region with Solus Lacus rotating on
20	Meridiani Sinus with Niliacus Lacus and Aurorea Sinus rotating on
27	Syrtis Major square and center

continued on p. 222

OPPOSITIONS OF MARS, 2010–2022

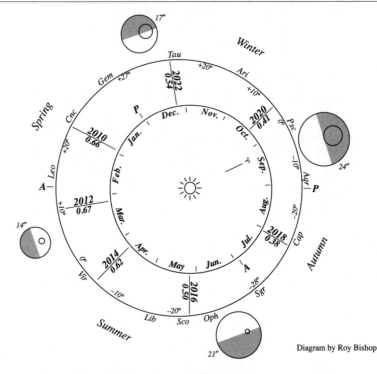

Diagram by Roy Bishop

The above diagram represents the orbits of Earth and Mars as viewed from the north ecliptic pole. Straight lines link simultaneous positions of the two planets for seven successive oppositions of Mars, beginning with that of the year 2010. The separation of the two planets (in astronomical units) at the various oppositions is indicated beside each of the connecting lines. The months inside of Earth's orbit indicate the position of Earth during the year (both planets orbit counterclockwise). For each orbit, two tick marks labelled A and P indicate the aphelion point and the perihelion point, respectively. The direction of the vernal equinox is shown (toward the late-September position of Earth). Around the orbit of Mars is indicated its declination (ranges between +27° and –28°) and the constellation in which Mars resides when at opposition.

Four views of Mars are shown: at its two equinoxes and two solstices. These views show the portion of Mars illuminated by the Sun, the location and approximate size of its north polar cap, and the apparent size of Mars (labelled in arcseconds) for oppositions occurring at these points in its orbit. The seasons of the Martian northern hemisphere are indicated around the outer margin of the diagram, and are very nearly one season ahead of those on Earth at the same orbital position. (For the southern hemisphere of Mars, the season and the configuration of the south polar cap are the same as those of the diametrically opposite view.) Note that the maximum angular diameter Mars can attain (25″) occurs near its perihelion, at a late-August opposition.

As an example of the information that can be read from this diagram: This year's opposition of Mars occurs in late July with Mars located near declination –25° in the constellation Capricornus, 0.38 au from Earth, and about 23″ in diameter. It will be autumn in the Martian northern hemisphere, and the south polar cap will be visible.

MAP OF MARS

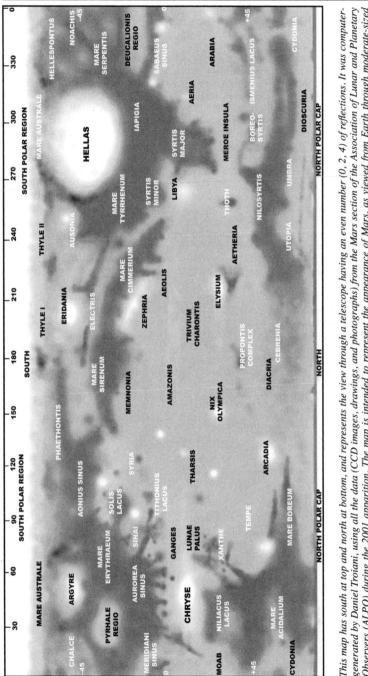

This map has south at top and north at bottom, and represents the view through a telescope having an even number (0, 2, 4) of reflections. It was computer-generated by Daniel Troiani, using all the data (CCD images, drawings, and photographs) from the Mars section of the Association of Lunar and Planetary Observers (ALPO) during the 2001 apparition. The map is intended to represent the appearance of Mars, as viewed from Earth through moderate-sized telescopes, during favorable apparitions, or electronic images that have been digitally processed. For recent observations of Mars, visit the Mars section of the ALPO website, alpo-astronomy.org.

JUPITER

Other than Venus when near inferior conjunction, Jupiter is the largest planet to view in a telescope, with an angular diameter ranging from 44″ to 50″ at opposition. Jupiter moves just over 30° per year in its orbit around the Sun, visiting a new constellation of the zodiac about every year.

Jupiter does not have a solid surface; however, unlike Venus, it has high-contrast, semistationary cloud features that have been observed for many centuries. Jupiter rotates on its axis in 9 h 51 m, slightly slower toward the poles, easily noticeable over a period of half an hour. In fact, when drawing Jupiter, sketch the major features in the first 10 min, because their locations will noticeably change if you dwell on it. Then fill in the details relative to the major features. A 50-mm telescope will show the equatorial belts, the polar hoods, and the four Galilean moons. A 75-mm aperture telescope will easily show the shadows of the moons and some structure in the various cloud belts. Fifty years ago, my old 50-mm refractor showed a brick-red Great Red Spot (GRS), but now the spot has faded to a very light salmon pink, so you need a 90-mm refractor just to see it, under good conditions. In recent years, it has been determined that the GRS has been shrinking for quite some time. In the 1800s, the spot was estimated to have been 41 000 km in its long axis, whereas present-day measurements by the *Hubble Space Telescope* show it to be only 16 500 km in length. It is notable that recent amateur observations have determined that the spot has experienced an acceleration in its rate of shrinkage. We may bear witness to the disappearance of the Great Red Spot in our lifetime. Jupiter's belts are dynamic and occasionally disappear only to reappear again a few year later. If the GRS disappears, it may be a long time before a similar long-lived major feature emerges. Stay tuned.

The views of Jupiter in 125-mm to 175-mm apochromatic refractors or high-quality 200-mm to 320-mm obstructed apertures are spectacular. Wait for those rare moments of excellent seeing, and you will be rewarded. These apertures (with high-quality optics, properly collimated) will reveal the ovals, festoons, and many structures recorded in the best images of Jupiter. With a 130-mm refractor at magnifications above 200x, the contrast on Jupiter starts to get soft. Larger apertures have a higher magnification threshold and will improve the contrast, color, and amount

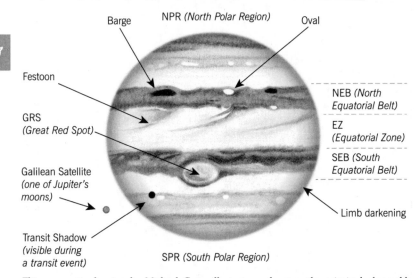

This composite drawing by Michael Gatto illustrates and names the principal observable features of Jupiter, including one of the Galilean satellites and its shadow.

of fine detail visible on Jupiter. In the last few years, several long-lived white ovals and additional red spots have been observed in Jupiter's southern regions, while the north equatorial belt has shown more dark markings along its margins. Because some of Jupiter's cloud features are colored, you can improve contrast and visibility by observing with color filters. The contrast of red spots and the belt features improves with a green filter, and the bluish festoons will darken with an orange or a red filter.

Jupiter is one of the better planets for imaging. The most recent generation of video imagers has improved the quality of amateur planet images. It is now easy to get images that push the limits of the optical system, and the dynamic range of the image can be stretched to reveal low-contrast details. Amateurs are producing images nearly as good as those from Hubble, and they are making discoveries such as "Red Spot, Jr." and impacts in Jupiter's atmosphere. As deep-sky observers search for locations with the darkest skies, leading imagers seek observing locations with stable atmospheres.

The year 2018 starts off with a close conjunction between Jupiter and Mars on the morning of Jan. 6, which is visible from Asia to eastern Europe. Mars is mag. 1.4 and Jupiter is mag. –1.8. Jupiter will show a 33.5″ disk, while Mars, far from opposition, will only show a 5″ disk. In the east coast of North America, we see them rise 21′ apart, narrowing as we cross the continent, until at the west coast, the gap has narrowed to 16′. The next morning, the east coast will see them as they separate at 15.5′, and the west coast at 21′. The Western Hemisphere gets two chances at this event, whereas in Asia, it closes to 12.1′. Jupiter spends most of 2018 in Libra, and on Mar. 9, it arrives at its easternmost stationary point, beginning to retrograde. We are not at the southernmost point of Jupiter's excursion on the ecliptic, but it only rises to –15° declination this year. Jupiter comes to opposition on May 9, where it will shine at mag. –2.5 and show a 45″ disk in the eyepiece.

At opposition in May, Jupiter's moons are at their largest apparent diameter for the year and readily recognizable in a telescope. Note the moons' subtle color differences, as well.

This year's data gives: Io 1.1″, Europa 1.0″, Ganymede 1.7″, and Callisto 1.5″.

On Jul. 11, Jupiter arrives at its second stationary point and returns to prograde motion. From here, it moves back toward α Lib and will be within a degree of it over the summer star parties. It will sit low in the sky and set a little more than an hour after the Sun. The fall ecliptic eats up Jupiter and it disappears from view. Jupiter's conjunction occurs on Nov. 26, then the gas giant passes into the morning sky. There is one more good event for 2018, on Dec. 21, Mercury joins Jupiter in the dawn sky, and the mag. –0.5 Mercury passes only 53′ north of mag. –1.8 Jupiter. It is a great close conjunction and worth getting up for. The closest approach of 50′ is visible in the western Pacific.

The Galilean moons of Jupiter are frequently involved in eclipses, occultations, and transits; these events are easy to observe in amateur telescopes. For a complete listing of events, see PHENOMENA OF THE GALILEAN SATELLITES on p. 230.

Experienced amateurs should consider trying to observe Himalia, a small body that shines dimly at mag. 15.1 (near opposition). Its orbit is highly inclined, with a 250-day period, and the satellite may be found as much as 1° away from Jupiter, so it is a bit of an observing challenge. Canadian amateur Alan Whitman has spotted Himalia in a 400-mm Newtonian reflector.

SATURN

Saturn is the second-largest planet in the Solar System, with a maximum equatorial angular diameter of 21″ (excluding the rings). The ringed planet takes 29.4 y to orbit the Sun, and moves only 12.2° per year in its eastward journey along the ecliptic. Saturn is the most oblate of the planets, with a polar/equatorial diameter ratio of 0.9.

With its incredible system of rings, Saturn is possibly the most spectacular planet in the Solar System. The rings subtend 42″–47″ near opposition, and are visible even in steadied (or image-stabilized) high-power binoculars and small spotting scopes.

JUPITER—TABLE OF DAILY CENTRAL MERIDIANS, 2018

Date 0h UT	System I	II	Date 0h UT	System I	II	Date 0h UT	System I	II	Date 0h UT	System I	II	Date 0h UT	System I	II
JANUARY			**MARCH**			**MAY**			**JULY**			**SEPTEMBER**		
1	222.7	75.7	1	177.3	300.1	1	96.1	113.5	1	12.2	284.1	1	73.7	232.6
2	20.5	225.9	2	335.2	90.4	2	254.2	263.9	2	170.0	74.3	2	231.4	22.7
3	178.3	16.1	3	133.2	240.7	3	52.2	54.3	3	327.9	224.6	3	29.1	172.7
4	336.1	166.3	4	291.1	31.1	4	210.2	204.7	4	125.7	14.8	4	186.7	322.8
5	133.9	316.4	5	89.1	181.4	5	8.3	355.1	5	283.6	165.0	5	344.4	112.8
6	291.7	106.6	6	247.1	331.7	6	166.3	145.5	6	81.5	315.2	6	142.1	262.9
7	89.6	256.8	7	45.0	122.1	7	324.3	295.9	7	239.3	105.5	7	299.8	52.9
8	247.4	47.0	8	203.0	272.4	8	122.4	86.3	8	37.1	255.7	8	97.5	203.0
9	45.2	197.2	9	1.0	62.7	9	280.4	236.7	9	195.0	45.9	9	255.2	353.0
10	203.0	347.3	10	159.0	213.1	10	78.4	27.1	10	352.8	196.1	10	52.8	143.1
11	0.8	137.5	11	316.9	3.4	11	236.5	177.5	11	150.6	346.3	11	210.5	293.1
12	158.6	287.7	12	114.9	153.8	12	34.5	327.9	12	308.5	136.5	12	8.2	83.2
13	316.5	77.9	13	272.9	304.1	13	192.5	118.3	13	106.3	286.7	13	165.9	233.2
14	114.3	228.1	14	70.9	94.5	14	350.5	268.7	14	264.1	76.9	14	323.5	23.3
15	272.1	18.3	15	228.9	244.9	15	148.6	59.1	15	61.9	227.1	15	121.2	173.3
16	70.0	168.5	16	26.9	35.2	16	306.6	209.5	16	219.7	17.2	16	278.9	323.4
17	227.8	318.7	17	184.9	185.6	17	104.6	359.9	17	17.5	167.4	17	76.5	113.4
18	25.6	108.9	18	342.8	335.9	18	262.6	150.3	18	175.4	317.6	18	234.2	263.4
19	183.5	259.1	19	140.8	126.3	19	60.6	300.6	19	333.2	107.8	19	31.9	53.5
20	341.3	49.4	20	298.8	276.7	20	218.6	91.0	20	131.0	257.9	20	189.6	203.5
21	139.2	199.6	21	96.8	67.0	21	16.6	241.4	21	288.7	48.1	21	347.2	353.5
22	297.0	349.8	22	254.9	217.4	22	174.6	31.8	22	86.5	198.3	22	144.9	143.6
23	94.9	140.0	23	52.9	7.8	23	332.6	182.1	23	244.3	348.4	23	302.5	293.6
24	252.7	290.2	24	210.9	158.2	24	130.6	332.5	24	42.1	138.6	24	100.2	83.7
25	50.6	80.5	25	8.9	308.6	25	288.6	122.9	25	199.9	288.7	25	257.9	233.7
26	208.4	230.7	26	166.9	98.9	26	86.6	273.2	26	357.7	78.9	26	55.5	23.7
27	6.3	20.9	27	324.9	249.3	27	244.6	63.6	27	155.5	229.0	27	213.2	173.8
28	164.2	171.2	28	122.9	39.7	28	42.6	214.0	28	313.2	19.2	28	10.9	323.8
29	322.0	321.4	29	280.9	190.1	29	200.6	4.3	29	111.0	169.3	29	168.5	113.8
30	119.9	111.6	30	79.0	340.5	30	358.6	154.7	30	268.8	319.5	30	326.2	263.8
31	277.8	261.9	31	237.0	130.9	31	156.6	305.0	31	66.5	109.6			
FEBRUARY			**APRIL**			**JUNE**			**AUGUST**			**OCTOBER**		
1	75.6	52.1	1	35.0	281.3	1	314.5	95.4	1	215.1	155.5	1	123.8	53.9
2	233.5	202.4	2	193.0	71.7	2	112.5	245.7	2	12.7	305.5	2	281.5	203.9
3	31.4	352.6	3	351.1	222.1	3	270.5	36.0	3	170.4	95.6	3	79.2	353.9
4	189.3	142.9	4	149.1	12.5	4	68.4	186.4	4	328.1	245.6	4	236.8	144.0
5	347.2	293.1	5	307.1	162.8	5	226.4	336.7	5	125.8	35.7	5	34.5	294.0
6	145.1	83.4	6	105.1	313.2	6	24.4	127.0	6	283.5	185.8	6	192.1	84.0
7	303.0	233.6	7	263.2	103.7	7	182.3	277.4	7	81.2	335.8	7	349.8	234.1
8	100.8	23.9	8	61.2	254.1	8	340.3	67.7	8	238.9	125.9	8	147.5	24.1
9	258.7	174.2	9	219.2	44.5	9	138.2	218.0	9	36.5	275.9	9	305.1	174.1
10	56.6	324.4	10	17.3	194.9	10	296.2	8.3	10	194.2	66.0	10	102.8	324.1
11	214.5	114.7	11	175.3	345.3	11	94.1	158.6	11	351.9	216.0	11	260.4	114.2
12	12.5	265.0	12	333.3	135.7	12	252.0	308.9	12	149.6	6.1	12	58.1	264.2
13	170.4	55.3	13	131.4	286.1	13	50.0	99.3	13	307.3	156.1	13	215.7	54.2
14	328.3	205.5	14	289.4	76.5	14	207.9	249.6	14	104.9	306.2	14	13.4	204.2
15	126.2	355.8	15	87.5	226.9	15	5.8	39.9	15	262.6	96.2	15	171.0	354.3
16	284.1	146.1	16	245.5	17.3	16	163.8	190.1	16	60.3	246.2	16	328.7	144.3
17	82.0	296.4	17	43.5	167.7	17	321.7	340.4	17	218.0	36.3	17	126.4	294.3
18	239.9	86.7	18	201.6	318.1	18	119.6	130.7	18	15.6	186.3	18	284.0	84.3
19	37.9	237.0	19	359.6	108.5	19	277.5	281.0	19	173.3	336.4	19	81.7	234.4
20	195.8	27.3	20	157.7	259.0	20	75.4	71.3	20	331.0	126.4	20	239.3	24.4
21	353.7	177.6	21	315.7	49.4	21	233.3	221.6	21	128.6	276.5	21	37.0	174.4
22	151.7	327.9	22	113.8	199.8	22	31.2	11.8	22	286.3	66.5	22	194.6	324.5
23	309.6	118.2	23	271.8	350.2	23	189.1	162.1	23	84.0	216.5	23	352.3	114.5
24	107.5	268.5	24	69.8	140.6	24	347.0	312.4	24	241.6	6.6	24	149.9	264.5
25	265.5	58.8	25	227.9	291.0	25	144.9	102.6	25	39.3	156.6	25	307.6	54.5
26	63.4	209.1	26	25.9	81.4	26	302.8	252.9	26	197.0	306.6	26	105.3	204.6
27	221.4	359.4	27	184.0	231.8	27	100.7	43.1	27	354.6	96.7	27	262.9	354.6
28	19.3	149.8	28	342.0	22.3	28	258.6	193.4	28	152.3	246.7	28	60.6	144.6
			29	140.0	172.7	29	56.4	343.6	29	310.0	36.8	29	218.2	294.6
			30	298.1	323.1	30	214.3	133.9	30	107.6	186.8	30	15.9	84.7
									31	276.0	82.5	31	173.6	234.7
												(too close to Sun)		

Saturn's rings are composed mostly of ice particles of sizes ranging from dust to boulders, in complex subsystems of rings within rings. The more you zoom in on the rings, the more structure there is to see. The *Cassini* probe has found fine structure right down to the limits of its image resolution.

Visually, in earthbound telescopes, the rings divide into three distinct sectors (see facing page). The outer (A) ring is separated from the first inner (B) ring by the Cassini Division, which J.D. Cassini discovered in 1675. The Cassini Division is visible in a 50-mm telescope, yet it is only 0.8″ wide at opposition. The A ring itself is divided by the Encke Gap, a very fine division about one-fifth of the way between the outer edge of the ring and the Cassini Division. The Encke Gap is extremely difficult to observe and requires a large aperture (250 mm or greater), high-quality optics, and high magnification (~500x), which in turn demands excellent atmospheric seeing. There is also a minimum in luminance called the Encke minimum, about halfway

---

JUPITER—DAILY CENTRAL MERIDIANS AND TIME OF TRANSIT OF GREAT RED SPOT

The table on the facing page can be used to calculate the longitude of the central meridian of the observed disk of Jupiter throughout 2018, except for the interval Nov. 1–Dec. 31, when Jupiter is too close to the Sun to observe. System I is the most rapidly rotating region, between the middle of the North Equatorial Belt and the middle of the South Equatorial Belt. System II applies to the rest of the planet, from the equatorial belts to the poles. The rotation rate of System I is 36.577 ± 0.008 °/h and that of System II is 36.259 ± 0.008 °/h. These figures, together with the closest tabular value, can be used to determine the longitude of a system's central meridian for any given date and time (UT) of observation. **Example:** At 9:00 p.m. CDT Jul. 18 = 2:00 UT Jul. 19, the longitude of the central meridian of System I is

333.2 + (36.577 × 2) = 406.4°;

putting this angle in the range 0°–360° by subtracting 360° leaves a longitude of 46.4°± 0.02°.

The table may also be used to estimate when the Great Red Spot (GRS) will cross the central meridian of Jupiter's disk. (Based on drift measurements, the GRS is predicted to be near longitude 103.0° in System II on 2018 Jan. 0, drifting by about +14.5° per year. See jupos.privat.t-online.de for an up-to-date value.)

Example: Suppose an observer in Albany is viewing Jupiter on the evening of Apr. 3 (time zone: EDT, –4h). At 0h UT Apr. 4 (20h EDT Apr. 3), the table gives 12.5° for the longitude of the central meridian in System II. Ignoring GRS drift, a further rotation of 103.0°– 12.5°= 90.5° will bring the GRS to the central meridian, which takes place 90.5°÷ 36.259°/h = 2.5 = 2 h 30 min later. Thus the GRS will transit at 2:30 UT Apr. 4 = 22:30 EDT Apr. 3. (Correcting for the annual drift in GRS longitude would add 14.5° × 3/12 ÷ 36.259°/h = 0.10 h, or 6 min to the transit time.) By timing a transit of the GRS and using the table, you can update its longitude for yourself. Alternatively, you can use a specialized GRS transit calculator, such as www.skyandtelescope.com/observing/objects/planets/3304091.html.

JUPITER AND SATURN IN 2018

	Jupiter		Saturn		
Date UT	Mag.	Equatorial Diameter ″	Mag.	Equatorial Diameter ″	Ring Inclination °
Jan. 1.0	−1.8	33	+0.5	15	26.5
Feb. 1.0	−2.0	36	+0.5	15	26.1
Mar. 1.0	−2.2	40	+0.6	16	25.7
Apr. 1.0	−2.4	43	+0.5	17	25.6
May 1.0	−2.5	45	+0.3	17	25.5
Jun. 1.0	−2.5	44	+0.0	18	25.7
Jul. 1.0	−2.3	41	+0.0	18	26.1
Aug. 1.0	−2.1	38	+0.2	18	26.4
Sep. 1.0	−1.9	35	+0.4	17	26.6
Oct. 1.0	−1.8	33	+0.5	16	26.6
Nov. 1.0	−1.7	31	+0.5	16	26.4
Dec. 1.0	−1.7	31	+0.5	15	26.0
Jan. 1.0	−1.8	31	+0.5	15	25.4

between the outer edge of the A ring and the Cassini Division. This is easier to see and is often confused with the Encke Gap.

The next ring inward is the B ring, which is the broadest and brightest of the rings. The inner edge of this ring fades a bit in brightness and often appears to have a stranded nature, like grooves in a vinyl record. The inner edge sometimes exhibits spokes in the ansae (the part of the rings seen on either side of the planet). You need high magnification and a very clean optical system to see these subtle features. They may only be visible on one side of the planet.

The innermost ring is the Crepe Ring (also called the C ring). It goes largely unnoticed because it is so dim in comparison to the outer two rings and the glare from Saturn. It is a ghostly ring about the same width as the A ring, and it appears dark where it passes in front of the planet. It looks like a shadow cast on the planet, but it is actually blocking the planet's reflected light from our view. A very clean optical system is essential to get a good view of the Crepe Ring. Contrast-robbing dust and debris on eyepiece and diagonal surfaces have a pronounced effect, because they are close to the eye. You know you have seen the Crepe Ring when you notice that the black space within the ansae next to the ball of the planet is only slightly darker than the Crepe Ring.

At a distance of 9.5 au from the Sun, Saturn does not receive enough solar energy to sustain as lively an atmosphere as that of Jupiter. There are a few belts, and the occasional storm or outbreak of activity. The average observer will see an equatorial-region belt and the dark polar hood, but not much else. The experienced observer may see much more, but the details are subtle. White spots have been seen in the south tropical zone, and a south equatorial disturbance was recorded in 2009. In late 2010, a dramatic storm appeared in the north temperate zone, and the white spot spread and was followed for many months in 2011. These subtle phenomena are more readily captured with a camera.

Saturn starts off 2018 just emerging from its winter-solstice conjunction with the Sun. It will perform its retrograde dance just above the lid of the Sagittarius Teapot, passing close to M21 and M22. The tilt of Saturn's rings will vary from 26.5° to 25.4° over the close apparition. We are over the peak of ring tilt, and the rings will start to tip down over the next number of years.

A close conjunction with Mercury may motivate you to hunt for the pair in the pre-dawn hours on Jan. 13, where the two planets rise 75 min before the Sun. On the east coast, the pair are separated by 42′ when they rise, and this expands to 49′ separation when the pair rise on the west coast. The closest approach is 38′, visible around longitude 0. Mercury shines at mag. –0.3, with a 5.5″ gibbous disk, and Saturn with a mag. 0.5, 15″ disk. You should be able to resolve both to disks in a medium-power telescope eyepiece.

The first of a sequence of close conjunctions between Saturn and the Moon is seen on the morning of Feb. 11. A rather late crescent Moon will pass 1.5° above Saturn in the morning twilight. Over the months of March and April, we see Mars and Saturn together in the morning sky. The closest approach is on Apr. 2, where Mars passes 1.3° below Saturn. Mars's 8.6″ disk will shine at mag. 0.3 with Saturn's 16.7″ disk at mag. 0.5. There will be a lovely color contrast between them. If you investigate with a telescope, you will notice M22 26′ below Mars. On Apr. 7, we get a last-quarter Moon joining the pair, a perfect photo opportunity. On Apr. 18, Saturn is at its stationary point and it starts retrograde motion. On Jun. 27, we are treated to a double header with Saturn coming to opposition at 13:28 UT, and the Moon joining in 7 h later. The closest approach of 45′ will be visible on the east coast, and the central regions of North America will see the Moon rise in daylight at closest approach. On the west coast, the pairing will separate to 1.2°. On Jul. 25, at 06:25, we get another close conjunction with the Moon, where it will pass 1° above Saturn.

As the summer closes, we see Saturn arrive at its second stationary point on

SATURN—MAIN RING FEATURES VISIBLE FROM EARTH

A   B   C

EARTH
(to same scale)

1.00 = 60 330 km = 9.74″ (at mean opposition distance)
---- 1.23
---- 1.52
---- 1.95
---- 2.02
---- 2.26

RADII

Appearance of rings
when "open" or "closed"

SATURN'S RING SYSTEM—MAIN STRUCTURAL REGIONS

Ring	Radius**	Discoverer
D	1.11 – 1.23	*Voyager 1* (1980)
C*	1.23 – 1.52	W.C. & G.P. Bond, W.R. Dawes (1850)
B*	1.52 – 1.95 }	{ Galileo (1610), C. Huygens (1659),
A*	2.02 – 2.26 }	{ J.D. Cassini (1675)
F	2.33	*Pioneer 11* (1979)
G	2.8	*Voyager 1* (1980)
E	3. – 8.	W.A. Feibelman (1966)

* Visible from Earth; also, the tenuous E ring can be
detected when Saturn's ring system appears edge-on.

** In units of Saturn's equatorial radius (60 330 km)

Diagram by
Roy Bishop/Michael Gatto

Sep. 6, and it returns to prograde motion eastward across Sagittarius. Saturn is on that shallow fall ecliptic and will sit low in the evening sky for the remainder of the year. The last of the good lunar conjunctions is on Oct. 15 at 03:43, well placed for North American viewing. From this point on, Saturn fades away into the twilight and ends the year heading for its New Year's Day conjunction with the Sun.

Saturn has 62 natural satellites, of which 8 are visible in amateur telescopes. Of those, only Titan shows a disk in large telescopes. At opposition this year, Titan presents a 0.8″ disk; the others, less than 0.25″.

The satellite Iapetus (mag. 10.5–12.7) is tidally locked to Saturn, with its leading hemisphere as dark as coal, and the other side quite white. (The actual albedos are 0.05 and 0.5, respectively.) Because of this, when Iapetus is near elongation on the west side of Saturn, it is about two magnitudes brighter than it is on the east side. The 79.3-day orbit of Iapetus takes it as far as 9.1′ from Saturn. It is directly north of Saturn on Jul. 2 and Sep. 19, and directly south on May 23 and Aug. 10. Since it is displaying both faces at these times, it will shine at an intermediate magnitude (see CONFIGURATION OF SATURN'S BRIGHTEST SATELLITES on p. 237).

URANUS

Uranus is the faintest of the planets visible to the naked eye and the third-largest overall, yet its tremendous distance means that its maximum angular diameter is only 4.0″. Uranus's orbital period is 84.4 y, and it moves along the ecliptic only about 4.3°/y. William Herschel discovered Uranus in 1781 with a 160-mm reflector, but it had been recorded by earlier observers, who charted it as a star. At mag. 5.7, it would require a clear and transparent sky for a successful naked-eye sighting. Binoculars easily reveal Uranus, and it blossoms into a pale blue-green disk under high magnification in a telescope. Some observers have reported seeing details on the planet, even with amateur-sized instruments. Fred Price, in *The Planet Observer's Handbook*, states that the only features seen on the planet are the two faint belts and that you need at least a 250-mm telescope to see these.

Uranus starts out 2018 3.5° west of mag. 4.2 o Psc and sets after 2 a.m. It has just turned back east from last year's retrograde and is well placed for winter observation. It shines at mag. 5.8 and displays a 3.6″ blue-green disk. On Mar. 29 [28 EDT], Uranus is joined by Venus in the evening sky in a fantastic conjunction. The bright mag. −3.9 beacon of Venus will help you find the pair (see p. 216). This is an extremely close conjunction, with closest approach of 4.1′ visible in eastern North America. The pair will spread apart moving westward, 5.4′ in Winnipeg, 7.6′ in Alberta, and 9′ on the west coast. Use high power on the pair. Venus shows a 10.5″ disk and Uranus is 3.4″. Uranus moves into conjunction with the Sun on Apr. 18, disappearing until late summer. Aug. 7 marks when Uranus starts retrograding west from its position southwest of Aries, 9° south of β Ari. The planet comes to opposition on Oct. 23, shines at mag. 5.7, and its disk will grow to 3.7″.

The Uranian satellite system is within reach of medium-to-large amateur telescopes, especially at opposition. This year at opposition, the moons Titania and Oberon are mag. 13.9 and 14.1, respectively, and their orbits describe an ellipse with the long axis 10° clockwise rotated from RA north. Titania's orbit is 33″ by 22″ and Oberon's is 44″ by 29″. These brighter, more-distant satellites may be seen in telescopes as small as 250 mm under good conditions. The inner moons suffer from Uranus's glare. The fainter moons, Ariel (mag. 14.3) and Umbriel (mag. 15.0), are

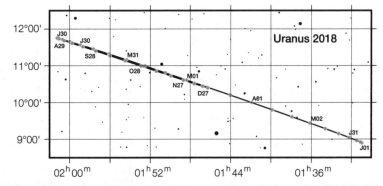

The two charts on this page and the next use the astrometric UCAC4 catalog. The UCAC4 lists model-fitted photometric magnitudes (579–642 nm). The bright star located near the chart lower center is o Psc, listed as mag. 4.25. Uranus is plotted as a gray circle of mag. ~5.8. The chart limiting magnitude is 9.5 according to the UCAC4. The charts' ephemerides are generated using the JPL Horizons Web-Interface. The chart limiting magnitude is 9.5 according to the UCAC4. The chart is generated using the open-source Generic Mapping Tools (GMT5.1.2) under Mac OS 10.10.5 (chart by Ian Cameron).

closer to Uranus (14″–22″ major axis), and a greater challenge. Use planetarium software to generate a finder chart for the evening you choose to search for these objects. To separate the satellites from the planet, use as much magnification as the conditions will bear; ensure a clean eyepiece. With these measures, and possibly an occulting-bar eyepiece, the observation should be possible in telescopes of aperture 300–430 mm.

NEPTUNE

Neptune is the outermost planet in the Solar System, with a maximum angular diameter of only 2.4″. It was found at Berlin Observatory by Johann Galle on 1846 Sep. 23, near a position calculated from irregularities in the motion of Uranus; credit for this prediction has historically been shared by Urbain le Verrier of France and John Couch Adams of England, but le Verrier is the real champion here (see tinyurl.com/j23quw3). Neptune was at aphelion in 1959, at mag. 7.9. Its next perihelion, at mag. 7.7, is in 2041, in Aries.

Neptune starts off the year ½° south of mag. 3.7 λ Aqr. It sets just after 11 local time and shines at mag. 7.9. Neptune comes to its conjunction with the Sun on Mar. 4, and it will disappear from view in the Northern Hemisphere until the summer star parties. Neptune begins to retrograde on Jun. 19 and sits 1° west of φ Aqr. Neptune comes to opposition on Sep. 7 and will shine at mag. 7.8. In the eyepiece, it will display a 2.4″ blue disk. This is a perfectly good time to hunt for Triton. On Nov. 25, Neptune is at its second stationary point, and it turns eastward in prograde motion. Mars and Neptune have close approach of 2.2′ on Dec. 7 at 14:08 UT. Asia through eastern Europe will see closest approach. Here in North America, we see the lead-up to the conjunction, with the west coast getting a 11.7′ separation as the two planets set; on the east coast, the pair are about 18′ apart as they set. Neptune ends the year 2.2° east of where it started off the year, 2.3° east of λ Aqr.

Neptune's one large moon, Triton, is within easy reach of medium-sized amateur telescopes (250+ mm). Triton is easier to find than any of the satellites of Uranus, primarily because it is brighter than those bodies, but also because Neptune is two magnitudes fainter than Uranus, so its glare is much reduced. At opposition, Triton is mag. 13.4, and from our perspective, its orbit describes a fat ellipse with a minor radius of 12″ and a major radius of 17″. Neptune's north pole is tipped away from Earth at -24.5°, so Triton appears to move in a counterclockwise direction around its primary.

Editor's note: Neptune is notoriously difficult to observe for most amateurs, as its great distance and blue color mean that not much reflected light reaches Earth. To see the planet's disk generally requires more magnification than binoculars provide, so a telescope is a must.

The bright star located near the chart edge is λ Aqr, listed as mag. 3.7. Neptune is plotted as a gray circle corresponding to mag. ~8. The chart limiting magnitude is 9.5 according to the UCAC4 (chart by Ian Cameron).

PHENOMENA OF THE GALILEAN SATELLITES
BY PATRICK KELLY

The table on the following six pages gives the various transits, occultations, and eclipses of the four great satellites of Jupiter during January–mid-October 2018. Jupiter is not well-placed for observing after mid-September, as it is in conjunction with the Sun on Nov. 26. Double-shadow transits are indicated in **bold**. Double-satellite transits are indicated in *italics*. When a bold and an italic event are close, that often indicates that two moons and two shadows can simultaneously be seen on Jupiter. Since the satellite phenomena are not instantaneous but take up to several minutes, the predicted times are for the middle of each event. The predictions were generated by the Institut de Mécanique Céleste et de Calcul des Ephémérides in Paris.

Satellites designations are: I = Io, II = Europa, III = Ganymede, IV = Callisto

Events abbreviations are:
Ec = eclipse   Oc = occultation   Tr = satellite transit   Sh = shadow transit
D = disappearance   R = reappearance   I = ingress   E = egress

The general motion of the satellites and the successive phenomena are shown in the diagram at right, which is a view of Jupiter and the orbit of one of its satellites, looking down from the north side. Satellites move from east to west across the face of the planet and from west to east behind it (here "east" and "west" are used in the sense of the observer's sky, not in the Jovian sense). Before opposition, shadows fall to the west, and after opposition, to the east (as in the diagram).

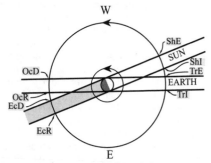

The sequence of phenomena for the outer satellite shown in the diagram, counterclockwise beginning at the lower right, is transit ingress (TrI), transit egress (TrE), shadow ingress (ShI), shadow egress (ShE), occultation disappearance (OcD), occultation reappearance (OcR), eclipse disappearance (EcD), and eclipse reappearance (EcR). The actual sequence will depend on the actual Sun–Jupiter–Earth angle and the size of the satellite's orbit.

Over 3/4 of the phenomena listed will **not** be visible from any one location because they occur when Jupiter is near or below the horizon or when daylight interferes. In practice, an observer usually knows when Jupiter will be conveniently placed in the night sky; if not, consult THE SKY MONTH BY MONTH section (p. 95). The table can then be scanned to see if there are any events during the intended observing period. For example, an observer in Washington, D.C. would know that Jupiter is well placed in April and May as Jupiter is at opposition on May 9. If planning to observe from 23:00 on Apr. 28 to 5:00 EDT on Apr. 29 (4 h behind UT), scanning the table for events in the interval Apr. 29 from 3:00 to 9:00 UT would find four events, beginning at 2:34 EDT on Apr. 29 when Io's shadow begins a transit, followed 16 min later by the moon itself appearing on Jupiter's surface. About two hours later, at 4:44 EDT, Io's shadow transit ends, and at 4:57 EDT, Io itself egresses. The configuration of the four Galilean satellites during that night is given in the diagram on the right-hand side of p. 105 in the THE SKY MONTH BY MONTH section.

A total of 1818 events (351 eclipses, 345 occultations, 562 shadows, and 560 transits) appear in the table, an average of one event every 3 h 46 min.

SATELLITES OF JUPITER, UT OF 2018 GEOCENTRIC PHENOMENA

JANUARY

0	16:53	I	ShI
	17:52	I	TrI
	19:03	I	ShE
	20:02	I	TrE
1	12:00	III	EcD
	13:17	II	ShI
	13:52	III	EcR
	14:07	I	EcD
	15:15	II	TrI
	15:33	II	ShE
	16:05	III	OcD
	17:17	I	OcR
	17:30	II	TrE
	17:51	III	OcR
2	11:21	I	ShI
	12:21	I	TrI
	13:31	I	ShE
	14:31	I	TrE
3	7:52	II	EcD
	8:36	I	EcD
	11:46	I	OcR
	12:14	II	OcR
4	5:50	I	ShI
	6:51	I	TrI
	7:59	I	ShE
	9:01	I	TrE
5	1:46	III	ShI
	2:34	**II**	**ShI**
	3:04	I	EcD
	3:37	III	ShE
	4:36	II	TrI
	4:49	II	ShE
	6:01	*III*	*TrI*
	6:15	I	OcR
	6:50	II	TrE
	7:44	III	TrE
6	0:18	I	ShI
	1:20	I	TrI
	2:28	I	ShE
	3:30	I	TrE
	21:10	II	EcD
	21:32	I	EcD
7	0:44	I	OcR
	1:36	II	OcR
	18:46	I	ShI
	19:50	I	TrI
	20:56	I	ShE
	21:59	I	TrE
8	15:50	II	ShI
	15:57	III	EcD
	16:00	I	EcD
	17:49	III	EcR
	17:57	II	TrI
	18:06	II	ShE
	19:14	I	OcR
	20:10	II	TrE
	20:21	III	OcD
	22:04	III	OcR
9	13:15	I	ShI
	14:19	I	TrI
	15:25	I	ShE
	16:29	I	TrE
10	10:28	II	EcD
	10:29	I	EcD
	13:43	I	OcR
	14:58	II	OcR
11	7:43	I	ShI
	8:49	I	TrI
	9:53	I	ShE
	10:58	I	TrE
12	4:57	I	EcD
	5:07	II	ShI
	5:45	**III**	**ShI**
	7:17	II	TrI
	7:22	II	ShE
	7:35	III	ShE
	8:12	I	OcR
	9:30	II	TrE
	10:17	III	TrI
	11:56	III	TrE
13	2:12	I	ShI
	3:18	I	TrI
	4:21	I	ShE
	5:27	I	TrE
	23:25	I	EcD
	23:46	II	EcD
14	2:04	II	EcR
	2:04	II	OcD
	2:41	I	OcR
	4:20	II	OcR
	20:40	I	ShI
	21:47	I	TrI
	22:50	I	ShE
	23:56	I	TrE
15	17:53	I	EcD
	18:23	II	ShI
	19:54	III	EcD
	20:37	II	TrI
	20:38	II	ShE
	21:10	I	OcR
	21:45	III	EcR
	22:50	II	TrE
16	0:34	III	OcD
	2:13	III	OcR
	15:08	I	ShI
	16:16	I	TrI
	17:18	I	ShE
	18:26	I	TrE
17	12:21	I	EcD
	13:04	II	EcD
	15:21	II	EcR
	15:25	II	OcD
	15:39	I	OcR
	17:40	II	OcR
18	9:37	I	ShI
	10:46	I	TrI
	11:47	I	ShE
	12:55	I	TrE
19	6:50	I	EcD
	7:40	II	ShI
	9:43	**III**	**ShI**
	9:55	II	ShE
	9:56	II	TrI
	10:08	I	OcR
	11:32	III	ShE
	12:09	II	TrE
	14:30	III	TrI
	16:05	III	TrE
20	4:05	I	ShI
	5:15	I	TrI
	6:15	I	ShE
	7:24	I	TrE
21	1:18	I	EcD
	2:22	II	EcD
	4:37	I	OcR
	4:40	II	EcR
	4:47	II	OcD
	7:01	II	OcR
	22:34	I	ShI
	23:44	I	TrI
22	0:43	I	ShE
	1:53	I	TrE
	19:46	I	EcD
	20:56	II	ShI
	23:06	I	OcR
	23:11	II	ShE
	23:16	II	TrI
	23:51	III	EcD
23	1:28	II	TrE
	1:42	III	EcR
	4:45	III	OcD
	6:21	III	OcR
	17:02	I	ShI
	18:13	I	TrI
	19:12	I	ShE
	20:22	I	TrE
24	14:14	I	EcD
	15:39	II	EcD
	17:34	I	OcR
	17:57	II	EcR
	18:07	II	OcD
	20:21	II	OcR
25	11:30	I	ShI
	12:42	I	TrI
	13:40	I	ShE
	14:51	I	TrE
26	8:42	I	EcD
	10:12	II	ShI
	12:03	I	OcR
	12:27	II	ShE
	12:34	II	TrI
	13:41	III	ShI
	14:46	II	TrE
	15:29	III	ShE
	18:40	III	TrI
	20:11	III	TrE
27	5:59	I	ShI
	7:11	I	TrI
	8:08	I	ShE
	9:19	I	TrE
28	3:11	I	EcD
	4:58	II	EcD
	6:32	I	OcR
	7:15	II	EcR
	7:28	II	OcD
	9:41	II	OcR
29	0:27	I	ShI
	1:39	I	TrI
	2:37	I	ShE
	3:48	I	TrE
	21:39	I	EcD
	23:29	II	ShI
30	1:00	I	OcR
	1:44	II	ShE
	1:53	II	TrI
	3:49	III	EcD
	4:05	II	TrE
	5:39	III	EcR
	8:52	III	OcD
	10:24	III	OcR
	18:55	I	ShI
	20:08	I	TrI
	21:05	I	ShE
	22:17	I	TrE
31	16:07	I	EcD
	18:15	II	EcD
	19:29	I	OcR
	20:33	II	EcR
	20:47	II	OcD
	23:00	II	OcR

FEBRUARY

1	13:24	I	ShI
	14:37	I	TrI
	15:33	I	ShE
	16:46	I	TrE
2	10:35	I	EcD
	12:45	II	ShI
	13:58	I	OcR
	15:00	II	ShE
	15:11	II	TrI
	17:22	II	TrE
	17:38	III	ShI
	19:26	III	ShE
	22:45	III	TrI
3	0:13	III	TrE
	7:52	I	ShI
	9:06	I	TrI
	10:02	I	ShE
	11:14	I	TrE
4	5:03	I	EcD
	7:34	II	EcD
	8:26	I	OcR
	9:51	II	EcR
	10:06	II	OcD
	12:20	II	OcR
5	2:21	I	ShI
	3:34	I	TrI
	4:30	I	ShE
	5:43	I	TrE
	23:32	I	EcD
6	2:02	II	ShI
	2:54	I	OcR
	4:16	II	ShE
	4:29	II	TrI
	6:39	II	TrE
	7:47	III	EcD
	9:36	III	EcR
	12:57	III	OcD
	14:25	III	OcR
	20:49	I	ShI
	22:03	I	TrI
	22:58	I	ShE
7	0:11	I	TrE
	18:00	I	EcD
	20:51	II	EcD
	21:23	I	OcR
	23:08	II	EcR
	23:25	II	OcD
8	1:37	II	OcR
	15:17	I	ShI
	16:31	I	TrI
	17:27	I	ShE
	18:40	I	TrE
9	12:28	I	EcD
	15:18	II	ShI
	15:51	I	OcR
	17:33	II	ShE
	17:46	II	TrI
	19:56	II	TrE
	21:36	III	ShI
	23:23	III	ShE
10	2:47	III	TrI
	4:11	III	TrE
	9:46	I	ShI
	11:00	I	TrI
	11:55	I	ShE
	13:08	I	TrE
11	6:56	I	EcD
	10:09	II	EcD
	10:19	I	OcR
	12:26	II	EcR
	12:43	II	OcD
	14:56	II	OcR
12	4:14	I	ShI
	5:28	I	TrI
	6:23	I	ShE
	7:37	I	TrE
13	1:24	I	EcD
	4:35	II	ShI
	4:47	I	OcR
	6:49	II	ShE
	7:02	II	TrI
	9:13	II	TrE
	11:44	III	EcD
	13:33	III	EcR
	16:57	III	OcD
	18:21	III	OcR
	22:42	I	ShI
	23:56	I	TrI
14	0:52	I	ShE
	2:05	I	TrE
	19:53	I	EcD
	23:16	II	OcR
	23:27	II	EcD

I = Io II = Europa III = Ganymede IV = Callisto

SATELLITES OF JUPITER, UT OF 2018 GEOCENTRIC PHENOMENA (cont.)

FEBRUARY (cont.)

Day	Time	Sat	Phen
15	1:44	II	EcR
	2:01	II	OcD
	4:13	II	OcR
	17:11	I	ShI
	18:25	I	TrI
	19:20	I	ShE
	20:33	I	TrE
16	14:21	I	EcD
	17:44	I	OcR
	17:51	II	ShI
	20:06	II	ShE
	20:19	II	TrI
	22:29	II	TrE
17	1:33	III	ShI
	3:20	III	ShE
	6:46	III	TrI
	8:06	III	TrE
	11:39	I	ShI
	12:53	I	TrI
	13:48	I	ShE
	15:01	I	TrE
18	8:49	I	EcD
	12:12	I	OcR
	12:45	II	EcD
	15:02	II	EcR
	15:18	II	OcD
	17:30	II	OcR
19	6:07	I	ShI
	7:21	I	TrI
	8:17	I	ShE
	9:29	I	TrE
20	3:17	I	EcD
	6:40	I	OcR
	7:07	II	ShI
	9:22	II	ShE
	9:34	II	TrI
	11:44	II	TrE
	15:41	III	EcR
	17:30	III	EcR
	20:52	III	OcD
	22:13	III	OcR
21	0:36	I	ShI
	1:49	I	TrI
	2:45	I	ShE
	3:57	I	TrE
	21:45	I	EcD
22	1:07	I	OcR
	2:02	II	EcD
	4:19	II	EcR
	4:34	II	OcD
	6:46	II	OcR
	19:04	I	ShI
	20:17	I	TrI
	21:14	I	ShE
	22:25	I	TrE
23	16:14	I	EcD
	19:35	I	OcR
	20:24	II	ShI
	22:39	II	ShE
	22:49	II	TrI
24	0:59	II	TrE
	5:31	III	ShI
	7:17	III	ShE
	10:39	III	TrI
	11:56	III	TrE
	13:32	I	ShI
	14:45	I	TrI
	15:42	I	ShE
	16:53	I	TrE
25	10:42	I	EcD
	14:03	I	OcR
	15:20	II	EcD
	17:37	II	EcR
	17:51	II	OcD
	20:02	II	OcR
26	8:01	I	ShI
	9:13	I	TrI
	10:10	I	ShE
	11:21	I	TrE
27	5:10	I	EcD
	8:31	I	OcR
	9:40	II	ShI
	11:55	II	ShE
	12:04	II	TrI
	14:13	II	TrE
	19:38	III	EcD
	21:27	III	EcR
28	0:43	III	OcD
	2:01	III	OcR
	2:29	I	ShI
	3:41	I	TrI
	4:38	I	ShE
	5:49	I	TrE
	23:38	I	EcD

MARCH

Day	Time	Sat	Phen
1	2:58	I	OcR
	4:38	II	EcD
	6:55	II	EcR
	7:06	II	OcD
	9:16	II	OcR
	20:57	I	ShI
	22:08	I	TrI
	23:07	I	ShE
2	0:16	I	TrE
	18:06	I	EcD
	21:26	I	OcR
	22:57	II	ShI
3	1:12	II	ShE
	1:18	II	TrI
	3:27	II	TrE
	9:29	III	ShI
	11:15	III	ShE
	14:29	III	TrI
	15:26	I	ShI
	15:42	III	TrE
	16:36	I	TrI
	17:35	I	ShE
	18:44	I	TrE
4	12:35	I	EcD
	15:53	I	OcR
	17:56	II	EcD
	20:13	II	EcR
	20:21	II	OcD
	22:31	II	OcR
5	9:54	I	ShI
	11:04	I	TrI
	12:04	I	ShE
	13:12	I	TrE
6	7:03	I	EcD
	10:21	I	OcR
	12:13	II	ShI
	14:28	II	ShE
	14:32	II	TrI
	16:41	II	TrE
	23:35	III	EcD
7	1:23	III	EcR
	4:22	I	ShI
	4:30	III	OcD
	5:31	I	TrI
	5:44	III	OcR
	6:32	I	ShE
	7:39	I	TrE
8	1:31	I	EcD
	4:48	I	OcR
	7:13	II	EcD
	9:30	II	EcR
	9:35	II	OcD
	11:45	II	OcR
	22:51	I	ShI
	23:59	I	TrI
9	1:00	I	ShE
	2:07	I	TrE
	19:59	I	EcD
	23:15	I	OcR
10	1:30	II	ShI
	3:45	II	ShE
	3:45	II	TrI
	5:54	II	TrE
	13:27	III	ShI
	15:13	III	ShE
	17:19	I	ShI
	18:14	III	TrI
	18:26	*I*	*TrI*
	19:24	III	TrE
	19:29	I	ShE
	20:34	I	TrE
11	14:28	I	EcD
	17:43	I	OcR
	20:31	II	EcD
	22:48	II	EcR
	22:49	II	OcD
12	0:58	II	OcR
	11:47	I	ShI
	12:53	I	TrI
	13:57	I	ShE
	15:01	I	TrE
13	8:56	I	EcD
	12:10	I	OcR
	14:47	II	ShI
	16:58	II	TrI
	17:01	II	ShE
	19:06	II	TrE
14	3:33	III	EcD
	5:20	III	EcR
	6:16	I	ShI
	7:20	I	TrI
	8:12	III	OcD
	8:25	I	ShE
	9:23	III	OcR
	9:28	I	TrE
15	3:24	I	EcD
	6:37	I	OcR
	9:49	II	EcD
	14:11	II	OcR
16	0:44	I	ShI
	1:48	I	TrI
	2:54	I	ShE
	3:56	I	TrE
	21:52	I	EcD
17	1:04	I	OcR
	4:03	II	ShI
	6:10	II	TrI
	6:18	II	ShE
	8:18	II	TrE
	17:25	III	ShI
	19:10	III	ShE
	19:12	I	ShI
	20:15	I	TrI
	21:22	I	ShE
	21:54	*III*	*TrI*
	22:23	I	TrE
	23:01	III	TrE
18	16:21	I	EcD
	19:31	I	OcR
	23:07	II	EcD
19	3:23	II	OcR
	13:41	I	ShI
	14:42	I	TrI
	15:50	I	ShE
	16:50	I	TrE
20	10:49	I	EcD
	13:58	I	OcR
	17:20	II	ShI
	19:21	II	TrI
	19:35	II	ShE
	21:30	II	TrE
21	7:30	III	EcD
	8:09	I	ShI
	9:09	I	TrI
	9:17	III	EcR
	10:19	I	ShE
	11:17	I	TrE
	11:49	III	OcD
	12:57	III	OcR
22	5:17	I	EcD
	8:25	I	OcR
	12:24	II	EcD
	16:35	II	OcR
23	2:38	I	ShI
	3:36	I	TrI
	4:47	I	ShE
	5:44	I	TrE
	23:45	I	EcD
24	2:51	I	OcR
	6:37	II	ShI
	8:33	II	TrI
	8:52	II	ShE
	10:41	II	TrE
	21:06	I	ShI
	21:22	**III**	**ShI**
	22:02	I	TrI
	23:07	III	ShE
	23:15	I	ShE
25	0:10	I	TrE
	1:29	III	TrI
	2:33	III	TrE
	18:14	I	EcD
	21:18	I	OcR
26	1:42	II	EcD
	5:46	II	OcR
	15:34	I	ShI
	16:29	I	TrI
	17:44	I	ShE
	18:37	I	TrE
27	12:42	I	EcD
	15:45	I	OcR
	19:54	II	ShI
	21:43	II	TrI
	22:09	II	ShE
	23:51	II	TrE
28	10:03	I	ShI
	10:56	I	TrI
	11:29	III	EcD
	12:12	I	ShE
	13:04	I	TrE
	13:16	III	EcR
	15:23	III	OcD
	16:29	III	OcR
29	7:10	I	EcD
	10:11	I	OcR
	14:59	II	EcD
	18:57	II	OcR
30	4:31	I	ShI
	5:23	I	TrI
	6:41	I	ShE
	7:31	I	TrE
31	1:39	I	EcD
	4:38	I	OcR
	9:11	II	ShI
	10:53	II	TrI
	11:26	II	ShE
	13:01	II	TrE
	22:59	I	ShI
	23:49	I	TrI

APRIL

Day	Time	Sat	Phen
1	1:09	I	ShE
	1:19	III	ShI
	1:57	I	TrE
	3:04	III	ShE
	4:59	III	TrI
	6:02	III	TrE
	20:07	I	EcD
	23:05	I	OcR
2	4:17	II	EcD
	8:07	II	OcR
	17:28	I	ShI
	18:16	I	TrI

I = Io II = Europa III = Ganymede IV = Callisto

SATELLITES OF JUPITER, UT OF 2018 GEOCENTRIC PHENOMENA (cont.)

APRIL (cont.)

Date	Time	Sat	Phen
2	19:37	I	ShE
	20:24	I	TrE
3	14:35	I	EcD
	17:31	I	OcR
	22:27	II	ShI
4	0:03	II	TrI
	0:43	II	ShE
	2:11	II	TrE
	11:56	I	ShI
	12:42	I	TrI
	14:06	I	ShE
	14:50	I	TrE
	15:26	III	EcD
	17:13	III	EcR
	18:51	III	OcD
	19:56	III	OcR
5	9:04	I	EcD
	11:57	I	OcR
	17:35	II	EcD
	21:16	II	OcR
6	6:24	I	ShI
	7:09	I	TrI
	8:34	I	ShE
	9:17	I	TrE
7	3:32	I	EcD
	6:24	I	OcR
	11:44	II	ShI
	13:12	II	TrI
	14:00	II	ShE
	15:20	II	TrE
8	0:53	I	ShI
	1:35	I	TrI
	3:03	I	ShE
	3:43	I	TrE
	5:17	III	ShI
	7:02	III	ShE
	8:25	III	TrI
	9:27	III	TrE
	22:00	I	EcD
9	0:50	I	OcR
	6:52	II	EcD
	10:26	II	OcR
	19:21	I	ShI
	20:01	I	TrI
	21:31	I	ShE
	22:09	I	TrE
10	16:29	I	EcD
	19:16	I	OcR
11	1:01	II	ShI
	2:21	II	TrI
	3:17	II	ShE
	4:29	II	TrE
	13:49	I	ShI
	14:28	I	TrI
	15:59	I	ShE
	16:36	I	TrE
	19:24	III	EcD
	21:11	III	EcR
	22:15	III	OcD
	23:20	III	OcR
12	10:57	I	EcD
	13:43	I	OcR
	20:10	II	EcD
	23:35	II	OcR
13	8:18	I	ShI
	8:54	I	TrI
	10:28	I	ShE
	11:02	I	TrE
14	5:25	I	EcD
	8:09	I	OcR
	14:19	II	ShI
	15:29	II	TrI
	16:34	II	ShE
	17:37	II	TrE
15	2:46	I	ShI
	3:20	I	TrI
	4:56	I	ShE
	5:28	I	TrE
	9:14	III	ShI
	10:59	III	ShE
	23:54	I	EcD
16	2:35	I	OcR
	9:28	II	EcD
	12:43	II	OcR
	21:15	I	ShI
	21:46	I	TrI
	23:25	I	ShE
	23:54	I	TrE
17	18:22	I	EcD
	21:01	I	OcR
18	3:36	II	ShI
	4:37	II	TrI
	5:51	II	ShE
	6:45	II	TrE
	15:43	I	ShI
	16:12	I	TrI
	17:53	I	ShE
	18:20	I	TrE
	23:22	III	EcD
19	1:08	III	EcR
	1:35	III	OcD
	2:41	III	OcR
	12:51	I	EcD
	15:27	I	OcR
	22:45	II	EcD
20	1:51	II	OcR
	10:12	I	ShI
	10:38	I	TrI
	12:21	I	ShE
	12:47	I	TrE
21	7:19	I	EcD
	9:53	I	OcR
	16:53	II	ShI
	17:45	II	TrI
	19:09	II	ShE
	19:54	II	TrE
22	4:40	I	ShI
	5:04	I	TrI
	6:50	I	ShE
	7:13	I	TrE
	13:13	III	ShI
	14:58	III	ShE
	15:07	III	TrI
	16:11	III	TrE
23	1:48	I	EcD
	4:19	I	OcR
	12:03	II	EcD
	14:59	II	OcR
	23:08	I	ShI
	23:30	I	TrI
24	1:18	I	ShE
	1:39	I	TrE
	20:16	I	EcD
	22:45	I	OcR
25	6:10	II	ShI
	6:53	II	TrI
	8:26	II	ShE
	9:01	II	TrE
	17:37	I	ShI
	17:56	I	TrI
	19:47	I	ShE
	20:05	I	TrE
26	3:19	III	EcD
	6:00	III	OcR
	14:44	I	EcD
	17:11	I	OcR
27	1:20	II	EcD
	4:07	II	OcR
	12:05	I	ShI
	12:22	I	TrI
	14:15	I	ShE
	14:31	I	TrE
28	9:13	I	EcD
	11:37	I	OcR
	19:28	II	ShI
	20:00	II	TrI
	21:43	II	ShE
	22:09	II	TrE
29	6:34	I	ShI
	6:48	I	TrI
	8:44	I	ShE
	8:57	I	TrE
	17:11	III	ShI
	18:24	III	TrI
	18:56	III	ShE
	19:30	III	TrE
30	3:41	I	EcD
	6:03	I	OcR
	14:38	II	EcD
	17:14	II	OcR

MAY

Date	Time	Sat	Phen
1	1:02	I	ShI
	1:14	I	TrI
	3:12	I	ShE
	3:23	I	TrE
	22:10	I	EcD
2	0:29	I	OcR
	8:45	II	ShI
	9:08	II	TrI
	11:01	II	ShE
	11:16	II	TrE
	19:31	I	ShI
	19:40	I	TrI
	21:41	I	ShE
	21:49	I	TrE
3	7:17	III	EcD
	9:18	III	OcR
	16:38	I	EcD
	18:55	I	OcR
4	3:55	II	EcD
	6:22	II	OcR
	13:59	I	ShI
	14:06	I	TrI
	16:09	I	ShE
	16:15	I	TrE
5	11:07	I	EcD
	13:21	I	OcR
	22:03	II	ShI
	22:15	II	TrI
6	0:19	II	ShE
	0:24	II	TrE
	8:28	I	ShI
	8:32	I	TrI
	10:38	I	ShE
	10:41	I	TrE
	21:09	III	ShI
	21:39	III	TrI
	22:49	III	TrE
	22:53	III	ShE
7	5:35	I	EcD
	7:47	I	OcR
	17:13	II	EcD
	19:29	II	OcR
8	2:56	I	ShI
	2:58	I	TrI
	5:06	I	ShE
	5:07	I	TrE
9	0:04	I	EcD
	2:14	I	EcR
	11:20	II	ShI
	11:22	II	TrI
	13:31	II	TrE
	13:36	II	ShE
	21:24	I	TrI
	21:25	I	ShI
	23:32	I	TrE
	23:35	I	ShE
10	11:16	III	EcD
	13:01	III	EcR
	18:30	I	OcD
	20:42	I	EcR
11	6:26	II	OcD
	8:46	II	EcR
	15:50	I	TrI
	15:53	I	ShI
	17:58	I	TrE
	18:03	I	ShE
12	12:56	I	OcD
	15:11	I	EcR
13	0:29	II	TrI
	0:38	II	ShI
	2:39	II	TrE
	2:54	II	ShE
	10:16	I	TrI
	10:22	I	ShI
	12:24	I	TrE
	12:32	I	ShE
14	0:53	III	TrI
	1:07	III	ShI
	2:07	III	TrE
	2:52	III	ShE
	7:22	I	OcD
	9:40	I	EcR
	19:34	II	OcD
	22:04	II	EcR
15	4:42	I	TrI
	4:50	I	ShI
	6:50	I	TrE
	7:00	I	ShE
16	1:48	I	OcD
	4:08	I	EcR
	13:37	II	TrI
	13:56	II	ShI
	15:47	II	TrE
	16:12	II	ShE
	23:08	I	TrI
	23:19	I	ShI
17	1:16	I	TrE
	1:29	I	ShE
	14:38	III	OcD
	17:00	III	EcR
	20:14	I	OcD
	22:37	I	EcR
18	8:41	II	OcD
	11:21	II	EcR
	17:34	I	TrI
	17:47	I	ShI
	19:42	I	TrE
	19:57	I	ShE
19	14:40	I	OcD
	17:05	I	EcR
20	2:44	II	TrI
	3:14	II	ShI
	4:55	II	TrE
	5:30	II	ShE
	12:00	I	TrI
	12:16	I	ShI
	14:08	I	TrE
	14:26	I	ShE
21	4:07	III	TrI
	5:05	III	ShI
	5:26	III	TrE
	6:50	III	ShE
	9:06	I	OcD
	11:34	I	EcR
	21:48	II	OcD
22	0:39	II	EcR
	6:26	I	TrI
	6:44	I	ShI
	8:35	I	TrE
	8:54	I	ShE
23	3:32	I	OcD
	6:03	I	EcR

I = Io II = Europa III = Ganymede IV = Callisto

SATELLITES OF JUPITER, UT OF 2018 GEOCENTRIC PHENOMENA (cont.)

MAY (cont.)

Day	Time	Sat	Phen
23	15:52	II	TrI
	16:32	II	ShI
	18:03	II	TrE
	18:47	II	ShE
24	0:52	I	TrI
	1:13	I	ShI
	3:01	I	TrE
	3:23	I	ShE
	17:54	III	OcD
	20:59	III	EcR
	21:59	I	OcD
25	0:31	I	EcR
	10:56	II	OcD
	13:56	II	EcR
	19:18	I	TrI
	19:42	I	ShI
	21:27	I	TrE
	21:51	I	ShE
26	16:25	I	OcD
	19:00	I	EcR
27	5:00	II	TrI
	5:50	II	ShI
	7:11	II	TrE
	8:06	II	ShE
	13:44	I	TrI
	14:10	I	ShI
	15:53	I	TrE
	16:20	I	ShE
28	7:23	III	TrI
	8:47	III	TrE
	9:04	III	ShI
	10:48	III	ShE
	10:51	I	OcD
	13:28	I	EcR
29	0:03	II	OcD
	3:14	II	EcR
	8:11	I	TrI
	8:39	I	ShI
	10:19	I	TrE
	10:48	I	ShE
30	5:17	I	OcD
	7:57	I	EcR
	18:08	II	TrI
	19:08	II	ShI
	20:20	II	TrE
	21:24	II	ShE
31	2:37	I	TrI
	3:07	I	ShI
	4:46	I	TrE
	5:17	I	ShE
	21:11	III	OcD
	22:39	III	OcR
	23:12	III	EcD
	23:44	I	OcD

JUNE

Day	Time	Sat	Phen
1	0:58	III	EcR
	2:26	I	EcR
	13:11	II	OcD
	16:31	II	EcR

Day	Time	Sat	Phen
1	21:03	I	TrI
	21:36	I	ShI
	23:12	I	TrE
	23:45	I	ShE
2	18:10	I	OcD
	20:54	I	EcR
3	7:17	II	TrI
	8:26	II	ShI
	9:29	II	TrE
	10:42	II	ShE
	15:30	I	TrI
	16:04	I	ShI
	17:38	I	TrE
	18:14	I	ShE
4	10:42	III	TrI
	12:11	III	TrE
	12:36	I	OcD
	13:02	III	ShI
	14:46	III	ShE
	15:23	I	EcR
5	2:20	II	OcD
	5:49	II	EcR
	9:56	I	TrI
	10:33	I	ShI
	12:05	I	TrE
	12:42	I	ShE
6	7:03	I	OcD
	9:52	I	EcR
	20:26	II	TrI
	21:44	II	ShI
	22:38	II	TrE
7	0:00	II	ShE
	4:22	I	TrI
	5:02	I	ShI
	6:31	I	TrE
	7:11	I	ShE
8	1:29	I	OcD
	3:11	III	EcD
	4:20	I	EcR
	4:56	III	EcR
	15:29	II	OcD
	19:06	II	EcR
	22:49	I	TrI
	23:30	I	ShI
9	0:58	I	TrE
	1:40	I	ShE
	19:56	I	OcD
	22:49	I	EcR
10	9:36	II	TrI
	11:03	II	ShI
	11:49	II	TrE
	13:18	II	ShE
	17:16	I	TrI
	17:59	I	ShI
	19:24	I	TrE
	20:08	I	ShE
11	14:05	III	TrI
	14:22	I	OcD
	15:38	III	TrE
	17:02	III	ShI
	17:18	I	EcR
	18:46	III	ShE

Day	Time	Sat	Phen
12	4:38	II	OcD
	8:23	II	EcR
	11:42	I	TrI
	12:27	I	ShI
	13:51	I	TrE
	14:37	I	ShE
13	8:49	I	OcD
	11:46	I	EcR
	22:46	II	TrI
14	0:21	II	ShI
	0:59	II	TrE
	2:36	II	ShE
	6:09	I	TrI
	6:56	I	ShI
	8:18	I	TrE
	9:05	I	ShE
15	3:16	I	OcD
	3:55	III	OcD
	5:32	III	OcR
	6:15	I	EcR
	7:09	III	EcD
	8:55	III	EcR
	17:47	II	OcD
	21:41	II	EcR
16	0:36	I	TrI
	1:25	I	ShI
	2:44	I	TrE
	3:34	I	ShE
	21:43	I	OcD
17	0:44	I	EcR
	11:56	II	TrI
	13:39	II	ShI
	14:10	II	TrE
	15:55	II	ShE
	19:02	I	TrI
	19:53	I	ShI
	21:11	I	TrE
	22:02	I	ShE
18	16:10	I	OcD
	17:31	III	TrI
	19:09	III	TrE
	19:13	I	EcR
	21:00	III	ShI
	22:45	III	ShE
19	6:57	II	OcD
	10:58	II	EcR
	13:29	I	TrI
	14:22	I	ShI
	15:38	I	TrE
	16:31	I	ShE
20	10:36	I	OcD
	13:41	I	EcR
21	1:07	II	TrI
	2:58	II	ShI
	3:21	II	TrE
	5:13	II	ShE
	7:56	I	TrI
	8:50	I	ShI
	10:05	I	TrE
	11:00	I	ShE
22	5:03	I	OcD
	7:22	III	OcD

Day	Time	Sat	Phen
22	8:10	I	EcR
	9:04	III	OcR
	11:08	III	EcD
	12:54	III	EcR
	20:08	II	OcD
23	0:16	II	EcR
	2:23	I	TrI
	3:19	I	ShI
	4:32	I	TrE
	5:28	I	ShE
	23:31	I	OcD
24	2:39	I	EcR
	14:19	II	TrI
	16:16	II	ShI
	16:34	II	TrE
	18:32	II	ShE
	20:50	I	TrI
	21:48	I	ShI
	22:59	I	TrE
	23:57	I	ShE
25	17:58	I	OcD
	21:01	III	TrI
	21:08	I	EcR
	22:43	III	TrE
26	0:59	III	ShI
	2:43	III	ShE
	9:19	II	OcD
	13:33	II	EcR
	15:18	I	TrI
	16:16	I	ShI
	17:26	I	TrE
	18:25	I	ShE
27	12:25	I	OcD
	15:36	I	EcR
28	3:31	II	TrI
	5:35	II	ShI
	5:46	II	TrE
	7:50	II	ShE
	9:45	I	TrI
	10:45	I	ShI
	11:54	I	TrE
	12:54	I	ShE
29	6:52	I	OcD
	10:05	I	EcR
	10:55	III	OcD
	12:41	III	OcR
	15:07	III	EcD
	16:53	III	EcR
	22:31	II	OcD
30	2:51	II	EcR
	4:12	I	TrI
	5:14	I	ShI
	6:21	I	TrE
	7:23	I	ShE

JULY

Day	Time	Sat	Phen
1	1:20	I	OcD
	4:34	I	EcR
	16:44	II	TrI
	18:54	II	ShI
	18:59	II	TrE
	21:09	II	ShE

Day	Time	Sat	Phen
1	22:39	I	TrI
	23:42	I	ShI
2	0:48	I	TrE
	1:51	I	ShE
	19:47	I	OcD
	23:03	I	EcR
3	0:35	III	TrI
	2:21	III	TrE
	4:58	III	ShI
	6:42	III	ShE
	11:43	II	OcD
	16:08	II	EcR
	17:07	I	TrI
	18:11	I	ShI
	19:16	I	TrE
	20:20	I	ShE
4	14:15	I	OcD
	17:32	I	EcR
5	5:57	II	TrI
	8:12	II	ShI
	8:13	II	TrE
	10:27	II	ShE
	11:34	I	TrI
	12:40	I	ShI
	13:43	I	TrE
	14:48	I	ShE
6	8:42	I	OcD
	12:00	I	EcR
	14:32	III	OcD
	16:22	III	OcR
	19:07	III	EcD
	20:53	III	EcR
7	0:55	II	OcD
	5:26	II	EcR
	6:02	I	TrI
	7:08	I	ShI
	8:11	I	TrE
	9:17	I	ShE
8	3:10	I	OcD
	6:29	I	EcR
	19:11	II	TrI
	21:27	II	ShI
	21:31	II	TrE
	23:46	II	ShE
9	0:29	I	TrI
	1:37	I	ShI
	2:38	I	TrE
	3:46	I	ShE
	21:38	I	OcD
10	0:58	I	EcR
	4:13	III	TrI
	6:03	III	TrE
	8:56	III	ShI
	10:40	III	ShE
	14:09	II	OcD
	16:25	II	OcR
	16:27	II	EcD
	18:43	II	EcR
	18:57	I	TrI
	20:06	I	ShI
	21:06	I	TrE
	22:14	I	ShE

I = Io II = Europa III = Ganymede IV = Callisto

SATELLITES OF JUPITER, UT OF 2018 GEOCENTRIC PHENOMENA (cont.)

JULY (cont.)

Day	Time	Sat	Phen
11	16:05	I	OcD
	19:27	I	EcR
12	8:26	II	TrI
	10:42	II	TrE
	10:49	II	ShI
	13:04	II	ShE
	13:25	I	TrI
	14:34	I	ShI
	15:34	I	TrE
	16:43	I	ShE
13	10:33	I	OcD
	13:56	I	EcR
	18:14	III	OcD
	20:07	III	OcR
	23:07	III	EcD
14	0:53	III	EcR
	3:22	II	OcD
	5:39	II	OcR
	5:44	II	EcD
	7:53	I	TrI
	8:00	II	EcR
	9:03	I	ShI
	10:02	I	TrE
	11:12	I	ShE
15	5:01	I	OcD
	8:24	I	EcR
	21:41	II	TrI
	23:58	II	TrE
16	0:08	II	ShI
	2:21	I	TrI
	2:23	II	ShE
	3:32	I	ShI
	4:29	I	TrE
	5:40	I	ShE
	23:29	I	OcD
17	2:53	I	EcR
	7:57	III	TrI
	9:50	III	TrE
	12:55	III	ShI
	14:40	III	ShE
	16:36	II	OcD
	18:54	II	OcR
	19:02	II	EcD
	20:49	II	TrI
	21:18	II	EcR
	22:00	I	ShI
	22:57	I	TrE
18	0:09	I	ShE
	17:57	I	OcD
	21:22	I	EcR
19	10:56	II	TrI
	13:13	II	TrE
	13:27	II	ShI
	15:17	II	TrI
	15:42	II	ShE
	16:29	I	ShI
	17:25	I	TrE
	18:37	I	ShE
20	12:25	I	OcD
	15:51	I	EcR

Day	Time	Sat	Phen
20	22:00	III	OcD
	23:56	III	OcR
21	3:06	III	EcD
	4:52	III	EcR
	5:51	II	OcD
	8:09	II	OcR
	8:19	II	EcD
	9:45	I	TrI
	10:35	II	EcR
	10:58	I	ShI
	11:54	I	TrE
	13:06	I	ShE
22	6:54	I	OcD
	10:20	I	EcR
23	0:13	II	TrI
	2:30	II	TrE
	2:46	II	ShI
	4:13	I	TrI
	5:01	II	ShE
	5:26	I	ShI
	6:22	I	TrE
	7:35	I	ShE
24	1:22	I	OcD
	4:49	I	EcR
	11:45	III	TrI
	13:40	III	TrE
	16:54	III	ShI
	18:39	III	ShE
	19:07	II	OcD
	21:25	II	OcR
	21:36	II	EcD
	22:41	I	TrI
	23:52	II	EcR
	23:55	I	ShI
25	0:50	I	TrE
	2:03	I	ShE
	19:50	I	OcD
	23:17	I	EcR
26	13:29	II	TrI
	15:47	II	TrE
	16:04	II	ShI
	17:09	I	TrI
	18:19	II	ShE
	18:24	I	ShI
	19:18	I	TrE
	20:32	I	ShE
27	14:19	I	OcD
	17:46	I	EcR
28	1:51	III	OcD
	3:49	III	OcR
	7:05	III	EcD
	8:22	II	OcD
	8:51	III	EcR
	10:41	II	OcR
	10:54	II	EcD
	11:38	I	TrI
	12:52	I	ShI
	13:10	II	EcR
	13:47	I	TrE
	15:01	I	ShE
29	8:47	I	OcD
	12:15	I	EcR

Day	Time	Sat	Phen
30	2:47	II	TrI
	5:05	II	TrE
	5:23	II	ShI
	6:06	I	TrI
	7:21	**I**	**ShI**
	7:39	II	ShE
	8:15	I	TrE
	9:29	I	ShE
31	3:16	I	OcD
	6:44	I	EcR
	15:39	III	TrI
	17:36	III	TrE
	20:54	III	ShI
	21:39	II	OcD
	22:39	III	ShE
	23:57	II	OcR

AUGUST

Day	Time	Sat	Phen
1	0:11	II	EcD
	0:34	I	TrI
	1:50	I	ShI
	2:27	II	EcR
	2:44	I	TrE
	3:58	I	ShE
	21:44	I	OcD
2	1:13	I	EcR
	16:05	II	TrI
	18:23	II	TrE
	18:42	II	ShI
	19:03	I	TrI
	20:18	**I**	**ShI**
	20:57	II	ShE
	21:12	I	TrE
	22:27	I	ShE
3	16:13	I	OcD
	19:42	I	EcR
4	5:45	III	OcD
	7:46	III	OcR
	10:55	II	OcD
	11:04	III	EcD
	12:51	II	EcR
	13:14	III	OcR
	13:29	II	EcD
	13:32	I	TrI
	14:47	I	ShI
	15:41	I	TrE
	15:45	II	EcR
	16:55	I	ShE
5	10:42	I	OcD
	14:10	I	EcR
6	5:23	II	TrI
	7:42	II	TrE
	8:00	I	TrI
	8:01	II	ShI
	9:16	**I**	**ShI**
	10:09	I	TrE
	10:16	II	ShE
	11:24	I	ShE
7	5:11	I	OcD
	8:39	I	EcR
	19:36	III	TrI
	21:35	III	TrE

Day	Time	Sat	Phen
8	0:13	II	OcD
	0:53	III	ShI
	2:29	I	TrI
	2:32	II	OcR
	2:38	III	ShE
	2:46	II	EcD
	3:44	I	ShI
	4:38	I	TrE
	5:02	II	EcR
	5:53	I	ShE
	23:40	I	OcD
9	3:08	I	EcR
	18:42	III	TrI
	20:58	*I*	*TrI*
	21:00	II	TrE
	21:19	II	ShI
	22:13	**I**	**ShI**
	23:07	I	TrE
	23:35	I	ShE
10	0:21	I	ShE
	18:09	I	OcD
	21:37	I	EcR
11	9:45	III	OcD
	11:47	III	OcR
	13:30	II	OcD
	15:03	III	EcD
	15:26	I	TrI
	15:49	II	OcR
	16:03	II	EcD
	16:42	I	ShI
	16:50	III	EcR
	17:36	I	TrE
	18:19	II	EcR
	18:50	I	ShE
12	12:37	I	OcD
	16:06	I	EcR
13	8:02	II	TrI
	9:55	*I*	*TrI*
	10:20	II	TrE
	10:39	II	ShI
	11:10	**I**	**ShI**
	12:04	I	TrE
	12:54	II	ShE
	13:19	I	ShE
14	7:07	I	OcD
	10:35	I	EcR
	23:37	III	TrI
15	1:38	III	TrE
	2:48	II	OcD
	4:24	I	TrI
	4:52	III	ShI
	5:08	II	OcR
	5:20	II	EcD
	5:39	**I**	**ShI**
	6:33	I	TrE
	6:37	III	ShE
	7:37	II	EcR
	7:48	I	ShE
16	1:36	I	OcD
	5:03	I	EcR
	21:21	II	TrI
	22:53	*I*	*TrI*
	23:40	II	TrE
	23:57	II	ShI

Day	Time	Sat	Phen
17	**0:08**	**I**	**ShI**
	1:02	I	TrE
	2:13	II	ShE
	2:16	I	ShE
	20:05	I	OcD
	23:32	I	EcR
18	13:48	III	OcD
	15:51	III	OcR
	16:07	II	OcD
	17:22	I	TrI
	18:26	II	OcR
	18:36	I	ShI
	18:38	II	EcD
	19:03	III	EcD
	19:31	I	TrE
	20:45	I	ShE
	20:50	III	EcR
	20:54	II	EcR
19	14:34	I	OcD
	18:01	I	EcR
20	10:42	II	TrI
	11:51	*I*	*TrI*
	13:01	II	TrE
	13:05	II	ShI
	13:16	**II**	**ShI**
	14:01	I	TrE
	15:14	I	ShE
	15:32	II	ShE
21	9:03	I	OcD
	12:30	I	EcR
22	3:41	III	TrI
	5:26	II	OcD
	5:43	III	TrE
	6:20	I	TrI
	7:34	I	ShI
	7:46	II	OcR
	7:55	II	EcD
	8:30	I	TrE
	8:50	**III**	**ShI**
	9:42	I	ShE
	10:11	II	EcR
	10:36	III	ShE
23	3:33	I	OcD
	6:59	I	EcR
24	0:02	II	TrI
	0:49	*I*	*TrI*
	2:02	I	ShI
	2:22	II	TrE
	2:35	**II**	**ShI**
	2:59	I	TrE
	4:11	I	ShE
	4:50	II	ShE
	22:02	I	OcD
25	1:28	I	EcR
	17:56	III	OcD
	18:45	II	OcD
	19:19	I	TrI
	20:00	III	OcR
	20:31	I	ShI
	21:05	II	OcR
	21:12	II	EcD
	21:28	I	TrE
	22:40	I	ShE

I = Io II = Europa III = Ganymede IV = Callisto

SATELLITES OF JUPITER, UT OF 2018 GEOCENTRIC PHENOMENA (cont.)

AUGUST (cont.)

Date	Time	Sat	Event
25	23:03	III	EcD
	23:29	II	EcR
26	0:51	III	EcR
	16:31	I	OcD
	19:56	I	EcR
27	13:24	II	TrI
	13:48	*I*	*TrI*
	15:00	I	ShI
	15:43	II	TrE
	15:54	**II**	**ShI**
	15:57	I	TrE
	17:08	I	ShE
	18:10	II	ShE
28	11:01	I	OcD
	14:25	I	EcR
29	7:49	III	TrI
	8:05	II	OcD
	8:17	*I*	*TrI*
	9:28	I	ShI
	9:52	III	TrE
	10:25	II	OcR
	10:27	I	TrE
	10:30	II	EcD
	11:37	I	ShE
	12:46	II	EcR
	12:49	III	ShI
	14:35	III	ShE
30	5:30	I	OcD
	8:54	I	EcR
31	2:45	II	TrI
	2:47	*I*	*TrI*
	3:57	I	ShI
	4:56	I	TrE
	5:05	II	TrE
	5:12	**II**	**ShI**
	6:06	I	ShE
	7:28	II	ShE

SEPTEMBER

Date	Time	Sat	Event
1	0:00	I	OcD
	3:23	I	EcR
	21:16	I	TrI
	21:25	II	OcD
	22:06	III	OcD
	22:26	I	ShI
	23:25	I	TrE
	23:45	II	OcR
	23:47	II	EcD
2	0:12	III	OcR
	0:34	I	ShE
	2:03	II	EcR
	3:02	III	EcD
	4:50	III	EcR
	18:29	I	OcD
	21:52	I	EcR
3	15:45	I	TrI
	16:07	*II*	*TrI*
	16:54	I	ShI
	17:55	I	TrE
3	18:27	II	TrE
	18:31	**II**	**ShI**
	19:03	I	ShE
	20:48	II	ShE
4	12:59	I	OcD
	16:21	I	EcR
5	10:15	I	TrI
	10:46	II	OcD
	11:23	I	ShI
	12:00	*III*	*TrI*
	12:24	I	TrE
	13:32	II	ShE
	14:04	III	TrE
	15:21	II	EcR
	16:48	III	ShI
	18:35	III	ShE
6	7:29	I	OcD
	10:49	I	EcR
7	4:44	I	TrI
	5:29	*II*	*TrI*
	5:52	I	ShI
	6:54	I	TrE
	7:49	II	TrI
	7:50	**II**	**ShI**
	8:00	II	ShE
	10:06	II	ShE
8	1:59	I	OcD
	5:18	I	EcR
	23:14	I	TrI
9	0:06	II	OcD
	0:20	I	ShI
	1:23	I	TrE
	2:19	III	OcD
	2:29	I	ShE
	4:26	III	OcR
	4:38	II	EcR
	7:01	III	EcD
	8:50	III	EcR
	20:28	I	OcD
	23:47	I	EcR
10	17:43	I	TrI
	18:49	I	ShI
	18:52	*II*	*TrI*
	19:53	I	TrE
	20:58	I	ShE
	21:09	II	ShI
	21:12	II	TrE
	23:25	II	ShE
11	14:58	I	OcD
	18:16	I	EcR
12	12:13	I	TrI
	13:18	I	ShI
	13:28	II	OcD
	14:23	I	TrE
	15:26	I	ShE
	16:14	III	TrI
	17:55	II	EcR
	18:19	III	TrE
	20:47	III	ShI
	22:34	III	ShE
13	9:28	I	OcD
	12:45	I	EcR
14	6:43	I	TrI
	7:46	I	ShI
	8:14	*II*	*TrI*
	8:52	I	TrE
	9:55	I	ShE
	10:27	II	ShI
	10:35	II	TrE
	12:44	II	ShE
15	3:58	I	OcD
	7:14	I	EcR
16	1:12	I	TrI
	2:15	I	ShI
	2:49	II	OcD
	3:22	I	TrE
	4:24	I	ShE
	6:35	III	OcD
	7:13	II	EcR
	8:42	III	OcR
	11:00	III	EcD
	12:49	III	EcR
	22:28	I	OcD
17	1:42	I	EcR
	19:42	I	TrI
	20:43	I	ShI
	21:38	*II*	*TrI*
	21:52	I	TrE
	22:52	I	ShE
	23:46	II	ShI
	23:58	II	TrE
18	2:03	II	ShE
	16:58	I	OcD
	20:11	I	EcR
19	14:12	I	TrI
	15:12	I	ShI
	16:11	I	OcD
	16:22	I	TrE
	17:21	I	ShE
	20:30	II	EcR
	20:32	III	TrI
	22:37	III	TrE
20	0:46	III	ShI
	2:34	III	ShE
	11:28	I	OcD
	14:40	I	EcR
21	8:41	I	TrI
	9:41	I	ShI
	10:51	I	TrE
	11:01	II	TrI
	11:50	I	ShE
	13:05	II	ShI
	13:22	II	TrE
	15:21	II	ShE
22	5:58	I	OcD
	9:09	I	EcR
23	3:11	I	TrI
	4:09	I	ShI
	5:21	I	TrE
	5:33	II	OcD
23	6:18	I	ShE
	9:47	II	EcR
	10:53	III	OcD
	13:00	III	OcR
	14:59	III	EcD
	16:48	III	EcR
24	0:28	I	OcD
	3:37	I	EcR
	21:41	I	TrI
	22:38	I	ShI
	23:51	I	TrE
25	0:25	II	TrI
	0:47	I	ShE
	2:24	II	ShI
	2:46	II	TrE
	4:40	II	ShE
	18:58	I	OcD
	22:06	I	EcR
26	16:11	I	TrI
	17:07	I	ShI
	18:21	I	TrE
	18:55	II	OcD
	19:16	I	ShE
	23:05	II	EcR
27	0:51	III	TrI
	2:56	III	TrE
	4:45	III	ShI
	6:33	III	ShE
	13:28	I	OcD
	16:35	I	EcR
28	10:41	I	TrI
	11:35	I	ShI
	12:51	I	TrE
	13:44	I	ShE
	13:49	II	TrI
	15:42	II	ShI
	16:09	II	TrE
	17:59	II	ShE
29	7:58	I	OcD
	11:04	I	EcR
30	5:11	I	TrI
	6:04	I	ShI
	7:21	I	TrE
	8:13	I	ShE
	8:17	II	OcD
	12:22	II	EcR
	15:14	III	OcD
	17:21	III	OcR
	18:58	III	EcD
	20:48	III	EcR

OCTOBER

Date	Time	Sat	Event
1	2:28	I	OcD
	5:33	I	EcR
	23:41	I	TrI
2	0:32	I	ShI
	1:51	I	TrE
	2:42	I	ShE
	3:13	II	TrI
	5:01	II	ShI
	5:34	II	TrE
2	7:18	II	ShE
	20:58	I	OcD
3	0:01	I	EcR
	18:11	I	TrI
	19:01	I	ShI
	20:21	I	TrE
	21:10	I	ShE
	21:40	II	OcD
4	1:40	II	EcR
	5:12	III	TrI
	7:17	III	TrE
	8:44	III	ShI
	10:33	III	ShE
	15:28	I	OcD
	18:30	I	EcR
5	12:41	I	TrI
	13:30	I	ShI
	14:51	I	TrE
	15:39	I	ShE
	16:37	II	TrI
	18:19	II	ShI
	18:58	II	TrE
	20:36	II	ShE
6	9:59	I	OcD
	12:59	I	EcR
7	7:11	I	TrI
	7:58	I	ShI
	9:21	I	TrE
	10:08	I	ShE
	11:03	II	OcD
	14:57	II	EcR
	19:36	III	OcD
	21:43	III	OcR
	22:57	III	EcD
8	0:48	III	EcR
	4:29	I	OcD
	7:27	I	EcR
9	1:41	I	TrI
	2:27	I	ShI
	3:51	I	TrE
	4:36	I	ShE
	6:02	II	TrI
	7:38	II	ShI
	8:23	II	TrE
	9:55	II	ShE
	22:59	I	OcD
10	1:56	I	EcR
	20:11	I	TrI
	20:55	I	ShI
	22:21	I	TrE
	23:05	I	ShE
11	0:26	II	OcD
	4:14	II	EcR
	9:34	III	TrI
	11:40	III	TrE
	12:42	III	ShI
	14:32	III	ShE
	17:29	I	OcD
	20:25	I	EcR

(too close to Sun)

I = Io   II = Europa   III = Ganymede   IV = Callisto

CONFIGURATIONS OF SATURN'S BRIGHTEST SATELLITES
BY LARRY D. BOGAN

The diagrams on the following three pages give the relative locations of Saturn's five brightest satellites for February through October 2018. Saturn resides in Sagittarius this year, is in opposition with the Sun on Jun. 27, and in conjunction on 2019 Jan. 2. The names and magnitudes of these satellites, in order of increasing distance from Saturn, are Enceladus 11.8, Tethys 10.3, Dione 10.4, Rhea 9.7, and Titan 8.4.

The curves in the diagrams show the elongations of the satellites from Saturn for day 0.0 UT to day 32.0 UT for each month. The dashed curves represent Enceladus and Dione, the first and third out from Saturn. The narrow, central, vertical band represents the disk of Saturn, and the wider band the outer edge of Saturn's A ring.

At the top of each monthly diagram is a scale drawing of Saturn, its rings, and the orbits of four of the five brightest satellites as seen through an inverting telescope (in the Northern Hemisphere). South is up. No orbit is shown for Enceladus, the innermost satellite, because of the small size of the scale drawing. Due to its faintness and proximity to the bright rings, Enceladus is best seen when near a maximum elongation, but even then good seeing, good optics, and an aperture of at least 200 mm are required.

During 2018, we see Saturn and its satellites from north of the ring plane. The apparent ring tilts for 2018 have a minimum of 25.5° in April and a maximum of 26.6° in September. The direction of motion of the satellites, as viewed with a telescope having an even number (0, 2, 4,…) of reflections in its optics, is counterclockwise. An arrow has been placed on the orbit of Titan to indicate all satellite orbit revolution directions.

A particular configuration of the satellites may be determined by drawing a horizontal line across the monthly curves at the time (UT) of interest. The intersection of this line with the curves gives the relative elongations of the satellites. Project these elongations onto the drawing of the orbits at the top of the diagram. The east side of the A ring vertical band has been extended up to the drawing to facilitate transfer of each elongation. A millimetre scale, a pair of dividers, or a strip of paper on which to mark enables one to do this quickly and accurately.

The direction of the orbital motion of a satellite determines on which side of its orbit (north or south) a satellite is located. Note the movement of the satellite along the diagram curves past elongation as it revolves around Saturn to determine whether to put the satellite on the north or south side of the orbit. The February diagram shows an example configuration for Feb. 4 at 9:00 p.m. EST (Feb. 5 at 2h UT).

Greatest Elongations and Conjunctions for Iapetus

The magnitude of Iapetus is comparable to the five plotted satellites, but it varies from 10.2 (western elongation) to 11.9 (eastern elongation). This satellite's orbit is about 2.9 times the size of Titan's and is tilted 15° to Saturn's ring plane; its period is 79.33 days. Iapetus is easiest to find near conjunctions when it is just north or south of Saturn. The table below lists times (UT) of greatest elongations and conjunctions during 2018. Use "east is least and west is best" to remember the brightest elongation.

Eastern Elong.	Inferior Conj.		Western Elong.	Superior Conj.	
			Jan. 23	Jan. 24	09 h
Feb. 13	Mar. 04	09 h	Mar. 25	Apr. 14	19 h
May 04	May 22	20 h	Jun. 12	Jul. 02	08 h
Jul. 21	Aug. 09	01 h	Aug. 29	Sep. 19	02 h
Oct. 08	Oct. 27	18 h	Nov. 17	Dec. 08	18 h

Note: Stellarium *for Mac, Linux, or Windows, a freeware computer program, displays the configuration of Saturn's satellites on your computer. It can be downloaded at* **www.stellarium.org**.

CONFIGURATIONS OF SATURN'S SATELLITES
2018 FEBRUARY–APRIL

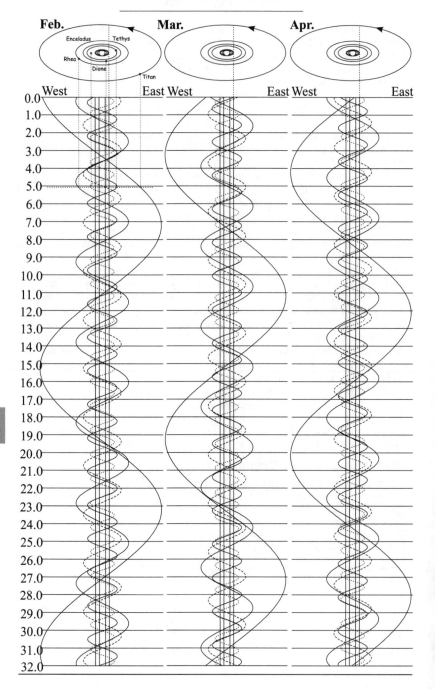

CONFIGURATIONS OF SATURN'S SATELLITES
2018 MAY–JULY

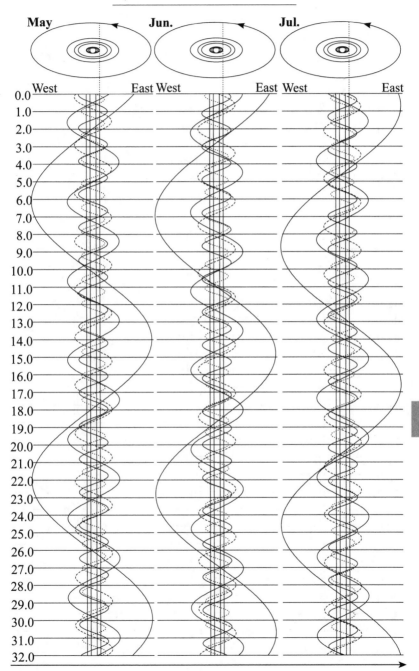

CONFIGURATIONS OF SATURN'S SATELLITES
2018 AUGUST–OCTOBER

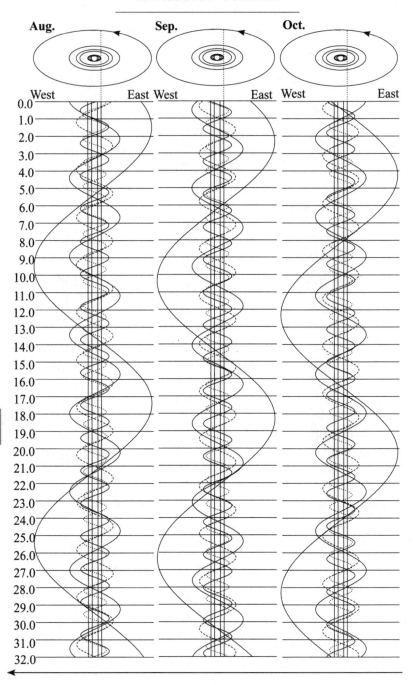

DWARF AND MINOR PLANETS

THE DWARF PLANETS

Classification of Solar System Bodies

The classification of Solar System bodies has been a rough ride on the pathway of astronomical history, and our destination may still be over the scientific horizon. At the start of the 19th century, the known Solar System included the Sun, the Earth and Moon, the classic five naked-eye planets, the "new" planet Uranus, a handful of natural satellites, and some comets. In quick succession, the "planets" 1 Ceres (1801), 2 Pallas (1802), 3 Juno (1804), and 4 Vesta (1807) were discovered between the orbits of Mars and Jupiter. In 1882, by which time many more small bodies had been discovered, these were reclassified as *asteroids*, numbered serially according to their discovery date. (Today, the designation *minor planet* is preferred over *asteroid*.)

Along the way, the planet Neptune (1846) was discovered and eventually Pluto (1930) became accepted as the ninth planet, even though it has a highly inclined and eccentric orbit relative to the other planets, and is smaller than the Moon and several natural satellites of other planets.

By 2006, the rate of discovery of Pluto-like *trans-Neptunian objects* (TNOs) prompted the International Astronomical Union (IAU) to controversially re-classify Pluto as a *dwarf planet*, numbered 134340 Pluto, followed by 1 Ceres; within two years these two were joined by three more TNOs (see below). The details may be found on the IAU webpage **www.iau.org/public/pluto/** and in Mike Brown's informative book *How I Killed Pluto and Why It had it Coming* (Random House, 2012).

Currently, the IAU recognizes three principal planetary categories: (1) planets, (2) dwarf planets, and (3) small Solar System bodies. The **planets** are the traditional eight bodies: Mercury, Venus, Earth, Mars, Jupiter, Saturn, Uranus, and Neptune. The **dwarf planets** are 1 Ceres, 134340 Pluto, 136199 Eris, 136108 Haumea, and 136472 Makemake (with 50000 Quaoar, 90377 Sedna, and 9040 Orcus being strongly considered). In plain terms, planets and dwarf planets are round, but dwarf planets are considered too small to have significant gravitational effect on other bodies (other than their satellites, if they have any). **Small Solar System bodies** are everything else, other than satellites: minor planets in the asteroid belt or elsewhere (including most TNOs), and comets. What distinguishes dwarf planets from minor planets is *roundness*: dwarf planets are round, while minor planets are irregular in shape. Such systems of classification are governed by scientific convention, and are subject to change.

1 CERES

Ceres was the first dwarf planet to be discovered, but it is the smallest, and the brightest, only because its orbit lies within the asteroid belt between Mars and Jupiter, while the others are all beyond Neptune. This close proximity makes Ceres readily observable, even in binoculars (at opposition). In early 2018, Ceres is retrograding in the evening sky in Cancer, eventually halting then prograding in Lynx, hovering at mag. 4.57 throughout the year. By August, the dwarf planet is lost in the Sun's glare. Much later in the year, Ceres appears in the morning sky in Virgo, then Libra (see the finder chart on the next page and the ephemeris on p. 245). In 2015, the *Dawn* spacecraft orbited Ceres and thoroughly mapped the surface, which appears to be largely water ice above a rocky core and possibly a liquid-water ocean. Interestingly, Ceres was found to be emitting water vapour from several locations, which is quite unusual for a rocky body.

FINDER CHART FOR 1 CERES

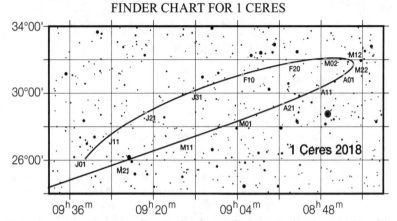

The bright star located near the path at the chart lower left is kappa Leo listed as mag. 4.5 and the bright star at center right is the visual binary iota Cnc at 4th mag. Ceres is plotted as a gray circle of mag. varying from 6.9 to 8.6. The chart limiting magnitude is 9.5 according to the UCAC4. The chart is generated using the open source Generic Mapping Tools (GMT5.1.2) under Mac OS 10.10.5. (chart by Ian Cameron).

134340 PLUTO
BY MURRAY PAULSON

Pluto's mean distance from the sun is 39.3 au, but its highly eccentric orbit currently locates it much closer, about 32.58 au in 2018. At its last perihelion in 1989, Pluto shone at mag. 13.6, a state it will not revisit until the 23rd century. As Pluto moves away from perihelion, it is slowly fading. Clyde Tombaugh discovered Pluto in 1930, when it was 42.3 au distant at mag 15.3. It will be another 38 years before Pluto becomes this faint again. In July of 2015 we looked in wonder at the first close-up views of Pluto's surface from the *New Horizons* spacecraft. Pluto once again basked in the spotlight and showed there were some interesting surprises out at the edge of the Kuiper belt.

Pluto is 2370 km in diameter, only twice that of its largest moon, Charon (1208 km). It has retrograde rotation of period 6.39 days, synchronous with Charon's revolution. Pluto also has four smaller satellites, Nix, Hydra, Kerberos, and Styx, the last discovered in July 2012. These four satellites are all less than 100 km in diameter and dimmer than mag. 23.

The year starts off with Pluto in conjunction with the Sun on Jan. 8. When I first viewed it in 1988, it was in conjunction on Nov. 4. It was also near perihelion and much easier to find at mag. 13.6. This year it is down in the deep south of Sagittarius, about 8° east of the handle of the Teapot. Pluto comes to opposition on Jul. 11 and will shine at mag. 14.4. It will sit just 11′ west of the mag.-5.6 star 50 Sgr. This is the only "bright" star in its neighborhood. It is a tough hunt, looking through all that atmosphere down near the horizon, so a 10″ scope or larger is needed to find distant Pluto, plus you need very good sky conditions. I encourage you to try a smaller aperture for the fun of the chase. The background stars are starting to thin out a bit, making the star hop somewhat more interesting. (Check the finder chart opposite.) Pluto will come to conjunction with the Sun early in the new year.

Now, if finding Pluto isn't enough of a challenge, see if you can spot it in a mid-sized refractor. The observation is possible in a 125–130-mm refractor, but the transparency and seeing must both be very good. One year, I challenged RASC Edmonton Centre member Alister Ling to find it in his 125-mm APO, and I tackled it with my 94-mm Brandon refractor. Pluto was much higher at that time. Alister achieved the observation with relative ease, but the smaller aperture of 94 mm made it a very tough hunt for me. I found it, but with great difficulty, eyestrain, and over an hour of painstaking star hopping. I welcome any comments or stories of your hunt.

FINDER CHART FOR 134340 PLUTO
BY Ian Cameron

This chart uses the astrometric UCAC4 catalog. The UCAC4 lists model fitted photometric magnitudes (579–642 nm). The brighter stars to mag. 9.5, indicated by the dark circles, are from Uranometria 2000 (Vol. 2, Chart 341). The bright star located at chart center is 50 Sgr and is listed as mag. 5.5. The Pluto ephemeris is generated using the JPL Horizons Web-Interface. Pluto is at opposition with mag. 14.20 on Jul. 10. The chart limiting magnitude is 15 according to the UCAC4. The chart is generated using the open source Generic Mapping Tools (GMT5.1.2) under Mac OS 10.10.5..

THE BRIGHTEST MINOR PLANETS

The following two pages contain ephemerides for those minor planets (identified by number and name) that reach mag. 10.1 or brighter during 2018 and are positioned more than 60° from the Sun. The table is ordered by opposition date, shown in the headers, along with the opposition magnitude. In the table, **Mag.** is visual magnitude. The ephemeris for the *dwarf planet* 1 Ceres is included here in keeping with tradition, but more information and a finder chart can be found in the THE DWARF PLANETS, on p. 241. See p. 23 for the current orbital elements of the 25 brightest minor planets (by absolute magnitude) and 3 dwarf planets.

Observers can make their own finder charts by plotting the coordinates on a suitable star atlas with equinox J2000.0. Those with computer planetarium software can obtain orbital elements in several popular electronic formats from the Minor Planet Center (www.minorplanetcenter.net/iau/MPEph/MPEph.html).

FEATURE MINOR PLANET: 15 EUNOMIA

The minor planet 15 Eunomia is by far the largest of all the stony S-type minor planets, and the Eunomian Family comprises the largest group found in the asteroid belt. The minor planet itself is ~300 km through its longest axis, with an average radius of ~250 km. A catastrophic impact that created the group is thought to have shattered a larger body that now makes up the bulk of the "family." Nearly 75% of the original parent body is in 15 Eunomia, leaving a group of much smaller bodies as the remainder. It is thought that some of these smaller bodies may have existed before the large impact, based on spectra of the smaller bodies and Eunomia itself. The collision creating the family was likely by a smaller body some 50 km in diameter, with a closing speed of ~22 000 km/h.

The bright star located near the path at chart center is 58 Hya listed at mag. 4.4. Eunomia is plotted as a gray circle of magnitude varying from 11.3 to 9.8. The chart limiting magnitude is 11.5 according to the UCAC4. The chart is generated using the open-source Generic Mapping Tools (GMT5.1.2) under Mac OS 10.10.5. (Chart by Ian Cameron.)

EPHEMERIDES FOR THE BRIGHTEST MINOR PLANETS IN 2018
BY DANIEL W.E. GREEN

Date 0h TT	RA (2000) h m	Dec ° '	Mag.	Date 0h TT	RA (2000) h m	Dec ° '	Mag.
2 Pallas	*2017 Oct. 29, mag. 8.2*			**1 Ceres* (continued)**			
Jan. 1	2 33.98	−25 52.8	8.7	Apr. 21	8 55.22	+29 22.2	8.3
11	2 37.49	−24 16.2	8.8	May 1	9 04.27	+28 17.8	8.4
21	2 43.56	−22 25.3	8.8	11	9 14.95	+27 06.2	8.5
31	2 51.95	−20 25.2	8.9	21	9 26.95	+25 48.0	8.6
Feb. 10	3 02.38	−18 19.4	9.0	31	9 39.98	+24 23.7	8.7
20	3 14.62	−16 11.1	9.0	Jun. 10	9 53.80	+22 53.8	8.7
Mar. 2	3 28.46	−14 02.8	9.0	**51 Nemausa**		*Feb. 25, mag 9.8*	
12	3 43.70	−11 56.7	9.1	Feb. 20	10 31.35	+02 23.6	10.0
	(Too close to the Sun)			Mar. 2	10 22.95	+04 09.7	9.9
Dec. 7	12 44.74	−06 37.5	9.1	**15 Eunomia**		*May 8, mag. 9.8*	
17	13 00.53	−06 35.2	9.0	Apr. 21	14 56.47	−33 12.0	10.0
27	13 15.35	−06 16.4	9.0	May 1	14 47.12	−32 41.6	9.8
7 Iris	*2017 Oct. 30, mag. 6.9*			11	14 37.41	−31 53.8	9.8
Jan. 1	2 08.84	+15 25.6	8.5	21	14 28.35	−30 52.5	9.8
11	2 20.86	+15 39.6	8.8	31	14 20.81	−29 43.8	10.0
21	2 35.08	+16 07.8	9.0	**9 Metis**		*Jun. 16, mag. 9.7*	
31	2 51.13	+16 45.8	9.2	Jun. 10	17 46.70	−25 43.8	9.8
Feb. 10	3 08.66	+17 29.5	9.3	20	17 35.81	−25 58.7	9.7
20	3 27.42	+18 15.3	9.5	30	17 25.25	−26 08.1	10.0
Mar. 2	3 47.20	+19 00.1	9.6	**4 Vesta**		*Jun. 19, mag. 5.3*	
12	4 07.79	+19 41.2	9.7	Jan. 31	16 24.97	−15 58.0	7.7
22	4 29.02	+20 16.3	9.9	Feb. 10	16 43.19	−16 32.5	7.6
Apr. 1	4 50.74	+20 43.6	10.0	20	17 00.64	−16 57.9	7.5
20 Massalia	*2017 Dec. 17, mag. 8.4*			Mar. 2	17 17.09	−17 14.9	7.4
Jan. 1	5 26.74	+22 01.7	8.8	12	17 32.30	−17 24.9	7.3
11	5 19.14	+21 55.8	9.1	22	17 45.98	−17 29.3	7.2
21	5 14.94	+21 53.7	9.3	Apr. 1	17 57.80	−17 30.1	7.0
31	5 14.60	+21 56.4	9.6	11	18 07.43	−17 29.6	6.9
Feb. 10	5 18.01	+22 03.4	9.8	21	18 14.47	−17 30.3	6.7
20	5 24.87	+22 13.4	10.0	May 1	18 18.54	−17 35.0	6.5
8 Flora		*Jan. 2, mag 8.2*		11	18 19.35	−17 45.9	6.2
Jan. 1	6 53.78	+20 57.6	8.2	21	18 16.73	−18 04.8	6.0
11	6 42.36	+21 54.2	8.5	31	18 10.87	−18 32.4	5.8
21	6 32.67	+22 45.0	8.8	Jun. 10	18 02.37	−19 07.5	5.5
31	6 26.17	+23 27.9	9.1	20	17 52.35	−19 48.0	5.3
Feb. 10	6 23.50	+24 02.7	9.4	30	17 42.30	−20 31.1	5.6
20	6 24.72	+24 29.8	9.7	Jul. 10	17 33.68	−21 14.6	5.8
Mar. 2	6 29.53	+24 49.7	10.0	20	17 27.64	−21 57.2	6.0
1 Ceres*		*Feb. 1, mag. 6.9*		30	17 24.89	−22 38.3	6.3
Jan. 1	9 32.99	+26 05.9	7.4	Aug. 9	17 25.60	−23 17.5	6.5
11	9 28.52	+27 26.6	7.2	19	17 29.66	−23 54.3	6.7
21	9 21.44	+28 49.7	7.0	29	17 36.78	−24 27.8	6.9
31	9 12.55	+30 06.1	6.9	Sep. 8	17 46.56	−24 56.8	7.1
Feb. 10	9 03.01	+31 07.3	7.0	18	17 58.64	−25 20.0	7.3
20	8 54.16	+31 47.6	7.2	28	18 12.66	−25 36.3	7.4
Mar. 2	8 47.21	+32 05.3	7.4	8	18 28.28	−25 44.4	7.5
12	8 42.95	+32 02.0	7.6	Oct. 18	18 45.22	−25 43.5	7.6
22	8 41.75	+31 40.9	7.8	28	19 03.19	−25 32.7	7.7
Apr. 1	8 43.59	+31 05.5	7.9	Nov. 7	19 21.96	−25 11.5	7.8
11	8 48.20	+30 18.6	8.1				

**dwarf planet; see p. 241*

EPHEMERIDES FOR THE BRIGHTEST MINOR PLANETS IN 2018

Date 0h TT	RA (2000) h m	Dec ° '	Mag.	Date 0h TT	RA (2000) h m	Dec ° '	Mag.
29 Amphitrite		**Jun. 15, mag 9.5**		**3 Juno** (continued)			
May 21	17 56.84	−32 32.8	10.0	Nov. 7	04 00.79	−01 54.8	7.5
31	17 48.50	−32 51.3	9.8	17	03 53.86	−03 20.1	7.4
Jun. 10	17 38.35	−32 59.4	9.6	27	03 46.34	−04 12.1	7.5
20	17 27.48	−32 54.9	9.5	Dec. 7	03 39.65	−04 25.9	7.7
30	17 17.20	−32 38.5	9.7	17	03 35.04	−04 02.0	7.9
Jul. 10	17 08.63	−32 13.0	9.9	27	03 33.29	−03 06.0	8.1
88 Thisbe		**Jul. 20, mag. 9.7**		**433 Eros**		**Dec. 7, mag. 9.7**	
Jul. 10	20 04.21	−17 30.7	10.0	Nov. 27	04 34.50	+62 10.2	10.0
20	19 55.38	−17 26.9	9.7	Dec. 7	04 23.00	+61 47.2	9.7
30	19 46.52	−17 25.5	9.9	17	04 12.89	+59 11.9	9.4
115 Thyra		**Sep. 2, mag. 9.9**		27	04 10.53	+54 16.1	9.2
Aug. 29	22 33.02	+02 35.8	9.9	2019 Jan. 6	04 17.90	+47 13.5	9.1
Sep. 8	22 21.98	+02 42.3	9.9	**40 Harmonia**		**Dec. 8, mag. 9.4**	
27 Euterpe		**Sep. 6, mag 9.8**		Nov. 17	05 24.62	+20 10.5	10.0
Sep. 8	22 59.68	−09 11.4	9.8	27	05 15.19	+20 17.4	9.7
30 Urania		**Sep. 19, mag. 9.6**		Dec. 7	05 03.93	+20 24.1	9.4
Sep. 8	23 49.91	+01 55.0	10.0	17	04 52.44	+20 30.9	9.7
18	23 41.02	+01 10.4	9.6	27	04 42.38	+20 39.0	10.0
28	23 32.02	+00 20.6	9.9	**6 Hebe**		**Dec. 28, mag. 8.4**	
3 Juno		**Nov. 17, mag. 7.4**		Aug. 9	04 56.58	+09 28.6	10.0
Jun. 20	01 34.18	+07 35.0	9.9	19	05 16.27	+09 21.4	10.0
30	01 52.41	+08 30.0	9.8	29	05 34.87	+09 02.9	9.9
Jul. 10	02 10.46	+09 14.1	9.7	Sep. 8	05 52.20	+08 34.0	9.8
20	02 28.17	+09 45.6	9.5	18	06 07.99	+07 56.5	9.8
30	02 45.37	+10 02.9	9.4	28	06 21.98	+07 12.3	9.7
Aug. 9	03 01.86	+10 04.3	9.3	Oct. 8	06 33.87	+06 23.9	9.6
19	03 17.35	+09 48.4	9.1	18	06 43.31	+05 34.2	9.4
29	03 31.50	+09 13.9	8.9	28	06 49.97	+04 46.9	9.3
Sep. 8	03 43.95	+08 20.2	8.7	Nov. 7	06 53.49	+04 06.5	9.2
18	03 54.21	+07 06.9	8.5	17	06 53.60	+03 38.0	9.0
28	04 01.87	+05 35.4	8.3	27	06 50.24	+03 26.8	8.8
Oct. 8	04 06.50	+03 48.4	8.1	Dec. 7	06 43.65	+03 37.8	8.6
18	04 07.78	+01 51.4	7.9	17	06 34.56	+04 14.0	8.5
28	04 05.74	+00 06.8	7.7	27	06 24.19	+05 15.1	8.4

1 2 3 4 5 6 7 8 9 10

Relative sizes of the Moon and the first 10 subplanets discovered: 1 Ceres, 2 Pallas, 3 Juno, 4 Vesta, 5 Astraea, 6 Hebe, 7 Iris, 8 Flora, 9 Metis, and 10 Hygeia (illustration by Michael Gatto, after Vystrix Nexoth).

PLANETARY OCCULTATIONS
BY DAVID W. DUNHAM, DAVID HERALD, STEVE PRESTON, AND DEREK BREIT

As major, dwarf, and minor planets and their moons move across the sky, they occasionally pass directly between an observer and a distant star, producing an occultation. Astronomers have learned much about Solar System bodies by carefully monitoring the changing apparent brightness of stars during the immersion and emersion phases of occultations. If the occulting body does not have an atmosphere, the occultation is virtually instantaneous; if there is an atmosphere, it causes the star's disappearance and reappearance to occur gradually. If a planet has rings or other debris in its environs, the extent and degree of transparency of this material can be precisely mapped. The rings of Uranus, the ring arcs of Neptune, and the atmosphere of Pluto were all discovered by occultation observations. If an occultation is observed at several distributed sites, the size and shape of the occulting body can be determined more accurately than by other Earth-based techniques.

Amateur astronomers can make important contributions to occultation observing campaigns. This is particularly true for minor-planet occultations, for which the paths across Earth are often very narrow and uncertain in location (due mainly to uncertainties in the ephemeris of the minor planet). By recording the times of the star's disappearance and reappearance as seen from several sites (i.e. by noting the edges of the minor planet's shadow as it sweeps across Earth), the object's profile can be directly determined. Often timings of adequate accuracy can be made by visual observers using modest telescopes.

When observing an occultation, it is important that an observer know his or her location to within a fraction of a kilometre. Geographic longitude and latitude as well as the altitude of an observing site can be determined with a GPS receiver, from a high-quality topographic map, or from some map websites. If observations are to be of maximum value, the times of immersion and emersion must be determined as accurately as possible—certainly to better than 0.5 s, and better than 0.2 s for the shortest events (those less than about 10 s in duration). Photoelectric equipment with high-speed digital recording systems is well-suited for this work. Attaching a low-light-level video camera to a telescope is a less-expensive method for accurate timing. Visual observers using audio recorders and shortwave time-signal receivers can also make useful contributions. Even simple measurements of the duration of an occultation made with an ordinary stopwatch can be of value. CCD observers should be aware that most of these systems are incapable of timing accuracies better than about 2 s; hence visual observation may be better. Some CCD observers use the trick of turning off the telescope clock drive shortly before the predicted time and let the images trail. The occultation will appear as a break in the trail that can be measured to about a tenth of a second if the moment the exposure is started (just after turning off the clock drive) is accurately timed.

Occultation observations are coordinated in North America by the International Occultation Timing Association (IOTA) (www.occultations.org). Whether an IOTA member or not, if you are able to locate stars to 11th magnitude, IOTA wants to inform you and others in your area of prediction updates. Please email the longitude and latitude (or location from the nearest town) of convenient observing sites, telescope size(s), and an indication of whether you are mobile to dunham@starpower.net. Individuals interested in joining IOTA should refer to LUNAR OCCULTATIONS, p. 162 in this Handbook, for membership information.

More information is in the *Solar System Photometry Handbook* (Willmann-Bell, Inc., 1983), *Sky & Telescope*, and occasional papers in the *Astronomical Journal*, *Icarus*, *Minor Planet Bulletin*, and other scientific journals.

Observations of occultations by major and minor planets, including negative observations, should be sent to reports@asteroidoccultation.com for analysis and publication by IOTA. When reporting timings, describe your geographic longitude, latitude, and altitude (to the nearest arcsecond and 30 m, respectively), telescope size, timing method, the start and end time of observation, an estimate of the observer's reaction time (if applicable) and the accuracy of the timing, and whether the reaction time correction has been applied. The report forms at www.asteroidocculation.com/observations are preferred; observational results are also posted there, as well as much more useful information.

Table of Planetary Occultations

The following two-page table (see p. 250) of planetary occultations by major, dwarf, and minor planets visible from North America and Hawaii for 2018 is based on predictions by Edwin Goffin, Scott Donnell, Steve Preston, Derek Breit, and David Herald. Preston and Breit assisted Dunham in the selection for the two-page table. Besides the two occultations by major planets listed (one by Saturn and one by Venus), there will be an occultation of a 12.9-mag. star by Pluto, the brightest star to be occulted by that dwarf planet since June 2015 (and since the *New Horizons* flyby a month later). Not included in the table is a difficult occultation of 6.9-mag. SAO 93148 = HIP 13358 by Venus, visible only from eastern Labrador and eastern Newfoundland at low altitude and in twilight at 23:25 UT of Apr. 12. Venus's 11″ disk will be 92% sunlit, so there will be less than 0.8″ of dark space between the star and Venus's terminator when the star will disappear.

The successive columns in the table list (1) the date and central time of the event; (2) the name of the occulting body; (3) the apparent magnitude of the major or minor planet; (4) the catalog and number of the occulted star; (5) the star's apparent visual magnitude; (6) the star's RA and (7) Dec; (8) the expected magnitude change from the combined brightness; (9) the predicted maximum duration of the occultation in seconds; and (10) the approximate region from which the occultation is predicted to be visible (locations are listed chronologically from first to last). Due to uncertainties mainly in the ephemerides of the minor planets from which these predictions are derived (most star positions are now accurately determined from the European Space Agency's Gaia mission), the region of visibility of an occultation is uncertain, by about half a path width for most of the minor-planet occultations listed. Errors may remain, so those near but outside the paths should try to observe. It's also useful, especially for the brighter stars that produce high signal-to-noise recordings, to observe even if you are located up to about 10 path widths from the predicted path, to check for the possibility of an occultation by a previously unknown satellite of the minor planet. Updated maps and more about these events is at www.poyntsource.com/New/RASC_Events.htm.

Note that the times are sometimes for the geocentric time of closest approach; for any specific location in North America or Hawaii, the event time can be several minutes earlier or later. A few weeks before each event, improved predictions and the latest path maps may be obtained from Steve Preston's minor-planet occultation website www.asteroidocccultation.com. Much other useful information, including interactive maps to zoom in on the path, circumstances for dozens of stations in and near the path, and lists of stars that can be used to prepoint telescopes to the target stars are at www.poyntsource.com/New/Global.htm. "Occult Watcher" finds many other minor-planet occultations visible from your site or region; it is a free download from www.hristopavlov.net/OccultWatcher/publish.htm. Since Occult Watcher works from an interactive website, IOTA uses it to coordinate minor-planet occultation observation plans.

Star catalogs are abbreviated as follows: SAO (Smithsonian Astrophysical Observatory); ZC (Robertson's Zodiacal Catalog); TYC (Tycho-2); PPM (Roeser Positions and Proper Motions); HIP (*HIPPARCOS*), and UCACx (xth U.S. Naval Observatory CCD Astrographic Catalog).

Some event stars, marked by * in the main table, have alternative star numbers, shown in the table on the facing page: Planet # is the minor-planet number and the alternative-star number (Alt. Star #) is from the *HIPPARCOS*-mission catalogs used for the predictions on IOTA's minor-planet occultation websites mentioned above. When known, spectral types (Sp.) are listed for the stars in the table.

Alternative star numbers for some events (*) in the main table (see next two pages):

Date	Planet #	Alt. Star #	Sp.	Date	Planet #	Alt. Star #	Sp.
Jan. 14	73	HIP 37989	K0	Jun. 14	168	HIP 99733	K0
Jan. 21	916	TYC 1749-00462-1	G5	Jul. 14	1015	TYC 6304-01603-1	G5
Feb. 16	57	TYC 0181-01123-1		Sep. 2	524	HIP 27092	G0
Feb. 17	20	TYC 1308-01348-1	A2	Oct. 2	213	TYC 6844-02124-1	B8
Feb. 19	978	TYC 6088-01506-1	A5	Oct. 7	439	HIP 80248	Mb
Feb. 22	1165	TYC 5517-00227-1		Oct. 30	350	HIP 8395	G0
Mar. 18	444	TYC 0796-01090-1	G0	Nov. 5	585	TYC 0657-00030-1	G5
Mar. 19	814	TYC 2521-00170-1	K0	Nov. 9	663	TYC 0177-00385-1	A2
Apr. 27	796	HIP 35093	G0	Dec. 16	663	TYC 0168-00862-1	A0
May 12	683	TYC 7281-01630-1	K0	Dec. 31	284	TYC 4929-00714-1	K0

Noteworthy events (marked in **bold** type in the main table on the next 2 pages):

Jan. 22: Jutta: The star is PPM 400129 = HIP 43950 = BD +22° 2029, spectral type G5.

Feb. 14: The star is SAO 92978 = HIP 11665 = BD +10° 330, spectral type G5.

May 11: On 2010 Jul. 8, in a path that crossed western Europe, asteroid (472) Roma occulted the 2.7-mag. red-giant star δ Ophiuchi, which has an angular size about one-third that of Roma. Dozens of observers recorded the event, but the gradual nature of the whole phenomena has so far thwarted attempts to comprehensively analyze the observations. An independently determined size and shape of Roma, from this and other occultations, could help the eventual analysis of the July 2010 data.

May 22: (201) Penelope is an M-class (metallic spectrum) minor planet that could support an unusual shape. The star is TYC 0278-00748-1, spectral type G0.

July 5: The star is TYC 6277-00323-1. The occultation by the rings will start around 4:10 UT (the times vary by a few minutes, depending on your location) and by the elliptical ball of Saturn, at about 5:17 UT. The star will reappear from behind the planet around 6:12 UT and from behind the rings around 6:36 UT. The star will appear in the Cassini Division for about 7 min around 4:30 UT and again around 6:18 UT (for most of North. America, the star will be in the Cassini Division when it reappears from behind Saturn). Large telescopes record the star's intensity as it passes behind the rings. There will be no occultations by Saturnian satellites, but the star will appear close to Tethys around 1:45 UT.

Aug. 3: (1461) Jean-Jacques is an M-class body with possibly an unusual shape. The star is HIP 107663, spectral type F5.

Aug. 15: Observations of this brightest star occulted by Pluto since the 2015 *New Horizons* flyby could tell how Pluto's atmosphere varies.

Sep. 7: ι (iota) Aquarii = ZC 3237 = SAO 164861 = HIP 109139, spectral type B8, the brightest star occulted by a sizable minor planet visible from North America in 2018.

Sep. 19: The star is SAO 77043 = HIP 24403, spectral type A2.

Sep. 29: (766) Moguntia is an MU-class minor planet that might support an unusual shape. The star is SAO 109560 = HIP 4526, spectral type K0. A past lunar occultation was reported as "gradual."

Oct. 28: Kleopatra is the largest M-class minor planet and the most elongated large one, about four times as long as it is wide. Radar observations around 2000 showed it to have a strange dog-bone shape, but later occultation and adaptive-optics observations indicate that it may be essentially two ellipsoids joined end-to-end. Observations of this occultation can help resolve the true shape of this strange asteroid.

Nov. 17: Eros: The body's size and shape was well-determined by the *NEAR Shoemaker* spacecraft that orbited Eros in 2000. Thus, the scientific value for this event will be more for astrometry, and determining if the star is binary.

Dec. 21: Venus: Venus's 30″ disk will be 41% sunlit. Only the dark-side reappearance can be seen, but it can be observed well since the sunlit parts of Venus will be at least 15″ away. Those with large telescopes may see the star faintly 1 or 2 min before the predicted reappearance, due to refraction of the star's light in the atmosphere. The central line of the occultation passes approximately from Wyoming to N. Carolina; a central flash should be visible along that line as the whole Venusian atmosphere focuses the star's light. ZC 2110 = SAO 158808 = HIP 72373, spectral type K0III.

IOTA-SELECTED LIST OF NORTH AMERICAN PLANETARY OCCULTATIONS FOR 2018

Date	UT	Occulting Body	Mag.	Star	Mag.	RA (2000) h m s	Dec ° ' "	ΔMag.	Dur. s	Nominal Path
Jan. 14	7:14	73 Klytia	12.2	*SAO 79687	10.2	07 47 09.6	+24 52 08	0.7	4.2	San Francisco to Oklahoma City to Savannah
21	22:54	916 America	15.3	*SAO 74826	9.6	01 37 07.2	+23 54 22	2.1	1.5	Cleveland to S New Hampshire
22	3:40	895 Helio	13.7	TYC 1751-01956-1	10.3	01 26 07.4	+26 16 32	3.5	5.4	Crescent City to St George, Utah to Corpus Christi
22	**13:27**	**1183 Jutta**	**15.3**	**ZC 1334**	**7.0**	**08 57 05.1**	**+21 51 38**	**8.3**	**2.4**	**Akiak and Kodiak to Eugene to Albuquerque**
25	0:23	430 Hybris	14.1	TYC 0145-01335-1	9.5	06 28 00.6	+07 19 14	4.6	5.7	Temple, Texas to Atlanta to Fayetteville
Feb. 7	8:43	50 Virginia	13.3	UCAC4 548-015983	11.0	05 32 04.5	+19 30 09	2.5	36.0	Los Angeles to Phoenix to Austin
10	7:59	303 Josephina	13.5	TYC 0842-01417-1	10.8	10 38 16.5	+10 47 32	2.8	8.3	Santa Maria, CA to Houston to Fort Lauderdale
12	8:05	218 Bianca	12.2	TYC 0262-00981-1	10.6	11 06 50.7	+00 07 28	1.8	5.8	Fairbanks to British Columbia to Helena to Dallas
14	**2:59**	**540 Rosamunde**	**15.6**	**ZC 396**	**8.6**	**02 30 28.8**	**+11 03 43**	**7.0**	**0.8**	**Baja Sur to Mexico to Laredo to Sarasota**
16	6:38	57 Mnemosyne	11.8	*PPM 153588	9.7	07 56 08.0	+00 02 10	2.2	10.9	NE Alaska to BC to Idaho Falls to Lubbock
17	1:50	20 Massalia	10.0	*SAO 77132	9.2	05 22 32.0	+22 10 15	1.2	18.7	Spokane to Winnipeg to Saint John's, NL
19	4:27	978 Aidamina	15.8	*SAO 156735	9.5	11 31 53.9	-18 14 26	6.3	5.9	Miles City, Montana to Myrtle Beach
20	3:34	468 Lina	15.1	TYC 1401-00740-1	11.0	09 09 25.9	+16 55 11	4.1	4.5	Temecula to Dallas to Jacksonville
20	11:25	1165 Imprinetta	16.0	*PPM 194811	10.2	11 44 47.6	-08 27 14	5.8	5.0	Kodiak to Bakersfield to Nogales to Havana, Cuba
27	12:43	282 Clorinde	13.8	TYC 0857-00770-1	10.2	11 37 35.1	+08 34 28	3.6	4.0	Whitehorse to Medford to Barstow to Hermosillo
28	1:00	1639 Bower	15.8	TYC 1209-01044-1	9.9	01 56 52.4	+19 31 27	5.9	1.1	Omaha to Marion, Indiana to Baltimore
Mar. 2	2:49	377 Campania	13.9	TYC 1267-01186-1	9.7	04 47 06.5	+15 43 41	4.2	5.4	Portland to Bemidji to Québec City
18	3:58	444 Gyptis	13.0	*SAO 116792	9.4	08 28 11.7	+07 52 16	3.7	23.9	Yellowknife to Saskatoon to Houston
19	7:19	814 Tauris	14.4	*SAO 62357	9.2	11 01 15.8	+36 03 58	5.3	8.1	Portland to Lincoln to Mrytle Beach
30	9:45	348 May	15.0	UCAC2 2440	10.9	17 40 33.1	-19 02 11	4.1	9.9	Calgary to Cedar Rapids to Richmond, Virginia
Apr. 2	10:11	313 Chaldaea	12.5	TYC 5610-00869-1	10.7	15 51 53.7	-01 38 24	2.0	14.3	Fort Hope to Rockford, Illinois to Biloxi to Cancun
10	5:58	424 Gratia	13.7	UCAC2 32376640	9.6	13 48 50.9	+01 38 24	3.2	5.7	Kamloops to Dickinson to Fort Wayne to DC
27	3:04	796 Sarita	14.8	*SAO 41642	10.2	07 15 26.8	+40 15 35	5.2	1.6	Battleford to Sioux City to Montgomery to Tampa
29	1:16	20 Massalia	10.9	TYC 1357-02401-1	10.2	07 08 51.5	+21 51 37	1.2	4.7	New Orleans, Louisiana to Tampa, Florida
May 6	1:29	50 Virginia	14.8	TYC 1356-03701-1	9.9	07 02 53.8	+20 43 35	4.9	3.1	Appleton, Wisconsin to Detroit to Philadelphia
11	**8:10**	**472 Roma**	**13.1**	**TYC 0371-00418-1**	**10.8**	**16 11 33.5**	**+02 19 29**	**2.4**	**4.2**	**Redding to Oklahoma City to Savannah**
12	2:36	683 Lanzia	13.1	*SAO 205255	9.4	14 10 21.1	-30 34 09	3.7	6.3	Jamestown, N. Dakota to Des Moines to Tampa
12	3:37	326 Tamara	15.0	TYC 2934-01541-1	9.6	16 17 15.6	+42 08 20	5.4	2.5	Billings to Oklahoma City to Beaumont, Texas
22	**5:22**	**201 Penelope**	**13.7**	**SAO 119044**	**9.9**	**11 46 48.4**	**+05 52 30**	**3.8**	**40.0**	**Medford to Las Vegas to Phoenix to Tampico**
Jun. 4	4:18	100 Hekate	14.3	TYC 1387-00270-1	9.8	08 26 57.0	+20 07 10	4.5	2.8	Seattle to Denver to Stillwater
14	9:46	168 Sibylla	13.3	*SAO 163368	8.9	20 14 11.3	-13 29 22	4.4	22.0	Baja Sur to Chihuahua to Victoria, Texas
24	1:33	739 Mandeville	12.4	TYC 0419-01405-1	10.0	17 40 08.6	+01 56 24	2.6	8.4	Tampico to Tampa
Jul. 5	**5:47**	**Saturn**	**0.1**	**PPM 733925**	**8.8**	**18 21 47.3**	**-22 29 57**	**0.0**	**6036.1**	**Americas**
11	10:22	656 Beagle	16.3	TYC 0614-00901-1	10.5	01 28 21.1	+09 13 53	5.8	2.8	Chico, California to Sun Valley, Idaho to Billings
14	6:49	1015 Christa	13.6	TYC 235777	9.3	19 17 46.8	-19 37 38	4.3	7.0	Santa Barbara to Cheyenne to Cohasset, Montana

† **Bold** = see the note for this event on p. 249   *See the alternate star name for this event at the top of p. 249.

IOTA SELECTED LIST OF NORTH AMERICAN
PLANETARY OCCULTATIONS FOR 2018 (continued)

Date	UT	Occulting Body	Mag.	Star	Mag.	RA (2000) h m s	Dec ° ' "	ΔMag.	Dur. s	Nominal Path
Jul. 16	9:21	38 Leda	13.7	TYC 1783-00572-1	10.0	03 12 31.4	+24 16 14	3.7	3.5	Mexico City to Jacksonville
Aug. 2	6:33	156 Xanthippe	12.1	TYC 5171-00647-1	10.4	20 26 60.0	-03 55 48	1.9	10.3	Seattle to Medicine Hat
3	9:25	**1461 Jean-Jacques**	14.7	SAO 190639	8.6	21 48 27.8	-26 14 09	6.1	3.0	Baja Sur to El Paso to St. Cloud
15	**5:29**	**134340 Pluto**	**14.2**	**UCAC4 341-187633**	**12.9**	**19 22 10.5**	**-21 58 49**	**1.6**	**122.6**	**Bermuda, E Cda, E & SW USA, Cuba, Mex, HI**
23	4:43	52 Europa	11.7	TYC 6306-01650-1	11.1	19 33 40.1	-20 34 50	1.1	39.2	Santa Maria, California to Provo to Winnipeg
27	9:12	365 Corduba	14.5	TYC 6058-00895-1	10.4	06 58 55.4	+12 18 35	4.1	2.4	Kansas City to Springfield to Providence
29	2:27	611 Valeria	14.7	TYC 5126-04083-1	10.2	18 45 19.5	-06 39 16	4.5	8.9	Mazatlan to Fort Davis to Dickinson, North Dakota
31	2:25	294 Felicia	14.3	TYC 6293-00594-1	10.7	18 52 06.9	-20 46 35	3.7	15.4	Duluth to Chattanooga to Daytona Beach
Sep. 2	8:29	524 Fidelio	14.7	*SAO 58387	8.9	05 44 41.6	+31 18 21	1.0	2.4	Baja to Phoenix to Pueblo to Minneapolis to Ameson
7	**0:34**	**633 Zelima**	**13.6**	**ι Aquarii**	**4.3**	**22 06 26.3**	**-13 52 12**	**9.3**	**3.8**	**San Antonio to Wilmington to Moncton**
16	8:54	80 Sappho	11.8	ZC 782	7.2	05 14 05.8	+21 13 25	4.6	5.0	Sacramento to Sioux Falls to Waterville, Maine
19	**1:14**	**156 Xanthippe**	**13.2**	**UCAC2 29554109**	**10.5**	**20 05 24.8**	**-06 59 30**	**2.8**	**28.0**	**Sioux Falls to Lebanon to Mobile**
29	**7:34**	**766 Moguntia**	**14.2**	**ZC 131**	**7.9**	**00 57 58.6**	**+07 36 42**	**6.3**	**3.8**	**Baja to El Paso to Shreveport to Atlanta**
Oct. 2	1:46	213 Lilaea	13.4	*SAO 186579	9.8	18 16 48.6	-22 58 42	3.6	3.8	Yarnell to Norman to Lexington to Providence
2	8:40	43 Ariadne	10.5	TYC 0619-00701-1	10.5	01 13 22.4	+14 09 27	0.7	7.6	Hawaii to Red Bluff to Idaho Falls to Thunder Bay
7	2:28	439 Ohio	16.2	*SAO 141133	7.5	16 22 59.4	-07 12 32	8.7	2.2	Eugene to Sioux Falls
7	12:26	524 Fidelio	14.3	TYC 2439-00311-1	10.4	06 36 41.2	+32 26 12	4.0	4.4	Seattle to Regina
20	8:10	1109 Tata	15.4	TYC 1798-00220-1	9.7	03 32 00.5	+22 47 37	5.7	5.9	Seattle to Saskatoon
22	7:06	863 Benkoela	14.3	TYC 5311-00158-1	10.3	04 01 57.8	-12 54 06	4.0	5.3	Close to Mexico City to Tampa and Orlando
28	**8:38**	**216 Kleopatra**	**11.4**	**TYC 0765-00506-1**	**11.1**	**07 32 57.1**	**+08 48 11**	**0.9**	**10.2**	**Kitsault to Thunder Bay to Syracuse**
30	3:59	350 Ornamenta	12.7	*SAO 167308	9.6	01 48 19.4	-26 06 02	3.2	8.3	Medford to Reno to El Paso and Laredo
Nov. 3	2:55	602 Marianna	12.1	UCAC2 47284751	10.2	04 33 22.8	+45 40 54	2.1	17.6	Puerto Vallarta to McAllen to Willmington
4	11:58	895 Helio	13.6	TYC 0220-01061-1	11.0	08 46 18.1	+04 14 25	2.7	5.7	San Francisco to Los Angeles to Mazatlan
5	4:20	585 Bilkis	13.7	*SAO 111335	9.1	03 40 07.1	+09 40 46	4.6	4.8	Redding to Great Falls to Tisdale
9	9:49	663 Gerlinde	14.5	*SAO 115431	9.7	07 25 53.5	+07 08 44	4.8	8.5	Toronto to Wilmington
17	**1:17**	**433 Eros**	**10.3**	**TYC 4078-00534-1**	**10.1**	**04 41 08.6**	**+60 51 51**	**0.9**	**7.3**	**Sacramento to St. Cloud to Kennebunkport**
17	2:18	148 Gallia	12.3	TYC 6958-01250-1	10.0	22 14 12.2	-25 19 01	2.4	6.4	Baja to Tucson to Madison
Dec. 16	4:44	38 Leda	11.5	TYC 2373-01454-1	10.7	04 33 46.4	+31 07 27	1.2	13.3	Santa Maria to Fargo to Gull Bay, Ontario
16	9:25	663 Gerlinde	13.8	*PPM 152237	9.7	07 15 11.3	+02 37 17	4.2	7.2	Baja Sur to El Paso to St Louis to Moncton
21	7:10	607 Jenny	14.3	TYC 1910-01297-1	10.4	07 24 48.4	+22 40 13	3.9	5.6	Baja to Tucson to Nashville to Virginia Beach
21	**12:00**	**Venus**	**-4.7**	**ZC 2110**	**5.9**	**14 47 55.0**	**-12 50 26**	**0.0**	**833.0**	**Mexico to SW and central USA to central Canada**
22	7:23	164 Eva	12.4	TYC 2957-00280-1	10.9	03 23 48.9	+38 46 59	1.7	7.2	Kitamat to Calgary to Des Moines to Charleston
24	7:13	526 Jena	14.0	TYC 1342-00465-1	10.4	06 47 29.9	+20 50 06	3.7	4.6	Baja to San Antonio to W Palm Beach
27	10:51	1004 Belopolskya	14.8	TYC 1306-00926-1	10.8	05 36 32.2	+19 29 16	4.0	5.4	Crescent City to Lawton, Oklahoma to Orlando
31	11:47	284 Amalia	15.0	*SAO 138174	9.7	11 23 01.2	-06 19 49	5.3	5.8	Regina to Topeka to New Orleans

† **Bold = see the note for this event on p. 249** *See the alternate star name for this event at the top of p. 249.

METEORS, COMETS, AND DUST

METEORS

BY MARGARET CAMPBELL–BROWN AND PETER BROWN

A *meteor* (from the Greek *meteoros*, meaning "high in the air") is the light, heat, ionization, and (occasionally) sound phenomena produced when a solid body (a *meteoroid*) collides with molecules in Earth's upper atmosphere. These collisions heat the surface of the object; then, at a height typically between 120 km and 80 km, the meteoroid begins to ablate, or lose mass. Typically, ablation takes the form of vapourization, although melting and quasicontinuous fragmentation may also contribute. It is these ablated meteoric atoms that collide with air molecules to produce atomic excitations, or ionization, leading to the emission of light we see in the night sky. Typical visual meteors are produced by meteoroids the size of a small pebble, although the relationship between mass, magnitude, and velocity is complex (Figure 1). The faintest meteors visible to the naked eye are due to meteoroids the size of the tip of a ballpoint pen; the brightest meteors are due to meteoroids whose diameters roughly match the thickness of a pen.

Larger and low-velocity meteoroids are favored to pass through Earth's atmosphere, although rarely as a single monolithic body. When these ponderable masses reach the ground, they are called *meteorites*. At the other extreme, very small meteoroids (micrometres in size) efficiently radiate heat from their surface and do not reach ablation temperatures; such particles reach Earth's surface without having been fully ablated, although most are heated many hundreds of degrees.

Meteoroids can be divided broadly into two groups: stream and sporadic meteoroids. *Stream* meteoroids follow similar orbits around the Sun, many of which can be linked to a particular parent object, in most cases a comet. When Earth intersects the orbit of a stream, a meteor shower occurs. Since all the meteoroids in a stream move along nearly identical orbits, their paths in the atmosphere are parallel. This creates a perspective effect: the meteor trails on the celestial sphere appear to radiate from a fixed location, called the meteor *radiant*. *Sporadic* meteoroids, in contrast, are much more loosely associated and are not part of tightly grouped streams.

Meteor showers are named for the constellation from which they appear to radiate. Official rules for naming showers have been adopted by IAU commission #22 and can be found at www.ta3.sk/IAUC22DB/MDC2007/Dokumenty/shower_nomenclature.php. When several showers have radiants in the same constellation, nearby bright stars are used in naming.

The sporadic complex as seen at Earth, however, is structured and shows definite directionalities as well as annual variations in activity levels. Sporadic meteor radiants are concentrated in six major source regions throughout the sky. These sources are in fixed locations with respect to the Sun. Variations in the strengths of these sources throughout the year have been observed; it is the elevation of these sources at a particular location plus the intrinsic strength of each source at a given time of the year that determine the average background sporadic rate. Figure 2 shows the distribution of sporadic radiants in Sun-centered coordinates. The expected sporadic rate varies as a function of the altitude of the apex of Earth's way throughout the year, but is generally in the range of 8–13 meteors per hour for visual observers. The apex is the instantaneous direction of travel of Earth around the Sun; it is the point on the ecliptic that transits at 6:00 local apparent solar time (see p. 40).

In general, meteoroid streams are formed when particles are ejected from comets as they approach the Sun. The parent objects of many showers have been identified from the similarity of the orbits of the object and the stream. Cometary associations include the η-Aquariids and Orionids, which are derived from 1P/Halley; the Leonids, which originate from 55P/Tempel–Tuttle; and the Perseids, from 109P/Swift–Tuttle. Several minor planets are known to be associated with meteor streams: 3200 Phaethon linked to the Geminid stream and 2003 EH1 linked to the Quadrantid shower are the most prominent examples. All of these particles have orbits that coincide closely with that of the parent object, but their orbits are gradually shifted through radiative effects and planetary perturbations. Such effects lead to a broadening of the stream over time, resulting in an increased duration of the meteor shower as seen from Earth—older streams tend to be more long-lived—and eventually transform stream meteoroids into sporadic meteoroids.

The visual strength of a meteor shower is measured by its Zenithal Hourly Rate (ZHR), defined as the number of meteors a single average observer would see if the radiant were directly overhead and the sky dark and transparent with a limiting stellar magnitude of +6.5 (conditions that are rarely met in reality). A more physical measure is the flux of a meteoroid stream, measured in numbers of meteors of absolute brightness (referenced to a range of 100 km) brighter than +6.5 per square kilometre per second perpendicular to the radiant direction. While an observer will tend to see the largest number of meteors by looking at the shower radiant, the most useful counts are obtained by looking some distance away from the radiant.

Most data on meteor showers are currently gathered visually by amateur observers. It is crucial to observe from a dark-sky location with a clear view of the sky, and to allow at least 20 min before the start of observations to allow dark adaptation of the eyes. One should choose an area of the sky to observe, preferably with an elevation

FIGURE 1 *Magnitude as a function of velocity for meteoroids of different sizes. Uncertainties in the mass scale are largest at high velocities and small masses, and may be as large as an order of magnitude in mass at the extremes.*

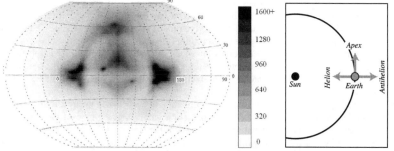

FIGURE 2 *Plot of the radiant distribution of meteors as seen by the Canadian Meteor Orbit Radar throughout the entire year, in Sun-centered ecliptic coordinates. The Sun is at (0,0), the helion, and the Earth's orbital velocity points to the center of the plot, the apex. The antihelion point is at (180,0). The small concentrations visible near the center of the plot are major showers (the Geminids and Eta Aquariids in particular). The intensity of the plot reflects the number of radiants per 2 deg². The rate of sporadic meteors as a function of time depends on which of the sporadic sources are above the horizon at the time of observation. The diagram at right shows the meaning of the coordinate system.*

greater than 40°. The limiting magnitude should be carefully recorded for each session, along with the UT and the center of the field of view of the observer. The most basic observations should include an estimate of the brightness of the meteor, the time of observation, and a shower association (based on the radiant and apparent speed of the meteor). Information on collecting and reporting scientifically useful observations can be found at the International Meteor Organization's website, www.imo.net.

TABLE OF METEOR SHOWERS FOR 2018

The table lists the major visual showers as well as those detectable by radio methods during the day. Of the strongest annual showers, the Moon is favorable for the **Perseids** and the **S Taurids**. Some models predict an enhancement in activity from a filament of the Perseid stream in 2018 about 5 hours before the traditional peak. There may also be a significant enhancement of the activity of the **Ursids** between one and two hours before the main peak, though the full Moon will make observing this shower more difficult.

Shower	Max Date UT	λ 2000	D	ZHR	θ ×10⁻⁶	R	Moon %	r	RA h m	Dec °	v km/s
Quadrantids	Jan. 3 20h	283.16	0.6	120	8.4	✓	96–	2.1	15 20	+49	43
April Lyrids	Apr. 22 18h	32.3	1.3	20	4.6	✓	48+	2.9	18 10	+34	48
η-Aquariids	May 6 8h	45.5	5	60	6.4	>03	66–	2.4	22 30	-2	66
S δ-Aquariids	Jul. 29 10h	126	8	20	6.2	>23	98–	3.2	22 44	-16	43
Perseids	**Aug. 13 1h**	**140.0**	**2**	**90**	**6.0**	✓	**4+**	**2.1**	**3 08**	**+58**	**60**
Orionids	Oct. 21 17h	208	2	20	2.2	>23	91+	2.4	6 20	+16	67
S Taurids	**Nov. 5 18h**	**223**	**15**	**10**	**1.0**	✓	**5–**	**2.3**	**3 34**	**+14**	**31**
N Taurids	Nov. 12 17h	230	15	15	1.4	✓	24+	2.3	4 00	+22	30
Leonids	Nov. 17 23h	235.3	1	20	1.9	>00	72+	2.5	10 12	+22	71
Geminids	Dec. 14 12h	262.2	1	120	11.0	✓	41+	2.3	7 28	+33	36
Ursids	Dec. 22 21h	270.7	0.5	10	2.2	✓	100	3.0	14 36	+75	35
S D ω-Cetids	May 6 20h	46	20	≈20	—	day	—	—	1 24	-6	36
N D ω-Cetids	May 9 23h	49	30	≈20	—	day	—	—	0 47	+19	36
D ζ-Perseids	Jun. 4 23h	74	19	≈25	—	day	—	—	3 47	+23	29
D Arietids	Jun. 9 16h	78.5	16	≈45	—	day	—	2.1	2 52	+26	41
D β-Taurids	Jun. 25 21h	94	9	≈20	—	day	—	—	5 31	+20	29
D Sextantids	Sep. 29 11h	186	12	≈20	—	day	—	—	10 17	-1	33

The column **Max Date** lists the date and hour (in Universal Time) when Earth intersects the densest part of the stream, based on the solar longitude λ (J2000.0) given in the third column.

The fourth column, **D**, gives the duration of the shower in days, which is the total number of days for which the activity level is over half the maximum activity.

The **ZHR**, or Zenithal Hourly Rate, is given for the peak of the shower. The θ column gives the meteoroid flux at the time of maximum (see text for explanation).

The **R** column gives the local times for which the radiant is above the horizon for an observer at 45°N latitude (and therefore meteors from the shower are visible); a ✓ symbol indicates that the radiant is up throughout the night hours, while "day" indicates that the shower is not visible at night.

The **Moon** column gives the percent illumination of the Moon at the time of the shower peak (+ for waxing, – for waning). The population index, **r**, at the time of the maximum is a measure of the size distribution of particles in the stream. A larger **r** value indicates an excess of small particles, while smaller **r** values indicate larger numbers of brighter meteors. A shower with a higher **r** value will therefore suffer more from background light such as moonlight or light pollution. Sporadic meteors at observable visual magnitudes have an **r** value near 3.0.

The **RA** and **Dec** columns show the position in the sky of the radiant at the time of the shower peak. The position of the radiant will vary from these values away from the time of the peak; tables published by IMO in their annual shower calendar provide details of radiant drift. The last column, **v**, gives the apparent atmospheric speed of the meteors in the shower.

FIREBALLS
BY PHILIP MCCAUSLAND

Fireballs are exceptionally bright meteors (at least mag. −5) that are spectacular enough to light up a wide area and attract public attention. Fireballs can occur as the brightest members of some annual meteor showers, but are more often part of the sporadic meteoroid flux and so can occur at any time. The brightest fireballs are sometimes termed bolides, being visible even in daylight.

Fireballs result from the collision of meteoroids ~1 cm or more in diameter with the Earth's atmosphere. The accurate reporting of such events is therefore of great interest for understanding this poorly known impactor population of Solar System material lying in the size range between dust and small asteroids. Fast-moving fireballs are typically destroyed in the upper atmosphere (>50 km altitude). Slower-moving fireballs with initial entry velocities typically <25 km/s can penetrate more deeply into the atmosphere and are capable of delivering meteorites. Reports of these slower type of fireballs are especially useful for assisting meteorite recovery efforts, and also critically for understanding the orbit of the object before it arrived on Earth. Excellent recent Canadian examples of meteorite-dropping fireballs with calculated orbits include Tagish Lake (2000), Buzzard Coulee (2008), and Grimsby (2009).

Systematic observations of fireballs are usually made by instruments in dedicated regional or global networks, using all-sky cameras, radar, and infrasound arrays (see meteor.uwo.ca). More information on all-sky camera networks in North America can be found at www.allsky.ca. More commonly, fireball observations are made by amateur observers and members of the public who are in the right place at the right time! Eyewitness and amateur camera observations are valuable and can be reported via the internet sites and phone numbers given below.

Fireball phenomena may include the development of a trail that persists after the event, the apparent fragmentation of the meteoroid during entry, flaring events, or a terminal burst in brightness, and occasionally reports of simultaneous "sizzling" sound that may be the result of transduced electromagnetic waves from the fireball. Meteorite-dropping fireballs in particular are often signified by reports of the persistence of "embers" after the main fireball and of a delayed sonic boom. These observations indicate that the meteoroid has likely penetrated into the lower atmosphere (<40 km altitude) and that portions of it may have survived entry to become meteorites. After entry to altitudes between ~30 and ~20 km, the meteoroid typically slows down to only 2–3 km/s, and fireball phenomena cease; thereafter any surviving fragments drop to the ground on ballistic trajectories over several minutes during a period called dark flight. Such falling objects may sometimes be heard producing whirring or popping noises by local witnesses within ~1 km of the meteorite fall. Fragments in dark flight can also often be detected in the troposphere by Doppler weather radar, which can thus assist in defining the approximate ground locations of the fallen meteorites.

The St. Thomas fireball of 2014 Mar. 19 (UT), widely seen over southern Ontario (all-sky image from Aylmer, Ontario). To date, no fragments have been recovered.

Rapid recovery of freshly fallen meteorites—as well as their careful handling and storage—before they have been exposed for long to the terrestrial atmosphere is highly desirable. Fresh recovery allows meteorite researchers to study water-soluble minerals (such as salt), organic phases, and physical properties (such as porosity and seismic velocities) before terrestrial alteration. Rapid meteorite recovery is also essential for the study of short-lived radioactive isotopes induced by pre-fall exposure to cosmic rays; this information is highly useful for estimating the true pre-fall size of the meteoroid as well as its dynamical history before encountering the Earth.

The scientific value of a freshly fallen meteorite is significantly greater when its pre-fall orbit is known. Under favorable circumstances, visual observer data can be used to obtain an approximate atmospheric trajectory, which, coupled with satellite or video observations, can be used to derive a pre-fall orbit.

The main reasons to report the observation of a fireball are: (1) to alert meteor researchers and all-sky camera network operators to the existence of a new event; (2) to add to the global database of observed fireball events, associated with meteor showers or not; (3) to assist with possible meteorite recovery from a slow fireball event; (4) to provide trajectory information that can be used to help calculate the orbit for a recovered meteorite; (5) to rule out catastrophic events such as airplane crashes and satellite re-entries; and, (6) to help calibrate atmospheric explosions detected by infrasound arrays deployed to monitor the Comprehensive Nuclear Test Ban Treaty.

The Meteorites and Impacts Advisory Committee (MIAC) maintains an informative website, including a fireball report form for Canadian events: www.uqac.ca/miac.

Other sites where fireballs may be reported include: USA and Canada (American Meteor Society) www.amsmeteors.org/fireball/report.html, North American Meteor Network (NAMN) www.namnmeteors.org/reports.html, and Global (International Meteor Organization) fireballs.imo.net/members/imo/report_intro.

The AMS site also offers smartphone users a fireball reporting app, allowing the user to automatically provide the observing location and indicate their fireball beginning and endpoint observations by phone orientation against the sky. This has proved to be very immediate and useful in recent fireball events and is recommended: www.amsmeteors.org/members/fireball/report-a-fireball.

Reports of fireballs seen over Canada can also be faxed to the Canadian Fireball Reporting Centre c/o Phil McCausland at 519-661-3198. Reports should include the following information (making notes immediately, at least of the precise time, is recommended):

(1) The name, telephone number/email, and address of the observer(s).

(2) The time of occurrence (and uncertainty in this time); an accurate time is required to search instrumental databases.

(3) The location of the observer at the time the fireball was seen (preferably in precise longitude and latitude).

(4) The beginning and ending points of the fireball, in terms of either astronomical RA and Dec, or azimuth and degrees elevation above the horizon. Indicate whether the true beginning was observed and whether the ending point was blocked by an object on the horizon.

(5) An estimate of the apparent magnitude; or compare the fireball brightness to that of the Moon. Was the ground lit up? Did the fireball cast shadows?

(6) The duration of the fireball event and the persistent trail (if any).

(7) A qualitative description of the event (e.g. color, flares, fragmentation, dust clouds persisting after the fireball, and sound). If sound was heard, report the time delay between the fireball and the arrival of the sound, or the precise time of the sound arrival as well as that of the fireball.

(8) The existence of any video, audio, or photographic records.

METEORITE IDENTIFICATION
BY RICHARD K. HERD AND CHRISTOPHER D.K. HERD

Meteorites are rocks from space that have fallen on Earth. Fossil meteorites are found in ancient strata; others, found at the surface, are recent arrivals or may have lain there for many thousands of years before discovery. Those witnessed to traverse Earth's atmosphere, and recovered based on those observations, are called meteorite *falls*; fewer than 1350 have ever been documented. Those with no record of arrival are meteorite *finds*, when recognized, and are far more numerous. Meteorites are named for where they are found. The Meteoritical Society (Met. Soc.) is the main worldwide organization for meteorite specialists, called *meteoriticists*. It is responsible for approval of new meteorites. Its nomenclature committee guidelines (meteoriticalsociety.org/?page_id=59) ensure that new meteorites are named to avoid confusion and ambiguity with existing meteorites, and that type specimens of all new meteorites are preserved in collections accessible to researchers.

Over 56 600 meteorites are known; many more probably exist. Over 33 000 are from Antarctica, over 10 000 are numbered meteorites from the Saharan and Arabian deserts, and about 13 600 (numbered and unnumbered) meteorites worldwide comprise the rest. See *Field Guide to Meteors and Meteorites* by O.R. Norton and L.A. Chitwood, Springer–Verlag, 2008; *Atlas of Meteorites* by M. Grady, B. Pratesi and V.M. Cecchi, Cambridge University Press, 2014; and the Meteoritical Bulletin database at: www.lpi.usra.edu/meteor. The latter allows a rapid search based on meteorite name, or any number of qualifiers.

Often there is confusion over when and where meteorites have fallen or have been preserved, and also over what they are and look like, even though websites now provide ready access to meteorite research, photos, and data. All are significantly different than Earth rocks. Samples sent to experts for identification, even by other scientists, are usually "meteorwrongs"—terrestrial rocks or minerals, human-made slag, metals, alloys, or concrete—that rarely resemble meteorites.

Meteorites probably begin as streams of fragments (*meteoroids*) that are debris from collisions between larger objects. The calculated orbits of several falls intersect the asteroid belt; their ultimate origin in space and time may be elsewhere. Links have been proposed between some types or groups of meteorites and specific asteroids or asteroid types, based on the meteorites' reflectance spectra and density. For example, results from the NASA Dawn mission have strengthened a connection between some howardite-eucrite-diogenite (HED) meteorites and minor planet 4 Vesta. New insights into the relationship between meteorites and asteroids are expected once the upcoming NASA *OSIRIS-REx* and JAXA *Hayabusa-2* asteroid sample return missions are complete. While the exact provenance of most meteorites is uncertain, they are an unparalleled source of information about the Solar System, from its primitive beginnings to its present. Many preserve pre-solar mineral grains made in stars that were part of our local stellar nursery. Decay products of short-lived radionuclides produced in the early Solar System and primordial organic compounds (possibly derived from cold, interstellar, molecular clouds) have been identified, yielding detailed information about the origin of the Solar System and the biological precursors of life.

The diversity of planetary bodies represented by meteorites is unmatched by planetary exploration missions. They are thus invaluable, and represent space exploration "without the commute," providing complementary information to planetary missions, and insights into the overall physical and chemical processes that have acted to form the Sun and its planets and their satellites. With increased space exploration, the current, somewhat arcane, classification schemes will undoubtedly change considerably to realistically reflect planetological contexts, as geological fieldwork provides for Earth rocks. In theory, any rocky Solar System body is a potential source of meteorites already in collections. About 140 meteorites are similar to Apollo samples, and are from the Moon (see curator.jsc.nasa.gov/antmet/lmc/index.cfm and www.meteorites.wustl.edu/lunar/moon_meteorites.htm). At least 107 meteorites are derived from Mars (see curator.jsc.nasa.gov/antmet/mmc/index.cfm and www.imca.cc/mars/martian-meteorites.htm). These meteorites, also known as the SNCs (shergottite-nakhlite-chassignite, after their main representatives, Shergotty, Nakhla, and Chassigny), are linked to the Red Planet by trapped gas within them that matches the composition of the unique Martian atmosphere, as measured by the 1976 *Viking* landers. The Martian meteorite of Tissint, Morocco, fell on 2011 Jul. 18, and represents only the 5th Martian meteorite fall and the first one in almost 50 years.

Popular ideas about when and where meteorites fall are connected with the observation of *meteors*, the brief streaks of light produced when high-speed, interplanetary particles enter Earth's upper atmosphere. Sporadic meteors and *meteor showers* do not produce meteorites; their fragile cometary debris fragments are reduced to dust high in the atmosphere. On average, Earth collects over 100 tonnes of cosmic debris per day. In contrast, stronger, larger space rocks can survive a fiery passage through the atmosphere and result in meteorites. These first appear as bright *fireballs*, are slowed to terminal speeds by atmospheric friction, and cease to show a bright trail long before they reach Earth's surface. Fireballs, which may seem very close, are usually quite high in the atmosphere, 50 km or more from the observer. Even if an extraterrestrial object does reach the surface, it is likely to plunge into the 70% that is water or to be lost among forests, jungles, or mountainous regions. In only uncommonly recorded cases have meteorites struck or landed within a few metres of humans (see "Possible Hazards of Meteorite Falls" by C.E. Spratt, *JRASC, 85* (October 1991), p. 263); the Chelyabinsk event of 2013 Feb. 15 is a rare case where the shock wave from the object's atmospheric entry caused widespread injuries. Rare meteoroids of masses exceeding many thousands of tonnes that are not slowed appreciably by Earth's atmosphere produce impact craters. Large impacts may have dramatically altered the history of life on our planet, but they do not result in meteorites—the kinetic energy is sufficiently high to vapourize the impacting body completely and to deform and melt the target area in seconds. Crater diameters are typically more than ten times the diameter of the impacting body. Glassy *tektites* found scattered over several continents may be evidence of such impacts, but they do not have meteorite compositions or characteristics, instead reflecting the composition of the target materials struck by the meteoroid.

Meteorites are divided into three groups that vary widely both in appearance and properties: *stones* or *stony meteorites*, *stony-irons*, and *irons* or *iron meteorites* (known in the past as *aerolites*, *siderolites*, and *siderites*, respectively). All usually contain metallic nickel-iron compounds (with traces of other metals) and are mildly to strongly magnetic, depending on the amount of nickel-iron relative to other minerals. Those that have lain on Earth's surface for long periods may be rusted almost beyond recognition; some require laboratory tests to confirm their identity.

Specimens generally have a quite soft, dull black to brown fusion crust formed by friction during atmospheric passage; more prevalent on stones and stony-irons, the crust may have partially flaked off or been weathered away. Meteorites only rarely contain bubble-like cavities; they are never almost perfectly spherical and smooth. During atmospheric entry, only their surface is affected. Surfaces of irons and stony-irons are dimpled rather than bulbous. They rust easily so there may be no bright metal showing. Stony meteorites do not show protuberances; weathered varieties are rusty, even on broken surfaces. Fresh stony meteorites may have a whitish "concrete-like" rock interior, with bright metal specks. Their crusts are black or smoky grey, varying from quite glassy to dull; telltale lines and bubbled patches orient their flight through the air. More metallic samples may have a shield-like shape, as a result of aerodynamic sculpting, and may therefore also be oriented.

Stones are the most abundant; they resemble some terrestrial rocks but are denser. Most (called *chondrites*) consist of spheres of silicate minerals (called *chondrules*) visible on broken, cut, or polished surfaces, and scattered grains of metal. The oldest, most primitive, and least altered meteorites are found among the chondrites. Rare stony meteorites without chondrules are called *achondrites*; these are thought to be melt products from chondrites, or samples of younger volcanic planetary surfaces. In August 1996, NASA scientists announced the discovery of fossil and chemical evidence of bacterial life in the Allan Hills 84001 meteorite—an ancient achondrite from Mars. Other scientists disagree that the weight of evidence points to ancient life on Mars; however, the rock retains evidence of the conditions necessary for life in the form of minerals precipitated by warm water. This controversy has resulted in renewed interest in missions to Mars and in finding water and life on Mars and elsewhere, even in extreme conditions on Earth. Irons and stony-irons are dense, with up to equal amounts of silicates and iron. Most irons are thought to be core material of planetary bodies formed by melting chondrites, whereas stony-irons (in particular the *pallasites*) may be samples of the core-mantle boundary of such planetary bodies.

Rare *carbonaceous chondrites* are grey to black, some resembling charcoal with silicate inclusions. The dark color is from iron oxides and sulphides. They contain a few percent carbon in very fine-grained carbonates, carbides, graphite, diamonds, and primitive organic molecules. They may have had biologically important roles in providing seeds for the origin of life. The study of these samples, along with interplanetary dust particles and samples of Comet Wild–2 from the NASA *Stardust* mission, has become important in deciphering the origins of meteorites and, therefore, of the Solar System and everything in it. We are all composed of recycled stardust.

Expertise in meteorite identification and classification exists at several government and university institutions, and museums. If a suspected meteorite passes initial criteria, such as magnetic character, presence of a fusion crust, etc., digital photos are typically requested for follow-up. Further examination and any analysis may be negotiated with the expert, but an expert opinion is usually free of charge. Experts can assist in enabling classification of any new meteorite: anyone who has found a meteorite should consult the Met. Soc. guidelines (see meteoriticalsociety.org/?page_id=59) to ensure that the proper name is assigned and that all other requirements are followed. Collectors, meteorite enthusiasts, and experts alike should be aware of local, regional, and national laws regarding meteorite collection and ownership. In some cases (e.g. Canada), meteorites may not be exported from the country without a permit.

METEORITE IMPACT CRATERS OF NORTH AMERICA
BY JOHN SPRAY

Earth has endured the hypervelocity impact of planetary bodies since its inception 4.6 billion years ago, as has every other planet in the Solar System. However, in contrast to the Moon, Mercury, Mars, many minor planets, and some satellites of the gas giants, the Earth shows relatively few impact craters on its surface. Currently, 188 are proven; see the Earth Impact Database (2015) at www.passc.net/EarthImpactDatabase.

The Moon's surface is saturated with craters, as is Mercury's, and over 42 000 craters have been named on Mars. Our planet's inventory is limited because Earth (like Venus) is an active planet. This means that most craters have been destroyed or buried due to plate tectonics, volcanic activity, or weathering. The interiors of the large gas planets (Jupiter, Saturn, Uranus, Neptune) are obscured, so we see no direct evidence of cratering—if there are indeed stable, solid surfaces on these planets.

Of the 188 known terrestrial craters, 60 occur in North America (see the following table), 31 of which are in Canada, 28 in the United States, and one in Mexico (see the map on p. 263). This total represents about one-third of the world inventory. North American craters range in diameter from as small as 36 m for the Whitecourt crater (Alberta), up to ~150 km for Chicxulub (Mexico). The principal criteria for determining if a geological feature is an impact structure formed by the hypervelocity impact of a meteorite or comet are listed below. Criteria are divided into megascopic (a bird's-eye/satellite scale), macroscopic (can be seen with the human eye), and microscopic (requiring a microscope):

1. Presence of *shatter cones* (conical-shaped fracture systems) that are in situ (macroscopic evidence);

2. Presence of multiple *planar deformation features* (PDFs) in minerals within in-situ rocks (microscopic evidence);

3. Presence of *high-pressure mineral polymorphs* within in-situ rocks (microscopic evidence, requiring proof via X-ray diffraction, etc.). Examples include the high-pressure polymorphs of $SiO2$ (e.g. stishovite);

4. *Morphometry*. On some planetary bodies, such as the Moon and Mars, we rely on the shape of the impact structure to determine its presence and type. This is a megascopic quality (i.e. too big to be seen by the unaided human eye, thus requiring remote sensing). On Earth, recognizing impact structures solely by their morphometry can be complicated by two factors: (a) weathering, erosion, burial processes, and tectonic deformation; and (b) certain terrestrial features having comparable shape (e.g. volcanoes, salt diapirs, glacial landforms), such that a circular structure alone is insufficient to claim impact-structure status;

5. Presence of an impact-generated *melt sheet* and/or *dikes*, and impact-melt *breccias* that were generated by hypervelocity impact (macroscopic). Melt sheets may be overlain by so-called fallback breccias, and material blasted out of the crater may form ejecta blankets about the original central cavity. For large impact events, ejecta can be distributed globally (e.g. Chicxulub);

6. *Pseudotachylyte* is a rock generated by frictional melting at the macroscopic scale. Some pseudotachylytes are associated with seismic faulting (earthquakes, due to isostatic rebound and plate tectonics), so they are not exclusively impact generated; however, in association with features 1–3 above, they can be contributory criteria.

In terms of relative importance, criteria 1–3 above are definitive, with supportive evidence being added by 4–6. For well-preserved buried structures, as revealed by detailed geophysical techniques (especially seismic data), some workers consider this as strong evidence in favor of an impact origin. Normally, buried craters are verified by drilling and sampling rock for evaluation using criteria 1–3 above.

TABLE OF METEORITE IMPACT CRATERS OF NORTH AMERICA

#	Name, Location	Lat. (N) ° '	Long. (W) ° '	Diam.* km	Age† My	Surface Expression	Visible Geologic Features
1	Ames, Oklahoma, USA	36 15	98 12	16	470. (30)	buried 3 km	none
2	Avak, Alaska, USA	71 15	156 38	12	3–95	buried 30 m	none
3	Barringer (Meteor), Arizona, USA	35 02	111 01	1.19	0.049 (0.003)	rimmed polygonal crater	fragments of meteorite, highly shocked sandstone
4	Beaverhead, Montana, USA	44 36	113 00	60	~600	oval area of crushed sandstone and shatter cones	shatter cones
5	Brent, Ontario	46 05	78 29	3.8	>453	sediment-filled shallow depression	fracturing
6	Calvin, Michigan, USA	41 50	85 57	8.5	450. (10)	buried 400 m	none
7	Carswell, Saskatchewan	58 27	109 30	39	115. (10)	discontinuous circular ridge	shatter cones, breccia, impact melt
8	Charlevoix, Québec	47 32	70 18	54	342. (15)	semicircular trough, central peak	breccia, shatter cones, impact melt
9	Chesapeake Bay, Virginia, USA	37 17	76 01	90	35.5 (0.3)	buried 400–500 m, ring structure	none
10	Chicxulub, Yucatan, Mexico	21 20	89 30	150	64.98 (0.05)	buried 1 km, ring of sink holes	none (related to the K/T mass-extinction event)
11	Clearwater East, Québec	56 05	74 07	26	290. (20)	circular lake	sedimentary float
12	Clearwater West, Québec	56 13	74 30	36	290. (20)	island ring in circular lake	impact melt, breccias
13	Cloud Creek, Wyoming, USA	43 07	106 45	7	190. (30)	buried 1.1 km	none
14	Couture, Québec	60 08	75 20	8	430. (25)	circular lake	breccia float
15	Crooked Creek, Missouri, USA	37 50	91 23	7	320. (80)	oval area of disturbed rocks, shallow marginal depression	breccia, shatter cones
16	Decaturville, Missouri, USA	37 54	92 43	6	<300	slightly oval depression	breccia, shatter cones
17	Deep Bay, Saskatchewan	56 24	102 59	13	99 (4)	circular bay	sedimentary float
18	Des Plaines, Illinois, USA	42 03	87 52	8	<280	buried, 15–100 m	none
19	Eagle Butte, Alberta	49 42	110 30	10	<65	minor structural disturbance	shatter cones
20	Elbow, Saskatchewan	50 59	106 43	8	395. (25)	buried, small mound	none
21	Flynn Creek, Tennessee, USA	36 17	85 40	3.8	360. (20)	sediment-filled shallow depression with small central peak	breccia, shatter cones
22	Glasford, Illinois, USA	40 36	89 47	4	<430	buried 350 m	none
23	Glover Bluff, Wisconsin, USA	43 58	89 32	8	<500	disturbed dolomite exposed	shatter cones
24	Gow, Saskatchewan	56 27	104 29	5	<250	lake and central island	breccia, impact melt
25	Haughton, Nunavut	75 22	89 41	23	39	shallow circular depression	shatter cones, breccia
26	Haviland, Kansas, USA	37 35	99 10	0.015	<0.001	excavated depression	fragments of meteorite
27	Holleford, Ontario	44 28	76 38	2.35	550. (100)	sediment-filled shallow depression	sedimentary fill
28	Ile Rouleau, Québec	50 41	73 53	4	<300	island is central peak of submerged structure	shatter cones, breccia dykes
29	Kentland, Indiana, USA	40 45	87 24	13	<97	central peak exposed in quarries, rest buried	breccia, shatter cones, disturbed rocks
30	La Moinerie, Québec	57 26	66 37	8	400. (50)	lake-filled depression	breccia float

*Approximate, apparent (post-erosion) rim-to-rim diameter, not including concentric features beyond the rim (e.g. both #31 and #52); also, not all craters are circular.
†Numbers in parentheses are uncertainties.

TABLE OF METEORITE IMPACT CRATERS OF NORTH AMERICA (cont)

#	Name, Location	Lat. (N) ° '	Long. (W) ° '	Diam.* km	Age† My	Surface Expression	Visible Geologic Features
31	Manicouagan, Québec	51 23	68 42	80–90	214. (1)	circumferential lake, central peak	impact melt, breccia
32	Manson, Iowa, USA	42 35	94 33	35	73.8 (0.3)	none, central elevation buried 30 m	none
33	Maple Creek, Saskatchewan	49 48	109 6	6	<75	buried, small mound	disturbed rocks
34	Marquez, Texas, USA	31 17	96 18	12.7	58. (2)	circular area of disturbed rock	shatter cones
35	Middlesboro, Kentucky, USA	36 37	83 44	6	<300	circular depression	disturbed rocks
36	Mistastin, Newfoundland/Labrador	55 53	63 18	28	36.4 (4)	elliptical lake and central island	breccia, impact melt
37	Montagnais, Nova Scotia	42 53	64 13	45	50.5 (0.8)	none, under water (115 m) and sediment	none
38	New Québec, Québec	61 17	73 40	3.44	1.4 (0.1)	rimmed, circular lake	raised rim, impact melt
39	Newporte, North Dakota, USA	48 58	101 58	3.2	<500	none, buried 3 km	none
40	Nicholson, NWT	62 40	102 41	12.5	<400	irregular lake with islands	breccia
41	Odessa, Texas, USA	31 45	102 29	0.168	<0.0635	sediment-filled depression with very slight rim, 4 others buried & smaller	fragments of meteorite
42	Pilot, NWT	60 17	111 01	6	445. (2)	circular lake	fracturing, breccia float
43	Presqu'ile, Québec	49 43	74 48	24	<500	none, heavily eroded	shatter cones
44	Red Wing, North Dakota, USA	47 36	103 33	9	200 (25)	none, buried 1.5 km	none
45	Rock Elm, Wisconsin, USA	44 43	92 14	6	<505	circular rim depression, central dome	shatter cones, breccia
46	Saint Martin, Manitoba	51 47	98 32	40	220 (32)	none, partially buried	impact melt
47	Santa Fe, New Mexico, USA	35 45	105 56	6–13	<1200	deeply eroded, large and extensive shatter cones	breccia, shatter cones
48	Serpent Mound, Ohio, USA	39 02	83 24	8	<320	circular area of disturbed rock, slight central peak	breccia, shatter cones
49	Sierra Madera, Texas, USA	30 36	102 55	13	~100	central hills, annular depression, outer ring of hills	breccia, shatter cones
50	Slate Islands, Ontario	48 40	87 00	30	~450	islands are central peak of submerged structure	shatter cones, breccia dykes
51	Steen River, Alberta	59 30	117 38	25	91 (7)	none, buried 200 m	breccia, impact melt,
52	Sudbury, Ontario	46 36	81 11	130	1850 (3)	deformed elliptical basin	shatter cones, breccia dykes
53	Tunnunik, NWT (see note below)	72 25	113 58	~25	130–450	heavily eroded	shatter cones
54	Upheaval Dome, Utah, USA	38 26	109 54	10	<170	circular area of disturbed rock	breccia dykes
55	Viewfield, Saskatchewan	49 35	103 04	2.5	190 (20)	buried 1 km	none
56	Wanapitei, Ontario	46 45	80 45	7.5	37.2 (1.2)	lake-filled depression	breccia float
57	Wells Creek, Tennessee, USA	36 23	87 40	12	200 (100)	basin with central hill, inner and outer annular valleys, ridges	breccia, shatter cones
58	West Hawk Lake, Manitoba	49 46	95 11	2.44	351 (20)	circular lake	none
59	Wetumpka, Alabama, USA	32 31	86 10	6.5	81 (1.5)	arcuate outer ridge, central depression	breccia
60	Whitecourt, Alberta	54 00	115 36	0.036	<0.0011	sediment-filled circular depression with raised rim obscured by trees	fragments of meteorite

* Approximate, apparent (post-erosion) rim-to-rim diameter, not including concentric features beyond the rim (e.g. both #31 and #52); also, not all craters are circular.
† Numbers in parentheses are uncertainties. *Note: Prince Albert crater, Victoria Island, NWT, discovered in 2012, has been renamed "Tunnunik."*

MAP OF NORTH AMERICAN METEORITE IMPACT STRUCTURES

Of the 188 known impact structures identified on Earth, 60 are in North America (31 in Canada, 28 in the United States, and 1 in Mexico). These are shown on the above map; the numbers correspond to the listing in the table on the previous pages. Although the oceans cover ~70% of Earth, only two impact structures have been identified on the seafloor (Mjølnir in the Barents Sea, and #37 off the coast of Nova Scotia). Also, with the exception of structure #52, all were formed within approximately the last 10% of Earth's history. Evidence of many earlier craters has been erased by geological processes. It is possible, however, to calculate a terrestrial cratering rate by focusing only on geologically stable areas of Earth (known as cratons), with low erosion and sedimentation rates. One such area is the North American craton. Calculations indicate that Earth has received at least 10 000 impacts generating craters greater than 20 km in diameter over the last 3.5 billion years. Very early in Earth history, the impactor flux was as high as 100 times the current rate. Some of these impacts had profound influence on the evolution of life on this planet. For example, Chicxulub (#10) is linked to a mass-extinction event 65 million years ago. Some impact craters are the source of considerable economic resources. In North America, hydrocarbons are extracted from #1, 2, 6, 34, 39, 44, 49, 51, 55; #7 produces uranium; #52 is the site of a world-class nickel-copper mining camp.

COMETS IN 2018
BY DANIEL W.E. GREEN AND SYUICHI NAKANO

Listed here are observable periodic comets predicted to return to perihelion in 2018 at about mag. 18 or brighter, those one-apparition comets expected to be recovered in 2018, and a few notable fainter comets. Favorable returns are indicated in **bold**, fair returns in regular type, and poor returns in *italic* (this scheme is intended as a rough guide only). The precision of the data should allow an ephemeris computation good to about 1'. The angular elements are referred to the ecliptic and mean equinox J2000.0.

Comet	Perihelion Date T TT	Perihelion Distance q au	Eccen. e	Siderial Period P a	Arg. Peri. ω °	Asc. Node Ω °	Incl. i °
74P/Smirnova-Chernykh	Jan. 26.70	3.5365	0.1493	8.5	87.14	77.06	6.65
185P/Petriew	27.67	*0.9338*	*0.6989*	*5.5*	*181.92*	*214.10*	*13.99*
250P/Larson	Feb. 2.22	2.2131	0.4068	7.2	45.09	73.68	13.29
235P/LINEAR	Mar. 17.46	2.7322	0.3155	8.0	333.74	204.46	8.90
169P/NEAT	Apr. 29.60	*0.6036*	*0.7680*	*4.2*	*218.09*	*176.09*	*11.30*
37P/Forbes	May 4.10	1.6103	0.5341	6.4	329.98	314.59	8.96
143P/Kowal-Mrkos	7.30	2.5323	0.4107	8.9	320.87	245.30	4.70
253P/PANSTARRS	7.75	2.0368	0.4129	6.5	230.73	146.88	4.94
240P/NEAT	16.22	2.1338	0.4490	7.6	352.10	74.93	23.50
66P/du Toit	19.14	1.2901	0.7869	14.9	257.21	21.90	18.67
159P/LONEOS	22.80	3.6252	0.3816	14.2	4.76	55.02	23.46
107P/Wilson-Harrington	23.53	*0.9699*	*0.6308*	*4.3*	*95.41*	*266.82*	*2.80*
187P/LINEAR	26.64	3.8806	0.1561	9.9	133.26	109.98	13.60
164P/Christensen	31.41	1.6853	0.5397	7.0	325.93	88.31	16.25
P/2001 T3 (NEAT)	Jun. 10.87	2.4853	0.6145	16.4	356.78	55.16	19.40
P/2011 CR42 (Catalina)	22.57	2.5217	0.2815	6.6	173.12	58.72	8.46
P/2013 CU129 (PANSTARRS)	24.35	0.7979	0.7227	4.9	211.93	46.23	12.16
49P/Arend-Rigaux	Jul. 15.50	1.4296	0.5994	6.7	332.89	118.82	19.04
P/2007 T2 (Kowalski)	21.91	0.6565	0.7846	5.3	359.63	3.41	9.74
105P/Singer Brewster	Aug. 10.32	2.0445	0.4105	6.5	46.47	192.43	9.18
48P/Johnson	12.20	2.0445	0.4270	6.5	216.56	110.13	12.21
243P/NEAT	26.04	2.4545	0.3593	7.5	283.56	87.66	7.64
125P/Spacewatch	27.95	1.5202	0.5136	5.5	87.18	153.18	9.99
21P/Giacobini-Zinner	Sep. 10.33	1.0128	0.7105	6.5	172.86	195.39	32.00
P/2005 R1 (NEAT)	14.32	2.0678	0.6258	13.0	118.80	257.98	15.48
59P/Kearns-Kwee	16.76	2.3588	0.4752	9.5	127.70	312.83	9.34
P/2011 V1 (Boattini)	30.88	1.7320	0.5502	7.6	269.24	46.79	7.38
P/2001 R6 (LINEAR-Skiff)	Oct. 4.25	2.1911	0.4759	8.5	308.48	67.34	17.38
P/2010 A1 (Hill)	14.02	1.9574	0.5541	9.2	13.30	47.31	10.31
P/2008 O2 (McNaught)	19.89	3.8152	0.1518	9.5	26.94	325.84	9.51
300P/Catalina	Nov. 2.08	*0.8328*	*0.6915*	*4.4*	*222.85*	*95.67*	*5.68*
64P/Swift-Gehrels	3.86	1.3932	0.6875	9.4	97.15	300.00	8.95
38P/Stephan-Oterma	10.97	1.5886	0.8593	38.0	359.58	78.00	18.35
247P/LINEAR	Dec. 2.10	1.4891	0.6250	7.9	47.45	54.01	13.66
P/2013 R3 (Catalina-PANSTARRS)	6.32	2.2002	0.2745	5.3	11.12	342.02	0.87
60P/Tsuchinshan	11.23	1.6226	0.5377	6.6	216.55	267.58	3.61
46P/Wirtanen	12.97	1.0554	0.6588	5.4	356.35	82.16	11.75
137P/Shoemaker-Levy	13.39	1.9302	0.5729	9.6	141.02	233.08	4.85
198P/ODAS	13.89	2.0059	0.4432	6.8	69.27	358.30	1.34

For an explanation of these elements, see p. 22; the elements are for an epoch within 20 days of perihelion. Visit the www.minorplanetcenter.net/iau/Ephemerides/Comets/ site for up-to-date ephemerides. For observers interested in monitoring the brightness of observable comets, visit www.icq.eps.harvard.edu/CometMags.html for comet magnitude updates. To make personalized finder charts using computer planetarium software, go to www.minorplanetcenter.net/iau/MPEph/MPEph.html to retrieve downloadable orbital elements in several popular electronic formats.

OBSERVING COMETS
BY DAVID H. LEVY

Each comet has its own unique, changing appearance. Observationally, comets are very much like deep-sky objects. Even in large telescopes, an observer can confuse a comet with a galaxy or a diffuse planetary nebula. Comets near a telescope's limit are virtually impossible to spot without an accurate position extracted from a detailed atlas, such as *Uranometria* or *Millennium*. It is difficult to define a telescope's limiting magnitude for comets, because the more diffuse a comet, the more difficult it is to find. Typically, under a dark sky, a 150-mm telescope will catch a 9th-mag. comet, a 200-mm telescope will see 10th, and a 400-mm should capture a 13th-mag. comet.

If you think you have found a new comet, after confirming the observation, file a *discovery report* according to the procedure in REPORTING OF ASTRONOMICAL DISCOVERIES, p. 7. For more information on comet observing and hunting, read *David Levy's Guide to Observing and Discovering Comets* (Cambridge, 2003).

Magnitude Estimates

The brightness of the coma can be estimated using a variety of methods, the most common of which is the "In-Out" method:

(1) Study the coma until you are familiar with its "average" brightness, an easy process if the coma is of uniform brightness, but rather difficult if there is a strong central condensation.

(2) With the help of a variable-star chart or some source in which star magnitudes are listed, find a comparison star at approximately the same altitude as the comet.

(3) Defocus the star to the size of the in-focus coma.

(4) Compare the star's out-of-focus brightness with that of the coma.

Repeat the last three steps with a second star, or more if needed, until an interpolation can be made.

Physical Characteristics

An estimate of a comet's magnitude is more useful if an estimate of the coma diameter is made at the same time. An observer seeing a 3′ coma, for example, will estimate much brighter than one who sees only a 1′ coma at the same time. The simplest way of estimating coma size is to draw the coma with the embedded and surrounding field stars, and then compare the drawing to an atlas, using its scale to determine the size.

A nightly measurement of a comet's degree of condensation is a good way of studying its changing behaviour. A comet undergoing an outburst of dust from its nucleus might begin its display by showing almost overnight the development of an increased condensation. Use an integer scale from 0 to 9, where 0 means a diffuse coma with absolutely uniform brightness, 3 means a diffuse coma with gradually increasing brightness toward the center, 6 involves a definite central condensation, and 9 refers to an almost stellar image.

Because of the changing Earth–Sun–comet geometry and the changing activity in a comet, the length and position angle of a tail should be measured. A rough way to measure the length of a tail is to sketch it and compare with a detailed atlas, as with the coma. Observers can also measure the position angle using an atlas and a protractor.

Visual Comet Hunting

The key ingredient to a successful comet search is perseverance, especially in this time of automated searches. The chances for a visual discovery have plummeted in the last few years. Although there are stories of people finding comets very quickly (Mark Whitaker discovered Comet Whitaker–Thomas 1968 V after three nights of comet hunting), these are the exception. Don Machholz searched for some 1700 hours for each of his first two comets, and I spent more than 917 hours before my first discovery. In contrast, neither Alan Hale nor Tom Bopp was comet hunting when they independently discovered what later became the Great Comet of 1997.

It is important to know the sky well before beginning a comet search program, but it is more important to know the difference between the fuzzy appearances of comets compared to galaxies, nebulae, and clusters. Observing all the objects in THE MESSIER CATALOGUE (see p. 314) provides an excellent education in what these distant objects look like, and observing as many known comets as possible is good preparation for recognizing an interloper. Generally, comets lack the bilateral symmetry of spiral galaxies and the mottled appearance of globular clusters. More important, they usually have unsharp edges, fading off into space so that it is often difficult to tell where the comet ends and the sky begins.

Although most comet hunters still use traditional star atlases to check their suspects, some are moving into a new mode of comet hunting. These hunters have attached encoders to their telescopes that allow an instant reading of the suspect's position in RA and Dec. If the telescope has been properly set up, this approach is faster. However, a sense of the nature of the fuzzy object in the field of view is still important since thousands of nonstellar objects dot the sky.

Comets may appear at any time, but they are usually found within 90° of the Sun. Good areas to search are in the evening western sky during the week after full Moon and in the morning eastern sky before dawn around new Moon. Although comet hunters differ in their approaches to searching, one way is to use an altazimuth mount and make horizontal sweeps. In the western sky, begin near the end of evening twilight at the horizon, sweep across, then return to the point of origin, move upward about half a field of view and sweep again, etc. In the morning, reverse the process.

Shortly after the discovery of Comet Okazaki-Levy-Rudenko (C/1989 Q1) in the summer of 1989, Steve Larson and David Levy imaged the comet with the 61-inch reflector atop Mt. Bigelow near Tucson, Arizona.

Photographic and Electronic Comet Hunting

While still possible, it is now very difficult to discover comets photographically because the sky is so well covered by the professional surveys. With film and a wide-angle camera like a Schmidt camera, take photographs of selected areas of sky, then repeat these exposures after at least 45 min. Using a stereomicroscope or a blink microscope, it is then possible to spot moving objects. Through a stereomicroscope, the comet will appear to "float" above or "sink" below the stellar background. If a blink microscope is used, the comet will appear to jump back and forth.

Using a CCD, take at least three images of each field, then examine either visually or using a moving-object detection program. Visual inspection is like blinking, so moving objects appear to move steadily through the three pictures, then jump back and begin moving again.

Finally, it is possible to discover comets over the internet. Since images from the *SOHO* spacecraft are made available soon after they are taken, amateur astronomers can scan these images for Sun-grazing comets. RASC member Michael Boschat won the 2001 Ken Chilton Prize for his discoveries of over 50 *SOHO* comets in this way.

Designation of Comets

The International Astronomical Union assigns each comet a unique designation that is similar to, although not identical to, the provisional designation system for minor planets (see www.minorplanetcenter.net/iau/lists/CometResolution).

The first component of the designation is a letter indicating the comet's status: C/ for a long-period comet, P/ for a periodic comet (defined as having a period of less than 200 years), X/ for a comet for which a reasonable orbit cannot be computed, and D/ for a disappeared comet. Then the year is stated, followed by the *half-month* letter. (The year is sub-divided into half-month intervals beginning with A (the first half of January) and concluding with Y (the last half of December), omitting the letter I.) Thus Comet Hale–Bopp, the first comet to be found in the second part of July 1995, is labelled C/1995 O1. Once the orbit of a periodic comet is well known, that comet receives a permanent number according to the order in which the comet's periodicity was recognized. Comet Halley—the first comet ever recognized to be periodic— is 1P/Halley. Comet Shoemaker–Levy 9, now disappeared, has the designation D/1993 F2, as it was discovered in the second half of March 1993.

Under a previous system, a comet was designated according to its order of discovery or recovery in a given year (e.g. 1982i, Comet Halley, was the ninth comet to appear in 1982). After cometary information was complete for a given year, each comet also received a Roman numeral designation based on the order of perihelion passage (e.g. Halley at its last return was also known as 1986 III). The current designation went into effect in January 1995, but it is retroactive to every previously discovered comet for which a reasonable orbit is available.

When a comet becomes well known, the vast majority of scientists, press, and public ignore the official designation, preferring instead to use more easily remembered names. Our experience with comets Hale–Bopp and Hyakutake (C/1996 B2) shows clearly that people are more comfortable with proper names. However, with two comets named Hyakutake, almost 1500 named *SOHO*, and well over 100 named LINEAR, we need to become familiar with the official designation in order to separate one comet from another (see www.cbat.eps.harvard.edu/cometnameg).

A handful of comets are named not for their discoverers, but for the persons who computed their orbits. The most famous of these is 1P/Halley, which has been well observed since at least 240 BC. It was finally identified as a comet appearing every 76 years or so by Edmund Halley in 1705. Two others are 2P/Encke and 27P/Crommelin.

In the event that the cometary nature of an object is established after it was originally given an minor planet designation, the original designation remains. When Gene and Carolyn Shoemaker and I discovered asteroid 1990 UL3 using the Palomar 18-in. telescope, for example, its orbit appeared to be more cometary than asteroidal. A few weeks after discovery, Steve Larson and I took a series of images through the Kuiper 61-in. telescope that clearly showed a tail, and the identification was changed to periodic comet Shoemaker–Levy 2. The mixed designation C/1990 UL3 applies.

Editor's Note: David Levy has discovered 23 comets: 9 by visual searches, 13 photo-graphically at Palomar Observatory under the combined name Shoemaker–Levy, and the latest, co-discovered with Wendee Levy and Tom Glinos, by Hyperion, an auto-mated telescope at Jarnac Observatory (at his home in Arizona): P/2010 E2 (Jarnac).

INTERPLANETARY DUST
BY ROY BISHOP

Outside of the astronomical community it is not generally realized that the inner Solar System contains a vast cloud of dust. The particles in this cloud are concentrated near the plane of the ecliptic and toward the Sun, their spatial particle density in the ecliptic falling off somewhat more rapidly than the reciprocal of their distance from the Sun. Measurements from spacecraft indicate that the cloud extends well beyond the orbit of Mars but is negligible in the vicinity of Jupiter's orbit and beyond.

The particles composing the cloud have a continuum of sizes, from pebble-sized clumps down to specks with diameters comparable to the wavelength of visible light and smaller. The smaller particles are the more numerous, although the mass distribution appears to peak near 10^{-8} kg, corresponding to a particle diameter of a few tenths of a millimetre. The total mass of the cloud is small, amounting to perhaps 10^{-14} of the mass of the Solar System. It is as if the satellites of Mars had been pulverized and spread throughout the inner Solar System.

Like the planetary system, the interplanetary dust cloud is not static; its particles generally move in orbits about the Sun. In addition, the particles undergo continual fragmentation due to collisions, sputtering associated with bombardment by the solar wind, electrostatic bursting, and sublimation. This progression toward smaller and smaller sizes is of crucial significance for the cloud, since particles with diameters appreciably less than a tenth of a millimetre have a sufficiently large surface-to-volume ratio that the radiation pressure of sunlight has a significant effect upon their motion—aberration of sunlight results in a small backward force, causing them to slowly spiral inward toward the Sun (the Poynting–Robertson Effect). During a total solar eclipse in 1983, instruments carried by a balloon detected a ringlike concentration of dust only a couple of solar diameters from the Sun. Its inner edge apparently marks the point at which solar heat vapourizes the infalling particles. The resulting tiny gas molecules, like the smallest particles of dust, are blown out of the Solar System by the dominant radiation pressure and interactions with the solar wind.

Because of the above-mentioned influences on the sizes and motions of the dust particles, the estimated mean life of a cloud particle is about 10^4 years. Since that is much less than the age of the Solar System, the cloud must be in a dynamic equilibrium—that is, it must be gaining new material as it loses the old. Part of the coma and tail of a comet is the result of significant quantities of dust ejected from its nucleus, and it is believed that short-period comets provide most of the new dust to the cloud (see *Sky & Telescope*, Jun. 2010, p. 16). Since comet nuclei are believed to consist of the undifferentiated matter from which the Solar System formed, much of the dust of the interplanetary cloud is most likely composed of this same low-density, fragile, primitive material.

To an observer on Earth the most noticeable aspect of the dust cloud is meteors—larger particles of the cloud that encounter Earth at high speeds and vapourize in the upper atmosphere. In addition, sunlight scattered by the dust cloud appears as a faint (fortunately!) glow in the vicinity of the ecliptic. The glow is brightest toward the Sun, is due primarily to particles with diameters between a few micrometres and a millimetre, and is referred to as the *zodiacal light*. A slight brightening in the sky opposite the Sun, called the *gegenschein* (German for "counterglow"), is due to a phase effect (analogous to full Moon) and also, possibly, to a concentration of dust at the L3 Lagrangian point of the Earth–Sun system. The integrated visual magnitude of the dust is about –8.5, making it the brightest Solar System object in the sky after the Sun and Moon. As astronomical objects the zodiacal light and the gegenschein are unusual in that they can be seen only with the unaided eye. Because of their large angular sizes and indistinct borders, both are invisible in binoculars or a telescope.

The Zodiacal Light

Poetic references to the zodiacal light go back several centuries (e.g. see *The Observatory, 108* (1988), p. 181). The 19th-century poet Edward FitzGerald is noted for his translation of the famous poem "Rubaiyat" by the Persian Omar Khayyam. In one of the stanzas Khayyam's reference to the morning was altered by FitzGerald into haunting references to the zodiacal light: "Dreaming when Dawn's Left Hand was in the Sky" (in mid-northern latitudes the zodiacal light and the first glow of the early autumn dawn combine to produce a large, glowing, ghostly figure having an upraised left arm); and "Before the phantom of False morning died" (the zodiacal light soon vanishes in the glow of the true dawn).

When conditions are favorable, the zodiacal light is indeed a mysterious and beautiful sight. Because the zodiacal light is brightest nearest the Sun, it is best seen within half an hour following the end of evening twilight and in the half hour prior to the beginning of morning twilight (for times of twilight, see p. 208), and when the ecliptic is at a steep angle relative to the horizon. In the tropics the ecliptic is always at a steep angle to the horizon. In mid-northern latitudes the optimum geometry occurs in the evening western sky in February and March, and in the morning eastern sky in September and October. The zodiacal light appears as a huge, softly radiant pyramid of white light with its base near the horizon and its axis centered on the zodiac (or better, the ecliptic). In its brightest parts it exceeds the luminance of the central Milky Way.

Despite its brightness, most people have not seen the zodiacal light. As mentioned above, certain times of night and year are more favorable than others. In addition, moonlight, haze, or light pollution rule out any chance of seeing this phenomenon. Even with a dark, transparent sky the inexperienced observer may confuse the zodiacal light with twilight and thus ignore it, or may not notice it because he or she is expecting a much smaller object.

The Gegenschein

The zodiacal light extends all around the zodiac with a shallow minimum in brightness some 120° to 150° from the Sun; nevertheless, this "zodiacal band" or "light bridge" is exceedingly faint and is visible only from high-altitude sites having very dark, transparent skies. However, the slight brightening in the vicinity of the antisolar point can be seen from most dark observing sites, provided the air is transparent.

The gegenschein is very faint. Haze, moonlight, bright nearby stars, planets, or light pollution will hide it completely. Most observers, including experienced ones, have not seen it. The gegenschein is sufficiently faint that, except from high-altitude sites with very dark skies, a person will not notice it without making a special effort to *look* for it. It is a ghostly apparition best seen near midnight, and in mid-northern latitudes, in the autumn or winter when the antisolar point is nearest the zenith. To avoid interference from bright stars or the Milky Way, the periods late September to early November and late January to early February are best. At these times the gegenschein is in Pisces and Cancer, respectively. It appears as a faint yet distinct, somewhat elliptical glow perhaps 10° in diameter. The luminance of the gegenschein is about 10^{-4} cd/m², some 10 orders of magnitude dimmer than the brightest light the human eye can tolerate.

Don't determine the antisolar point before you look—imagination is too powerful. Find the antisolar point by locating the gegenschein, and *then* check your star charts!

STARS

CONSTELLATIONS—NAMES AND ABBREVIATIONS

Nominative & Pronunciation	Genitive & Pronunciation	Abbr.	Meaning
Andromeda, ăn-drŏm′ē-dȧ	Andromedae, ăn-drŏm′ē-dē′	And	Daughter of Cassiopeia
Antlia, ănt′lĭ-ȧ	Antliae, ănt′lē-ē′	Ant	The Air Pump
Apus, ā′pŭs	Apodis, ăp′ȧ-dĭs	Aps	Bird of Paradise
Aquarius, ȧ-kwâr′ē-ŭs	Aquarii, ȧ-kwâr′ē-ī′	Aqr	The Water Bearer
Aquila, ȧ-kwĭl′ȧ	Aquilae, ȧ-kwĭl′e	Aql	The Eagle
Ara, ā′rȧ	Arae, ā′rē	Ara	The Altar
Aries, âr′ēz	Arietis, ȧ-rī′ē-tĭs	Ari	The Ram
Auriga, ô-rī′gȧ	Aurigae, ô-rī′gē	Aur	The Charioteer
Boötes, bō-ō′tēz	Boötis, bō-ō′tĭs	Boo	The Herdsman
Caelum, sē′lŭm	Caeli, sē′lī	Cae	The Chisel
Camelopardalis kȧ-měl′ō-pȧr′dȧ-lĭs	Camelopardalis kȧ-měl′ō-pȧr′dȧ-lĭs	Cam	The Giraffe
Cancer, kăn′sēr	Cancri, kăn′krē	Cnc	The Crab
Canes Venatici kā′nēz vē-năt′ĭ-sī	Canum Venaticorum kā′nŭm vē-năt′ĭ-kôr′ŭm	CVn	The Hunting Dogs
Canis Major, kā′nĭs mā′jēr	Canis Majoris, kā′nĭs mā-jôr′ĭs	CMa	The Big Dog
Canis Minor, kā′nĭs mī′nēr	Canis Minoris, kā′nĭs mī-ñôr′ĭs	CMi	The Little Dog
Capricornus, kăp′rĭ-kôr-nŭs	Capricorni, kăp′rĭ-kôr-nī	Cap	The Goat
Carina, kȧ-rī′-nȧ	Carinae, kȧ-rī′-nē	Car	The Keel
Cassiopeia, kăs′ĭ-ō-pē′yȧ	Cassiopeiae, kăs′ĭ-ō-pē′yē	Cas	The Queen
Centaurus, sěn-tôr′ŭs	Centauri, sěn-tôr′ī	Cen	The Centaur
Cepheus, sē′fē-ŭs	Cephei, sē′fē-ī′	Cep	The King
Cetus, sē′tŭs	Ceti, sē′tī	Cet	The Whale
Chamaeleon, kȧ-mē′lē-ŭn	Chamaeleontis, kȧ-mē′lē-ŏn′tĭs	Cha	The Chameleon
Circinus, sûr′sĭ-nŭs	Circini, sûr′sĭ-nī	Cir	The Compasses
Columba, kō-lŭm′bȧ	Columbae, kō-lŭm′bē	Col	The Dove
Coma Berenices kō′mȧ běr′ē-nī′sēz	Comae Berenices kō′mē běr′ē-nī′sēz	Com	Berenice's Hair
Corona Australis kō-rō′nȧ ôs-trā′lĭs	Coronae Australis kō-rō′nē ôs-trā′lĭs	CrA	The Southern Crown
Corona Borealis kō-rō′nȧ bôr′ē-ăl′ĭs	Coronae Borealis kō-rō′nē bôr′ē-ăl′ĭs	CrB	The Northern Crown
Corvus, kôr′vŭs	Corvi, kôr′vī	Crv	The Crow
Crater, krā′tēr	Crateris, krā-tēr′ĭs	Crt	The Cup
Crux, krŭks	Crucis, kroo′sĭs	Cru	The Cross
Cygnus, sĭg′nŭs	Cygni, sĭg′nī	Cyg	The Swan
Delphinus, děl-fī′nŭs	Delphini, děl-fī′nī	Del	The Dolphin
Dorado, dō-rȧ′dō	Doradus, dō-rȧ′dŭs	Dor	The Swordfish
Draco, drā′kō	Draconis, drā′kō′nĭs	Dra	The Dragon
Equuleus, ē-kwoo′lē-ŭs	Equulei, ē-kwoo′lē-ī′	Equ	The Little Horse
Eridanus, ē-rĭd′ȧ-nŭs	Eridani, ē-rĭd′ȧ-nī′	Eri	The River
Fornax, fôr′năks	Fornacis, fôr-năs′ĭs	For	The Furnace
Gemini, jěm′ĭ-nī	Geminorum, jěm′ĭ-nôr′ŭm	Gem	The Twins
Grus, grŭs	Gruis, groo′ĭs	Gru	The Crane (bird)
Hercules, hûr′kū-lēz	Herculis, hûr′kū-lĭs	Her	The Son of Zeus
Horologium, hŏr′ō-lō′jĭ-ŭm	Horologii, hŏr′ō-lō′jĭ-ī	Hor	The Clock
Hydra, hī′drȧ	Hydrae, hī′drē	Hya	The Water Snake (♀)
Hydrus, hī′drŭs	Hydri, hī′drī	Hyi	The Water Snake (♂)
Indus, ĭn′dŭs	Indi, ĭn′dī	Ind	The Indian

CONSTELLATIONS—NAMES AND ABBREVIATIONS (continued)

Nominative & Pronunciation	Genitive & Pronunciation	Abbr.	Meaning
Lacerta, là–sûr′tà	Lacertae, là–sûr′tē	Lac	The Lizard
Leo, lē′ō	Leonis, lē′ō′nǐs	Leo	The Lion
Leo Minor, lē′ō mī′nēr	Leonis Minoris lē′ō′nǐs mī–nôr′ǐs	LMi	The Little Lion
Lepus, lē′pǔs	Leporis, lĕp′ôr–ǐs	Lep	The Hare
Libra, lē′brà	Librae, lē′brē	Lib	The Balance
Lupus, lōō′pǔs	Lupi, lōō′pī	Lup	The Wolf
Lynx, lǐnks	Lyncis, lǐn′sǐs	Lyn	The Lynx
Lyra, lī′rà	Lyrae, lī′rē	Lyr	The Lyre
Mensa, mĕn′sà	Mensae, mĕn′sē	Men	The Table
Microscopium mī′krō–skō′pē–ǔm	Microscopii mī′krō–skō′pē–ī′	Mic	The Microscope
Monoceros, mō–nŏs′ēr–ŏs	Monocerotis, mō–nŏs′ēr–ō′tǐs	Mon	The Unicorn
Musca, mǔs′kà	Muscae, mǔs′ē	Mus	The Fly
Norma, nôr′mà	Normae, nôr′mē	Nor	The Square
Octans, ŏk′tănz	Octantis, ŏk′tăn′tǐs	Oct	The Octant
Ophiuchus, ō′fē–ū′kǔs	Ophiuchi, ō′fē–ū′kī	Oph	The Serpent Bearer
Orion, ō–rī′ŏn	Orionis, ôr′ē–ō′nǐs	Ori	The Hunter
Pavo, pā′vō	Pavonis, pà–vō′nǐs	Pav	The Peacock
Pegasus, pĕg′à–sǔs	Pegasi, pĕg′à–sī	Peg	The Winged Horse
Perseus, pûr′sē–ǔs	Persei, pûr′sē–ī′	Per	Rescuer of Andromeda
Phoenix, fē′nǐks	Phoenicis, fē–nī′cǐs	Phe	The Phoenix
Pictor, pǐk′tēr	Pictoris, pǐk–tor′ǐs	Pic	The Painter
Pisces, pī′sēz	Piscium, pǐsh′ē–ǔm	Psc	The Fishes
Piscis Austrinus, pī′sǐs ôs–trī′nǔs	Piscis Austrini, pī′sǐs ôs–trī′nī	PsA	The Southern Fish
Puppis, pǔp′ǐs	Puppis, pǔp′ǐs	Pup	The Stern
Pyxis, pǐk′sǐs	Pyxidis, pǐk′sǐ–dǐs	Pyx	The Compass
Reticulum, rē–tǐk′–ū–lǔm	Reticuli, rē–tǐk′–ū–lī	Ret	The Reticle
Sagitta, sà–jǐt′à	Sagittae, sà–jǐt′ē	Sge	The Arrow
Sagittarius, săj′ǐ–târ′ē–ǔs	Sagittarii, săj′ǐ–târ′ē–ī′	Sgr	The Archer
Scorpius, skôr′pē–ǔs	Scorpii, skôr′pē–ī	Sco	The Scorpion
Sculptor, skǔlp′tēr	Sculptoris, skǔlp′tôr′ǐs	Scl	The Sculptor
Scutum, skū′tǔm	Scuti, skōō′tī	Sct	The Shield
Serpens, sûr′pĕnz	Serpentis, sûr–pĕn′tǐs	Ser	The Serpent
Sextans, sĕks′tănz	Sextantis, sĕks–tăn′tǐs	Sex	The Sextant
Taurus, tôr′ǔs	Tauri, tôr′ī	Tau	The Bull
Telescopium tĕl′à–skō′pē–ǔm	Telescopii, tĕl′à–skō′pē–ī	Tel	The Telescope
Triangulum, trī–ăng′gū–lǔm	Trianguli, trī–ăng′gū–lī′	Tri	The Triangle
Triangulum Australe trī–ăng′gū–lǔm ôs–trā′lē	Trianguli Australis trī–ăng′gū–lī′ ôs–trā′lǐs	TrA	The Southern Triangle
Tucana, tōō–kăn′à	Tucanae, tōō–kăn′ē	Tuc	The Toucan
Ursa Major, ûr′sà mā′jēr	Ursae Majoris, ûr′sē mà–jôr′ǐs	UMa	The Great Bear
Ursa Minor, ûr′sà mī′nēr	Ursae Minoris, ûr′sē mī–nôr′ǐs	UMi	The Little Bear
Vela, vē′là	Velorum, vē–lôr′ǔm	Vel	The Sails
Virgo, vûr′gō	Virginis, vûr′jǐn–ǐs	Vir	The Maiden
Volans, vō′lănz	Volantis, vō–lăn′tǐs	Vol	The Flying Fish
Vulpecula, vǔl–pĕk′ū–là	Vulpeculae, vǔl–pĕk′ū–lē′	Vul	The Fox

ā dāte; ă tăp; â câre; à gàgà; ē wē; ĕ mĕt; ē makēr; ī īce; ǐ bǐt; ō gō; ŏ hŏt; ô ôrb; ōō mōōn; ū ūnite; ŭ ŭp; û ûrn

In terms of area (based on the official IAU boundaries), of the 88 constellations the 3 largest are Hydra (1303 square degrees), Virgo (1294), and Ursa Major (1280); the 3 smallest: Sagitta (80), Equuleus (72), and Crux (68). A complete list of the areas of the constellations appears in the 1972 edition of *The Handbook of the British Astronomical Association*, and was reproduced in the June 1976 issue of *Sky & Telescope* (p. 408).

HERCULES

BY CHRIS BECKETT & RANDALL ROSENFELD

> Right there in its orbit wheels a Phantom form, like to a man that strives at a task. That sign no man knows how to read clearly, nor on what task he is bent, but men simply call him On His Knees [Engonasin]. Now that Phantom, that toils on his knees, seems to sit on bended knee, and from both his shoulders his hands are upraised and stretch, one this way, one that, a fathom's length. Over the middle of the head of the crooked Dragon, he has the tip of his right foot; Aratus (*fl.* ca. 390–240 BC), *Phaenomena*, Mair trs. 1921, 384–387.

The keystone star pattern of Hercules keeps the celestial sphere of summer suspended overhead for northern observers and just fits in a 9° binocular. The Romans associated the "Kneeling One" to the mythical strongman Hercules, now known as home to one of the first deep-sky objects observers learn to locate by heart, Messier 13. However, there is much more worth taking a gaze at as the constellation passes through zenith.

Rasalgethi represents the "head of the kneeler" and means northern observers imagine Hercules upside down. William Herschel discovered the variability of Rasalgethi, which changes from an eye-catching 2.7 magnitude to a 4.0 over a six-year period, greatly altering the region of the sky. Small telescopes split it into two components, a brilliant red-orange primary and rare blue-green secondary. For those more interested in star patterns than variables, DoDz 7's sailboat-shaped pattern of stars is a low-power telescope field to the north. According to Bratton, Herschel also discovered 33 deep-sky objects within Hercules with deep-sky gems 6106, 6181, and 6207 appearing as large, faint spirals with core details visible through big instruments. Hercules also includes globular cluster 6229 plus galaxy 6364, discovered by Édouard Stephan of Stephan's Quintet fame, requiring significant aperture to appear nonstellar. Herschel also determined the approximate position for the solar apex in Hercules, the direction to which our Solar System is heading in space, as close to Lambda Herculis, only 10° or one fist at arm's length away from today's accepted position. The apex cannot be visually observed, but 4° south is Webb's Wreath, a suitable replacement.

Flanked by two mag. 6 stars, M13 is visible to the naked eye as a faint, fuzzy star that went unnoticed, until Edmund Halley's observation in 1714. Messier observed the "nebula without stars" much like modern binoculars reveal it as a bright, yet fuzzy star, while telescopes show a sugar pile spilling onto black velvet. Under certain conditions a "propeller" pattern is glimpsed, discovered by Lord Rosse as a "Y"-shaped void or depression stretching across the cluster. From the darkest locations, some observers have reported glimpsing another globular cluster, M92, without optical aid, while observers with large instruments report spiral structure. Another showpiece is NGC 6210, the Turtle Nebula, a blue star-like planetary nebula visible in small telescopes.

Many objects fell out of catalogs as they were discovered to be unassociated stellar groupings, yet Hercules is rich ground for observers wishing to explore asterisms once thought to reside in the realm of the nebulae. Ptolemy cataloged z Herculis as the "rearmost star in the left foot" and it appears as a nebulous star in Bayer's *Uranometria*. At nearly 7th mag., it is the faintest star charted during pretelescopic times, making an excellent test for determining the best observing nights from dark locations. Another "nebulous star in the left shin" is how Hevelius cataloged f Herculis, fuzzier to the unaided eye than M13 and with beautiful star chains, when viewed through small instruments.

The region between Hercules and Lyra once was home to Ramus Pomifer, the apple branch, and later the obsolete Cerberus, a multiheaded snake, each held by Hercules during brief appearances on early charts. While these constellations have passed into obscurity, low-power wide-field observing can retrace the crooked tree branches and snake bodies of star trails once thought to be a nebula. One such object is the Sudor Ophiuchi asterism (TL-2), Lorenzin's interpretation and coining of a discovery attributed to Hevelius; it contains the stars 32, 33, and 34 Oph (near 60 Her) and is a great hunting ground in the boundary of the visible Milky Way Galaxy.

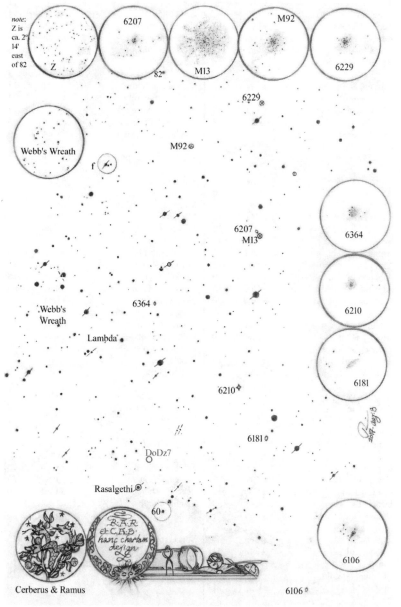

note:
Z is
ca. 2°
14'
east
of 82

Diagram by Randall Rosenfeld

FINDING LIST OF SOME NAMED STARS

Name & Pronunciation	Con.	RA	Name & Pronunciation	Con.	RA
Acamar, ā′kà-màr	θ Eri	2	Gienah, jē′nà	γ Crv	12
Achernar, ā′kēr-nàr	α Eri	1	Hadar, hăd′ar	β Cen	14
Acrux, ā′krŭks	α Cru	12	Hamal, hăm′al	α Ari	2
Adhara, à-dā′rà	ε CMa	6	Izar, ē′zar	ε Boo	14
Alnair, ăl-nâr′	α Gru	22	Kaus Australis, kôs ôs-trā′lĭs	ε Sgr	18
Albireo, ăl-bĭr′ē-ō	β Cyg	19	Kochab, kō′kăb	β UMi	14
Alcor, ăl-kôr′	80 UMa	13	Markab, màr′kăb	α Peg	23
Alcyone, ăl-sī′ō-nē	η Tau	3	Megrez, me′grĕz	δ UMa	12
Aldebaran, ăl-dĕb′à-ràn	α Tau	4	Menkar, mĕn′kàr	α Cet	3
Alderamin, ăl-dĕr′à-mĭn	α Cep	21	Menkent, mĕn′kĕnt	θ Cen	14
			Merak, mē′răk	β UMa	11
Algieba, ăl-jē′bà	γ Leo	10	Merope, mĕr′ō-pē	23 Tau	3
Algenib, ăl-jē′nĭb	γ Peg	0	Miaplacidus, mē′à-plăs′ĭ-dŭs	β Car	9
Algol, ăl′gŏl	β Per	3	Mintaka, mĭn-tà′kà	δ Ori	5
Alioth, ăl′ĭ-ŏth	ε UMa	12	Mira, mē′rà	o Cet	2
Alkaid, ăl-kād′	η UMa	13	Mirach, mī′răk	β And	1
Almach, ăl′măk	γ And	2	Mirfak, mir′făk	α Per	3
Alnilam, ăl-nī′lăm	ε Ori	5	Mizar, mē′zàr	ζ UMa	13
Alphard, ăl′fàrd	α Hya	9	Nunki, nŭn′kē	σ Sgr	18
Alphecca, ăl-fĕk′à	α CrB	15	Peacock, pē′kŏk	α Pav	20
Alpheratz, ăl-fē′răts	α And	0	Phecda, fĕk′dà	γ UMa	11
Altair, ăl-târ′	α Aql	19	Polaris, pō-lâr′ĭs	α UMi	2
Ankaa, ăn′kà	α Phe	0	Pollux, pŏl′ŭks	β Gem	7
Antares, ăn-tā′rēs	α Sco	16	Procyon, prō′sĭ-ŏn	α CMi	7
Arcturus, ark-tū′rŭs	α Boo	14	Rasalgethi, ràs′ăl-jē′thē	α Her	17
Atria, ā′trē-a	α TrA	16			
Avior, ă-vē-ôr′	ε Car	8	Rasalhague, ràs′ăl-hāg	α Oph	17
Bellatrix, bĕ-lā′trĭks	γ Ori	5	Regulus, rĕg′ū-lŭs	α Leo	10
Betelgeuse, bĕt′ĕl-jūz	α Ori	5	Rigel, rē′gĕl	β Ori	5
Canopus, kà-nō′pŭs	α Car	6	Rigil Kentaurus, rē′gĭl kĕn-tô′rŭs	α Cen	14
Capella, kàp-pĕl′à	α Aur	5			
Caph, kăf	β Cas	0	Sabik, sā′bĭk	η Oph	17
Castor, kàs′tĕr	α Gem	7	Scheat, shē′ăt	β Peg	23
Cor Caroli, kôr kăr′ō-lē	α CVn	12	Schedar, shĕd′àr	α Cas	0
Deneb, dĕn′ĕb	α Cyg	20	Shaula, shō′là	λ Sco	17
Denebola, dĕ-nĕb′ō-la	β Leo	11	Sirius, sēr′ē-ŭs	α CMa	6
Diphda, dĭf′dà	β Cet	0	Spica, spē′kà	α Vir	13
Dubhe, dŭb′ē	α UMa	11	Suhail, sŭ-hāl′	λ Vel	9
Elnath, ĕl′năth	β Tau	5	Thuban, thoo′ban	α Dra	14
Eltanin, ĕl-tā′nĭn	γ Dra	17	Vega, vey′gà	α Lyr	18
Enif, ĕn′ĭf	ε Peg	21			
Fomalhaut, fō′măl-ôt	α PsA	22	Zubenelgenubi, zoo-bĕn′ĕl-jĕ-nū′bē	α Lib	14
Gacrux, gà′krŭks	γ Cru	12			

Key to pronunciation at the foot of p. 271.

THE BRIGHTEST STARS
BY TOOMAS KARMO, CHRIS CORBALLY, AND RICHARD GRAY

This table has the 286 brightest stars (allowing for variability). An extended table-with-essay is in **www.rasc.ca/handbook/supplements**. We flag known companions of substellar mass (~"planets") as "+n" (n = 1, 2, …). Data for visual doubles are for the brighter component (A), with the last column describing companion(s). Where the double is too close to be resolved conveniently, data are for combined light (AB).

Apparent Visual Magnitude ($m_V = V$): Apparent magnitudes, with "v" appended for variables, are from *HIPPARCOS*. (For variables, these data are occasionally in mild conflict with published magnitude ranges.) The photoelectric system is from H.L. Johnson and W.W. Morgan, *Ap. J., 117* (1953). The (yellow) *V* filter corresponds roughly to the response of the eye. The probable error of a *V* value is at most 0.03.

Color Index ($B - V$): Since B on this system is the brightness of a star through a blue filter, the difference $B - V$, here taken from *HIPPARCOS*, measures apparent color (as possibly reddened by interstellar dust; although, in general, $B - V$ and spectral type are well correlated). The probable error of a $B - V$ value is at most 0.02.

Spectral Classification (**MK Type**): The "temperature type" (O, B, A, F, G, K, M) is given first, followed by a finer subtype (0–9) and a "luminosity class" (Roman numerals I–V, with "a" or "b" added occasionally to indicate slightly brighter or fainter stars within the class). O stars are hottest, M stars coolest; Ia stars are the most luminous supergiants, III stars are giants, and V stars are dwarfs. (V stars form the largest class in the cosmos, comprising the main sequence.) Other MK symbols include "e" for hydrogen emission; "f" for broad, nonhydrogen emission in hot stars; "m" for strong metallic absorption; "n" or "nn" for unusually broad absorption (a signature of rotation); "p" for peculiarities; "s" for a mixture of broad and sharp lines; and ":" for a minor uncertainty. The types are the best available from Garrison's unpublished spectrograms and the literature. Where a single star (e.g. α CMa A) is given two types (e.g. A0 and A1), with the second type flagged "m", the first is the type that best characterizes the hydrogen lines, the second the type that best characterizes the metal lines.

Parallax (π), *Proper Motion* (μ), and *Position Angle* (**PA**): Parallaxes, in milliarcseconds (mas), proper-motion vector norms ("/y), and vector position angles (degrees, from N through E) are derived from the *HIPPARCOS* 2007 data reduction, with a few exceptions.

Absolute Visual Magnitude (M_V) and *Distance in Light-Years* (**D**): Absolute magnitudes and distances are determined from parallaxes, except where a colon follows the absolute magnitude; in these cases, both quantities are determined from a calibration of the spectral classification. The absolute magnitude is left uncorrected for interstellar absorption. The appropriate correction is typically ~0.06 mag. per 100 ly outside the Local Bubble, i.e. beyond ~100 ly.

Radial Velocity (V_{rad}): Radial velocities are from BSC5. "SB" indicates a spectroscopic binary, an unresolved system whose duplicity is revealed by periodic Doppler oscillations in its spectrum and for which an orbit is possibly known. If the lines of both stars are detectable, "SB2" is used; "+" and "–" indicate, respectively, motion away from and toward the observer. "V" indicates a variable velocity in a star not observable as a spectroscopic binary. (In most "V" cases, the orbit is unknown.)

Remarks: Remarks include data on variability and spectra, and particulars on companions which are stars. Our principal source for variability ranges is P.N. Kholopov et al., *Combined General Catalogue of Variable Stars*, 4.1 ed., 1998 (online as VizieR GCVS4). We follow the IAU rules, as promulgated from 2016 onward, for star names, but adding **boldface** for navigation-star names.

We thank the late Professor Emeritus R.F. Garrison (University of Toronto), lead author of this article for editions 1984 through 2015, for the guidance and encouragement he generously gave to us and the wider RASC family.

TABLE OF BRIGHTEST STARS

Star Name	RA (2018.5) h m	Dec ° '	m_v	B–V	MK Type	π mas	M_v	D ly	μ "/y	PA °	V_{rad} km/s	Remarks	Name
Sun+8P			−26.75		G2 V		4.8	8 lm					
α And	0 09.3	+29 12	2.07	−0.04	B9p IV: (HgMn)	34	−0.3	97	0.214	140	−12 SB	var.: 2.25–2.31, 0.10 d	Alpheratz
β Cas	0 10.2	+59 15	2.28v	0.38	F2 III	60	1.2	55	0.554	109	+12 SB		Caph
γ Peg	0 14.2	+15 17	2.83v	−0.19	B2 IV	8	−2.6	400	0.009	168	+4 SB	var.: 2.78–2.89, 0.15 d	Algenib
β Hyi	0 26.7	−77 09	2.82	0.62	G1 IV	134.1	3.5	24.3	2.243	82	+23		
α Phe	0 27.2	−42 12	2.40	1.08	K0 IIIb	38.5	0.3	~85	0.426	147	+75 SB		Ankaa
δ And A	0 40.3	+30 58	3.27	1.27	K3 III	~30.9	0.7	106	0.142	126	−7 SB		
α Cas	0 41.6	+56 38	2.24	1.17	K0 IIIa	~14.3	−2.0	230	0.060	122	−4 V?		Schedar
β Cet	0 44.5	−17 53	2.04	1.02	K0 III	~33.9	−0.3	96	0.235	82	+13 V?		Diphda
η Cas A	0 50.2	+57 55	3.46	0.59	G0 V	168	4.6	19.4	1.222	117	+9 SB	B:7.51, K4 Ve, 12.9", PA:62°→324°, 1779→2016	
γ Cas	0 57.8	+60 49	2.15v	−0.05	B0 IVnpe (shell)	5	−4.2	600	0.026	98	−7 SB	var.:1.6–3.0; B: 8.8, 2.1", PA:255°→259°, 1888→2002	
β Phe AB	1 06.9	−46 37	3.32	0.88	G8 III	16	0.3:	150	0.088	293	−1	AB similar, 0.7", PA:26°→84°, 1891→2016	
η Cet+2P	1 09.5	−10 05	3.46	1.16	K1.5 III CN1	26.3	0.6	124	0.257	123	+12V		
β And	1 10.8	+35 43	2.07	1.58	M0 IIIa	17	−1.8	200	0.209	123	+3 V		Mirach
δ Cas	1 27.0	+60 20	2.66v	0.16	A5 IV	32.8	0.2	99	0.301	99	+7 SB	ecl.? 2.68–2.76, 759 d	Ruchbah
γ Phe	1 29.2	−43 13	3.41v	1.54	K7 IIIa	14	−0.9	230	0.209	185	+26 SB	irreg. var.: 3.39–3.49	
α Eri	1 38.4	−57 09	0.45	−0.16	B3 Vnp (shell?)	23	−2.7	140	0.095	114	+16 V		Achernar
α Tri	1 54.1	+29 40	3.42	0.49	F6 IV	52	2.0	63	0.234	177	−13 SB		Mothallah
β Ari	1 55.7	+20 54	2.64	0.16	A4 V	56	1.4	59	0.148	138	−2 SB		Sheratan
ε Cas	1 55.7	+63 46	3.35	−0.15	B3 IV:p (shell)	8	−2.2	400	0.037	121	−8 V		
α Hyi	1 59.4	−61 29	2.86	0.29	F0n III–IV	45	1.1	72	0.265	84	+1 V		
γ And A	2 05.0	+42 25	2.10	1.37	K3 IIb	9	−3.1	400	−0.065	~139	−12 SB	B: 5.4, B9 V, 9.8"; C: 6.2, A0 V; BC 0.2"	Almach
α Ari+1P	2 08.2	+23 33	2.01	1.15	K2 IIIab	49.6	0.5	66	0.240	128	−14 SB	calcium weak?	Hamal
β Tri	2 10.7	+35 04	3.00	0.14	A5 IV	26	0.1	130	0.154	105	+10 SB2		
ο Cet Aa	2 20.3	−2 54	6.47v	0.97	M5–10 IIIe	11	1.7	300	0.238	178	+64 V	LPV, 2–10; Ab(VZCet): WD, 10.4, 0.5", ~400y	Mira
γ Cet AB	2 44.3	+3 19	3.47	0.09	A2 Va	41	1.5	80	0.207	225	−5 V	A: 3.57; B: 6.23, 2.0", PA:283°→299°, 1825→2015	
α UMi A	2 55.0	+89 21	1.97v	0.64	F5–8 Ib	7.5	−3.6	430	−0.046	~105?	−17 SB	low-amp. Cep., 4.0 d; B: 9.1, F3 V, 18"(2013)	Polaris
θ Eri A	2 59.0	−40 14	3.28	0.17	A5 IV	30	0.5	100	0.057	293	+12 SB2	B: 4.35, A1 Va, 8.6", PA:82°→91°, 1835→2013	Acamar
α Cet	3 03.2	+4 10	2.54	1.63	M2 III	13	−1.9	250	0.078	188	−26 V		Menkar
γ Per	3 06.1	+53 35	2.91	0.72	G8 III + A2 V	13	−1.5	240	0.006	175	+3 SB2	composite spectrum; orbit 14.6 y, next eclipse 2019	
ρ Per	3 06.4	+38 55	3.32v	1.53	M4 III	11	−1.6	310	0.167	129	+28	semiregular var.: 3.3–4.0	
β Per	3 09.4	+41 02	2.09v	0.00	B8 V + F:	36	−0.1	90	0.003	119	+4 SB	ecl.: 2.12–3.39, 2.9 d; composite	Algol
α Per	3 25.7	+49 56	1.79	0.48	F5 Ib	~6.4	−4.2	510	0.035	138	−2 V	in open cluster	Mirfak
δ Per	3 44.2	+47 51	3.01	−0.12	B5 IIIn	6	−3.0	500	0.050	149	+4 SB		
γ Hyi	3 47.0	−74 11	3.26	1.59	M2 III	15.2	−0.8	~214	0.126	24	+16		
η Tau	3 48.6	+24 10	2.85	−0.09	B7 IIIn	8	−2.6	400	0.048	156	+10 V?	in Pleiades	Alcyone

TABLE OF BRIGHTEST STARS (continued)

Star Name	RA (2018.5) h m	Dec ° ′	m_v	B−V	MK Type	π mas	M_v	D ly	μ ″/y	PA °	V_{rad} km/s	Remarks
ζ Per A	3 55.3	+31 56	2.84	0.27	B1 Ib	4	−4.0	800	0.011	150	+20 SB	B: 9.16, B8 V, 12.9″, PA:205°→209°, 1824→2012
γ Eri	3 58.9	−13 27	2.97	1.59	M1 IIIb	16	−1.0	200	0.129	151	+62	calcium, chromium weak — **Zaurak**
ε Per A	3 59.1	+40 04	2.90	−0.20	B0.5 IV	5	−3.6	600	0.028	149	+1 SB2	B: 7.39, B9.5 V, 8.7″, PA:10°→10°, 1821→2012
λ Tau A	4 01.7	+12 32	3.41v	−0.10	B3 V	7	−2.4	480	0.017	209	+18 SB2	ecl.: 3.37−3.91, 4.0 d; B: A4 IV
α Ret A	4 14.7	−62 26	3.33	0.92	G8 II−III	20.2	−0.1	162	0.065	40	+36 SB?	
θ² Tau	4 29.7	+15 55	3.40	0.18	A7 III	22	0.1	150	0.112	104	+40 SB	in Hyades
α Dor AB	4 34.4	−55 00	3.30	−0.08	A0p V: (Si)	19	−0.3	169	−0.059	161	+26	A: 3.8; B: 4.3, B9 IV; 0.3″ (2014); orbit 12 y
α Tau A	4 37.0	+16 33	0.87v	1.54	K5 III	49	−0.7	67	0.199	161	+54 SB	irregular var.: 0.75−0.95 — **Aldebaran**
π³ Ori	4 50.8	+7 00	3.19	0.48	F6 V	124	3.7	26.3	0.464	89	+24 SB2	
ι Aur	4 58.2	+33 12	2.69v	1.49	K3 II	7	−3.2	500	0.016	155	+18 V	var.: 2.63−2.78
ε Aur A	5 03.3	+43 51	3.03v	0.54	F0Iab? + ~B5V	<2?	−8.0:	~2000	−0.003	170	−3 SB	ecl.: 2.92−3.83, 9892 d (dimmed ~700d) — **Almaaz**
ε Lep	5 06.2	−22 21	3.19	1.46	K4 III	15	−0.9	210	0.076	164	+1	
η Aur	5 07.8	+41 15	3.18	−0.15	B3 V	13	−1.2	240	0.075	155	+7 V?	
β Eri	5 08.8	−5 04	2.78	0.16	A3 IVn	36	0.6	89	0.112	228	−9	var.: 2.97−3.41, 2 d — **Cursa**
μ Lep	5 13.8	−16 11	3.29v	−0.11	B9p IV: (HgMn)	18	−0.5	190	0.050	109	+28	
β Ori A	5 15.4	−8 11	0.18	−0.03	B8 Ia	4	−6.9	900	0.001	69	+21 SB	B: 6.8, B5 V, 9.5″(2014); C: 7.6; BC: 0.1″ — **Rigel**
α Aur Aa+Ab	5 18.1	+46 01	0.08	0.80	G6:III + G2:III	76	−0.5	43	0.433	170	+30 SB2	composite; Aa: 0.7; Ab: 0.9, 0.0–0.1″ — **Capella**
η Ori AB	5 25.4	−2 23	3.35v	−0.24	B0.5 V + B	3	−4.0	1000	−0.004?	n.a.	+20 SB2	ecl.: 3.31−3.60, 8.0 d; A: 3.6; B: 5.0, 1.8″ (2015)
γ Ori	5 26.1	+6 22	1.64	−0.22	B2 III	13	−2.8	250	0.015	212	+18 SB?	**Bellatrix**
β Tau	5 27.5	+28 37	1.65	−0.13	B7 III	24	−1.4	130	0.175	173	+9 V	**Elnath**
β Lep A	5 29.0	−20 45	2.81	0.81	G5 II	~20.3	−0.6	160	0.086	183	−14 V?	B: 7.5, 2.7″, PA:268°→8°, 1875→2015 — **Nihal**
δ Ori A	5 33.0	−0 17	2.25v	−0.18	O9.5 II	5	−4.4	700	0.001	137	+16 SB	ecl.: 2.14−2.26, 5.7 d — **Mintaka**
α Lep	5 33.5	−17 49	2.58	0.21	F0 Ib	1.5	−6.6	2000	0.004	72	+24	**Arneb**
λ Ori A	5 36.2	+9 57	3.39	−0.16	O8 IIIf	3	−4.2	~1100	0.004	216	+34	B: 5.61, B0 V, 4.5″, PA:45°→44°, 1779→2015 — **Meissa**
ι Ori	5 36.3	−5 54	2.75	−0.21	O9 III	~1.4	−6.5	2000	0.001	108	+22 SB2	B: 7.3, B7 IIIp (He wk), 11.6″, PA:134°→141°, 1779→2012
ε Ori	5 37.2	−1 11	1.69	−0.18	B0 Ia	2	−7.2	2000	0.002	118	+26 SB	**Alnilam**
ζ Tau	5 38.8	+21 09	2.97v	−0.15	B2 IIIpe (shell)	8	−2.7	400	0.020	175	+20 SB	
α Col A	5 40.3	−34 04	2.65	−0.12	B7 IV	12	−1.9	260	0.025	176	+35 V?	ecl., var.: 2.88−3.17, 133 d; B: 5.0, 0.007″, 0.36 y — **Phact**
ζ Ori A	5 41.7	−1 56	1.74	−0.20	O9.5 Ib	4	−5.0	700	0.005	58	+18 SB	B: 4.2, B0 III, 2.4″, PA:152°→167°, 1822→2013 — **Alnitak**
κ Ori	5 48.6	−9 40	2.07	−0.17	B0.5 Ia	5	−4.4	600	0.002	131	+21 V?	**Saiph**
β Col	5 51.6	−35 46	3.12	1.15	K1.5 III	37.4	1.0	87	0.408	8	+89 V	**Wazn**
α Ori	5 56.2	+7 25	0.45v	1.50	M2 Iab	7	−5.5	500	0.030	68	+21 SB	semiregular var.: 0.0−1.3 — **Betelgeuse**
β Aur AB	6 00.9	+44 57	1.90v	0.08	A1 IV	40.2	0.0	81	0.056	269	−18 SB2	ecl.: 1.89−1.98, 4.0 d (mags. equal) — **Menkalinan**
θ Aur	6 01.0	+37 13	2.65	−0.08	A0p II: (Si)	19.7	−0.9	166	−0.086	149	+30 SB	B: 7.2, G2 V, 4.0″, PA:7°→304°, 1871→2014
η Gem	6 16.0	+22 30	3.31v	1.60	M3 III	8	−2.0	380	−0.064	259	+19 SB	var.: 3.2−3.9, 233 d; B: 6.2, 1.7″ (2012) — **Propus**
ζ CMa	6 21.0	−30 04	3.02	−0.16	B2.5 V	9.0	−2.2	360	0.008	61	+32 SB	**Furud**

TABLE OF BRIGHTEST STARS (continued)

Star Name	RA (2018.5) h m	Dec ° '	m_V	B–V	MK Type	π mas	M_V	D ly	μ "/y	PA °	V_{rad} km/s	Remarks	
β CMa	6 23.5	−17 58	1.98v	−0.24	B1 II–III	7	−3.9	~490	0.003	256	+34 SB	var.: 1.93–2.00, 0.25 d	Mirzam
μ Gem	6 24.1	+22 30	2.87v	1.62	M3 IIIab	14	−1.4	230	0.124	153	+55 V?	irregular var.: 2.75–3.02	Tejat
α Car	6 24.4	−52 42	−0.62	0.16	A9 Ib	11	−5.5	~310	0.031	41	+21		**Canopus**
ν Pup	6 38.3	−43 13	3.17	−0.10	B8 IIIn	9	−2.1	370	0.004	186	+28 SB		
γ Gem	6 38.8	+16 23	1.93	0.00	A1 IVs	30	−0.7	110	0.057	166	−13 SB		Alhena
ε Gem	6 45.1	+25 07	3.06	1.38	G8 Ib	4	−4.0	800	0.014	204	+10 SB		Mebsuta
α CMa A	6 46.0	−16 45	−1.44	0.01	A0mA1 Va	~379	1.5	8.6	−1.339	−204	−8 SB	B: 8.5, WDA; 10.7" (2016); orbit 50.1 y	**Sirius**
ξ Gem	6 46.3	+12 52	3.35	0.44	F5 IV	56	2.1	58.7	0.223	211	+25 V?		
α Pic	6 48.4	−61 58	3.24	0.22	A6 Vn	~34	0.9	100	0.252	345	+21		
τ Pup	6 50.4	−50 38	2.94	1.21	K1 III	18	−0.8	180	0.077	154	+36 SB		
ε CMa A	6 59.4	−29 00	1.50	−0.21	B2 II	8.0	−4.0	410	0.004	68	+27		**Adhara**
ο² CMa	7 03.8	−23 52	3.02	−0.08	B3 Ia	1	−6.6	3000	0.004	329	+48 SB		
δ CMa	7 09.1	−26 25	1.83	0.67	F8 Ia	2	−6.6	2000	0.005	317	+34 SB		Wezen
π Pup	7 17.8	−37 08	2.71	1.62	K3 Ib	4	−4.3	800	0.012	303	+16		
η CMa	7 24.8	−29 20	2.45	−0.08	B5 Ia	2	−6.5	2000	0.007	325	+41 V		Aludra
β CMi	7 28.2	+8 15	2.89	−0.10	B8 V	~20.2	−0.6	~162	0.064	234	+22 SB		Gomeisa
σ Pup A	7 29.8	−43 20	3.25	1.51	K5 III	17	−0.6	190	0.198	342	+88 SB	B: 8.6, G5: V, 21.5", PA:90°→73°, 1826→2011	
α Gem A	7 35.8	+31 51	1.93	0.03	A1mA2 Va	63	0.9	52	−0.254	−234	+6 SB	orbit 445 y; max = 6.5" in 1880; min = 1.8", in 1965; 5.0" (2016)	
α Gem B	7 35.8	+31 51	2.97	0.03	A2mA5 V:	63	2.0	52	−0.254	−234	−1 SB		Castor
α CMi A	7 40.3	+5 11	0.40	0.43	F5 IV–V	285	2.7	11.5	−1.259	−215	−3 SB	B: 10.3, WD; 3.8" (2014); orbit 41 y	**Procyon**
α Gem +1P	7 46.4	+27 59	1.16	0.99	K0 IIIb	97	1.1	33.8	0.628	266	+3 V		**Pollux**
ξ Pup	7 50.1	−24 54	3.34	1.22	G6 Iab–Ib	3	−4.5	1200	0.005	260	+3 SB		
χ Car	7 57.2	−53 02	3.46	−0.18	B3 IVp	7	−2.3	500	0.035	304	+19 V	Si II strong	
ζ Pup	8 04.2	−40 03	2.21	−0.27	O5 Iafn	3.0	−5.4	1080	0.034	299	−24 V?		Naos
ρ Pup	8 08.3	−24 22	2.83v	0.46	F2mF5 II: (var)	51.3	1.4	64	0.095	299	+46 SB	var.: 2.68–2.87, 0.14 d	Tureis
γ² Vel	8 10.1	−47 24	1.75v	−0.14	O9 I: + WC8	3	−5.9	1100	0.012	330	+35 SB2	var.: 1.81–1.87	
ε Car	8 22.9	−59 34	1.86v	1.20	K3:III + B2:V	5	−4.5	600	0.034	311	+2	ecl.?: 1.82–1.94	**Avior**
ο UMa A+1P	8 31.8	+60 39	3.35v?	0.86	G5 III	~18.2	−0.3	~179	0.172	231	+20	var.?: 3.30?–3.36?	Muscida
δ Vel AB	8 45.2	−54 47	1.93	0.04	A1 Va	40	0.3	81	−0.107	−164	+ 2 V?	B: 5.0, 0.4", PA:177°→263°, 1894→2013	
ε Hya ABC	8 47.8	+6 21	3.38	0.68	G5:III + A:	25	0.4	130	−0.232	−259	+36 SB	composite A: 3.8; B: 4.7, 0.3"(2014); C: 7.8, 2.8"(2016)	
ζ Hya	8 56.4	+5 52	3.11	0.98	G9 II–III	~19.5	−0.4	~167	0.101	279	+23		
ι UMa A	9 00.5	+47 58	3.12	0.22	A7 IV	~68.9	2.3	47.3	−0.491	−244	+9 SB	BC: 10.8, M1 V, 2.4", PA:349→82°, 1831→2012	Talitha
λ Vel	9 08.7	−43 30	2.23v	1.66	K4 Ib–IIa	6.0	−3.9	540	0.028	299	+18	var.: 2.14–2.30	**Suhail**
a Car	9 11.5	−59 03	3.43v	−0.19	B2 IV–V	7	−2.3	500	0.022	312	+23 SB2	ecl.2: 3.41–3.44	HR 3659
β Car	9 13.4	−69 48	1.67	0.07	A1 III	28.8	−1.0	113	0.191	305	−5 V?		**Miaplacidus**
ι Car	9 17.6	−59 21	2.21v	0.19	A7 Ib	4.3	−4.6	800	0.022	302	+13	var.: 2.23–2.28	Aspidiske

TABLE OF BRIGHTEST STARS (continued)

Star Name	RA (2018.5) h m	Dec ° ′	m_v	B–V	MK Type	π mas	M_v	D ly	μ ″/y	PA °	V_{rad} km/s	Remarks
α Lyn	9 22.2	+34 19	3.14	1.55	K7 IIIab	16	–0.8	203	0.224	274	+38	
κ Vel	9 22.7	–55 05	2.47	–0.14	B2 IV–V	6	–3.8	600	0.016	315	+22 SB	
α Hya	9 28.5	–8 44	1.99	1.44	K3 II–III	18	–1.7	180	0.038	336	–4 V?	**Alphard**
N Vel	9 31.8	–57 07	3.16	1.54	K5 III	13.6	–1.2	240	0.033	280	–14	**HR 3803**
θ UMa	9 34.1	+51 36	3.17	0.48	F6 IV	74.2	2.5	44.0	1.088	241	+15 SB	
ε Leo	9 46.9	+23 41	2.97	0.81	G1 II	13.2	–1.4	250	0.047	259	+4 V?	
υ Car AB	9 47.6	–65 09	2.92	0.29	A6 II	2.3	–5.3	~1400	0.028	307	+14	A: 3.01; B: 5.99, B7 III, 5.0″, PA:126°→126°, 1836→2010
η Leo	10 08.3	+16 40	3.48	–0.03	A0 Ib	3	–4.5	1300	~0.003	n.a.	+3 V	B: 4.5, 0.1″, PA:84°→309°, 1937→1993
α Leo A	10 09.4	+11 53	1.36	–0.09	B7 Vn	41	–0.6	79	0.249	271	+6 SB	**Regulus**
ω Car	10 14.2	–70 08	3.29	–0.07	B8 IIIn	9.5	–1.8	340	0.037	281	+7 V	**HR 4050**
q Car	10 17.7	–61 26	3.39v	1.54	K3 IIa	5.0	–3.1	660	0.026	286	+8	irregular var.: 3.36–3.44
ζ Leo	10 17.7	+23 19	3.43	0.31	F0 IIIa	12	–1.2	270	0.020	110	–16 SB	**Adhafera**
λ UMa	10 18.2	+42 49	3.45	0.03	A1 IV	24	–0.3	140	0.186	256	+18 V	**Tania Borealis**
γ Leo A+1P	10 21.0	+19 45	2.61	1.13	K1 IIIb Fe-0.5	26	–0.3	130	–0.333	~118	–37 SB	4.7″ (2016), PA:99°→126°, 1820→2016 (510.3 y)
γ Leo B	10 21.0	+19 45	3.16	1.42	G7 III Fe-1	26	–0.2	130	–0.346	~118	–36 V	max ~5″, around 2100 — **Algeiba**
μ UMa	10 23.4	+41 24	3.06	1.60	M0 IIIp	14	–1.2	230	0.089	293	–21 SB	**Tania Australis**
p Car	10 32.7	–61 47	3.30v	–0.09	B4 Vne	7	–2.6	500	0.021	304	+26	Ca II emission; irregular var.: 3.27–3.37
θ Car	10 43.6	–64 30	2.74	–0.22	B0.5 Vp	7	–3.0	460	0.022	303	+24 SB	**HR 4140**; nitrogen enhanced
μ Vel AB	10 47.6	–49 31	2.69	1.07	G5 III + F8:V	28	–0.1	~117	0.083	131	+6 SB	A: 2.72; B: 5.92, 2.3″, PA:55°→57°, 1880→2016
ν Hya	10 50.5	–16 17	3.11	1.23	K2 III	23	–0.1	144	0.220	25	–1	
β UMa	11 02.9	+56 17	2.34	0.03	A0mA1 IV–V	~40.9	0.4	80	0.088	68	–12 SB	**Merak**
α UMa AB	11 04.9	+61 39	1.81	1.06	K1 III	27	–1.1	120	0.139	255	–9 SB	**Dubhe**; A: 1.86; B: 4.8, A8 V, 0.7″ (2014)
ψ UMa	11 10.7	+44 24	3.00	1.14	K1 III	22.6	–0.2	145	0.068	246	–4 V?	
δ Leo	11 15.1	+20 25	2.56	0.13	A4 IV	56	1.3	58	0.193	132	–20 V	**Zosma**
θ Leo	11 15.2	+15 20	3.33	0.00	A2 IV	~19.8	–0.2	165	0.099	217	+8 V	**Chertan** (K-line var.)
λ Cen	11 36.6	–63 07	3.11	–0.04	B9.5 IIn	8	–2.4	400	0.034	258	–1 V	
β Leo	11 50.0	+14 28	2.14	0.09	A3 Va	91	1.9	36	0.511	257	0 V	**Denebola**
γ UMa	11 54.8	+53 36	2.41	0.04	A0 Van	39	0.4	83	0.108	84	–13 SB	**Phecda**
δ Cen	12 09.3	–50 50	2.58v	–0.13	B2 IVne	8	–2.9	400	0.050	262	+11 V	irregular var.: 2.51–2.65
ε Crv	12 11.1	–22 43	3.02	1.33	K2 III	~10.3	–1.9	320	0.072	278	+5	
δ Cru	12 16.1	–58 51	2.79v	–0.19	B2 IV	9.4	–2.3	350	0.037	254	+22 V?	var.: 2.78–2.84, 0.15 d
δ UMa	12 16.3	+56 56	3.32	0.08	A2 Van	40.5	1.4	81	0.104	86	–13 V	**Megrez**
γ Crv	12 16.8	–17 39	2.58	–0.11	B8 III	21	–0.8	154	0.160	278	–4 SB	**Gienah** sp. var.?
α Cru A	12 27.6	–63 12	1.25	–0.20	B0.5 IV	10	–3.7	~320	0.037	251	–11 SB	**Acrux** 5.4″ (1826); 4.2″ (2016)
α Cru B	12 27.6	–63 12	1.64	–0.18	B1 Vn	10	–3.3	~320	0.037	251?	–1	PA: 114°→112°, 1826→2016
δ Crv A	12 30.8	–16 37	2.94	–0.01	B9.5 IVn	~37.6	0.8	87	0.252	237	+9 V	B:8.26, K2 V, 24.6″, PA: 216°→213°, 1782→2012 **Algorab**

TABLE OF BRIGHTEST STARS (continued)

Star Name	RA (2018.5) h m	Dec ° ′	mv	B–V	MK Type	π mas	Mv	D ly	μ ″/y	PA °	Vrad km/s	Remarks	Name
γ Cru	12 32.2	−57 13	1.59v	1.60	M3.5 III	37	−0.6	89	0.267	174	+21	var: 1.60–1.67	**Gacrux**
β Crv	12 35.4	−23 30	2.65	0.89	G5 II	22	−0.6	146	0.057	179	−8 V		
α Mus	12 38.3	−69 14	2.69v	−0.18	B2 IV–V	10.3	−2.2	320	0.042	252	+13 V	var: 2.68–2.73, 0.090 d	
γ Cen A	12 42.5	−49 04	2.95	−0.02	A1 IV	25	−0.1	130	~0.194	~267	−6	orbit 84 y; min = 0.2″; 0.4″ (2010),	
γ Cen B	12 42.5	−49 04	2.85	−0.02	A0 IV	25	−0.2	130	~0.194	~267	−6	0.2″ (2014) max = 1.7″	
γ Vir AB	12 42.6	−1 33	2.74	0.37	F1 V + F0mF2 V	85	2.4	39	0.619	~276	−20	A: 3.48; B: 3.50; 0.8″ (2007); 2.5″ (2016)	**Porrima**
β Mus AB	12 47.4	−68 13	3.04	−0.18	B2 V + B2.5 V	~9.6	−3.1	340	~0.043	~258	+42 V	A: 3.51; B: 4.00, 1.1″, PA:317°→53°, 1880→2016	
β Cru	12 48.8	−59 47	1.25v	−0.24	B0.5 III	12	−3.4	300	0.046	249	+16 SB	var: 1.23–1.31, 0.24 d	**Mimosa**
ε UMa	12 54.8	+55 52	1.76v	−0.02	A0p IV: (CrEu)	~39.5	−0.3	83	0.112	94	−9 SB?	var: 1.76–1.78, 5.1 d	**Alioth**
δ Vir	12 56.5	+3 18	3.39	1.57	M3 III	16	−0.5	~198	0.473	264	−18 V?		
α² CVn A	12 56.9	+38 13	2.85	−0.06	A0p (SiEu)	28	0.1	110	0.241	283	−3 V	B:5.6, F0 V, 20.0″, PA:234°→229°, 1777→2016	**Cor Caroli**
ε Vir	13 03.1	+10 52	2.85	0.93	G9 IIIab	29.8	0.2	110	0.275	274	−14 V?		**Vindemiatrix**
γ Hya	13 19.9	−23 16	2.99	0.92	G8 IIIa	~24.4	−0.1	134	0.081	121	−5 V?		
ι Cen	13 21.6	−36 49	2.75	0.07	A2 Va	55	1.5	59	0.352	256	0		
ζ UMa A	13 24.7	+54 50	2.23	0.06	A1 Va	40	0.1	83	0.123	100	−6 SB2	B:3.94, A1mA7 IV–V, 14.4″; period >5000 y?	**Mizar**
α Vir	13 26.2	−11 15	0.98v	−0.24	B1 V	13	−3.4	250	0.052	234	+1 SB2		**Spica**
ζ Vir	13 35.6	−0 41	3.38	0.11	A2 IV	44	1.6	74	0.285	280	−13		
ε Cen	13 41.1	−53 34	2.29	−0.17	B1 III	8	−3.3	400	0.019	233	+3		
η UMa	13 48.3	+49 13	1.85	−0.10	B3 V	31	−0.7	104	0.122	263	−11 SB?		**Alkaid**
ν Cen	13 50.6	−41 47	3.41	−0.22	B2 IV	~7.5	−2.2	440	0.034	233	+9 SB		
μ Cen	13 50.7	−42 34	3.47v	−0.17	B2 IV–Vpne	~6.4	−2.5	510	0.031	232	+9 SB	variable shell: 2.92–3.47	
η Boo	13 55.6	+18 18	2.68	0.58	G0 IV	88	2.4	37	0.361	190	0 SB		**Muphrid**
ζ Cen AB	13 56.7	−47 23	2.55	−0.18	B2.5 IV	8.5	−2.8	380	0.073	232	+7 SB2		
β Cen AB	14 05.1	−60 28	0.58v	−0.23	B III	8	−4.8	400	0.041	235	+6 SB	B:3.94, A1mA7 IV–V, 0.4″; period 1500y?	**Hadar**
π Hya	14 07.4	−26 46	3.25	1.09	K2 IIIb	~32.3	0.8	101	0.148	163	+27 V		
θ Cen	14 07.8	−36 28	2.06	1.01	K0 IIIb	55	0.8	59	0.734	225	+1		**Menkent**
α Boo	14 16.5	+19 05	−0.05	1.24	K1.5 III Fe−0.5	89	−0.3	37	2.279	209	−5 V	high space velocity	**Arcturus**
γ Boo	14 32.8	+38 14	3.04	0.19	A7 III	37.6	0.9	87	0.190	323	−37 V		**Seginus**
η Cen	14 36.7	−42 14	2.33v	−0.16	B1.5 IVpne	11	−2.5	310	0.048	227	−21 V?	variable shell: 2.30–2.41	
α Cen B	14 40.9	−60 55	1.35	0.9	K1 V	750	5.7	4.3	3.703	283	−22 SB	AB 4.1″ (2016); orbit 79.9 y; min = 2″(1955); max 22″	
α Cen A	14 40.9	−60 55	−0.01	0.71	G2 V	750	4.4	4.3	3.710	~277	+5 SB	C: Proxima, 12.4, M5c, 212°	**Rigil Kentaurus**
α Lup	14 43.2	−47 28	2.30v	−0.15	B1.5 III	7	−3.5	460	0.032	221	+7 SB?	var: 2.29–2.34, 0.26 d	
α Cir	14 44.0	−65 03	3.18	0.26	A7p (Sr)	60.4	2.1	54.1	0.303	220	−17 V	B: 8.6, K5 V, 15.7″, PA:263°→224°, 1826→2016	
ε Boo AB	14 45.8	+27 00	2.35	0.97	K0 II–III+A0 V	16	−1.6	200	0.044	288	−17 V	A:2.50; B:4.66, 2.9″; PA:318°→343°, 1822→2015	**Izar**
β UMi +1P	14 50.7	+74 05	2.07	1.46	K4 III	24.9	−0.9	131	0.035	289	+17 V		**Kochab**
α² Lib	14 51.9	−16 07	2.75	0.15	A3 III–IV	43	0.9	76	0.126	237	−10 SB		**Zubenelgenubi**

TABLE OF BRIGHTEST STARS (continued)

Star Name	RA (2018.5) h m	Dec ° '	mv	B–V	MK Type	π mas	Mv	D ly	μ "/y	PA °	Vrad km/s	Remarks
β Lup	14 59.8	−43 12	2.68	−0.18	B2 IV	9	−2.7	380	0.054	222	0 SB	
κ Cen	15 00.4	−42 11	3.13	−0.21	B2 V	9	−2.2	400	0.029	218	+8 SB	
σ Lib	15 05.2	−25 21	3.25v	1.67	M2.5 III	11	−1.5	290	0.083	239	−4	semiregular var.: 3.20–3.46
ζ Lup	15 13.6	−52 10	3.41	0.92	G8 III	~27.8	0.6	117	0.133	238	−10	
δ Boo	15 16.2	+33 15	3.46	0.96	G8 III Fe−1	~26.8	0.6	122	0.140	143	−12 SB	
β Lib	15 18.0	−9 27	2.61	−0.07	B8 IIIn	~17.6	−1.2	190	0.100	259	−35 SB	Zubeneschamali
γ TrA	15 20.7	−68 45	2.87	0.01	A1 IIIn	17.7	−0.9	184	0.074	244	−3 V	
γ UMi	15 20.7	+71 46	3.00	0.06	A3 III	6.7	−2.9	490	0.025	315	−4 V	Pherkad
δ Lup	15 22.6	−40 43	3.22	−0.23	B1.5 IVn	4	−3.9	900	0.032	218	0 V?	
ε Lup AB	15 23.9	−44 45	3.37	−0.19	B2 IV−V	6	−2.6	500	~0.030	~230	+8 SB2	A: 3.56; B: 5.04, 0.2", PA:285°→95°, 1883→2014
ι Dra +1P	15 25.3	+58 54	3.29	1.17	K2 III	32.2	0.8	101	0.019	334	−11	Edasich
α CrB	15 35.5	+26 39	2.22v	0.03	A0 IV (composite)	43	0.4	75	0.150	127	+2 SB	ecl.: 2.21–2.32, 17 d Alphecca
γ Lup AB	15 36.4	−41 14	2.80	−0.22	B2 IVn	8	−2.8	400	~0.030	~212	+2 V	A: 3.5; B: 3.6; similar spectra 1.0" (2016)
α Ser	15 45.2	+6 22	2.63v?	1.17	K2 IIIb CN1	44	0.9	74	0.141	71	+3 V?	var.? Unukalhai
α TrA	15 56.8	−63 29	2.83	0.32	F0 IV	~80.8	2.4	40.4	0.444	205	0	
π Sco A	16 00.0	−26 10	2.89	−0.18	B1 V + B2 V	6	−3.4	600	0.029	203	−3 SB2	3.4 + 4.5, 1.57 d; system resembles β Lyr
T CrB	16 00.3	+25 52	10.08v	1.34	gM3: + Bep	-	0.6	2500?	0.011	329	−29 SB	recurrent nova 1866 (mag. 3), 1946 (mag. 2)
η Lup A	16 01.4	−38 27	3.42	−0.21	B2.5 IVn	7	−2.2	440	0.033	211	+8 V	A: 3.47; B: 7.70, 15.0", PA:22°→15°, 1834→2016
β Sco AB	16 01.4	−22 40	2.29	−0.12	B0.3 IVe+B3V	7	−3.6	500	−0.037	~196	−7 SB	AB: 10.8 y, 0.2"(2015), periastron outbursts 2000, 2011
δ Sco AB	16 06.5	−19 51	2.56	−0.06	B0.5 V	8	−2.9	400	0.025	192	−1 SB	A: 2.78; B: 5.04, ~0.3"; C: 4.93, 14" Acrab
δ Oph	16 15.3	−3 44	2.73	1.58	M1 III	~19.1	−0.9	171	0.150	198	−20 V	Yed Prior
ε Oph	16 19.3	−4 44	3.23	0.97	G9.5 IIIb	31	0.7	106	0.093	64	−10 V	Yed Posterior
σ Sco A	16 22.3	−25 38	2.91v	0.13	B1 III	3	−3.7	700	0.019	213	+3 SB	var.: 2.86–2.94, 0.25 d; B: 8.3, B9 V, 20.3" (2016)
η Dra A	16 24.2	+61 28	2.73	0.91	G8 IIIab	35.4	0.5	92	0.059	343	−14 SB?	B: 8.7, 4.4", PA:150°→143°, 1843→2015
α Sco A	16 30.5	−26 28	1.06v	1.86	M1.5 Iab	6	−5.1	600	0.026	207	−3 SB	irregular var.: 0.88–1.16; B: 5.37, 3.2"(2016) **Antares**
β Her	16 31.0	+21 27	2.78	0.95	G7 IIIa	23	−0.4	140	0.100	261	−26 SB	Kornephoros
τ Sco	16 37.0	−28 15	2.82	−0.21	B0 V	7	−3.0	500	0.025	203	+2 V	
ζ Oph	16 38.2	−10 36	2.54	0.04	O9.5 Vn	9	−2.7	370	0.029	32	−15 V	
ζ Her AB	16 42.0	+31 34	2.81	0.65	G1 V	93	2.7	35	−0.575	~307	−70 SB	A: 2.90; B: 5.53, G7 V, 1.5" (2016), orbit 34 y
η Her	16 43.5	+38 53	3.48	0.92	G7.5 IIIb Fe−1	30.0	0.9	109	0.092	157	+8 V?	
α TrA	16 50.6	−69 04	1.91	1.45	K2 IIb−IIIa	~8.4	−3.5	390	0.036	150	−3	**Atria**
ε Sco	16 51.4	−34 20	2.29	1.14	K2 III	51	0.8	64	0.666	247	−3	
μ¹ Sco	16 53.1	−38 05	3.00v	−0.20	B1.5 IVn	7	−2.9	500	0.024	206	−25 SB2	ecl.: 2.94–3.22, 1.4 d
κ Oph	16 58.5	+9 21	3.19	1.16	K2 III	36	1.0	91	0.292	268	−56 V	
ζ Ara	17 00.2	−56 01	3.12	1.55	K4 III	7	−2.7	490	0.041	206	−6	
ζ Dra	17 08.8	+65 42	3.17	−0.12	B6 III	10	−1.8	330	0.028	314	−17 V	

TABLE OF BRIGHTEST STARS (continued)

Star Name	RA (2018.5) h m	Dec ° ′	m_v	B–V	MK Type	π mas	M_v	D ly	μ ″/y	PA °	V_{rad} km/s	Remarks
η Oph AB	17 11.4	−15 45	2.43	0.06	A2.5 Va	37	0.3	90	−0.107	~22	−1 SB	A: 3.0; B: 3.5, A3 V, 0.6″ (2016), orbit 87.6 y **Sabik**
η Sco	17 13.5	−43 16	3.32	0.44	F2 V:p (Cr)	~44.4	1.6	73	0.290	175	−28	
α Her AB	17 15.5	+14 22	2.78v	1.16	M5 Ib–II	9	−2.4	400	0.032	347	−33 V	semiregular var.: 2.7–4.0; B: 5.4, 4.8″(2016) **Rasalgethi**
π Her	17 15.7	+36 47	3.16	1.44	K3 IIab	8.7	−2.2	380	0.027	276	−26 V?	
δ Her	17 15.8	+24 49	3.12	0.08	A1 Vann	43.4	1.3	75	−0.158	~188	−40 SB	**Sarin**
θ Oph	17 23.1	−25 01	3.27v	−0.19	B2 IV	~7.5	−2.4	440	0.025	197	−2 SB	B: 8.8, 12.7″(2013) is optical companion
β Ara	17 26.8	−55 33	2.84	1.48	K3 Ib–IIa	5	−3.6	600	0.027	199	0	occ. bin.: 3.4, 5.4; var.: 3.25–3.31, 0.14 d
γ Ara A	17 27.0	−56 24	3.31	−0.15	B1 Ib	~2.9	−4.4	1100	0.016	182	−3 V	
β Dra A	17 30.9	+52 17	2.79	0.95	G2 Ib–IIa	8.6	−2.5	380	0.020	308	−20 V	broad lines for Ib; B:10.0,18.1″,PA:324°→326°, 1835→2016 **Rastaban**
υ Sco	17 32.0	−37 19	2.70	−0.18	B2 IV	6	−3.5	600	0.030	185	+8 SB	B: 11.5, 4.4″, PA:13°→12°, 1889→1934 **Lesath**
α Ara	17 33.3	−49 53	2.84	−0.14	B2 Vne	12	−1.7	300	0.075	206	0 SB	
λ Sco	17 34.9	−37 07	1.62v	−0.23	B1.5 IV	6	−4.6	600	0.032	195	−3 SB2	**Shaula**
α Oph	17 35.8	+12 33	2.08	0.16	A5 Vnn	67	1.2	49	0.247	154	+13 SB?	ecl.?, var: 1.62–1.68, 0.21 d **Rasalhague**
θ Sco	17 38.6	−43 00	1.86	0.41	F1 III	~11	−3.0	300	0.006	119	+1	**Sargas**
κ Sco	17 43.8	−39 02	2.39v	−0.17	B1.5 III	7	−3.5	480	0.026	193	−14 SB	var.: 2.41–2.42, 0.20 d
β Oph	17 44.4	+4 34	2.76	1.17	K2 III	~39.8	0.8	82	0.165	345	−12 V	**Cebalrai**
μ Her A	17 47.2	+27 43	3.42	0.75	G5 IV	~120.3	3.8	27.1	0.804	201	−16 V	BC: 9.78, 35.5″, PA:240°→249°, 1781→2015
ι¹ Sco	17 48.9	−40 08	2.99	0.51	F2 Ia	2	−5.9	2000	0.006	180	−28 SB	
G Sco	17 51.1	−37 03	3.19	1.19	K2 III	25.9	0.3	126	0.049	56	+25	**HR 6630**
γ Dra	17 57.0	+51 29	2.24	1.52	K5 III	21.1	−1.1	154	0.024	200	−28	**Eltanin**
ν Oph +2P	18 00.0	−9 46	3.32	0.99	G9.5 IIIa	22	0.0	150	0.117	185	+13	
γ² Sgr	18 07.0	−30 25	2.98	0.98	K0 III	34	0.6	97	0.189	197	+22 SB	**Alnasl**
η Sgr A	18 18.9	−36 45	3.10v	1.5	M3.5 IIIab	22	−0.2	~146	0.211	218	+1 V?	irreg. var.: 3.05–3.12; B: 8.33, G8: IV:, 3.5″ (2016)
δ Sgr	18 22.2	−29 49	2.72	1.38	K2.5 IIIa	9	−2.4	350	0.041	128	−20 V?	**Kaus Meridionalis**
η Ser	18 22.3	−2 54	3.23	0.94	K0 III–IV	54	1.9	~60.5	0.890	218	+9 V?	
ε Sgr	18 25.4	−34 22	1.79	−0.03	B9.5 III	23	−1.4	~143	0.130	198	−15	**Kaus Australis**
λ Sgr	18 29.1	−25 25	2.82	1.02	K1 IIIb	~41.7	0.9	78	0.191	194	−43 V?	**Kaus Media**
α Lyr	18 37.6	+38 48	0.03	0.00	A0 Va	130	0.6	25.0	0.350	35	−14 V	protoplanetary debris? **Vega**
φ Sgr	18 46.8	−26 58	3.17	−0.11	B8 III	14	−1.2	240	0.051	89	+22 SB	apparent duplicity now discounted
σ Sgr	18 56.4	−26 16	2.05	−0.13	B2.5 V	14	−2.2	230	0.056	164	−11V	**Nunki**
γ Lyr	18 59.6	+32 43	3.25	−0.05	B9 II	5	−3.1	600	0.003	290	−21 V	**Sulafat**
ζ Sgr AB	19 03.0	−29 51	2.60	0.06	A2 IV–V + A4:V:	37	0.4	90	n.a.	n.a.	+22 SB	A: 3.2; B: 3.5, 0.6″ (2016), orbit 21.1 y **Ascella**
ζ Aql A	19 06.3	+13 54	2.99	0.01	A0 Vann	~39.3	1.0	83	0.096	184	−25 SB	
λ Aql	19 07.2	−4 51	3.43	−0.10	B9 Vnp (kB7HeA0)	26	0.5	120	0.093	192	−12 V	
τ Sgr	19 08.1	−27 38	3.32	1.17	K1.5 IIIb	27	0.5	120	0.255	191	+45 SB	
π Sgr ABC	19 10.9	−21 00	2.88	0.38	F2 II–III	6	−3.1	500	0.036	182	−10	A: 3.7; B: 3.8 0.1″ (1989); C: 6.0, AB-CD<1″?

TABLE OF BRIGHTEST STARS (continued)

Star Name	RA (2018.5) h m	Dec ° '	m_v	B–V	MK Type	π mas	M_V	D ly	μ "/y	PA °	V_{rad} km/s	Remarks	Name
δ Dra	19 12.6	+67 42	3.07	0.99	G9 III	33.5	0.7	97	0.133	46	+25 V		Altais
δ Aql	19 26.4	+3 09	3.36	0.32	F2 IV	64	2.4	51	0.268	72	–30 SB		
β Cyg A	19 31.5	+28 00	3.36	1.09	K3 II + B9.5 V	8	–2.3	430	0.009	229	–24 V	B: 5.11, 35", Aa, Ac: Δm = 1.5, 0.4" (2008)	Albireo
δ Cyg AB	19 45.6	+45 11	2.86	0.00	B9.5 III	20	–0.7	160	~0.066	~42	–20 SB	B: 6.4, F1 V; 2.7", PA:41°→215°, 1826→2016	
γ Aql	19 47.1	+10 40	2.72	1.51	K3 II	~8.3	–2.7	390	0.017	100	–2 V		Tarazed
α Aql	19 51.7	+8 55	0.76	0.22	A7 Vnn	195	2.2	16.7	0.660	54	–26		**Altair**
θ Aql	20 12.3	–0 46	3.24	–0.07	B9.5 III	11	–1.5	290	0.036	81	–27 SB2		
β Cap A	20 22.0	–14 43	3.05	0.79	K0: II: + A5: V:n	10	–2.0	300	0.046	81	–19 SB	A: mult.: 4.0 + 4.3 + 4.8 + 6.7, <1"	Dabih
γ Cyg	20 22.9	+40 19	2.23	0.67	F8 Ib	2	–6.5	2000	0.003	111	–8 V		Sadr
α Pav	20 27.1	–56 40	1.94	–0.12	B2.5 V	18	–1.8	180	0.086	175	+2 SB		**Peacock**
α Ind	20 38.9	–47 14	3.11	1.00	K0 III CN–1	33	0.7	98	0.083	37	–1		
α Cyg	20 42.1	+45 21	1.25	0.09	A2 Ia	2	–6.9	~1400	0.003	47	–5 SB		**Deneb**
η Cep	20 45.7	+61 55	3.41	0.91	K0 IV	70.1	2.6	46.5	0.823	6	–87	B(75"): optical; C: shared p-motion, 78"	
β Pav	20 46.6	–66 08	3.42	0.16	A6 IV	~24.1	0.3	135	0.044	283	+10		
ε Cyg	20 47.0	+34 02	2.48	1.02	K0 III	44.9	0.7	73	0.486	47	–11 SB?		
ζ Cyg	21 13.7	+30 18	3.21	0.99	G8 IIIa Ba 0.5	23	0.0	140	0.069	175	+17 SB		
α Cep	21 19.0	+62 40	2.45	0.26	A7 Van	66.5	1.6	49.1	0.158	72	–10 V	var: 3.16–3.27, 0.19 d; B: 7.8; 13.5" (2016)	Alderamin
β Cep	21 28.9	+70 39	3.23v	–0.20	B1 III	5	–3.4	700	0.015	56	–8 SB		Alfirk
β Aqr	21 32.5	–5 29	2.9	0.83	G0 Ib	6	–3.2	500	0.020	114	+7 V?		Sadalsuud
ε Peg	21 45.1	+9 58	2.38v	1.52	K2 Ib	5	–4.2	700	0.027	89	+5 V	irregular var.: 0.7–3.5 (flare in 1972)	**Enif**
δ Cap	21 48.1	–16 03	2.85v	0.18	A3mF2 IV:	84	2.5	38.7	0.396	139	–6 SB	occ. bin.: 2.81–3.05, 1.0 d, 3.2 + 5.2	Deneb Algiedi
γ Gru	21 55.0	–37 17	3.00	–0.08	B8 IV-Vs	15	–1.1	210	0.099	98	–2 V?		
α Aqr	22 06.0	–0 14	2.95	0.97	G2 Ib	6	–3.1	~520	0.021	117	+8 V?		Sadalmelik
α Gru	22 09.4	–46 52	1.73	–0.07	B7 Vn	32	–0.7	101	0.194	139	+12		**Alnair**
ζ Cep	22 11.5	+58 18	3.39	1.56	K1.5 Ib	3.9	–3.7	800	0.014	69	–18 SB		
ζ Tuc	22 19.8	–60 10	2.87	1.39	K3 III	16	–1.1	200	0.081	241	+42 SB		
ζ Peg	22 42.4	+10 56	3.41	–0.09	B8.5 III	16	–0.6	210	0.078	98	+7 V?	irregular var.: 2.0–2.3	Homam
β Gru	22 43.8	–46 47	2.07v	1.61	M5 III	18	–1.6	180	0.135	92	+2		
η Peg	22 43.9	+30 19	2.93	0.85	G8 II + F0 V	15	–1.2	210	0.029	153	+4 SB		Matar
δ Aqr	22 55.6	–15 43	3.27	0.07	A3 IV-V	20	–0.2	160	0.051	237	+18 V	(wk λ4481)	Skat
α PsA +1P	22 58.7	–29 31	1.17	0.14	A3 Va	130	1.7	25.1	0.36	117	+7	exoplanet image published 2008	**Fomalhaut**
β Peg	23 04.7	+28 11	2.44v	1.66	M2 II-III	16.6	–1.5	~196	0.232	54	+9 V	irregular var.: 2.31–2.74	Scheat
α Peg	23 05.7	+15 18	2.49	0.00	A0 III-IV	24	–0.6	133	0.073	124	–4 SB		**Markab**
γ Cep +1P	23 40.1	+77 44	3.21	1.03	K1 III-IV	71	2.5	46	0.135	339	–42 V?		Errai

SPECTROSCOPY OF STARS
BY CHRIS CORBALLY, RICHARD GRAY, AND TOOMAS KARMO

An important column is included in the table of Brightest Stars. This is the classification of the star's spectrum in terms of MK Type, after Morgan and Keenan who first developed this primary system in 1943. Its symbols are explained in the introduction to the table. The MK type is really a compact description of the star's spectrum in relation to a grid of standard stars, first covering the two dimensions of temperature type and luminosity, and then including common peculiarities that stars may show.

The MK types are useful in estimating the physical parameters of stars, along with their ages, distances, and reddenings (the amount of dust in their line of sight), which are important for galactic astronomy. The classifications identify the more astrophysically interesting stars.

Classifying spectra: The classification process for normal stars is straightforward, matching as close as possible the "look" of a star's spectrum with how it fits into a "library of standard spectra." You can either build up that library through your own spectra, which is the best way eventually, or find a library that suits the resolution of your spectra on the internet.[1] For precise work, be careful that the stars you are using as standards are genuine MK system standards. The matching of unknown to standard spectra is made easier and more precise by using ratios of spectral features, traditionally called "absorption lines." The best features to use change, depending on the temperature type of the star. Richard Gray's Digital Spectral Classification Atlas[2] points out these features in the blue-green region of the spectrum, where the criteria are the most sensitive, while *winmk* and *xmk* are programs for comparing digital spectra on screen.[3]

Observing spectra: Slitless spectroscopy is a simple way to start obtaining one's own spectra. This involves putting a prism or diffraction grating in front of a DSLR lens or the digital imager on a telescope.[4] The spectra are of low resolution, but are sufficient to distinguish the broad MK "letter classes" of stars, to monitor variable stars, and get novae and supernovae, emission nebulae, and comets.[5] There are plenty of bright examples of these. For more detailed spectra, a spectrograph matching your telescope needs to be bought or made.[6]

Processing spectra: While a picture of a spectrum, or group of them in a crowded field, is beautiful, the science comes alive when one displays the intensity of the signal against wavelength. Extracting a 1-D digital spectrum from the 2-D image on the detector is both a science and an art, but there is abundant help on the internet.[7] The other step for science is calibrating the pixel position against actual wavelength along the spectrum. Again look to the internet for help in this.

What to observe: Examples of spectral interest are given under Resources 5 and 6 below. The AAVSO posts campaigns for observing objects, which often include the need for spectral data.[8] There are also interesting, bright variable stars, like Miras and B-type shell stars, that repay long-term spectroscopic observing. As John Martin remarks, "interesting" is a matter of individual taste and scientific curiosity. As these develop, you will surely become delighted with looking at your spectra and very knowledgeable about them.

A Few Resources
1 pendientedemigracion.ucm.es/info/Astrof/invest/actividad/spectra.html
2 ned.ipac.caltech.edu/level5/Gray/frames.html
3 www.appstate.edu/~grayro/MK/winmk.htm (for MS Windows)
  www.appstate.edu/~grayro/spectrum/ftp/download.html
  (see Auxiliary X-Windows programs for Linux and iOS versions)
4 The Star Analyzer is one such grating www.rspec-astro.com/star-analyser
  John Martin's page comprehensively describes slitless spectroscopy
  go.uis.edu/gratingspectra
5 Examples are at www.rspec-astro.com/sample-projects
6 Modest off-the-shelf spectrographs include the Shelyak ALPY-600, while both Christian Buil's and John Menke's websites offer advice on building your own and show their inspiring images
  www.astrosurf.com/buil and www.menkescientific.com/johnspage.html
7 Start at go.uis.edu/gratingspectra
8 www.aavso.org/observing-campaigns#current

THE 50 BRIGHTEST STARS BY MAGNITUDE

This table contains the Sun and 50 other stars with an apparent magnitude brighter than mag. 2.0 that appear in the previous table. A subset of data from that table is included, although the spectral classifications have been simplified. As in the previous table, the components of visual binary stars are listed separately; their combined magnitudes appear in footnotes. Where more than one star has the same apparent magnitude, they have been sorted by right ascension. Navigation star names are **bold**.

Rank	Star Name	RA (2018.5) h m	Dec ° '	m_V	$B-V$	MK Type	M_V	D ly	
	Sun			−26.75	0.63	G2	4.8	8 lm	
1	α CMa A	6 46.0	−16 45	−1.44	0.01	A0	1.5	8.6	**Sirius**
2	α Car	6 24.4	−52 42	−0.62	0.16	A9	−5.5	~310	**Canopus**
3	α Boo	14 16.5	+19 05	−0.05	1.24	K1.5	−0.3	37	**Arcturus**
4	α Cen A	14 40.9	−60 55	−0.01	0.71	G2	4.4	4.3	**Rigil Kentaurus A**[1]
5	α Lyr	18 37.6	+38 48	0.03	0.00	A0	0.6	25.0	**Vega**
6	α Aur Aa+Ab	5 18.1	+46 01	0.08	0.80	G6+G2	−0.5	43	**Capella**
7	β Ori A	5 15.4	−8 11	0.18	−0.03	B8	−6.9	900	**Rigel**
8	α CMi A	7 40.3	+5 11	0.40	0.43	F5	2.7	11.5	**Procyon**
9	α Eri	1 38.4	−57 09	0.45	−0.16	B3	−2.7	140	**Achernar**
10	α Ori	5 56.2	+7 25	0.45v	1.50	M2	−5.5	500	**Betelgeuse**
11	β Cen AB	14 05.1	−60 28	0.58v	−0.23	B1	−4.8	400	**Hadar**
12	α Aql	19 51.7	+8 55	0.76	0.22	A7	2.2	16.7	**Altair**
13	α Tau A	4 37.0	+16 33	0.87v	1.54	K5	−0.7	67	**Aldebaran**
14	α Vir	13 26.2	−11 15	0.98v	−0.24	B1	−3.4	250	**Spica**
15	α Sco A	16 30.5	−26 28	1.06v	1.86	M1.5	−5.1	600	**Antares**
16	β Gem	7 46.4	+27 59	1.16	0.99	K0	1.1	33.8	**Pollux**
17	α PsA	22 58.7	−29 31	1.17	0.14	A3	1.7	25.1	**Fomalhaut**
18	α Cru A	12 27.6	−63 12	1.25	−0.20	B0.5	−3.7	~320	**Acrux A**[2]
19	β Cru	12 48.8	−59 47	1.25v	−0.24	B0.5	−3.4	300	**Mimosa**
20	α Cyg	20 42.1	+45 21	1.25	0.09	A2	−6.9	~1400	**Deneb**
21	α Cen B	14 40.9	−60 55	1.35	0.88	K1	5.7	4.3	**Rigil Kentaurus B**[1]
22	α Leo A	10 09.4	+11 53	1.36	−0.09	B7	−0.6	79	**Regulus**
23	ε CMa A	6 59.3	−29 00	1.50	−0.21	B2	−4.0	410	**Adhara**
24	γ Cru	12 32.2	−57 13	1.59v	1.60	M3.5	−0.6	89	**Gacrux**
25	λ Sco	17 34.9	−37 07	1.62v	−0.23	B1.5	−4.6	600	**Shaula**
26	γ Ori	5 26.1	+6 22	1.64	−0.22	B2	−2.8	250	**Bellatrix**
27	α Cru B	12 27.6	−63 12	1.64	−0.18	B1	−3.3	~320	**Acrux B**[2]
28	β Tau	5 27.5	+28 37	1.65	−0.13	B7	−1.4	130	**Elnath**
29	β Car	9 13.4	−69 48	1.67	0.07	A1	−1.0	113	**Miaplacidus**
30	ε Ori	5 37.2	−1 11	1.69	−0.18	B0	−7.2	2000	**Alnilam**
31	α Gru	22 09.4	−46 52	1.73	−0.07	B7	−0.7	101	**Alnair**
32	ζ Ori A	5 41.7	−1 56	1.74	−0.20	O9.5	−5.0	700	**Alnitak**
33	γ² Vel	8 10.1	−47 24	1.75v	−0.14	WC8+O9	−5.9	1100	[no IAU name]
34	ε UMa	12 54.8	+55 52	1.76v	−0.02	A0	−0.3	83	**Alioth**
35	α Per	3 25.7	+49 56	1.79	0.48	F5	−4.2	510	**Mirfak**
36	ε Sgr	18 25.4	−34 22	1.79	−0.03	A0	−1.4	~143	**Kaus Australis**
37	α UMa AB	11 04.9	+61 39	1.81	1.06	K0	−1.1	120	**Dubhe**
38	δ CMa	7 09.1	−26 25	1.83	0.67	F8	−6.6	2000	**Wezen**
39	η UMa	13 48.3	+49 13	1.85	−0.10	B3	−0.7	104	**Alkaid**
40	θ Sco	17 38.6	−43 00	1.86	0.41	F1	−3.0	300	**Sargas**
41	ε Car	8 22.9	−59 34	1.86v	1.20	K3+B2	−4.5	600	**Avior**
42	β Aur	6 00.9	+44 57	1.90v	0.08	A1	−0.1	81	Menkalinan
43	α TrA	16 50.6	−69 04	1.91	1.45	K2	−3.5	390	**Atria**
44	γ Gem	6 38.8	+16 23	1.93	0.00	A1	−0.7	110	**Alhena**
45	α Gem A	7 35.8	+31 51	1.93	0.03	A1	0.9	52	**Castor A**
46	δ Vel AB	8 45.2	−54 47	1.93	0.04	A1	0.0	81	[no IAU name]
47	α Pav	20 27.1	−56 40	1.94	−0.12	B2.5	−1.8	180	**Peacock**
48	α UMi A	2 55.0	+89 21	1.97v	0.64	F5–8	−3.6	430	**Polaris**
49	β CMa	6 23.5	−17 58	1.98v	−0.24	B1	−3.9	~490	**Mirzam**
50	α Hya	9 28.5	−8 44	1.99	1.44	K3	−1.7	180	**Alphard**

[1] To the unaided eye, the combined visual magnitude of Rigil Kentaurus A and B is −0.28.
[2] To the unaided eye, the combined visual magnitude of Acrux A and B is 0.68.

THE NEAREST STARS
BY TODD J. HENRY

The nearest stars hold a special fascination for any of us who have gazed skyward. Astronomers study the Sun's neighbors because they are the nearest, and therefore brightest, examples of their types. For many kinds of stars, the fundamental framework of stellar astronomy is built upon direct measurements of luminosities, colors, temperatures, and masses of nearby stars. Their surrounding environments are remote destinations to explore from Earth, and any planets orbiting them could someday become outposts of humankind because the nearest stars are the first step beyond our own Solar System.

The definition of a "nearby" star system is that its distance is accurately known to be within a designated horizon. Distances may be measured geometrically, via astrometry using the technique of trigonometric parallax, or estimated using myriad combinations of photometric and spectroscopic data. Here we adopt distances based on trigonometric parallaxes only, as they are the most reliable and are independent of assumptions about the type of star under scrutiny. With modern techniques, we now know the distances to a few hundred stars to better than 1% accuracy.

The list presented here includes the Sun's 51 nearest stellar neighbors and their companions within the astonomically convenient horizon of 5.0 parsecs, or 16.3 light-years (ly). The definition of a parsec, which is equivalent to 3.26 ly, is based upon the radius of the Earth's orbit: as the Earth swings around the Sun, nearby stars shift back and forth relative to more distant, background objects because of our changing perspective, much as a thumb held at arm's length will seem to shift relative to a distant background when you close one eye, then the other. This shift is called parallax. The size of the shift depends entirely upon the star's distance, and astronomers have defined the distance at which a star's parallax is $1.00''$ to be 1.00 parallax-second (parsec). As the distance increases, the shift decreases inversely, i.e. parallax = 1/distance. Thus, a star at 5.00 parsecs will exhibit a trigonometric parallax of 0.200 arcseconds, or 200 milliarcseconds (mas). The shifts are slight—the parallax of the nearest star, Proxima Centauri, is 769 mas and is only about 1/2300th the width of the full Moon.

To be included in the list, a stellar system must have a trigonometric parallax of at least 200 mas with an error of less than 10 mas published in the refereed literature, meaning that the distance is known to 5% or better. There are, effectively, four broad categories of nearby star parallaxes: (1) A wonderful compendium of ground-based parallax efforts through 1995 is *The General Catalogue of Trigonometric Stellar Parallaxes* (a.k.a. the *Yale Parallax Catalog*, or *YPC*) by van Altena et al. The *YPC* includes nearly 16 000 parallax measurements of more than 8 000 stars. Stars as bright as Sirius and as faint as mag. 20 can be found in the *YPC*, with most parallaxes accurate to 3–13 mas. (2) ESA's *HIPPARCOS* space astrometry mission targeted nearly 120 000 relatively bright stars at a precision of typically 0.5–4 mas, with a compendium of results published in 1997. In 2007, van Leeuwen published a new reduction of the *HIPPARCOS* data, and those results have been used to generate the parallaxes given here. (3) Since then, several teams have continued using traditional telescopes on the ground to measure parallaxes for both new and known stars within 5 parsecs, primarily by the Allegheny, Dartmouth, RECONS, Torino, and USNO groups. (4) In space, the *Hubble Space Telescope* has been used to determine parallaxes of several of the Sun's neighbors, while measuring stellar masses or searching for exoplanets (primarily by the U. Texas group). The list presented here uses a comprehensive combination of trigonometric parallaxes from various sources to arrive at a weighted mean parallax for each system, which simply means that higher-quality parallaxes are mathematically given more weight in the averaging process. Individual component parallaxes have been combined for all systems except for the nearest one, which is, in fact, a triple including Proxima and the two components of α Centauri, A and B. The *YPC* includes 43 of the 51 extrasolar systems, while *HIPPARCOS* improved upon many of those, but added no new systems. RECONS added five of the eight remaining systems, with the latest three additions having parallaxes measured by other teams. In total, 133 different parallaxes have been used to generate the distances given. The RECONS group (www.recons.org) is keeping a tally of all trigonometric parallax efforts since the *YPC* and *HIPPARCOS*, and the reader is encouraged to contact the author about any overlooked publications (thenry@astro.gsu.edu).

Including the Sun, there are 52 known systems in the 5-parsec sphere, made up of 66 stars, 8 brown dwarfs, and 15 extrasolar planets (plus, of course, the 8 planets in the Solar System). Curiously, there are one-third more systems in the southern sky (30) than in the north (21), even though historically far more astronomical observations have been made in the northern sky. Seventeen of the systems include stellar or brown-dwarf companions, while an additional ten (including the Solar System) have planets. The smallest type of star, known as red dwarfs of spectral type M, dominate our galaxy, accounting for 73% of the 5-parsec sample (48 of 66 stars—all stars without types in the list are type M, but individual spectral types are not available because of close separations in multiple systems, hence the "J" for joint in some spectral types). None of these red dwarfs is visible with the unaided eye. In some ways, our galaxy mimics an ocean full of creatures, large and small, but it is the smallest fish that dominate the population. Missing from the nearby waters are the largest whales, the most massive stars of spectral types O and B. Such stars are exceedingly rare and have lifetimes of only a few million years. The visually brightest star in the night sky is Sirius, which is the brighter star in the sixth-nearest system, and the only A-type star listed. Near Sirius in the sky is Procyon (the 15th-nearest system), nearly as bright and the only F-type star listed. Both Sirius and Procyon have white-dwarf companions that are the leftover embers of more-massive counterparts. These stars have already reinvented themselves, having changed from stars larger than Sirius and Procyon to reveal only their cores as white dwarfs by sloughing off their outer layers long ago. In the past, the light of Sirius and Procyon would be lost in the glare of their much larger, and brighter, components. In all, there are five white dwarfs, denoted by "D" in the list, nearer than 5 parsecs. The two stars most similar to our Sun are the only other two G dwarfs, α Centauri A and τ Ceti. Finally, eight stars are of K type, including α Centauri B, 61 Cygni A and B, and the naked-eye stars ε Indi, o^2 Eridani A, and ε Eridani. The latter star is particularly interesting because it is circled by a band of cold dust and at least one planet, with reports of two additional planets inferred because of gaps in the dusty disk. Also worthy of note is Kapteyn's Star, which is a rare subdwarf—an ancient, subluminous star of spectral luminosity class VI—that is moving quickly through the solar neighborhood. It has the largest radial velocity of the systems in the list, and has the second-fastest proper motion, only surpassed by Barnard's Star, the second-nearest system.

We continue to find more of the Sun's neighbors, even so close to home. Recent and ongoing sky surveys provide a wealth of solar neighborhood candidates for those who cleverly dig through the databases for gems. DENIS (DEep Near-Infrared Survey) has provided two recent additions, the red dwarf DENIS 1048–3956 and the brown dwarf DENIS 0255–4700. Following in the footsteps of Giclas and Luyten, who both did breakthrough work in studies of nearby stars via proper-motion searches, the SCR (SuperCOSMOS–RECONS) effort trawls an electronic database generated by scanning glass plates of the entire sky. The 27th-nearest system, an M/T dwarf pair known as SCR 1845–6357, was found during an early SCR search, and efforts are continuing.

In the following table, names are given in the first column with emphasis on discovery names or variable-star names, the latter if for no other reason than it gives some idea as to the system's location in the sky. Component designations within a single system are listed as A, B, or C, and are enclosed by parentheses if there are different names for individual members. Presumed planets are listed as "+nP" in the companion column, where n is the number of planets. Astrometric information is given next, including **RA** and **Dec** for equinox J2000.0, the weighted mean parallax (π) and its estimated error (**err**) in mas, the derived distance (**D**) in light-years, and the proper motion (μ) in mas/y with the position angle of the motion (**PA**) (north is 0°, east is 90°). Spectroscopic information is then listed, including the systemic radial velocity (V_{rad}) and spectral type (**Sp.**) for each component, when known. Photometric information is provided in the form of the visual magnitude (m_v), where it may be useful to know that the human eye can see to about mag. 6. The list closes with the derived absolute magnitude (M_v), which is a valuable measurement of an object's intrinsic brightness, and reflects how bright an object would appear if it were at a standard distance of 10 parsecs.

In the past few years, brown dwarfs very near the Sun have been found, including WISE 1049–5319AB, which currently ranks as the third-nearest system. Eight brown dwarfs are now known within 5 parsecs. Nonetheless, the stars still outnumber the brown dwarfs by 8:1, and there are more extrasolar planets known than brown dwarfs. GJ 1061, now ranked as the 21st-nearest system, remains the closest new star found to the Sun since the YPC and *HIPPARCOS* compendia. In the next few years, additional brown dwarfs will likely enter the sample—WISE 0855–0714 and DENIS 0817–6155 are the leading contenders, but require accurate parallaxes for inclusion—and now that *Gaia* observations are underway, new stars may be added as well.

In 1999, the first planet around Ross 780 was announced, and thus the first reliable exoplanet discovery within 5 parsecs made it into the *Observer's Handbook* in 2000. Other than the Sun, there are now 9 systems within 5 parsecs that are *reported* to have planets. Research on individual nearby stars has recently been reinvigorated because the nearest stellar systems are prime targets for more-sensitive exoplanet searches and, ultimately, life. The population of nearby stars remains a compelling area of research because we have yet to answer the fundamental questions, what types of stars form at what rates? and, how much mass in our galaxy can be found in stars? That so many faint, yet nearby, objects have slipped through previous surveys of our neighborhood hints at more to come. Undoubtedly, the more complete our reconnaissance of the solar neighborhood, the better we will understand the nature of stars that make up our galaxy, and our Sun's place among them.

* (See entry 2 at right.) For the fastest-moving star in the sky, Barnard's Star, the 2018.0 coordinates are RA 17h 40m 23s, Dec +4° 46′ 48″, steadily moving northward in eastern Ophiuchus.

TABLE OF NEAREST STARS

Name		RA (2000) Dec h m ° '	π mas	err mas	D ly	μ mas/y	PA °	V_{rad} km/s	Sp.	m_V	M_V
Sun	+8P								G2V	−26.71	4.84
1 Proxima Cen (C)+1P		14 30 −62 41	768.69	0.29	4.24	3853	281.5	−16	M5.0V	11.13	15.56
α Cen	A	14 40 −60 50	747.23	1.17	4.36	3710	277.5	−26	G2V	0.01	4.38
	B	14 40 −60 50				3724	284.8	−18	K0.0V	1.34	5.71
2 Barnard's		17 58 +04 42*	545.52	0.29	5.98	10358	355.6	−111	M3.5V	9.54	13.22
3 WISE 1049−5319	A	10 49 −53 19	495.02	4.56	6.59	2787	277.5		L8.0V	23.25	26.72
	B	10 49 −53 19							T1.0V	24.07	27.54
4 Wolf 359		10 56 +07 01	414.35	1.08	7.87	4696	234.6	+19	M5.5V	13.61	16.70
5 Lalande 21185		11 03 +35 58	393.25	0.57	8.29	4802	186.9	−85	M2.0V	7.46	10.43
6 Sirius	A	6 45 −16 43	380.02	1.28	8.58	1339	204.1	−9	A1V	−1.43	1.47
	B	6 45 −16 43							DA2	8.44	11.34
7 BL Cet	(A)	1 39 −17 57	373.70	2.70	8.73	3368	80.4	+29	M5.5V	12.63	15.49
UV Cet	(B)	1 39 −17 57						+32	M6.0V	13.08	15.94
8 Ross 154		18 50 −23 50	337.22	1.97	9.67	666	106.8	−10	M3.5V	10.50	13.14
9 Ross 248		23 42 +44 11	316.04	0.55	10.31	1617	177.0	−78	M5.5V	12.29	14.79
10 ε Eri	+1P	3 33 −09 27	311.22	0.09	10.48	977	271.1	+16	K2.0V	3.73	6.20
11 CD −36 15693		23 06 −35 51	305.08	0.70	10.69	6896	78.9	+9	M1.0V	7.34	9.76
12 Ross 128		11 48 +00 48	298.14	1.37	10.94	1361	153.6	−31	M4.0V	11.15	13.52
13 EZ Aqr	A	22 39 −15 18	289.50	4.40	11.27	3254	46.6	−50	M5.0VJ	13.03	15.34
	B	22 39 −15 18								13.27	15.58
	C	22 39 −15 18								15.07	17.38
14 61 Cyg	A	21 07 +38 45	286.08	0.48	11.40	5281	51.9	−66	K5.0V	5.21	7.49
	B	21 07 +38 45				5172	52.6	−64	K7.0V	6.03	8.31
15 Procyon	A	7 39 +05 13	285.17	0.64	11.44	1259	214.7	−4	F5 IV–V	0.37	2.65
	B	7 39 +05 13							DQZ	10.70	12.98
16 BD +59 1915	A	18 43 +59 38	283.83	1.46	11.49	2238	323.6	−1	M3.0V	8.90	11.17
	B	18 43 +59 38				2313	323.0	+1	M3.5V	9.69	11.96
17 GX And	(A)+1P	0 18 +44 01	280.00	0.59	11.65	2918	81.9	+12	M1.5V	8.09	10.32
GQ And	(B)	0 18 +44 01						+11	M3.5V	11.07	13.30
18 ε Ind	A	22 03 −56 47	276.07	0.28	11.81	4704	122.7	−40	K3.0V	4.68	6.89
	B	22 04 −56 47				4823	121.1		T1.0V		
	C	22 04 −56 46							T6.0V		
19 DX Can		8 30 +26 47	275.63	2.42	11.83	1290	242.2	−5	M6.0V	14.96	17.16
20 τ Cet		1 44 −15 56	273.97	0.17	11.91	1922	296.4	−17	G8.5V	3.49	5.68
21 GJ 1061		3 36 −44 31	269.08	0.53	12.21	831	118.8	−20	M5.0V	13.09	15.24
22 YZ Cet		1 13 −17 00	269.08	2.99	12.12	1372	61.9	+28	M4.0V	12.16	14.31
23 Luyten's	+2P	7 27 +05 14	266.23	0.66	12.25	3738	171.2	+18	M3.5V	9.88	12.01
24 SO 0253+1652		2 53 +16 53	259.90	0.62	12.55	5050	137.9		M6.5V	15.14	17.21
25 Kapteyn's		5 12 −45 01	255.67	0.91	12.76	8670	131.4	+245	M2.0VI	8.85	10.89
26 AX Mic		21 17 −38 52	253.44	0.80	12.87	3455	250.6	+28	K9.0V	6.67	8.69
27 SCR 1845−6357	A	18 45 −63 58	250.30	0.53	13.03	2558	74.7		M8.5V	17.40	19.39
	B	18 45 −63 58							T6.0V		
28 Kruger 60	A	22 28 +57 42	248.06	1.39	13.15	990	241.6	−34	M3.0V	9.79	11.76
	B	22 28 +57 41							M4.0V	11.41	13.38
29 DENIS 1048−3956		10 48 −39 56	247.20	0.41	13.19	1530	229.2		M8.5V	17.39	19.36
30 UGP 0722−0540		7 22 −05 40	242.80	2.40	13.43	970	291.3		T10.0V		
31 Ross 614	A	6 29 −02 49	241.54	0.37	13.50	930	131.7	+17	M4.0V	11.18	13.09
	B	6 29 −02 49							M5.5V	14.26	16.17
32 Wolf 1061	+2P	16 30 −12 40	234.38	1.50	13.92	1189	184.5	−21	M3.5V	10.07	11.92
33 Wolf 424	A	12 33 +09 01	233.34	2.45	14.31	1811	277.4		M5.0VJ	13.25	15.09
	B	12 33 +09 01								13.24	15.08
34 van Maanen's		0 49 +05 23	232.70	1.81	14.02	2978	155.5	+54	DZ7	12.40	14.23
35 CD −37 15492		0 05 −37 21	230.32	0.90	14.16	6100	112.5	+23	M1.5V	8.54	10.35
36 TZ Ari		2 00 +13 03	221.82	0.69	14.70	2097	147.8	−29	M4.0V	12.35	14.08
37 BD +68 946	+1P	17 36 +68 20	220.47	0.83	14.79	1309	194.2	−29	M3.0V	9.17	10.89

TABLE OF NEAREST STARS (continued)

Name		RA (2000) h m	Dec ° '	π mas	err mas	D ly	μ mas/y	PA °	Vrad km/s	Sp.	mV	MV
38 G 208–44	(A)	19 54	+44 25	220.13	0.44	14.82	731	143.1		M5.5VJ	13.46	15.17
G 208–45	(B)	19 54	+44 25							M6.0V	14.01	15.72
G 208–44	(C)	19 54	+44 25								16.75	18.46
39 CD –46 11540	+1P	17 29	–46 54	220.11	1.39	14.82	1050	146.9	–10	M2.5V	9.39	11.10
40 LHS 292		10 48	–11 20	218.16	0.59	14.95	1644	158.5	–7	M6.5V	15.73	17.42
41 L 145–141		11 46	–64 50	216.12	1.09	15.09	2688	97.4		DQ6	11.50	13.17
42 Ross 780	+4P	22 53	–14 16	214.45	0.57	15.21	1174	125.1	–2	M3.5V	10.18	11.84
43 G 158–27		0 07	–07 32	208.00	1.16	15.68	2041	203.6	–42	M5.0V	13.77	15.36
44 LHS 288		10 44	–61 13	206.35	0.77	15.81	1657	348.1		M5.5V	13.90	15.47
45 DENIS 0255–4700		2 55	–47 01	205.75	0.53	15.85	1149	119.5		L7.5V	22.92	24.49
46 BD +44 2051	(A)	11 05	+43 32	205.67	0.93	15.86	4511	282.1	+69	M1.0V	8.77	10.34
WX UMa	(B)	11 06	+43 31				4531	281.9		M5.5V	14.44	16.01
47 BD +50 1725		10 11	+49 27	205.53	0.49	15.87	1452	249.7	–26	K7.0V	6.59	8.15
48 BD +20 2465		10 20	+19 52	204.60	2.80	15.94	506	264.0	+12	M2.5V	9.29	10.84
49 WISE 1639–6847		16 39	–68 47	202.30	3.10	16.11	3156	169.3		brown dwarf		
50 CD –49 13515	+2P	21 34	–49 01	202.03	1.00	16.14	819	183.2	+4	M1.5V	8.66	10.19
51 o² Eri	A	4 15	–07 39	200.65	0.23	16.26	4088	213.2	–42	K0.5V	4.43	5.94
	B	4 15	–07 39				4073	212.4		DA4	9.52	11.03
	C	4 15	–07 39							M4.0V	11.24	12.75

Editor's Note: For more information, see A.H. Batten, "Our Changing Views of the Solar Neighborhood," *JRASC, 92* (1998), pp. 231–237, at www.rasc.ca/sites/default/files/jrasc1998-10.pdf.

SOME EASILY OBSERVABLE NEARBY STARS

This table lists some of the nearby stars from the main table that may be of interest to the observer, including all those of mag. 6 and brighter, plus three of historical interest (all red dwarfs). The stars have been reordered by magnitude of the primary component. The table data have been simplified—consult the original table for details.

Name		RA (2000) h m	Dec ° '	π mas	D ly	μ "/y	PA °	Sp.	mV
Sun	+8P							G2	–26.7
Sirius[1]	A	6 45	–16 43	380	8.6	1.3	204	A1	–1.4
α Cen[2, 3]	A	14 40	–60 50	747	4.4	3.7	278	G2	0.0
	B	14 40	–60 50			3.7	285	K0.0	1.3
Procyon[4]	A	7 39	+5 13	285	11.4	1.3	215	F5	0.4
τ Cet[5]		1 44	–15 56	274	11.9	1.9	296	G8.5	3.5
ε Eri[5]	+1P	3 33	–09 27	311	10.5	1.0	271	K2.0	3.7
o² Eri[6]	A	4 15	–07 39	201	16.3	4.1	213	K0.5	4.4
	B	4 15	–07 39			4.1	212	DA4	9.5
ε Ind	A	22 3	–56 47	276	11.8	4.7	123	K3.0	4.7
61 Cyg[7]	A	21 7	+38 45	286	11.4	5.3	52	K5.0	5.2
	B	21 7	+38 45			5.2	53	K7.0	6.0
Kapteyn's		5 12	–45 1	256	12.8	8.7	131	M2.0	8.9
Barnard's[8]		17 58	+4 42	546	6.0	10.4	356	M3.5	9.6
Luyten's[9]		7 27	+5 14	266	12.3	3.7	171	M3.5	9.9

[1] α CMa, see note on facing page.
[2] Rigil Kentaurus, similar to Sun, see note on p. 292.
[3] The star system nearest to Sun reported to have at least one planet.
[4] α CMi, see note on p. 292
[5] Similar to Sun, the nearest such star visible to observers at north-temperate latitudes.
[6] B is the nearest white-dwarf star that is easily observable, see p. 304.
[7] First star to have its stellar parallax measured (Bessel, 1838).
[8] Star with the largest proper motion; second-closest star system to Sun (Barnard, 1916).
[9] Only 1.2 ly from Procyon.

DOUBLE AND MULTIPLE STARS
BY BRIAN D. MASON

Approximately 85% of stars are found in double or multiple systems. While the first detection of double systems dates back to the early 17th century, it was not until systematic work with large-aperture telescopes was done (notably by William Herschel) that the physical rather than optical nature of these systems was ascertained. The larger the aperture of the telescope, the closer the stars that can be separated under good conditions. The resolving power in arcseconds can be estimated as $120/D$, where D is the diameter of the telescope objective in millimetres. Astronomers using long-baseline optical interferometry have measured double-star separations less than a milliarcsecond $(0.001'')$.

The *Journal of Double Star Observations* (hereafter *JDSO*) is a good source for free information on double and multiple stars (see www.jdso.org). The double stars in the following table were selected to cover a wide variety of interests. Wide or slowly moving pairs are good for evaluating optical performance or estimating seeing. With the preponderance of inexpensive, large-aperture telescopes, the availability of interferometry for the amateur (see R. Caloi, *JDSO 4*, 111, 2008), and access to systems with larger magnitude differences (see J. Daley, *JDSO 3*, 159, 2007), closer systems have been included. The list covers many decades of separation with small and large Δm. Of the 136 listed systems, 19 have separations of $1''$ or less and 23 between $1''$ and $2''$. At more moderate separations, there are 19 between $2''$ and $3''$, 19 between $3''$ and $5''$, 24 between $5''$ and $7''$, 19 between $7''$ and $10''$, and 13 with separations greater than $10''$. Of these more moderate separations, those with both small and large magnitude differences are well represented. The pairs are well distributed in RA. One-third of the objects are found south of the equator, giving adequate coverage of southern declinations. Sissy Haas (*Sky & Telescope*, September 2012) provides some excellent test objects for determining your Δm limit at a range of separations. Also, an article by Dirk Terrell (*Sky & Telescope*, August 2012) is ideal for those looking at eclipsing binaries, including pairs much closer than those listed in these tables.

Since many of the stars selected exhibit significant motion, the predicted position angles (PA) and separations are given for both 2018.0 and 2019.0. PA is the angular direction of the fainter star (B) from the brighter (A), measured counterclockwise from north (*clockwise* in an optical system having an *odd* number of reflections). Note that data for 2018.0 have been changed for some systems, due to improvements in orbit calculations or more recent measurements. Also included are notes on selected systems. If no 2018.0 data are provided, there is no calculation (orbital or linear) of the motion (if any) of this double. The 2018.0 data are the most recently published.

Notes on some double and multiple stars in the table (marked with a *):

γ And BC: parameters for BC, which recently went through periastron, are based on the new orbit by Docobo et al.

τ Per Aa, Ab: The parameters given here are from an unpublished orbit determined with extensive observing done by the Navy Precision Optical Interferometer. A long-period eclipsing binary—a total eclipse period of about a week is predicted for Feb. 4. Coverage of the eclipse with accurate and precise photometry in many wavelengths could assist the determination of important astrophysical parameters for this system.

40 Eri BC: One of the closest systems, BC is the closest white-dwarf–M-dwarf pair, and the A component, a K dwarf, is physically sharing the same very large proper motion. B is the second brightest and easiest to observe white dwarf. The orbit of the BC pair has recently been recalculated by Mason et al., resulting in masses of 0.575 ±0.018 and 0.204 ±0.006 solar masses for B and C, respectively.

α CMa AB: The companion to Sirius is a difficult target, usually observable only during periods of exceptional seeing, when you can use the highest magnification and move the primary off the field of view. The white-dwarf secondary, predicted by Bessel and first observed by Alvan Clark, remains a challenging target for visual observers. The recent book by Jay Holberg, *Sirius: Brightest Diamond in the Sky*, is excellent. Based on archival and unpublished ground-based observations as well as observations with the *Hubble Space Telescope*, masses of 2.063 ±0.023 and 1.018 ±0.011 solar masses for A and B, respectively, have been determined based on a new orbit by Bond et al.

α CMi AB: Like Sirius, Procyon has a white-dwarf companion. It was first detected in 1840 by the variation in the proper motion of the star, but not resolved until 1896, by Shaeberle with the 91-cm refractor of Lick Observatory. Based on archival ground-based observations as well as observations with the *Hubble Space Telescope*, masses of 1.478 ±0.012 and 0.592 ±0.006 solar masses for A and B, respectively, have been determined based on a new orbit by Bond et al.

HR 3752: Although it has only moved slightly in position angle, the pair has closed since its first measure by John Herschel while at the Cape nearly two centuries ago.

ξ UMa AB: Many "firsts" are associated with this system. It was one of the first discovered systems (Herschel), one of the first systems whose motion led to the discovery of the physical (rather than optical) nature of double stars (Struve), and the first to have an orbit calculated for it (Savary). Always relatively wide, with an obvious position-angle change of 6° per year, this is a system that will never fail to please, observing season to observing season.

α Cen AB: Our closest neighbor is a quick-moving double star. The brighter component is a near twin of the Sun, while the B component is cooler. According to R.G. Aitken, this pair was discovered by Father Richaud while observing a comet at Pondicherry, India, in December 1689. In 2015, AB went through a close approach from Nov. 20 to Dec. 9 (this is due to the geometry of the orbit; periastron is not until June 2035). The C component, Proxima, slightly closer to the Sun, is an extremely faint red dwarf, separated from the A component by 2.2°.

44 Boo: This close, but small, Δm pair is relatively easy to observe and has a very precise orbit. It passed through periastron in 2012, but is expected to get closer in angular separation until 2021, when it will begin opening up again.

ρ Oph AB: Fit equally well by both a linear solution and a long-period orbit; it is unclear which gives better predictions for future positions. The very similar proper motions argue for an orbital solution ultimately, but it may not resemble the one used here. The C and D components, both between 2″ and 3″ away, have approximately the same parallax so may be physical as well, if only tenuously connected.

ε Lyr AB, CD: The AB (ϵ^1) and CD (ϵ^2) pairs of the Double-Double are 3.47′ apart at PA 172°. Listed in the list of "20 Fun Naked-Eye Double Stars" (Sep. 2014 *Sky & Telescope*, p. 64). The parameters for AB are the mean values from two preliminary orbits.

16 Vul: While one node of the apparent ellipse is well covered, there are only a few points near periastron. Now begins the long, slow slog to apastron. The orbital elements may see significant change before we even get an approximately correct solution.

λ Oct: This pair, only accessible in the Southern Hemisphere, has seen little change in separation but 20° in motion since its first resolution 180 years ago.

TABLE OF DOUBLE AND MULTIPLE STARS

Star	RA (2000) h	m	Dec °	′	Magnitudes comb.	A	B	2018.0 PA °	Sep. ″	2019.0 PA °	Sep. ″	Period y
36 And AB	00	55.0	+23	38	5.6	6.1	6.5	333	1.15	334	1.17	168
ζ Phe AB, C	01	08.4	−55	15	4.0	4.0	8.2	239	6.76			
θ Psc AB	01	13.7	+24	35	4.6	4.7	9.1	221	7.80			
κ Tuc AB	01	15.8	−68	53	4.9	5.0	7.7	316	4.96	316	4.95	857
γ Ari AB	01	53.5	+19	18	3.8	4.5	4.6	1	7.39			
α Psc AB	02	02.0	+02	46	3.8	4.1	5.2	262	1.84	261	1.84	3267
γ And A, BC	02	03.9	+42	20	2.2	2.3	5.0	63	9.80			
γ And BC*	02	03.9	+42	20	5.0	5.3	6.5	128	0.11	123	0.14	63
ι Tri	02	12.4	+30	18	5.0	5.3	6.7	69	3.73			
ι Cas AB	02	29.1	+67	24	4.5	4.6	6.9	228	2.63	227	2.63	620
ι Cas AC	02	29.1	+67	24	4.5	4.6	9.1	117	6.67			
α UMi AB	02	31.8	+89	16	2.1	2.1	9.1	233	18.12			
ν Cet	02	35.9	+05	36	5.0	5.0	9.1	80	8.41			
84 Cet	02	41.2	−00	42	5.8	5.8	9.7	301	3.63			
γ Cet AB	02	43.3	+03	14	3.4	3.5	6.2	299	2.03			
τ Per Aa, Ab*	02	54.3	+52	46	4.0	4.2	5.9	98	0.02	276	0.06	4
ε Ari AB	02	59.2	+21	20	4.6	5.2	5.6	210	1.33	210	1.32	1216
γ Per Aa, Ab	03	04.8	+53	30	2.7	2.9	4.4	244	0.15	244	0.09	15

* See note in text.

TABLE OF DOUBLE AND MULTIPLE STARS (continued)

Star	RA (2000) h	m	Dec °	'	Magnitudes comb.	A	B	2018.0 PA °	Sep. "	2019.0 PA °	Sep. "	Period y
α For	03	12.1	−28	59	3.9	4.0	7.2	301	5.42	301	5.43	269
94 Cet AB	03	12.8	−01	12	5.1	5.1	11.0	189	2.12	188	2.12	1420
HR 997	03	18.7	−18	34	5.8	5.9	8.2	122	8.08	122	8.10	linear
32 Eri AB	03	54.3	−02	57	4.5	4.8	5.9	349	6.91			
HR 1230	04	10.0	+80	42	5.2	5.6	6.3	156	0.67	157	0.67	372
40 Eri A, BC	04	15.3	−07	39	4.4	4.4	9.8	102	83.74			
40 Eri BC*	04	15.3	−07	39	9.8	10.0	11.5	331	8.22	331	8.15	230
ε Aur AB	05	02.0	+43	49	3.0	3.0	14.0	226	28.93			
14 Ori	05	07.9	+08	30	5.4	5.8	6.7	286	0.97	285	0.98	197
β Ori A, BC	05	14.5	−08	12	0.3	0.3	6.8	202	9.52			
14 Aur AB	05	15.4	+32	41	5.0	5.0	9.0	11	9.75			
16 Aur	05	18.2	+33	22	4.8	4.8	10.6	55	4.14			
HR 1771 AB	05	21.8	−24	46	5.1	5.4	6.6	99	3.50			
118 Tau AB	05	29.3	+25	09	5.4	5.8	6.7	209	4.66			
33 Ori AB	05	31.2	+03	18	5.4	5.7	6.7	27	1.85			
λ Ori AB	05	35.1	+09	56	3.3	3.5	5.5	44	4.46			
ζ Ori AB	05	40.7	−01	57	1.7	1.9	3.7	167	2.18	168	2.17	1509
52 Ori	05	48.0	+06	27	5.3	6.0	6.0	220	1.00	221	1.00	1140
β Mon AB	06	28.8	−07	02	4.0	4.6	5.0	137	7.15			
β Mon AC	06	28.8	−07	02	4.2	4.6	5.4	130	9.91			
β Mon BC	06	28.8	−07	02	4.4	5.0	5.4	113	2.93			
HR 2384 AB	06	29.8	−50	14	5.3	6.0	6.2	249	0.32	245	0.28	53
α CMa AB*	06	45.1	−16	43	−1.5	−1.5	8.5	72	10.94	70	11.08	50
12 Lyn AB	06	46.2	+59	27	4.8	5.4	6.0	66	1.91	66	1.91	908
12 Lyn AC	06	46.2	+59	27	4.8	5.4	7.1	307	9.30			
38 Gem AB	06	54.6	+13	11	4.7	4.8	7.8	143	7.32	142	7.33	1898
HR 2674	07	03.3	−59	11	5.5	5.8	6.8	86	1.41			
δ Gem	07	20.1	+21	59	3.5	3.6	8.2	229	5.45	229	5.44	1200
α Gem	07	34.6	+31	53	1.6	1.9	3.0	53	5.25	53	5.31	460
HR 2949 AB	07	38.8	−26	48	3.8	4.4	4.6	318	9.93			
α CMi AB*	07	39.3	+05	14	0.4	0.4	10.8	310	4.48	317	4.62	41
χ Gem	07	44.4	+24	24	3.7	3.7	8.2	241	7.24			
ζ Cnc AB	08	12.2	+17	39	4.9	5.3	6.3	10	1.13	7	1.13	60
ζ Cnc AB, C	08	12.2	+17	39	4.6	4.9	6.3	65	5.93	65	5.93	1115
HR 3432	08	37.3	−62	51	5.5	5.5	11.0	237	5.76			
ι Cnc	08	46.7	+28	46	4.0	4.1	6.0	308	31.30			
ε Hya AB, C	08	46.8	+06	25	3.4	3.5	6.7	309	2.82	310	2.82	589
ι UMa A, BC	08	59.2	+48	03	3.1	3.1	9.2	106	1.94	109	1.92	2084
σ² UMa AB	09	10.4	+67	08	4.8	4.9	8.9	347	4.43	347	4.46	970
38 Lyn AB	09	18.8	+36	48	3.8	3.9	6.1	222	2.61			
HR 3752*	09	25.5	−61	57	5.8	5.8	9.6	330	8.77			
ψ Vel	09	30.7	−40	28	3.6	3.9	5.1	129	1.08	133	1.06	34
11 LMi	09	35.7	+35	49	4.8	4.8	12.5	50	6.52	50	6.56	201
γ Sex AB	09	52.5	−08	06	5.1	5.4	6.4	39	0.51	38	0.49	·78
γ Leo AB	10	20.0	+19	50	2.1	2.4	3.6	127	4.73	127	4.74	554
μ Vel	10	46.8	−49	25	2.7	2.8	5.7	57	2.40	57	2.41	149
54 Leo	10	55.6	+24	45	4.3	4.5	6.3	112	6.56			
ξ UMa AB*	11	18.2	+31	32	3.8	4.3	4.8	161	2.01	157	2.10	60
ν UMa AB	11	18.5	+33	06	3.5	3.5	10.1	145	7.77			
57 UMa AB	11	29.1	+39	20	5.3	5.4	10.7	355	5.46			
α¹ Cru AB	12	26.6	−63	06	0.6	1.3	1.6	112	4.20			
24 Com	12	35.1	+18	23	4.8	5.1	6.3	272	20.37			
γ Vir AB	12	41.7	−01	27	2.8	3.5	3.5	0	2.69	359	2.81	169
β Mus	12	46.3	−68	06	3.0	3.5	4.0	63	0.84	65	0.82	194
θ Vir AB	13	09.9	−05	32	4.4	4.4	9.4	342	6.82			
α Com AB	13	10.0	+17	32	4.4	4.9	5.5	192	0.51	192	0.52	26
ζ UMa AB	13	23.9	+54	56	2.0	2.2	3.9	152	14.40			
84 Vir	13	43.1	+03	32	5.5	5.6	8.3	228	2.64			
τ Boo	13	47.3	+17	27	4.5	4.5	11.1	74	1.43	79	1.37	964
HR 5386 A, BC	14	23.4	+08	27	4.8	5.0	6.8	195	6.03			
φ Vir AB	14	28.2	−02	14	4.9	4.9	10.0	112	5.26			

* See note in text.

TABLE OF DOUBLE AND MULTIPLE STARS (continued)

	RA (2000)		Dec		Magnitudes			2018.0 PA	Sep.	2019.0 PA	Sep.	Period
Star	h	m	°	′	comb.	A	B	°	″	°	″	y
α Cen AB*	14	39.6	−60	50	−0.3	0.0	1.3	327	4.46	337	4.92	80
π¹ Boo	14	40.7	+16	25	4.5	4.9	5.8	113	5.42			
ζ Boo AB	14	41.1	+13	44	3.8	4.5	4.6	286	0.33	283	0.29	125
ε Boo AB	14	45.0	+27	04	2.4	2.6	4.8	343	2.89			
ξ Boo AB	14	51.4	+19	06	4.6	4.8	7.0	299	5.39	298	5.30	152
44 Boo*	15	03.8	+47	39	4.8	5.2	6.1	80	0.53	91	0.39	210
π Lup	15	05.1	−47	03	3.8	4.6	4.6	65	1.82			
η CrB AB	15	23.2	+30	17	5.0	5.6	6.0	238	0.46	256	0.39	42
δ Ser AB	15	34.8	+10	32	3.8	4.2	5.2	172	3.97	172	3.97	1038
ζ² CrB	15	39.4	+36	38	4.6	5.0	5.9	307	6.24			
ι¹ Nor AB	16	03.5	−57	47	4.7	5.2	5.8	67	0.16	26	0.19	27
ξ Sco AB	16	04.4	−11	22	4.3	5.2	4.9	9	1.11	10	1.12	46
ξ Sco AC	16	04.4	−11	22	5.0	5.2	7.3	43	7.53	43	7.53	1514
11 Sco AB	16	07.6	−12	45	5.7	5.8	9.8	263	3.34			
χ Her AB	16	08.1	+17	03	4.8	5.1	6.2	14	27.00	14	26.98	linear
σ CrB AB	16	14.7	+33	52	5.2	5.6	6.5	239	7.23	239	7.24	726
ρ Oph AB*	16	25.6	−23	27	4.6	5.1	5.7	337	2.86	337	2.86	2398
α Sco	16	29.4	−26	26	0.9	1.0	5.4	277	2.57	277	2.56	1218
λ Oph AB	16	30.9	+01	59	3.8	4.2	5.2	44	1.41	44	1.41	129
HR 6246 AB	16	49.6	+13	16	5.7	5.7	10.0	44	5.21			
μ Dra AB	17	05.3	+54	28	4.9	5.7	5.7	0	2.56	359	2.58	812
η Oph AB	17	10.4	−15	44	2.4	3.1	3.3	229	0.53	229	0.51	88
α Her AB	17	14.6	+14	23	3.3	3.5	5.4	103	4.64	103	4.64	3600
36 Oph AB	17	15.3	−26	36	3.9	4.3	5.1	140	5.06	139	5.07	471
HR 6426 AB	17	19.0	−34	59	6.0	6.4	7.4	80	0.53	23	0.52	42
41 Ara AB	17	19.1	−46	38	5.6	5.6	8.9	258	10.62	258	10.69	953
95 Her	18	01.5	+21	36	4.3	4.9	5.2	259	6.43			
τ Oph AB	18	03.1	−08	11	4.8	5.3	5.9	288	1.51	289	1.49	257
70 Oph AB	18	05.5	+02	30	4.1	4.2	6.2	123	6.50	123	6.56	88
HR 6749–50	18	06.8	−43	25	4.9	5.7	5.7	359	1.74	358	1.74	450
59 Ser AB	18	27.2	+00	12	5.3	5.4	7.6	320	3.70			
HR 6997 AB	18	36.6	+33	28	5.4	5.4	9.4	201	6.85			
ε¹ Lyr AB*	18	44.3	+39	40	4.8	5.2	6.1	345	2.28	345	2.27	1765
ε² Lyr CD*	18	44.3	+39	40	4.6	5.3	5.4	75	2.39	74	2.40	724
β Cyg AB	19	30.7	+27	58	2.9	3.2	4.7	54	34.72			
16 Cyg AB	19	41.8	+50	32	5.3	6.0	6.2	133	39.78	133	39.79	13513
δ Cyg AB	19	45.0	+45	08	2.8	2.9	6.3	216	2.75	216	2.76	918
ε Dra	19	48.2	+70	16	3.9	4.0	6.9	21	3.24			
π Aql AB	19	48.7	+11	49	5.8	6.3	6.8	106	1.48			
ζ Sge AB, C	19	49.0	+19	09	5.0	5.0	9.0	311	8.44			
ψ Cyg AB	19	55.6	+52	26	4.9	5.0	7.5	177	2.78			
16 Vul*	20	02.0	+24	56	5.2	5.8	6.2	127	0.85	127	0.85	1201
χ Cep AB	20	08.9	+77	43	4.4	4.4	8.3	120	7.21			
β Cap AB	20	21.0	−14	47	3.1	3.2	6.1	267	205.40			
β Del AB	20	37.5	+14	36	3.7	4.1	5.0	199	0.26	220	0.22	27
52 Cyg	20	45.6	+30	43	4.2	4.2	8.7	70	6.02			
γ Del	20	46.7	+16	07	3.9	4.4	5.0	265	8.92	265	8.9	3249
HR 8040 AB	20	58.5	+50	28	5.5	5.9	6.8	25	2.00			
ε Equ AB	20	59.1	+04	18	5.4	6.0	6.3	274	0.06	140	0.02	101
12 Aqr AB	21	04.1	−05	49	5.6	5.8	7.5	197	2.47			
τ Cyg AB	21	14.8	+38	03	3.7	3.8	6.6	192	0.98	188	0.99	50
μ Cyg AB	21	44.1	+28	45	4.5	4.8	6.2	324	1.50	325	1.48	789
λ Oct*	21	50.9	−82	43	5.4	5.6	7.3	63	3.48			
30 Peg AB	22	20.5	+05	47	5.4	5.4	11.5	17	6.37			
Kruger 60 AB	22	28.0	+57	42	9.7	9.9	11.4	244	1.60	230	1.73	45
ζ² Aqr AB	22	28.8	−00	01	3.7	4.3	4.5	157	2.24	156	2.26	540
δ Cep AB	22	29.2	+58	25	4.0	4.2	6.1	282	21.75			
ο Cep AB	23	18.6	+68	07	4.8	5.0	7.3	223	3.37	223	3.38	1505
72 Peg	23	34.0	+31	20	5.1	5.7	6.1	106	0.58	107	0.58	492
σ Cas AB	23	59.0	+55	45	4.9	5.0	7.2	328	3.35			

* See note in text.

CARBON STARS
BY RON OSTROMECKI AND RICHARD HUZIAK

Carbon stars are variable, late-stage red giants with periodicities ranging from around 70 days to over 400 days. Carbon in the outer atmosphere of the star absorbs blue light, resulting in the red appearance. Magnitude estimation can be tricky because of a phenomenon called the Purkinje effect, which can lead to overstating the brightness of the star. The newer spectral classification C encompasses the older classifications J, N, and R.

Star	RA (2000) h m	Dec ° '	Tycho 2 Δm$_v$	B–V	Spec.
WZ Cas	0 01.3	+60 21	6.8–7.7	2.8	C9,2JLi
SU And	0 04.6	+43 33	8.0–8.5	2.81	C6,4
ST Cas	0 17.5	+50 17	9.0–10.0	2.48	C4,4
VX And	0 19.9	+44 43	7.5–9.7	5.59	C4,5J
NQ Cas	0 24.6	+54 18	9.1–9.8	1.83	C4,5J
AQ And	0 27.5	+35 35	7.7–9.5	3.65	C5,4
W Cas	0 54.9	+58 34	7.8–12.5	3.6	C7,1e
Z Psc	1 16.1	+25 46	6.4–7.5	2.86	C7,2
WW Cas	1 33.5	+57 45	9.1–11.7	2.1	C5,5
R Scl	1 27.0	–32 33	5.7–8.1	4.4	C6,5ea
V Ari	2 15.0	+12 14	8.2–8.9	2.15	C5p,5
R For	2 29.3	–26 06	7.5–13.0	2.21	C4,3e
HD 16115	2 35.1	–9 27	8.15	1.21	C2,3
DY Per	2 35.3	+56 09	10.5–16.0	2.0	C4,5
V623 Cas	3 11.4	+57 54	7–3–8.0	2.3	C4,5J
Y Per	3 27.7	+44 11	8.1–11.3	2.52	C4,3e
V466 Per	3 41.5	+51 30	7.6–9.1	4.25	C5,5
U Cam	3 41.8	+62 39	7.5–9.0	3.95	C5.5e
AC Per	3 45.1	+44 47	9.0–9.6:	3.09	C6,3
UV Cam	4 05.9	+61 48	7.5–7.7	2.26	C5,3
T Cae	4 47.3	–36 13	7.7–8.7	2.59	C6,4
ST Cam	4 51.2	+68 10	6.7–8.0	3.38	C5,4
TT Tau	4 51.5	+28 32	7.9–9.0	2.3	C7,4
SU Tau	5 49.1	+19 04	9.1–18.0	1.1	C1,0
V346 Aur	4 52.6	+38 30	9.3–9.8	3.56	C8,1J
R Lep	4 59.6	–14 48	5.5–11.7	4.93	C7,6e
EL Aur	5 03.4	+50 38	8.7–9.2	3.4	C5,4
W Ori	5 05.4	+1 11	5.5–6.9	3.81	C5,4
TX Aur	5 09.1	+39 0	8.5–9.2	3.71	C5,4
SY Eri	5 09.8	–5 31	7.8–9.1	2.62	C6,3
UV Aur	5 21.8	+32 31	7.3–10.9	2.1	C7,2Jep
S Aur	5 27.1	+34 09	8.2–13.3	1.81	C4–5
RT Ori	5 33.2	+7 09	7.6–8.6	2.97	C6,4
SZ Lep	5 35.8	–25 44	7.4–7.9	2.4	C7,3
S Cam	5 41.0	+68 48	8.1–10.9	2.95	C7,3e
TU Tau	5 45.2	+24 25	7.7–8.8	2.75	C5,4
Y Tau	5 45.7	+20 42	6.4–7.3	3.44	C6.5,4e
FU Aur	5 48.1	+30 38	8.5–9.2	2.77	C7,2
TU Gem	6 10.9	+26 01	6.9–8.0	3.36	C6,4
GK Ori	6 17.7	+8 31	9.5–11	2.0	C4–5
V Aur	6 24.0	+47 42	8.5–13	3.87	C6,2e
BL Ori	6 25.5	+14 43	5.9–6.6	2.55	C6,3
RV Aur	6 34.7	+42 30	9.9–10.4:	3.47	C4,5
UU Aur	6 36.5	+38 27	5.1–6.6	3.1	C6,3
VW Gem	6 42.1	+31 27	8.1–8.5	2.68	C5,4
GY Mon	6 53.2	–4 35	8.1–9.1:	2.64	C6,3
NP Pup	6 54.4	–42 22	6.2–6.5	2.5	C-R3
RV Mon	6 58.4	+6 10	6.9–7.7	3.2	C5,3
V614 Mon	7 01.0	–3 15	7.0–7.4	1.96	C4,5J
RY Mon	7 06.9	–7 33	7.5–9.2	4.38	C6,5:
W CMa	7 08.1	–11 55	6.3–7.1	2.66	C6,3
R CMi	7 08.7	+10 01	7.5–11.6	2.55	C7,1Je
BM Gem	7 21.0	+24 60	8.9–10.0:	2.8	C5,4J
RU Cam	7 21.7	+69 40	8.1–9.8	1.16	C2,2e
BE CMa	7 23.6	–22 58	9.3–9.8:	2.46	C5,5J
NQ Gem	7 31.9	+24 30	7.4–8.2:	2.27	C6,2e
W CMi	7 48.8	+5 24	8.7–9.0	3.23	C7,2
RT Pup	8 05.3	–38 47	8.2–9.1	2.43	C6,2
RU Pup	8 07.5	–22 55	8.3–8.5:	3.61	C5,4
RY Hya	8 20.1	+2 46	8.3–11.1	3.77	C6,4e
AC Pup	8 22.7	–15 55	8.9–10.1	3.04	C5,4
YY Pyx	8 28.2	–27 15	9.0–9.7	4.52	C
UZ Pyx	8 46.6	–29 44	7.0–7.6	2.39	C5,5J
X Cnc	8 55.4	+17 14	5.7–6.9	3.37	C5,4
T Cnc	8 56.7	+19 51	7.6–10.5	4.32	C4,7
RT UMa	9 18.4	+51 24	8.6–9.6	3.69	C4,4
Y Hya	9 51.1	–23 01	6.2–7.4	4.17	C5,4
SZ Car	9 59.9	–60 13	7.2–7.8	2.81	C
AB Ant	10 11.9	–35 19	6.6–7.1	2.47	C6,3
U Hya	10 37.6	–13 23	4.6–5.4	2.8	C6.5,3
VY UMa	10 45.1	+67 25	5.7–6.3	2.59	C6,3
TZ Car	10 46.1	–65 37	8.7–9.1	2.43	C
V Hya	10 51.6	–21 15	6.0–12.3	5.55	C6,3e
SY Car	11 15.6	–57 56	8.8–9.0	2.48	C
S Cen	12 24.6	–49 26	8.1–8.6	2.04	C4,5
SS Vir	12 25.2	+0 46	6.0–9.6	4.2	C6,3e
Y CVn	12 45.1	+45 26	4.9–5.9	3.4	C5,4J
RU Vir	12 47.3	+4 09	8.1–14.2	4.5	C8,1e
RY Dra	12 56.4	+65 60	5.9–8.0	3.7	C4,5J
TT CVn	12 59.4	+37 49	8.0–8.6	1.99	C3,5CH
R CrB	15 48.6	+28 09	5.7–15.2	1.9	C0,0
V CrB	15 49.5	+39 34	6.9–12.6	3.12	C6,2e
RR Her	16 04.2	+50 30	8.1–9.4	3.0	C6.5e
V Oph	16 26.7	–12 26	7.3–11.6	4.38	C6,3e
SU Sco	16 40.6	–32 23	8.6–<13.0:	3.36	C5,5
TW Oph	17 29.7	–19 28	8.5–9.4	4.34	C5,5
SZ Sgr	17 44.9	–18 39	8.4–8.8	2.89	C7,3
SX Sco	17 47.5	–35 42	8.7–9.8	3.82	C5,4
T Dra	17 56.4	+58 13	7.2–13.5	2.7	C7,2e
FO Ser	18 19.4	–15 37	8.4–8.7	2.03	C4,5
SS Sgr	18 30.4	–16 54	9.6–10.2	3.82	C3,4
T Lyr	18 32.3	+36 60	7.5–9.2	5.46	C6,5
HK Lyr	18 42.8	+36 58	7.5–8.4	3.5	C7,4
RV Sct	18 44.4	–13 13	8.7–9.1	2.63	C4,4
S Sct	18 50.3	–7 54	6.6–7.3	3.32	C6,4
UV Aql	18 58.5	+14 22	8.6–9.8:	4.39	C5,4–5
V Aql	19 04.4	–5 41	6.7–7.2	4.0	C5,4
V1942 Sgr	19 19.2	–15 55	6.7–7.2	2.73	C6,4
UX Dra	19 21.6	+76 34	5.9–7.1	2.91	C7,3
AW Cyg	19 28.8	+46 03	8.2–9.2	3.87	C4,5
AQ Sgr	19 34.3	–16 22	7.0–7.4	3.26	C7,4
TT Cyg	19 41.0	+32 37	7.2–8.0	2.6	C5,4e
AX Cyg	19 57.2	+44 16	7.7–8.9	4.4	C4,5
V1469 Aql	20 01.1	+9 31	8.4–8.5:	2.04	C
SV Cyg	20 09.5	+47 52	8.5–9.8	3.15	C7.4
RY Cyg	20 10.4	+35 57	8.5–10.3	2.82	C5,5
RS Cyg	20 13.4	+38 44	6.5–9.5	2.8	C8,2e
RT Cap	20 17.1	–21 19	6.8–8.0	4.42	C6,4
WX Cyg	20 18.6	+37 27	8.8–13.2	2.59	C8,2JLi
U Cyg	20 19.6	+47 54	5.9–12.1	2.81	C8,2e
V778 Cyg	20 36.1	+60 05	10.2–11.4	3.2	C4,5J
BD Vul	20 37.3	+26 29	9.3–12.7	3.74	C7,3e
CY Cyg	20 41.3	+48 08	7.7–13.9	4.04	C6,3e
S Cep	21 35.2	+78 37	7.4–12.9	4.45	C7,4e
V460 Cyg	21 42.0	+35 31	5.6–6.5	2.75	C6,4
RV Cyg	21 43.3	+38 01	7.8–8.4	4.52	C6,4e
RX Peg	21 56.4	+22 52	8.6–9.8	3.18	C4,4J
RZ Peg	22 05.9	+33 30	7.6–13.6	2.65	C9,1e
DG Cep	22 44.2	+61 44	8.7–9.7	3.17	C6,4
TV Lac	22 56.1	+54 14	8.7–9.5:	2.94	C4,5
VY And	23 01.8	+45 53	9.6–11.8	3.81	C4,4J
EW And	23 27.0	+49 31	8.8–9.4	3.33	C7,3
ST And	23 38.8	+35 46	7.7–11.8	3.53	C5,3e
TX Psc	23 46.4	+3 29	4.8–5.2	2.78	C7,2

COLORED DOUBLE STARS

BY MICHEL DUVAL

The list of *colored* double stars in the following table is limited to the most beautiful pairs and those pairs most easily viewed by beginning observers in small instruments (75-mm to 150-mm objective diameter).

Subjective appreciations are suggested regarding beauty (!!!—very beautiful, !!—beautiful, !—nice) and the difficulty of visually separating the pairs in the telescope (T—tight, VT—very tight, F—faint).

The abbreviations used for colors are: B—Blue, E—Emerald, G—Green, Gd—Gold, L—Lilac, O—Orange, R—Red, T—Topaz, V—Violet, W—White, and Y—Yellow. Different observers may perceive colors differently depending on their eye physiology, telescope optics, and local seeing conditions.

The colored double stars β Cyg, α CVn, and ε Boo are better known as Albireo, Cor Caroli ("Heart of Charles"), and Izar, respectively.

An online supplement to this table at **www.rasc.ca/handbook/supplements** contains pairs that may be easier to observe with higher magnifications and/or larger instruments. A section was added to this supplement for the 2017 edition showing the differences between perceptions of colors by our eyes and by photos taken at various sensitivities and time exposures. François Chevrefils of the Centre francophone de Montréal de la SRAC and Alan Whitman are thanked for reviewing this table and its supplement.

TABLE OF COLORED DOUBLE STARS

Star	SAO	RA (2000) h	m	Dec °	′	Magnitudes A	B	Sep. ″	Color A	B	Notes Beau.	Diff.
WINTER												
Σ 163 Cas	12006	1	51	+64	51	6.8	9.1	34	O	B	!!	F
λ Ari	75051	1	58	+23	36	5.0	6.7	37	Y	B	!!	
γ And	37734	2	04	+42	19	2.3	5.4	10	O	B	!!!	
66 Cet	129752	2	13	−2	24	5.7	7.7	16	O	B	!	F
59 And	55330	2	11	+39	02	6.0	6.7	17	Y	B	!!	
η Per	23655	2	51	+55	53	3.8	8.5	28	O	B	!!	F
32 Eri	130806	3	54	−2	57	4.8	5.9	7	T	B	!!!	T
ε Per	56840	3	58	+40	01	3.0	9.0	9	Y	G		VT
φ Tau	76558	4	20	+27	21	5.1	7.5	49	Y	B		F
χ Tau	76573	4	22	+25	38	5.4	8.5	19	Y	G		F
Σ 627 Ori	112305	5	00	+3	37	6.6	7.0	21	Y	G	!!	
ρ Ori	112528	5	13	+2	52	4.6	8.5	7	O	B	!	F
Σ 680 Tau	77098	5	19	+20	08	6.0	10.0	9	Y	B		F
σ Ori	132406	5	39	−2	37	3.9	6.5	42	O	B	!!	
26 Aur	58280	5	39	+30	30	6.0	8.0	12	Y	B	!	F
ε Mon	113810	6	24	+4	36	4.5	6.5	13	Y	B	!	F
5 Lyn	25733	6	27	+58	25	5.2	9.8	32	Y	B	!	F
20 Gem	95795	6	32	+17	47	6.3	6.9	20	Y	B	!	
38 Gem	96265	6	54	+13	11	5.0	7.8	7	Y	B	!!	T
h3945 CMa	173349	7	17	−23	19	4.8	5.8	27	Y	B	!!!	
δ Gem	79294	7	20	+21	59	3.5	8.5	6	Y	R	!!	T
κ Gem	79653	7	44	+24	24	3.6	8.1	7	O	B		F, VT
Σ 1149 CMi	115981	7	49	+3	13	7.8	9.2	22	Y	B	!	F
Σ 1183 Mon	135505	8	06	−9	14	6.2	7.8	31	Y	G	!	F
ι Cnc	80416	8	47	+28	46	4.0	6.6	31	Y	B	!!	

Note: The Smithsonain Astrophysical Observatory (SAO) numbers in column 2 are provided for use with Go To telescope databases. The SAO Star Catalog contains details on 258,996 stars, see tdc-www.harvard.edu/catalogs/sao.html. The SAO and Harvard College Observatory are joined as the Harvard–Smithsonian Center for Astrophysics (CfA).

TABLE OF COLORED DOUBLE STARS (continued)

Star	SAO	RA (2000) h	m	Dec °	'	Magnitudes A	B	Sep. "	Color A	B	Notes Beau.	Diff.
SPRING												
Σ 1321 UMa	27178	9	14	+52	41	8.0	8.0	18	Y	B		
Σ 1360 Leo	98615	9	30	+10	36	8.0	9.0	14	B	G		
6 Leo	117751	9	32	+9	43	5.4	9.3	37	O	G		
γ Leo	81298	10	20	+19	50	2.4	3.6	5	O	Y		VT
35 Sex	118449	10	43	+04	45	6.9	8.4	7	O	B		
54 Leo	81583	10	56	+24	45	4.3	6.3	6	Y	B	!	T
88 Leo	99648	11	32	+14	22	6.4	9.1	15	Y	B	!	F
2 CVn	44097	12	16	+40	40	5.9	8.7	11	Gd	B		
17 Vir	119360	12	22	+05	18	6.6	10.0	21	B	O		
24 Com	100160	12	35	+18	23	5.1	6.3	20	Gd	B	!!	
32 Cam	2102	12	49	+83	25	5.0	6.0	21	Y	B		
35 Com	82550	12	53	+21	15	5.2	9.8	28	Y	B		
α CVn	63257	12	56	+38	19	2.9	5.6	19	B	G	!!!	
ε Boo	83500	14	45	+27	04	2.6	4.8	3	O	B		VT
ξ Boo	101250	14	51	+19	06	4.8	7.0	6	Y	O		VT
ζ CrB	64834	15	39	+36	38	5.0	6.0	6	Y	B	!!!	
SUMMER												
β Sco	159682	16	05	−19	48	2.6	4.9	14	B	O	!	
κ Her	101951	16	08	+17	03	5.0	6.0	28	Y	R	!	
α Her	102680	17	15	+14	23	3.5	5.4	5	R	G	!	VT
ψ Dra	8890	17	42	+72	09	4.9	6.1	30	Y	L	!	
95 Her	85648	18	01	+21	36	5.0	5.1	6	G	B	!!	T
59 Ser	123497	18	27	+0	12	5.4	7.7	4	Y	G	!!	VT
ζ Lyr	67321	18	45	+37	36	4.3	5.9	44	Y	G	!!	
o Dra	31219	18	51	+59	23	4.8	7.8	34	Gd	L	!!	F
11 Aql	104308	18	59	+13	37	5.3	9.3	19	Y	B	!!	
β Cyg	87301	19	31	+27	58	3.1	5.1	35	Y	B	!!!	
57 Aql	143898	19	54	−8	14	6.0	6.0	36	Y	G	!!	
17 Cyg	68827	19	46	+33	44	5.0	9.0	26	R	B	!	F
OΣ 394 Cyg	69238	20	00	+36	25	7.0	10.0	11	O	B		
26 Cyg	49098	20	01	+50	06	5.0	9.0	41	Y	B		F
31 Cyg	49337	20	13	+46	44	4.0	7.0	107	O	B	!!	
σ Cap	163445	20	19	−19	07	5.4	9.4	56	O	B	!	F
52 Cyg	70467	20	45	+30	43	4.0	9.0	6	Y	B		
AUTUMN												
γ Del	106475	20	47	+16	07	4.4	5.0	9	O	G	!	T
1 Peg	107073	21	22	+19	48	4.2	7.6	36	O	V		
h 1647 Peg	89737	21	29	+22	11	6.1	10.2	41	O	B		
β Cep	10057	21	29	+70	34	3.2	8.6	13	W	B	!	T
41 Aqr	190986	22	14	−21	04	5.6	6.7	5	Y	B		VT
δ Cep	34508	22	29	+58	25	4.2	6.1	41	Y	B	!!	
Σ 2978 Peg	73010	23	07	+32	50	6.4	7.5	8	Y	B	!	
57 Peg	128001	23	10	+8	41	5.1	9.7	32	Y	B		F
Σ 2991 Peg	108463	23	13	+11	04	6.0	10.0	33	Y	B	!	F
Ψ¹ Aqr	146598	23	16	−9	05	4.5	10.0	49	Y	B	!	
94 Aqr	165625	23	19	−13	27	5.3	7.0	12	Y	G	!!	
OΣΣ 254 Cas	21002	00	01	+60	21	7.6	8.7	57	R	B	!!	
Σ 3053 Cas	10937	00	02	+66	06	5.9	7.3	15	O	B		
42 Psc	91866	00	22	+13	29	6.4	10.3	29	T	E		
12 Cet	128791	00	30	−3	57	6.0	10.8	12	Y	B		
55 Psc	74182	00	39	+21	26	5.6	8.5	7	O	B	!!	F
η Cas	21732	00	49	+57	49	3.5	7.2	13	W	G	!	
Σ 80 Cet	109577	00	59	+0	47	8.0	9.0	28	Y	B		

VARIABLE STARS

BY STELLA KAFKA AND ELIZABETH O. WAAGEN

Variable stars are stars whose brightness changes on timescales from minutes to years. They reveal many stellar properties. Depending upon their type, variables can tell us their age, mass, radius, temperature, luminosity, internal and external structure, composition, and evolutionary history. Systematic observation of variable stars is an area in which amateur astronomers can make a valuable contribution to astronomy.

For beginning observers, simplified charts of the fields of four different types of bright variable stars are shown below (see **www.aavso.org** for authoritative versions). On each chart the magnitudes (with decimal point omitted) of several suitable comparison stars are shown. A brightness estimate of the variable is made using two comparison stars, one brighter, one fainter than the variable. The magnitude, date, and time of each observation are recorded. When a number of observations have been made, a graph of magnitude versus date can be plotted. The shape of this *light curve* depends upon the type of variable. Further information about variable-star observing is available from the American Association of Variable Star Observers (AAVSO), 49 Bay State Road, Cambridge MA 02138, USA (email: aavso@aavso.org).

Table 1 is a list of long-period variables, brighter than mag. 8.0 at maximum and north of –20°. The first column (the Harvard designation of the star) gives the position for the year 1900: the first four characters give the hours and minutes of right ascension, the next three the declination in degrees. The **Max.** column gives the mean maximum magnitude. The **Min.** column gives the mean minimum magnitude. The period (**Per.**) is in days. **Epoch** gives the predicted date of the earliest maximum occurring this year; by adding multiples of the period to this epoch, the dates of subsequent maxima can be found. These variables may reach maximum two or three

TABLE 1—LONG-PERIOD VARIABLE STARS NORTH OF –20°

Variable		Max. m_v	Min. m_v	Per. d	Epoch 2018	Variable		Max. m_v	Min. m_v	Per. d	Epoch 2018
0017+55	T Cas	7.9	11.9	445	Jun. 21	1425+39	V Boo	7.0	11.3	260	Jul. 8
0018+38	R And	6.9	14.3	409	Jul. 25	1432+27	R Boo	7.2	12.3	223	Feb. 22
0211+43	W And	7.4	13.7	396	Mar. 10	1517+31	S CrB	7.3	12.9	361	Aug. 18
0214–03a	o Cet	3.4	9.3	332	Jan. 14	1546+39	V CrB	7.5	11.0	358	Oct. 11
0228–13	U Cet	7.5	12.6	235	Aug. 4	1546+15	R Ser	6.9	13.4	356	Jun. 13
0231+33	R Tri	6.2	11.7	267	May 16	1606+25	RU Her	8.0	13.7	485	No Max
0430+65	T Cam	8.0	13.8	373	Oct. 24	1621+19	U Her	7.5	12.5	406	Aug. 22
0455–14	R Lep	6.8	9.6	427	Jul. 21	1621–12	V Oph	7.5	10.2	297	Feb. 15
0509+53	R Aur	7.7	13.3	458	Mar. 19	1632+66	R Dra	7.6	12.4	246	Aug. 30
0549+20a	U Ori	6.3	12.0	368	Apr. 21	1647+15	S Her	7.6	12.6	307	Apr. 5
0617–02	V Mon	7.0	13.1	340	Jun. 27	1702–15	R Oph	7.6	13.3	306	May 30
0653+55	R Lyn	7.9	13.8	379	Sep. 20	1717+23	RS Her	7.9	12.5	220	Jul. 15
0701+22a	R Gem	7.1	13.5	370	Mar. 8	1805+31	T Her	8.0	12.8	165	Jan. 26
0703+10	R CMi	8.0	11.0	338	Apr. 7	1811+36	W Lyr	7.9	12.2	198	May 23
0727+08	S CMi	7.5	12.6	333	Mar. 28	1833+08	X Oph	6.8	8.8	329	Mar. 14
0811+12	R Cnc	6.8	11.2	362	Jul. 21	1901+08	R Aql	6.1	11.5	270	Aug. 2
0816+17	V Cnc	7.9	12.8	272	Feb. 28	1910–17	T Sgr	8.0	12.6	395	Apr. 16
0848+03	S Hya	7.8	12.7	257	Jan. 1	1910–19	R Sgr	7.3	12.5	270	Jan. 4
0850–08	T Hya	7.8	12.6	289	Sep. 20	1934+49	R Cyg	7.5	13.9	426	Jun. 26
0939+34	R LMi	7.1	12.6	372	May 5	1940+48	RT Cyg	7.3	11.8	190	Jun. 13
0942+11	R Leo	5.8	10.0	310	Mar. 27	1946+32	X Cyg	5.2	13.4	408	Dec. 14
1037+69	R UMa	7.5	13.0	302	Apr. 15	2016+47	U Cyg	7.2	10.7	463	No Max
1214–18	R Crv	7.5	13.8	317	Sep. 5	2044–05	T Aqr	7.7	13.1	202	Jan. 2
1220+01	SS Vir	6.8	8.9	364	Mar. 19	2108+68	T Cep	6.0	10.3	388	Jun. 11
1231+60	T UMa	7.7	12.9	257	Feb. 19	2137+53	RU Cyg	8.0	9.4	233	May 5
1233+07	R Vir	6.9	11.5	146	May 16	2301+10	R Peg	7.8	13.2	378	May 12
1239+61	S UMa	7.8	11.7	226	Apr. 16	2307+59	V Cas	7.9	12.2	229	Aug. 11
1315+46	V CVn	6.8	8.8	192	Jan. 8	2315+08	S Peg	8.0	13.0	319	Jul. 25
1327+06	S Vir	7.0	12.7	375	Apr. 29	2338–15	R Aqr	6.5	10.3	387	Jun. 9
1344+40	R CVn	7.7	11.9	329	Sep. 26	2353+50	R Cas	7.0	12.6	430	Jul. 14
1425+84	R Cam	8.3	13.2	270	Jun. 6	2357–15	W Cet	7.6	14.4	351	Apr. 11

weeks before or after the epoch and may remain at maximum for several weeks. This table has been prepared with AAVSO observations.

Table 2 lists stars that are representative of some other types of variables. Elements for preparation of predicted maxima of Cepheids and minima of eclipsing binaries are from www.aavso.org/vsx, the International Variable Star Index (VSX). Data and elements for the predicted maximum of RR Lyr are from the GEOS RR Lyr Database (http://rr-lyr.irap.omp.eu/dbrr/index.php), using the Le Bourne et al. 2014 elements therein.

DESCRIPTION OF VARIABLE-STAR TYPES

Variable stars can be divided into two main classes: intrinsic variables, in which the variation is due to changes of a single star, and extrinsic variables, in which the variation is due to interaction of multiple stars or objects within a stellar system. There are many cases of overlapping variability types, such as a Mira pulsating variable as part of an eclipsing binary system. Intrinsic variables fall into three main classes: (1) pulsating stars, in which periodic expansion and contraction of the stellar surface occur; (2) eruptive variables, in which solarlike flares occur; and (3) rotating stars, in which shape distortion or star spots cause variation. Extrinsic variables consist of two main classes: (4) binary systems, in which variability is caused by orbital motion or mass transfer; and (5) cataclysmic variables, in which accretion onto a compact object can cause it to go into outburst. With modern detectors, about 1% of all stars are found to be variable. Brief and general descriptions of the major types in each class are given below.

TABLE 2—OTHER TYPES OF VARIABLE STARS

Variable		Max. m_v	Min. m_v	Type	Spectral Class	Period d	Epoch 2018 UT
0053+81	U Cep	6.7	9.8	Ecl.	B7Ve+G8III-IV	2.493087#	Jan. 3.47*
0301+40	β Per	2.1	3.3	Ecl.	B8V+G8III	2.86736	†
0355+12	λ Tau	3.5	4.0	Ecl.	B3V+A4IV	3.9529478#	Jan. 1.61*
0416+19	T Tau	9.6	10.8	INT	F8Ve-K1IV-Ve(T)		
0530–05	T Ori	9.5	12.3	INA	B8-A3EpV		
0539+09	FU Ori	8.7	9.8	FU	F2peI-II		
0619+07	T Mon	5.6	6.6	Cep	F7Iab-K1Iab+A0V	27.024649	Jan. 16.20
0658+20	ζ Gem	3.6	4.2	Cep	F7Ib-G3Ib	10.149806	Jan. 8.79
0749+22	U Gem	8.6	15.5	UGSS	Pec(UG)+M4.5V		
1846+33	β Lyr	3.4	4.3	Ecl.	B8II-IIIep	12.94061713	Jan. 7.95*
1922+42	RR Lyr	6.9	8.0	RR Lyr	A5.0-F7.0	0.5668#	Jan. 1.04
1946+35	CI Cyg	8.9	12.2	ZAND	Pec Bep+M5III		
1947+00	η Aql	3.5	4.3	Cep	F6Ib-G4Ib	7.17679#	Jan. 6.08
2138+43	SS Cyg	8.0	12.5	UGSS	K5V+(Pec)UG		
2225+57	δ Cep	3.5	4.4	Cep	F5Ib-G1Ib	5.36627	Jan. 1.57

* Minimum   # Changing period; revised for 2018.

† Algol; predictions for all minima in 2018 are given in THE SKY MONTH BY MONTH section (p. 98).

(1) Pulsating Variables

δ *Scuti* stars are variables that have both radial and nonradial pulsation modes with periods of 0.01–0.2 day and amplitudes from barely measurable to nearly a full magnitude. They are of A–F spectral types. Typical representative: CY Aquarii.

Cepheids are variables that pulsate with periods of 1–70 days. They have high luminosity, and the amplitude of light variation ranges from 0.1 to 2 magnitudes. The prototypes of the group, classical Cepheids, are located in open clusters and obey the well-known period-luminosity relation. They are of late F spectral class at maximum and G to K at minimum. The later (cooler) the spectral class of a classical Cepheid at minimum, the longer is its period. Typical representative of classical Cepheids: δ Cephei.

RR Lyrae stars are giant variables with periods of 0.2–1.2 days and amplitude of light variation between 0.5 and 2 magnitudes. They are usually of spectral class A. About 20% of RR Lyrae stars exhibit the Blazhko effect (a long-term variation in period and amplitude), including the prototype of the class itself, RR Lyrae.

RV Tauri stars are supergiant variables with a characteristic light curve of alternating deep and shallow minima. The periods, defined as the interval between two deep minima, range from 30 to 150 days. The amplitude of light variation may be as much as 3 magnitudes. Many show long-term cyclic variation of 500 to 9000 days. Generally, the spectral classes range from F–G at maximum to K–M at minimum light. Typical representative: R Scuti.

Long-period (Mira Ceti) variables are giants that vary with visual amplitudes from 2.5 to 5 magnitudes or more. They have well-defined periodicity, ranging from 80 to 1000 days. They show characteristic emission spectra of late spectral classes M, C, and S. Typical representative: o Ceti (Mira).

Semiregular variables are giants or supergiants showing appreciable periodicity accompanied by intervals of irregularities in light variation. The periods range from 30 to 1000 days with visual amplitudes not more than 1 to 2 magnitudes in general. Typical representative: R Ursae Minoris.

(2) Eruptive Variables

Eruptive variables are those with flares occurring in their chromospheres, along with shell mass ejections and other stellar-wind phenomena. The ejected matter can cause brightness increases or drops.

FU Orionis variables are young stars embedded in nebulae. Usually they have large-amplitude fluctuations that may take years to complete. Typical representative: FU Orionis.

T Tauri variables are young stars that have not yet reached the Zero Age Main Sequence. They are characterized by irregular variations of several magnitudes, often accompanied by emission lines and brightness fadings, probably due to dust. Typical representative: T Tauri.

UV Ceti stars are late-type dwarfs that display flare activity. The flares can range from several tenths of a magnitude to many magnitudes in size, lasting a few minutes. Typical representative: UV Ceti.

R Coronae Borealis stars are highly luminous variables that have nonperiodic drops in brightness from 1 to 9 magnitudes due to the formation of "carbon soot" in the star's atmosphere. The duration of minima varies from a few months to years. Members of this group fall into the F–K and R spectral classes. Typical representative: R Coronae Borealis.

Irregular variables are stars that at times show only a trace of periodicity or none at all. Often, poorly studied stars are placed in this category. Typical representative: RX Leporis.

(3) Rotating Variables

Rotating variables are stars with nonuniform surface brightness, caused by star spots, mass outflow, or even shape distortion.

γ Cassiopeiae variables are rapidly rotating B stars with mass outflow, forming equatorial rings or disks that can cause temporary fading episodes. Typical representative: γ Cassiopeiae.

RS Canum Venaticorum variables are rapidly rotating stars, usually close binary systems that undergo small amplitude changes in light that may be due to dark or bright spots on their surface. Eclipses may also be present in such systems (due to binarity). Typical representative: RS Canum Venaticorum.

(4) Binary Systems

Binary systems are composed of two stars or a planet around a star, in which the orbital plane is oriented such that one object crosses the disk of another object. These are usually divided into four main classes: detached, semi-detached, contact, and transitting. The first three relate to whether two stars overfill their Roche lobes or are completely isolated from one another.

Detached systems are those in which the two stars are completely isolated from one another. Light curves usually show constant light between eclipses; eclipse depth can be quite large, depending on the relative brightness of the stellar pair. Typical representative: β Persei (Algol).

Semi-detached systems have one member (the donor) overflowing its Roche lobe, with mass accreting onto the other star. Typical representative: U Cephei.

Contact binaries have both members within a common envelope. These stars often exhibit ellipsoidal variations, with the light curves continuously varying throughout the orbit. Typical representative: β Lyrae.

Transitting systems are a new class of binary, in which a planet crosses the disk of the parent star. These variations are quite small (a few hundredths of a magnitude at best), but give a great deal of information about the host star and about the transitting planet. Typical representative: HD 209458.

(5) Cataclysmic Variables

These are semi-detached binaries that typically show outbursts caused by thermonuclear runaway on either the star surface or on an accretion disk. They are a product of accretion from one star of a binary system onto the other star, usually a compact object such as a white dwarf or neutron star.

Novae consist of a normal star and a white dwarf, whose combined magnitude increases 7 to 16 magnitudes in brightness in one to several hundred days. After the outburst, the star fades slowly, returning to initial brightness in several years or decades. Near maximum brightness, the spectrum is generally similar to A or F giants. Typical representative: CP Puppis (Nova 1942).

Supernovae increase in brightness by 20 or more magnitudes due to a gigantic stellar explosion that destroys the system. The general appearance of the light curve is similar to novae. Typical representative: CM Tauri (supernova of 1054 CE, and now the central star of the Crab Nebula).

U Geminorum types are dwarf novae that have long intervals of quiescence at minimum with sudden rises to maximum. Depending upon the star, the amplitude of eruptions ranges from 2 to 6 magnitudes, and the duration between outbursts can be tens to thousands of days. Most of these stars are spectroscopic binaries with periods of a few hours. Typical representative: SS Cygni.

SU Ursae Majoris types are dwarf novae similar to U Gem and Z Cam stars in their physical and spectroscopic properties. They have frequent, faint, and narrow eruptions that last from one to a few days, along with infrequent, bright, and long eruptions—superoutbursts—that last 10 to 20 days. During superoutbursts, there are small-amplitude, periodic variations—superhumps—that are 2% to 3% longer than the orbital period of the system. Typical representative: SU Ursae Majoris.

Z Camelopardalis types are variables similar to U Gem stars in their physical and spectroscopic properties. They show brightness variations interrupted by intervals of constant brightness—standstills—lasting for several cycles, approximately one-third of the way from maximum to minimum. Typical representative: Z Camelopardalis.

VARIABLE STAR OF THE YEAR: TYC 2505-672-1

BY JOSEPH E. RODRIGUEZ, JOSHUA PEPPER, KEIVAN STASSUN, STELLA KAFKA, AND ELIZABETH O. WAAGEN

Eclipsing binaries (EBs), where two stars orbit each other and their orbit is aligned to our line of sight, allow us to precisely measure the fundamental properties of each star (Mass, Radius, Effective Temperature) without the need of stellar models. Therefore, they provide a natural astrophysical laboratory to directly test theoretical models. One of the most famous EB systems is ε Aur. As a result of its very deep eclipse depth (0.8 – 1.0 mag.) and being very bright (V~3), it has become an ideal target for detailed characterization by both the professional and amateur community (Carroll et al. 1991). From an analysis of the system's spectral energy distribution (SED), it was proposed that ε Aur consisted of an asymptotic-giant-branch F star eclipsed every 27.1 years by a main-sequence B5 star embedded in a large semi-opaque circumstellar disk (Hoard et al. 2010). This interpretation was later confirmed by directly imaging the shadow of the companion's disk during the last eclipse (Kloppenborg et al. 2010).

From combining ground-based photometric observations of TYC 2505-672-1 spanning ~120 years, astronomers have discovered another remarkable eclipsing system,

TYC 2505-672-1 (RA=09h 53m 10.0043s, Dec=+33° 53′ 52.734″ (2000), V=10.7). The first eclipse occurred in the early to mid-1940s, and a second eclipse recently ended in late 2014 (Lipinov et al. 2010). Each eclipse occurs every ~69.1 years, lasts ~3.5 years, and has a maximum depth of 4.5 magnitudes (Rodriguez et al. 2016) (Figure 1). From analysis of optical spectra taken during the recent eclipse, it was determined that the primary star in the system is an evolved M giant (Afanasiev et al. 2013). Later that year, at the American Astronomical Society's Giants of Eclipse conference, it was first proposed that TYC 2505-672-1 could be an EB, similar to ε Aur (Tang et al. 2013).

From analyzing the SED, both during and prior to the most recent eclipse, it was determined that the system not only contains an M giant but also a small, hot (~8000K) star embedded in a very large opaque circumstellar disk (Rodriguez et al. 2016). From the measured luminosities of each star, it was determined that the small, hot companion was likely 0.1–0.5 R_{sun}. For a star with T_{eff}~8000K, that would be too large for it to be a cool white dwarf, but too small to be a main A-star, the common types of stars with that temperature. It was proposed that the companion is likely a "stripped red giant" subdwarf-B type star, likely to become a helium white dwarf. A possibly explanation for the system's architecture is that there were originally two red-giant stars and the outer hydrogen envelope of one was stripped away, possibly creating the observed large opaque disk around the companion (Rodriguez et al. 2016). However, a puzzle remains since it is unknown how the star could have been tidally stripped at such a far orbital separation (~24 AU). The next eclipse is predicted to begin in early 2080 and end in late 2083. This very rare system is poised to be the next archetype for understanding post-main-sequence evolution, and is expected to become a top target for detailed characterization.

Although the next eclipse is not expected for many decades, general multi-band (UBVRI & u′g′r′i′z′) photometric monitoring may provide evidence of an additional component in the system and alert the community if TYC 2505-672-1 goes into an unexpected eclipse. If the companion is indeed a star (as expected), the radial-velocity motion of the primary star should be many kilometres per second, easily detectable by low-resolution spectroscopy. Therefore, we recommend low-cadenced (2–3 times a month) spectroscopic observations over the next decade to measure the mass of the companion.

During the next eclipse, multi-band photometric observations will provide crucial information about the possible grain properties in the disk around the small, hot companion. Currently, optical interferometric observations are not possible for a target as faint as TYC 2505-672-1. However, it is expected that these observations will be possible by the next expected eclipse. Please submit observations promptly to the AAVSO via the website **www.aavso.org/WebObs**.

References:
Afanasiev, V., Denisenko, D., Krushinsky, V., et al. 2013, *The Astronomer's Telegram*, 4834, 1
Carroll, S.M., Guinan, E.F., McCook, G.P., & Donahue, R.A. 1991, *ApJ, 367*, 278
Kloppenborg, B., Stencel, R., Monnier, J.D., et al. 2010, *Nature, 464*, 870
Lipunov, V., Kornilov, V., Gorbovskoy, E., et al. 2010, *Advances in Astronomy*, 2010, 30
Rodriguez, J.E., Stassun, K.G., Lund, M.B., et al. 2016, *The Astronomical Journal, 151*, 123
Tang, S., Grindlay, J.E., Bildsten, L., & collaborators, m. 2013, in *Giants of Eclipse*, 20302

The KELT-North, DASCH, CRTS, AAVSO, and ASAS-SN observations plotted from 1890 to 2015. The line represents an LC model of the combined photometric data. KELT-North observations during eclipse are below the faintness limit of KELT and are therefore only upper limits.

EXPIRED STARS
BY ROY BISHOP

Stars are where the action is, and the action is fuelled by gravitation and thermonuclear fusion. Gravitation, the midwife and undertaker, forms a star, heats it to the temperatures necessary to ignite successive stages of fusion reactions, and when nuclear fuel runs out, crushes the ashes of the star into one of three final states: white dwarf, neutron star, or black hole. Thermonuclear fusion, powered by the strong nuclear interaction between protons and neutrons, merely delays the onset of further collapse and higher temperatures. In the case of our Sun, the first and by far the longest delay, the "hang-up" provided by hydrogen-to-helium fusion, is already half over.

White Dwarfs

Stars comparable to our Sun have insufficient gravity to reach the temperatures necessary to form nuclei heavier than carbon or oxygen. When the thermal support pressure generated by fusion wanes, gravity gradually crushes the central portion of the star. If the mass of this core is less than 1.4 solar masses (a limit discovered by a leading astrophysicist of the 20th century, Subramanyan Chandrasekhar), the collapse halts at a very hot, Earth-sized remnant known as a white dwarf. At this point, the squeeze of gravity is offset by *electron degeneracy pressure*, an intrinsic aspect of the wave–particle nature of matter and the same pressure responsible for the stability and size of an atom. However, in the case of a white dwarf, the pressure is such that the electrons are not tied to individual atomic nuclei but occupy the whole star. In this sense, the star has become a giant atom. In physics jargon: electrons are fermions (i.e. they obey Fermi–Dirac quantum statistics) and hence abide by the Pauli Exclusion Principle, which dictates that no two electrons can occupy the same quantum state. That results in an immense pressure, sufficient to prevent further collapse, provided the mass is less than the Chandrasekhar limit. White-dwarf diameters are about 1% that of our Sun, which has a nearly water-like average density (1 g/cm^3). Thus a cubic centimetre of white-dwarf material has a mass near 100^3 g or one tonne (like a Honda Fit crushed into a sugar cube).

Because of their immense thermal energy and small surface area, white dwarfs cool extremely slowly. The Universe is not yet old enough for any white dwarf to have cooled sufficiently to become a "black dwarf." Also, white dwarfs are intrinsically very faint; thus only those close to the Solar System can be seen.

Only one white dwarf is easily observable with a small telescope: **Omicron 2 Eridani B** (also designated 40 Eridani B), located 16.3 light-years from Earth. Omicron 2 Eridani A, the bright (mag. 4.4) companion to the dim (mag. 9.5) white dwarf, is shown on the JANUARY ALL-SKY MAP on p. 340: o^2 Eri A is the eastern (left-hand) member of the close pair of stars located due west of the word "Rigel." Omicron 2 Eridani B, the white dwarf, is located only 83″ east-southeast of o^2 Eri A (position angle ≈110°). Remarkably, stars A and B are accompanied by a third star, a faint (mag. 11.2) red-dwarf star, o^2 Eri C, which resides only 9″ north of B. (There is a brighter and closer white dwarf, the companion of Sirius, α CMa B, but it is usually lost in the glare of Sirius. See THE NEAREST STARS (p. 286) and DOUBLE AND MULTIPLE STARS (p. 291) for more information on both of these stellar systems.)

For the observer with a small telescope, o^2 Eri B is the only Earth-sized object visible in the depths of interstellar space, the only visible object with a mass density far exceeding that of ordinary matter, the only accessible star no longer powered by nuclear reactions, and the only star that has expired and can still be seen.

Neutron Stars

For a large star of about eight or more solar masses, energy-releasing reactions end in its center with the fusion of silicon nuclei into iron. Iron has the most tightly bound nucleus (per nuclear particle) and hence is no good as a fuel for further fusion. Electron degeneracy pressure supports the inert iron core until silicon fusion in a surrounding shell supplies enough additional iron to push the inert core over the Chandrasekhar limit. Gravity then overwhelms electron degeneracy pressure, and the core collapses in less than a second, so quickly that, momentarily, the outer layers of the star stay where they were. Gravitation-induced temperatures in the core rise past 10^{10} K, sufficient to disassemble heavy nuclei synthesized over the life of the star. That absorbs energy, accelerating the collapse. Also, electrons attain sufficient energy to combine with protons to form neutrons and neutrinos, another energy-absorbing reaction that also removes electrons, further hastening the collapse.

Provided the infalling mass is less than about three solar masses, like a hammer striking an anvil, when the core reaches a diameter of about 20 km, the infall is violently arrested by *neutron degeneracy pressure*, the same pressure that, in the case of both neutrons and protons, governs the size and structure of the nuclei of atoms of ordinary matter. With a diameter 500 times smaller than that of a white dwarf, the density at this stage is 500^3 larger, 100 million tonnes per cubic centimetre (like an aircraft carrier crushed to the size of the ball of a ballpoint pen). That is the density of ordinary atomic nuclei. The star's core has effectively become a gigantic nucleus, composed primarily of neutrons.

The abrupt rebound of the nearly rigid central core reverses the infall of the adjacent layers, turning the implosion into a spectacular explosion, a Type II supernova. The explosion mechanism is complex and not yet well understood, but appears to involve interactions with the immense numbers of neutrinos generated in the neutron production, and possibly acoustic waves generated by vibrations of the core as it is pummeled by infalling material within a second of its formation. The gravitational energy released in the sudden collapse of the couple of solar masses now locked in the central neutron star is about 10^{46} J. That is far more energy than our Sun will produce in its entire 10-billion-year lifetime.

Over the next several thousand years, the remnants of the outer layers of the star form an expanding, glowing cloud of gas and dust, seeding interstellar space with the heavy chemical elements (oxygen, silicon, iron, uranium, etc.) synthesized in its outer layers both before and during the supernova explosion. The potassium ions moving in the neurons of your brain as you read these words emerged from such a conflagration some 5 billion years ago.

No neutron stars are visible in a small telescope, although one is *indirectly* visible in the **Crab Nebula**, M1. The Crab supernova was a bright, naked-eye star in the skies of Earth in the year 1054 AD, although it had taken 6000 years for the light of the explosion to reach our planet. The nebula we see today is the expanding debris cloud as it was nearly 1000 years after the initial explosion.

The Crab Nebula glows across the electromagnetic spectrum, from radio waves to gamma rays, powered by the rapid but decreasing spin of the neutron star at its center. The glow of the debris cloud is like the glow of a red-hot disk brake slowing the spin of a wheel. The visible light from the cloud is *synchrotron radiation* emitted by electrons as they spiral in the tangled magnetic field of the neutron star. Nowhere else in the heavens is such an exotic light visible in a small telescope, polarized light with the brilliance of a thousand suns, emitted not by atoms but by free electrons being flung about by a spinning neutron star. The neutron star itself is known as a *pulsar* because it flashes (30 times per second!) in step with its spin. Even if the Crab pulsar were bright enough to be visible in a small telescope, the flashing would not be apparent because, as in a motion picture or cathode-ray-tube monitor, the flicker is too rapid for the eye to follow.

Color photographs of the Crab Nebula reveal a celestial gift: a package of bluish synchrotron radiation wrapped in the loops of a tattered red ribbon—fragments of the shattered star, fluorescing in hydrogen-alpha light. Unfortunately, the luminance of the fluorescence is below the threshold for vision in the red part of the spectrum. Thus all we see is the ghostly cloud of synchrotron radiation.

The Crab Nebula is located 1° northwest of the star ζ Tau, at the tip of the east horn of Taurus. In the JANUARY ALL-SKY MAP on p. 340, the nebula is the tiny circle of dots 5 mm to the right of the cross marking the summer solstice (SS). In a telescope, the nebula appears merely as a small glowing cloud, but to the knowledgeable observer, this synchrotron radiation brake of a spinning neutron star is an object for profound contemplation.

Black Holes

Stars whose masses are greater than about 20 solar masses likely retain more than 3 solar masses in their imploding cores. This is sufficient that gravitation will overwhelm not only the degeneracy pressure of electrons, but also the highly incompressible nature of nuclear matter. Within seconds, spacetime itself closes around the imploding stellar core, removing all but the core's gravitational field from the observable Universe. The star has become a black hole.

The earliest and best candidate for a stellar black hole is **Cygnus X-1**. Discovered by Dr. Tom Bolton of the University of Toronto, using the 1.88-m telescope at the David Dunlap Observatory (see p. 11), it is one of the strongest galactic X-ray sources in the sky. Cygnus X-1 is the invisible companion of a star that can be seen in a small telescope: HDE 226868, an O9.7Iab star, a very luminous, very hot supergiant located about 8000 ly from the Sun. It orbits its nearby, unseen companion with a 5.6-day period. The mass of the companion is between 10 and 16 solar masses, far too large for it to be a white dwarf or neutron star. X-rays are generated as material from the supergiant falls toward the invisible companion. The X-rays extend to energies of 100 keV and vary on time scales as short as milliseconds, indicative of a very compact companion.

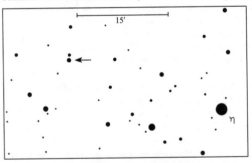

At 9th magnitude, the supergiant HDE 226868 is visible in any small telescope. It is less than half a degree from the 4th-magnitude star η Cygni, which is the star in the neck of the swan, next to the "C" in CYGNUS on the SEPTEMBER ALL-SKY MAP on p. 344. Any low magnification will more than encompass the field shown in the **finder chart** above. North is upward, η Cygni is at the lower right, and HDE 226868 is indicated by the small arrow. The chart magnitude limit is about 13. Although HDE 226868 is a blue supergiant, in telescopes of sufficient aperture this star appears orange because of interstellar dust between us and the star.

All that is to be seen is the hot supergiant, but the view will be worth the search if you know that at this same location in the field of your telescope lurks one of the most likely candidates for a black hole, a knot in the fabric of spacetime where a giant star has vanished. No painting, computer simulation, or Hollywood movie can match this observation.

A DEEP-SKY SELECTION—FROM NEAR TO FAR

NGC	M	Type^A	Con	RA h	OH List^B	Size^C '	S^C mag/arcsec^2	m^D	Distance	Remarks
	45	OC	Tau	3	M, OC	100	20	(1.4)	0.44 kly	Pleiades Cluster
1435		RN	Tau	3	DSCO	20×15	21.6	4	0.44	Merope Nebula in above
ρ Oph area		GMC	Oph	16	WFW^E	5.5°			0.46	EN+DN complex
6726–7		E/RN	CrA	19	SHS	2		11v	0.5	complex region
		DN	Cru	12	SHS	7°×5°	—	—	0.6	Coalsack
7293		PN	Aqr	22	FNGC	16×12	20.8	14.6	0.7	Helix Nebula
ζ Ori		GMC	Ori	5	various^F	2°		2	1.2	Flame, Horsehead, etc.
6853	27	PN	Vul	19	M	8×6	20.8	13	~1.2	Dumbbell Nebula
1976	42	EN	Ori	5	M	65	15–22	4	1.34	Orion Nebula
6960		SNR	Cyg	20	FNGC	70×6	23.2		1.5	Veil Nebula (west)
2068	78	RN	Ori	5	M	8×6	20.8	10	1.6	many young var. stars
7000		EN	Cyg	20	FNGC	100	23.6		~1.9	North America Nebula
3132		PN	Vel	10	SHS	1.4	17.6	10	2.0	Eight-Burst Nebula
B142–3		DN	Aql	19	DN	80×50	—	—	2	Barnard's "E"
6720	57	PN	Lyr	18	M	1.5×1	17.9	14.8	2.3	Ring Nebula
2261		E/RN	Mon	6	FNGC	2	20.1	11v	2.5	Hubble's Variable Nebula
3587	97	PN	UMa	11	M	2.5	21.6	13	~2.8	Owl Nebula
2392		PN	Gem	7	FNGC	0.7	16.2	10	2.9	Clown Face (Eskimo)
7009		PN	Aqr	21	FNGC	0.4	14.6	12	3.0	Saturn Nebula
7129		RN	Cep	21	FNGC	7	22.5	10	3.3	small OC imbedded
6514	20	EN	Sgr	18	M	28	24.4		~4.7	Trifid Nebula
188		OC	Cep	0	OC	15	24.5	(10)	5.0	oldest OC
IC 443		SNR	Gem	6	DSCO	50×40			5	Jellyfish Nebula
2237–9		EN	Mon	6	FNGC	80×60	26.8	5	5.2	Rosette Nebula
2244		OC	Mon	6	OC	40	22.1	(4.8)	5.2	OC in above
1952	1	SNR	Tau	5	M, RS	5×3	20.6	16v	6.5	Crab and central pulsar
4755		OC	Cru	12	SHS, OC	10	17.8	(4.2)	6.8	Jewel Box
3372		EN	Car	10	SHS	85×80		4.5v	8	Carina Nebula
6838	71	GC	Sge	19	M	6	21.5	(9)	13	looks like OC
5139		GC	Cen	13	SHS, GC	30	19.6	(3.6)	17	ω Centauri GC
6205	13	GC	Her	16	M, GC	23	21.1	(5.7)	21	Hercules Cluster
6715	54	GC	Sgr	18	M, GC	6	21.5	(9)	89	core of Sgr Dwarf Gal.?
2070		EN	Dor	5	SHS	20	20	13	160	Tarantula Nebula in LMC
		G	Dor	5	SHS, G	6°×5°	22.4	(1)	163	Large Magellanic Cloud
224	31	G	And	0	M, G	150×50	22.3	(4)	2.6 Mly	Andromeda Galaxy
598	33	G	Tri	1	M, G	60	22.8	(5.3)	2.8	Triangulum Galaxy
3031	81	G	UMa	9	M, G	18×10	22.3	(8)	12	paired with M82
5128		G	Cen	13	SHS, RS	10×8	20.6	(7.2)	12	Centaurus A radio source
5236	83	G	Hya	13	M, G	10×8	21.4	(8)	15	Southern Pinwheel
5427		G	Vir	14	DSG	2.0×1.7	22.0	(12.0)	110	interacting with 5426
Abell 1367		G	Leo	11	DSCO	1°		(13–16)	380	Leo Galaxy Cluster
3C 273		Q	Vir	12	DSCO, RS	stellar		(12.8)	2440	brightest quasar

^A **DN**–dark nebula, **EN**–emission nebula (HII), **G**–galaxy, **GC**–globular cluster, **GMC**–giant molecular cloud, **OC**–open cluster, **PN**–planetary nebula, **Q**–quasar, **RN**–reflection nebula, **SNR**–supernova remnant

^B **DN**–DARK NEBULAE, **DSG**–DEEP SKY GEMS, **DSCO**–DEEP-SKY CHALLENGE OBJECTS, **FNGC**–THE FINEST NGC OBJECTS, **G**–GALAXIES: BRIGHTEST AND NEAREST, **GC**–GLOBULAR CLUSTERS, **M**–THE MESSIER CATALOGUE, **OC**–OPEN CLUSTERS, **RS**–RADIO SOURCES, **SHS**–SOUTHERN HEMISPHERE SPLENDOURS, **WFW**–WIDE-FIELD WONDERS (*Use a combination of* **NGC** *or* **M** *catalog number,* **Con***, and* **RA** *hour to locate an object in one of the lists in this chapter.*)

^C Approximate observable **Size** and surface brightness (*S*) from R.N. Clark, *Visual Astronomy of the Deep Sky* (Sky Publishing, 1990) available online at www.clarkvision.com. These values are not definitive!

^D *m* is the mag. of the associated star for nebulae; v = variable; (*m*) is the total mag. for G, GC, OC, and Q.

^E 1° south of ρ Oph, RA 16h 28m, Dec –24° 3.3', star cloud and several ICs, see WIDE-FIELD WONDERS

^F See FNGC (2024), DSG (2023), DSCO (IC 434), WFW, and DN (B33)

STAR CLUSTERS

BY PETER JEDICKE AND ANTHONY MOFFAT

The study of star clusters is crucial to the understanding of stellar structure and evolution. For most purposes, it can be assumed that the stars in a given cluster formed nearly simultaneously from the same parent cloud of gas and dust. Thus the basic factor that distinguishes one star in a cluster from another is the quantity of matter each contains. When comparing clusters, it is essentially only the age and the chemical composition of their stars that differ. But what makes one cluster *appear* different from another is mainly the degree of concentration and regularity, the spread in magnitude and color of the member stars (all of which vary mainly with age), and the total number of stars. Extremely young clusters are often irregular in shape, with clumps of newly formed stars pervaded by lanes of obscuring dust and bright nebulosity (e.g. the Orion Nebula around the Trapezium Cluster). The oldest clusters, which have not yet dissipated, and those that have not been torn apart by external forces, tend to be symmetrical in shape, with only the slower-burning, low-mass stars remaining visible; the massive stars will have spent their nuclear fuel and passed to the degenerate graveyard of white dwarfs, neutron stars, or black holes, depending upon their original mass.

The star clusters in the following tables were selected as the most conspicuous. Two types can be recognized: *open* and *globular*. Open clusters often appear as irregular aggregates of tens to thousands of stars, sometimes barely distinguishable from random fluctuations of the general field. Ranging in age from very young to very old, open clusters are concentrated toward the disk of the Milky Way and generally contain stars of chemical abundance similar to the Sun.

Sometimes we observe loose, extended groups of very young stars. Using precise methods of photometry, spectroscopy, and kinematics, we see that these stars often have a common, but not necessarily strictly coeval, origin. Such loose concentrations are called *associations*. Dynamically, both open clusters and associations are generally unbound over time scales of the order of 10 million years, being subject to the strong tidal forces of passing clouds and the background Milky Way Galaxy. Often, associations contain subconcentrations of young open clusters (e.g. the double cluster h and χ Persei of slightly different ages despite their proximity, in the association Per OB1, which stretches over 6° of the sky), with a strong gradient in age as the star-formation process rips through them from one edge to another. In view of their sparse nature, we do not include any of the 100-plus cataloged Milky Way associations.

Globular clusters, on the other hand, are highly symmetric, extremely old and rich agglomerations of up to several million stars, distributed throughout the galactic halo but concentrated toward the center of the galaxy. Compared to the Sun and other disk stars, they tend to be much less abundant in elements heavier than hydrogen and helium. For the larger and brighter globular clusters, the observer's goal is to see them well enough to distinguish a generous sprinkling of individual stars against a diffuse glowing background. Large telescope apertures and good skies will help resolve globular clusters. Higher powers are helpful for identification of smaller, more distant globular clusters.

The following table lists all well-defined open clusters in the Milky Way Galaxy with angular diameters* greater than 40′ and/or integrated magnitudes brighter than 5.0, as well as the richest clusters and some of special interest. The apparent integrated photographic magnitude (m_{pg}) is from Collinder, the angular diameter (**Diam.**) is generally from Trumpler, and the photographic magnitude of the fifth-brightest star (m_5) is from Shapley, except where in *italics*, which are new data. The distance (**Dist.**) is mainly from Becker and Fenkart (*Astr. Astrophys. Suppl. 4* (1971), p. 241). The earliest spectral type

---

* Note that the apparent angular diameter of a cluster may underestimate the full cluster diameter and may be closer to the nuclear diameter, excluding the corona (see David Turner, tinyurl.com/3uaulcb).

of cluster stars (**Sp**) is a measure of the age as follows: expressed in millions of years, O5 = 2, B0 = 8, B5 = 70, A0 = 400, A5 = 1000, F0 = 3000, and F5 = 10 000. Complete source lists of open clusters can be found at **www.univie.ac.at/webda/navigation.html**.

OPEN CLUSTERS

NGC/ other†	RA (2000) h m	Dec ° '	Mag. m_{pg}	Diam. '	m_5	Dist. 10^3 ly	Sp	Remarks
188	0 44.0	+85 21	9.3	14	14.6	5.0	F2	Oldest known
752	1 57.8	+37 41	6.6	45	9.6	1.2	A5	
869	2 19.0	+57 10	4.3	30	9.5	7.0	B1	h Per
884	2 22.4	+57 07	4.4	30	9.5	8.1	B0	χ Per, M supergiants
Perseus	3 22	+48 36	2.3	240	5	0.6	B1	Moving cl.; α Per
Pleiades	3 47.1	+24 08	1.6	120	4.2	0.41	B6	M45, best known
Hyades	4 20	+15 38	0.8	400	3.9	0.15	A2	Moving cl. *, in Taurus
1912	5 28.6	+35 50	7.0	18	9.7	4.6	B5	M38
1976/80	5 35.4	−5 23	2.5	50	5.5	1.3	O5	Trapezium, very young
2099	5 52.4	+32 32	6.2	24	9.7	4.2	B8	M37
2168	6 08.8	+24 21	5.6	29	9.0	2.8	B5	M35
2232	6 26.5	−4 45	4.1	20	7	1.6	B1	
2244	6 32.4	+4 52	5.2	27	8.0	5.3	O5	Rosette, very young
2264	6 41.0	+9 53	4.1	30	8.0	2.4	O8	S Mon
2287	6 47.1	−20 44	5.0	32	8.8	2.2	B4	M41
2362	7 18.8	−24 56	3.8	7	9.4	5.4	O9	τ CMa
2422	7 35.6	−14 30	4.3	30	9.8	1.6	B3	
2437	7 41.8	−14 49	6.6	27	10.8	5.4	B8	M46**
2451	7 45.4	−37 58	3.7	37	6	1.0	B5	
2516	7 58.3	−60 54	3.3	50	10.1	1.2	B8	
2546	8 12.5	−37 39	5.0	45	7	2.7	B0	
2632	8 40.1	+20 00	3.9	90	7.5	0.59	A0	Praesepe, M44
IC 2391	8 40.3	−53 03	2.6	45	3.5	0.5	B4	
IC 2395	8 41.0	−48 11	4.6	20	10.1	2.9	B2	
2682	8 50.4	+11 50	7.4	18	10.8	2.7	F2	M67, very old
3114	10 02.6	−60 07	4.5	37	7	2.8	B5	
IC 2602	10 43.3	−64 23	1.6	65	6	0.5	B1	θ Car
Tr 16	10 45.2	−59 42	6.7	10	10	9.6	O3	η Car and Nebula
3532	11 06.4	−58 39	3.4	55	8.1	1.4	B8	
3766	11 36.1	−61 37	4.4	12	8.1	5.8	B1	
Coma	12 25.1	+26 06	2.9	300	5.5	0.3	A1	Very sparse
4755	12 53.6	−60 20	5.2	12	7	6.8	B3	κ Cru, "Jewel Box"
6067	16 13.3	−54 13	6.5	16	10.9	4.7	B3	Classic Cepheids
6231	16 54.0	−41 48	3.5	16	7.5	5.8	O9	O supergiants, WR stars
Tr 24	16 57.0	−40 40	3.5	60	7.3	5.2	O5	
6405	17 40.1	−32 13	4.6	26	8.3	1.5	B4	M6
IC 4665	17 46.7	+5 44	5.4	50	7	1.1	B8	
6475	17 53.9	−34 48	3.3	50	7.4	0.8	B5	M7
6494	17 56.9	−19 01	5.9	27	10.2	1.4	B8	M23
6523	18 03.1	−24 23	5.2	45	7	5.1	O5	M8, Lagoon Nebula
6611	18 18.9	−13 47	6.6	8	10.6	5.5	O7	M16, nebula
IC 4725	18 31.7	−19 15	6.2	35	9.3	2.0	B3	M25, Cepheid U Sgr
IC 4756	18 39.3	+5 27	5.4	50	8.5	1.4	A3	
6705	18 51.1	−6 17	6.8	12.5	12	5.6	B8	M11, very rich
Mel 227	20 11.2	−79 19	5.2	60	9	0.8	B9	
IC 1396	21 38.9	+57 30	5.1	60	8.5	2.3	O6	Tr 37
7790	23 58.4	+61 13	7.1	4.5	11.7	10.3	B1	Cepheids CEa, CEb, and CF Cas

† IC = Index Catalogue, Tr = Trumpler, Mel = Melotte. * Basic for distance determination.
** Appears to contain planetary nebula NGC 2438, but this is not a cluster member.

The table below lists all the globular clusters in the Messier list and most of the globular clusters with a total apparent visual magnitude brighter than about 8.0. A table of Milky Way Galaxy globular-cluster data is available on W.E. Harris's website **physwww.mcmaster.ca/~harris/WEHarris.html**. The apparent diameter (**Diam.**) is from Cragin, Lucyk, and Rappaport (*Deep Sky Field Guide To Uranometria 2000.0*, Willmann-Bell, 1993). The concentration class (**CC**) is from I to XII, where I is the most compact and XII the least. The integrated spectral type (**Int. Sp. T.**) varies mainly with the abundances. An observer who can see stars down to the magnitude given in the *V*(**HB**) ("horizontal-branch") magnitude) column has a good chance of being able to resolve the globular cluster; this information is from Djorgovski and Meylan (*Structure and Dynamics of Globular Clusters*, Astronomical Society of the Pacific, 1993, p. 341).

GLOBULAR CLUSTERS

NGC	M/ other	RA (2000) h m	Dec ° '	Mag. m_V	Diam. '	CC	Int. Sp. T.	Dist. 10^3 ly	V(HB)
104	47 Tuc	0 24.0	−72 04	3.95	30.9	III	G4	13	14.06
288		0 52.8	−25 35	8.09	13.8	X		29	15.44
362		1 03.2	−70 50	6.40	12.9	III	F9	28	15.40
1851		5 14.0	−40 02	7.14	11.0	II	F7	46	16.10
1904	79	5 24.1	−24 31	7.73	8.7	V	F5	42	16.20
2808		9 11.9	−64 51	6.20	13.8	I	F7	30	16.19
3201		10 17.6	−46 24	6.75	18.2	X	F6	17	14.75
4590	68	12 39.5	−26 44	7.84	12.0	X	F2	33	15.60
4833		12 59.5	−70 52	6.91	13.5	VIII	F3	20	15.45
5024	53	13 12.9	+18 10	7.61	12.6	V	F6	60	16.94
5139	ω Cen	13 26.8	−47 28	3.68	36.3	VIII	F5	17	14.52
5272	3	13 42.2	+28 22	6.19	16.2	VI	F6	35	15.65
5904	5	15 18.5	+2 04	5.65	17.4	V	F7	26	15.11
6093	80	16 17.0	−22 58	7.33	8.9	II	F6	33	15.86
6121	4	16 23.6	−26 31	5.63	26.3	IX	F8	14	13.35
6171	107	16 32.5	−13 03	7.93	10.0	X	G0	21	15.70
6205	13	16 41.7	+36 27	5.78	16.6	V	F6	21	14.95
6218	12	16 47.1	−1 56	6.70	14.5	IX	F8	24	14.90
6254	10	16 57.1	−4 05	6.60	15.1	VII	F3	20	14.65
6266	62	17 01.2	−30 06	6.45	14.1	IV	F9	22	15.90
6273	19	17 02.6	−26 16	6.77	13.5	VIII	F7	28	16.95
6333	9	17 19.2	−18 30	7.72	9.3	VIII	F5	27	16.10
6341	92	17 17.1	+43 08	6.44	11.2	IV	F2	26	15.05
6356		17 23.6	−17 49	8.25	7.2	III	G4	50	17.50
6388		17 36.3	−44 44	6.72	8.7	III	G2	37	16.90
6397		17 40.7	−53 40	5.73	25.7	IX	F4	9	12.90
6402	14	17 37.6	−3 14	7.59	11.7	VIII	F4	29	17.50
6541		18 08.0	−43 42	6.30	13.1	III	F6	13	15.10
6626	28	18 24.5	−24 52	6.79	11.2	IV	F8	19	15.68
6637	69	18 31.4	−32 20	7.64	7.1	V	G2	28	16.20
6656	22	18 36.3	−23 54	5.10	24.0	VII	F5	10	14.15
6681	70	18 43.2	−32 17	7.87	7.8	V	F5	29	15.60
6715	54	18 55.0	−30 28	7.60	9.1	III	F7	89	17.71
6752		19 10.9	−59 58	5.40	20.4	VI	F4	17	13.85
6779	56	19 16.6	+30 11	8.27	7.1	X	F5	33	16.20
6809	55	19 40.1	−30 57	6.32	19.0	XI	F4	20	14.35
6838	71	19 53.8	+18 46	8.19	7.2	†	G1	13	14.44
6864	75	20 06.0	−21 55	8.52	6.0	I	F9	61	17.45
6981	72	20 53.5	−12 32	9.27	5.9	IX	F7	55	16.99
7078	15	21 30.1	+12 10	6.20	12.3	IV	F3	34	15.86
7089	2	21 33.5	−0 50	6.47	12.9	II	F4	40	16.05
7099	30	21 40.4	−23 10	7.19	11.0	V	F3	26	15.10

† Originally thought to be an open cluster; never assigned a concentration class

FEATURE CLUSTER—47 TUCANAE CONTAINS A BLACK HOLE WITH A MASS OF 2300 SUNS.

Nestled among the glories of the sky that are forever buried below the horizon for North American and European observers is the globular cluster called 47 Tucanae. We all call it 47 Tuc, and it usually gets a nod any time someone mentions the view of Omega Centauri. Although Omega Centauri is widely held to be the brightest and most beautiful of all the globular clusters, it is more likely the core of a former dwarf galaxy and no longer considered a true globular cluster at all. This leaves 47 Tuc with a claim to being the most stupendous sight among the more than 100 globular clusters of the Milky Way.

There are two misconceptions about 47 Tuc, the first being that it belongs to the Small Magellanic Cloud, (mostly) within the constellation of Tucana. In fact, the SMC is at least ten times further away than the globular cluster. This means 47 Tuc is a bit closer even than M13, the favorite target of Northern Hemisphere observers, or M4, which lies above the galactic center. Like all the visible globular clusters, it is part of the Milky Way's galactic halo. The second misconception is that 47 Tuc was assigned a Flamsteed number. Sir John Flamsteed (1646–1719) was the first Astronomer Royal, but he never traveled to the Southern Hemisphere and certainly never observed this southern gem. Moreover, Flamsteed did not even assign numbers to the stars in his published catalogue. Our subject here did not receive the appellation "47 Tuc" until it was included in Johann Bode's extended list of the stars in Tucana. Bode's *Beschreibung* was published in 1801.

So, who was first to recognize 47 Tuc? It was Nicolas Louis de La Caille (1713–1762), a French astronomer who was invited to set up an observatory at the Cape of Good Hope along Africa's south coast. La Caille did not observe the cluster long enough to decide if it was a comet or a "nebula." Along with charting about 10 000 stars, La Caille provided a list of some 42 nebulae, clusters, and asterisms in the southern skies. But La Caille and most 18th-century astronomers of course did not appreciate globular clusters as such. We owe the distinction of globular clusters as a separate category to William Herschel (in 1785), and it was his son Sir John Herschel who (in 1847) correctly put 47 Tuc among them. Finally, it was late in the 19th century that J.L.E. Dreyer drew up the *New General Catalogue* and assigned 47 Tuc the current scientific designation NGC 104.

For scientific studies, the capabilities of modern telescopes across the electromagnetic spectrum deliver a target like 47 Tuc right into our arms, so to speak. Whereas fewer than 400 stars were individually identified down to visual mag. 18.8 in the chart presented by Gonzalo Alcaino in 1973's *Atlas of Globular Clusters*, the 2006 paper that improved the distance measurement used 14 366 stars measured by the *Hubble Space Telescope*, and positions of 130 000 stars in total! Also remarkable is the long-term observation of millisecond pulsars in 47 Tuc by the Parkes Radio Telescope in Australia, at 20-cm wavelength. Analyzing these data, Bulent Kiziltan, Holger Baumgardt, and Abraham Loeb concluded in 2017 (*Nature*, *542*, 203–205) that the motions of these pulsars—there are about 30 of them—only make sense if there is a black hole at the center of the cluster. They used an innovative statistical technique to calculate that the black hole is probably 2300 times the mass of the Sun, and that makes it an example of an intermediate-mass black hole (IMBH), much bigger than any individual star but far smaller than those found in the cores of galaxies and active galactic nuclei. What's remarkable about this 2300-solar-mass black hole is that there seems to be very little matter falling into it, because there is no persuasive evidence from X-ray observations of an accretion disk to accompany the black hole.

There may also be at least one less-massive black hole in the core of 47 Tuc. Measurements of nine fairly weak X-ray sources there go back to the *Einstein* and *ROSAT* satellites and more recently *Chandra* and *NuSTAR*. One of these sources exhibits the signature of a white-dwarf object circling around a very compact object and dumping gas into it. Combining these data with more measurements by another radio telescope in Australia have led the University of Alberta's Craig Heinke and his collaborators to the conclusion, reported early in 2017 (MNRAS), that this compact object is a modest black hole with a mass comparable to a single star. These various results give 47 Tuc a special significance, showing the fascinating complexity of a globular cluster, to go along with the breathtaking view.

THE MESSIER CATALOGUE
BY ALAN DYER

Charles Messier's Catalogue provides a selection of the best and brightest deep-sky wonders for Northern Hemisphere viewers. Messier compiled his list in the late 1700s to aid prospective comet hunters. Some of these objects he discovered himself, some were first seen by other astronomers of the day, while a few (the Pleiades and the Beehive) were known since antiquity. The Messier numbers do not follow an ordered sequence across the sky. Rather, they are numbered in the order he discovered and cataloged them. Although he intended to, Messier never did publish a list with entries renumbered in order of right ascension.

In our version of THE MESSIER CATALOGUE, we've listed the objects by season *for the evening observer*, grouping the objects within their respective constellations. The constellations are then listed roughly in order of increasing right ascension, that is, constellations farther to the east and that rise later in the night are farther down the list. This is to help plan the sequence of an evening's Messier hunt.

The identity of some Messier objects is controversial. There is evidence that M91 and M102 are mistaken observations of M58 and M101, respectively. M104 and M109 were found by a colleague, Pierre Mechain, and reported to Messier for inclusion in his catalogue. NGC 205, one of the companion galaxies to M31, the Andromeda Galaxy, was apparently found by Messier but never included in his catalogue. Modern-day observers have dubbed this object M110. In our list, we have included 110 entries, including two objects that some have suggested as alternative candidates for M91 and M102.

Modern-day Messier hunters often wonder what telescopes Messier used. The largest were 190-mm and 200-mm reflectors. However, their speculum metal mirrors would have had the equivalent light-gathering power of a modern 80-mm to 100-mm reflector. He also used a number of 90-mm refractors. Today, a dark site and a good 80-mm refractor or 100-mm reflector should be sufficient for completing the entire list. Objects M6 and M7 are the most southerly, while M74 and M76 are often considered the faintest and most difficult. M83's low altitude and diffuse appearance make it a challenge for Canadian observers north of 50° latitude.

The columns contain the Messier number, the equivalent NGC (New General Catalogue) number, the constellation, the type (see below), the equinox J2000.0 coordinates, the visual magnitude m_v, the angular size in arcminutes (arcseconds for planetary nebula), and observing remarks. Entries marked "!!" are showpiece objects. Data are taken from *The Deep Sky Field Guide to Uranometria 2000.0* (Willmann-Bell, Inc., 1993), compiled by Murray Cragin, James Lucyk, and Barry Rappaport from a variety of contemporary catalogs. Some sizes have been rounded to two significant figures. Also recommended as an excellent guide is *The Messier Objects*, by Stephen James O'Meara (Cambridge University Press, 1998).

MESSIER AND NGC OBJECT TYPES

OC = open cluster	GC = globular cluster
EN = emission nebula	RN = reflection nebula
E/RN = EN + RN	
PN = planetary nebula	SNR = supernova remnant
G-SA *or* G-S = spiral galaxy	G-SB = barred spiral galaxy
G-E = elliptical galaxy	G-S0 = lenticular galaxy
G-I = irregular galaxy	(alphanumeric suffixes denote galaxy sub-types)

NUMERICAL LISTING OF MESSIER OBJECTS

M#	Sky	Con	M#	Sky	Con	M#	Sky	Con	M#	Sky	Con	M#	Sky	Con
1	WIN	Tau	23	SUM	Sgr	45	WIN	Tau	67	SPR	Cnc	89	SPR	Vir
2	AUT	Aqr	24	SUM	Sgr	46	WIN	Pup	68	SPR	Hya	90	SPR	Vir
3	SPR	CVn	25	SUM	Sgr	47	WIN	Pup	69	SUM	Sgr	91	SPR	Com
4	SUM	Sco	26	SUM	Sct	48	WIN	Hya	70	SUM	Sgr	92	SUM	Her
5	SPR	Ser	27	SUM	Vul	49	SPR	Vir	71	SUM	Sge	93	WIN	Pup
6	SUM	Sco	28	SUM	Sgr	50	WIN	Mon	72	AUT	Aqr	94	SPR	CVn
7	SUM	Sco	29	SUM	Cyg	51	SPR	CVn	73	AUT	Aqr	95	SPR	Leo
8	SUM	Sgr	30	AUT	Cap	52	AUT	Cas	74	AUT	Psc	96	SPR	Leo
9	SUM	Oph	31	AUT	And	53	SPR	Com	75	SUM	Sgr	97	SPR	UMa
10	SUM	Oph	32	AUT	And	54	SUM	Sgr	76	AUT	Per	98	SPR	Com
11	SUM	Sct	33	AUT	Tri	55	SUM	Sgr	77	AUT	Cet	99	SPR	Com
12	SUM	Oph	34	AUT	Per	56	SUM	Lyr	78	WIN	Ori	100	SPR	Com
13	SUM	Her	35	WIN	Gem	57	SUM	Lyr	79	WIN	Lep	101	SPR	UMa
14	SUM	Oph	36	WIN	Aur	58	SPR	Vir	80	SUM	Sco	102	SPR	Dra?
15	AUT	Peg	37	WIN	Aur	59	SPR	Vir	81	SPR	UMa	103	AUT	Cas
16	SUM	Ser	38	WIN	Aur	60	SPR	Vir	82	SPR	UMa	104	SPR	Vir
17	SUM	Sgr	39	SUM	Cyg	61	SPR	Vir	83	SPR	Hya	105	SPR	Leo
18	SUM	Sgr	40	SPR	UMa	62	SUM	Oph	84	SPR	Vir	106	SPR	CVn
19	SUM	Oph	41	WIN	CMa	63	SPR	CVn	85	SPR	Com	107	SUM	Oph
20	SUM	Sgr	42	WIN	Ori	64	SPR	Com	86	SPR	Vir	108	SPR	UMa
21	SUM	Sgr	43	WIN	Ori	65	SPR	Leo	87	SPR	Vir	109	SPR	UMa
22	SUM	Sgr	44	SPR	Cnc	66	SPR	Leo	88	SPR	Com	110	AUT	And

SEASONAL LISTING OF MESSIER OBJECTS

M#	NGC	Con	Type	RA (2000) Dec h m ° '		m_v	Size '	Remarks
The Winter Sky								
1	1952	Tau	SNR	5 34.5	+22 01	8.4	6 × 4	!! famous Crab Neb. supernova remnant
45	—	Tau	OC	3 47.0	+24 07	1.2	110	!! Pleiades; look for subtle nebulosity
36	1960	Aur	OC	5 36.1	+34 08	6.0	12	bright but scattered group; use low pow.
37	2099	Aur	OC	5 52.4	+32 33	5.6	20	!! finest of three Auriga clusters; very rich
38	1912	Aur	OC	5 28.7	+35 50	6.4	21	look for small cluster NGC 1907 0.5° S
42	1976	Ori	E/RN	5 35.4	−5 27	—	65 × 60	!! Orion Nebula; finest in northern sky
43	1982	Ori	E/RN	5 35.6	−5 16	—	20 × 15	detached part of Orion Nebula
78	2068	Ori	RN	5 46.7	+0 03	—	8 × 6	bright featureless reflection nebula
79	1904	Lep	GC	5 24.5	−24 33	7.8	8.7	200-mm telescope needed to resolve
35	2168	Gem	OC	6 08.9	+24 20	5.1	28	!! look for sm. cluster NGC 2158 0.25° S
41	2287	CMa	OC	6 47.0	−20 44	4.5	38	4° south of Sirius; bright but coarse
50	2323	Mon	OC	7 03.2	−8 20	5.9	16	between Sirius & Procyon; use low mag
46	2437	Pup	OC	7 41.8	−14 49	6.1	27	!! contains planetary nebula NGC 2438
47	2422	Pup	OC	7 36.6	−14 30	4.4	29	coarse cluster 1.5° west of M46
93	2447	Pup	OC	7 44.6	−23 52	≈6.2	22	compact, bright cluster; fairly rich
48	2548	Hya	OC	8 13.8	−5 48	5.8	54	former "lost" Messier; large, sparse cl.

SEASONAL LISTING OF MESSIER OBJECTS (continued)

M#	NGC	Con	Type	RA (2000) Dec h m ° '		m_v	Size '	Remarks
The Spring Sky								
44	2632	Cnc	OC	8 40.1	+19 59	3.1	95	!! Beehive or Praesepe; use low power
67	2682	Cnc	OC	8 50.4	+11 49	6.9	29	one of the oldest star clusters known
40	—	UMa	2 stars	12 22.4	+58 05	8.0	—	double star Winnecke 4; separation 50″
81	3031	UMa	G-SAab	9 55.6	+69 04	6.9	24 × 13	!! bright spiral visible in binoculars
82	3034	UMa	G-I0	9 55.8	+69 41	8.4	12 × 6	!! the "exploding" galaxy; M81 0.5° S
97	3587	UMa	PN	11 14.8	+55 01	9.9	194″	!! Owl Nebula; distinct grey oval
101	5457	UMa	G-SABcd	14 03.2	+54 21	7.9	26 × 26	!! Pinwheel Gal.; diffuse face-on spiral
108	3556	UMa	G-SBcd	11 11.5	+55 40	10.0	8.1 × 2.1	nearly edge-on; paired with M97 0.75° SE
109	3992	UMa	G-SBbc	11 57.6	+53 23	9.8	7.6 × 4.3	barred spiral near γ UMa
65	3623	Leo	G-SABa	11 18.9	+13 05	9.3	8.7 × 2.2	!! bright elongated spiral
66	3627	Leo	G-SABb	11 20.2	+12 59	8.9	8.2 × 3.9	!! M65 and NGC 3628 in same field
95	3351	Leo	G-SBb	10 44.0	+11 42	9.7	7.8 × 4.6	bright barred spiral
96	3368	Leo	G-SABab	10 46.8	+11 49	9.2	6.9 × 4.6	M95 in same field
105	3379	Leo	G-E1	10 47.8	+12 35	9.3	3.9 × 3.9	bright elliptical near M95 and M96
53	5024	Com	GC	13 12.9	+18 10	7.5	12.6	150-mm telescope needed to resolve
64	4826	Com	G-SAab	12 56.7	+21 41	8.5	9.2 × 4.6	!! Black Eye Gal.; eye needs big scope
85	4382	Com	G-SA0⁺	12 25.4	+18 11	9.1	7.5 × 5.7	bright elliptical shape
88	4501	Com	G-SAb	12 32.0	+14 25	9.6	6.1 × 2.8	bright multiple-arm spiral
91	4548	Com	G-SBb	12 35.4	+14 30	10.2	5.0 × 4.1	some lists say M91 = M58, not NGC 4548
98	4192	Com	G-SABab	12 13.8	+14 54	10.1	9.1 × 2.1	nearly edge-on spiral near star 6 Com. B.
99	4254	Com	G-SAc	12 18.8	+14 25	9.9	4.6 × 4.3	nearly face-on spiral near M98
100	4321	Com	G-SABbc	12 22.9	+15 49	9.3	6.2 × 5.3	face-on spiral with starlike nucleus
49	4472	Vir	G-E2	12 29.8	+8 00	8.4	8.1 × 7.1	very bright elliptical
58	4579	Vir	G-SABb	12 37.7	+11 49	9.7	5.5 × 4.6	bright barred spiral; M59 and M60 1° E
59	4621	Vir	G-E5	12 42.0	+11 39	9.6	4.6 × 3.6	bright elliptical paired with M60
60	4649	Vir	G-E2	12 43.7	+11 33	8.8	7.1 × 6.1	bright elliptical with M59 and NGC 4647
61	4303	Vir	G-SABbc	12 21.9	+4 28	9.7	6.0 × 5.9	face-on two-armed spiral
84	4374	Vir	G-E1	12 25.1	+12 53	9.1	5.1 × 4.1	!! w/ M86 in Markarian's Chain
86	4406	Vir	G-E3	12 26.2	+12 57	8.9	12 × 9	!! w/ many NGC galaxies in Chain
87	4486	Vir	G-E0-1	12 30.8	+12 24	8.6	7.1 × 7.1	the one with famous jet and black hole
89	4552	Vir	G-E	12 35.7	+12 33	9.8	3.4 × 3.4	elliptical; resembles M87 but smaller
90	4569	Vir	G-SABab	12 36.8	+13 10	9.5	10 × 4	bright barred spiral near M89
104	4594	Vir	G-SA	12 40.0	–11 37	8.0	7.1 × 4.4	!! Sombrero Galaxy; look for dust lane
3	5272	CVn	GC	13 42.2	+28 23	5.9	16.2	!! contains many variable stars
51	5194/5	CVn	G-SABc	13 29.9	+47 12	8.4	8 × 7	!! Whirlpool Galaxy; superb in big scope
63	5055	CVn	G-SABc	13 15.8	+42 02	8.6	14 × 8	!! Sunflower Galaxy; bright, elongated
94	4736	CVn	G-SAab	12 50.9	+41 07	8.2	13 × 11	very bright and comet-like
106	4258	CVn	G-SABbc	12 19.0	+47 18	8.4	20 × 8	!! superb large, bright spiral
68	4590	Hya	GC	12 39.5	–26 45	7.7	12	150-mm telescope needed to resolve
83	5236	Hya	G-SABc	13 37.0	–29 52	7.6	16 × 13	large and diffuse; superb from far south
102	5866?	Dra	G-SA0⁺	15 06.5	+55 46	9.9	6.6 × 3.2	or is M102 = M101? (look for 5907)
5	5904	Ser	GC	15 18.6	+2 05	5.7	17.4	!! one of the sky's finest globulars
The Summer Sky								
13	6205	Her	GC	16 41.7	+36 28	5.7	16.6	!! Hercules Cluster; NGC 6207 0.5° NE
92	6341	Her	GC	17 17.1	+43 08	6.4	11.2	9° NE of M13; fine but often overlooked
9	6333	Oph	GC	17 19.2	–18 31	7.6	9.3	smallest of Ophiuchus globulars
10	6254	Oph	GC	16 57.1	–4 06	6.6	15.1	rich globular cluster; M12 is 3° NW
12	6218	Oph	GC	16 47.2	–1 57	6.8	14.5	loose globular cluster near M10
14	6402	Oph	GC	17 37.6	–3 15	7.6	11.7	200-mm telescope needed to resolve
19	6273	Oph	GC	17 02.6	–26 16	6.7	13.5	oblate globular; M62 4° S
62	6266	Oph	GC	17 01.2	–30 07	6.7	14.1	asymmetrical; in rich field

SEASONAL LISTING OF MESSIER OBJECTS (continued)

M#	NGC	Con	Type	RA (2000)	Dec	m_v	Size	Remarks
Summer Sky (cont)				h m	° '		'	
107	6171	Oph	GC	16 32.5	−13 03	8.1	10.0	small, faint globular
4	6121	Sco	GC	16 23.6	−26 32	5.8	26.3	bright globular near Antares
6	6405	Sco	OC	17 40.1	−32 13	4.2	33	!! Butterfly Cluster; best at low power
7	6475	Sco	OC	17 53.9	−34 49	3.3	80	!! excellent in binocs or rich-field scope
80	6093	Sco	GC	16 17.0	−22 59	7.3	8.9	very compressed globular
16	6611	Ser	EN + OC	18 18.6	−13 58	—	35 × 28	Eagle Neb. w/ open cl.; use neb. filter
8	6523	Sgr	EN	18 03.8	−24 23	—	45 × 30	!! Lagoon Nebula w/ open cl. NGC 6530
17	6618	Sgr	EN	18 20.8	−16 11	—	20 × 15	!! Swan or Omega Nebula; use neb. filter
18	6613	Sgr	OC	18 19.9	−17 08	6.9	10	sparse cluster; 1° south of M17
20	6514	Sgr	E/RN	18 02.3	−23 02	—	20 × 20	!! Trifid Nebula; look for dark lanes
21	6531	Sgr	OC	18 04.6	−22 30	5.9	13	0.7° NE of M20; sparse cluster
22	6656	Sgr	GC	18 36.4	−23 54	5.1	24	spectacular from southern latitude
23	6494	Sgr	OC	17 56.8	−19 01	5.5	27	bright, loose open cluster
24	—	Sgr	starcloud	18 16.5	−18 50	4.6	95 × 35	rich star cloud; best in big binoculars
25	IC 4725	Sgr	OC	18 31.6	−19 15	4.6	32	bright but sparse open cluster
28	6626	Sgr	GC	18 24.5	−24 52	6.8	11.2	compact globular near M22
54	6715	Sgr	GC	18 55.1	−30 29	7.6	9.1	not easily resolved
55	6809	Sgr	GC	19 40.0	−30 58	6.4	19.0	bright, loose globular cluster
69	6637	Sgr	GC	18 31.4	−32 21	7.6	7.1	small, poor globular cluster
70	6681	Sgr	GC	18 43.2	−32 18	8.0	7.8	small globular 2° east of M69
75	6864	Sgr	GC	20 06.1	−21 55	8.5	6	small and distant; 59 000 ly away
11	6705	Sct	OC	18 51.1	−6 16	5.8	13	!! Wild Duck Cl.; the best open cluster?
26	6694	Sct	OC	18 45.2	−9 24	8.0	14	bright, coarse cluster
56	6779	Lyr	GC	19 16.6	+30 11	8.3	7.1	within a rich starfield
57	6720	Lyr	PN	18 53.6	+33 02	8.8	>71″	!! Ring Nebula; an amazing smoke ring
71	6838	Sge	GC	19 53.8	+18 47	8.0	7.2	loose globular; looks like an open cluster
27	6853	Vul	PN	19 59.6	+22 43	7.3	>348″	!! Dumbbell Nebula; a superb object
29	6913	Cyg	OC	20 23.9	+38 32	6.6	6	small, poor open cluster 2° S of γ Cygni
39	7092	Cyg	OC	21 32.2	+48 26	4.6	31	very sparse cluster; use low power

The Autumn Sky

M#	NGC	Con	Type	RA (2000)	Dec	m_v	Size	Remarks
2	7089	Aqr	GC	21 33.5	−0 49	6.4	12.9	200-mm telescope needed to resolve
72	6981	Aqr	GC	20 53.5	−12 32	9.3	5.9	near the Saturn Nebula, NGC 7009
73	6994	Aqr	OC	20 59.0	−12 38	8.9p	2.8	group of four stars only; an "asterism"
15	7078	Peg	GC	21 30.0	+12 10	6.0	12.3	rich, compact globular
30	7099	Cap	GC	21 40.4	−23 11	7.3	11	toughest in one-night Messier marathon
52	7654	Cas	OC	23 24.2	+61 35	6.9	12	young, rich cl.; faint Bubble Neb. nearby
103	581	Cas	OC	1 33.2	+60 42	7.4	6	three NGC open clusters nearby
31	224	And	G-SAb	0 42.7	+41 16	3.4	185 × 75	!! Andromeda Gal.; look for dust lanes
32	221	And	G-E2	0 42.7	+40 52	8.1	9 × 7	closest companion to M31
110	205	And	G-S0/E5 pec	0 40.4	+41 41	8.1	22 × 11	more distant companion to M31
33	598	Tri	G-SAcd	1 33.9	+30 39	5.7	67 × 42	large, diffuse spiral; requires dark sky
74	628	Psc	G-SAc	1 36.7	+15 47	9.4	11 × 11	faint, elusive spiral; tough in small scope
77	1068	Cet	G-SABab	2 42.7	−0 01	8.9	8.2 × 7.3	a Seyfert galaxy; with starlike nucleus
34	1039	Per	OC	2 42.0	+42 47	5.2	35	best at low power
76	650/51	Per	PN	1 42.4	+51 34	10.1	>65″	Little Dumbbell; faint but distinct

THE FINEST NGC OBJECTS

BY ALAN DYER

Those looking for an observing project beyond THE MESSIER CATALOGUE turn to the New General Catalogue (NGC). The NGC contains 7840 entries and forms the core database of today's computerized backyard telescopes. To match THE MESSIER CATALOGUE, this list contains 110 of the finest NGC objects visible from mid-northern latitudes. The seasonal order is similar to that used in THE MESSIER CATALOGUE, and there is no overlap. While the brightness of the best NGCs rivals many Messier targets, at least a 200-mm telescope is required to see all 110 objects on this list. Most are easy; a few are challenging.

The NGC was originally published by J.L.E. Dreyer in 1888, a work that expanded upon Sir John Herschel's 1864 "General Catalogue." Supplementary "Index Catalogues" were published by Dreyer in 1895 and 1908. The first IC extends the NGC with another 1529 objects discovered visually between 1888 and 1894. Most are faint, elusive targets. (To provide a flavor of this extension to the NGC, one entry from the first IC is included on this list, IC 289.) The Second Index Catalogue contains 3857 entries, most discovered photographically between 1895 and 1907.

The *Sky Atlas 2000.0*, the sets of index card charts called *AstroCards*, *The Night Sky Observer's Guide Vols. 1 and 2* by Kepple and Sanner, and the *Uranometria 2000.0 Deep Sky Atlas* are recommended finder aids. Most planetarium and deep-sky charting computer programs, as well as computerized telescopes, include all the objects on this list and many more.

Notation below is as in THE MESSIER CATALOGUE. Magnitudes (m_v) are visual, with the exception of those marked "p," which are photographic, or blue, magnitudes. Most galaxies appear smaller than the sizes listed. For open clusters, the number of stars (*) is also given. Data are taken from *The Deep Sky Field Guide to Uranometria 2000.0* (see the introduction to THE MESSIER CATALOGUE), with some sizes rounded to two significant figures.

SEASONAL LISTING OF FINEST NGC OBJECTS

#	NGC	Con	Type	RA (2000) Dec		m_v	Size	Remarks
				h m	° ′		′	
The Autumn Sky								
1	7009	Aqr	PN	21 04.2	−11 22	8.3p	>25″	!! Saturn Nebula; small bright oval
2	7293	Aqr	PN	22 29.6	−20 48	7.3	>769″	!! Helix Nebula; large, diffuse; use filter
3	7331	Peg	G-SAb	22 37.1	+34 25	9.5	10 × 4	!! large, bright spiral galaxy
4	7635	Cas	EN	23 20.7	+61 12	—	15 × 8	Bubble Neb.; very faint; 0.5° SW of M52
5	7789	Cas	OC	23 57.0	+56 44	6.7	15	!! 300*; faint but very rich cluster
6	185	Cas	G-E3	0 39.0	+48 20	9.2	14 × 12	companion to M31; small and faint
7	281	Cas	EN	0 52.8	+56 37	—	35 × 30	!! large faint nebulosity near η Cas
8	457	Cas	OC	1 19.1	+58 20	6.4	13	80*; rich; one of the best Cas. clusters
9	663	Cas	OC	1 46.0	+61 15	7.1	16	80*; look for NGCs 654 and 659 nearby
10	IC 289	Cas	PN	3 10.3	+61 19	13.3	>34″	dim oval smudge; use a nebular filter!
11	7662	And	PN	23 25.9	+42 33	8.3	>12″	!! Blue Snowball; annular at high power
12	891	And	G-SAb	2 22.6	+42 21	9.9	13 × 3	!! faint, classic edge-on with dust lane
13	253	Scl	G-SABc	0 47.6	−25 17	7.6	30 × 7	!! very large and bright but at low altitude
14	772	Ari	G-SAb	1 59.3	+19 01	10.3	7.3 × 4.6	diffuse spiral galaxy
15	246	Cet	PN	0 47.0	−11 53	10.9	225″	large and faint with mottled structure
16	936	Cet	G-SB	2 27.6	−1 09	10.2	5.7 × 4.6	near M77; NGC 941 in the same field

SEASONAL LISTING OF FINEST NGC OBJECTS (continued)

#	NGC	Con	Type	RA (2000) h m	Dec ° '	m_v	Size '	Remarks
Autumn Sky (continued)								
17	869/884	Per	OC	2 21.0	+57 08	≈5	30/30	!! Double Cluster; 315*; use low power
18	1023	Per	G-SB0⁻	2 40.4	+39 04	9.3	8.6 × 4.2	bright lens-shaped galaxy near M34
19	1491	Per	EN	4 03.4	+51 19	—	25 × 25	visually small and faint emission nebula
20	1501	Cam	PN	4 07.0	+60 55	11.5	52″	faint; dark center; look for NGC 1502
21	1232	Eri	G-SABc	3 09.8	−20 35	10.0	6.8 × 5.6	face-on spiral; look for NGC 1300 nearby
22	1535	Eri	PN	4 14.2	−12 44	9.6p	>18″	bright planetary with blue-grey disk

The Winter Sky

#	NGC	Con	Type	RA (2000) h m	Dec ° '	m_v	Size '	Remarks
23	1514	Tau	PN	4 09.2	+30 47	10.9	>114″	faint glow around 9.4ᵐ central star
24	1931	Aur	E/RN	5 31.4	+34 15	—	4 × 4	haze surrounding four close stars
25	1788	Ori	RN	5 06.9	−3 21	—	5 × 3	fairly bright but diffuse reflection nebula
26	1973+	Ori	E/RN	5 35.1	−4 44	—	≈20 × 10	NGC 1973-5-7 just N. of M42 and M43
27	2022	Ori	PN	5 42.1	+9 05	11.9	>18″	small, faint & distinct with annular form
28	2024	Ori	EN	5 41.9	−1 51	—	30 × 30	bright but masked by glow from ζ Ori
29	2194	Ori	OC	6 13.8	+12 48	8.5	8	80*, fairly rich; look for 2169 nearby
30	2371/2	Gem	PN	7 25.6	+29 29	11.3	>55″	faint double-lobed planetary; use filter
31	2392	Gem	PN	7 29.2	+20 55	9.2	>15″	!! Clown Face or Eskimo Nebula
32	2237+	Mon	EN	6 32.3	+5 03	—	80 × 60	!! Rosette Nebula; very large; use filter
33	2261	Mon	E/RN	6 39.2	+8 44	var	3.5 × 1.5	Hubble's Variable Nebula; comet-shaped
34	2359	CMa	EN	7 18.6	−13 12	—	9 × 6	bright; look for 2360 & 2362 nearby
35	2440	Pup	PN	7 41.9	−18 13	9.4	>14″	almost starlike; irregular at high power
36	2539	Pup	OC	8 10.7	−12 50	6.5	21	50*; rich cluster; near M46 and M47
37	2403	Cam	G-SABc	7 36.9	+65 36	8.5	26 × 13	!! very large & bright; visible in binocs.
38	2655	Cam	G-SAB0	8 55.6	+78 13	10.1	6.0 × 5.3	bright ellipse with starlike nucleus

The Spring Sky

#	NGC	Con	Type	RA (2000) h m	Dec ° '	m_v	Size '	Remarks
39	2683	Lyn	G-SAb	8 52.7	+33 25	9.8	8.4 × 2.4	nearly edge-on spiral; very bright
40	2841	UMa	G-SAb	9 22.0	+50 58	9.2	6.8 × 3.3	!! classic elongated spiral; very bright
41	3079	UMa	G-SBc	10 02.2	+55 41	10.9	8.0 × 1.5	edge-on spiral; NGC 2950 nearby
42	3184	UMa	G-SABc	10 18.3	+41 25	9.8	7.8 × 7.2	large, diffuse face-on spiral
43	3877	UMa	G-SAc	11 46.1	+47 30	11.0	5.1 × 1.1	edge-on; same field as χ UMa
44	3941	UMa	G-SB0°	11 52.9	+36 59	10.3	3.7 × 2.6	small, bright. and elliptical
45	4026	UMa	G-S0	11 59.4	+50 58	10.8	4.6 × 1.2	lens-shaped edge-on near γ UMa
46	4088	UMa	G-SABbc	12 05.6	+50 33	10.6	5.4 × 2.1	nearly edge-on; NGC 4085 in same field
47	4157	UMa	G-SABb	12 11.1	+50 29	11.3	7.1 × 1.2	a thin sliver; NGC 4026 and 4088 nearby
48	4605	UMa	G-SBcp	12 40.0	+61 37	10.3	6.4 × 2.3	bright, distinct edge-on spiral
49	3115	Sex	G-S0⁻	10 05.2	−7 43	8.9	8.1 × 2.8	Spindle Galaxy; bright and elongated
50	3242	Hya	PN	10 24.8	−18 38	7.8	>16″	!! Ghost of Jupiter; small but bright
51	3003	LMi	G-Sbc?	9 48.6	+33 25	11.9	5.2 × 1.6	faint elongated streak
52	3344	LMi	G-SABbc	10 43.5	+24 55	9.9	6.9 × 6.4	diffuse face-on barred spiral
53	3432	LMi	G-SBm	10 52.5	+36 37	11.2	6.9 × 1.9	nearly edge-on; faint flat streak
54	2903	Leo	G-SABbc	9 32.2	+21 30	9.0	12 × 6	!! very large, bright elongated spiral
55	3384	Leo	G-SB0⁻	10 48.3	+12 38	9.9	5.5 × 2.9	same field as M105 and NGC 3389
56	3521	Leo	G-SAb	11 05.8	−0 02	9.0	12 × 6	very large, bright spiral
57	3607	Leo	G-SA0°	11 16.9	+18 03	9.9	4.6 × 4.1	NGC 3605 & 3608 in same field
58	3628	Leo	G-Sb pec	11 20.3	+13 36	9.5	14 × 4	large edge-on; same field as M65 & M66
59	4111	CVn	G-SA0⁺	12 07.1	+43 04	10.7	4.4 × 0.9	bright lens-shaped edge-on spiral
60	4214	CVn	G-I AB	12 15.6	+36 20	9.8	10 × 8	large irregular galaxy
61	4244	CVn	G-SAcd	12 17.5	+37 49	10.4	17 × 2	!! large distinct edge-on spiral

SEASONAL LISTING OF FINEST NGC OBJECTS (continued)

#	NGC	Con	Type	RA (2000) Dec		m_v	Size	Remarks
				h m	° ′		′	
Spring Sky (continued)								
62	4449	CVn	G-I Bm	12 28.2	+44 06	9.6	5.5 × 4.1	bright with odd rectangular shape
63	4490	CVn	G-SBd p	12 30.6	+41 38	9.8	6.4 × 3.3	Cocoon Gal.; bright spiral; 4485 in field
64	4631	CVn	G-SBd	12 42.1	+32 32	9.2	16 × 3	!! large edge-on; with companion 4627
65	4656/7	CVn	G-SBm p	12 44.0	+32 10	10.5	20 × 3	!! in field with 4631; NE end curves up
66	5005	CVn	G-SABbc	13 10.9	+37 03	9.8	5.8 × 2.8	bright elongated spiral near α CVn
67	5033	CVn	G-SAc	13 13.4	+36 36	10.2	10 × 5	large bright spiral near NGC 5005
68	4274	Com	G-SBab	12 19.8	+29 37	10.4	6.7 × 2.5	NGCs 4278/83/86 in same field
69	4414	Com	G-SAc	12 26.4	+31 13	10.1	4.4 × 3.0	bright spiral with starlike nucleus
70	4494	Com	G-E1-2	12 31.4	+25 47	9.8	4.6 × 4.4	small bright elliptical
71	4559	Com	G-SABc	12 36.0	+27 58	10.0	12 × 5	large spiral with coarse structure
72	4565	Com	G-SAb	12 36.3	+25 59	9.6	14 × 2	!! superb edge-on spiral with dust lane
73	4725	Com	G-SABab	12 50.4	+25 30	9.4	10 × 8	very bright, large spiral
74	4038/9	Crv	G-SB/IB	12 01.9	−18 52	~10.4	~5 × 3 ea.	"Antennae" interacting galaxies
75	4361	Crv	PN	12 24.5	−18 48	10.9	>45″	small and bright; with 13ᵐ central star
76	4216	Vir	G-SABb	12 15.9	+13 09	10.0	7.8 × 1.6	nearly edge-on; with NGC 4206 and 4222
77	4388	Vir	G-SAb	12 25.8	+12 40	11.0	5.7 × 1.6	with M84 and M86 in Markarian's Chain
78	4438	Vir	G-SA0/a	12 27.8	+13 01	10.2	8.9 × 3.6	paired w/ NGC 4435 to form the "Eyes"
79	4517	Vir	G-Scd	12 32.8	+0 07	10.4	9.9 × 1.4	edge-on spiral; often mislabelled NGC 4437
80	4526	Vir	G-SAB0°	12 34.0	+7 42	9.7	7.1 × 2.9	between two 7ᵐ stars
81	4535	Vir	G-SABc	12 34.3	+8 12	10.0	7.1 × 6.4	near M49 and 0.75° N of NGC 4526
82	4567/8	Vir	G-SAbc	12 36.5	+11 15	~11	~3 × 2 ea.	"Siamese Twins" interacting galaxies
83	4699	Vir	G-Sab	12 49.0	−8 40	9.5	4.4 × 3.2	small & bright; look for NGC 4697 3°N
84	4762	Vir	G-SB0°?	12 52.9	+11 14	10.3	9.1 × 2.2	flattest galaxy known; 4754 in same field
85	5746	Vir	G-SA?b	14 44.9	+1 57	10.3	6.8 × 1.0	fine edge-on near 109 Virginis
86	5466	Boo	GC	14 05.5	+28 32	9.0	11	loose class XII; like rich open cl.; faint
87	5907	Dra	G-SAc	15 15.9	+56 20	10.3	12 × 2	!! fine edge-on with dust lane; near 5866
88	6503	Dra	G-SAcd	17 49.4	+70 09	10.2	7.3 × 2.4	bright elongated spiral
89	6543	Dra	PN	17 58.6	+66 38	8.1	>18″	Cat's Eye Nebula; with 10.9ᵐ central star
The Summer Sky								
90	6210	Her	PN	16 44.5	+23 49	8.8	>14″	blue starlike planetary
91	6369	Oph	PN	17 29.3	−23 46	11.4	>30″	"Little Ghost"; look for 6309 nearby
92	6572	Oph	PN	18 12.1	+6 51	8.1	8″	tiny bright blue oval
93	6633	Oph	OC	18 27.7	+6 34	4.6	27	sparse wide field cluster; IC 4756 nearby
94	6712	Sct	GC	18 53.1	−8 42	8.2	7.2	small globular; look for IC 1295 in field
95	6781	Aql	PN	19 18.4	+6 33	11.4	>109″	pale version of the Owl Nebula, M97
96	6819	Cyg	OC	19 41.3	+40 11	7.3	9.5	150*; faint but rich cluster in Milky Way
97	6826	Cyg	PN	19 44.8	+50 31	8.8	>25″	!! Blinking Planetary; 10.6ᵐ central star
98	6888	Cyg	EN	20 12.0	+38 21	—	18 × 13	Crescent Nebula; faint; use nebular filter
99a	6960	Cyg	SNR	20 45.7	+30 43	—	70 × 6	!! Veil Nebula west half; use filter!
99b	6992/5	Cyg	SNR	20 56.4	+31 43	—	72 × 8	!! Veil Nebula east half; use filter!
100	7000	Cyg	EN	20 58.8	+44 20	—	120 × 100	!! North America; use filter & low power
101	7027	Cyg	PN	21 07.1	+42 14	8.5	15″	unusual protoplanetary nebula
102	6445	Sgr	PN	17 49.2	−20 01	11.2	>34″	small, bright and annular; near M23
103	6520	Sgr	OC	18 03.4	−27 54	7.6p	6	60*; small; dark nebula B86 in same field
104	6818	Sgr	PN	19 44.0	−14 09	9.3	>17″	"Little Gem"; annular; NGC 6822 0.75°S
105	6802	Vul	OC	19 30.6	+20 16	8.8	3.2	50*; at east end of Brocchi's Cluster
106	6940	Vul	OC	20 34.6	+28 18	6.3	31	60*; fairly rich cluster in Milky Way
107	6939	Cep	OC	20 31.4	+60 38	7.8	7	80*; very rich; NGC 6946 in same field
108	6946	Cep	G-SABcd	20 34.8	+60 09	8.8	13 × 13	faint, diffuse face-on spiral near 6939
109	7129	Cep	RN	21 42.8	+66 06	—	7 × 7	faint reflection neb. around sparse cluster
110	40	Cep	PN	0 13.0	+72 32	12.4	>37″	unusual red planetary; 11.6ᵐ central star

DARK NEBULAE
BY PAUL GRAY

Dark nebulae, often appearing as "holes in the sky," are fascinating to observe. The following is a representative selection of visually observable dark nebulae. The **minimum aperture** in millimetres is what observers have found to be necessary to see each nebula; however, many may be observable with smaller apertures under excellent skies. Quality of optics, the observer's experience, and full dark adaptation are often more important than the aperture. Some objects will also benefit from the use of a filter because they are superimposed upon a bright nebula.

Nebulae are listed in order of RA. Column **B** lists the *Barnard Catalogue* number; two objects (L 889 and L 906) are from the *Lynds Catalogue*, one (LG 3) is from the *Le Gentil Catalogue*, and one is uncataloged. The column **Chart #** lists the chart in *Uranometria 2000.0 Deep Sky Atlas* (2nd Ed., 2001) that contains the object; *italic* numbers indicate that the object is not actually marked on the given chart. The **opacity** is based on a scale of 1 to 6, with 6 being the easiest to observe; no objects of opacity 1 or 2 are listed, since these objects are very difficult to observe visually. Showpiece objects are marked "!!". For further information, including finder charts, images, and observation reports, visit **www.rasc.ca/handbook/supplements**.

#	B	Con	RA (2000) h m	Dec ° '	Chart #	Size '	Opa-city	Min. Aper. mm	Remarks
1	5	Per	3 48	+32 54	60	22×9	5	200	1° NE of ο Per
2	211/3	Tau	4 17.2	+27 48	78	12×110	3	200–250	narrow NW–SE lanes, faint bkgd starfield
3	33	Ori	5 40.9	−2 28	116	6×4	4	100–150	Horsehead Nebula; use Hβ filter
4	34	Aur	5 43.5	+32 39	59	20	4	200	2° W of M37; spider-like appearance
5	35	Ori	5 45.5	+9 03	96	20×10	5	150–200	near FU Ori and bright nebula Ced 59
6	37	Mon	6 33	+1100	96	3°	5	150 RFT	near NGC 2245, 2247; try binoculars
7	40	Sco	16 14.7	−18 59	147	15	3	250	in bright nebula IC 4592; 50′ NE of ν Sco
8	44	Oph	16 40	−24 04	146	35×300	6	10×70	large dark rift; naked-eye in superb sky
9	59	Oph	17 11.4	−27 29	146	60	6	10×70	3° SW of θ Oph; part of stem of Pipe Nebula
10	64	Oph	17 17.2	−18 32	146	20	6	150–200	30′ W of M9; causes darkening of M9
11	68	Oph	17 22.6	−23 44	146	3	6	200	small; near B72; region rich in dark nebulae
12	70	Oph	17 23.6	−23 58	146	4	4	200	small; near B72; region rich in dark nebulae
13	72	Oph	17 23.6	−23 38	146	30	6	80–125	!! the Snake; "S" shape; 1.5° N of θ Oph
14	78	Oph	17 33	−26 00	146	3°	6	eye	!! Pipe bowl, "Prancing Horse" hindquarters
15	84A	Sgr	17 57.5	−17 40	146	16	5	150–200	1.5° N of M23; try for extensions to S
16	85	Sgr	18 02.6	−23 02	145	5	4	100	!! dark lanes inside Trifid Nebula (M20)
17	86	Sgr	18 02.7	−27 50	145	4	5	200	!! Ink Spot; nice pair with NGC 6520 5′ E
18	87	Sgr	18 04.3	−32 30	163	12	4	200	Parrot's Head; 2° S of γ Sgr
19	88	Sgr	18 04.4	−24 07	145	2	4	200	on edge of M8; *not* Burnham's "Dark Comet"
20		Sgr	18 04.5	−24 14	*145*	2×1	4	200	Burnham's "Dark Comet"; use filter
21	303	Sgr	18 09.5	−24 00	145	1	5	200–250	inside IC 4685; use filter; challenging
22	92/3	Sgr	18 15.5	−18 11	145	12×6	6	7×50	!! on NW edge of Small Sgr Star Cloud, M24
23	103	Sct	18 39.2	−6 37	126	40×40	6	10×0	on NW side of Scutum star cloud
24	104	Sct	18 47.3	−4 32	105	16×1	5	150–200	20′ N of β Sct; a checkmark shape
25	108	Sct	18 49.6	−6 19	125	3	3	200	30′ W of M11; rich region
26	112	Sct	18 51.2	−6 40	125	20	4	200	30′ S of M11; also look for B114, B118
27	133	Aql	19 06.1	−6 50	125	10×3	6	100	on Scutum star cloud; very dark spot!
28	142/3	Aql	19 40.7	+10 57	85	80×50	6	10×50	!! Barnard's famous "E" cloud
29	145	Cyg	20 02.8	+37 40	48	6×35	4	200	triangular shape
30	L 889	Cyg	20 24.8	+40 10	48	100×20	–	7×50	within γ Cygni Nebula, IC 1318
31	L 906	Cyg	20 37	+42 00	48	6°	–	eye	"Northern Coalsack"
32	150	Cep	20 00.6	+60 18	20	60×3	5	250	curved filament 1.6° S of η Cep
33	353	Cyg	20 57.1	+45 32	32	20×10	5	100	in N of North America Nebula; B352 in field
34	LG 3	Cyg	21 00	+53 00	*32*	12°	–	eye	!! "Funnel Cloud Nebula"; best after Coalsack
35	361	Cyg	21 12.9	+47 22	32	20	4	100	cluster IC 1369 to N; try for 1° tendril to W
36	365	Cep	21 34.9	+56 43	19	22×3	4	200	in IC 1396; indistinct "S" shape; use filter
37	163	Cep	21 42.2	+56 42	19	4	4	200	in IC 1396; use filter
38	168	Cyg	21 49	+47 29	31	100×20	5	7×50	large E–W lane; Cocoon Nebula at E end

DEEP-SKY CHALLENGE OBJECTS

BY ALAN DYER AND ALISTER LING

The beauty of the deep sky extends well past the best and brightest objects. The attraction of observing is not the sight of an object itself but our intellectual contact with what it *is*. A faint, stellar point in Virgo evokes wonder when you try to fathom the depths of this quasar billions of light-years away. The eclectic collection of objects below is designed to introduce some "fringe" catalogs while providing challenging targets for a wide range of apertures. Often more important than sheer aperture are factors such as the quality of sky, quality of the optics, use of an appropriate filter, and the observer's experience. Don't be afraid to tackle some of these with a smaller telescope.

Objects are listed in order of right ascension. Abbreviations are the same as in THE MESSIER CATALOGUE and THE FINEST NGC OBJECTS, with the addition of DN = dark nebula and Q = quasar. **Chart #** indicates the chart in which the object can be found in *Uranometria 2000.0 Deep Sky Atlas* (2nd Ed., 2001). The last column suggests the minimum aperture, in millimetres, needed to see that object. Most data are taken from *Sky Catalogue 2000.0, Vol. 2*. Some visual magnitudes are from other sources.

#	Object	Con	Type	RA (2000) h m	Dec ° ′	m_v	Size ′	Chart #	Minimum Aperture mm
1	NGC 7822	Cep	E/RN	0 03.6	+68 37	—	60 × 30	8	300

large, faint emission nebula; rated "eeF"; also look for E/R nebula Ced 214 (associated w/ star cluster Berkeley 59) 1° S

2	IC 59	Cas	E/RN	0 56.7	+61 04	—	10 × 5	18	200–250

faint emission/reflection nebula paired with IC 63 very close to γ Cas.; requires clean optics; rated as "pF"

3	NGC 609	Cas	OC	1 37.2	+64 33	11.0	3.0	17	250–300

faint patch at low power; high power needed to resolve this rich cluster (also look for Trumpler 1 cluster 3° S)

4	IC 1795	Cas	EN	2 24.7	+61 54	—	27 × 13	29	200

brightest part of a complex of nebulosity that includes IC 1805 and IC 1848; use a nebular filter

5	Maffei I	Cas	G-E3	2 36.3	+59 39	≈14	5 × 3	29	300

heavily reddened galaxy; very faint; requires large aperture and black skies; nearby Maffei II for extremists

6	NGC 1049	For	GC	2 39.7	−34 29	11.0	0.6	175	250–300

Class V globular in dwarf "Fornax System" Local Group galaxy 630 000 ly away; galaxy itself invisible?

7	Abell 426	Per	G cl.	3 19.8	+41 31	12–16	≈30	43, A4	200–400

Perseus galaxy cluster 300 million ly away; mag. 11.6 NGC 1275 Perseus A at center; see close-up chart A4

8	NGC 1432/35	Tau	RN	3 46.1	+23 47	—	30 × 30	78, A12	100–150

Pleiades nebulosity (also includes IC 349); brightest around Merope; requires transparent skies and clean optics

9	IC 342	Cam	G-SBc	3 46.8	+68 06	≈12	17 × 17	16	200–300

large and diffuse face-on spiral; member of UMa–Cam cloud (Kemble's Cascade of stars also on this chart)

10	NGC 1499	Per	EN	4 00.7	+36 37	—	145 × 40	60	80–125 RFT

California Nebula; very large and faint; use a wide-field telescope or big binoculars plus Hβ filter

11	IC 405	Aur	E/RN	5 16.2	+34 16	—	30 × 19	59	200

Flaming Star Nebula associated with runaway star AE Aurigae; see Burnham's Handbook p. 285 (also look for IC 410)

12	HH 1	Ori	E	5 36.3	−06 45	≈14.5	8″	136	250

Herbig–Haro 1; best with no filter at 250× or more; bipolar jets from forming star; not plotted; 2.5′ SW NGC 1999

13	IC 434 / B 33	Ori	E/DN	5 40.9	−2 28	—	60 × 10	116	100–150 in dark sky!

B 33 is the Horsehead Nebula, a dark nebula superimposed on a very faint emission nebula IC 434; use Hβ filter

14	Sh 2-276	Ori	EN	5 48.0	+1 —	—	600 × 30!	116	100–150 RFT

Barnard's Loop; SNR or interstellar bubble? difficult to detect due to size; use filter and sweep with wide field

15	Abell 12	Ori	PN	6 02.4	+9 39	≈13	37″	96	250–300

plotted in *Uranometria* as PK 198.6–6.3; on NW edge of μ Orionis; OIII filter required

16	IC 443	Gem	SNR	6 16.9	+22 47	—	50 × 40	76	250–300

faint supernova remnant very close to η Gem.; use filter (also look for NGC 2174 and Sh 2–247 on this chart)

17	J 900	Gem	PN	6 25.9	+17 47	12.2	8″	76	200

Jonckheere 900; bright starlike planetary; plotted as PK 194.2+2.5 in *Uranometria*; use OIII filter & high power

18	IC 2177	Mon	E/RN	7 05.1	−10 42	—	120 × 40	135	200–300

Seagull Nebula; large, faint; contains bright patches Gum 1 (−10°28′), NGC 2327 (−11°18′) & Ced 90 (−12°20′)

DEEP-SKY CHALLENGE OBJECTS (continued)

#	Object	Con	Type	RA (2000) h m	Dec ° '	m_v	Size '	Chart #	Minimum Aperture mm
19	PK 205 +14.2	Gem	PN	7 29.0	+13 15	≈13	≈700"	95	200–250

Medusa Nebula or Abell 21; impressive in large aperture w/ OIII filter

| 20 | PK 164 +31.1 | Lyn | PN | 7 57.8 | +53 25 | ≈14 | 400" | 26 | 250 |

Jones–Emberson 1; faint with two small components; use OIII filter; sometimes confused with nearby NGC 2474–75

| 21 | Leo I | Leo | G-E3 | 10 08.4 | +12 18 | 9.8 | 10.7×8.3 | 93 | 300 |

dwarf elliptical; satellite of Milky Way; very low surface brightness; 0.3° N of Regulus! requires clean optics

| 22 | Abell 1367 | Leo | G cl. | 11 44.0 | +19 57 | 13–16 | ≈60 | 72, A11 | 300–400 |

cluster of some 30 or more galaxies within a 1° field near 93 Leonis; Copeland's Septet nearby

| 23 | NGC 3172 | UMi | G-Sb | 11 50.2 | +89 07 | 13.6 | 0.7×0.7 | 1 | 250 |

"Polarissima Borealis"—closest galaxy to the north celestial pole; small, faint, and otherwise unremarkable

| 24 | NGC 4236 | Dra | G-SBb | 12 16.7 | +69 28 | 9.6 | 18.6×6.9 | 13 | 200–250 |

very large, dim barred spiral; a diffuse glow (NGC 4395 on Chart #54 a similar large diffuse face-on)

| 25 | Mrk 205 | Dra | Q | 12 21.6 | +75 18 | 14.5 | stellar | 5 | 300 |

Markarian 205; a faint star on SW edge of NGC 4319; center of redshift controversy

| 26 | 3C 273 | Vir | Q | 12 29.1 | +2 03 | 12–13 | stellar | 111 | 250–300 |

at 2–3 billon ly away, one of the most distant objects visible in amateur telescopes; magnitude variable

| 27 | NGC 4676 | Com | G cl. | 12 46.2 | +30 44 | 14.1p | 2×1 | 53 | 250 |

"The Mice" or VV 224—two classic interacting galaxies; very faint double nature detectable at high power

| 28 | Abell 1656 | Com | G cl. | 13 00.1 | +27 58 | 12–16 | ≈60 | 71, A8 | 250–300 |

Coma Berenices galaxy cluster; very rich; 400 million ly away; brightest member NGC 4889; see close-up chart A8

| 29 | NGC 5053 | Com | GC | 13 16.4 | +17 42 | 9.8 | 10.5 | 71 | 100–200 |

faint and very loose globular 1° SE of M53; requires large aperture to resolve; difficult in hazy skies; class XI

| 30 | NGC 5897 | Lib | GC | 15 17.4 | –21 01 | 8.6 | 12.6 | 148 | 150–200 |

large and loose; easily hidden in hazy skies at higher latitude; brightest stars mag. 13.3, main branch mag. 16.3

| 31 | Abell 2065 | CrB | G cl. | 15 22.7 | +27 43 | ≈16 | ≈30 | 69 | 500 in superb sky! |

Corona Borealis galaxy cluster; perhaps the most difficult object for amateur telescopes; 1.5 billion ly away

| 32 | NGC 6027 | Ser | G cl. | 15 59.2 | +20 45 | ≈15 | 2×1 | 69 | 400 |

Seyfert's Sextet (6027 A–F); compact group of 6 small and very faint galaxies; see Burnham's Handbook p. 1793

| 33 | B 72 | Oph | DN | 17 23.5 | –23 38 | — | 30 | 146 | 80–125 RFT |

Barnard's dark S-Nebula or "The Snake"; opacity of 6/6; 1.5° NNE of θ Ophiuchi; area rich in dark nebulae

| 34 | NGC 6791 | Lyr | OC | 19 20.7 | +37 51 | 9.5 | 16 | 48 | 200–250 |

large, faint but very rich open cluster with 300 stars; a faint smear in smaller instruments; Type II 3 r

| 35 | PK 64 +5.1 | Cyg | PN | 19 34.8 | +30 31 | 9.6 | 8" | 48 | 200 |

Campbell's Hydrogen Star; very bright but very starlike; also cataloged as star BD +30°3639

| 36 | M 1-92 | Cyg | RN | 19 36.3 | +29 33 | 11.0 | 12"×6" | 48 | 250–300 |

Minkowski 1-92 or Footprint Nebula; bright, starlike reflection nebula; double at high mag; associated star invisible

| 37 | NGC 6822 | Sgr | G-I | 19 44.9 | –14 48 | ≈11 | 10.2×9.5 | 125 | 100–150 |

Barnard's Galaxy; member of the Local Group; large but very low surface brightness; requires transparent skies

| 38 | Palomar 11 | Aql | GC | 19 45.2 | –8 00 | 9.8 | 3.2 | 125 | 200–300 |

brightest of 15 heavily reddened GCs found on Sky Survey; magnitude is misleading; 11 Terzan GCs more challenging

| 39 | IC 4997 | Sge | PN | 20 20.2 | +16 45 | 10.9 | 2" | 84 | 200 |

bright but starlike planetary; the challenge is to see the disk! blink the field with and without a nebular filter

| 40 | IC 1318 | Cyg | EN | 20 26.2 | +40 30 | — | large | 32, A2 | 80–150 RFT |

complex of nebulosity around γ Cygni; multitude of patches in rich starfield; use a very wide field plus filter

| 41 | PK 80 –6.1 | Cyg | PN? | 21 02.3 | +36 42 | 13.5 | 16" | 47 | 250 |

the "Egg Nebula"; a very small proto-planetary nebula; can owners of large telescopes detect polarization?

| 42 | IC 1396 | Cep | EN | 21 39.1 | +57 30 | — | 170×140 | 19 | 100–125 RFT |

extremely large and diffuse area of emission nebulosity; use nebular filter and very wide-field optics in dark sky

| 43 | IC 5146 | Cyg | E/RN | 21 53.5 | +47 16 | — | 12×12 | 31 | 200–250 |

Cocoon Nebula; faint and diffuse; use Hβ filter; at the end of the long filamentary dark nebula Barnard 168

| 44 | NGC 7317–20 | Peg | G cl. | 22 36.1 | +33 57 | 13–14 | ≈1 ea. | 46 | 250–300 |

Stephan's Quintet; 0.5° SSW of NGC 7331; easy to pick out 3 or 4 (also look for "companions" to 7331)

| 45 | Jones 1 | Peg | PN | 23 35.9 | +30 28 | 12.1 | 332" | 45 | 250–300 |

plotted as PK 104.2 –29.6 in *Uranometria*; large dim glow; OIII filter required

DEEP-SKY GEMS
BY DAVID H. LEVY

The 154 objects in this personal list are selected from nearly 400 deep-sky objects that I assembled over forty-plus years of comet-hunting. My observing program, called CN-3, began on 1965 Dec. 17 and has continued without interruption since then (see www.rasc.ca/david-h-levy-logbooks). The objects are numbered chronologically (L#) in the order I first located them in the night sky, and these numbers match those in my book, *Deep Sky Objects: The best and brightest from four decades of comet chasing* (Prometheus Books, New York, 2005, 262 pp). **UI** refers to the charts in *Uranometria 2000.0*. **UII** refers to charts in *Uranometria 2000.0 Deep Sky Atlas* (the 2nd edition of **UI**). Chart numbers in parentheses indicate unlabelled objects.

This selection complements the other Handbook deep-sky observing lists. Specifically, the following objects are not included here: all objects that appear in THE MESSIER CATALOGUE, THE FINEST NGC OBJECTS, and THE DEEP-SKY CHALLENGE OBJECTS; also, several double stars and variable stars, a few asterisms, some photographic objects, and the gegenschein are not included, though observing them is strongly encouraged; finally, several objects with southern declinations are left out to ensure that the Deep-Sky Gems observing certificate can be earned without travel by the typical RASC member. Levy 384 deserves special note: Just as the terms "Plaskett's Star" and "Kemble's Cascade" recognize Canadian astronomers from the past, "Levy 384" has become the recognized name for a previously unnamed asterism.

On a final, personal note, the late Leo Enright deserves great credit and thanks for the amount of time and effort he invested since he originated this project in 2007. A dear and special friend, Leo devoted his life to inspiring people to take up skywatching. He was one of my closest friends and I miss him deeply.

The main list is grouped by season and ordered by RA. The list below is a cross-reference aid.

NUMERICAL LISTING OF DEEP-SKY GEMS

L#	Sky RA	L#	Sky RA	L#	Sky RA	L#	Sky RA	L#	Sky RA	L#	Sky RA	L#	Sky RA
5	Spr 14	59	Aut 1	133	Spr 9	171	Spr 12	205	Sum 16	239	Aut 0	279	*Sum 18*
6	Sum 16	62	Aut 2	134	Spr 12	172	Spr 12	206	Sum 16	240	Aut 0	280	Aut 23
8	Win 4	64	Aut 1	135	Spr 12	178	Spr 12	207	Sum 17	243	Sum 17	281	Aut 23
19	Sum 16	81	Aut 0	136	Spr 11	181	Spr 11	208	Sum 17	247	Aut 22	282	Aut 22
27	Spr 13	82	Spr 14	137	Spr 11	182	Spr 12	209	Spr 9	249	Aut 23	284	Aut 1
28	Spr 14	83	Spr 14	138	Spr 11	183	Spr 12	210	Spr 12	255	Spr 13	286	Win 3
29	Spr 14	95	Win 5	140	*Spr 12*	184	Spr 13	211	Spr 12	256	Win 8	296	Win 7
31	Aut 1	96	Win 8	145	Spr 12	185	Spr 13	212	Spr 12	257	Spr 12	300	Spr 10
34	Aut 1	98	Sum 18	147	Sum 18	186	Spr 13	213	Spr 12	259	Spr 12	315	Spr 13
35	Win 7	99	Aut 2	149	Sum 18	187	Spr 13	214	Spr 12	260	Spr 12	317	Spr 15
36	Sum 17	110	Sum 19	156	Sum 20	188	Spr 12	215	Spr 12	261	Spr 13	324	*Win 3*
37	Spr 9	112	Aut 21	158	Win 7	189	Spr 13	217	Spr 11	262	Sum 19	326	Spr 12
38	Aut 23	114	Win 4	159	Win 6	190	Spr 13	219	Spr 10	263	Aut 21	331	Spr 10
41	Spr 11	116	Win 6	160	Win 6	191	Spr 12	220	Sum 20	266	Spr 15	334	Sum 17
42	Spr 12	120	*Sum 17*	161	Win 6	192	Spr 12	223	Aut 0	267	Spr 13	337	Spr 10
44	Win 3	121	Spr 15	162	Win 6	193	Spr 12	224	Aut 2	268	Spr 14	338	Aut 2
50	Win 4	123	Win 4	163	Spr 9	195	Win 7	225	Win 3	270	Sum 18	340	Aut 2
51	Spr 9	124	Win 6	164	Spr 11	196	Spr 14	226	Win 8	271	Sum 17	341	Aut 2
53	Aut 1	125	Win 5	165	Spr 10	201	Spr 11	231	Spr 13	273	Win 5	342	Aut 0
55	Aut 23	129	Spr 10	167	Spr 10	202	Spr 14	232	Spr 13	276	Aut 0	367	Aut 1
56	Aut 0	130	Spr 10	169	Spr 9	203	Spr 14	236	Sum 16	277	Aut 22	382	Spr 11
57	Aut 23	131	Spr 9	170	Spr 12	204	Spr 14	238	Aut 1	278	Aut 1	384	Win 8

Editor's note: for certificate purposes, this list was revised in late 2011 by introducing Levy 120, 140, 279, and 324 (see entries in italics) in place of previous duplicates Levy 1, 245, 325, and 381.

DEEP-SKY GEMS (continued)

L#	NGC	RA (2000) Dec		m_v	Size	UI	UII	Remarks
		h m	° ′		(′)			
The Autumn Sky								
112	7023	21 00.5	+68 10	7.0	10 × 8	32	9	Unusual-looking nebula in Cepheus
263	7006	21 01.5	+16 11	10.5	2.8	209	83	Globular cluster in Delphinus
277	7184	22 02.7	−20 49	11.2	6.5 × 1.4	346	142	Very elongated galaxy in Aquarius
247	7217	22 07.9	+31 22	10.1	3.5 × 3.0	122	46	Round galaxy in Pegasus
282	7314	22 35.8	−26 03	10.9	4.2 × 1.7	347	142	Elongated galaxy in Piscis Austrinus
249	7457	23 01.0	+30 09	11.2	4.1 × 2.5	124	46	Elongated galaxy in Pegasus
55	7664	23 26.6	+25 04	12.7	3.0 × 1.7	169	63	Galaxy in Pegasus
57	7723	23 38.8	−12 58	11.2	2.8 × 1.9	304	121	Galaxy in Aquarius
280	7721	23 38.8	−06 31	11.6	3.3 × 1.3	304	121	Elongated galaxy in Aquarius
281	7727	23 39.9	−12 18	10.6	5.6 × 4.0	304	121	Round galaxy in Aquarius
38	7753	23 47.1	+29 20	12.0	3.2 × 1.7	89	45	Slightly elongated galaxy in Pegasus
276	7814	00 03.3	+16 09	10.6	6.0 × 2.5	170	81	Elongated galaxy in Pegasus
342	91	00 21.8	+22 25	13.7	2.2 × 0.8	126	63	Galaxy in And, in galaxy cluster
81	147	00 33.2	+48 30	9.5	15.0 × 9.4	60	30	Comet-like galaxy; satellite of M31
223	150	00 34.3	−27 48	11.3	3.4 × 1.6	306	141	Elongated galaxy in Sculptor
240	157	00 34.8	−08 24	10.4	4.0 × 2.4	261	121	Elongated "Amoeba Galaxy" in Cetus
239	247	00 47.1	−20 46	9.2	19.0 × 5.5	306	158	Very elongated galaxy in Cetus
56	270	00 50.6	−08 39	12.1	2.0 × 1.7	262	140	Galaxy in Cetus
64	404	01 09.4	+35 43	10.3	6.1 × 6.1	91	62	Round galaxy near β Andromedae
278	474	01 20.1	+03 25	11.5	10.0 × 9.2	217	120	Galaxy near NGC 470 in Pisces
34	488	01 21.8	+05 15	10.3	5.5 × 4.0	217	100	Elongated galaxy in Pisces
31	514	01 24.1	+12 55	11.7	3.9 × 2.9	173	100	Easily seen galaxy in Pisces
59	524	01 24.8	+09 32	10.2	3.5 × 3.5	173	100	Round galaxy in Pisces
238	578	01 30.5	−22 40	11.0	3.9 × 2.2	308	158	Elongated galaxy in Cetus
367	613	01 34.3	−29 25	10.0	5.2 × 2.6	352	158	Special galaxy in Sculptor
284	718	01 53.2	+04 12	11.7	2.4 × 2.0	218	119	Round galaxy in Pisces
341	755	01 56.4	−09 04	12.6	2.8 × 1.1	264	139	Elongated galaxy in Cetus
53	752	01 57.8	+37 41	5.7	50	92	61	Very large open cluster in Andromeda
62	898	02 23.3	+41 57	12.9	1.8 × 0.5	91	43	Elongated galaxy in Andromeda
99	949	02 30.8	+37 08	11.8	3.3 × 2.1	93	61	Very cometary galaxy in Triangulum
224	IC 1830	02 39.1	−27 27	11.9	1.9 × 1.5	310	157	Galaxy in Fornax
338	1042	02 40.4	−08 26	11.0	4.2 × 3.3	215	139	Galaxy in Cetus
340	1134	02 53.6	+13 00	12.1	2.3 × 0.8	175	99	Round galaxy in Aries
The Winter Sky								
225	1187	03 02.6	−22 52	10.7	5.2 × 3.0	311	157	Round galaxy in Eridanus
44	1333	03 29.2	+31 25	—	6 × 3	94	60	A weird reflection nebula in Perseus
286	1360	03 33.3	−25 51	9.4	6.5	312	156	Beautiful planetary nebula in Fornax
324	Tom* 5	03 47.8	+59 03	8.4	14.0	28	39	*Open cluster in Camelopardalis*
50	1579	04 30.2	+35 16	—	12 × 8	96	60	Reflection nebula in Perseus
123	1600	04 31.7	−05 05	10.9	2.3 × 1.5	223	117	Round, diffuse galaxy in Eridanus
8	1624	04 40.4	+50 27	13.0	5 × 5	40	42	Cluster with nebulosity in Perseus
114	1637	04 41.5	−02 51	10.8	3.4 × 2.6	224	117	Comet-like round galaxy in Eridanus
273	1746	05 03.6	+23 49	6.1	42	134	77	Beautiful open cluster in Taurus
95	1999	05 36.5	−06 42	10.0	2 × 2	271	136	Diffuse nebula in Orion
125	2023	05 41.6	−02 14	—	10 × 10	226	116	Nebula near ζ Orionis
116	2158	06 07.5	+24 06	8.6	5	136	76	Compact cluster near M35 in Gemini
124	2174	06 09.7	+20 30	—	40 × 30	137	76	Large field of dust in Orion
161	2245	06 32.7	+10 10	—	5 × 4	182	95	Comet-like bright nebula in Mon
162	2252	06 35.0	+05 23	7.7	20	227	95	Open cluster like rope of stars, in Mon
160	2254	06 36.6	+07 40	9.1	4	182	95	Open cluster and star chain in Mon
159	2264	06 41.1	+09 53	3.9	20	183	95	"Christmas Tree Cluster" in Mon
296	2362	07 18.8	−24 57	4.1	8	319	153	Open cluster in Canis Major
158	IC2194/6/7	07 33.7	+31 19	(12.5)	—	(100)	57	Three of the "Castor Cluster" galaxies
195	2419	07 38.1	+38 53	10.3	4.1	100	95	"Intergalactic Wanderer" in Lynx
35	2420	07 38.5	+21 34	8.3	10	139	75	Open cluster in Gemini

* "Tom" refers to the catalog of 5 open clusters discovered by Clyde Tombaugh, better known as the discoverer of Pluto.

DEEP-SKY GEMS (continued)

L#	NGC	RA (2000) Dec h m ° '	m_v	Size (')	UI	UII	Remarks
The Winter Sky (continued)							
384	Levy384	08 15.6 −13 58	—	2	(275)	(134)	Compact asterism in Puppis (special!)
256	IC 2367	08 24.2 −18 46	12.5	2.3 × 0.5	321	153	Galaxy in Puppis
226	2613	08 33.4 −22 58	10.5	7.6 × 1.9	321	153	Edge-on galaxy in Pyxis
96	2681	08 53.5 +51 19	10.3	5.3 × 3.5	44	39	Galaxy in Ursa Major
The Spring Sky							
163	2775	09 10.3 +07 02	10.1	4.6 × 3.7	187	93	Round galaxy in Cancer
51	Arp 321	09 38.9 −04 52	(12.5)	—	(233)	113	"Larry, Moe, & Curly" galaxies in Hya
131	2964	09 42.9 +31 51	11.3	3.2 × 1.8	103	56	Galaxy contains Mrk 404 in Leo
169	2986	09 44.3 −21 17	10.6	4.1 × 3.4	323	152	Round galaxy in Hydra
209	3049	09 54.8 +09 16	12.1	2.3 × 1.5	188	93	Comet-like galaxy in Leo
37	3055	09 55.3 +04 16	12.1	2.0 × 1.1	234	113	Comet-like galaxy in Sextans
133	3070	09 58.0 +10 22	12.3	1.6 × 1.6	189	93	Round galaxy near NGC 3069, in Leo
129	U 5373	10 00.0 +05 20	11.3	5.5 × 3.7	234	113	Sextans B galaxy; Local Group member
337	0957 +561A/B	10 01.3 +55 54	15.5	—	45	25	Famous double quasar in Ursa Major (gravitational lens; distinct in 16" scope)
130	3198	10 19.9 +45 33	10.3	9.2 × 3.5	72	39	Very elongated galaxy in Ursa Major
300	3226	10 23.4 +19 54	11.4	2.5 × 2.2	144	73	Galaxy in Leo
165	3245	10 27.3 +28 30	10.8	2.9 × 2.0	105	73	Elongated galaxy in Leo Minor
219	3309	10 36.6 −27 31	11	4.4 × 3.1	325	151	Hydra I galaxy cluster (five members)
	+ 3311	10 36.7 −27 32	10.9	4.0 × 3.6			
	+ 3312	10 37.0 −27 34	11.8	3.4 × 1.1			
	+ 3314	10 37.4 −27 41	12.8	1.5 × 0.8			(actually two spirals!!)
	+ 3316	10 37.6 −27 36	12.6	1.4 × 1.2			
167	3310	10 38.7 +53 30	10.8	3.5 × 3.2	46	25	Round galaxy in Ursa Major
331	3319	10 39.2 +41 41	11.1	6.9 × 4.0	72	38	Graceful spiral galaxy in Ursa Major
164	3486	11 00.4 +28 58	10.5	6.6 × 4.7	106	73	Round galaxy in Leo Minor
382	U 6253	11 13.5 +22 10	12	15.0 x12.5	146	73	Galaxy in Leo
137	3718	11 32.6 +53 04	10.8	10.0x 4.7	47	24	Elongated galaxy in Ursa Major
136	3738	11 35.8 +54 31	11.7	3.2 × 2.8	47	24	Galaxy near M97 in Ursa Major
41	3810	11 41.0 +11 28	10.8	3.8 × 2.6	192	91	Round galaxy in Leo
201	3865	11 44.9 −09 14	12.0	2.0 × 1.6	282	131	Diffuse galaxy in Crater
181	3887	11 47.1 −16 51	10.6	3.5 × 2.4	292	131	Round galaxy in Crater
217	3923	11 51.0 −28 48	9.6	6.9 × 4.8	368	150	Elongated galaxy in Hydra
138	3953	11 53.8 +52 20	10.1	6.0 × 3.2	47	24	Very elongated galaxy in Ursa Major
193	4129	12 08.9 −09 02	12.5	2.3 × 0.7	283	131	Elongated galaxy in Virgo
135	4256	12 18.7 +65 54	11.9	4.1 × 0.8	25	13	Edge-on galaxy in Draco
134	4319	12 21.7 +75 19	11.9	2.8 × 2.1	9	5	Galaxy near 4291 & 4386 in Draco
42	4340	12 23.0 +16 43	11.2	3.7 × 3.1	193	91	Galaxy near NGC 4350 in Coma
171	4450	12 28.5 +17 05	10.1	5.0 × 3.4	148	72	Elongated galaxy in Coma
145	4473	12 29.8 +13 26	10.2	3.7 × 2.4	193	91	Very elongated galaxy in Coma
140	4485	12 30.5 +41 42	11.9	2.0 × 1.3	37	75	*Elong. galaxy N of NGC 4490 in CVn*
260	4519	12 33.5 +08 39	11.8	3.5 × 2.3	194	90	Galaxy in Virgo
192	4536	12 34.5 +02 11	10.6	6.4 × 2.6	239	110	Very elongated galaxy in Virgo
326	4570	12 36.9 +07 15	10.9	4.3 × 1.3	194	90	Comet-like elongated galaxy in Virgo
188	4591	12 39.3 +06 01	13.0	1.6 × 0.8	194	90	Elongated galaxy in Virgo
178	4596	12 39.9 +10 11	10.4	4.6 × 4.1	194	90	Elongated galaxy in Virgo
213	4623	12 42.2 +07 41	12.2	2.0 × 0.7	194	90	Very elongated galaxy in Virgo
182	4636	12 42.8 +02 41	9.5	7.1 × 5.2	239	110	Galaxy with bright core in Virgo
170	4651	12 43.7 +16 24	10.8	3.5 × 2.3	194	90	Round galaxy in Coma
210	4685	12 47.1 +19 28	12.6	1.5 × 0.9	149	71	"Winking Galaxy" in Coma
172	4689	12 47.8 +13 46	10.9	3.7 × 3.2	194	90	Elongated galaxy in Coma
215	4688	12 47.8 +04 20	11.9	4.0 × 4.0	239	110	Very large galaxy in Virgo
214	4713	12 50.0 +05 19	11.7	2.9 × 1.8	194	90	Elongated galaxy in Virgo
259	4722	12 51.5 −13 19	12.9	1.5 × 0.7	284	130	Round galaxy in Corvus

DEEP-SKY GEMS (continued)

L#	NGC	RA (2000) Dec	m_v	Size	UI	UII	Remarks
		h m ° ′		(′)			

The Spring Sky (continued)

L#	NGC	RA (2000) Dec	m_v	Size	UI	UII	Remarks
191	4772	12 53.5 +02 10	11.0	2.7 × 1.3	239	110	Galaxy in Virgo
211	4779	12 53.8 +09 44	12.4	1.9 × 1.7	194	90	Round galaxy in Virgo
212	4795	12 55.0 +08 04	12.1	1.9 × 1.7	194	90	Round galaxy in Virgo
183	4818	12 56.8 −08 31	11.1	3.4 × 1.4	284	130	Very elongated galaxy in Virgo
257	4866	12 59.5 +14 10	11.2	5.5 × 1.2	194	90	Elongated galaxy in Virgo
190	4956	13 05.1 +35 11	12.4	1.5 × 1.5	109	53	Round galaxy in Canes Venatici
255	5016	13 12.1 +24 06	12.8	1.7 × 1.3	150	71	Round galaxy in Coma
187	5020	13 12.6 +12 36	11.7	3.0 × 2.6	195	90	Elongated galaxy in Virgo
232	5068	13 18.9 −21 02	9.6	7.1 × 6.6	330	149	Very large galaxy in Virgo
189	5127	13 23.8 +31 34	11.9	2.3 × 1.7	109	53	Round galaxy in Canes Venatici
184	5147	13 26.3 +02 06	11.8	1.6 × 1.5	240	110	Round galaxy in Virgo
315	5146	13 26.5 −12 19	12.3	1.8 × 1.2	285	130	Round galaxy in Virgo
185	5248	13 37.5 +08 53	10.3	6.2 × 4.6	196	90	Round galaxy in Boötes
267	5247	13 38.1 −17 53	10.1	5.2 × 3.2	331	130	Beautiful, diffuse spiral in Virgo
261	5350	13 53.4 +40 22	11.3	3.1 × 2.5	76	36	Galaxy in Canes Venatici
186	5371	13 55.7 +40 28	10.6	4.1 × 3.2	76	36	Round galaxy in Canes Venatici
231	5364	13 56.2 +05 01	10.5	6.6 × 5.1	196	89	Elongated galaxy in Virgo
27	5377	13 56.3 +47 14	11.3	4.1 × 2.3	76	36	Galaxy near Big Dipper's handle
202	5427	14 03.4 −06 02	11.4	2.6 × 1.8	286	129	Galaxy, interacting with 5426, in Vir
28	5473	14 04.7 +54 54	11.4	2.2 × 1.7	49	23	Comet-like galaxy near M101 in UMa
29	5474	14 05.0 +53 40	10.8	6.0 × 4.9	49	23	Galaxy near M101 in Ursa Major
82	5634	14 29.6 −05 59	9.4	4.9	287	109	Globular cluster in Virgo
83	5638	14 29.7 +03 14	11.2	2.3 × 2.1	242	109	Comet-like galaxy in Virgo
5	5676	14 32.8 +49 28	11.2	3.7 × 1.6	77	36	Small elliptical galaxy in Boötes
203	5668	14 33.4 +04 27	11.5	3.2 × 2.8	242	109	Comet-like galaxy in Virgo
268	5690	14 37.7 +02 17	11.8	3.3 × 1.0	242	109	Very elongated galaxy in Virgo
196	5694	14 39.6 −26 32	9.2	3.6	332	148	"Tombaugh's Cluster" in Hydra
317	5838	15 05.4 +02 06	10.9	3.5 × 1.6	242	108	Elongated galaxy in Virgo
121	5846	15 06.4 +01 36	10.0	3.0 × 3.0	243	108	Galaxy in Virgo
204	5850	15 07.1 +01 33	10.8	4.6 × 4.1	243	108	Comet-like galaxy in Virgo
266	5962	15 36.5 +16 37	11.3	2.6 × 1.8	199	88	Round galaxy in Serpens

The Summer Sky

L#	NGC	RA (2000) Dec	m_v	Size	UI	UII	Remarks
205	6106	16 18.8 +07 25	12.2	2.3 × 1.2	201	87	Galaxy in Hercules
206	6118	16 21.8 −02 17	11.7	4.6 × 1.9	246	107	Galaxy in Serpens
236	6181	16 32.3 +19 50	11.9	2.3 × 0.9	156	69	Galaxy in Hercules
19	6207	16 43.1 +36 50	11.5	3.0 × 1.1	114	50	Spiral galaxy near M13 in Hercules
6	6229	16 47.0 +47 32	9.4	4.5	80	34	Compact globular cluster in Hercules
271	6287	17 05.2 −22 42	9.3	5	337	146	Globular cluster in Ophiuchus
334	6342	17 21.2 −19 35	9.8	3	338	146	Globular cluster near M9 in Ophiuchus
36	6364	17 24.5 +29 24	12.9	1.5 × 1.2	115	50	Comet-like galaxy in Hercules
207	6384	17 32.4 +07 04	10.4	6.4 × 4.3	203	86	Galaxy in Ophiuchus
208	6426	17 44.9 +03 00	11.1	3.2	248	106	Globular cluster in Ophiuchus
243	6440	17 48.9 −20 22	9.1	5.4	338	146	Globular cluster in Sagittarius
120	*6451*	17 50.7 −30 13	8.2	7.0	164	377	*"Tom Thumb Cluster,"* OC in Scorpius
279	*6522*	18 03.6 −30 02	8.3	16.4	163	377	*"Baade's Window,"* two faint GCs
	+ 6528						*close to the galactic center in Sgr*
270	6535	18 03.8 −00 18	10.5	3.6	249	106	Globular cluster in Serpens
149	6553	18 09.3 −25 54	8.1	8.1	339	145	Faint globular cluster in Sagittarius
147	6638	18 30.9 −25 30	9.1	5	340	145	Globular cluster in Sagittarius
98	6709	18 51.5 +10 21	6.7	13	205	85	Open cluster in Aquila
110	6760	19 11.2 +01 02	9.1	6.6	251	105	Globular cluster in Aquila
262	6814	19 42.7 −10 19	11.2	3.0 × 3.0	297	125	Round galaxy in Aquila
220	6910	20 23.1 +40 47	7.4	7	84	32	Open cluster in Cygnus
156	6934	20 34.2 +07 24	8.7	5.9	208	84	Globular cluster in Delphinus

WIDE-FIELD WONDERS
BY CHRIS BECKETT

In recent years, wide-field eyepieces, short-tube refractors, fast (sub-f/4) reflectors, and large, imaged-stabilized binoculars have increased in popularity. Dark-Sky Preserves with transparent skies have become attractive observing destinations for amateur astronomers. Such equipment and sites lend themselves to viewing a host of wonderful wide-field deep-sky objects that exceed typical telescopic fields of view. Observing large objects such as star clouds, open clusters, diffuse nebulae, giant molecular clouds, and supernova remnants—often with multiple objects in the same field of view—allows the observer to gain an appreciation for the structure of our home galaxy, the Milky Way. Although many objects in the following list are visible under light-polluted skies, they are best observed from the darkest sites with the aid of a good selection of nebula filters. All you need to begin is a pair of handheld binoculars—try experimenting with a filter taped over one objective. Several objects are visible using this technique in a dark location—in fact, some become invisible once you move to large apertures or high power! In the following list, **RA** and **Dec** identify the brightest portions. Most object types are defined on p. 314; in addition, DN = dark nebula, GMC = giant molecular cloud, and Ast = asterism.

Object	Con	Type	RA (2000) Dec h m ° ′		Size ′	Remarks
NGC 206	And	starcloud	00 41	+40 49	5	star cloud within dark lanes of M31
best seen in wide fields with M31 dust lanes to SW; use M32 and mag. 7 star to locate						
Collinder 463	Cas	OC	01 47	+71 52	57	Crescent Cluster
4 dozen stars scattered in a crescent						
Stock 2	Cas	OC	02 16	+59 33	60	Mushroom Cluster
try to see the Double Cluster and Stock 2 in same field; note star chain leading to Stock 2						
IC 1805 & 1848	Cas	EN	02 34	+61 29	4.5°	Heart and Soul Nebulae
large complex of nebulae and star clusters; use filter; IC 1795 is brightest part of IC 1805						
Cosmic ? Mark	Cet	Ast	02 37	+06 56	2.5°×1°	asterism known as the "Question Mark"
looks exactly like a large question mark, best seen in binoculars						
Melotte 20	Per	OC	03 25	+49 54	5°	Perseus OB3 Association
large cluster for small binoculars; look for a miniature "Draco" asterism, including 4 stars denoting the head						
Kemble's Cascade	Cam	Ast	03 59	+63 06	3°	asterism: colorful chain of 20+ stars
terminates at NGC 1502; named by Walter Scott Houston in honour of Father Lucian Kemble (1922–1999)						
Taurus Cloud	Tau	GMC	4h–5h	+16–31	25°×15°	part of the Taurus Molecular Cloud
M45, NGC 1435, IC 353/349/1995; many dark nebulae; "haze" over background star field						
NGC 1499	Per	EN	04 02	+36 39	145×40	California Nebula
use magnification of 15× to 30× to detect wave detail and to train for fainter objects						
Sh2-245	Tau	EN	04 03	+03 06	15×90	Eridanus Arc
use Hβ filter; look for brightest section 3° S of ν Tau						
NGC 1647	Tau	OC	04 47	+19 10	40	large binocular cluster, 5° NE of Hyades
bright; often overlooked; telescope reveals many "double" stars; may be glimpsed without aid in a dark sky						
NGC 1746	Tau	OC	05 05	+23 50	42	NGC 1750 and NGC 1758 superimposed
15× binoculars show a nice cluster embedded in a chain of meandering stars						
IC 2118	Eri	RN	05 08	–07 12	3°×1°	Witch Head Nebula
use low-power, wide-field binoculars or telescope on best nights.						
Collinder 65	Tau	OC	05 27	+16 43	6°	Giant Mushroom
binocular cluster, beautiful, but often not marked on charts; large mushroom-shaped arrow						
Sh2-264	Ori	EN	05 36	+09 56	4.5°×4°	Angelfish Nebula
use Hβ filter in vicinity of λ Ori to see this huge nebula						
Collinder 70	Ori	OC	05 36	–01 06	3°	Orion OB1 Association
3-D view of Ori belt stars over distant field; look for S-shaped star chain W of ε Ori						
Simeis 147	Tau	SNR	05 41	+28 06	3.5°	Taurus supernova remnant
look for "Skates Egg" knot, 10′ E of mag. 8 star SAO 77397						

Object	Con	Type	RA (2000) Dec		Size	Remarks
			h m	° '	'	
Orion GMC	Ori	GMC	05 42	−02 24	1°×2°	Orion Molecular Cloud bright section
use low-power binoculars and filters; look for wave and gap SW of ε Orionis.						
Collinder 89	Gem	OC	06 19	+23 38	60	
large, loose cluster						
Collinder 132	CMa	OC	07 16	−30 42	80	large cluster
beautiful sprinkling of colorful stars visible even during full Moon						
MW 3	UMa	IFN	09 30	+70 11		Volcano Nebula
Mandel Wilson 3 Integrated Flux Nebula; use low power, dark sky, and luck						
Mel 111	Com	OC	12 26	+26 02	3°	Coma Star Cluster
best with very wide-field binoculars						
ρ Oph Complex	Sco		16 26	−23 27	60×25	star cloud with triple star and nebulae
IC 4604 surrounds ρ Oph (mag. 4.6); IC 4603 at HD147889 (mag. 7.9); IC 4605 at 22 Sco (mag. 4.8)						
Sh2-27	Oph	EN	16 33	−10 08	10°×7°	very large emission nebula
use UHC filter and best sky possible; brightest section NW of M107; some uncertainty over classification						
LBN 1103	Sco	EN	16 34	−28 08	4°×3°	SE of Antares
large sprawling nebula, 15× binoculars give best view in dark sky						
Prancing Horse	Oph	DN	17 30	−24 00	10°×7°	large, delicate, dark nebula
B59, B78, B77, B262, B63, B64, B268; observe dark rift in Cyg to Aql as warmup						
IC 4665	Oph	OC	17 47	+05 43	70	Summer Beehive
overlooked large star cluster; best in binoculars; fuzzy patch with the unaided eye						
NGC 6455	Sco		17 52	−35 20	2°	starcloud often mistaken as small OC
starcloud visible without optical aid; SW of M7, which is possibly superimposed						
Taurus Poniatovii	Oph	Ast	17 57	+05 10	10°×5°	asterism: Poniatowski's Bull in NE Oph
main stars 72, 66, 67, 68, and 70 Oph; extends into Ser; Barnard's Star currently resides here; defunct const.						
NGC 6526	Sgr	EN	18 06	−23 41	40	nebula N of M8
large U-shaped nebula and star cloud N of a dark rift, look for NGC 6546 to NE						
IC 4685	Sgr	EN	18 10	−23 49	60	large complex
use nebular filters; look for: NGC 6559, CR 367, IC 1274/5						
IC 1284	Sgr	EN	18 18	−19 40	17×15	eye of M24
use Hβ filter; sweep SW of IC 1284 to detect 120'×30' nebulous region						
Sh2-54	Ser	EN	18 19	−11 58	60×30	nebula & starcloud
large nebular haze N of M16; look for open cluster NGC 6604 & Simeis 3-132						
NGC 6633	Oph	OC	18 28	+06 31	27	Circular Cloud
large cluster sitting over top of apparent star cloud						
IC 4756	Ser	OC	18 40	+05 28	52	Graff's Cluster
visible without optical aid with NGC 6633 as "duelling clusters"						
Basel 1	Sct	OC	18 49	−05 49	55	W of M11
small cluster in the bowl of a dipper-shaped asterism						
B111	Sct	DN	18 51	−04 56	2°	Half-Moon Nebula
large kidney-shaped dark nebula N of M11, superimposed on Scutum star cloud						
B138	Aql	DN	19 15	+0 52	140×20	Barnard's Black Lizard
huge dragon-shaped dark nebula below Altair; use binoculars						
NGC 6774	Sgr	OC	19 17	−16 18	60	Ram's Head
a "true cluster"; contains G2 stars; look for star chains running SE and SW						
Collinder 399	Vul	Ast	19 26	+20 15	89	Coathanger or Brocchi's Cluster
3 dozen orange and blue stars in the pattern of a coathanger; look E for NGC 6802						
Stock 1	Vul	OC	19 36	+25 15	52	halfway between β Cyg and Coathanger
50 stars mag. 7 and brighter; best seen in binoculars						
Sh2-119	Cyg	EN	21 17	+43 46	2.5°×2°	NE of North America Nebula complex
use large binoculars or RFT with nebular filter; sweep past 68 Cyg; visible if Pelican can be seen						
IC 1396	Cep	EN	21 40	+57 34	170×140	large emission nebula
locate μ Cep, then add nebular filter; attempt van den Bergh 142, Elephant Trunk Nebula						
Stock 12	Cas	OC	23 37	+52 36	40	
very large, loose, binocular cluster; look for star chain to SE						
Great Rift		DNs/GMCs			120°	overlapping dark nebulae and GMCs
huge naked-eye rift splitting the Milky Way from Cyg, through Aql, Oph, and Sco, to Cen						

SOUTHERN HEMISPHERE SPLENDOURS
BY ALAN WHITMAN

Any serious deep-sky observer yearns to experience the far-southern sky, the home of the finest emission nebula (the Carina Nebula), the most obvious dark nebula (the Coalsack), arguably the best open cluster (NGC 3532), the most impressive globular cluster (47 Tucanae), the biggest and brightest globular cluster (Omega Centauri, although it is likely the core of a small galaxy absorbed by the Milky Way), the galaxy that offers amateur telescopes hundreds of targets within it (the Large Magellanic Cloud), and the closest naked-eye star in the night sky (α Centauri), just to name a few. Here is a checklist of "must-see" splendours, rated with one to three exclamation marks, plus 16 other significant objects. The author has observed all of these objects under fine, dark skies.

Dec −35° was chosen as the northern cutoff for this list. However, three slightly more northerly objects that greatly benefit from being viewed higher in the sky were included, notably M83, because it is one of the finest face-on spiral galaxies in the southern sky, but its three spiral arms are not well seen from Canada. Countries like Australia, Chile, and Namibia offer the best views of these magnificent objects. However, most objects on the list can be viewed from the southern Caribbean; many are visible from Hawaii or from the Florida Keys; some, including Omega Centauri, Centaurus A, and the many glorious clusters in the tail of Scorpius, can be appreciated from the American Southwest. February through April are the preferred months for a southern observing run, since there are no far-southern splendours (those with exclamation marks) located between 20h and 0h of right ascension.

Data for open and globular clusters are from Archinal and Hynes's 2003 reference book *Star Clusters*, with the two noted exceptions. Data for other objects are mostly from Malin and Frew's highly recommended 1995 guidebook *Hartung's Astronomical Objects for Southern Telescopes*, 2nd ed. The dimensions of galaxies and nebulae and a few other numbers are mostly from various lists in the *Observer's Handbook* or from Sinnott's 1988 work, *NGC 2000.0*. Various sources, including private communications, have provided some difficult-to-obtain data.

Notation used below is mostly as defined on p. 314; in addition, * = star or stars, CC = concentration class of a globular cluster (see p. 312), and DN = dark nebula. Numbers without a prefix in the **NGC** column are NGC numbers.

#	NGC	Con	Type	RA (2000) h m	Dec ° ′	m_V	Size″ ′	Remarks
1	55	Scl	G-SBm	0 14.9	−39 12	7.9	32×6	! in 100-mm scope: diffuse splinter
2	104	Tuc	GC	0 24.1	−72 5	4	50	!!! 47 Tuc; yellow core in 370-mm scope
3	β	Tuc	Dbl*	0 31.5	−62 58	4.3, 4.5	27″	! both blue-white
4	SMC	Tuc	G-SBm	0 52.7	−72 50	2.3	5°×3°	!!! many NGCs included
5	362	Tuc	GC	1 3.2	−70 51	6.8	14	! Milky Way GC beside SMC; CC III
6	p	Eri	Dbl*	1 39.8	−56 12	5.8, 5.8	12″	! both yellow-orange dwarfs
7	1097	For	G-SBb	2 46.3	−30 17	9.3	13×8	! in 300-mm scope: bar and tough arms
8	θ	Eri	Dbl*	2 58.3	−40 18	3.2, 4.1	8.4″	! both white
9	1313	Ret	G-SBd	3 18.3	−66 30	8.9	9×7	in 370-mm scope: bar, one spiral arm
10		For	Gal Cl.	3 22.7	−37 12	—		position is for bright 1316, Fornax A
11	1365	For	G-SBc	3 33.6	−36 8	9.5	14×10	!! in 300-mm scope: bar with 2 spiral arms
12	f	Eri	Dbl*	3 48.6	−37 37	4.9, 5.4	8.1″	! yellowish stars
13	1566	Dor	G-Sc	4 20	−54 56	9.4	13×9	!! in 250-mm scope: two classic spiral arms
14	ι	Pic	Dbl*	4 50.9	−53 28	5.6, 6.5	12.5″	! very nice yellow pair
15	1851	Col	GC	5 14.1	−40 3	7.1	12	! brightest center of any GC; CC II
16	LMC	Dor	G-SBm	5 23.6	−69 45	0.1	11°×9°	!!! many nights' work for large apertures
17	2070	Dor	EN/OC	5 38.7	−69 6	5.4	20	!!! Tarantula Nebula; "spider legs" easy
18	γ	Vol	Dbl*	7 8.7	−70 30	3.9, 5.4	14.4″	! gold and light-green pair
19	2451	Pup	OC	7 45.4	−37 57	2.8	50	! two OCs in radial line, 400 ly apart

SOUTHERN HEMISPHERE SPLENDOURS (continued)

#	NGC	Con	Type	RA (2000) h m	Dec ° '	m_v	Size '	Remarks
20	2477	Pup	OC	7 52.2	−38 32	5.8	20	!! 300*; arcs of 12th-mag. −13th-mag. stars
21	2516	Car	OC	7 58	−60 45	3.8	22	!! 100*; resembles the Beehive but richer
22	γ	Vel	Dbl*	8 9.5	−47 20	1.8, 4.1	41″	! 4*; 1.8-mag. star is brightest Wolf–Rayet
23	2547	Vel	OC	8 10.2	−49 14	4.7	25	! The Heart Cluster (description by Dyer)
24	IC 2391	Vel	OC	8 40.3	−52 55	2.6	60	! o Vel Cluster; bright stars; fine in binocs
25	2736	Vel	SNR	9 0.4	−45 54	—	20x0.5	! Pencil Nebula, part of Vela SNR; use filter
26	2808	Car	GC	9 12	−64 52	6.2	14	! brightest CC I; like a pile of sand
27	3114	Car	OC	10 2.7	−60 6	4.2	35	! 120*; four arcs of stars in binocs
28	3132	Vel	PN	10 7.7	−40 26	9.2	0.8	Eight-Burst Nebula; colorless
29	3199	Car	EN	10 17.1	−57 55	9	22	! crescent formed by Wolf–Rayet star
30	3201	Vel	GC	10 17.6	−46 25	6.9	20	star chains right through core; CC X
31	3293	Car	OC	10 35.8	−58 14	4.7	5	!! Gem Cluster; EN/RN/DN involved
32	3324	Car	EN	10 37.3	−58 38	6.7	15	two-lobed nebula
33	IC 2602	Car	OC	10 43	−64 24	1.6	100	! θ Car Cl, a.k.a. the Southern Pleiades
34	3372	Car	EN	10 45.1	−59 52	2.5	80	!!! Carina Nebula[A]
35	3532	Car	OC	11 5.5	−58 44	3	50	!!! Football Cluster; finest OC?; 55′ across
36	3699	Cen	PN	11 28	−59 57	11.3	1.1	dark rift visible in 200-mm scope
37	3766	Cen	OC	11 36.3	−61 37	5.3	15	! triangular; 60*; λ Cen Nebula nearby
38	3918	Cen	PN	11 50.3	−57 11	8.1	0.2	! the Blue Planetary; round
39	—	Mus	DN	12 25	−72	—	3°×12′	! the Dark Doodad; near 4372 and γ Mus
40	4372	Mus	GC	12 25.8	−72 39	7.2	19	! CC XII (size is from NGC 2000.0)
41	α	Cru	Dbl*	12 27.6	−63 12	1.3, 1.6	4.2″	! blue-white pair; 3rd star 4.9 mag. at 90″
42	DY	Cru	Red*	12 47.4	−59 42	9v	—	! Ruby Crucis; 3′ W of β Cru; B−V is 5.8
43	—	Cru	DN	12 51	−63	—	6°	!!! Coalsack; forms head of the Emu DN
44	4755	Cru	OC	12 53.6	−60 21	4.2	10	! Jewel Box; sparse in small apertures
45	4833	Mus	GC	12 59.6	−70 52	6.9	14	! CC VIII (magnitude is from W.E. Harris)
46	4945	Cen	G-SBcd	13 5.5	−49 28	8.4	20×4	! in 500-mm scope: dark lane on SW edge
47	5128	Cen	G-S0pec	13 25.5	−43 1	6.8	26×20	!! Cen A; merging spiral and elliptical[B]
48	5139	Cen	GC	13 26.8	−47 29	3.9	55	!!! Omega Cen; huge rich oval; CC VIII
49	5189	Mus	PN	13 33.5	−65 59	9.5	2.6	! the Spiral Planetary; use OIII filter
50	M83	Hya	G-SABc	13 37	−29 52	7.6	16×13	!! in 200-mm: bar, 1 arm; 370-mm: 3 arms
51	5286	Cen	GC	13 46.4	−51 22	7.4	11	! CC V; bluish PN 5307 nearby
52	5460	Cen	OC	14 7.6	−48 18	5.6	35	25 straggling*; trapezoidal asterism in S
53	α	Cen	Dbl*	14 40.9	−60 55	0.0, 1.3	4.5″	!! rapidly changing yellow pair: 22″−1.7″
54	5822	Lup	OC	15 4	−54 20	6.5	35	! triangular; stars are in discrete clumps
55	5927	Lup	GC	15 28	−50 40	8	6	CC VIII; pair with Nor GC 5946
56	B228	Lup	DN	15 45	−34	—	4°×20′	! an unknown wonder; opacity 6
57	5986	Lup	GC	15 46.1	−37 47	7.6	10	200-mm resolves large core; CC VII
58	6025	TrA	OC	16 3.6	−60 25	5.1	15	! triangular, in three clumps
59	6067	Nor	OC	16 13.2	−54 13	5.6	15	! 100*; many pairs
60	6087	Nor	OC	16 18.9	−57 54	5.4	15	! 40*; embedded in Norma Star Cloud
61	6124	Sco	OC	16 25.3	−40 40	5.8	40	100*; many trios around circumference
62	6231	Sco	OC	16 54.2	−41 50	2.6	14	!! ζ, 6231, and Tr 24 form the False Comet
63	6242	Sco	OC	16 55.5	−39 28	6.4	9	23*; good for small scopes
64	6259	Sco	OC	17 0.7	−44 39	8	15	like a fainter M11; 120*
65	6281	Sco	OC	17 4.8	−37 53	5.4	8	25*; shines in modest scopes
66	6302	Sco	PN	17 13.7	−37 6	9.6	1.5×0.5	Bug Nebula; bright core; knots at tips
67	IC 4651	Ara	OC	17 24.7	−49 55	6.9	10	! loops and chains of 70 equal-mag. stars
68	6388	Sco	GC	17 36.3	−44 44	6.8	10	450-mm scope resolves faint stars; CC III
69	6397	Ara	GC	17 40.7	−53 40	5.3	31	!! easily resolved 10th-mag. stars; CC IX
70	6541	CrA	GC	18 8	−43 42	6.3	15	! huge outer halo; CC III
71	6723	Sgr	GC	18 59.6	−36 38	6.8	13	! CC VII; part of fine complex below
72	6726–7	CrA	RN	19 1.7	−36 54	—	9×7	! 7th-mag. stars involved[C]
73	6752	Pav	GC	19 10.9	−59 59	5.3	29	!! easily resolved 11th-mag. stars; CC VI[D]
74	7582	Gru	G-SBb	23 18.4	−42 22	10.2	4×1	brightest member of Grus Quartet

[A] Chevron-shaped dark lane, many other DN involved, including Keyhole Nebula; tiny orange mag. 5 (variable) Homunculus Nebula at center; four OC involved

[B] Prominent broad dark lane; 370-mm scope reveals thin bright streak within the dark lane

[C] Part of !! complex with GC 6723, DN SL 40+41 (55′ long, opacity 6), variable RN 6729 (involved with R CrA), headlight Dbl* Brs 14 (mags. 6.6, 6.8 at 13″), and Dbl* γ CrA (both yellow-white, mags. 4.9, 5.0 at 1.3″ and widening)

[D] Curving star chains converge to a tiny central peak; very tight group of four 12th-mag. galaxies 1° SE

GALAXIES: BRIGHTEST AND NEAREST
BY BARRY F. MADORE AND IAN STEER

External galaxies are generally of such low surface brightness that they often prove disappointing objects for the amateur observer. However, it must be remembered that many of these galaxies were discovered with very small telescopes and that the enjoyment of their discovery can be recaptured. In addition, the central concentration of light varies from galaxy to galaxy, making a visual classification of the types possible at the telescope. Indeed, the *Hubble galaxy classification* (**Type**) given in Table 1 (facing page) is in part based on the fraction of light coming from the central bulge of the galaxy as compared to the contribution from a disk component. Disk galaxies with dominant bulges are classified as **Sa**; as the nuclear contribution declines, types of **Sb**, **Sc**, and **Sd** are assigned until the nucleus is absent at type **Sm**. Often the disks of these galaxies show spiral symmetry, the coherence and strength of which is denoted by Roman numerals **I** through **V**, smaller numbers indicating well-formed global spiral patterns. Those spirals with central bars are designated **SB**, while those with only a hint of a disk embedded in the bulge are called **S0**. A separate class of galaxies that possess no disk component are called ellipticals and can only be further classified numerically by their apparent flattening, with **E0** being apparently round and **E7** being the most flattened.

Environment appears to play an important role in determining the types of galaxies we see at the present epoch. Rich clusters of galaxies, such as the system in Coma, are dominated by ellipticals and gas-free S0 galaxies. The less-dense clusters and groups tend to be dominated by the spiral, disk galaxies. Remarkably, pairs of galaxies are much more frequently of the same Hubble type than random selection would predict. Encounters between disk galaxies may in some cases result in the instabilities necessary to form the spiral structure we often see. M51 (the Whirlpool) and its companion, NGC 5195, are an often-cited example of this type of interaction. In the past, when the Universe was much more densely packed, interactions and collisions may have been sufficiently frequent that entire galaxies merged to form a single large new system; it has been suggested that some elliptical galaxies formed in this way.

Table 1 on the facing page lists the 40 brightest galaxies taken from the *Revised Shapley–Ames Catalog*. As well as their designations, positions, and types, the table lists the total blue magnitudes, major and minor axis lengths (to the nearest minute of arc), the latest estimate of their distances in 10^6 ly, and their radial velocities corrected for the motion of our Sun about the galactic center. Although the Universe as a whole is in expansion, there are parts that are still bound together (or at the very least,

The Hubble "tuning fork" diagram of galaxy classification, using actual galaxy images, with the Messier, NGC (N), or UGC (U) number indicated below the type. (Diagram created by Ian Steer.)

held back in their expansion) by gravity. These groups and clusters are, in essence, representative of the largest material structures in the Universe. Recently, large-scale flows of material have been reported, far in excess of the velocities expected due to the perturbing presence of other galaxies and clusters of galaxies. Either there are exceedingly large concentrations of matter yet to be discovered just beyond our limited view of the world, or the Universe has had a much more interesting history than our present theories indicate. The brightest and nearest galaxies in Table 1 may be moving not only as a result of the universal expansion, but also through very complex interactions with distant parts as yet only postulated but not seen. A selection of nearest galaxies, listed on the following page in Table 2, form what is known as the Local Group of Galaxies. **(Data in Tables 1 and 2 have been updated for 2018.)**

TABLE 1—THE 40 OPTICALLY BRIGHTEST SHAPLEY-AMES GALAXIES

NGC	Other	RA (2000) Dec h m	° ′	Type	Magnitude B_T	Size ′	Distance 10^6 ly	Rad. Vel. km/s
55		0 14.9	−39 11.8	SBm	8.84	32 × 6	6.29	129
205	M110	0 40.4	+41 41.1	E5 pec	8.92	22 × 11	2.64	−241
221	M32	0 42.7	+40 51.9	E2	9.03	9 × 7	2.51	−200
224	M31	0 42.7	+41 16.2	Sb I–II	4.36	190 × 60	2.54	−300
247		0 47.1	−20 45.6	SBd III–IV	9.86	21 × 7	11.7	156
253		0 47.6	−25 17.3	SBc	7.09	28 × 7	10.3	243
292	SMC	0 52.7	−72 49.7	SBm IV–V pec	2.70	320 × 185	0.196	158
300		0 54.9	−37 41.1	Sd III	8.95	22 × 16	6.39	144
598	M33	1 33.8	+30 39.6	Scd II–III	6.27	71 × 42	2.87	−179
628	M74	1 36.7	+15 47.0	Sc I	9.95	11 × 10	29.1	657
1068	M77	2 42.7	−00 00.8	Sb II	9.61	7 × 6	41.2	1137
1291		3 17.3	−41 06.5	SB0/a	9.39	10 × 8	28.0	839
1313		3 18.3	−66 29.9	SBd III–IV	9.20	9 × 7	12.9	470
1316	Fornax A	3 22.7	−37 12.5	S0 pec	9.40	12 × 9	65.1	1760
	LMC	5 23.6	−69 45.4	SBm III	0.90	645 × 550	0.163	278
2403		7 36.9	+65 36.2	SBcd III	8.11	22 × 12	11.3	131
2903		9 32.2	+21 30.1	SBbc I–III	9.68	13 × 6	28.4	556
3031	M81	9 55.6	+69 03.9	Sab I–II	7.89	27 × 14	12.1	−34
3034	M82	9 55.9	+69 40.8	I0	9.30	11 × 4	13.1	203
3521		11 05.8	−00 02.2	SBbc II–III	9.83	11 × 5	38.6	801
3627	M66	11 20.3	+12 59.5	SBb II	9.65	9 × 4	31.9	727
4258	M106	12 19.0	+47 18.2	SBbc II	8.41	19 × 7	24.3	448
4449		12 28.2	+44 05.6	IBm IV	9.99	6 × 4	12.2	207
4472	M49	12 29.8	+08 00.0	E2	9.37	10 × 8	51.5	997
4486	M87	12 30.8	+12 23.5	E0	9.59	8 × 7	54.2	1307
4594	M104	12 40.0	−11 37.4	Sa	8.98	9 × 4	36.3	1024
4631		12 42.1	+32 32.5	SBd	9.75	16 × 3	19.0	606
4649	M60	12 43.7	+11 33.2	E2	9.81	7 × 6	53.9	1117
4736	M94	12 50.9	+41 07.2	Sab	8.99	11 × 9	16.4	308
4826	M64	12 56.7	+21 41.0	Sab II	9.36	10 × 5	16.8	408
4945		13 05.5	−49 28.1	SBcd	9.30	20 × 4	13.3	563
5055	M63	13 15.8	+42 01.8	Sbc II–III	9.31	13 × 7	26.1	484
5128	Cen A	13 25.5	−43 01.2	S0 pec	7.84	26 × 20	12.0	547
5194	M51	13 29.9	+47 11.7	Sbc I–II pec	8.96	11 × 7	27.9	463
5236	M83	13 37.0	−29 52.0	SBc II	8.20	13 × 12	22.2	513
5457	M101	14 03.2	+54 20.9	SBcd I	8.31	29 × 27	22.2	241
6744		19 09.8	−63 51.5	SBbc II	9.14	20 × 13	27.5	841
6822		19 45.0	−14 48.2	IBm IV–V	9.31	16 × 14	1.63	−57
6946		20 34.9	+60 09.2	SBcd II	8.23	12 × 10	18.5	40
7793		23 57.8	−32 35.5	Sd IV	9.98	9 × 6	12.8	227

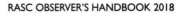

TABLE 2—THE NEAREST GALAXIES—OUR LOCAL GROUP

Name	RA (2000.0) h m	Dec ° '	Type	Magnitude B_T	Distance 10^6 ly
Milky Way Galaxy			Sb/c		
IC 10	0 20.3	+59 18	IBm	11.80	2.90
NGC 147	0 33.2	+48 31	dE5 pec	10.47	2.51
And III	0 35.6	+36 30	dE	15.00	2.41
NGC 185	0 39	+48 20	dE3 pec	10.10	2.41
M110 = NGC 205	0 40.4	+41 41	E5 pec	8.92	2.64
M32 = NGC 221	0 42.7	+40 52	E2	9.03	2.51
M31 = NGC 224	0 42.7	+41 16	Sb I–II	4.36	2.54
And I	0 45.7	+38 02	dE3 pec	13.60	2.51
SMC	0 52.7	–72 50	SBm IV–V pec	2.70	0.196
Sculptor	1 0.2	–33 43	dE	8.60	0.261
LGS 3	1 3.9	+21 53	Irr	14.20	3.91
IC 1613	1 4.8	+02 07	IBm V	9.88	2.41
And II	1 16.5	+33 25	dE	13.50	2.09
M33 = NGC 598	1 33.8	+30 40	Scd II–III	6.27	2.87
Fornax	2 40	–34 27	dE4	9.28	0.456
LMC	5 23.6	–69 45	SBm III	0.90	0.163
Carina	6 41.6	–50 58	dE3	11.30	0.326
Antlia	10 4.1	–27 20	IBm	16.19	4.30
Leo I	10 8.5	+12 18	dE3	11.18	0.815
Sextans	10 13.1	–01 37	dE	10.40	0.261
Leo II	11 13.5	+22 09	dE0	12.60	0.717
Ursa Minor	15 9.1	+67 13	E	11.90	0.228
Draco	17 20.2	+57 55	E pec	10.90	0.261
Sagittarius	18 55.3	–30 33	IBm:	4.50	0.098
NGC 6822	19 45	–14 48	IBm IV–V	9.31	1.63

Editor's Notes:

(1) Aside from those famous companions of the Milky Way Galaxy, the Large Magellanic Cloud (LMC) and the Small Magellanic Cloud (SMC), there is only one galaxy beyond our own that is easily visible to unaided human eyes: M31, the Andromeda Galaxy (2.58 Mly distant). M33, the Triangulum Galaxy, can also be seen, but this is a difficult observation. To locate M31, see the NOVEMBER ALL-SKY MAP on p. 345, where the tiny cluster of six dots above the first "A" of "ANDROMEDA" indicates its location. With modest optical aid (e.g. binoculars) a dozen or more of the galaxies listed in Table 1 can be seen by experienced observers under dark skies. With a 250-mm telescope, the quasar 3C 273, at 1000 times the distance of M31, can elicit a noticeable signal in the visual cortex (see p. 323).

(2) An interesting article by G. Lake entitled "Cosmology of the Local Group" appears in *Sky & Telescope*, December 1992, p. 613.

(3) The National Aeronautics and Space Administration/Infrared Processing and Analysis Center (NASA/IPAC) Extragalactic Database (NED) is a comprehensive compilation of extragalactic data for 215 million distinct extragalactic objects. The database includes most major catalogs and offers references to and abstracts of articles of extragalactic interest that have appeared in most major journals. Also online are 1.9 billion photometric measurements, 5 million redshifts, over 2.6 million images, and more than 400 thousand detailed classifications. It is possible to search the main NED database for objects selected by catalog prefix, position, type, or redshift. The database is available at ned.ipac.caltech.edu. See ned.ipac.caltech.edu/level5 for a knowledgebase of review articles and basic information.

GALAXIES WITH PROPER NAMES
BY BARRY F. MADORE

Below are the catalog designations and positions of galaxies known to have proper names, which usually honour the discoverer (e.g. McLeish's Object), identify the constellation in which the galaxy is found (e.g. Andromeda Galaxy), or describe the galaxy in some easily remembered way (e.g. Whirlpool Galaxy).

Galaxy Name	Other Names / Remarks	RA (2000) h m	Dec ° '
Ambartsumian's Knot	NGC 3561, UGC 06224, ARP 105	11 11.2	+28 42
Andromeda Galaxy	M31, NGC 224, UGC 00454	0 42.7	+41 16
Andromeda I		0 45.7	+38 01
Andromeda II		1 16.5	+33 26
Andromeda III		0 35.3	+36 31
Antennae Galaxy	Ring Tail, NGC 4038/39, ARP 244	12 01.9	−18 52
Antlia Dwarf	AM 1001-270	10 04.0	−27 20
Aquarius Dwarf	DDO 210	20 46.9	−12 51
Arp's Galaxy		11 19.6	+51 30
Atoms For Peace	NGC 7252, ARP 226	22 20.8	−24 41
Baade's Galaxies A & B	MCG+07-02-018/19	0 49.9	+42 35
Barbon's Galaxy	Markarian 328, ZWG 497.042	23 37.7	+30 08
Barnard's Galaxy	NGC 6822, IC 4895, DDO 209	19 44.9	−14 48
Bear's Paw (Claw)	NGC 2537, UGC 04274, ARP 6	8 13.2	+46 00
BL Lacertae		22 02.7	+42 17
Black Eye Galaxy	M64, NGC 4826, UGC 08062	12 56.7	+21 41
Bode's Galaxies	M81/82, NGC 3031/4, UGC 05318/22	9 55.7	+69 23
Burbidge Chain	MCG-04-03-010 to 13	0 47.5	−20 26
BW Tauri	UGC 03087, MCG+01-12-009	4 33.2	+05 21
Carafe Galaxy	Cannon's Carafe, near NGC 1595/98	4 28.0	−47 54
Carina Dwarf		6 41.6	−50 58
Cartwheel Galaxy	Zwicky's Cartwheel, MCG-06-02-022a	0 37.4	−33 44
Centaurus A	NGC 5128, ARP 153	13 25.5	−43 01
Circinus Galaxy		14 13.2	−65 20
Coddington's Nebula	IC 2574, UGC 05666, DDO 81	10 28.4	+68 25
Copeland Septet	MCG+04-28-004/05/07 to 11, UGC 06597, UGC 06602, ARP 320, NGC 3745/46/48/50/51/53/54†	11 37.8	+21 59
Cygnus A	MCG+07-41-003	19 59.4	+40 43
Draco Dwarf	UGC 10822, DDO 208	17 20.2	+57 55
Exclamation Mark Galaxy		0 39.3	−43 06
The Eyes	NGC 4435/8, UGC 07574/5, ARP 120a/b	12 27.7	+13 03
Fath 703	NGC 5892	15 13.7	−15 29
Fornax A	NGC 1316, ARP 154	3 22.7	−37 12
Fornax Dwarf	MCG-06-07-001	2 39.9	−34 32
Fourcade–Figueroa	MCG-07-28-004	13 34.8	−45 33
The Garland	S of NGC 3077 = UGC 05398	10 04.2	+68 40
Grus Quartet	NGC 7552/82/90/99	23 17.8	−42 26
GR 8 (Gibson Reaves)	UGC 08091, DDO 155	12 58.7	+14 13
Hardcastle's Galaxy	MCG-05-31-039	13 13.0	−32 41
Helix Galaxy	NGC 2685, UGC 04666, ARP 336	8 55.6	+58 44
Hercules A	MCG+01-43-006	16 51.2	+04 59
Hoag's Object		15 17.2	+21 35

† Position errors caused these to be historically marked as nonexistent in the NGC and RNGC.

GALAXIES WITH PROPER NAMES (continued)

Galaxy Name	Other Names / Remarks	RA (2000) h m	Dec ° '
Holmberg I	UGC 05139, DDO 63	9 40.5	+71 11
Holmberg II	UGC 04305, DDO 50, ARP 268	8 19.3	+70 43
Holmberg III	UGC 04841	9 14.6	+74 14
Holmberg IV	UGC 08837, DDO 185	13 54.7	+53 54
Holmberg V	UGC 08658	13 40.6	+54 20
Holmberg VI	NGC 1325a	3 24.9	−21 20
Holmberg VII	UGC 07739, DDO 137	12 34.7	+06 17
Holmberg VIII	UGC 08303, DDO 166	13 13.3	+36 12
Holmberg IX	UGC 05336, DDO 66	9 57.6	+69 03
Horologium Dwarf	Schuster's Spiral	3 59.2	−45 52
Hydra A	MCG-02-24-007	9 18.1	−12 06
Integral Sign Galaxy	UGC 03697, MCG+12-07-028	7 11.4	+71 50
Keenan's System	NGC 5216/16a/18, UGC 08528/9, ARP 104	13 33.2	+62 43
Kowal's Object		19 29.9	−17 41
Large Magellanic Cloud	Nubecula Major	5 23.6	−69 45
Leo I	Regulus Dwarf, UGC 05470, DDO 74, Harrington–Wilson #1	10 08.5	+12 18
Leo II	Leo B, UGC 06253, DDO 93, Harrington–Wilson #2	11 13.4	+22 10
Leo III	Leo A, UGC 05364, DDO 69	9 59.3	+30 45
Lindsay–Shapley Ring	Graham A	6 42.8	−74 15
Lost Galaxy	NGC 4535, UGC 07727	12 34.3	+08 11
McLeish's Object		20 09.7	−66 13
Maffei I	UGCA 34	2 36.3	+59 39
Maffei II	UGCA 39	2 42.0	+59 37
Malin 1		12 37.0	+14 20
Mayall's Object	MCG+07-23-019, ARP 148	11 03.9	+40 50
Mice	NGC 4676a/b, UGC 07938/9, IC 819/20, ARP 242	12 46.1	+30 44
Miniature Spiral	NGC 3928, UGC 06834	11 51.8	+48 41
Minkowski's Object	ARP 133 (NE of NGC 541)	1 25.8	−01 21
Pancake	NGC 2685, UGC 04666, ARP 336	8 55.6	+58 44
Papillon	IC 708, UGC 06549	11 33.9	+49 03
Pegasus Dwarf	UGC 12613, DDO 216	23 28.5	+14 44
Perseus A	NGC 1275/6, UGC 02669	3 19.8	+41 31
Phoenix Dwarf Irregular		1 51.1	−44 26
Pinwheel Galaxy	see also Triangulum Galaxy	1 33.9	+30 39
Pinwheel Galaxy	M99, NGC 4254, UGC 07345	12 18.8	+14 25
Pinwheel Galaxy	M101, NGC 5457, UGC 08981, ARP 26	14 03.3	+54 22
Pisces Cloud	NGC 379/80/82-85, UGC 00682/3/6-9, ARP 331	1 07.5	+32 25
Pisces Dwarf	LGS 3	0 03.8	+21 54
Polarissima Australis	NGC 2573	1 42.0‡	−89 20
Polarissima Borealis	NGC 3172, ZWG 370.002	11 50.3‡	+89 07
Reinmuth 80	NGC 4517a, UGC 07685	12 32.5	+00 23
Reticulum Dwarf	Sersic 040.03	4 36.2	−58 50
Sagittarius Dwarf		19 30.0	−17 41
Sculptor Dwarf	MCG-06-03-015	1 00.2	−33 42
Sculptor Dwarf Irregular		0 08.1	−34 34

‡ The high declination of these objects makes the RA particularly uncertain.

GALAXIES WITH PROPER NAMES (continued)

Galaxy Name	Other Names / Remarks	RA (2000) h m	Dec ° '
Seashell Galaxy	Companion to NGC 5291	13 47.4	−30 23
Sextans A	UGCA 205, MCG-01-26-030, DDO 75	10 11.0	−04 41
Sextans B	UGC 05373, DDO 70	10 00.0	+05 19
Sextans C	UGC 05439	10 05.6	+00 04
Sextans Dwarf		10 13.1	−01 37
Seyfert's Sextet	Serpens Sextet, NGC 6027/6027a-e, UGC 10116	15 59.2	+20 46
Shapley–Ames 1		1 05.1	−06 13
Shapley–Ames 2	NGC 4507	12 35.1	−39 55
Shapley–Ames 3	MCG-02-33-015	12 49.4	−10 07
Shapley–Ames 4	UGC 08041	12 55.2	+00 07
Shapley–Ames 5	MCG-07-42-001	20 24.0	−44 00
Shapley–Ames 6		21 23.2	+45 46
Siamese Twins	NGC 4567/4568	12 36.5	+11 15
Silver Coin	Sculptor Galaxy, NGC 253, UGCA 13	0 47.6	−25 18
Small Magellanic Cloud	Nubecula Minor	0 52.7	−72 50
Sombrero Galaxy	M104, NGC 4594	12 39.9	−11 37
Spider	UGC 05829, DDO 84	10 42.6	+34 27
Spindle Galaxy	NGC 3115	10 05.2	−07 42
Stephan's Quintet	NGC 7317-20, UGC 12099-102, ARP 319	22 36.0	+33 58
Sunflower Galaxy	M63, NGC 5055, UGC 08334	13 15.8	+42 02
Triangulum Galaxy	Pinwheel, M33, NGC 598, UGC 01117	1 33.9	+30 39
Ursa Minor Dwarf	UGC 09749, DDO 199	15 08.8	+67 12
Virgo A	M87, NGC 4486, UGC 07654, ARP 152	12 30.8	+12 23
Whirlpool Galaxy	Rosse's Galaxy, Question Mark Galaxy, M51, NGC 5194/5, UGC 08493/4, ARP 85	13 29.9	+47 12
Wild's Triplet	MCG-01-30-032 to 34, ARP 248	11 46.8	−03 49
Wolf–Lundmark–Melotte	MCG-03-01-015, DDO 221	0 02.0	−15 28
Zwicky #2	UGC 06955, DDO 105	11 58.4	+38 03
Zwicky's Triplet	UGC 10586, ARP 103	16 49.5	+45 30

Catalogs:

AM *Catalogue of Southern Peculiar Galaxies and Associations*, by H.C. Arp and B.F. Madore, Cambridge University Press (1987).

ARP *Atlas of Peculiar Galaxies*, H. Arp, *Ap. J. Suppl. 14*, 1 (1966).

DDO *David Dunlap Observatory Publ.*, S. van den Bergh, II, No. 5, 147 (1959).

IC *Index Catalogue*, J.L.E. Dreyer, *Mem. R.A.S.* (1895–1910).

MCG *Morphological Catalogue of Galaxies*, B.A. Vorontsov–Velyaminov et al., Moscow State University, Moscow (1961–1974).

NGC *New General Catalogue of Nebulae and Clusters of Stars*, J.L.E. Dreyer, *Mem. R.A.S.* (1888).

RNGC *The Revised New General Catalogue of Nonstellar Astronomical Objects*, J.W. Sulentic and W.G. Tifft, University of Arizona Press (1973).

UGC *Uppsala General Catalogue of Galaxies*, P. Nilson, *Nova Acta Regiae Societatis Scientiarum Upsaliensis*, Ser. V: A, Vol. 1, Uppsala, Sweden (1973).

UGCA *Catalogue of Selected Non-UGC Galaxies*, P. Nilson, Uppsala Astronomical Observatory (1974).

ZWG *Catalogue of Galaxies and Clusters of Galaxies*, F. Zwicky et al., Vol. 1–6, California Institute of Technology (1961–1968).

RADIO ASTRONOMY AND RADIO SOURCES
BY KEN TAPPING & HUGH PETT

Cosmic radio sources fall into two broad classes: "Continuum Sources," which emit over much of the radio spectrum and extend well beyond the frequency band used by any particular radio telescope, and "Spectral Sources," which emit radio spectral lines, such as the 1420.406 MHz (21-cm wavelength) spectral line from cosmic, neutral hydrogen. The continuum emissions are produced by high-energy electrons in magnetic fields, hot plasmas, or by plasma waves. These emissions are broadband but vary with frequency.

Frequency Bands Allocated for Radio Astronomical Use

The list below shows the frequency bands up to 31.5 GHz allocated by international treaty for use by radio observatories.

Band (MHz)	Primary Lines	Band (GHz)	Primary Lines
322.0–328.6	deuterium, D	4.8–5.0	formaldehyde, HCHO
406.1–410.0	continuum-only	10.6–10.7	continuum-only
608–614	continuum-only	14.47–14.50	formaldehyde, HCHO
1400–1427	hydrogen, H (21 cm)	15.35–15.40	continuum-only
1610.6–1613.8	hydroxyl, OH	22.21–22.50	water, H_2O
1660–1670	hydroxyl, OH	23.6–24.0	ammonia, NH_3
2670–2700	continuum-only	31.3–31.5	continuum-only

Cosmic Radio Sources

The sources listed below are among those observable using small radio telescopes. Flux densities are given for 0.1, 0.5, 1, and 4 GHz (wavelengths of 3 m, 60 cm, 30 cm, and 7.5 cm, respectively) because equipment for these wavelengths is widely available.

Source	RA (2000) Dec h m ° '	Flux Densities (0.1, 0.5, 1, and 4 GHz) Jy	Remarks
Sun		20k/250k/450k/800k	"quiet" values; short, intense emissions from flares
Moon		2/50/210/3350	225 K thermal; plus near-surface emissions at <3 cm
Jupiter			Strong bursts at dekametre wavelengths
W3	2 25.4 +62 06	—/80/150/134	IC 1795; complex, bright HII region; OH emission
Taurus A	5 34.5 +22 01	1450/1250/1000/360	Crab Nebula; remnant of 1054 CE supernova
Orion A	5 35.3 −5 25	90/200/360/330	Orion Neb.; HII star-forming region; OH, IR source
IC 443	6 17.0 +22 34	350/140/80/20	Jellyfish Nebula; supernova remnant
Virgo A	12 30.8 +12 23	1950/150/300/120	M87; elliptical galaxy (E0) with jet; mag. +8.6
Centaurus A	13 25.4 −43 02	8500/5000/1900/200	NGC 5128; galaxy (S0 pec); mag.. +6.8, $z = 0.002$
3C 295	14 11.4 +52 12	95/60/28/10	radio galaxy; mag. +20.5, $z = 0.461$
Galactic center	17 42.0 −28 50	4400/2900/1800/800	strong, diffuse emission from galactic center
Sagittarius A*	17 42.5 −28 55	100/250/200/336	compact source at gal. ctr.; assoc. with black hole?
Cygnus A	19 59.5 +40 44	15500/4000/2100/370	strong radio galaxy (E); mag. +16.2, $z = 0.056$
Cygnus X	20 22.6 +40 23	400/150/30/70	complex region
Cassiopeia A	23 23.4 +58 49	25000/4500/2800/810	supernova remnant

Technology is advancing too quickly for printed books to be very useful. However, for background radio-astronomy information, see *Radio Astronomy*, by J.D. Kraus (Cygnus-Quasar Books, Powell, Ohio, 1986). A number of small, simple radio telescopes and some projects to try are described in *Radio Astronomy Projects*, by William Lonc, Radio-Sky Publishing, 1997. Organizations focusing on amateur radio astronomy include the Society of Amateur Radio Astronomers—SARA (sara.org) and the UK Amateur Radio Astronomy Network (**www.ukaranet.org.uk**). The RASC Okanagan Centre (**okanagan-radio-astronomy.org/index.html**) has an active radio-astronomy group.

MAPS OF THE NIGHT SKY
BY ROY BISHOP

The maps on the following seven pages cover the entire sky. Stars are shown down to a magnitude of 4.5 or 5, that is, those that are readily apparent to the unaided eye on a reasonably dark night.

The first six maps are drawn for latitude 45°N but are useful for latitudes several degrees north or south of this. They show the hemisphere of sky visible at various times of year. Because the aspect of the night sky changes continuously with both longitude and time, while time zones change discontinuously with both longitude and time of year, it is not possible to state simply when a particular observer will find that his or her sky fits exactly one of the six maps. The month indicated above each map is the time of year when the map will match the *late evening* sky. On any particular night, successive maps will represent the sky as it appears every four hours later. For example, at 2:00 or 3:00 on a March morning, the May map should be used. Just after mealtime on a January night, the November map will be appropriate. The center of each map is the *zenith*, the point directly overhead; the circumference is the horizon. To identify the stars, hold the map in front of you so that the part of the horizon you are facing (west, for instance) is downward. (The four letters around the periphery of each map indicate compass directions.)

The southern-sky map is centered on the south celestial pole and extends to Dec 20°S at its periphery. Thus there is considerable overlap with the southern areas of the other maps. Note that the orientation of the various names is generally inverted compared to that on the first six maps, as most users of this Handbook will be residents of the Northern Hemisphere and will make use of the southern-sky map when they make trips to the tropics. Thus in "normal" use this map will be read in an area above its center, unlike the first six maps, which are normally read below their centers. The months indicated around the edge of the map may be used to orient it to each of the preceding six maps and have the same "late evening" significance as explained above. Tick marks around the edge of the map indicate hours of right ascension, with hours 0, 3, 6, etc., labelled. Starting at the center of the map, the series of small crosses along RA 0h indicates southern declinations 90°, 80°, 70°,..., 20°. With the aid of a drawing compass, an observer in the Northern Hemisphere can quickly locate a circle, centered on the south celestial pole, that represents the southern limit of his or her sky.

On all seven maps, stars forming the usual constellation patterns are linked by straight lines, constellation names being given in uppercase letters. Three constellations (Horologium, Mensa, and Microscopium) consist of faint stars; hence no patterns are indicated and the names are placed in parentheses. Small clusters of dots indicate the positions of bright star clusters, nebulae, or galaxies. The pair of wavy dotted lines indicates roughly the borders of the Milky Way. Small asterisks locate the directions of the galactic center (GC), the north galactic pole (NGP), and the south galactic pole (SGP). LMC, SMC, and CS signify, respectively, the Large Magellanic Cloud, the Small Magellanic Cloud, and the Coal Sack. Two dashed lines appear on each of the first six maps. The one with more dashes is the celestial equator. Tick marks along this indicate hours of right ascension, the odd hours being labelled. The line with fewer dashes is the ecliptic, the apparent annual path of the Sun across the heavens. Letters along this line indicate the approximate position of the Sun at the beginning of each month. Also located along the ecliptic are the Northern Hemisphere vernal equinox (VE), summer solstice (SS), autumnal equinox (AE), and winter solstice (WS).

The epoch of the maps is 1950.0. Because of the small scale of the maps, the effect of precession is not yet significant.

JANUARY ALL-SKY MAP

MARCH ALL-SKY MAP

MAY ALL-SKY MAP

JULY ALL-SKY MAP

SEPTEMBER ALL-SKY MAP

NOVEMBER ALL-SKY MAP

THE SOUTHERN SKY

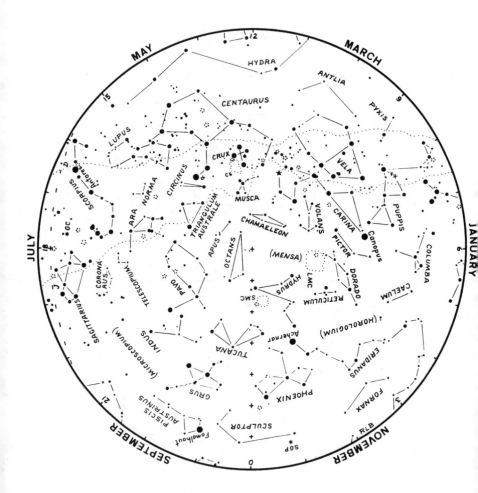

Editor's Note: A Glossary can be found online at **www.rasc.ca/handbook/supplements**.

RASC OBSERVER'S HANDBOOK 2018

INDEX
(**bold** = primary pages)

"MM" denotes the monthly pages of THE SKY MONTH BY MONTH starting on p. 98.

"MM" denotes the monthly pages of THE SKY MONTH BY MONTH starting on p. 98.

"MM" denotes the monthly pages of THE SKY MONTH BY MONTH starting on p. 98. ⟶

"MM" denotes the monthly pages of THE SKY MONTH BY MONTH starting on p. 98.

"MM" denotes the monthly pages of THE SKY MONTH BY MONTH starting on p. 98.

2018 HOLIDAYS AND SPECIAL DATES

New Year's Day .... Mon. Jan. 1
Martin Luther King Jr. Day .... Mon. Jan. 15

Winter Star Party, Florida Keys .... Mon. Feb. 12 – Sun. Feb. 18
Ash Wednesday (beginning of Lent) .... Wed. Feb. 14
Chinese New Year (Year of the Dog) .... Fri. Feb. 16
Washington's Birthday / Presidents Day .... Mon. Feb. 19

Daylight Saving Time starts (see p. 45) .... Sun. Mar. 11
Staunton River Star Party, Staunton River, Virginia ... Wed. Mar. 14 – Sun. Apr. 18
Naw-Rúz (Bahá'í New Year)* .... Wed. Mar. 21
Good Friday .... Fri. Mar. 30
First Day of Passover* .... Sat. Mar. 31

Easter Sunday .... Sun. Apr. 1
Midsouth Star Gaze, French Camp, Mississippi .... Wed. Apr. 11 – Sat. Apr. 14
International Astronomy Week .... Mon. Apr. 23 – Sun. Apr. 29
International Astronomy Day .... Sat. Apr. 28

Texas Star Party, Fort Davis, Texas .... Sun. May 6 – Sun. May 13
First day of Ramadân* .... Wed. May 16
RTMC Astronomy Expo, Riverside, California .... Thu. May 24 – Mon. May 28
Memorial Day .... Mon. May 28

Apollo Rendezvous, Dayton, Ohio .... Sat. Jun. 9
Rocky Mountain Star Stare, Gardner, Colorado .... Thu. Jun. 13 – Mon. Jun. 1 7
Cherry Springs Star Party, Coudersport, Pennsylvania ... Thu. Jun. 14 – Mon. Jun. 17
Harrisburg Star Party, Harrisburg, Pennsylvania ..... Thu. Jun. 14 – Mon. Jun. 17
RASC General Assembly, Calgary, Alberta .... Thu. Jun. 28 – Mon. Jul. 2

Independence Day .... Wed. Jul. 4
Golden State Star Party, Bieber, California .... Wed. Jul. 11 – Sun. Jul. 15
Green Bank Star Quest, Green Bank, West Virginia ... Wed. Jul. 11 – Sat. Jul. 14

Nebraska Star Party, Valentine, Nebraska .... Sun. Aug. 5 – Fri. Aug. 10
Oregon Star Party, Ochoco National Forest, Oregon ... Tue. Aug. 7 – Sun. Aug. 12
Stellafane Convention, Springfield, Vermont .... Thu. Aug. 9 – Sun. Aug. 12

Labor Day .... Mon. Sep. 3
Acadia Night Sky Festival, Bar Harbor, Maine .... Thu. Sep. 6 – Sun. Sep. 9
Rosh Hashanah (Jewish New Year)* .... Mon. Sep. 10
Islamic New Year* .... Wed. Sep. 12
Yom Kippur (Day of Atonement)* .... Wed. Sep. 19
Craters of the Moon Star Party, Arco, Idaho .... Sat. Sep. 22 – Sun. Sep. 23

Heart of America Star Party, Butler, Missouri .... Thu. Oct. 4 – Sun. Oct. 7
Illinois Dark Sky Star Party, Jim Edgar Panther Creek FWA ... Thu. Oct. 4 – Sat. Oct. 6
Okie-Tex Star Party, Camp Billy Joe, Oklahoma ...... Sat. Oct. 6 – Sun. Oct. 14
Columbus Day .... Mon. Oct. 8
Halloween .... Wed. Oct. 31

Daylight Saving Time ends (see p. 45) .... Sun. Nov. 4
Veterans Day .... Sun. Nov. 11
Thanksgiving Day .... Thu. Nov. 22

Christmas Day .... Tue. Dec. 25

*Begins at sunset the previous evening.

See p. 11 for websites and geographical coordinates for the listed *star parties*.